Too
Secret
Too
Long

Other books by Chapman Pincher:

Not with a Bang

Dirty Tricks

Inside Story

Their Trade Is Treachery

The Private World of St. John Terrapin

Too Secret Too Long

Chapman Pincher

St. Martin's Press
New York

Library of Congress Cataloging in Publication Data

Pincher, Chapman.
    Too secret too long.

    Includes index.
    1. Espionage—Great Britain—History—
20th century.   I. Title.
UB271.G7P56   1984   327.1'2'0941   84-18199
ISBN 0-312-80902-6

First published in Great Britain by Sidgwick & Jackson Ltd.
First U.S. Edition

10   9   8   7   6   5   4   3   2   1

To my helpers, overt and covert,
and to my wife, family and friends
who have sustained me
in the long haul

Contents

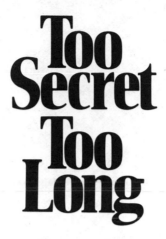

Too Secret Too Long

Introduction

Between the two world wars, the reputations of the British Intelligence and Security Services were legendary and were, justifiably, held as examples of undercover efficiency throughout the world, so much so that any apparent failure was regarded as more probably a hidden success for the wily British. During the Second World War the performance of both the Secret Intelligence Service (MI6) and the Security Service (MI5) against the German, Italian, and Japanese enemies was outstandingly brilliant.

MI6, roughly the equivalent of the U.S. Central Intelligence Agency (CIA), essentially an espionage and intelligence-gathering service operating mainly overseas, was responsible for the operation known as Ultra/Enigma, which broke the "uncrackable" German codes and made a tremendous contribution to the Allied victory.[1]

MI5, which is comparable to the FBI in its assignment as a domestic counter-espionage agency, ran the incredibly successful "Double Cross" operation, which detected German spies as fast as they were intruded and turned them against their own country.[2] Since the Second World War, however, the reputations of both services have plummeted, not only in Britain but abroad, and particularly in the U.S., as well as—one would imagine—in the Soviet Union, following a succession of disgraceful spy scandals.

What is the reason for the apparently sudden change in performance after the Second World War? The basic answer is straightforward: the Germans and their allies were almost totally unable to penetrate the British secret services[3], but the Soviets, who became the main adversary almost immediately after the Allied victory, have deeply penetrated both MI6 and MI5, and associated departments like Government Communications Headquarters, known as GCHQ (the British equivalent of the U.S. National Security Agency), the Foreign Office (equivalent of the U.S. State Department) and the Defence Ministry (equivalent to the U.S. Department of Defense and the Pentagon combined).

The list of proven major spies alone, with their places and years of

3

treachery, is a shameful record by any standard: Alan Nunn May (atom-bomb project), Klaus Fuchs (atom and H-bomb projects), Donald Maclean (Foreign Office and atom-bomb project), Kim Philby (MI6), Guy Burgess (MI6, MI5, and Foreign Office), Anthony Blunt (MI5), Leo Long (Military Intelligence), John King (Foreign Office), George Blake (MI6), John Vassall (Admiralty), John Cairncross (Foreign Office, Treasury, MI6), Frank Bossard (Aviation Ministry), Douglas Britten (Royal Air Force), Nicholas Prager (Royal Air Force), Geoffrey Prime (GCHQ-NSA), Michael Bettaney (MI5). Their combined treachery totals more than 140 active spy-years. If the less proven spies are included the spy-years total exceeds 200.

Secret Service officers whom I have consulted have attempted to explain the difference by stating that the German Intelligence Service (the *Abwehr*) was manned by amateurs who were easy to counter, whereas the Soviet Intelligence Service consists of polished professionals backed by unlimited resources. There is truth in that but it savours more of an excuse than a justification. A detailed study of Soviet penetrations, all of which I covered journalistically as they were exposed during the last thirty-nine years, together with inside information about other cases which I present in this book, has left me in no doubt that the real reason for the long run of Soviet successes has been the *ineffectiveness* of all the British departments concerned with security, and especially of the main department, MI5.

The Soviet threat has come from two fronts. Many of the agents discussed in this book were not recruited by what is now called the KGB but by the other main arm of Soviet intelligence, the GRU, which began as a branch of the Red Army.[4] Most books about Soviet espionage, including my own previous work, have failed to draw a sufficient distinction between the GRU and the KGB, which began as completely separate services and still retain considerable independence. My researches have convinced me that the British Security and Intelligence services have been similarly remiss, and that as a result highly significant clues to Soviet clandestine activities have not been appreciated early enough or, in some cases, at all. If this sounds condescending on the part of an unofficial investigator I leave it to the facts as they unfold to convince the reader of the truth of my claim.

An extensive study of the Soviet intelligence and espionage networks undertaken by the CIA and published in 1982 concludes that Britain was the main target country of the GRU until 1940, when greater effort was devoted to Germany, although Britain remained important.[5] There can be no doubt that separate GRU and KGB networks were built up in Britain before the last war, during it, and since. While much has come to light about parts of the KGB network, such as the Cambridge Ring, little has been revealed about the British section of the so-called "Red Orchestra" of 5,000 GRU spies and agents operating in Europe—though it has been established by MI5 that it recruited successfully at Cambridge and Oxford, the identities of some of the Britons being known. One of the purposes of this book is to draw attention to the relatively unknown GRU operations in Britain, which were probably every bit as damaging as those of the KGB and still continue on a large scale.

The recent conviction of the MI5 officer Michael Bettaney for actively volunteering his services as a Soviet "mole" demonstrated that the so-called "climate of treason," the circumstances of which are said to have induced Cambridge undergraduates and others to become traitors to their own country, persists after half a century.

This book is much more about the " climate of security," the even more peculiar circumstances that permitted so many men, and some women, to betray their country for long periods before being detected, and, in too many instances, without being brought to justice when they were detected.

The lack of any ongoing outside supervision of Great Britain's intelligence establishment has certainly enabled this situation to continue. Such a supervisory or "oversight" body, to use the current term, has been frequently advocated on the grounds that the secret services should be more accountable to Parliament mainly to ensure that they do not excessively infringe civil liberties. I advocate it in the conviction that it could greatly improve the efficiency of the secret services and reduce the risk of their being penetrated by more traitors. I make these claims having critically examined each serious incident of espionage, penetration, and suspected penetration and after weighing the advantages and disadvantages of oversight had it then been in existence. In this examination and in the analysis of the cases, which has not been attempted publicly before, I have been assisted by highly experienced security and intelligence officers. If I am accused of just being wise after the various events then I simply ask the security authorities to follow suit. Meanwhile, with the aid of brief summaries entitled "The Potential Value of Oversight" appended to each case, readers can form their own conclusions about the virtue or otherwise of independent supervision of the secret services.

Previous proposals for oversight of the secret services have been summarily rejected on the assumption that it would inevitably decrease security—a view which I formerly supported. In fact, a degree of oversight far more embracing than anything likely to be accepted in Britain has been operating successfully and safely in the U.S. for the past seven years, through the agency of Select Commit-

5

tees on Intelligence in the Senate and Congress, each committee being served by a full-time professional staff.

Effective oversight also offers the only deterrent to another outrageous situation—the extent to which Parliament, the British and American publics, and even the CIA and FBI have been systematically misled by official statements and reports on security and espionage affairs. As part of my survey I have examined every relevant Parliamentary statement, debate and official report and, as the reader will see, the truth has been repeatedly suppressed, distorted, manipulated and, on occasion, falsified on spurious grounds of "national interest," while the real purpose was to prevent embarrassment of departments and individuals, and of Britain herself before her American and other allies.

When a secret department is in difficulties and questions have to be answered in Parliament or a report has to be published, the information can only come from the department itself because it is secret. The opportunity and the temptation for misrepresentation or deception are, therefore, unrivalled and are uncontrollable save by the department itself. On a security issue any minister or prime minister is only as reliable as the brief provided by officials. While they are within their rights in denying information which would genuinely damage national security, it is iniquitous that they should distort and falsify history by producing misleading documents or providing misleading statements for Parliament which then become the historical record. British governments hate to be accused of cover-ups, but there is nothing of which they are consistently more guilty, largely because of their dependence on the advice and testimony of officials over whom there is no effective oversight. If this book is an indictment of the past behavior of the Whitehall and Westminster machinery it is also a plea for more honesty, not only in the interests of the public and Parliament but of those in secret departments themselves.

My researches have produced examples of another heinous activity on the part of the secret services—the deliberate misleading of their American counterparts purely to save loss of professional face. Oversight could well prevent this practice which could hardly be more counter-productive in view of the high degree of British dependence on the U.S. intelligence services.

This book, therefore, has three major purposes: to demonstrate the urgent need for oversight of the activities of the secret services by some independent body in the interests of the security services themselves; to place on record a mass of new information about espionage and subversion which makes the extent of Soviet penetration of

6

secret departments even more alarming; to show the appalling degree to which Parliament and the world have been misled about the secret services by information originating from the secret services. The intention is not to challenge the integrity of the officers of these services, most of whom are professionally beyond reproach, but to expose the extent to which they and their managers have deluded themselves into believing that concealment or falsification of security disasters is in the interests of the nation and of the services.

It is also to tell the astonishing, infuriating, and sometimes heartbreaking story of two people—the man who, if he was a spy, may without exaggeration or melodrama be called the Spy of the Century, and the woman who was the most successful agent-runner of all time.

CHAPTER ONE

A Soviet Agent Called Sonia

THE slim, dark-haired woman with Slavic features and a foreign accent seemed all that she professed to be when she knocked on the door of the rectory at Glympton, a tiny Oxfordshire village some three miles from the nearest landmark, the mighty Palace of Blenheim, seat of the Dukes of Marlborough. She told the vicar, the Reverend Charles Henry Cox, that she was a German refugee married to an Englishman called Len Beurton who, sadly, was still unable to get out of Switzerland. She herself had just made the hazardous journey with her two children whom she had been forced to place in a boarding school. The kindly Mr Cox and his wife offered her a bedroom and board until she could find permanent accommodation and hoped that she would play cards with them in the long evenings, and that she would pray with them, for the date was February 1941.[1]

In fact Mrs Beurton, who had given her correct name, was not only an atheistic, case-hardened communist but a regular major in the intelligence branch of the Soviet Red Army, the G.R.U., with ten years of espionage behind her in China, Poland and Switzerland – courageous, dedicated effort which had earned her the coveted Order of the Red Banner. Within days of being installed in the rectory, and between prayers and card games, Mrs Beurton, whose G.R.U. code-name was Sonia , began constructing the radio transmitter she was to use in the nine-year British chapter of her career which would qualify her as the most successful female spy in history.

Sonia did not let the Revd and Mrs Cox see any evidence of the radio transmitter she was building in her bedroom. Had they done so they might have connected this activity with the fact that within the previous few months a large part of Blenheim Palace and its grounds had been requisitioned by Britain's Security Service, commonly known as MI5.

What Sonia did and whom she saw when she left the rectory for exercise is not known, but that she had been sent by Moscow on an urgent assignment is beyond question. The probability that her target was an important officer inside MI5 seems overwhelming, not only to the author but to security and intelligence officers involved in the belated study of her case.[2] The nature and extent of her daring exploits, presented here in detail for the first time after rigorous cross-checks, are almost impossible to explain without the existence of a powerful protective hand inside MI5; she and her collaborators could hardly have survived otherwise. The manner of her defection to East Germany, where she still lives at the time of writing, is further evidence of this protection.

Historically, and because of the effects of her activities on Western security, which continue to the present day, the story of Sonia is a natural starting point for a study of the Soviet assault on the security and intelligence services of the West and particularly on those of Britain, the United States, Canada and Australia. The rot in British security, which was to ruin its reputation and inflict incalculable damage on the institutions it was designed to protect, took hold during the Second World War, but the germs of it were sown among British traitors in the 1930s and, earlier still, among certain Germans, like Sonia, who were to enter Britain on the pretext of being political or Jewish refugees.

Sonia was born in Berlin in 1907. Her father, Dr Robert René Kuczynski, a Jew of Polish origin, was an economist of some wealth and distinction. Sonia's given name was Ursula, but her parents called her Ruth and that was the name she always preferred. Dr Kuczynski was deeply involved in left-wing politics, especially after the First World War, and became an ideological communist. It was inevitable that his daughter and his older son, Juergen, who witnessed the effects of the gross inflation in Germany, should become committed communists at an early age.[3] Sonia was only seventeen when she joined the Communist Youth Union. Within two years she was an Agitation and Propaganda (Agitprop) leader for the German Communist Party (K.P.D.) in Berlin. By the following year she had a job with Ullstein Brothers, the well-known German publishing house, which gave her literary ambitions, but she was dismissed when her over-enthusiastic communist activities were discovered. She therefore joined her father and brother, who were doing research work in the U.S., leaving behind her boy-friend, Rudolf (Rolf or Rudi) Hamburger, whom she had done her best to convert to the cause. With the enterprise which was to characterize her life, she obtained a post in a bookstore in New York and in 1929 she returned to Germany to marry Rolf. Meanwhile her father had cemented his adherence to the communist system by visiting Moscow where he may have been recruited to

9

Soviet Intelligence, though this may have happened later in England.

German communists who, like the Kuczynskis, happened to be Jews, later attempted to explain their allegiance to Moscow as having originated in their opposition to Hitler and his racial policies. In fact, when Sonia and many others were recruited to pro-Soviet communism Hitler was not a force of consequence. Their allegiance derived from the fact that they were dedicated to communism for its own sake.

In 1930 Rolf applied for an architect's post with the Shanghai Municipal Council at the suggestion of a friend there, and secured it. By that time the German Communist Party had become virtually a section of the Soviet Intelligence and subversion service and it is possible that the Hamburgers were under instructions to get to China, where Moscow believed the revolutionary prospects were very promising. Sonia records in her memoirs: 'I was thrilled by the prospect, as a German Communist, of cooperating with the persecuted comrades in China.'[4] She advised the Central Committee of the K.P.D. about her move, and in what she regularly refers to as 'good conspiratorial practice' she was told that she would be contacted there.

The young couple – Sonia was then twenty-three – left Germany in July 1930 travelling to China via Moscow on the Trans-Siberian Express. They secured accommodation in the Shanghai International Settlement, a commercial and residential area under British control, where there were about 500 other Germans, some 4,500 Britons and about 1,100 Americans, along with many Chinese. They quickly met influential Germans and, because they were both fluent in English, Britons and Americans too. They were soon part of the international social scene there, which Sonia disliked but accepted as necessary until they could be selective about friends.

Among the Americans who instantly appealed to Sonia was an extraordinary woman journalist and revolutionary called Agnes Smedley who was to have a profound effect on her life. There are letters to Miss Smedley from Sonia recording the warmth of their friendship.[5] Sonia remembers the date of their first meeting as 7 November because it was the thirteenth anniversary of the Russian Revolution.

Miss Smedley, who had been briefly married, had arrived in Shanghai in May 1929 having previously attended the Sixth World Congress of the Comintern in Moscow. A woman of great determination and physical courage, then aged thirty-four, she was already something of a veteran in the service of the Comintern, the agency for promoting revolution worldwide, which had been taken over by Stalin as an instrument of Soviet aggrandizement and subservience to Moscow. Miss Smedley was fluent in German, having lived in Berlin, and her overt function was to serve as Far Eastern correspondent of the *Frankfurter Zeitung*. Her covert objective was to assist the Chinese Communist Party to achieve eventual control of the country. She quickly established a reputation as the most radical writer in China, burning with class hatred; she was a prominent member of the International Union of Revolutionary Writers, to which she actively recruited journalists. One of her revolutionary tasks was to organize writers to stir up trouble with press articles which were usually written under pseudonyms, her own being 'Mary Rogers'.

While dedicating her life mainly to Chinese communism, she was an ardent supporter of the Soviet Union, carrying out many conspiratorial services for the Fourth Bureau of the Red Army, the military intelligence arm which was to develop into the G.R.U.[6] At that stage there was no general conflict of interest between the Communist Parties of the Soviet Union (C.P.S.U.) and China. Stalin believed that the C.P.S.U. would always be regarded as the senior and dominant party and, with an eye on India and the expulsion of the British from there, he argued that once that country was sandwiched between two communist giants like the U.S.S.R. and China, a communist revolution there was inevitable.[7]

Some writers have insisted that Agnes Smedley was not an active espionage agent, but it has recently been established that she most certainly was.

Like most Europeans working in Shanghai, which was an exciting beat for any journalist and especially for a revolutionary, Miss Smedley lived either in the International Settlement, run by the British, or in the French Concession, changing her lodgings frequently because of extended visits to Peking and other areas of China. Being gregarious, she ran something of a salon in her various homes, providing a rendezvous for other journalists, communists and fellow-agents. Though not particularly attractive she seems to have been highly sexed and had affairs with several communist colleagues. Among these was a German journalist and dedicated communist whose daring exploits in espionage were probably to be crucial in the forthcoming war between Germany and the Soviet Union. His name was Richard Sorge and his efforts on Stalin's behalf were to cost him his life.[8]

Sorge, who had been sent to Britain from Germany in 1928 on conspiratorial work for the Comintern, was transferred to the service of the Fourth Bureau of the Red Army, the intelligence service, and was posted to Shanghai early in 1930, when he was

11

thirty-five.[9] Almost immediately he met Smedley by previous arrangement and she virtually became his assistant, as well as his mistress, even introducing him to the man who was to be his main aide in Tokyo, a Japanese journalist called Ozaki Hotsumi who was working in Shanghai.[10] The German who was to be Sorge's radio-transmitting link with Moscow, Max Klausen, was also a visitor to Smedley's flat. Smedley's assistance was to be acknowleged by Sorge in the confession he wrote before being executed by the Japanese in 1944.[11] As Major-General Charles Willoughby, intelligence chief to General Douglas MacArthur, observed on Smedley in 1953: 'It is reasonable to assume that she recruited other Soviet agents before and has recruited others since.'[12] The recently published memoirs of two professional Soviet agents, Otto Braun and Ruth Werner (Sonia's pen-name), have shown that the major-general was correct.

Otto Braun was another communist colleague and lover of Agnes Smedley and was as eminent in Comintern history as Sorge. Braun was involved in military work with the Chinese Red Army and was known to the Chinese as 'Li Teh'.[13] The very senior Comintern official Arthur Ewert was a frequent visitor to the Smedley gatherings, together with his wife who was also an active Soviet agent and recruiter. Left-wing American journalists like Harold Isaacs, who edited *China Forum*, a local paper printed in English, sought her company and support.[14] Rewi Alley, the New Zealand writer who acquired such strong Marxist leanings while working in Shanghai that he is now domiciled in Peking, was another acquaintance.[15]

Among other occasional visitors to the Smedley 'salon' was a young English journalist and tobacco company employee called Roger Henry Hollis, then in his late twenties. While confirming much later in his life that he had known Agnes, he claimed to be unable to recall how he had come to meet her. It could have been through membership of some Shanghai club, such as the Press Club or American Club. He may have sought her out for journalistic assistance or he might have been directed towards her by some mutual friend such as Arthur Ewert, who seems to have known Smedley in Germany. Hollis's connection with her is important, not only because of the kind of people he was likely to meet in her company, but because Miss Smedley was a 'very dynamic person and influenced a number of young men'.[16] According to Miss Smedley's biographers, she normally disliked Englishmen because of her involvement in the Indian nationalist movement and her continuing harassment in Shanghai by the Municipal Police, who were mainly British. So to have been a welcome visitor to her house

Hollis was somewhat special.[17] He was special in another way too because, although the idea would have been ridiculed at the time, he was to become the chief of Britain's most secret and, at one time, most prestigious Security Service, MI5. He was also to become deeply suspected of being a long-serving Soviet agent who had been recruited in China.

CHAPTER TWO

A 'Good Bottle Man'

HOLLIS, the third child and third son of the Right Reverend George Arthur Hollis, was born in Wells, Somerset, on 2 December 1905. His father, who at that time was Priest Vicar of Wells, was to become Resident Canon of Wells, Principal of the Theological College attached to Wells Cathedral, and later Suffragan Bishop of Taunton, the county town of Somerset.[1] Roger's mother was the daughter of a Canon of Wells Cathedral. His eldest brother, Michael, who was six years older and is still alive at the time of writing, entered the Church, married a daughter of the Dean of Salisbury and became Bishop of Madras. Christopher, the best known of the three, was born in 1902. He became a Member of Parliament and an excellent speaker, a considerable historian, a contributor to humorous magazines, and a convert to Roman Catholicism. Roger had a younger brother, Marcus, who is still alive but remains a very private person and little is known about him beyond the fact that he worked for a few years in the Secret Intelligence Service.

Roger was educated at Clifton College, Bristol, a public school with a good reputation, though not to be compared with Eton, to which Christopher had won his way. In 1924 Roger entered Worcester College, Oxford, a university with which his father and elder brothers had happy and fruitful associations.[2] His father had been a distinguished member of Keble College; his brother Michael had been a scholar of Trinity College; while Christopher enjoyed and distinguished himself at Balliol. Roger's achievements at university, where he read English, were to be in sharp contrast. His closest friend in later life, Sir Dick White, who was a brief contemporary at Oxford, said that Hollis had a reputation there of wasting his time on 'wine, women and golf', a view reiterated by another contemporary, Sir Harold Acton.[3] Sir Harold described him to me as 'rather hearty and young for his age. I think he became a member of our boisterously bohemian Hypocrites Club, which was eventually closed down by the proctors. He was a drinking friend of Evelyn Waugh.'

In his diaries Waugh recorded lunching at Worcester College in November 1924 with Roger Hollis, whom he described as 'a good bottle man'. Also present were Roger Fulford, who was later to join Hollis in MI5, and Tom Driberg, the left-winger who was to work as an outside agent for MI5 and as a double agent for the K.G.B. In the following month Waugh had dinner with Hollis and Claud Cockburn, who was to become a prominent communist. Waugh recorded that he, Hollis and Cockburn then went on a pub-crawl which 'after sundry indecorous adventures ended up at the Hypocrites, where another blind was going on' Next day he gave lunch to Hollis, Cockburn and others at the New Reform Club with 'more solid drinking'.[4]

All this was normal enough, perhaps, for an undergraduate of the 1920s but it was to contrast sharply with the reserved and withdrawn personality which Hollis was to project only a few years later.

Sir Harold Acton also noted that Roger was 'overshadowed at Oxford by his brilliant brother, Christopher'. A search of the available records in the Oxford Union Library shows that Christopher was a regular and popular debater while there is no mention whatever of Roger ever having spoken at a debate. I have been told that in later life Roger mentioned to friends that he had represented the university in a debating team which toured abroad, but it was Christopher who achieved that distinction. Hollis's friends have claimed that he was non-political and the fact that he did not speak at debates is evidence of that, but there are no signs of activity in that respect on the part of Tom Driberg either, and he became chairman of the Labour Party. There is no evidence that Hollis showed any interest in communism at Oxford, but that also applied to many of the most dedicated who were required by the Party to conceal their political views against the day when overt communism might keep them out of employment useful to the cause.

Claud Cockburn, who was to become a correspondent for the communist *Daily Worker* (now *Morning Star*) and was suspected of being a Soviet agent by MI5 because he published a newsletter containing accurate secret intelligence, described Hollis as having been 'apolitical' at Oxford.[5] It seems certain that Hollis was never a member of the British Communist Party, and his supporters have taken some comfort from this, but neither was Philby. Many of those recruited for active service to the Comintern were required to avoid all contact with the Party and even to appear to be right wing, as Philby's case demonstrates. If Hollis was talent-spotted at

15

Oxford, which seems doubtful, he was in a different category from the Cambridge recruits who were all intellectually bright. Hollis appeared to be singularly lacking in attributes likely to provide access to secrets. He left Oxford without a degree in 1926, after less than two years of attendance and four terms short of his final examinations.

MI5 colleagues and Whitehall friends of Roger Hollis have told me that, while he never expressed any love for Oxford, he was proud of his half-blue in golf. He never won a half-blue, however. He was a keen and capable golfer but the university golfing authorities have confirmed that he never represented the university at golf.[6] Such a deceitful boast may be common enough but it is odd behaviour for a Director-General of MI5 and, perhaps, indicative of his feelings of inferiority at Oxford.

Hollis's decision to become what today would be called a drop-out seems to have been linked with his friendship with another left-wing student, Maurice Richardson, who later joined the Communist Party and remained a convinced Marxist for many years. According to him they both decided to quit Oxford and go to Mexico. The writer D. H. Lawrence had drawn attention to that country, and while Hollis seemed to show no interest in such literary efforts, Richardson did. Mexico also happened to be a centre of Comintern activity because of its inherent political instability and its convenience as a base for infiltrating Central and Latin American countries considered ripe for revolution. Richardson, however, backed down from the precipitous path to Mexico and remained at Oxford to take his degree, becoming a journalist and writer of some distinction. Hollis, on the other hand, faced his parents' anger and disappointment by announcing his intention to go to China and, hopefully, work there as a journalist.[7] It seemed an odd decision for a young man with no apparent connections with that country and it continues to puzzle people who have studied his case. Merlyn Rees, the former Home Secretary, who knew about the Hollis case because of his responsibility for MI5 in the late 1970s, regards the decision to quit Oxford to go to China as its most puzzling aspect, especially as Hollis did not even wait until the end of an academic year, so pressing was his determination to leave.[8] Sir Harold Acton, who was rich, was soon to go from Oxford to Peking, but he assured me that he was not responsible for firing Hollis's interest. 'I was drawn to it by my love of Chinese art and I cannot believe that Roger was interested in that,' he told me.

It remains conceivable, but improbable, that Hollis had been recruited by the G.R.U., which was certainly active at Oxford at that time, and accepted the exciting prospect of going to China in preference to failing his finals, for which he had done insufficient work. Almost all the Comintern agents being sent to China then were Europeans or Americans, and the fact that no funds were provided has no significance because recruits were supposed to find their own way to their posts as a measure of their determination.[9] It would seem more likely that Hollis simply rebelled against the cloying atmosphere of both Wells Cathedral and Oxford. When called back from retirement in 1970 to be interrogated, he said that he had gone to China 'to get away from the family and from the Church'.[10]

There was the additional factor that he was unable or unwilling to compete with his gifted elder brothers. He was also to suffer from a severe spinal problem which, as it progressed, was to lead some of his colleagues to describe him as a hunchback, though that was an exaggeration. Sir Harold recalled that Hollis was already noticeably round-shouldered at Oxford and this could have been an additional psychological burden contributing to his determination to get away from relatives and friends.

The degree of Hollis's determination to go to China was demonstrated by his behaviour when his parents declined to finance his journey. He worked for a year as a clerk in the Standard Bank in London to earn his passage. A school friend from Clifton College recalled seeing him then, posting late letters at a City post office. 'He did not seem pleased to be caught doing such a menial task,' the friend remarked.

According to statements made by Hollis himself in 1970 when, aged sixty-four, he professed poor recollection of the events, he travelled to China by boat via Malaya, leaving Britain early in 1927. Having seriously underestimated his running costs, he said that he had found himself in Penang with no more than £10 but had found a modest job as a stringer – a part-time journalist – with a newspaper said, by one MI5 source, to have been the *South China Times*. He appears to have arrived in China in the spring of 1927.

Hollis had told his parents that he would earn his livelihood through journalism and there is no doubt that he did so during his first year in China.[11] Then on 1 April 1928 he secured a post with the British American Tobacco Company (B.A.T.) which, with its subsidiary, the British Cigarette Company, owned factories in Shanghai, Hankow, Tientsin, Mukden and Harbin. This move suggests that he had been unable to earn enough for his requirements through writing, but he continued his journalism on a freelance basis throughout his stay in China.[12]

The fact that Hollis was primarily a journalist during his first year in China and remained an active freelance helps to explain his

17

friendship with Agnes Smedley and makes it likely that he would have met fellow-journalists and writers and others frequenting her 'salon'. He certainly met Arthur Ewert and Rewi Alley, probably met Harold Isaacs, and may have met Sorge in the latter's capacity as a journalist. Whether or not he met and knew Sonia is of crucial importance to a study of treachery in Britain in view of the strange way in which their paths were to cross in the years ahead.

According to Sonia's memoirs she became such a close friend of Agnes Smedley that hardly a day passed when they did not speak to one another, either in person or on the telephone. Harold Isaacs, who lives in the U.S. and is now in his middle seventies, remembers Sonia in Smedley's circle as Ruth Hamburger; he also remembers Arthur Ewert and his friendship with Sonia.[13] Rewi Alley, in his late eighties, remembers Ruth and Rudi Hamburger, and Hollis.

There is no doubt that Hollis and Sonia had mutual friends who were ardent left-wingers. When considering Hollis's activities in China there has been a tendency, even inside MI5, to think of him as the rather remote, asocial person he appeared to be to most people during his service in the security world, but when he went to China he had only recently left Oxford, and his fondness there for 'wine, women and golf' and his reputation as a 'good bottle man' are more likely to have characterized his behaviour in China. In that light Sonia would have been likely to appeal to him. They were about the same age, were both from upper-middle-class homes and, from the photographs and incidents recorded in her book, Sonia seems to have been full of energy and fun. She was also sexually attractive in a Slavic way, black-haired with a trim figure and good legs; one fellow-spy described her as tall, slender, almost fragile-looking with movements which were 'smooth and a trifle languid'.[14] She was also described as an amusing companion, as she appears to have been from the photographs, and she played tennis, which was one of Hollis's regular sports.

When one of Hollis's closest friends in MI5 wrote to me about what was known about Sonia in China, he said that 'in her younger days in the Far East she, no doubt, obliged the comrades with some easy sex', a reference to her known affair with Sorge and with another Soviet agent known as 'Ernst'.[15]

In view of the circumstances it would seem likely that Hollis and Sonia did know one another in China and while, as yet, there is no proof of this, their later extraordinary contiguity in Britain makes it difficult to believe that they did not.

Sonia was one of many young people who dedicated themselves so completely to the Communist Party, with its ready answers to all problems, that they found life empty and difficult if forced to live outside it, and she was soon chafing for an opportunity to serve the cause. Smedley already knew, through a representative of the Soviet T.A.S.S. agency whom Sonia had met, that her new German friend was anxious to establish contact with other communists. Smedley wasted no time in assisting her. She told Sonia that a communist whom she could trust would visit her flat. A few days later Richard Sorge knocked on her door and, without revealing his identity at that stage, talked her into working as an 'illegal' – having no diplomatic cover – agent for the Fourth Bureau of the Red Army, though she did not discover the true nature of her employer for some time.[16] As other Soviet agents have recorded, or admitted when interrogated, it was standard Soviet practice to recruit young people to the cause of peace or to undercover work for the 'communist ideal', and only later would they discover that they were operating for Soviet Intelligence. Sorge warned Sonia of the dangers and gave her some elementary instruction, including an admonition against contacting the Communist Party in Shanghai, or anyone else, in order to preserve her cover.

Sonia recalls the excitement of being recruited to an international conspiracy and how 'the conspiratorial way of conduct and behaviour became second nature'. Her memoirs and other accounts of her activities reveal that both she and Smedley were much more deeply involved in Sorge's espionage activities than was previously suspected. She records having at least eighty clandestine meetings with Sorge over their two-year period together in Shanghai. Her first 'illegal' function was to allow her flat to be used as a meeting place for Sorge and his group, which included Otto Braun, Ewert and his wife, as well as spies like Klausen and Ozaki Hotsumi. She records that Sorge was sometimes accompanied by one or two unnamed European friends. Sonia also acted as a courier for Sorge's China spy-ring, especially with the spymaster, Manfred Stern, who was chief military adviser to the Central Committee of the Chinese Communist Party during 1932.

As a further cover and to help the general cause, Sonia began active work as a freelance journalist, probably with Smedley's assistance, writing in journals like the *Red Flag* under the initials 'A.Z.' She also became a keen photographer, a useful accomplishment for a spy, and her memoirs contain several photographs she took with her Leica camera during her espionage career in several countries.

Sonia's now well-documented record shows that she was an avid recruiter of pro-Soviet agents, though in her early years in China she was probably essentially a talent-spotter who would not go further without first consulting Sorge, who would have taken advice from Moscow. Later she was a highly successful agent-runner, courier and radio operator and, in Britain, probably a case officer.

Did Sonia or Smedley talent-spot Hollis and was any effort made to recruit him? Before that question is considered it is necessary to examine an extraordinary relationship which has not been revealed before and which puts the whole Hollis case in a new light.

CHAPTER THREE

An Unsuspected Communist Connection

EARLY in 1931 the Smedley entourage had been enlarged by the arrival from Moscow of a major figure in the history of international communism, a pioneer of world revolution called Arthur Ewert. With him was his wife Elise, also a seasoned Soviet revolutionary known in conspiratorial circles as 'Mrs Szabo', from her maiden name, Sabrowski. As Sonia and Otto Braun record, Ewert and his wife were received rapturously in Shanghai because of their standing in Moscow and wide revolutionary experience.[1] Ewert, who was of German origin, is of the greatest significance to this book because I have established that he was a friend of Roger Hollis, a fact that has been unknown to the British security authorities and to those who have claimed that Hollis had no certain contacts with the communists, apart from his admission of a casual acquaintanceship with Agnes Smedley. Because of this relationship, and because so much about Ewert is scattered in relatively inaccessible books and documents, I shall describe his extraordinary career in some detail.

The Ewerts had been posted to Shanghai from Moscow as Comintern emissaries to the Chinese Communist Party. Their German friend, Gerhardt Eisler, had arrived there in 1929, under cover of being a salt merchant, and between them they ran the secret Far East Bureau of the Comintern, centred in Shanghai.[2] Ewert had not been there long when the bureau had to cease operations because of the Japanese occupation of Shanghai. He moved to Peking, where Hollis had also been temporarily posted and was sharing accommodation with a British army officer who was later to reveal the friendship between the 26-year-old journalist and employee of the British American Tobacco Company and a full-blown international revolutionary.[3]

Arthur Ernst Ewert was born in East Prussia in 1890 and, after training in communist and conspiratorial affairs, emigrated to Canada in 1914 with Elise. Immediately after the Russian Revolution of 1917 they were involved in setting up a communist party in

Canada. He first achieved public prominence on 23 March 1919, when Toronto police raided a boarding house and arrested him and Elise, who had been using the pseudonym Annie Bancourt, while he had used the alias Arthur Brown. The police reported finding four pistols and ammunition in Ewert's rooms along with literature aimed at the overthrow of the Canadian Government. They believed Ewert to be the main instigator of the undercover, subversive organization.[4] After internment in a camp for enemy aliens, Ewert was deported to the U.S., whence, presumably, he had entered Canada. His wife remained in prison for a few months longer and then joined Ewert in Detroit, an important centre of communist activity in the U.S.

The Ewerts returned to Germany where he became a prominent member of the Communist Party of Germany (K.P.D.) and, eventually, communist member of the Reichstag during the Weimar Republic. In 1923 he was elected to the K.P.D. Politburo and began his career with the Comintern. He was seconded to Moscow where he was one of a specially selected group of multilingual international instructors with plenipotentiary powers to guide the various sectors of the Comintern working to Moscow's orders after the Comintern had been 'Bolshevized'.[5] Ewert was considered senior enough to be an instructor in the International Division of the Communist University of Leningrad. The communist agent, Richard Krebs, has described how Ewert was 'popular because of his robust warmth and rollicking humour' and that he taught 'aspects of class war and the struggle for communism' leading to the seizure of power through revolution.[6] Known in the Soviet Union as 'A. Braun', Ewert was particularly close to Nikolai Bukharin, a leading Bolshevik who was nominally head of the Comintern.[7]

In 1927 Ewert, who spoke good English, was sent to the U.S. under the pseudonym 'Grey' to give guidance to the quarrelling American Communist Party, in which various groups were struggling for control. He remained there for only a few months, chairing a commission detailed to settle the dispute in Stalin's interests.[8] After the implementation of an agreement he returned to Germany, where a similar dispute had developed in the K.P.D. There he tried to resolve the difficulty by securing the leadership for himself, using a scandal about the mishandling of Party funds to bring down the leader, Ernst Thaelmann. In this bid for power Ewert was abetted by Gerhardt Eisler, another 'international socialist' who was to have an equally colourful career as a communist subversive.[9]

In the following year Ewert and Eisler's handling of Thaelmann was overruled by Moscow and, to the misfortune of both of them,

Stalin began to undermine their protector Bukharin, who was expelled, first from the Comintern and then from the Soviet Politburo. Ewert, too, was expelled and exiled from Germany by the K.P.D. but, early in 1930, he acknowledged his errors and was readmitted to Comintern work.[10] He was summoned to Moscow to work for the Comintern's Latin American section and was sent to South America, under the name of Harry Berger, with his wife.[11] Then he was posted to China. After a sojourn in Peking, where he was friendly with Hollis, visiting the latter's apartment on several occasions, he was recalled to Moscow and sent to Montevideo to bring out a Brazilian revolutionary called Luis Carlos Prestes, who had angered the Kremlin by attracting more loyalty to himself than to the Party.[12] Prestes was to remain in Moscow for four years while Ewert and his wife returned to China and the company of Miss Smedley and of Sonia. In 1932 Sonia records that she spent three days 'during a nice trip to the country' with Arthur Ewert, Mrs Szabo and Agnes Smedley.[13] By that time, according to former employees of the British American Tobacco Company, Hollis was working in the advertising department and had moved more permanently to Shanghai where, it seems likely, he and Ewert continued to meet.

Part of Ewert's task was to end the Chinese Communist Party's revolt against Stalin's pact with Chiang Kai-shek, which the Kremlin was still pursuing in spite of the massacre of communists. In this connection Ewert's activities were recorded by Otto Braun, who contacted him within days of his arrival in Shanghai, and recalled that he met him in the presence of Agnes Smedley.[14] Ewert remained in Shanghai, with occasional visits elsewhere, until July 1934, when he moved hastily to Moscow via Vladivostok.

In April of the following year it was decided in Moscow that Prestes, the revolutionary whom Ewert had pulled out of South America to be disciplined, should return to Brazil surreptitiously and that Ewert would join him to stage a revolt against the Vargas Government and replace it with a 'Soviet government of workers and peasants'. A woman member of the Red Army, an ex-German who happened to be a friend of the ubiquitous Sonia, and went by name of Olga Benario, was detailed to accompany Prestes, posing as his wife but acting as his bodyguard, prepared to 'sacrifice her life for him', though she had never met him before. Her main function was probably to serve as his political officer and report back to Moscow on his activities and real attitude to Stalin. The pair arrived in Rio de Janeiro under the name Mr and Mrs Antonio Vilar and were soon joined by the Ewerts, using the name Berger.[15]

The revolt, staged in November 1935, was a fiasco and the main participants, including the Ewerts, were arrested. Prestes, described in *The Times* on that occasion as a pathetic figure lacking in leadership, was sentenced to sixteen years' imprisonment, and Ewert to fourteen.[16] Ewert was tortured in gaol to induce him to incriminate the Soviet Government and disclose his contacts. According to a letter in *The Times* written by his sister, Minna, who was then living in London, he was burned with cigarettes, beaten, and given electric shocks.[17] He certainly became mentally deranged and never fully recovered his sanity.

Ewert's wife and Olga Benario, together with Olga's baby daughter who had been born in Brazil, were deported to Germany and incarcerated in Ravensbrück concentration camp, where they were eventually exterminated. Ewert was freed in May 1945 and arrived in East Germany by Soviet ship in August 1947, living there in various medical institutions until his death in July 1959, in his seventieth year. The Central Committee of the East German Communist Party paid tribute to his work and the funeral oration was delivered by his old co-conspirator, Gerhardt Eisler.[18]

Ewert's record of extraordinarily dedicated service to the cause of Soviet communism shows him to have been a far more formidable and politically important revolutionary figure than anyone known to have been associated with Philby, Burgess, Blunt or Maclean, all of whose previous links with communism had been grossly underestimated by the security authorities. Ewert's association with Hollis should, therefore, have been of high significance when MI5 came to examine the suspicions against him, but it was missed entirely, in a way which seems all too typical of the inquiries made into the background of former members of the secret services.

While trying to secure evidence of Hollis's left-wing affiliations during his years in China, an MI5 officer involved in the case in the late 1960s discovered that while Hollis had been in Peking in 1930 and 1931 he had shared a flat with a British army officer who had been posted there to learn Chinese. This soldier was still alive and living in retirement in the Cotswolds where the MI5 officer, whose identity is known to me, interviewed him. The MI5 man learned that most of Hollis's friends whom the officer was able to list had been diplomats and businessmen, with some of whom he played golf. The army man expressed concern about one of them, whose name was Arthur Ewert and whom he described as an 'international socialist'. He remembered meeting Ewert, a big, shambling man with powerful shoulders, a large head and red hair, and said that Hollis saw him frequently, so that they were more than casual aquaintances. He said that he found the relationship difficult to understand because Hollis's politics appeared to be so conserva-

24

tive. He did not suggest that Hollis might have been seeing him for journalistic purposes, which presumably he may have been doing.[19]

Unfortunately the MI5 man noted Ewert's last name as Ewart, believing him to be British. After failing to find any trace of him in the MI5 records he took no further action, having convinced himself that the army officer would probably have considered anyone with even moderate left-wing views as being dangerous.[20]

Because of the fortuitous way in which the information about the friendship between Hollis and Ewert reached me, there can be no doubt of its authenticity. In 1982 I acquired a copy of Sonia's memoirs, which had proved very difficult to obtain outside East Germany. I showed translations of relevant extracts to certain people with specialist knowledge, including Sonia's references to Arthur Ewert, of whom I had never previously heard. Among the comments I received was the information I have recorded, together with an admission by the officer who had failed to follow up the Ewert lead that he had 'certainly missed something'. My researches into the Comintern literature soon showed that what the officer had missed would have completely altered MI5's attitude to the Hollis case. A routine check with the F.B.I. or with Canadian records should have produced enough on Ewert to have sounded louder alarm bells and have led to more rigorous inquiries.

There can be little doubt, especially in view of Ewert's visits to Moscow, that he would have reported on his association with Hollis, because such reports were a routine requirement for Comintern officials. As a result, if not previously on his own initiative, he would have been required to try to recruit Hollis who, as the son of an important cleric and likely to return to Britain one day, could have his uses. Hollis's journalistic activities would have been likely to have reinforced that requirement.

With Ewert, Smedley and probably some of their friends such as Sorge and Sonia, Hollis was in touch not only with zealous communists but with professional Soviet agents and inveterate recruiters. The allegation that Hollis never associated with communists and left no 'spoor', as the Cambridge Ring did, therefore has no substance.

Supporters of Hollis, including a most senior MI5 officer, are prepared to admit that he may well have been friendly with Ewert, Smedley and even with Sonia, but they claim that such associations would have been entirely out of journalistic interest. 'Wouldn't you, as a journalist, have tried to cultivate such people?' the officer asked me. It would seem to be a fair question but the documentary evidence shows that neither I nor Hollis would have had much

25

success in interviewing Ewert or cultivating him as a usable source. Ewert was in China surreptitiously on subversive Comintern business and in considerable danger of arrest by the Chinese authorities or the Shanghai Municipal Police. As Harold Isaacs has stated recently, whenever he saw Ewert it was 'conspiratorially', meaning for Comintern purposes with all security precautions being taken.[21] The odds are that the same circumstances applied to Hollis's meetings with Ewert and perhaps for the same reasons.

There is an even more potent factor which vitiates the assumption that their relationship was entirely innocent. When Hollis was questioned about his Chinese days during his interrogation in 1970 he avoided any mention of Ewert.[22] As he was then only sixty-four and in good health it would seem to be most unlikely that he could have forgotten such a forceful and larger-than-life figure who impressed his personality on so many others. The much older Harold Isaacs, whose memory for most of his Shanghai comrades has dimmed, remembers Ewert: 'A stout man with a florid complexion I knew as a representative of the Comintern. We met conspiratorially from time to time...'[23]

There can be no doubt that if the MI5 and MI6 officers who were eventually to investigate Hollis had known of his association with such a powerful Comintern official as Ewert they would have delved more deeply into his past and interrogated him in greater detail. With people like Ewert and Smedley, whom Sonia describes as a recruiter for the G.R.U., Hollis was not in contact with just communists but with Soviet agents of the highest calibre and strongest determination to secure recruits.

Hollis's friends and supporters have asked, 'How could a young man with his stable, ecclesiastical background and being so English have been recruited as a Soviet spy?' Had Hollis ever written his memoirs then the following extracts from the account by Sonia's fellow-agent, Alexander Foote, of how he became a Soviet agent could possibly have flowed from his pen: 'A psycho-analyst would be hard put to find anything in my early life which would indicate that one day I should be running part of a Soviet network. My upbringing was as ordinary as that of any child of middle-class parentage brought up between the wars. It was not really political sense or political education which shaped my decisions, leading me from the Industrial Midlands to Switzerland to post-war Russia and ultimately back to England again. From a restless sales manager to a Russian spy is a difficult game of Consequences. However, it was almost inevitable that my early discontent, restlessness and desire for something new and preferably exciting would lead me towards the Communist Party. While still in business I had attended Communist Party discussion groups and gradually was led to believe that International Communism was the panacea for all the world's ills. The outbreak of the Spanish Civil War crystallised my somewhat inchoate thoughts on the whole matter. I was convinced that the Rebels were inspired and supported by the German-Italian Fascists with the idea of their gaining control first of the Peninsula and ultimately of Europe.'[24]

For the 'Industrial Midlands' read 'Somerset': for 'Switzerland' read 'China': for 'the Spanish Civil War' read 'the savage conflicts in China': for 'German-Italian Fascists' read 'the forces of Chiang Kai-shek and the Japanese'.

Whittaker Chambers, the American communist traitor who achieved notoriety as the main witness against Alger Hiss, the State Department official imprisoned for perjury, described in his testimony why he became a communist and Soviet recruiter: 'Marxism, Leninism offers an oversimplified explanation of the causes of world economic crisis and a program for action. The very vigor of the project particularly appeals to the more or less sheltered middle-class intellectuals who feel that there the whole context of their lives has kept them from the world of reality.'[25] Hollis was no intellectual but neither was Foote. Regarding such people, Alexander Orlov, the Soviet diplomat who defected during the late 1930s, put the Soviet position more directly when he wrote that the recruiters 'based their appeal to young men who were tired of a tedious life in the stifling atmosphere of their privileged class'.[26]

Hollis's possible susceptibility to recruitment to communism and the Soviet cause appears to have been closely parallelled by that of Whittaker Chambers. Both were university drop-outs. During Chambers' university days he became friendly with aspiring writers and followed their example. When he quit before taking a degree he had a wanderlust. His decision to become a communist came during a period of personal failure. If Hollis was 'getting away from the Church' by going to China, as he was to claim, communism offered some kind of faith, of which the Hollis family seemed in need.

The recent case of the MI5 officer, Michael Bettaney, showed that continuing Christian belief can co-exist with dedication to pro-Soviet communism. His background was similar to that of Hollis. He was an unremarkable Oxford student with strong religious belief and found himself, in his early twenties, in the turmoil and violence of Northern Ireland, where, if he is to be believed, the seeds of his conversion to communism were sown.

27

Shanghai in the late 1920s and 1930s was more conducive to the recruitment of a young man to the apparent cause of social and political justice than anywhere in Britain or the United States. It was a city of appalling poverty for the Chinese masses who made it the sixth largest city in the world. Many of them were driven to make a starvation-level living as pack-animals. The streets thronged with beggars, some of whom were found dead on the pavements almost every morning. By contrast, the Shanghai International Settlement, where Hollis lived, was an enclave of prosperity, a major centre of commerce and, with the French Concession, had a night-life which gave the city a scandalous reputation. There were splendid hotels and exclusive clubs, including four golf clubs where Hollis played. Outside the European settlements organized labour and the communists in particular were brutally suppressed by various secret societies and by the troops of Chiang Kai-shek. Chiang had gangs of special police called Blue Shirts who behaved more atrociously than Hitler's Brown Shirts. About 100,000 communists and alleged communists are said to have been killed by the Blue Shirts.[27]

Jack Tilton, in the 1930s a Detective Inspector with the Shanghai Municipal Police, which he served with distinction, has written to me describing how he witnessed executions in the streets and saw severed heads in trees. The tough shoot-to-kill methods which the Municipal Police found it necessary to use against subversives in the International Settlement itself could have generated resentment in a young man's mind. The later Japanese atrocities against the whole Chinese nation were appalling, and Hollis may well have witnessed the direct attack on the Chapei district of Shanghai made by the Japanese in January 1932, when there was furious fighting and a curfew had to be enforced in the International Settlement. Some of the Cambridge recruits to the Soviet service have explained how they were incensed by their reading of the distant cruelties and injustices of the Spanish Civil War and Hitler's repression of the Jews. The effects of on-the-spot observation of the cruelties and injustices in Shanghai are likely to have been more urgently persuasive.

Throughout Hollis's nine-year stay in China the country was in a continuous state of ferment which was eventually to lead to the post-war communist victory. He was there during the Long March of the communists which seemed, and indeed was, heroic. He was there during the student revolutions in Peking in 1935 and 1936 and, in the latter year, wrote to his parents expressing some sympathy with the Chinese communist cause: 'One can't really help but sympathise with them in a way, though really they are playing into Japan's hands.'[28]

Such ferment was, inevitably, exploited by Soviet intelligence officers and political activists using the cosmopolitan population of the Settlement as a recruitment pool. Many books and records testify to the extent of this activity.

The newly established fact that Hollis began as a journalist in China and remained an active freelance is of the greatest significance in any consideration of the possibility that he was recruited to Soviet Intelligence there. The common belief that he had quickly secured a post with B.A.T., and might even have gone there having already been appointed, led to the reasonable question:'Why would the Soviets have any interest in a young Englishman working for a tobacco company?' The question becomes irrelevant in view of Hollis's journalistic interests and connections. Not only did these bring him into contact with communist recruiters, as described, but at that time both the G.R.U. and K.G.B. were making a point of recruiting journalists. Sorge, Smedley, Sonia, Ozaki Hotsumi and several highly suspect Americans in Shanghai were journalists. So were Philby, Burgess, and others in Britain. Journalists are a sound investment because they tend to secure access to important people, who do not always guard their tongues, and because the nature of their work provides an excellent cover for any clandestine activities.

If Hollis was recruited, his B.A.T. position would have been helpful in improving contacts. It is known, for instance, that he was friendly with several young diplomats both in Peking and Shanghai.[29] His B.A.T. work would also have been useful in any courier tasks he was asked to perform as it regularly gave him a reason for moving about in China, with all expenses paid. His letters, together with some evidence supplied by B.A.T. show him to have been in Peking, Chungking, Hankow and Dairen as well as Shanghai, where he was certainly based in 1932.

Even with MI5's limited knowledge of Hollis's activities in China – for, as will be seen, the efforts made in that direction were feeble – the officers who investigated him were in little doubt that Smedley or one of her entourage would have tried to recruit him on ideological grounds, which have always been preferred by Soviet Intelligence as being more reliable and more durable.

Confessions by proven Soviet spies confirm that the recruitment procedure is well established. A target like Hollis would be asked by a communist friend, such as Ewert, Smedley or Sonia, to work on behalf of 'peace', a Soviet euphemism for subversion. Having agreed to do that he would have been passed to a professional controller, like Sonia in her later days, or someone like Ewert, who as both a friend and a recruiter could have served both purposes. The recruit would then be told that the work would not only be secret but dangerous, exciting factors which increased the appeal for many young people. He might be told that he would be working for the Comintern to encourage the rule of the proletariat throughout the world, bringing peace and goodwill everywhere. Only later, sometimes much later, when irretrievably committed, would he learn that his real master was the Soviet Intelligence Service. One of the controller's first tasks was to secure some form of written, preferably handwritten, commitment through which the recruit could be blackmailed later, if necessary. This could be a receipt for a small payment as expenses or for a token gift.

A senior C.I.A. source, who seems convinced that Hollis was recruited in China, has referred to the presence there of a known and particularly brutal Soviet recruiter who was active then, suggesting that Hollis might have been put under pressure through sexual blackmail or bribery. Hollis was certainly susceptible to women, but sex seems an unlikely lever with Hollis, save for the possibility that it could have brought him into closer contact with a recruiter like Agnes Smedley or Sonia. If Hollis arrived in China almost penniless, as he alleged, and then had to scratch a living mainly as a freelance journalist for a year he might have been open to bribery, but all the signs from his subsequent behaviour suggest that, if he was recruited, it was as an ideological spy.

Whatever method might have been used he would have been warned, if recruited, to keep away from the Communist Party and not to display any overt affiliations, but to present a right-wing image. It is also crucial to appreciate that if Hollis was recruited by any of his known or likely pro-Soviet friends in China it would have been to the service of the Fourth Bureau of the Red Army, the G.R.U., and not to the organization which became the K.G.B.

To Soviet recruiters Hollis would not have been any less of a candidate than Blunt who, in 1934, looked like spending his life as an academic. The Soviet practice was to recruit as widely as possible and then to insinuate those with qualifications into positions where they would have access to information. Sonia herself had no particular attributes, apart from unflinching loyalty to the Party, and when she attended an espionage course in Moscow she found the other recruits were unqualified people such as a German seaman and a Czech labourer.[30] It was not, of course, by chance that Soviet Intelligence preferred to recruit foreigners as agents. If they were caught, any direct link with the Soviet Union could be denied. Hollis fits easily into the pattern of young people of little or no immediate value who were eventually to secure of little or no immediate value who were eventually to secure positions with access to secrets of the highest value. There would have been nothing unusual about such an overseas recruitment. Sonia, a German, was certainly recruited in China, as were several of the Sorge spy-ring which was to operate in Japan, while Philby was recruited in Vienna.

The improbability of Hollis being recruited as a Soviet agent, which has been greatly stressed by most of his friends, is therefore no greater than that applicable to many proven spies, while the circumstances surrounding Hollis were more conducive to recruitment.

CHAPTER FOUR

Fully Trained Agent

AN event which brought the Smedley *galère* even closer was the arrest, in June 1931, of the 'organization secretary' of the Comintern's Far East Bureau in Shanghai. He called himself Hilaire Noulens and evidence that he and his wife were Soviet agents had reached the Shanghai Municipal Police from two sources. Noulens, who had arrived in the city in 1930, first insisted that he was a Belgian engaged in straightforward trade union work and was earning his livelihood as a teacher of French and German, but he was found to have several passports and several addresses in Shanghai. The police established that he was a communist who had lived in Switzerland under the name Paul Ruegg, and that he and his wife Gertrud, also a communist, had established 'legends' there supporting their claim to be Swiss citizens. A search of Noulens' apartment revealed three large boxes containing the accounts of the Comintern's Far East Bureau; this and other evidence convinced the police that he was the head of the Comintern branch in Shanghai, which was controlling pro-Soviet subversive activities in other areas of the Far East as well. It helped to fund the Chinese Communist Party, recruited students for training in Moscow, liaised with the Chinese Red Army, and operated a regular courier service to Europe.[1]

Noulens was later shown to be a Russian Jew called Luft, who had previously been on the staff of the Soviet Embassy in Vienna as an intelligence officer, while his wife was a Russian from Leningrad and had been a secretary in the Soviet Embassy in Rome.[2] Both were Soviet as well as Comintern agents. They were handed over for trial by the Chinese Government in Nanking. A communist lawyer, Dr Jean Vincent, who was later to reappear in Sonia's clandestine life, was sent from Switzerland to help defend them.

In standard Soviet pattern the prisoners lied and blustered but were unable to account for their activities or their aliases and were handed over to the military authorities for trial by court martial.[3]

The Comintern had an apparatus for defending important

members whose cover might be broken and, under the guidance of a clever European communist called Willi Muenzenberg, it was brought into action. A Noulens Defence Committee was established to secure their release and worldwide sympathy was drummed up for the two 'trade unionists'. Agnes Smedley and Sonia assisted behind the scenes but, like all others directly associated with the G.R.U., they were not permitted to be involved publicly.[4] They and other clandestine organizers did not sign the numerous petitions which appeared in issue after issue of *China Forum*, the left-wing paper produced by the American journalist Harold Isaacs.

Examination of the enormous publicity generated on behalf of the two Soviet agents manifests the extreme gullibility of the left-inclined. 'Intellectuals' in America, France, Germany, Australia and Britain lent their names to petitions demanding the release of the couple. In the British Parliament left-wing M.P.s urged intervention by the Government and asked why it condoned political conditions in the International Settlement in Shanghai which made it necessary for a trade union official to have several aliases![5]

Sonia records how she and Smedley quarrelled over who should have custody of the Noulens' five-year-old son while the parents were in prison. It seems that Smedley won, apparently because Sorge objected to any involvement by Sonia which might become overt while she was serving as a Red Army agent.[6]

After a hunger strike by the accused, the case came to trial and they were sentenced to death, which was quickly commuted to life imprisonment. Later they were released. For many years it was believed that the Chinese authorities had bowed to the international outrage and to pressure from Moscow.[7] The truth is more sordid, as the Soviet agent Otto Braun has revealed. He learned that the prisoners would be saved and eventually released only if a Chinese judge was bribed with $20,000. Moscow provided the money, which Braun took to Shanghai where he handed it to Sorge, who succeeded in bribing the judge, while sedulously avoiding public involvement with the affair.[8]

The deportation of the couple to the safety of the Soviet Union was not fortunate for them. Noulens had been a supporter of Trotsky and he was almost certainly liquidated in Stalin's purge of G.R.U. agents. As one of his former associates, Elizabeth Poretsky, has recorded, none of his friends ever heard of him again.

Hollis's name does not appear among those of Shanghai journalists who openly supported the Noulens campaign but Jack Tilton, the Shanghai Municipal Police Detective Inspector who was involved in the Noulens case claims to recall seeing Hollis lunching with Isaacs in a Shanghai restaurant at the time. Tilton was lunching there with a friend, Harry Lee, the British owner of a tobacco concern who had met Hollis through business and told Tilton who it was sitting with Isaacs.[9] Isaacs cannot remember Hollis but says that he may have known him under a different name and that if they were having lunch it would have been 'conspiratorially' and 'not to talk about golf', as he put it.[10] It is possible, or perhaps even likely, that Hollis wrote under a different name in deference to his employers, B.A.T., who may not have known of this extra-mural activity. Isaacs, who admits that he was something of a notorious character because of his political activities, concedes that if he was lunching with Hollis it is likely that the event would have been noticed by the Municipal Police because they kept him under some degree of surveillance.

In December 1932 Sorge was ordered to Moscow, where he discussed Sonia's future with the Red Army Intelligence Centre. Clearly, he gave a good report on her because shortly afterwards she was invited to visit Moscow for six months' professional training. She accepted, though this meant leaving her small son because of the danger that he might learn to speak Russian and so reveal her Soviet connections at some later date. To such a dedicated communist as Sonia even her children came second to the Party, and the boy was left with her husband's parents in Czechoslovakia.[11]

She was received with great enthusiasm and was instructed in wireless telegraphy and in the techniques of repairing and constructing 'music boxes', as radio transmitters were called then by the G.R.U. She was also taught micro-photography. She learned that she was on the regular strength of the Red Army with the rank of captain, and was to use the code-name Sonia in her future radio contacts with Moscow. As far as is known, she continued to use that code-name throughout her long career.

While in Moscow Sonia met Agnes Smedley, who was there on other business, and they resumed their friendship, though Sonia claims that she was never to meet Agnes again because after her course was completed she was posted to Mukden in Manchuria at the beginning of April 1934, being seen off from Moscow by no less a person than General Davidov of the G.R.U. Working under a new controller, whom she knew by the code-name 'Ernst' and by whom she was to have a second child, a daughter, she continued her espionage activities, paying visits to Shanghai and elsewhere.[12] Her marriage to Rolf Hamburger had already been in difficulties, perhaps because of her closeness to Sorge, for whom women were a weakness.

It is worth recording, in view of her possible relationship with Hollis, that Sonia goes out of her way to remark that it is not improper to break the rules of conspiracy occasionally by more intimate association with a fellow-agent as human relations are also important.

In Mukden Sonia secured a job as representative of an American firm of booksellers as cover for being there and for visiting Shanghai, where the firm had its Chinese headquarters. Her G.R.U. purpose was to use her transmitter to maintain contact between Moscow and Chinese partisans fighting the Japanese, who were occupying Manchuria. It could be of significance that the British American Tobacco Company and its subsidiary, the British Cigarette Company, owned a factory in Mukden. Hollis may have visited there, as it seems to have been part of his duties to visit other factories.[13] Sonia was posted to Peking in May 1935, where she could certainly have met Hollis because he was often in the capital city on business.

In the meantime, Hollis had moved about in China visiting many other cities in the course of his work. The army officer with whom he had shared a flat in Peking said that Hollis had worked as a freelance writer for the *Peking Times*, which he regarded as very anti-British, and this may have increased the interest of Arthur Ewert in Hollis.[14] Hollis's letters home show that he bought a Leica camera in Shanghai and during his trips in China he took many photographs. One letter is of particular interest because it dates a visit he paid in the latter half of 1934, to Moscow while travelling back to China on the Trans-Siberian Railway after spending the summer on leave in England. It describes how he and a schoolmaster called Tebbs, who was making the same journey, were met in Moscow by a representative of Intourist who drove them to the National Hotel in a 'very luxurious Lincoln car with a charming young lady as a guide'. Hollis told his parents that Moscow depressed him 'unutterably' and his description of it as a 'huge drab slum' has been construed as evidence that he could not possibly have been a communist.[15] In fact, such comments were common among Soviet supporters who visited Moscow at that time, and since. Even Sonia, who could never bring herself to criticize the Soviet system, described the deplorable condition of family homes in Moscow, even those belonging to high-level people.

Hollis's visit to Moscow was an event of considerable interest to those who were eventually to investigate and interrogate him about his possible recruitment to the Soviet cause. It was standard procedure for those recruited elsewhere to visit Moscow for personal appraisal and instruction, if that ever proved to be feasible, and Hollis would have needed an excuse like an Intourist trip. The records show that Ewert was in Moscow during Hollis's visit and, if they had remained in touch, it is not unlikely that Ewert may have met him. It may or may not be significant that Sonia had been in Moscow on one of her instructional visits to G.R.U. headquarters a few months previously that year.

Further letters home written from Chungking reveal that in December 1934, shortly after his twenty-ninth birthday, Hollis suffered a haemorrhage, his second, which X-ray examination revealed to be due to tuberculosis of the left lung. One of his letters stated: 'I'm now resting in the Canadian mission hospital before being shipped down river...' When the doctors decided that he needed urgent treatment he was flown to Hankow. Having recuperated in the mountains he subsequently went to Dairen for a holiday.

Hollis's prosaic letters home have been construed as denoting a typical English public school product who could not possibly have been a communist, much less a Soviet agent.[16] However, with ecclesiastical parents sheltered in a cathedral close in Somerset, it is unlikely that Hollis would have been prepared to write about such known friends as Arthur Ewert and Agnes Smedley or to proclaim any untraditional political interests. On 22 October 1935 Hollis wrote to his mother, Meg, requesting her to send him two Old Cliftonian ties because it was difficult to get decent ties in China and he was in the habit of wearing an 'OC tie almost continuously'. This has also been put forward as evidence that Hollis was so English that he could never betray his country, but Guy Burgess, whose terrible treachery is known, sported an Old Etonian tie when living in Moscow and often drew attention to it. Hollis also wrote home about golf and this, too, has been taken as denoting a solid Englishman, but Philby had been keen on cricket and, in exile in the Soviet Union, has said that one of the things he misses most is Lords!

On 28 November 1935 Hollis asked his mother for a statement about his British shares, suggesting that it would be a good idea if some of his Chinese earnings could be invested. This has been taken as a capitalistic move hardly compatible with communist leanings. There are many known communists, however, who are not averse to exploiting the system they profess to detest to their own advantage. I have been assured by a B.A.T. official that as a young employee Hollis would not have earned much and his investments must have been modest, even counting what he made from journalism.

Hollis's description of Russians in China in a further letter home as 'blousy' and 'flamboyant', wearing attenuated bathing costumes on the beach, has been construed as suggesting that he did not like them, but that is thin evidence of any attitude to the Soviet Union as a whole and his main invective was reserved for the Japanese, whom he described as 'filthy little people' who would move the British out of north China unless something was done to stop them.

Hollis told his parents that in addition to writing for Chinese papers he was doing freelance articles for *The Times* of London. He wrote to his mother, with some pride, urging her to look for an article which appeared on 14 December 1935. This was a column-length report about widespread flooding of the Yellow River, the refugee problem it created, and the privations of those made homeless. Despite a search on my behalf by *Times* staff, no record of any contribution by Hollis then or at any other time could be found in the paper's very substantial archives.[17] Hollis may have been misleading his parents in a Walter Mittyish way, as he did his friends about his half-blue for golf. The special correspondent responsible for the Yellow River report may have been one of his journalist friends for whom he may have worked as a researcher.

Hollis's career in China was cut short by a worsening of his tuberculosis. The family letters show that in June 1936, when he was in Shanghai, B.A.T. decided that he needed treatment abroad and he left China in July for ever, apparently with some regret. He returned to Britain either via the Trans-Siberian Railway and Moscow, as his MI5 colleagues believed, or via Canada, as his family maintains.

Sonia, too, left China for ever, in the second half of 1935. The man who had succeeded Sorge as head of the G.R.U. ring in Shanghai was arrested and there were fears – unfounded as it transpired – that he might name his accomplices. In addition, Sonia's husband had been given his first European leave, after five years in Shanghai, with all expenses for himself and his family paid by the Municipal Council. The G.R.U. wanted to exploit the situation and called Sonia to Moscow to give her her next espionage posting and new instructions. She explained that her parents, the Kuczynskis, had emigrated to London – which the G.R.U. almost certainly knew already – and that she wanted to see them. It suited the Centre for Sonia to reach her next post, in Poland, from Britain rather than direct from the Soviet Union so she was given permission to visit her parents, travelling by steamer from Leningrad. Though she was already pregnant by Comrade

'Ernst', her husband agreed to pretend that the child was his.[18]

They were met by her parents at London Docks and stayed with them in a smallish house at 25a Upper Park Road, off Haverstock Hill, N.W.3. Her father, Dr Robert René Kuczynski, had arrived as a political refugee and, as described more fully in Chapter 8, had been awarded a research fellowship at the London School of Economics. Also living with the Kuczynskis was Sonia's old German nanny, Olga 'Ollo' Muth, who had looked after her younger sisters and was part of the family. Early in 1936 Ollo accompanied the Hamburgers back to Poland where Rolf, Sonia's husband, had also secured a Soviet Intelligence posting, having by that time been fully recruited to the service of the G.R.U. In April of that year Sonia's daughter, Nina, by her Mukden co-spy 'Ernst' was born.[19]

In June 1937 Sonia was summoned to Moscow again for advance training at the radio school and, as the G.R.U. did not want the Polish authorities to know of her Soviet connections, she was instructed to travel by an indirect route. She travelled via London where she obtained a visa for Moscow from the Soviet Consulate on a false passport. She appears to have stayed two or three weeks in England and, while she had a legitimate excuse for visiting there because her parents were in London, her journey would have been much shorter had she travelled from Poland via Stockholm, which would have been just as safe and much cheaper. As the G.R.U. was always mean with money, some additional purpose may have been served by the London visit.[20] Hollis is believed to have been in England in June 1937 and there might have been some contact.

While in Moscow Sonia was decorated for her espionage services with the Order of the Red Banner, the highest then available to a non-Soviet citizen.[21] This must have been mainly for her work in China because she complains in her memoirs about the undemanding nature of the work in Poland, to which she returned in the autumn of 1937, leaving her cherished medal behind in Moscow as it would reveal her true work should anybody outside the U.S.S.R. ever see it.

CHAPTER FIVE

A Strange Appointment

SHORTLY after Hollis arrived back in England, and presumably while staying in the West Country, he met his future wife, Evelyn Swayne, the daughter of a well-off solicitor from Burnham-on-Sea in Somerset, not far from his home town of Wells. His former colleagues in the British American Tobacco Company recall that he was sent, at the company's expense, to a sanatorium in Switzerland, which was the usual place for the treatment of tuberculosis in those days, when effective drugs against the disease were unknown.[1] The timing and duration of this treatment is in some doubt and his surviving relatives appear to have no record or recollection of it. It might be expected that B.A.T. would have wasted no time in sending him to Switzerland, but a letter to his fiancée shows that he was in England during the winter of 1936.[2] It is possible that he went to Switzerland after his marriage in July 1937; MI5 officers who questioned him distinctly remember being told by Hollis that he went there.[3] Inquiries in Switzerland on my behalf have failed to discover any information about him, as foreign patients there for relatively short periods were not required to register and the records of the main sanatoria at Davos and Leysin appear to have been destroyed.[4]

It has also been impossible to discover whether he had left B.A.T.'s employment before his marriage. The company continued to employ him for a while after his return to England from China but regarded his health as being too delicate for regular work. The date is important to those MI5 officers still interested in the case because Sonia is known to have visited London during June and July of 1937 on what was probably a recruiting mission and, if she was sent to approach Hollis, the fact that he was out of work, in poor health and with few qualifications at a time of deep recession when jobs were scarce, even for graduates, could have significance.[6]

Hollis was certainly in England on 17 July because on that day he married Miss Swayne in Wells Cathedral, his father performing the ceremony with the assistance of his other clergyman son. About

400 guests attended the reception in the Town Hall which the local paper described as 'including many personages well known in ecclesiastical and social circles of the county'.[7] It described Hollis as 'assistant manager of the Ardath Tobacco Company'; he described himself rather more grandiosely on the marriage certificate as a 'Merchant'. The Ardath Tobacco Company, which was owned by B.A.T., was very successful in the late 1930s and it seems doubtful that Hollis would have been its assistant manager unless this was a nominal post while a decision about his future was made.[8] He may, in fact, have already left B.A.T. According to MI5 sources, and apparently confirmed by Hollis's relatives, he was employed in 'clerk-type' posts and was learning shorthand and typing. He was said to be very depressed at his failure to secure a decent job in England because, though his wife had some money, he desperately needed work. His sad situation could be of significance because bitter disappointment has often been a factor in inducing young men to rebel against the system and to feel less compunction about betraying their country. Hollis was certainly deeply disappointed at being deprived of what looked like a promising career in B.A.T.[9]

While his marriage gave him comfort, friends were soon saying that he had married the wrong girl because their natures were incompatible. The marriage was to last for thirty-one years, but only because Hollis kept it intact mainly for professional reasons, as his behaviour following his retirement showed.

In spite of his health Hollis managed to play golf and tennis, which were the family recreations at Wells, and his tennis connections were to establish his new career. Early in 1938 he was living in London and through regular appearances at a local tennis club he met an army major called 'Tiny' Meldrum. According to MI5 officers who were to investigate Hollis he told Meldrum that he was very keen to join MI5, an organization then so secret and so little known that it is surprising that he was even aware of it. Hollis's supporters, however, say that Meldrum talent-spotted Hollis for MI5, though in view of his health, this would seem doubtful. Meldrum happened to be a friend of a woman MI5 officer called Jane Sissmore (later Archer) and drew her attention to Hollis at a time when MI5 was beginning to expand to cope with the war which seemed inevitable. She decided to arrange an informal interview, using a social occasion as the excuse without revealing her identity. Meldrum invited Hollis to play tennis at Miss Sissmore's club in Ealing. She was to be the third player; the fourth was a fairly recent recruit to MI5 called Dick Goldsmith White (now Sir Dick). White, who had joined MI5 in 1936, believed he had been invited because he had been a near contemporary of Hollis at Oxford, though he had never met him. Being an athlete in training, White, who won a blue as a miler in his first year, was never a 'bottle man' and was not interested in the rumbustious company which Hollis kept.[10]

At first sight Miss Sissmore and White were not impressed. Hollis was shy and distinctly frail physically. They were aware that he had by no means recovered from his tuberculosis. They knew of his poor record at Oxford, where his failure to take his degree was hardly evidence of the patient application needed for security work. Nevertheless, White thought that there was something 'gritty and hard-headed' about him and he and Miss Sissmore decided to recommend him for further consideration.[11] Hollis was interviewed by an MI5 board which rejected him but suggested that in view of his foreign experience he might try the Secret Intelligence Service (MI6). He duly applied in writing and was rejected, ostensibly on the grounds that his health was not reliable enough for service abroad, an essential requirement for an agency which operates mainly overseas.[12]

When questioned by both MI5 and MI6 Hollis did not divulge his past association with communists such as Cockburn at Oxford or, more importantly, his more recent connection with Smedley, Ewert and others in China, though a document dated 19 January 1937 shows that MI5 was interested in Smedley's subversive activities and those of her friends.[13] He could, perhaps, have presented his former friendship with Ewert, in particular, as useful experience of communism but chose to remain silent about it.[14] There was no positive vetting of candidates then. Had any special search into his background been attempted, there could have been easy consultation with the Shanghai authorities. Files were still being kept on almost every resident of the International Settlement there and particularly on those consorting with Smedley and her communist entourage.[15] Instead, the fact that Hollis had been a public schoolboy and Oxford undergraduate with a father who was a bishop was taken as sufficient evidence of his loyalty and integrity.

The MI6 recruitment board's rejection of Hollis was also influenced by his lack of a university degree and his deficiency in languages. Hollis had no facility with foreign languages and never acquired any. Such rebuffs would have disenchanted most candidates but Hollis persisted to an extent which would now arouse suspicion. On his behalf Miss Sissmore and White pressed the MI5 chief, Sir Vernon Kell, to take him on.[16] When the staff had been as small as twenty-five officers, Kell had insisted on interviewing every potential recruit, but in 1938 the service was expanding too rapidly for this to be practicable so he agreed to the recruitment of Hollis provided that Miss Sissmore would take responsibility for him, which she agreed to do. It remains strange that MI5 should have taken on such a frail young man knowing that he was not fully recovered from tuberculosis, a highly infectious disease, to work in a post for which he had no vocational qualifications. His unsuitability for work abroad was also a disadvantage to MI5, which had many overseas commitments in those days.

It has been suggested that Hollis owed his success in entering MI5 and his later promotions to being a Freemason, which the same sources believe he joined in Shanghai.[17] Kell seems to have been a Mason but there is no evidence that he met Hollis before his recruitment, and there is no firm evidence that Hollis was a Mason; his close relatives and friends say that he was not.

It has also been suggested to me that Hollis's wife knew Miss Sissmore and assisted in her husband's recruitment, but Meldrum's great stress on the candidate's 'highly honourable and stable family background' probably carried greater weight. Whatever the reasons for his acceptance, if Hollis was a Soviet agent then he had achieved the top priority target set by his recruiters.

I have been unable to establish the precise date when Hollis joined MI5 but an existing letter shows that he was in by July 1938; the date of entry probably lies between March and July.[18] There were no regular terms and conditions of service and no pension rights then. Sir Dick White recalls that Hollis was worried about the low pay and says that he might not have accepted the job had he not been so poorly off, but another MI5 source insists that Hollis often expressed his relief at getting into MI5, not only because it meant regular employment, but it enabled him to dispense with the shorthand and typing lessons. This latter view accords with a letter which Hollis wrote to his mother-in-law in July 1938: 'Married for one year... a crazy year, dragged from place to place but these days are over now for this job is really splendid and I'm enjoying it enormously.' The reference to 'dragged from place to place' may refer to his tuberculosis treatment, in which case his sojourn in Switzerland could be dated as after his marriage.[19]

Those who knew Hollis professionally soon after he had joined MI5 describe him as shy, reserved, colourless and withdrawn. One woman who spent several years in the organization during the war recalled him as 'unutterably dull and unmemorable. I could hardly put a face to him now.' She laughed derisively when I told her of his 'wine, women and golf' image at Oxford, exclaiming, 'What! That shrinking violet!' This impression has been confirmed to me by others. One woman who served Hollis as an occasional secretary during his early days describes him as 'dull, unimaginative and, perhaps, too stupid to have been a spy'. Another believes that in the early years of his marriage he was sexually repressed and that this had something to do with his buttoned-up nature. In fact, the character change when he entered MI5 may simply have been the product of maturity and responsibility, but it could also be attributed to instruction in the self-effacing requirements of the 'conspiratorial life' described by both Sonia and Alexander Rado, who ran the famous 'Lucy Ring' in Switzerland, in their memoirs.

The reputation for being apolitical to the point of ignorance, which Hollis had left with his Oxford contemporaries, could no longer be true, though he may have continued to give a similar impression. He could not have been familiar with people like Smedley and Ewert and have witnessed the events in Shanghai and elsewhere in China without becoming well informed about the nature and aims of pro-Soviet communism. So it cannot be justifiably pleaded that any blame he bore for MI5's failure to detect the operations of Soviet agents was the result of his naivety about Soviet intentions or about the means which the Kremlin was prepared to adopt to achieve them. According to contemporaries in MI5 Hollis was soon giving the impression of being a serious and knowledgeable student of Marxism and international communism, though he had not volunteered any such knowledge before he was recruited.[20]

CHAPTER SIX

The Dangerous Dr Kuczynski

In the context of Hollis's entry into MI5 it should be appreciated that if he was a spy there was no safer place to be. A study of the known cases of Philby, Blunt, Burgess, Cairncross and others who were deep inside the secret services shows that they could not have been better placed to avoid and escape serious suspicion. As a built-in bonus for any spy there was, and probably still is, an enormous reluctance on the part of the senior managements of MI5 and MI6 to begin to consider that any of their colleagues, senior or junior, could possibly have infiltrated their organizations or have been recruited since joining them. When evidence of a double agent's activities arose or threatened to arise he was poised to neutralize it. Undue nosiness in seeking additional information through the unauthorized perusal of files or the questioning of colleagues could be excused as zeal, and repeatedly was. Habits which would appear suspicious could be passed off to close relatives, friends and colleagues as being in line of the peculiar duty. The event most dangerous to a spy, the sudden appearance of a defector from the G.R.U. or K.G.B., could be neutralized either by ensuring the defector's elimination before arrival by a timely warning to Moscow or by undermining his credibility if he did arrive.

Through internal knowledge of the organization and its counter-espionage methods, and especially of its weaknesses in that direction, an insider knew which paths were the safest to tread. Through his experience he was best fitted to resist interrogation if subjected to it and knew enough about the legal weaknesses to realize that he had the right to refuse interrogation, a step likely to result in his dismissal but nothing worse.

In the nature of things, the higher an agent rose in the organization and the more trusted he became the less likely was he to become suspect and the more likely was evidence against him to be ignored.

Hollis was to reach the summit.

The headquarters of MI5 was in Thames House, Millbank, when Hollis joined the service, but in 1939 it moved to 57 St James's Street. By virtue of being on the permanent staff, Hollis was classed as a professional, in contrast to those recruited later for wartime service, but, like many others, he had no professional training for the work and simply learned as he went along. If he worked at first for Miss Sissmore, which seems to have been the arrangement when he was taken on, it would have been in connection with Soviet counter-espionage in what was then B Division. He was soon transferred, however, to that part of F Division responsible for overseeing communists, where, according to Sir Dick White, he was to become the accepted authority on international communism, a strange coincidence in view of his connections with important international communists in China and his failure to mention them during his recruitment.

As Hollis was to remain in what is usually referred to as Section F throughout the war and to be appointed acting head of it in 1940 with the rank of Assistant Director, it is of the utmost importance in any consideration of MI5's operations against Soviet agents that his responsibilities in that direction should be properly established. It has been widely accepted in the past that he was responsible only for overseeing the subversive activities of members of the British Communist Party and this has led to a gross misunderstanding of the true requirements with which his superiors charged him.

I have established, with difficulty but beyond question in view of the sources, that Hollis was also responsible for the investigation of Comintern and other pro-Soviet activities in the United Kingdom. Further, with B Division's counter-espionage activities being concentrated against the Germans and their allies, Hollis's area of responsibility also included the activities of Soviet spies. This has been confirmed to me by former MI5 officers. When the Radio Security Service intercepted messages which appeared to originate with illegal Soviet agents operating in Britain, they passed them to Hollis.[1] There are also confirmatory statements by Philby and Blunt. In his book, *My Silent War*, Philby, referring to the time when he was head of Soviet counter-espionage in MI6, states: 'My opposite number in MI5 was Roger Hollis, the head of its section investigating Soviet and Communist affairs.' Blunt, in his statement to *The Times* after his public exposure, said in answer to the question 'Was MI5 concerned about Soviet activity in Britain?' that '...there was a section technically looking after Soviet activities and the Communist Party...'[2]

To appreciate what was required of Hollis and his section in these capacities it is necessary to examine the true nature and strength of the Soviet and communist threats, which were virtually the same because of the total subservience to Moscow of the British communists and of members of foreign communist parties sheltering in Britain.

In 1938, when Hollis entered MI5, the United Kingdom was the main target of Soviet Intelligence operations in Western Europe and by 1939 there was an effective illegal radio-transmission network operating there.[3] Germany became the main target once the Soviet Union had been attacked, but by then Britain had been infiltrated by many German and Czech communists, some of whom were professional Soviet Intelligence agents who had entered the country as political or Jewish refugees, or both. Among the last, one of the most dangerous and most successful was Dr Juergen Kuczynski, Sonia's elder brother, some of whose nefarious espionage activities have been admitted in his memoirs and in those of his sister.

Kuczynski, who was born in Germany in 1904, had joined the German Communist Party (K.P.D.) in 1930 and visited the U.S.S.R. in the same year. He was soon recruited to the G.R.U., through friendship with a Soviet G.R.U. officer in Berlin called Bessonov, and in the second half of 1936 he was posted to Britain. His cynical cover was that of being anti-fascist on two counts, being Jewish and a communist, but his purpose, in Moscow's eyes, was to further the Soviet cause rather than oppose Nazism. He was to do that by feeding back information in the economic field, which was his academic speciality, by assisting other spies and agents in the military and scientific fields, and by organizing communist German exiles so that, after the Nazis had been overthrown, they would return to Germany and help to convert it into a communist satellite of the Soviet Union.[4]

About 50,000 German refugees found asylum in Britain before the Second World War and the great majority consisted of Jews escaping racial persecution. Some 700 were political refugees, and of these about 400 were members of the K.P.D., while about 160 belonged to the German Social Democratic Party, which was also on Hitler's 'hit list'.[5] Juergen Kuczynski stood at the summit of the communist group and while functioning in secret as a G.R.U. agent, as did several of his comrades, he was overtly involved in most of the K.P.D's activities. In London he was among the founders of the Free German League of Culture, a centre for German refugees with the prime purpose of securing new adherents to the pro-Soviet communist cause. Its club house was in Upper Park Road, N.W.3, near the home of Juergen and Sonia's parents, and Juergen's wife, Marguerite, also an ardent communist, was the librarian there. Until the fall of France, Kuczynski frequently visited Paris for conspiratorial discussions with Gerhardt Eisler, the notorious agent who had been in Shanghai, and others based there. In August 1939 he was prominent at a conference of Communist Party delegates in London and through organizations like the Left Book Club he fostered relations with the British Communist Party.[6]

Most of the German communists found work in Britain, but Kuczynski, like others among the political leaders, were helped financially by the British Communist Party and by Quaker organizations.[7] This left him free to organize communist groups in Birmingham, Manchester, Liverpool and Glasgow. He was friendly with British communists such as Hollis's university friend Claud Cockburn who, Kuczynski recalls, 'knew thousands of diplomatic secrets'. After the German occupation of France had forced the Comintern agents out of Paris, Kuczynski lived in the same small London hotel as Gerhardt Eisler and his wife, better known as Hilda Massing, a Soviet agent in her own right. In recalling these clandestine associations Kuczynski underlines the importance of the 'rules of conspiracy'. He certainly needed to observe them for, as another Soviet spy posing as a German refugee was later to confess, Kuczynski was regarded as the head of the underground section of the K.P.D. in England.[8]

I stress the activities of Juergen Kuczynski at this point to show that it is extremely unlikely that Hollis, being responsible for overseeing communist and Comintern agents, could have been unaware of them. There is documentary evidence to show that Hollis's section was aware of the subversive activities of several of Kuczynski's equally dangerous German comrades, like Hans Kahle, Wilhelm Koenen, Heinz Schmidt, Eva Kolmer and Karl Kreibich, who were working for Moscow against British interests long before the Soviet Union entered the war. Their names are in a 'List of Foreign Communists Considered Dangerous' supplied by MI5 to the U.S. Embassy in London in December 1940.[9] Some were interned in the general round-up of aliens, but when they were released little or nothing was done to curb their activities.

The history of internments provides further evidence that Hollis should have been aware of Kuczynski and his anti-British activities. As spies might have been infiltrated among people seeking asylum, the Home Office decided that the credentials of all enemy aliens should be examined with a view to interning those who might be dangerous. With assistance from the records of MI5 and Special Branch, the German-speaking refugees were grouped into three categories. Most, who were non-political and considered friendly to the British cause, were in Category C, while some 7,000 who were believed to be anti-fascist but politically active were in Category B. A hard core of about 600 were graded Category A because they were regarded as security risks dangerous to the state. They included some suspected of being Nazis but also many communists likely to put the interests of the Soviet Union before those of Britain.[10]

Kuczynski was among those listed as dangerous and, after appearing before a tribunal on 20 January 1940, he was interned in a camp in Devon. He must have been regarded as a particular risk because this was well before the mass internment of Germans consequent on the fall of France in May 1940 and the expected invasion of Britain. He would normally have been moved to a safer camp in Canada or Australia, as some of his comrades were, but persistent representations by the pro-communist lawyer D.N.Pritt and other agitators secured his release after three months and he immediately returned to active propaganda and espionage,[11] becoming President of the German-Soviet Friendship Society. Indeed, he records that he was active inside the camp in Devon, recruiting to the communist cause, and delayed his release for an extra three days so that he could hand over his pro-Soviet work to another internee. He was never re-interned, in spite of his constant subversion. If MI5 was consulted concerning his release, the record of its reaction could be informative, especially if its advice derived from Hollis's section.

After his release Kuczynski was quickly in touch with the Soviet Ambassador. He became friendly with Anatoli Gromov, otherwise known as 'Henry', a Soviet Intelligence officer posing as a diplomat in the Soviet Embassy.[12] Gromov, who visited Kuczynski's home, was actively controlling Maclean, Philby, Burgess and the rest of the Cambridge Ring of spies and should have been under some degree of surveillance by MI5, though there is no evidence that he ever was. Kuczynski was, in fact, an active G.R.U. agent throughout the war yet never seems to have been subject to any interference by MI5 or anybody else once he had been freed from internment.

Dr Anthony Glees, who has examined most, and possibly all, of the MI5 documents concerning wartime German exiles which have so far been made available, has noted that the Kuczynskis, who were probably the most important among the communists, are never mentioned.[13] This omission suggests the possibility of a protective hand inside MI5. The origin of any references to such communists would have been Hollis's Section F and, probably, Hollis himself.

Kuczynski and the rest of the German communists who were

Soviet agents had almost all been recruited into the G.R.U. Simultaneously there was an active K.G.B. network, the best known section of which was the Cambridge Ring. Philby, Maclean, Burgess, Blunt and the rest had all been ostensibly recruited into the Comintern and then been taken over by Soviet Intelligence before Hollis entered MI5 but, as they continued to serve the Soviet interest throughout the war, they clearly fell into his sphere of responsibility. Again, there is no evidence that anything was ever done by Hollis or anyone else in the secret services to interfere with their activities or cause them the slightest concern.

Admittedly, Hollis was no less perceptive than anyone else in the secret services in his failure to suspect or detect the treachery of the Cambridge Ring. So, perhaps, in fairness, it should be asked if the attitude to communists in general, before the Soviet Union was unexpectedly forced into the war in 1941, was such as to make it reasonable that he should have failed to take notice even of the overt activities of people like Kuczynski.

I was myself a student in the 1930s at London University where communist agitators and propagandists were probably more active than at Cambridge, and where pro-communist rallies and demonstrations were everyday events. Later, in Liverpool, I witnessed the communist propaganda on behalf of the International Brigade in the Spanish Civil War and recall the differing accounts of Stalin's purges and show-trials of his former comrades in the general Press and the pro-Soviet *Daily Worker*. I find it impossible to believe than a person like Hollis, who had been perceptive enough to make a living as a journalist, could have failed to appreciate that Stalin's Soviet Union was a dictatorship based on terror and every bit as dangerous to democratic freedom as Hitler's Germany. Only those totally committed to the patently absurd Stalinist ideology could continue to blind themselves to the truth. It is of course, possible that Hollis was one of these, as was his MI5 colleague Blunt, and his counterpart in MI6, Philby. In addition to his background experience of communism in action in China, Hollis had the professional appreciations of the true situation in the Soviet Union fed into MI5 from the Foreign Office, MI6 and elsewhere. So, unless he was completely blinkered by ideological adherence, he must have known the full nature of the Soviet threat to establish communist régimes wherever possible, and he must have appreciated that the communists in Britain, both home-grown and imported, as well as the professional Soviet spies who were, inevitably, active, were working to that end. In Hollis's case in particular, the excuse of ignorance of the extent and nature of the threat, which he was supposed to counter, cannot be pleaded.

There remains the question of whether, being aware of the threat, he ever had the resources at his command to counter it in any effective way. Hollis's section was small, as was the whole of MI5 when he joined it, and the manpower under his command when he became head of Section F was nowhere near large enough to deal with the threat adequately. There was a sub-section responsible for running the agents intruded into the Communist Party, and there were field officers like the MI5 agent-runner Maxwell Knight, who were attached to other sections and fed in information from their agents and sub-agents.[14] Hollis also had regular reports from the Metropolitan Police Special Branch which, at that stage and since, did much of the leg-work in maintaining surveillance over subversives and suspects. Like any other section, Hollis's had access to ancillary departments of MI5, such as the watcher service, which undertakes surveillance, and the technical services, which provide electronic and other forms of non-human surveillance, but as the German threat mounted such access inevitably became more limited. Nevertheless, Hollis's achievement against the pro-Soviet communist threat was appallingly meagre, even after all allowances are made for his second-priority position. The activities of the pro-Soviet German communist refugees have now been heavily documented in various German bibliographical encyclopaedias and they show that the counter-espionage effort against them was so ineffective as to have been negligible. That the effort against British spies who had been recruited by the Soviet Union was equally negative is beyond question. That stricture will be seen to apply, with even more suspicious force, to Sonia when she became British at a later date.

Is it possible that Hollis and his section were efficient and that some higher authority nullified his efforts through lack of interest or for some other reason? Such an argument applies to Philby's subordinates in MI6, but Hollis was quickly made acting head of his section and there is no evidence to suggest that anyone at higher level in MI5 was stifling his efforts. They may, of course, have been stifled at the political level, but before the U.S.S.R. was forced into the war in June 1941, Churchill, who was aware of the extent to which the Soviet Union was helping Germany to beat the naval blockade with supplies of oil, grain and other materials, expressed concern at the danger of Soviet subversion in Britain. During Chamberlain's premiership there was certainly deep suspicion of Soviet motives, even in the normally credulous Foreign Office, as the diaries of Sir Alexander Cadogan, the chief official there, clearly show.[15] It would be reasonable to suppose, therefore, that the political leaders expected MI5 to make an effective effort against the pro-Soviet threat and that Hollis's superiors would have been keen to please their political masters.

I cannot believe that before the Nazi-Soviet pact the British Government was turning a blind eye to MI5 evidence about Soviet espionage and subversion simply to avoid offending Stalin in the hope that he might make a non-aggression pact with Britain. Nor can I believe that it did so after the Nazi-Soviet pact was signed in the hope of encouraging Stalin to repudiate it.

Early in September 1939, Cadogan received a secret telegram from Washington which gave the first lead to a Soviet spy who had been operating in Britain for several years and may have provided Hollis with his first experience of an espionage case resulting in a trial.[16] The spy was a Captain John King, a cipher clerk in the Communications Department. He was put under surveillance, arrested, and the following month he was tried in camera because Britain was then at war. He pleaded guilty and was sentenced to ten years' imprisonment. He confessed to having been recruited, while serving in Geneva, by a Dutchman operating as an 'illegal' Soviet agent. In his diary, Cadogan reveals that the Foreign Office had been aware of leaks over the past few years but had been unable to trace the culprit. King had been exposed only because a defector from Soviet Intelligence, being interrogated in Washington, had revealed his name. This situation, in which a damaging spy was to be exposed only through chance information provided by a defector or an intercept, was to be repeated again and again throughout Hollis's twenty-seven years in MI5.

The defector who exposed King and gave leads to other British spies was a Polish Jew who called himself Walter Krivitsky but whose real name was Ghinsburg. He had been recruited to the Fourth Bureau of the Red Army (G.R.U.) in 1924, had been transferred to the K.G.B. in 1934, and had defected in October 1937 believing, correctly, that unless he did so he would be killed in Stalin's paranoid purge of non-Russians 'plotting against him'. Though never holding the rank of general, as has been claimed, Krivitsky had been virtually West European Inspector-General for both Soviet espionage agencies and his knowledge was so vast that when he defected in Paris the information he divulged to French security, in return for protection, filled eighty large volumes, which were stored with other documents in a barge on the Seine. The French did not share the information, even with an ally in wartime, and according to French officials the documents were all lost because the bottom of the barge rotted away. It seems more likely, however, in view of the known penetration of the French secret

51

services by Soviet agents, that this was an excuse to cover the deliberate destruction of the records.[17]

In January 1940, after being based in the U.S. and in Canada, Krivitsky was invited by MI5 to visit London under the pseudonym Walter Thomas. In the course of an interrogaion, mainly by Miss Sissmore, spread over three weeks, he revealed that Soviet Intelligence was receiving information from several British sources but claimed that he did not know their names. He described one as a young aristocrat who had been educated at Eton and Oxford, had gone into the Foreign Office in 1936 or 1937 and had then been able to hand over copies of the minutes of the 'Imperial Council' to the Soviets. This was identified as the Committee of Imperial Defence. He also mentioned a British journalist who had been sent to Spain to spy for the K.G.B. during the Spanish Civil War, and also to France. He said that a White Russian called von Petrov, who was known to have been working for the British secret service, had really been a Soviet agent of the G.R.U. and had been particularly valuable because he had a wonderful source inside the secret service (MI6) who fed him with information for the Russians.[18]

It is now certain that the journalist was Philby and the secret serviceman spying for von Petrov was Charles Howard Ellis. The identity of the young aristocrat remains in doubt. It almost certainly was not Donald Maclean, though he was already spying then for the Soviet Union in the German section of the Foreign Office. Another defector, the diplomat Alexander Orlov, independently confirmed that complete sets of the minutes of the Committee of Imperial Defence were available to Moscow, but Maclean never saw complete sets.[19] However, Krivitsky may have known about Maclean. According to an American lawyer, a former Ukrainian called Isaac Don Levine who assisted Krivitsky in writing his memoirs, the defector described a young spy in the Foreign Office who had a Scottish name and bohemian habits.[20]

All this information was, presumably, passed to Hollis's section as well as to other people in MI5, but nothing of any consequence was done about the leads.

I have spoken to a Mrs Beryl Edwards who knew the Krivitskys well. She recalled that he had been very depressed after his visit to MI5 and had said: 'They just didn't want to listen.'[21] The failure to follow up Krivitsky's leads has been a matter of adverse comment by many authors and has been dismissed by the authorities as facile criticism based on hindsight, but the von Petrov lead, which was clear-cut, should surely have been pursued; the general reluctance was to be repeated with other defectors.

The least that Krivitsky's evidence, and especially his exposure of King, should have done was to alert MI5, and Hollis in particular because of his specific responsibilities, to the persistent effort being made by Soviet Intelligence to penetrate the secret departments of Whitehall. There is little evidence that it had any such effect.

It has been suggested to me that if Hollis had been recruited as a G.R.U. spy Krivitsky would have known about him and would have exposed him, but the dates show that to be incorrect. Krivitsky would not have known about an agent recruited in China and he had defected before Hollis could have been of any interest to any European spy-ring. Sonia, the only European spy operator likely to have known anything about Hollis, did not know Krivitsky.

As he had predicted might happen, Krivitsky died violently, in Washington in February 1941, in what is generally believed to have been a K.G.B. assassination. I have established that following a further study of his report to MI5 and of his later statements to an American committee of inquiry, it had been intended to ask him back to London for more intense interrogation or, failing that, to send an MI5 officer to see him.[22] He was also due to give further evidence to the American committee. It is possible that the timing of his death was associated with these intentions; Donald Maclean has been accused of 'signing Krivitsky's death warrant' by informing the K.G.B. of the threat to himself if the defector was questioned again. It seems unlikely, however, that Maclean would have known about Krivitsky's movements and the information to Moscow may have originated from another source with closer access. Any spy inside MI5 at any time could be guaranteed to take every practicable step to neutralize any defector and his evidence as a matter of routine self-protection.

CHAPTER SEVEN

Swiss Interlude

IN June 1938, around the time that Hollis was entering MI5, Sonia, who was still based in Poland, was ordered to Moscow to prepare for another assignment, but before going there she made a further visit to England, taking the two children there with their nanny Ollo and leaving them in accommodation which she found, or was found for her, in Felpham, near Bognor in Sussex. While in Moscow during August it was decided that she should go to Switzerland to set up a new G.R.U. network because the old one had been destroyed in Stalin's purges. Her main intelligence target was to be Germany and, having been promoted to major, it was decided that she should travel first to Britain, not only to pick up Ollo and the children, but to recruit some Englishmen to serve as spies in Germany under her control. She claims that her idea was to recruit former communists who had proved their loyalty by service in the International Brigade in Spain. The G.R.U. Centre was such a law unto itself that this seems unlikely, however, for how would Sonia have known where to find acceptable people on a flying visit? She certainly travelled to England, though, leaving Moscow in September and reaching London by a roundabout route to cover her Soviet connections.[1]

In London she contacted a man believed to be Fred Copeman, formerly of the International Brigade, and asked for the names of possible G.R.U. recruits to operate in Germany. Mr Copeman, who died towards the end of 1983 in his late seventies, told me that he remembered the occasion but had no documentary record of it. I sent him photographs of Sonia, and his wife Kitty, a former Treasurer of the Young Communist League, telephoned me to say that he was in no doubt that he had met her. Copeman had been in Spain until about the first week in April when he had returned to London. The first recruit whom he recommended was a Liverpudlian called Alexander Foote. This man, who was to be of some importance in Sonia's career and should have ended it ignominiously had the British security authorities been really alert, was

54

sent back from Spain, ostensibly to be present at the Communist Party Congress in Birmingham though really for the purpose of facilitating his recruitment to Soviet Intelligence.[2] By the time Foote reached England Sonia had been required to leave for Switzerland and his recruitment was eventually accomplished in October by another woman who was, almost certainly, one of Sonia's sisters.[3]

Swiss police records show that Sonia arrived in Montreux on 23 September 1938 under the name Ursula Hamburger.[4] By revealing that she was Jewish, giving her father's name and her place of birth correctly, she provided sound reasons for her presence in Switzerland.[5] According to her memoirs the Centre had agreed that her husband, Rolf, should accompany her until she had established herself. He wanted to return to China for active espionage operations there and Moscow had agreed that he should. Her record of Rolf's movements could be K.G.B. disinformation to cover his real whereabouts, for the Montreux authorities have no record of him. On the other hand, if he intended to remain in Switzerland for less than three months, he would not have needed to register. Sonia claimed that they had come direct from Shanghai which, as usual, was false.

Sonia and her family, including Ollo, stayed in a boarding house before finding a chalet at Caux, a health resort above Montreux, where she set up her clandestine radio, keeping in regular touch with Moscow. In the late autumn of 1938 Foote was instructed to travel from London to Geneva where he would be approached by a woman who would be carrying an orange in her right hand and a string bag containing a green parcel in her left, while he was to carry a leather belt.[6] The woman was Sonia, and having carefully established Foote's identity to her satisfaction, she instructed him to go to Munich, posing as a tourist, to learn to speak German and to make as many German contacts as possible. Sonia was also the paymaster for the embryo spy-ring and she gave Foote sufficient funds for his purpose. Sonia's money supply originated from an account in the Irving Bank in New York and reached her via the communist Swiss lawyer Dr Jean Vincent, whom she had met in Shanghai when he was defending the Noulens.[7]

Foote returned to Geneva, on instructions, after three months and was then told that his employers were not the Comintern, as he had believed, but Red Army Intelligence – the G.R.U. He went back to Munich and in April 1939 was visited by another Englishman, whom Sonia had met two months previously and was also to be important in her career.[8] He was a former comrade of Foote's in the Spanish Civil War and his real name was Leon ('Len') Charles

Beurton.[9] He was a British subject, born of a naturalized French father in the Romford district of London on 19 February 1914. Like Sonia, he was to use several aliases, such as John Miller and Fenton. The addition of Beurton to the Swiss network had been suggested to Sonia by Foote but his actual recruitment had been accomplished in London by her sister, Brigitte. Beurton's mission in Germany was as vague as Foote's and they achieved virtually nothing before returning to Switzerland shortly before the outbreak of war between Britain and Germany in September 1939. The two young men – Beurton was twenty-five – installed themselves in a pension in Montreux, not far from Sonia's chalet, and she continued to instruct them in codes, transmissions, the construction and repair of radio sets and other espionage skills.[10]

Sonia repeatedly told her co-conspirators that she was completely entrusted by Moscow to build up her own espionage network in Switzerland and was left to her own resources. In fact, she was under the firm control of the G.R.U. Centre, like any other agent. She was controlled by the woman who had preceded her in Switzerland, a most able spymaster called Maria Poliakova (codename 'Vera'), who had been promoted to G.R.U. headquarters in Moscow.[11] Sonia was required by standing orders to mislead her colleagues in case they were ever captured and interrogated. Sonia was also able to keep in close touch with her family, most of whom were active Soviet agents. Her father, brother and some of her sisters made visits to her in Switzerland, Rolf having left for China early in 1939.[12]

In December 1939 the G.R.U. Centre ordered Sonia to contact the leaders of another quite separate spy-ring already functioning in Switzerland. This group, later to become famous as the 'Lucy Ring', was run by a Hungarian called Alexander Rado, who was based in Geneva.[13] From then on, the two rings were ordered to work together. This move, together with the training of Foote as a radio operator and the recruitment of Beurton, was a prelude to Sonia's transfer to a much more important role in England. In preparation for this posting, which she kept secret from the other members of her ring, she began to complain, openly, about Stalin's pact with Hitler, claiming to be disenchanted with him because the pact would enable Hitler to attack in Western Europe without fear of having to fight on two fronts. In fact, it is abundantly clear from Sonia's subsequent behaviour and from her memoirs that she never wavered in her dedication to the Soviet cause, whatever the political ploys Stalin might exploit. Her faith in the Party line was unshakeable and she was one of many who could not have borne to live outside the Communist Party. Her true reaction to Stalin's pact with Hitler was probably more like that of her brother Juergen who, already being in England, handed out expensive cigars to his comrades 'to celebrate the pact which will keep the U.S.S.R. out of the war', as he records in his memoirs.

Foote was completely taken in by Sonia's claim that her faith in communism had been shattered and, once war had been declared, she reinforced her apparently spontaneous desire to leave Switzerland and to give up intelligence work by claiming to be worried about her children. Being Jewish, they could have been in grave danger if Hitler invaded Switzerland which, at that stage, seemed quite possible. In fact, as she repeatedly records with pride in her memoirs, Sonia was on active service as a Red Army major in the G.R.U. and, children or not, she knew she would have to go wherever she was posted. As she was unable to keep her eventual destination secret from her close conspiratorial colleagues, she did her best to deny them knowledge of its purpose by pretending to sever her connections with espionage. This was a sensible routine precaution in case Foote or any others of the Swiss ring should be caught and interrogated, as they were, but the lengths to which she went suggest that the Centre had particularly sensitive reasons for ensuring, as far as possible, that nobody should know that she was being posted to espionage duties in England.

Her claim that the Centre was allowing her to leave Switzerland because she was in extra danger through being Jewish was transparently false. Rado, who remained in Switzerland, and many other members of the 'Red Orchestra' operating in countries which were to be occupied by the Germans, were Jews.

To expedite her posting to Britain, Sonia had received an order from Moscow earlier in 1939 to secure British nationality, and thereby a British passport, by divorcing her husband and marrying Foote. In the line of duty, and realizing that his marriage was in hopeless disarray following the birth of Sonia's illegitimate daughter, Rolf agreed to the divorce, which became final at the end of 1939.[14] Sonia preferred to marry Len Beurton, who though seven years younger may have been having an affair with her. As he too was British, the Centre had no objections. She and Len married in Montreux on 23 February 1940, a date they chose because it was the 'birthday of the Red Army'. Immediately after her marriage Sonia applied to the British Consulate in Geneva for a passport, which she received on 2 May 1940.

Presumably Sonia appreciated the greater danger to which she was being exposed by the transfer from neutral Switzerland, which was soft on spies, to Britain. The Soviet Union was an ally of the Nazis, supplying them with the petrol, food and other materials that enabled them to withstand blockade. If, as a British subject, she was caught spying for the U.S.S.R. in England during war she faced a possible death sentence. Further, following the defeat of France and the evacuation from Dunkirk in May and June 1940, Britain seemed a more certain target than Switzerland for invasion and occupation. Irrespective of whether she knew she would enjoy some special protection in Britain, Sonia was, unquestionably, a most courageous woman. As Leopold Trepper, the 'Grand Chief' of the 'Red Orchestra', wrote in his memoirs, communists like Sonia and Sorge 'regarded themselves not as spies but as fighters in the vanguard of world revolution'.[15]

The German victories in Western Europe meant the G.R.U. spy network in Britain, which consisted largely of 'illegal' agents such as Sonia's brother, could no longer be controlled from Paris, Brussels or The Hague as it had been under the general G.R.U. preference for having its 'residents' stationed in a nearby country rather than in the target country itself. Sonia had clearly been earmarked to act as one of the couriers, paymasters and radio operators for the British network. As she admits in her memoirs, she already had money for these purposes paid into three bank accounts in London by the Moscow Centre, probably through some other British paymaster.

Before leaving for Britain, Sonia had a narrow escape from exposure and arrest which would have been to Britain's great benefit. Ollo, the diminutive, grey-haired nanny, knew that she would not be accompanying the family to England but did not want to be parted from the children, so to ensure their stay in Switzerland she denounced her mistress and Len as spies to the British Consular representative in Montreux. No notice was taken of her.[16]

The Centre did not give Sonia permission to travel to Britain until October 1940 when she applied for a visitor's permit to move to Geneva, in anticipation of leaving the country.[17] There she remained busy instructing another radio operator for the Lucy Ring and transmitting some messages herself. The Centre then decided that her new husband was not to accompany her to Britain, where he would be called up for military service, but to remain in Switzerland until further orders. As C.I.A. records show, he was to do little work there and it may be that the Centre had other reasons for wanting Sonia to begin her service in Britain without a man by her side.[18]

She left her temporary abode in Geneva with her children on 18 December 1940, travelling by bus to Barcelona, thence to Madrid and then on to Lisbon, which she reached on Christmas Eve.[19]

CHAPTER EIGHT

Target – MI5

In the summer of 1939 it had been decided that in the event of war MI5 would move from central London to Wormwood Scrubs prison in North Hammersmith, an odd choice because as the bomber flies or mis-aims it was not far removed from the centre of the metropolis. Early in 1940 a further decision was taken to evacuate the greater part of the organization from the prison to the much safer location of Blenheim Palace at Woodstock, about nine miles north of Oxford. Colonel Sir Eric St Johnston, then Chief Constable of Oxfordshire, recalled the move for me: 'We discussed certain security aspects and, in particular, the concern felt about moving the secret files. In September, when one of the first incendiary bombs fell on Wormwood Scrubs there was a sudden decision to move overnight to Woodstock. I was asked to provide twelve policemen to help move the secret files. I cannot be sure of the date but I think it would have been in the last week of September.' The date is significant.[1]

The incendiary bomb that had fallen on the prison set fire to part of the Registry, the heart of MI5 where the records were held. Fortunately, the records had already been duplicated by photography and the charred documents were also kept for reference. According to Mrs Yvonne Macpherson, who was at Blenheim for five years, and other witnesses, most of the staff were installed there by October 1940, 'from a prison to a palace', as one employee put it.[2] Mr Derek Tangye, who was an officer at Blenheim, remembers Hollis and his section as being among the first arrivals.[3]

At the time of the move Hollis had been living alone at 18 Elsham Road, W.14, between Holland Park and Kensington High Street, which had been convenient for Wormwood Scrubs. His wife, who had previously been with him, had gone to the safety of the West Country for the birth of what was to be their only child, Adrian Swayne Hollis, born on 2 August 1940. On the birth certificate Hollis gave his occupation as 'Civilian attached to the War Office Staff'. He had already been appointed acting head of

Section F, with all the responsibilities I have described, and this also made him a key member of a political sub-committee chaired by Lord Swinton, which was supposed to monitor Soviet espionage activities. The promotion had surprised some of Hollis's colleagues, especially in view of his total inability to speak or read any foreign language, particularly German, which was then in common use in Comintern communications.[4]

As acting head of Section F, which was also responsible for over-seeing British and foreign fascists – Germans, Italians, Spaniards and others who might be active in Britain – Hollis could, presumably, have switched to specializing in that area. In 1940 it would have had more direct application to the war effort and should, therefore, have offered greater chance of further promotion, but Hollis chose to remain in charge of overseeing communists and other real and potential Soviet agents.

Having vacated his London house, Hollis moved into accommodation at 29a Charlbury Road in Oxford. Number 29 was then owned by Hugh Cairns, Professor of Surgery at Balliol College, and 29a seems to have been an annexe to the house, which still exists.[5] It is not known when his wife joined him with their infant son but she eventually did so, paying frequent visits to her parents in the safety of the West Country, Oxford being a likely target for the Luftwaffe because of the nearby motor works.[6] After about a year the Hollis family moved to a house in Garford Road, which is next to Charlbury Road. They remained there until February 1943.[7]

These locations and the proximity of the MI5 out-station at Blenheim Palace would seem to be of considerable significance in view of the contemporary moves of Sonia (see map page 63).

After a three-week wait in Lisbon, following her departure from Switzerland, Sonia secured a steamship passage to Britain via Gibraltar, arriving in Liverpool early in February 1941. After a routine interrogation by immigration officials, she spent one night in a Liverpool hotel with her two children and, next day, she travelled straight to Oxford, a city with which she had no known associations.[8] Why did she go to Oxford where, as events showed, she intended to settle for the duration of the war at least?

It was assumed – all too readily – by MI5 officers who later investigated her movements that she went to Oxford because her parents were living there. Her father, Dr Robert René Kuczynski, the distinguished demographer, was believed to be attached to one of the Oxford colleges.[9] The truth is very different.

Sonia's father, who had been born in Berlin in 1876 and was of Polish–Jewish origin, was involved in radical German politics after the First World War and became a leading member of the German communists in exile. After six years at the Brookings Institution, a research organization in Washington promoting public understanding of economic and foreign policies and related issues, he entered Britain in 1933 as a political refugee and was awarded a research fellowship at the London School of Economics, becoming the first Reader in Demography there in 1938.[10] I have established that he remained in that post until August 1941, when he reached the compulsory retiring age of sixty-five.[11] The L.S.E. was evacuated to Cambridge at the outbreak of the war but Dr Kuczynski did not accompany it there and his daughter's memoirs make it clear that her parents maintained their London home. He was, however, researching a British colonial populations project, for which purpose he had reading facilities at the Rhodes Library and the Bodleian Library in Oxford.[12] From time to time, therefore, he visited Oxford for brief periods, taking advantage, as many other academics did, of some respite from the London bombing.

In October 1940 he secured accommodation in a smallish semi-detached house at 224 Headington Road, then held in the name of a Mr John Bedding.[13] From that address he wrote to a friend saying that he would be staying there only a few days, having secured more suitable occasional lodgings. These proved to be in a large Victorian house at 78 Woodstock Road to which he moved some time after 13 November, when Dr Stella Churchill, a physician and surgeon, acquired the lease.[14] Dr Kuczynski remained there, at intervals, until mid-1942, when he returned permanently to London.[15] He was certainly using a room or rooms in the house when Sonia arrived in Oxford in February 1941 but was not a regular sub-tenant, as Dr Churchill was required to list sub-tenants on her lease.[16]

Sonia claims that there was no room for her and her children with her parents 'who had squeezed in with friends', but 78 Woodstock Road is so large that it is now student accommodation for St Hugh's College.

Juergen Kuczynski published a detailed biography of his father in 1957 and made no mention of any post or stay in Oxford.[17] Nor is there any such mention in his own memoirs or in the German biographical dictionaries which record Dr René Kuczynski's career in considerable detail. His obituary notice in *The Times*, which was written by his daughter Brigitte, traces his academic career and does not mention Oxford.[18] My inquiries at the colleges where he was most likely to have worked have all produced negative results. Academic acquaintances of his, one of whom was at Oxford himself during the war, cannot recall any connection between Dr Kuczynski and any Oxford college.[19] Sonia herself records that he spent most of his time in London because she travelled there twice a month to speak with him, not only for family reasons but 'conspiratorially'. Dr Kuczynski knew what Sonia was doing and did all he could to help her by giving her confidential information from high-level friends such as Sir Stafford Cripps, the Labour politician. As she records, she passed it on to the G.R.U. Centre in Moscow.

It would seem to be more than coincidence that the Moscow Centre delayed its instructions to Sonia to start arrangements for her move from Switzerland to Oxford until the very month, October 1940, that her father had secured his *pied-à-terre* in Oxford and his cover for being there. His presence then gave Sonia her own cover for being in Oxford if she was ever questioned about that, which she never was. In view of the undoubted fact that Juergen Kuczynski and his father already had G.R.U. connections and, as Sonia herself was in touch with her family by letter from Switzerland, her parents must have known of her intention to move to Oxford and her father may well have been instructed to be there to assist with money as well as with parental welcome.

Sonia had certainly not chosen Oxford because her parents were living there, as MI5 itself has assumed. What, then, was her real reason for going there rather than anywhere else in Britain? Unwittingly, she answers the question herself in her memoirs by stating, in a reference to her husband's eventual departure from Switzerland, that like herself, he received instructions from headquarters – the Centre – to move to England. She confirms it, more forcibly, by revealing that she was a regular officer in the Red Army with the rank of major, later to be colonel. No serving officer of any army decides where he or she will live. When Sonia left Shanghai she was posted to Mukden and then ordered to move to Peking. She was assigned to Warsaw – not just anywhere she chose in Poland – and then ordered to move to Danzig.[20] She was posted to the Lausanne area of Switzerland – not to any place of her choice in that country. And, in view of her subsequent behaviour, she was posted to Oxford. The 'legend' with which she deluded her Swiss replacement, Alexander Foote – that she was giving up espionage to live in the safety of England – is disposed of by Sonia herself in her account of her immediate resumption of Soviet intelligence work and her continuation of it throughout the war and afterwards. Her account of her arrival in Oxford because her parents were living there is part of that legend, which the G.R.U. authorities wished to preserve in the interests of her real activities there. Those activities must have been important to warrant the posting of such an experienced officer, who had already earned the high distinction

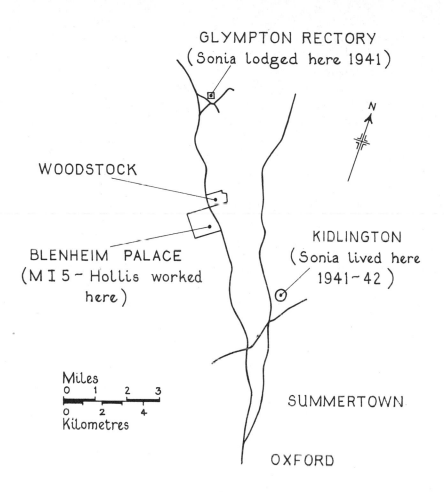

GLYMPTON RECTORY
(Sonia lodged here 1941)

N

WOODSTOCK

KIDLINGTON
(Sonia lived here
1941-42)

BLENHEIM PALACE
(M I 5 – Hollis worked
here)

Miles
0 1   2   3

0   2   4
Kilometres

SUMMERTOWN

OXFORD

of the Order of the Red Banner, and would be awarded another.[21]

In furtherance of her legend, Sonia tries to convince her readers, probably on instructions from Soviet officials who vetted her book, that she was given *carte blanche* to go to Oxford to recruit a completely new network of spies, but as already mentioned this would have been totally out of character for the G.R.U. Centre, which always insisted on controlling its agents in fine detail. Sonia knew little about Britain and nothing about the Oxford area. Further, she had been forbidden by Moscow, for conspiratorial safety, to approach the Communist Party or any overt British communists who might have assisted her in securing recruits. She eventually met several German communists who were spying for the Soviet Union, but they already had effective arrangements for transmitting their information to Moscow and, as none of them was a major spy, it is unlikely that an agent-runner as experienced as

63

Sonia would have been uprooted from Switzerland just to assist them. It is also known now, from some of her radio traffic which has been identified, that she was transmitting substantial amounts of material to Moscow soon after her arrival in the Oxford area, making it nearly certain that she either had advance knowledge of how to contact a productive source or that she was quickly given it.[22]

Sonia records that she had great difficulty in finding lodgings in Oxford and had to place her children in boarding school, though this may really have been a move to give her greater freedom of action while she was making her preparations. The first address where she found proper accommodation for herself – 'Glympton Rectory, near Woodstock', as she describes it – is intriguing in the extreme, as I have already pointed out, and offers an indication of her likely mission in the Oxford area. Woodstock is a small town adjacent to Blenheim Palace, where the major part of MI5, including the section headed by Hollis, had been evacuated. It is stretching belief in coincidence rather far to accept that Sonia, a highly professional G.R.U. agent, posted to the area for a specific purpose, happened to have MI5 on her doorstep purely by chance. I have established that the rector of Glympton, the late Reverend Charles Cox, did take in such refugees in 1941, but regrettably the visitors' book no longer exists.[23]

The probability is that Sonia's target was some MI5 officer who had already been recruited. Could this have been Anthony Blunt who is known to have been spying for the Soviet Union at that time? There are three compelling reasons why it could not. First, Blunt was based in London throughout the war, visiting Blenheim only occasionally. Secondly, Blunt was always an agent of the K.G.B., not the G.R.U., to which Sonia belonged. Thirdly, Blunt's controllers when Sonia was active in the Oxford area have been positively identified through information which he provided, and on other grounds could not have included Sonia.[24] They were all men, K.G.B. officers with 'legal' status, posing as diplomats in the Soviet Embassy in London and able to use the Embassy's radio transmitting facilities. It would have made no sense to have a controller based in and around Oxford to service such a productive spy as Blunt in London, especially when Sonia had no motor car. On the other hand, to service a spy working in or near Oxford, an 'illegal' operator like Sonia with her own transmitter, made excellent sense, and several counter-espionage officers have told me that it would have been standard practice for the G.R.U. to have used an 'illegal' in such circumstances. A 'legal' controller based in London at the Embassy would have needed to make frequent visits to Oxford, not always easy during the war and likely to arouse suspicion.

If it is accepted as likely that her target was MI5 – Bletchley, the only alternative target of note, was too remote for someone with no transport – it follows that the spy she was servicing had been recruited by the G.R.U., for in the early 1940s the two Soviet intelligence agencies operated so independently that no G.R.U. officer would have been permitted to run a K.G.B. spy. Again, it seems oddly coincidental that if Hollis, who was living in Oxford and commuting to Blenheim, had been recruited to the Soviet service either in China or later through his Chinese connections, it would have been by the G.R.U. because all the known recruiters he may have met were involved with the G.R.U.

Sonia remained a paying guest of the rector of Glympton for only a few weeks, but that would have been long enough for her to have established contact with her target and, as she herself records, to build a radio transmitter.[25] The haste with which she built a transmitter in her bedroom at Glympton, which was not without the risk of discovery, suggests that she knew she would have information to transmit and does not accord with her story that she had to build up her own network of contacts. When an 'illegal' agent is establishing cover in a new country every precaution is taken, usually over many months, to avoid arousing suspicion, but Sonia's behaviour showed a sense of urgency suggesting that she knew that important secret material would soon be in her hands.

In order to be able to transmit she needed privacy and a place where she could construct an aerial in safety. She found this in April, after only a few weeks at Glympton, in the form of a furnished bungalow in Kidlington, which she describes as a 'suburb' four kilometres from Oxford. It was, in fact, half way between Blenheim Palace and Oxford (see map p.63) and ideally placed for servicing a spy inside MI5, especially one who could call at a convenient dead-letter box on the way home from Oxford by car. Sonia recalls how, being alone, she had to climb on to the bungalow roof to fix up a radio aerial for her transmissions to Moscow. She claims that Moscow did not contact her until May 1941, but some of her earliest traffic was picked up and recorded by a foreign intelligence service and when MI5 was able to secure this, many years later, it left no doubt that she had begun to transmit in April at the latest.[26]

Before leaving Switzerland she had been instructed on how to meet a senior G.R.U. officer whom she would need to contact on occasion when in possession of documents which needed to be transported to Moscow rather than transmitted. After a number of abortive attempts she made contact with the man. She was to know him only as 'Sergei'; his name was Simon Kremer, a secretary to the Military (G.R.U.) Attaché at the Soviet Embassy in London.[27] His espionage activities have been confirmed by the decipherment of G.R.U. traffic between himself and Moscow, but only long after he had returned to the Soviet Union. Kremer supplied Sonia with ample funds and she quickly had enough important information to use her transmitter twice a week.

Once she had secured a permanent home for herself her cover was secure, for she could pose as a British housewife and mother waiting for her British husband to return from Switzerland, where he had been delayed because of the sudden outbreak of war. Her British nationality made her immune to possible internment and as long as she obeyed the conspiratorial rules and her transmissions went undetected she could look forward to a long spell of constructive effort for her beloved Soviet Union. Her hundreds of transmissions did indeed go undetected by British counter-intelligence, or at least appeared to do so, and in view of that it is necessary to consider her transmitting methods and the hazards she faced, or should have faced.

CHAPTER NINE

A British Bonus for Soviet Spies

SONIA gives some details of her transmitting and receiving methods in her memoirs, but greater insight into the system used by the G.R.U. during the war is provided by Alexander Foote in his *Handbook for Spies*, first published in 1949. As he had been taught by Sonia, and both were operating as 'illegals' at relatively equal distances from the Centre in Moscow, it is reasonable to assume that their methods were broadly the same. It is certain, from what both reveal, that the system was bilateral. Sonia not only transmitted to Moscow but received messages in reply. Such a system should be easier to detect than the alternative blind system in which the Centre replied later by a coded signal sent over Moscow radio or by some other concealed device.

On average, Sonia transmitted twice a week at prearranged times so that the Centre would be listening, and in the small hours of the night so that local interference with the radio sets of nearby residents, which might have aroused suspicion, would be minimal. Using a hand morse key, with which she was an above-average performer, she first sent out her call sign which probably consisted of three letters – Foote's, for example, was FRX – repeated. The Centre then acknowledged receipt by sending its call sign for Sonia, Foote's being NDA. In addition the Centre would give some indication, using a number, of the strength with which the signal was being received. These call signs were varied according to a prearranged plan in Sonia's possession. Once communication had been established on a certain wavelength, both Sonia and the Centre then switched to a different wavelength for the transmission of her messages to reduce the risk that it might be monitored.[1]

Sonia sent all her messages in a cipher which she had brought with her from Switzerland or had been supplied to her by 'Sergei' in Britain. By the time she called Moscow she would have enciphered her messages and would get them off as rapidly as possible. This encipherment might take several hours, depending on the amount of material.

Whatever the method of encipherment which Sonia used it was certainly very safe. In addition to her regular transmissions she would have been required to listen for her call sign on other days in case the Centre needed to contact her, and there would also have been days when the Centre listened for her in case she had urgent information. Such a bilateral system ensures the maximum receipt of information from both sides and the minimum time on the air, but if it is being monitored by counter-intelligence it is not only more detectable than a blind system but more likely to lead to the location of the agent.

In the spring of 1941, when Sonia started her regular transmission from the Oxford area – of which there is no doubt – an organization called the Radio Security Service (R.S.S.) had the responsibility for detecting, monitoring and locating such clandestine transmitters. This service, which was part of a section of MI5 called MI8c, was centred on Hanslope Park in Buckinghamshire, about thirty-five miles from Oxford. It had listening stations at strategic points and the services of about 1,500 amateur radio operators, known as Voluntary Interceptors, working in their homes. Foreign transmissions which might be of interest were recorded by hand, as there were no magnetic tapes then, and passed to Bletchley Park for possible deciphering.[2]

The R.S.S. was able to work out the nationality of the traffic and its likely destination by processes collectively called 'discrimination'. When relevant, Bletchley Park fed back any deciphered material to the R.S.S. to assist it in tracking down further messages. Bletchley dealt with MI5 and MI6 directly, but there was also direct liaison between the R.S.S. and MI5 and MI6 concerning traffic which was believed to be Soviet and illegal, in other words, not emanating from the Soviet Embassy or a consulate but from a possible spy. A former officer who was very senior in the R.S.S. has told me that such coded messages, which had not been deciphered, were passed personally to Hollis in MI5, as head of the section responsible for Soviet counter-espionage. After 1944, when Philby became responsible for Soviet counter-espionage in MI6, they also went to him personally.[3] The R.S.S. then waited for instructions from MI5 or MI6 if they felt there was any need to locate the source of the illegal traffic.[4] For that purpose the R.S.S. had mobile detector vans which could be sent out to pinpoint the transmitter by taking bearings, a process called radio-goniometry.

The decision as to whether the R.S.S. should take further action was taken by a committee, and the advice of Hollis and Philby regarding illegal Soviet traffic would have been commanding. If the decision was negative or there was no response at all the R.S.S did not send out vans or attempt any other direction-finding on its own initiative.

I have been assured by R.S.S officers that Sonia's messages must almost surely have been recorded at some stage and that the traffic analysts to whom they should have been passed would have had no difficulty in realizing that they were intended for the G.R.U. Centre in Moscow and that it was replying. Yet Sonia escaped without detection for at least six years, and according to my evidence for eight. Why?

My senior R.S.S. informant well remembers giving details of illegal Soviet traffic to Hollis and that it was not received with much enthusiasm.[5] When he inquired about the results and whether any further action was needed he was told that it had proved impossible to break the cipher, implying that further action would be not worth while. He remembers receiving similar responses from Philby. My informant is certain that because of MI5 and MI6's close collaboration and proximity, once Hollis had returned to London from Blenheim they would have made a joint decision, so the circumstances offer an obvious explanation of Sonia's immunity from detection.

The lack of enthusiasm on Hollis's part caused no surprise at Hanslope Park but was rather welcome because by the time that Sonia had arrived in England the 'phoncy' war had been terminated by the Blitzkrieg on France and the Low Countries and Britain awaited invasion by Germany. The R.S.S., like Bletchley Park, was therefore concentrating its efforts on German radio traffic and the detection of any German agents already operating in Britain or trying to enter. On 22 June 1941, the day Germany attacked the Soviet Union, this policy was reinforced by a decision which presented Sonia and every other Soviet agent with an incredible bonus and gave Hollis further reason for ignoring any Soviet traffic drawn to his attention by the R.S.S.

When Churchill decided that the Soviets should be treated as allies, in spite of their previous assistance to the Nazis, a group called the Y Board, consisting of the Chief of the Secret Intelligence Service (MI6) and the Directors of Intelligence of the Navy, Army and R.A.F., ruled that all deciphering of coded Soviet signals should cease for the duration of the war.[6] As Professor F.H. Hinsley puts it in his official history, *British Intelligence in the Second World War,* 'all work on Russian codes and ciphers was stopped from 22 June 1941...'[7]

The importance of this event to the ease with which Soviet agents, both British and foreign, were able to continue their espionage and subversion activities throughout the war, and probably for a year or two afterwards, does not seem to have been appreciated before. There may even have been a touching belief in certain areas, including MI6, that as the Soviets were allies, however reluctantly, they would desist from any clandestine operations against British interest. As the activities of Sonia, Fuchs, the Cambridge Ring and a host of other Soviet agents were to show, nothing could have been further from the truth.

I have been unable to discover if the Soviets were officially told of this decision as a gesture of friendship but they must soon have learned of it from their spies in MI6, MI5 and the Government Code and Cipher School, the forerunner of G.C.H.Q., at Bletchley. Whether agents like Sonia ever learned of it may never be known. It is unlikely that Moscow would have informed them of this gratuitous contribution to their safety for it might have induced them to ignore the conspiratorial procedures by which it set such store. And there is no certainty that the G.R.U. and K.G.B. chiefs would have believed the Y Board's decision, as, to them, it must have seemed incredible. It continues to be incredible to some academics like Professor Bradley Smith, the eminent American historian, who do not believe that the decision was really taken or, if taken, observed.[8] Professor Hinsley, however, has assured me that it was and this has been confirmed by Sir Dick White, who held an important position in the relevant branch of MI5 at the time.[9]

With Winston Churchill's well-known distrust of the Kremlin it might be wondered why he agreed with the Y Board's decision. There appears to be no record that he was ever told of it, though the MI6 chief or one of the Service chiefs may have mentioned it to him verbally.[10]

The decision clearly applied to Soviet Intelligence messages passing between Moscow and the 'legal' controllers of agents operating in Britain from the Soviet Embassy. It must, therefore, have been a major contribution to the charmed life enjoyed by Philby, Blunt, Maclean, Burgess and others who were serviced that way. In the case of Philby and Blunt, who almost certainly knew of the decision through their work, it may help to explain why they were able to operate with little fear of exposure.

Hollis in MI5 and later Philby in MI6, as the officers responsible, could also interpret it as applying to messages transmitted to and from 'illegal' Soviet agents like Sonia so that they too received a major degree of protection.

While the R.S.S. became, understandably, less inclined to pursue Russians', to quote an informant, following the Y Board's edict, there was no ban on the recording of Soviet traffic which seemed illegal, and it was in fact continued, though on a reduced scale.[11] As a result, some Soviet traffic, which may have included some of Sonia's, was passed from time to time to Hollis for decipherment then or later, as already indicated. If Hollis was a spy he was in a position to stifle work on intercepts which might contain information that he had provided to Sonia, just as Philby stifled information threatening his own situation in MI6. Since it is certain that Philby was a Soviet agent throughout the war, an examination of MI5 and MI6 records might reveal the degree of collusion between Hollis and Philby on the action taken about Soviet intercepts in general. Indeed, the whole professional relationship between Hollis and Philby would seem to merit more detailed examination than has been devoted to it. Their offices in London were very close, Hollis's at 57 St James's Street and Philby's in Ryder Street, as were the clubs in Pall Mall where they sometimes lunched. It would also have been convenient for them to have met at their homes when Philby moved into Carlyle Square in Chelsea.

As a result of the activities of the R.S.S. many thousands of Soviet messages were recorded during the war and passed to MI5, MI6, and to Foreign Office establishments, and should have been available for possible decipherment when the war was over and a backtrack became necessary as the Soviet Union replaced Germany as the main future adversary. A major source has told me that much of this material was destroyed round about the time that it was due to be handed over, or was actually handed over, to G.C.H.Q., probably in 1946. No work was done on the remainder for many years because of the influence of Philby in MI6 and Hollis and Mitchell in MI5. These three recommended that the intercepts should be kept on a 'care and maintenance basis', meaning that they would be stored but that no work would be done on them on the grounds that the decoders would be better occupied on other activities. Serious decipherment of what remained of this wartime traffic was not begun until 1960, as will be described later.[12]

Philby and Hollis could have been responsible for the destruction of Soviet intercepts in their possession, but who would have ordered the destruction of material once it had reached G.C.H.Q., if it ever did? A knowledgeable informant who was working in G.C.H.Q. at the time has told me that such a decision could have been taken only 'from some exalted position in MI5 or MI6' and that G.C.H.Q. would never have initiated it because it was trying to develop the maximum amount of information about Soviet codes and ciphers as soon as the war ended.[13]

Fortunately, the American authorities did not take such a

trustful view of the Soviets and many thousands of clandestine messages between the U.S. and Moscow were recorded, some of them becoming decipherable, as described in Chapter 18. The extent to which these deciphered messages contributed to the exposure of wartime Soviet spies like Fuchs, Maclean and the Rosenbergs underlines what might have been lost as a result of the Y Board's decision and its consequences.

Whatever the details of what happened in Whitehall, the German attack on the Soviet Union on 22 June 1941 had immediate effects of the greatest advantage to the pro-Soviet agents operating in Britain. Apart from the major bonus of the ban on decipherment, there appears to have been a complacent assumption all round that as the Soviet Union had become an ally, subversive activities on the Soviets' behalf were of little account. Hollis's responsibilities were not formally changed but the priority accorded to his work must, inevitably, have been diminished. As for the agents themselves, Blunt is on record in MI5 as having said that he and his fellow-spies 'felt better' about their continuing treachery once the Soviet Union was in the war.[14] They could have taken heart that, if caught, they could claim that they were only assisting an ally to defeat Hitler, which was the secret services' main objective. Indeed, to those spies operating inside the secret services the whole 'climate' of security would seem to have changed, though a specialist like Hollis should have remained aware that any diminution in Soviet subversion, if it occurred at all, would be temporary. In fact, as will be seen, there was no diminution and Sonia was to be the recipient of technical information of such importance that it could not be transmitted by radio but had to be handed in to the Soviet Embassy for onward passage to Moscow in the diplomatic pouch which, once the U.S.S.R. had become an ally, was not subject to search. On one of these visits to 'Sergei' she was given an advanced miniature transmitter to replace the cumbersome one she had built herself at Glympton Rectory.[15]

Sonia's relatives gave her good reason for visiting London when she needed to: 'When in London I stayed with my parents,' she writes, referring to a period quite early in 1941, which is further evidence that their stay in Oxford had been short. Both her father and Juergen knew that she was a G.R.U. agent and served her as sources when they could, though they had other outlets for their information. No doubt she told them the disturbing news she had received from the G.R.U. Centre concerning her husband Rolf. He had been arrested for espionage in Chungking where he and 'Ernst', the father of her daughter, had moved, being unable to operate their transmitter safely from Shanghai. According to Sonia,

Rolf was sentenced to death but was eventually released as the Noulens had been, perhaps after the provision of a bribe.[16]

In the flush of enthusiasm to help the Soviets resist the German onslaught the British Intelligence chiefs decided to form a liaison link with the N.K.V.D., the forerunner of the K.G.B. The task was allotted to the Special Operations Executive (S.O.E.) which had been set up in the previous year to subject the Germans to sabotage and subversion in the occupied territories. In August 1941 a liaison mission was sent to Moscow with the cover-name 'Sam', under the leadership of Brigadier George Hill, a former MI6 officer who spoke fluent Russian. The selection of Hill was extraordinary because the Soviets knew that he had been involved with another spy, Sidney Reilly, in an abortive effort to assassinate members of the Bolshevik Committee after the Russian Revolution. Nevertheless, an N.K.V.D. officer was assigned to London, but while Britain seems to have given considerable intelligence assistance to the Kremlin, little was received in return. The Soviets demanded everything and offered nothing, and by the end of 1941 the British Government was protesting at the highest diplomatic level about the obstructiveness of the Soviet authorities. They were unwilling to exchange even technical intelligence about captured German equipment.[17] Alexander Foote related how one of his colleagues in Switzerland secured documents and plans which would have been of great value to the British as well as to the Russians but were so bulky that their contents could not be transmitted by radio. It was suggested that the material should be handed to the British through a secure cut-out, but the Centre ordered that the documents should be burned immediately.[18]

Pursuing its own interests with almost unrelieved selfishness, Moscow suggested that the R.A.F. should be used to drop selected N.K.V.D. agents by parachute to work behind the German lines for espionage and sabotage purposes.[19] The British agreed and several agents were brought to Britain by submarine and dropped into occupied Europe. Best known of these was Wilhelm Kruyt, who was dropped into Belgium in June 1942, and his son John, who was dropped into Holland. Their main purpose was to bolster branches of the G.R.U. 'Red Orchestra', which was working against British interests as well as those of Nazi Germany. As the C.I.A. handbook on the 'Red Orchestra' states, 'The British High Command may not have been aware of Kruyt's true role.' A later variation of this operation was to involve Sonia, her brother Juergen, and probably Hollis in a way which does little credit to British security, however relaxed the 'climate' may have become.[20]

In the autumn of 1942 Sonia was required to vacate her

bungalow in Kidlington and found a larger, unfurnished cottage in Oxford itself. This suited her better because the tempo of her radio transmissions was increasing. The cottage, at 50a George Street in the Summertown district of Oxford, used to be a coachman's dwelling belonging to an elegant Regency house called The Avenue at 302 Woodstock Road. The house was occupied by Neville Laski, a judge who, together with his wife, was very active in the Jewish community and especially in the assistance of refugees. The location of Avenue Cottage, in which Sonia remained for three years, is shown on the map on page 85. It was approximately one mile from Hollis's home in a residential area covering about thirty square miles and this, again, is rather difficult to accept as sheer coincidence.[21]

Neville Laski's daughter, Mrs Pamela Anderson, who remembers Sonia well as Mrs Beurton, thinks it almost certain that she heard of the cottage through her mother, who was the daughter of a rabbi, or through some agency concerned with Jewish refugees which her mother was running. Mr and Mrs Laski may have been friendly with Sonia's father, who was working at the London School of Economics with Neville's brother, Professor Harold Laski, the left-wing socialist, and lodged at intervals at 78 Woodstock Road. Mrs Anderson has no recollection of this but points out that the house was always full of visitors from London and elsewhere. Neville Laski may also have been friendly with Hollis during their simultaneous residence in Oxford. Both had been educated at Clifton College and were keen members of the Old Cliftonian Society.[22] Mr Harry Edwards, the current secretary of the Old Cliftonian Society and an ex-master of the school, told one of my researchers that Laski was a very active member of the Old Cliftonians and made it his business to keep in touch with those living in his area. If Hollis visited Laski's home he could well have run into Sonia socially because, as Mrs Anderson recalls, 'Mrs Beurton, who called herself Ruth, managed to insinuate herself into my mother's friendship. I always disliked her and I had a row with her.' Mrs Anderson also remembers a request by Sonia to her mother for permission to string her aerial from the cottage to one of the sheds in the Laskis' large garden. 'I am not a bit surprised to find that my suspicions of Mrs Beurton have turned out to be justified,' she told me.[23]

Her suspicions were indeed justified. By that time Sonia's husband, Len, had secured Moscow's permission to return to Britain and, from July 1942, was with his wife in George Street for a year before being called up for military service. Their transmitter was concealed in a cavity in a stone wall surrounding the Laski property and was taken out for regular transmissions of what Sonia describes as 'large quantities of top-secret material of a military, technical and political nature provided by a number of English sources, some quite high-level'.[24]

Sonia records that she acquired a bicycle which she used extensively for her clandestine meetings with the spies supplying her with information. This is a highly significant piece of information, confirmed by Mrs Anderson, because it means that such spies were being serviced locally, either through meetings or through messages left in hiding places. Sonia records that in 1942 and 1943 her clandestine meetings — '*treffs*', as she calls them — became more numerous and to keep her nocturnal transmissions secret from her children, who were becoming curious, she lodged them in boarding school again.[25]

Mrs Anderson made a further intriguing suggestion during a conversation with me and I record it in case harder evidence ever accrues: 'I believe that Mrs Beurton used to attend some of the parties put on at Woodstock by the MI5 staff, of whom many were women.' She recalled that Sonia had a lot of male visitors which surprised her because she did not find Mrs Beurton very attractive, either in appearance or manner. These took place when her husband, whom she remembers as being 'very good-looking and rather nice', was away serving in the Coldstream Guards. In the context of her possible attendance at parties it could be relevant to record that Sonia refers in her memoirs to being fond of dancing.

To summarize, I contend, from the circumstances already described, that there can be little, if any, doubt that Sonia was deliberately sent to Oxford by the G.R.U. to serve at least one important agent who was based in that area and for whom an 'illegal' courier with an independent radio transmitter to Moscow, and great skill in using it, was essential. This is supported by the fact that Sonia was of German origin, because such 'illegals' were almost always non-Soviets to limit the risk of direct connections with the Soviet Union if they were caught. Further, the agent concerned must have been recruited by the G.R.U. and not the K.G.B. The target would seem to have been in MI5 at Blenheim Palace and the timing of Sonia's final order to move from Switzerland to Oxford, together with the preliminary arrangements for it, suggest that the G.R.U. Centre in Moscow knew of the impending Blenheim move. In that case they could have been informed of it by a spy inside MI5 who, then being based in London, was presumably being serviced there. It would seem to be more than coincidence that in October 1940, MI5 moved to Blenheim, Sonia was ordered to arrange to move from Switzerland to Oxford and Sonia's father secured lodgings in Oxford with a professional reason for being there.

The transfer of Sonia would have been in line with Soviet practice if, as I contend, she was already acquainted with a spy inside MI5. When Donald Maclean knew that he was to be posted to Washington he informed his controller, the K.G.B. diplomat who called himself Anatoli Gromov. Gromov was then switched to the Soviet Embassy in Washington so that he could continue to service such an established source.[26] The transfer of Alger Hiss to the U.S. State Department coincided with the arrival in America of Boris Bykov to direct the unit of Soviet military intelligence being run by Whittaker Chambers.[27]

On the evidence so far adduced the likeliest candidate for an MI5 spy serviced by Sonia in Oxford is Roger Hollis.

CHAPTER TEN

In Post at Blenheim Palace

WHILE the MI5 Registry and some of the officers were housed inside Blenheim, most of the accommodation was anything but palatial and Hollis's office was in a Nissen hut in the grounds.[1] Soon after his arrival MI5 was asked for a secret list of the foreign communists residing in Britain who were considered to be dangerous security risks because of their allegiance to the Soviet Union. The request had come from the U.S. Embassy in London, where the Immigration Department had received warnings from a Briton who had been dealing with communist refugees that some who were no longer anti-Hitler, following their approval of the Nazi-Soviet pact, might apply to enter the U.S. A letter, declassified from 'Secret' by the U.S. authorities in July 1983, shows that the request for the list was sent to Guy Liddell, then head of B Division responsible for counter-espionage. Liddell's reply, dated 26 December 1940, included a list of foreign communists whom, to quote Liddell, 'we do consider to be dangerous'.[2]

The MI5 department responsible for overseeing the dangerous activities of all such communists was Section F, headed by Hollis, and there can be little doubt that it sent the list on to Liddell. The list contained only twenty names and they all appear to have been Germans, including some Sudeten Germans from Czechoslovakia. At least three had become well known to the security authorities through their public pursuit of pro-Soviet interests – Heinz Schmidt, Wilhelm Koenen and Hans Kahle. As published documents have shown, these men, and some of the others, were Soviet espionage agents.[3] Several of them had openly associated with Juergen Kuczynski and had been interned, as he had, as dangerous security risks. Kuczynski, however, was noticeably absent from the list though he had been released from internment only nine months previously and had lost no time in resuming his pro-Soviet activities. The fact that he had been released from internment under the pressure of communist propaganda should not have influenced MI5, had it really been alert, particularly as most, if not all, of those on the list were also to be released .[4]

Evidence presented by Dr Anthony Glees in his informative book *Exile Politics During the Second World War* shows that MI5 had to make some effort to oversee the activities of German communists sheltering in Britain if only to satisfy the requirements of the Foreign Office which needed reports on them from time to time. Hollis's section was involved in the production of a dossier about the attitude of left-wing German exile groups towards the question of uniting themselves. In a second attempt MI5's inquiries appeared to support the view that the communists, of whom there were about 300 known in London, were taking over the leadership of the German anti-Nazi exiles. As regards the German Social Democrats (the S.P.D.) MI5 'could not convey the significance which the party had possessed and was determined to possess again'. Dr Glees suggests that information favourable to the Social Democrats may have been suppressed by Philby and others attached to the Foreign Office, or in it, who wished the German communists to prosper.[5] It is also possible that such information was withheld by people with similar interests in MI5.

At Blenheim, Section F remained small and Hollis was extremely fortunate in being promoted to the rank of Assistant Director after only two years' experience and with his health still in doubt.[6] His position as acting head of the section was to be of some significance in view of information which was to reach MI5 later.

The speed of Hollis's promotion throughout his career continued to be a subject for comment among his colleagues, who attributed it mainly to the influence of Dick White. It was not the result of any display of insight or leadership on Hollis's part, nor to general popularity because most of his colleagues known to me regarded him as shy and dull or disliked him as being suspicious and shifty. One who watched him over many years described him as 'terribly self-effacing – the sort of man who would hide behind a mushroom. He had little to say and it was difficult to hear what he did say.' Derek Tangye, who knew him well at Blenheim, found him 'austere, remote. I did not think him very bright.'[7] Colonel Sir Eric St Johnston, who knew Hollis at Blenheim and later at Curzon Street, described him as 'stooping, rather lop-sided with a permanent half-smile and no aura of leadership whatever'.[8] Colonel 'Tar' Robertson, godfather to Hollis's son, was more complimentary in describing him as 'very round-shouldered', while Mrs Betty Morris, another Blenheim contemporary who later knew Hollis socially, called him 'shrunken and always looking older than his years'.[9] As already mentioned, from an early age Hollis suffered from a progressive spinal problem which may have been associated with his tuberculosis. His friend Commander Courtney, who once accompanied him on a trip to the East German border, described him as 'dark and stooping so that you might almost have thought he had a slight hump-back', while other later contemporaries, like John Drew and Colonel Noel Wild, referred to him as 'a hunchback'.[10]

Apart from Sir Dick White I found one wartime contemporary who is said to have admired Hollis – Sir Roger Fulford, the writer who had been with him at Worcester College, but my efforts to secure an appraisal produced only a brief letter stating that he would 'be ashamed to write anything that was disloyal to him'.[11]

Hollis was essentially a desk operator, the field work being carrried out by officers who were running penetration agents. The most productive of these, and the one about whom most is known, was Maxwell Knight, who was a distinguished naturalist and broadcaster. Knight, who used the code-letter 'M', from which his friend Ian Fleming may have derived his initial for James Bond's chief, operated in secrecy and considerable independence from a flat in Dolphin Square, which meant that his agents and assistants did not have to visit headquarters. One of these assistants, Miss Joan Miller (now Phipps), has told me of Knight's relationship with Hollis before and during the war.[12]

The results of Knight's efforts in discovering evidence of suspicious activity by communists eventually filtered to Hollis, and both Knight and Miss Miller found that very rarely was anything done about it. 'Once a report ended up on Hollis's desk that was usually the end of it,' she told me. Knight was deeply concerned rightly as it proved – with the activities of agents of the Comintern whom he believed to be operating in Britain not just against Germany but on behalf of the Soviet Union. He submitted a two-page report to Hollis entitled 'The Comintern Is Not Dead'. Miss Miller typed it out and she remembers that it recommended a course of action against suspected Comintern agents. Hollis rejected the report as being 'exaggerated' and took no known action on its suggestions. Miss Miller dates the report as having been submitted to Hollis in 1942. There may have been personal reasons why he was opposed to any hunt for Comintern agents, especially those of German origin, when Sonia, who was one of those who should have been on his list of suspects, was operating round the corner from his home. Knight repeatedly voiced his belief that MI5 itself had been penetrated by Soviet Intelligence agents but no effective notice was taken.[13]

After Miss Miller married in 1943 she left MI5 and took a job in another secret department located in Bush House in the Strand.

Her job was to read incoming telegrams and ensure that they were passed to the relevant departments. She noticed that an army major was copying some of the telegrams and reported the fact to her old colleague, Knight. An inquiry showed that the contents of some of the telegrams had been leaking to communist sources, but when Hollis was told of the situation he was prepared to do no more than have the major transferred, without any interrogation, to a post in Germany.[14]

Miss Miller remembers Hollis, at that stage, as being 'withdrawn, dull, uninspiring and already quite hunched'. While compiling a book in the late 1970s about her experiences, Miss Miller claims that she had concluded that he must have been a Soviet agent.[15] This was before I had revealed the official suspicions concerning Hollis, about which she had heard nothing. Miss Miller's view is currently held by at least two other women who worked with Hollis at Blenheim, though I have been unable to establish when they reached that opinion.[16]

Whatever the truth about Hollis's loyalty there is no escaping the fact that the efforts of his department against Soviet espionage during the war were lamentably ineffective. The Cambridge Ring operated by the K.G.B. is now known to have been more numerous than the original Ring of Five, with many ancillary supporters, and there were other K.G.B. spies and agents whose activities were never seriously hindered. Prominent among these was Philby's estranged Austrian wife, Lizi. After travelling back to Vienna to bring her Jewish parents to the safety of London, she lived in London, or close by, throughout the war, cohabiting with a German communist called Georg Honigmann.[17] Both were open communists and Lizi served for some time as a courier between Burgess, Blunt and the Soviet Embassy.[18] MI5, and Hollis's section in particular, seem to have had no knowledge of this or even of Lizi's relationship with Philby.

There is still much to be learned about the G.R.U. network in Britain, as the large C.I.A. handbook on its general activities indicates. Sonia is listed as a member, but there is little else. The C.I.A. may have been limited by objections from MI5 against further publicity, as the British security authorities have complete power of veto regarding the release of information concerning British security affairs, even when the U.S. Freedom of Information Act is invoked. But my inquiries suggest that the G.R.U. has been able to conceal most of its wartime work in the U.K. because MI5 discovered so little about it. Dark hints that MI5 had splendid triumphs against Sonia and other G.R.U. operators which must remain concealed for ever have no substance in fact.

CHAPTER ELEVEN

A Dubok in a Graveyard

SOME time late in 1942 or possibly early in 1943 a Red Army cipher clerk called Lieutenant Igor Gouzenko, then in his early twenties, was on the night shift in the Moscow headquarters of the G.R.U. on Krapoykinskaya Boulevard. The cipher room of the Special Communications Division was located in half of the ballroom on the second floor of a palace, which had formerly belonged to a millionaire called Riabushinsky, the other half being used as the office of the Chief of Main Intelligence. Beneath a ceiling decorated with nymphs and flowers were rows of tables where cipher clerks, most of whom had junior officer rank, were busy throughout the night with coded dispatches from the various fronts and with information from intelligence agents.[1]

Gouzenko, a short, stocky, fair-haired student of architecture who had been drafted into the Red Army and then selected for training in the deciphering of secret telegrams, shared a table with a pre-war friend, Lieutenant Lubimov. To further the security of valuable spies it was strictly forbidden for one officer to share any information about his work with another, but because the work tended to be so boringly routine, Gouzenko and Lubimov somtimes did so. Gouzenko, who was later to defect and impressed Western security authorities with his powers of detailed recall, told me on more than one occasion what happened on a particular night when Lubimov was handed a telegram from a G.R.U. source in England: 'Lubimov leaned towards me and said: "This is material from a spy working for us inside MI5. He has the code-name 'Elli' and he is so important that he must never be contacted personally but only through *duboks*." A *dubok* is the G.R.U. name for a hiding-place – what you call a dead-letter box. Lubimov then passed the deciphered telegram to me. I read it and saw the name "Elli" in it with my own eyes. I cannot remember all the contents of the telegram and they might not have meant much to me as I never handled "Elli" messages, but Lubimov went on to tell me about the spy. He said that the favourite *dubok* was a split between the stones of a certain grave. The name on the headstone was Brown.'[2]

As various authorities, apart from Gouzenko himself, have confirmed, all *duboks* suggested for use by Soviet agents and agent-runners must first be approved by Moscow and the fact that the details had been sent to the G.R.U. Centre indicated that the agent-runner or courier supplying them was a G.R.U. person and that 'Elli' was a G.R.U. recruit.[3] At that time the G.R.U. tended to use 'illegal' agent-runners and couriers for servicing spies as well placed and as valuable as 'Elli', rather than using officials with diplomatic status. And they tended to be non-Soviets, a precaution which limited the diplomatic damage if they were caught. It was essential for the Centre to know all the details of a *dubok* in the case of a lone 'illegal' so that somebody else could be sent to empty it in the event of illness or an accident. To leave a package in a *dubok* for any unnecessary length of time could endanger the spy because somebody might find it accidentally and hand it to the police. A 'legal' agent operating inside the Soviet Embassy could always make local arrangements for such an emergency without involving Moscow.

Gouzenko went on to tell me: 'Lubimov also said that "Elli" had something Russian in his background but this could have meant no more than that he had visited Russia, had a wife with some Russian relative or had a job to do with Russia. There is not the slightest doubt in my mind that there was a Soviet agent inside MI5 during the period 1942–43 and probably later on.'[4]

According to an informant eventually concerned with investigations into the identity of 'Elli', Lubimov had also told Gouzenko that the spy was able to bring out MI5 files about Soviet Intelligence officers serving in London so that those officers could see exactly how much MI5 knew about them.[5] In 1942/43 those files were located in the Registry at Blenheim Palace, so the person with ready access to them must have been based there or have been a regular visitor. As will be seen, no visitor fits the requirement and if 'Elli' was located in Blenheim the odds are that the G.R.U. agent who serviced him would be lodged not far away, particularly in wartime when petrol was rationed and transport services, especially those from London, were subject to disruption from bombing.

As will be established more fully in Chapter 14, the person who best fits the known information about 'Elli' is, unquestionably, Hollis. He had regular and authorized access to the files mentioned by Gouzenko. He had been to the Soviet Union at least once and at the time when Gouzenko saw the 'Elli' telegram he was in charge of anti-communist and anti-Soviet security. He also had previous associations with Soviet agents such as Arthur Ewert, which would have been reported back to Moscow and be on record there. His known and likely associates in China were all linked with the G.R.U.

The person who best fits the requirements for the agent-runner who serviced 'Elli' is unquestionably Sonia. She is a self-confessed G.R.U. agent-runner and clandestine radio operator working throughout the war in the Oxford area close to Blenheim. When Gouzenko saw the 'Elli' telegram she was installed in Avenue Cottage and Hollis was in Garford Road, only about a mile away. She was an 'illegal' with independent means for transmitting most of her material. As her memoirs testify, she had wide experience of servicing *duboks* and describes several which she selected, such as 'under a protruding root of the fourth tree on the left-hand side, after a railway bridge over the Oxford–Banbury Road'.[6] Further, there is no evidence of any other Soviet agent-runner or controller operating in the Oxford area in the 1940s.[7]

As regards the particular *dubok* mentioned in the 'Elli' telegram – a split between the stones of a certain grave, the name on the headstone being Brown – one would imagine that there must be scores of such graves in the Oxford area belonging to people called Brown or Browne. Nevertheless I thought it worthwhile to investigate any graveyard which could have been mutually convenient to Hollis and Sonia late in 1942 or early in 1943. Before doing so I rechecked my records of telephone conversations I had had with Gouzenko. Originally Gouzenko had described the *dubok* as a split in a tomb. He had then told me that the grave had belonged to somebody called Brown and I recorded this in the paperback edition of *Their Trade is Treachery*, published in 1982, long before I made any searches in the Oxford area.[8] In a further telephone conversation, however, Gouzenko said that the name had been on the 'headstone', suggesting a grave rather than a tomb. In a letter dated 6 March 1983, Gouzenko's widow Svetlana confirmed that her husband had told her in 1945 that the name Brown was in the telegram and that he had seen it.

The map on p.85 and the general size of the City of Oxford would suggest that there must be several graveyards in the area, but investigations carried out on my behalf by my son, who is a professional researcher, showed that there is only one, and this was also the case in the war years. The graveyard is called St Sepulchre's Cemetery, situated off Walton Street, and before it ceased to be used shortly after the end of the Second World War it served six churches, none of which had a functional graveyard of its own.[9] From Hollis's house it was one and a quarter miles; from Sonia's a mile and a half. When it is remembered that Sonia had only a bicycle for transport and that Hollis was working six days a week at Blenheim, such convenience would have been essential if visits to the *dubok* had to be frequent.

Though most of the graves in St Sepulchre's were already old in the early 1940s, people were still being buried there in the 'new' area of the cemetery, so it would not have been difficult to have had apparent reason for visiting it. As Gouzenko pointed out to his wife, however, a grave used as a *dubok* would have to be so old that there was no risk of it still being attended by relatives.[10] This condition would have to apply to any other graves in the immediate vicinity as well. The grave should also be quickly accessible.

Not far from the entrance to the cemetery proper, and only a few yards from the path, there is a grave with a very distinctive headstone bearing the words 'In loving memory of Emily Browne' and 'Died 1883'. Because the headstone is the only one cut away by the stonemason to form a cross, while retaining the curved, conventional shape, it could very easily be spotted by anybody, such as 'Elli', who had been given a description of it. The grave is also one of several with two apparent headstones, a small one inserted in the ground at the base of the large one. This was almost certainly the original footstone to the grave. It is the custom in many cemeteries to move these old footstones close to the head-stones for convenience of graveyard maintenance. While a number of graves in St Sepulchre's have been treated in this way, the Browne grave is the only one with a gap between the two stones large enough – about three inches – for a document or small package to be concealed in it. The other graves' footstones have been set so hard up against the headstones that there is no space between them. Though the Browne grave is easily accessible in the dark or in bad weather, being just left of the last yew tree by the path, no small package placed between the stones would have been visible except to somebody looking for it, as my tests showed. The gap between the stones is slightly overgrown with ivy and may have been more so in the past. Further, all the graves in the area are so old that they are most unlikely to have been tended in the early 1940s. The graves which were then recent were at the far end of the cemetery.

The existence of this grave does not necessarily mean that it was the *dubok* mentioned by Gouzenko as having been used by 'Elli' and his agent-runner, but it remains of some interest that it conforms in all respects to the requirements. Had no such grave existed in the area it would have been evidence against the probability that 'Elli' and his agent-runner operated there. I also put these facts on record because Svetlana Gouzenko has suggested, tantalizingly,

84

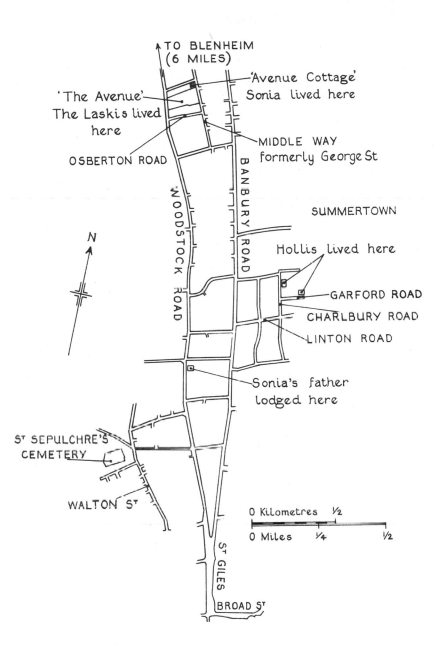

TO BLENHEIM
(6 MILES)

'Avenue Cottage'
Sonia lived here

'The Avenue'
The Laskis lived
here

MIDDLE WAY
formerly George St

OSBERTON ROAD

BANBURY ROAD

WOODSTOCK ROAD

SUMMERTOWN

N

Hollis lived here

GARFORD ROAD

CHARLBURY ROAD

LINTON ROAD

Sonia's father
lodged here

St SEPULCHRE'S
CEMETERY

St GILES

WALTON St

0 Kilometres   ½

0 Miles   ¼   ½

BROAD St

*The remarkable proximity of Hollis, Sonia and her father to each other and to
St Sepulchre's Cemetery, the possible site of the secret hiding place for
messages described by Gouzenko*

that the first name, and therefore the sex, of the person buried in the grave might have been in the telegram and that if her late husband made a note of it, it might still be among his voluminous papers.[11]

Meanwhile it is intriguing to contemplate the possibility that Lubimov was deciphering a message sent by Sonia from her transmitter in Avenue Cottage. As the map shows, it would have been convenient for Hollis, or any other MI5 officer living in Oxford, to have walked there or have stopped nearby if driving home from Blenheim. I have established that while the ancillary staff, mainly women who were housed in Oxford colleges, were transported to and from Blenheim by bus, the officers used private cars.

It could be significant that on the occasions when Sonia's father stayed in Oxford he was only about half a mile from the cemetery and, as he knew about her activities and approved of them, he could have served as a courier. The grave would, of course, have been only one of several *duboks* used by 'Elli' and on his behalf.

CHAPTER TWELVE

The Two-faced Dr Fuchs

ANOTHER German communist refugee who repaid the hospitality extended to him with treachery of such a degree that it was to be of major historic significance was the 'atomic bomb spy' Klaus Fuchs, whose proven association with Sonia puts her in the front rank of female agents on that count alone. The involvement of MI5, and of Hollis's section in particular, in the successive security clearances of Fuchs make it difficult to disbelieve that there was not someone inside MI5 with an interest in ensuring that he remained in the bomb project.

Fuchs, who was the son of a German Quaker preacher, was born in Russelheim, near Frankfurt, in 1911. While at Kiel University, where he studied physics, he became a communist, working in the underground movement against the Nazis. In March 1933 he attended a secret conference of anti-Nazis in Berlin, where he learned that the Gestapo was looking for him. He went into hiding for five months and seems to have spent part of the time in Berlin, where he may have met Sonia's brother, Juergen, who was active in communist affairs there. In September of that year, on the advice of the Communist Party that he should leave Germany to complete his studies and return to help build the new communist Germany when the Nazis had been overthrown, he arrived in England as a political refugee.[1]

Fuchs had chosen England after hearing from a German girl to whom he had written and who was living as an au pair with an English family. The girl's fiancé, who was German, was Fuchs's cousin and it so happened that the head of the English family, who lived in the village of Clapton-in-Gordano, near Bristol, was a Soviet sympathizer. It has been stated in several books that the family were Quakers and this was the reason why they invited Fuchs to join them when their au pair told them of Fuchs's plight. This is, however, quite incorrect; they were not Quakers and never had been.[2]

The family was headed by the late Ronald Gunn, who was

related by marriage to the Wills family, of cigarette fame, and had a position with the company in Bristol.

Close relatives of Mr Gunn have assured me that he and his family were not Quakers but that he was 'very well known for his communist leanings'. He had made Intourist trips to the Soviet Union, and was greatly concerned when a diary he had dropped in the street in England during the war was found to contain names and addresses connected with his communist interests.[3] It would seem likely that the au pair had not only told Fuchs about these interests but had told Gunn that Fuchs was a communist. The story that it was a Quaker connection which had brought Fuchs to the Gunn household may have been fabricated later by Fuchs himself to protect the Gunns from interrogation by the security authorities. MI5 officers seem to have accepted this, as they accepted other lies which Fuchs was to tell them.

Fuchs lied from the moment he arrived in Britain. He told the immigration authorities that he was going to study physics at Bristol University, but at that stage he had no prospects of doing so. He also said that the Gunn family were friends of his father, which was untrue.[4]

He remained with the Gunns in Clapton-in-Gordano for about a year, learning English, and when they moved to a house in Bristol he went with them, remaining there for about two years before acquiring lodgings of his own. Ronald Gunn did him a further service by introducing him to Sir Nevill Mott, who had recently taken the chair in Theoretical Physics at Bristol University and who spoke German.[5] At Gunn's request Mott took Fuchs on as a research assistant, a position he held for four years before moving to Edinburgh University to work with Professor Max Born, a naturalized German scientist, in 1937.

At some stage Fuchs made secret contact with other German communists in Britain, including Juergen Kuczynski. He was later to admit that though as a refugee he was not supposed to take part in political activities, he had associated freely with other communists and Marxists for six years in Britain before the war.[6] He confessed that he was considered to be a member of the 'underground section' of the German Communist Party operating in Britain and had probably filled out a biography and given it to officials of that section, of which he knew Juergen Kuczynski to be the head.[7]

In June 1940 Fuchs was subjected, like most Germans and Italians, to internment, in his case in Canada, until inquiries had established that it was safe to release him. In 1934 the Chief Constable of Bristol had been informed by the German Consul there that Fuchs was a dangerous communist who had escaped abroad when wanted for questioning. A copy of the police report was passed to the Home Office and thence to the records of MI5, which were available to Hollis's section when it came to examine his case in 1940. As there was no way of confirming the report, and both the police and MI5 were ignorant of Fuchs's connections with other communists in Britain, it was recommended that Fuchs should be released from detention, which he was in January 1941. While in detention he had cemented relations with Soviet-committed German communists like Hans Kahle, and it is likely that under their tutelage his own commitment was fortified.[8]

By the time Fuchs was released Britain had embarked on the project to design and manufacture atomic bombs and, having established something of a reputation in the increasingly important discipline of theoretical physics, he was invited to join one of the research teams which was working at Birmingham University. Having no adverse information from MI5, the responsible ministry gave the necessary security clearance.[9]

For any understanding of how Fuchs was able to spy so damagingly for so long it is essential to appreciate that the man most responsible for his successive security clearances was Roger Hollis. This can be stated categorically because of the release in the U.S. of the British minutes of a Conference on Security Standards held in Washington in June 1950. Hollis took it upon himself to review the British aspects of the Fuchs case and the minutes state that 'Mr Hollis...had, throughout, been concerned with all the security clearance aspects of the case and was confident that the facts as he would report them were substantially correct and represented all that was known at the times in question'.[10] He was also confident, no doubt, that the minutes would remain secret for ever.

Fuchs joined the Birmingham team in May 1941 (not 'at the end of 1941', as Hollis told the Conference) and signed the Official Secrets Act in the following month.[11]

Fuchs was to claim that when he discovered the nature of his work, which was to develop a highly secret system of producing the nuclear explosive uranium 235, he made a spontaneous decision to pass all the information he could to the Soviets in furtherance of his communist principles, the U.S.S.R. at that time having been attacked by the Germans.[12] He claimed that he achieved this by going to London to make contact with Kuczynski who promised to assist him.[13] At a further meeting, by which time Kuczynski would undoubtedly have alerted the G.R.U. Centre, either through his Embassy contacts or through Sonia, Fuchs made clandestine contact with a Russian he knew only as 'Alexander' but whom he was to identify later, from a photograph, as Simon Kremer, secretary of the Military Attaché's staff at the Soviet Embassy and a G.R.U. officer already known to Sonia as 'Sergei'.[14]

Kuczynski has disclosed that he was involved in underground work among German communist exiles in Birmingham, and it may be that his first knowledge that Fuchs had become involved in atomic weapons work reached him there and that after consultation with Moscow he pressured Fuchs into becoming a spy. In his *Dialog mit meinem Urenkel*, published in 1983, Kuczynski was permitted to admit that Fuchs had been 'his friend in England'.

The first meeting between Fuchs and Kremer is believed to have taken place in the summer of 1941, probably in August. They had no more than three meetings – one in the Soviet Embassy – at which Fuchs handed over written information about his work.[15] After a few months he was passed on to Sonia who, being based in Oxford, was much more conveniently placed for Birmingham.[16] He might already have met Sonia socially through his underground communist connections, though that would have been in breach of the 'conspiratorial practice' to which she paid such attention.

Later in 1941 an informer inside German refugee circles told MI5 that Fuchs was well known as a communist, though it was not certain that he was a Party member. MI5 – and again it must have been Hollis's section – passed the information to the ministry concerned, observing that any leakage from Fuchs would be more likely to be to the Soviets than to the Germans. The only known result of this warning was advice to Birmingham University urging the minimum disclosures to Fuchs, a condition which it was impossible to observe.[17] Soon afterwards, when responsibility for atomic energy passed to the Department of Scientific and Industrial Research (D.S.I.R.), that department asked for more definitive information concerning the clearance of Fuchs, clearly indicating that some doubt existed. MI5 supplied all the information it claimed to have and left any action to the D.S.I.R.'s chief, Sir Edward Appleton, who took the view that Fuchs could not be spared. He therefore became a full member of the atomic team with no restrictions on information.[18] This failure by MI5 to give clear-cut guidance to Appleton was the crucial error which led to the great betrayal of nuclear secrets to the Soviet Union. It was inevitable that as a scientist with an international outlook Appleton, who was a friend of mine, would interpret MI5's lack of decisive advice as reasonable grounds for employing Fuchs. Hollis had a double responsibility for the failure. He was not only head of the section responsible for overseeing German communists like

Fuchs, he was also on a special committee giving guidance on the internment of enemy aliens, as he had been at the time of Fuchs's release from internment in Canada.[19] This was a sub-committee of the Security Executive set up by Churchill under Lord Swinton. The official papers of that sub-committee would, therefore, be instructive, if they still exist.

In 1942 Fuchs was naturalized by a particularly rapid process pushed through, as Hollis explained at the Washington Conference, 'to avoid the administrative difficulties involved in getting access for an enemy alien to prohibited places' where atomic work was in progress.[20] The standard investigation must have involved data supplied by MI5, and since none of this was adverse, as the Conference minutes state, Fuchs took the Oath of Allegiance.

Over the next two years Fuchs met Sonia at regular intervals in country lanes and other places near Banbury, which was convenient for both of them and to which they could travel by train.[21] This means that though MI5 had doubts about Fuchs and knew that he was in an extremely sensitive position it made no effort, or at least no effective effort, to put him under surveillance. As a result of that omission, Fuchs and Sonia were able to perpetrate some of the most damaging espionage of the war, for although the Soviets may have become reluctant allies, there was never any intention to share atomic secrets with them. There was no unfairness about that. The Soviets were making no contribution to the nuclear effort, and from the start of the war to the end they refused to provide any information about Soviet or captured German weapons unless it chanced to suit them.[22]

Whether Sonia was Fuchs's case officer or just a courier at that stage is uncertain, but he supplied her with details of what became the gaseous diffusion process for separating uranium 235 from ordinary metallic uranium and was to be the basis of a huge production plant in America. He also fed her with the results of work he was doing on the physics of the atomic bomb itself.[23] She either transmitted this by radio to Moscow or, in the case of documents, handed them over to 'Sergei' and his successors. Between them they gave enormous assistance to the Soviet scientists who were already engaged on research to make atomic weapons. All this was happening after the N.K.V.D., the predecessor of the K.G.B., had promised British Intelligence that in return for assistance it would not mount subversive missions in Britain.[24] It could be argued, of course, that this promise did not apply to the G.R.U.!

While Fuchs was handing over secrets, the informer in the German refugee circles came up with further information claiming that Fuchs had definitely belonged to the German Communist Party and was taking active part in communist affairs in Birmingham, though discreetly. MI5 took no effective notice of this allegedly because the police could not corroborate it.[25]

The timing of Fuchs's first act of treachery in the summer of 1941 and the fact that Sonia was not involved with him as a courier until the end of 1941 prove that she was not posted to Oxford to serve him. When the G.R.U. Centre ordered Sonia to Britain Fuchs was interned in Canada and there was no certainty that he would be released. It was not until after his release that he was invited to join the atomic bomb project, which he did in May 1941, by which time Sonia was well established in the Oxford area. When the G.R.U. posted Sonia to Oxford it could have had no idea that Fuchs would ever be involved in military work, would be based in Birmingham or would be willing to spy. Fuchs was an unforseeable bonus so there must have been some other agent, established or about to be established in the Oxford area, who merited Sonia's transfer there. What she achieved through her service to Fuchs alone, however, was sufficient to establish her place in the annals of espionage.

In December 1943 Fuchs was made a temporary Government official and posted to the U.S. to work with American nuclear scientists in what had become a joint crash programme to develop atomic weapons.[26] The U.S. authorities were told that he had been through the security clearance procedures and they accepted the British assurance that Fuchs was 'clean'.[27] Sonia had produced a third child, a son, Peter, only a few weeks previously but that did not stop her from meeting Fuchs in October to give him instructions, sent to her by the Centre, for a clandestine meeting with his new American courier. The instructions were typically conspiratorial and reminiscent of Sonia's meeting with Alexander Foote in Geneva. On a certain date in January 1944 Fuchs was to go to a street corner in New York, where he was first based. He should hold a tennis ball in his left hand. He would recognize his contact, whom he would know only as 'Raymond', because he would be wearing gloves and would be carrying a book with green binding and another pair of gloves.[28]

While Fuchs was meeting his new controller the chief of the British atomic project asked for the latest and most detailed security opinion on him because it was vital to avoid any damage to the atomic link-up with the U.S. by sending someone who was a security risk.[29] Hollis's section was instrumental in producing the reassurance that there were no security objections to Fuchs. The fact that suspicion had existed and that there had been further reports of his active links with communism were not passed to

American security. When U.S. security chiefs were later to claim that they had been misled, the British were to argue that the stricture was unfair because security clearance for the atomic project had been the most comprehensive ever applied in Britain.[30] Nevertheless, at the secret Washington Conference on Security Standards in 1950 Hollis admitted that 'a serious mistake had undoubtedly been made'. He excused the error by claiming that Fuchs had been involved in a type of espionage which 'necessitated positive action only during a few periods in a year, each of which might not last more than half an hour'. This was a lame excuse because it was typical of many spies.

While the British minutes record that Hollis's explanation was 'sympathetically received', Dr Henry D. Smyth, author of the famous official report on the atomic bomb, asked whether the American authorities had been told of 'the adverse information about Fuchs and the British reasons for discounting it, and whether Fuchs's security clearance was re-examined immediately before his transfer to the U.S. or whether the original decision was reported'. Hollis said that Fuchs's security clearance had been carefully reviewed by MI5 immediately before his transfer but claimed that 'it was never the practice to report from one country to another the details of a security investigation as each Government must take responsibility for its own employees'.[31]

Making all allowances for the small size and resources of Hollis's section, its performance was lamentable and was to be reponsible for damage to Anglo-American relations which has still never been fully repaired. Because the U.S. security authorities took Britain's word that Fuchs was secure, he was free from any check in America, where he became part of a spy-ring which was to give the Soviet Union details of the structure of the atomic bomb itself.

Though Fuchs was never told so, his move to America marked his transfer from control by the G.R.U. to the K.G.B. which, on Stalin's instructions, was beginning to take over the G.R.U.'s more important assets.[32] None was more important at that stage than Fuchs. During his time in America, first at Columbia University in New York and then at Los Alamos, New Mexico, Fuchs was under the overall control of a highly successful K.G.B. officer who used the name Anatoli Yakovlev and posed as Soviet Vice-Consul in New York. Yakovlev ran several highly productive agents, operating through couriers who did not know who he was. In accordance with good conspiratorial practice, the couriers were non-Russians, as Sonia was in Britain.[33]

Through Fuchs and other members of his ring Yakovlev was able to provide his country with details of the structure of the first atomic bombs as well as technical information about the production of uranium and plutonium explosives – a stupendous espionage achievement.

A memorandum from J.Edgar Hoover, the F.B.I. chief, to the White House dated June 1950 indicates the damage.[34] Fuchs gave 'Raymond' documents and information about the production of fissionable materials and their potential use. He outlined the nature of the plants to be built to produce them and the plans for the construction of an atomic bomb. He described the plutonium bomb, its detonation mechanism, and provided a sketch of the weapon. He also revealed the rate of production of the atomic explosives.

Another F.B.I. document reveals that for some unspecified reason the F.B.I. officer in London sent the Gestapo list which included Fuchs's name to headquarters in Washington in 1945,[35] but no notice seems to have been taken of it. So while Hoover did all he could to pin the blame entirely on the British, there was some degree of incompetence in the U.S.

By August 1945, or thereabouts, Fuchs knew that the U.S. Government was anxious to end the Anglo-American partnership and that he would be posted back to London. He told his courier 'Raymond' this in September and expressed his fear that the British security authorities might learn that he was a communist because the British had captured Kiel and might have found the Gestapo dossier about him.[36] He was not aware that MI5 had already dismissed the Gestapo evidence as 'tainted'. Towards the end of November, during a trip to Montreal, he was interviewed for a senior appointment at the new Atomic Energy Research Establishment to be built on a disused R.A.F. airfield at Harwell, Berkshire.[37]

The previous record of the British security authorities regarding Fuchs would suggest that any fear was unfounded and that he might even have had the benefit of a protective hand. He was to continue to enjoy what looks like a charmed life until the security authorities were forced to take action by an event outside their control – the deciphering of a K.G.B. radio message by American Intelligence.

Sonia's own memoirs and the little of her recorded traffic which has since been examined show that she remained very active during Fuchs's absence. In November 1944 'Sergei' of the Soviet Embassy had brought her greetings from the Director in Moscow, as well he might considering the worth of her services. After having received from 'Sergei' a more advanced and smaller transmitter, she was able to dismantle her old set which she kept for emergencies in an espionage operation which must easily rank as one of the most extraordinary of the war, especially in terms of the involvement of MI5.

In June 1942 President Roosevelt had established an intelligence and special operations organization called the Office of Strategic Services (O.S.S.) under the command of Colonel William 'Wild Bill' Donovan, who already had intelligence and military connections with Britain.[38] As the O.S.S. was to operate against Germany, its major base in that theatre had to be London. By the early spring of 1943 the O.S.S. had established a close working relationship on security and counter-intelligence with both MI5 and MI6. To carry out its tasks the O.S.S. wanted to infiltrate agents into Germany and the occupied territories and, for this purpose, had set up a section called the Labour Branch, 'Labour' in that context referring to trade unions. The branch had arisen out of the concept that German trade unionists who had fled Hitler's Reich for political reasons would be so staunchly anti-Nazi that they would make trustworthy recruits for anti-German intelligence work. An O.S.S. officer called George Pratt was sent to London to seek out and recruit such people.[39]

The political German refugees in Britain were known to be of two main categories – genuine democratic socialists and dedicated pro-Soviet communists. At that stage the communists were, quite rightly, not regarded as reliable and only German socialists were selected for recruitment. As the Germans had been resident in Britain for some years the British security authorities required some control over their selection for intelligence purposes, especially as it involved some degree of indoctrination into secret matters. A Co-ordination Committee was established and there seems to be no doubt that MI5 was one of the vetting authorities, possibly the only one.[40] The O.S.S. intended to drop the Germans by parachute, as Soviet spies had been dropped in the previous year. The selected Germans were warned that as there was no established underground resistance in Germany, those dropped would be in particular danger. Nevertheless, volunteers came forward and the first of them were parachuted from an R.A.F. Lancaster bomber at night in September 1944.[41] This involvement of the R.A.F. implies further British interest and some control of the operation.

Understandably, the number of recruits available for such missions was limited, especially as young able-bodied men could not be used because they would have attracted the attention of the German authorities since they should have been in the German forces. In the second half of 1944, therefore, it was decided to extend the catchment area to German communists sheltering in

95

Britain. What then occurred would be struck out of any film script or novel as being too incredible.

CHAPTER THIRTEEN

The Kuczynski Parachutists

FOR the special recruitment of the German communists the O.S.S. Labour Branch detailed a young army lieutenant called Joseph Gould, a former film industry public relations official who had already been assigned to London. I have had the good fortune to find Mr Gould, who lives in Washington, and to receive first-hand assistance from him.[1] He claims that the Germans whom he recruited were not known to him to be communists as such but to be 'pro-Soviet or communist-orientated' and to be involved with the Free German Movement. This was an organization set up in London in September 1943 on the initiative of the German communists to induce the German socialists to join with them in forming a united workers' party front to exert influence in post-war Germany.[2] Two months previously German exiles in Moscow, including some captured *Wehrmacht* officers, had set up a Free German Committee which was officially recognized by Stalin and looked like the nucleus of a communist German government in exile. It is surely no coincidence that the person in London selected by the German Communist Party (the K.P.D.) to approach the German Socialist Party (S.P.D.) should have been a Soviet agent – Dr René Kuczynski, Sonia's father.[3] As the invitations to the foundation meeting in Trinity Church Hall, Finchley Road, show, he was also the chairman on that occasion.[4] The socialists realized from the start, that this was a typical communist ploy and that the K.P.D. really regarded true democratic socialists as their enemies, but the Foreign Office was so concerned by this apparent bid to ensure that post-war Germany would be pro-Soviet that it asked MI5 to carry out investigations into British exile politics.[5] This must have involved Hollis and his department. Indeed it would be reasonable to assume that MI5 had penetrated the K.P.D. In addition to printed invitations there were posters about the meeting and the Free German Movement was reported in the communist Press. Hollis must have been aware of the overt activities of Sonia's father and brother even if ignorant of their clandestine work.

97

Relations between the American O.S.S. and the British secret services had become strained because after being given access to British secret intelligence Colonel Donovan had established his own, direct, contacts in London with the intelligence services of the governments in exile, like the Free French, which were riddled with Soviet agents.[6] Lieutenant Gould, therefore, disdained seeking British assistance. He sought out a left-wing bookshop in London and asked the owners if they knew any important figure in the Free German Movement whom they could approach. They suggested a certain Dr Juergen Kuczynski.[7]

Kuczynski was approached by Gould at his flat in August 1944 and remarked that the American was the first intelligence officer of any Allied nation to approach him. Kuczynski asked for a week in which to produce a list of potential agents to be dropped in Germany, and when the two met again in a London restaurant some of them were with him, ready to be introduced to Gould. Neither Gould nor the British security authorities were aware that during the interval the Moscow Centre had been informed of the operation through the services of Sonia and had insisted on approving the volunteers for political suitability.[8] Kuczynski had consulted other leading German communists and Soviet agents in London such as Hans Kahle, Erich Henschke and Wilhelm Koenen, who had compiled the list of volunteers and passed it to Sonia for onward transmission to Moscow. According to Sonia, the volunteers were told that Moscow approved of their action and that part of their purpose was to assist in the setting up of a German communist state.

Gould chose seven who, in his view, had the physical stamina and resourcefulness to undertake such a dangerous mission.[9] He believed that they had all been living in London, but some had been rustled up from as far afield as Scotland. Their names were passed to the requisite British security authority which, according to Gould, was MI5. The MI5 section most likely to have been involved was that responsible for overseeing the German communists being recruited, namely Section F commanded by Hollis. Whether or not Hollis was on the Co-ordinating Committee his counsel would almost certainly have been sought. In that case the part played by Kuczynski should have been known to him. If MI6 was involved in any way the likeliest officer to have been concerned would have been Philby, who was then head of Soviet counter-espionage.

As Kuczynski was known to both the British and American security authorities as a pro-Soviet communist committed to the establishment of Moscow's concept of a 'Free' Germany, it would be instructive to know MI5's reaction to his involvement. Regrettably, MI5 did not seem to be aware of the involvement of Kahle and Koenen, who both figured on the list of foreign communists considered dangerous supplied by MI5 to the U.S. Embassy three years previously.

The vetting of the communist volunteers would appear to have been perfunctory. Two of the men approved by the Moscow Centre had previously been regarded as so dangerous to security that one, Paul Land, had been deported for internment in Canada, while another, Tony Ruh, had been sent to Australia, both being allowed to return following persistent representations by pro-Soviet Britons like the lawyer D.N. Pritt who had also lobbied on behalf of Kuczynski when he had been interned.[10] Mr Gould has assured me that he was never told that Land and Ruh had previously been interned as dangerous aliens.

Gould did not see Kuczynski again nor, in keeping with Sonia's good conspiratorial practice, did he ever meet her or know of her existence. Kuczynski handed over the Soviet interest in the operations to Henschke whom Sonia had known from her earliest Party activities in Berlin and who used his G.R.U. code-name Karl Castro.[11] Mr Gould has confirmed that he knew him only by this pseudonym and that he was liaison man for Kuczynski.[12]

The seven selected agents were taken on the O.S.S. payroll and underwent eight weeks of intensive training in espionage techniques in London and in parachute jumping on an airfield. They were supplied with cover stories, German clothes and forged papers.[13] They repeatedly asked Gould what political part the Free German Movement was to play in post-war Germany but were given no undertakings. Throughout their training everything they were told, including secret codes, went to Henschke who passed it to Sonia for onward transmission to Moscow.[14] In return, the Soviets reacted in their typically co-operative manner. On one occasion a mission required the dropping aircraft to land and refuel in territory occupied by Soviet troops. Moscow refused permission and the flight had to be re-routed.[15]

Five main missions were mounted code-named after tools: 'Hammer', 'Chisel', 'Mallet', 'Pickaxe' and 'Buzzsaw'. In the first mission, 'Hammer', Land and Ruh were dropped on 1 March 1945 from an American Air Force A26 about thirty miles west of Berlin and made their way into the shattered capital. Eleven days later they were to pass their first assessments of the state of life in Berlin to the O.S.S. This was achieved by Land speaking into a walkie-talkie radio to an aircraft flying high above him. 'Chisel' mission, with one agent aboard, was shot down on its way to the Ruhr, but

'Hammer' continued to be productive, providing assessments of Berlin's defences.[16]

When the Russians entered Berlin, Land and Ruh gave themselves up to a Russian commander saying that they were American Intelligence officers. They were held captive for two months and when they were returned to American army control it was feared that they might have been turned into double agents, working primarily for the Soviet Union. They had, in fact, been working for the Russians all the time since Henschke had managed to get access to their reports and had fed them all to Sonia. The same had happened with the reports from two agents dropped in 'Buzzsaw' near Bavaria, the area which was believed to have been earmarked as the 'redoubt' where the Nazis would mount their last stand. They reported no signs of activity. In 'Pickaxe' a single agent was dropped near the Czech border, while in 'Mallet', the last operation, the agent who had been dropped into Berlin during an air raid was seized by the Russians, who believed he was a Gestapo man. [17]

Sonia records that her work with these agents continued until a few weeks after the end of the war, and those who survived, brave men that they were, returned to their country of origin to play their part in the establishment of a communist dictatorship and Soviet client state – the German Democratic Republic.

Even before her work with the parachutists terminated, Sonia was busy with a fresh espionage venture in partnership with her brother. In September 1944, Juergen Kuczynski, a recognized authority on economic conditions in Germany, was asked by the U.S. Embassy in London to take part in the American Strategic Bombing Survey to help assess the damage caused by the Allied bombing policy to the German war effort.[18] In the established routine manner he asked for time to consider the offer, which required his appointment to the U.S. Army in the rank of lieutenant-colonel, so that he could take advice from G.R.U. headquarters. Through her transmitting facilities in Oxford Sonia obtained a quick response, indicating that Moscow was enthusiastic and looked forward to receiving the Bombing Survey results, which were to be tightly held by the Allied authorities. Juergen supplied her with this information on a regular basis and, in addition, passed on even more secret data which came his way because he was on the distribution list for other reports of greater value to the G.R.U. Through O.S.S. contacts he became friendly with Professor Richard Ruggles, an American who had devised a secret system for measuring German armaments production. The results were so secret that they went to very few people, but Sonia soon became one of them and has recorded how she transmitted the results of Ruggles's researches to Moscow, where they were quickly 'on the desk of the Commander-in-Chief of the Soviet Army'.[19] When interviewed by a newspaper correspondent in East Berlin in 1980, Kuczynski said: 'I worked with men like Kenneth Galbraith, Paul Nitze and George Ball in assessing the damage to Germany's industry. Through my sister I passed to Moscow every piece of information I received.'[20]

It remains a matter for wonder that all these clandestine and highly illegal transmissions were never detected, even taking into account the ban on the decipherment of Soviet radio traffic.

Evidence that while Sonia and her brother were operating so effectively under MI5's nose, MI5 remained tasked to prevent Soviet espionage in Britain, in spite of the wartime alliance with the Soviet Union, became public in July 1943 with the sentencing of Douglas Frank Springhall, a well-known British communist, to seven years' penal servitude under the Official Secrets Act.[21] Springhall, then forty-two and described in the contemporary newspaper reports as 'thick-set, broad-shouldered and clean-shaven with a florid complexion', was accused by the judge of 'worming secrets from a Government department by means of a little woman clerk'. The woman was Olive Sheehan, a clerk in the Air Ministry who had given Springhall information about jet propulsion developments on the understanding that it would be passed straight to Moscow. She was sentenced to three months' imprisonment and agreed to testify against Springhall when his case was heard in camera.

A 'Strictly Confidential' document passed by MI5 to the U.S. Embassy in August 1943 and released in 1983 makes it even more clear that MI5 was fully aware of the treachery being perpetrated by Russians and by British communists on their behalf. It reads: 'Our friends stated that they were aware that the Soviet Government was actively engaged at the present time in obtaining espionage information concerning the British Government. It was stated that the Soviet espionage organisations seemed to operate in two channels: One, directly through the Communist Party of England, utilising the Party organisation and English Communists who are employed in the armed services and the Government to collect espionage data. According to our friends, the second Soviet espionage group is apparently completely separated from the Communist Party of England and operates on what he described as a diplomatic level. This, of course, would include the Russian Embassy in London, as well as their various consular offices throughout the United Kingdom and the various Russian Trade Commissions which are accredited to the British Government and enjoy a pseudo-diplomatic immunity.'[22]

This documentary evidence surely disposes of any suggestion that MI5 was encouraged by the Government or by the circumstances to relax its interest in Soviet espionage once the U.S.S.R. became an ally and that the ineffectiveness of people like Hollis was, therefore, understandable and excusable. On the contrary, a further statement by MI5 to the U.S. Embassy, released in the same document, reads: 'Our friends further advised the Legal Attaché [of the American Embassy] that it was the intention of the Security Services and the British Government to prosecute these Communists for violation of the Official Secrets Act and not as Communists engaged in subversive activities against the British Government.'

This alleged determination makes it even more difficult to understand why so few traitorous communists and their Soviet controllers were detected. Springhall was detected only because his activities as a communist organizer and close links with Moscow were so well known that he was under regular surveillance and was seen visiting Mrs Sheehan's home.

Springhall had been a G.R.U. agent for years and had not only come to the notice of MI5 after being expelled from the Navy for sedition but had been sent to prison for two months during the 1926 General Strike when he was a Young Communist League agitator, having been a delegate to a Communist Congress in Moscow two years previously. As a political commissar to the British Battalion of the International Brigade in Spain he recruited Alexander Foote, Sonia's trainee radio operator, to the G.R.U.[23] He had visited Moscow again in 1939, almost certainly on G.R.U. business, for he was to run a G.R.U. network of agents of whom Mrs Sheehan was only one.[24] As is now appreciated, most of the rest, who went undetected, were part of the British section of the 'Red Orchestra'. In common with G.R.U. practice at that time Springhall was essentially an illegal agent-runner but had some connections with the Soviet Embassy, being in touch with Simon Kremer ('Sergei'), of the G.R.U. Military Attaché's office.

Unusually, Springhall used his overt communism as the Party's national organizer as cover for his numerous communist contacts. He lived in a Communist Party flat almost next door to its London headquarters and was therefore an easy subject for regular surveillance by Special Branch police. When it was decided to arrest him MI5 had hoped to induce him to give leads to his other agents and controllers. True to his training he declined any help whatever, gave no evidence at his trial, and after his eventual release died in exile in Moscow, after a sojourn in China. The Communist Party also behaved according to standing instructions. It expelled Springhall ignominiously, claiming to know nothing of his espionage.[25]

Only one of Springhall's other sources was identified, again as a result of routine surveillance. This was Ormond Uren, a 23-year-old officer in the Highland Light Infantry working in the Special Operations Executive in London. He had secretly joined the Communist Party in 1940 after being commissioned and had volunteered to supply the Party with information about his secret work. He was seen talking to Springhall and was kept under surveillance after Springhall's conviction. When confronted two months later he confessed all he knew. In October 1943 he was court-martialled, cashiered and sentenced to seven years' penal servitude. Ill-advised attempts have been made to link Uren and Springhall with the Cambridge Ring of spies. Both, in fact, were G.R.U. agents and there was no connection with the Cambridge group or any other K.G.B. ring.[26]

Further evidence that the Government was alert to the Soviet threat, in spite of the current alliance, originated from Churchill himself in April 1944 when he ordered a purge of communists in secret establishments.[27] He probably had weapons research and development mainly in mind, but if MI5 and MI6 were supposed to be included they either ignored the edict or did nothing that was effective, and the Soviet spies in those agencies continued to prosper.

A chance event which would have greatly disturbed Sonia had she heard of it, and Hollis even more so if he was a spy, occurred at Blenheim early in 1945 when Jack Tilton, former Detective Inspector with the Shanghai Municipal Police, called there. His purpose was to pick up some secret papers concerning his recent appointment to an R.A.F. security post. He wished to join MI5 and while he was there he took the opportunity to hand in testimonials and an eight-page record of his Shanghai activities, including his operations against communists there. As with a further attempt to join MI5 soon after the war, Tilton found his application completely ignored without even an acknowledgement. Understandably, he wonders why.[28]

Though communists of several nationalities continued to spy or serve as agents in Britain throughout the war, no more were prosecuted until early in 1946, when MI5's hand was forced through an event over which it had no control – the defection of a Soviet member of the G.R.U. in another country.

103

CHAPTER FOURTEEN

A Mole Called 'Elli'

On the night of 5 September 1945, one month after the atomic bomb had ended the Second World War, Igor Gouzenko, the G.R.U. cipher clerk defected from the Soviet Embassy in Ottawa with more than 100 carefully selected secret documents and a mass of memorized information.[1] He had been posted there from Moscow in June 1943 as code cipher clerk and translator to the G.R.U. chief in the Embassy. In the desperate hours after his defection, when he was being hunted by strong-arm men from the Embassy and could find no Canadian to listen to his story, Gouzenko told his wife, Swetlana, three things which she was to tell the Royal Canadian Mounted Police (R.C.M.P.) if he was captured. One of them was the existence of a G.R.U. spy, code-named 'Elli', inside MI5 in Britain. [2]

Gouzenko was nearly handed back to the Soviets because the jittery Canadian Prime Minister, Mackenzie King, was more concerned with preserving relations with the Kremlin, but wiser counsels prevailed and Gouzenko was interviewed at length by the security authorities who were then part of the R.C.M.P.

As Gouzenko named a British atomic scientist, Dr Alan Nunn May, as a traitor, in addition to making the 'Elli' allegation, the nearest available British Intelligence officer was flown to Ottawa to take part in the initial debriefing of the defector, which was led by Superintendent Charles Rivett-Carnac of the R.C.M.P. The British officer was Peter Dwyer who represented MI6 and was, at that time, working on secondment with the British Security Co-ordination Agency directed by Sir William Stephenson – well known through his code-name 'Intrepid' – in New York.[3]

Gouzenko could not remember being questioned by Dwyer, an able officer about whom there have never been any official doubts, when I spoke with him. This was almost certainly because he was interrogated by a small group including Dwyer who would ask questions relating to the British interest and would not, necessarily, have been identified as being British. A Russian-speaking member of the R.C.M.P. was present but the cross-examination was greatly facilitated by Gouzenko's grasp of English.[4]

Dwyer immediately sent a telegram to MI6 headquarters in Broadway, London, summarizing the information relating to the British and including what Gouzenko had alleged about 'Elli'. The telegram still exists in the MI6 archives. I have been assured by someone who had reason to examine it that it contains all the details about 'Elli' which Gouzenko could remember having been given by his colleague Lubimov, as described in Chapter 11. These were that 'Elli' was so important that he was normally contacted only through messages left in dead-letter boxes, that he was able to bring out files about Soviet Intelligence officers serving in Britain, and that he had something Russian in his background. The telegram also contained the important clue that 'Elli' was operated by the G.R.U., not the K.G.B., and had presumably been recruited by that organization.[5]

During the war years, and afterwards, some degree of rivalry existed between MI6 and MI5 and there was a dangerous tendency for the two agencies to withhold information from each other. The reaction of the MI6 chief, Sir Stewart Menzies, to the telegram was to keep the 'Elli' information inside his service and for his own men to continue the inquiries, at least for a while, though MI5, which then had no representative in North America, would eventually have to be informed. Menzies called in the chief of his Soviet counter-espionage section, who was Kim Philby, and suggested that he should fly out to Canada to interview Gouzenko and bring back further, and more detailed, information. Philby would have liked to have gone in order to be able to report everything to his K.G.B. controller, who had no direct information from the G.R.U., which was keeping as quiet as possible about the disaster inflicted on it by Gouzenko's defection. At that moment, however, Philby was in a highly dangerous situation following the attempted defection of another Soviet Intelligence officer, Konstantin Volkov (see Chapter 21). He therefore played for time and asked Menzies for a couple of days to enable him to decide whether he could spare the time from several other cases which seemed to be of high priority. Menzies deferred to Philby's judgement, as he usually did.[6]

What Philby really wanted was advice from his K.G.B. controller, with whom he remained in regular contact, either by dead-letter box messages or directly. If the controller decided that it would be unsafe for him to go to Canada then Philby wanted the next best thing – the dispatch of some agent of the controller's choice or one to whom he did not object.

Significantly, the copy of the telegram from Dwyer which Menzies had handed to Philby is creased as it would have been if it had been folded into four and taken out of the office in somebody's pocket. Firm evidence that Philby immediately consulted his controller is an urgent radio message which was sent from K.G.B. headquarters in Moscow to the K.G.B. chief in London that week and was deciphered much later. It mentions the original report concerning Gouzenko's defection which had been supplied by 'Stanley', which is now known to have been the K.G.B.'s code-name for Philby. The report was received during the interval when Philby was deciding whether he should go to Canada or send somebody else. The message also confirmed that 'Stanley's' information was correct, suggesting that the K.G.B. chief in London had asked Moscow to verify with the G.R.U. what Philby had told his controller.[7]

In the event, Philby told Menzies that in his judgement he would be more effectively occupied in London and he suggested that his MI5 counterpart on Soviet-espionage, Roger Hollis, shold be sent instead. Clearly, Philby was confident that he could induce Hollis to accept the mission.[8] As he was to record later: 'We both served on the Joint Intelligence Sub-Committee, which dealt with Communist affairs, and never failed to work out an agreed approach to present to the less well-informed representatives of the Service departments and the Foreign Office.'[9] In this instance Philby's chief was among the 'less well-informed'. Menzies concurred with his suggestion and a note from Philby to Hollis suggesting that the Gouzenko case was more in his line of business apparently still exists in the MI5 files.[10]

Supporters of Hollis have suggested that the fact that this note about the hand-over of the case from MI6 to MI5 has remained in the official records is evidence that Philby and Hollis could not have been collaborating because, in that case, one of them would have removed it. The clutching of such a straw makes no sense anyway because it is highly unlikely that if both men were traitors either knew anything about the other in 1945. There is no evidence that they did and while Philby may have suspected that Hollis was a Soviet agent following Moscow's agreement that he should, if possible, be sent to deal with Gouzenko, it would have been in breach of established conspiratorial practice for him to have been told so.

Menzies' agreement to the choice of Hollis, which presumably must also have had the support of the MI5 chief, is further evidence that Hollis was actively involved in Soviet counter-espionage. It was, nevertheless, unusual. Former MI6 officers have told me that normal practice would have been for Philby to have suggested somebody else inside MI6. Further, Hollis had no experience in the specialized field of interrogation. Nor was his unfriendly, buttoned-up manner conducive to persuading a defector to talk.

On the other hand, if Hollis was 'Elli' then it was completely in Moscow's interest that he should be sent out to deal, as summarily as possible, with the dangerous situation created by Gouzenko. Gouzenko had already stated that he had no knowledge of 'Elli's' identity so there was no danger of recognition, but nothing is more likely to threaten the safety of a spy than the arrival of a defector who knows anything about him. As will be seen in Chapter 21, when Philby was plunged into what appeared to be a similarly dangerous situation by another defector he took advice from Moscow and ensured that he himself was sent out to deal with it.

Hollis flew to Ottawa via New York early in September 1945 and called first at the headquarters of British Security Co-ordination in New York.[11] Sir William Stephenson has told me that he had been warned by Guy Liddell, then head of MI5 counter-espionage, to be careful about what he said to Hollis who was 'violently anti-American'. Sir William volunteered that Liddell had given him the impression that he suspected Hollis, and because anyone who was anti-American was dangerous to his organization, he steered clear of him.

Hollis made his way to Ottawa and it is possible that on that first visit he did not see Gouzenko. The defector's revelations were so astounding and the R.C.M.P. was so afraid that he might be snatched back by the Soviets or assassinated that he and his wife and child were hidden in various cottages for three weeks and then transferred to a safe and secret location, 'Camp X', near Toronto, where he stayed on and off foreight months.[12] Because of the involvement of Nunn May, the atomic scientist, who was due to return to Britain to a university post, Hollis found himself immediately involved in discussions with high-level Canadian and British officials regarding the possible arrest of Nunn May and other spies, and the publicity about them. The main meetings were held in the office of the British High Commissioner, the late Malcolm MacDonald.[13] Hollis was always reserved in conversation and his only contribution recorded by Mackenzie King was the statement, 'The Russians have got a lot of information on the atomic bomb.'[14]

Gouzenko's disclosures had by that time revealed the existence of a G.R.U. spy-ring inside Canada involving at least twenty non-

Soviet residents of Canada, together with leads to a spy-ring in the United States. It so happened that one member of the Canadian ring, Kathleen Willsher, who had been working for the Soviet Union inside the British High Commissioner's office in Ottowa, also had the code-name 'Elli'.[15] There was nothing surprising in this because the two 'Ellis' were in different rings, operating in different countries and would not be confused in coded radio traffic. The existence of the two 'Ellis' was attested by Gouzenko under secret questioning in 1945 and early in 1946 following the establishment of a Royal Commission to examine the whole treacherous effort by the Soviets to subvert one of its wartime allies, which had done all it could to help them. The Royal Commission took its evidence in camera and restricted its report, published in June 1946, to the Canadian spy-ring, so while Miss Willsher, who eventually received three years' imprisonment, was named as 'Elli', there was no mention of the other 'Elli' in MI5 in England.

Svetlana Gouzenko has told me that when her husband mentioned MI5 to the R.C.M.P. and to the Commission there was great concern that he even knew of its existence which in those days was supposed to be secret.[16] She also recalls that Gouzenko was advised by the Canadian authorities not to mention the English 'Elli' in any public statements he might make, which is why he remained silent about the matter in his book.[17] Because of the tremendous embarrassment felt by the Canadian Government by Gouzenko's revelations, for which there was then no precedent, he was also advised to restrict his evidence to names which he could substantiate through the documents he had removed from the Soviet Embassy in Ottawa.[18] As he had learned about the MI5 'Elli' before leaving Moscow for Canada he could not produce any documentary proof of it.

I disclosed Gouzenko's evidence on the English 'Elli' in *Their Trade is Treachery*. Those who found it difficult, or inconvenient, to believe that Soviet Intelligence would ever have used two agents with the same code-name, even in different rings, were confounded when, later in 1981, the Canadian Government unexpectedly released Gouzenko's original evidence to the Royal Commission.[19] It showed that Gouzenko had been very clear indeed about the existence of the two 'Ellis' – one being Miss Willsher, the other being in England.

Hollis returned to England in time to meet the *Queen Mary* when the ship docked at Southampton on 7 October 1945 bringing the Canadian Prime Minister, Mackenzie King, and his chief civil servant from the Foreign Affairs Department, Norman

Robertson.[20] Hollis went aboard with a telegram from Washington which said that President Truman was in favour of delaying the arrest of Nunn May until more could be discovered about the spy-ring affecting atomic secrets. Hollis had brought back from Canada the translation of a document provided by Gouzenko revealing the arrangements whereby Nunn May was to establish contact with the Soviets on his return to London so that he could continue his espionage. Nunn May, who had already returned to take up his academic appointment at King's College, London, was to meet an unknown agent in front of the British Museum, having exchanged the usual 'conspiratorial' recognition signals and passwords. Neither Nunn May nor the contact kept any of the proposed meetings, indicating that both had been warned of the danger. This could have been the result of a tip-off or of Soviet wariness following the disappearance of Gouzenko. At that stage, however, the Soviets could not be certain that he had defected, as the Canadians were pretending to know nothing about him – unless, of course, they had been told that he was in R.C.M.P. hands by an informer. Nunn May's arrest was delayed until 4 March 1946.

Early in 1946 Gouzenko was taken from Camp X to the Justice Building in Ottawa where he gave evidence to the Royal Commission over a lengthy period.[21] Hollis then made a further visit to Ottawa and personally questioned Gouzenko there on behalf of MI5. For reasons which will become apparent, the apologists for Hollis have done all they can to suggest that Hollis never interrogated Gouzenko, but I have proof from several prime sources that he did so. Those MI5 and MI6 investigators who became involved in the inquiries about Hollis and have seen the records are in no doubt that he did see and speak with Gouzenko. A former Director-General of MI5 has confirmed to me in writing that Hollis saw Gouzenko and reported on him. After consulting the R.C.M.P., Robert Kaplan the Solicitor-General of Canada has stated publicly that Gouzenko was interrogated by Hollis.[22]

Finally, in talks with me Gouzenko described his interrogator in terms which could apply only to Hollis: 'When he interviewed me in the Justice Department he was introduced only as a "gentleman from England". He was only about forty but he was so stooped that he approached me in a crouching way as though anxious that his face should not be seen. I was surprised that this man, who seemed almost afraid to talk to me, asked me very little when I told him that the G.R.U. had a spy inside MI5 in England, known by the code-name "Elli". We talked in English but for such a short time that we did not even sit down. He behaved as though he wanted to get away from me as quickly as possible.'[23] Later, Gouzenko was to say that the interview lasted only three minutes.

As several witnesses have testified, Hollis was already hunched at that time. Later, after realizing that his interrogator had been Hollis and that he was under suspicion of being a spy, Gouzenko believed that he understood his anxiety and need to keep the encounter short. 'I wondered if he was worried that I might recognize him from some photograph he thought I might have seen in Moscow but, as a cipher clerk, I had no opportunity to see photographs of G.R.U. spies.'[24]

Mrs. Gouzenko has assured me recently that 'the gentleman from England' was definitely not Dwyer. 'Igor saw newspaper pictures of Dwyer later when he took a public post in Canada. "The gentleman from England" was definitely Roger Hollis.'[25]

Because of subsequent curious events it is important to any assessment of the Hollis case that his interrogation of Gouzenko and its brevity should be firmly established in the reader's mind. One of Hollis's former colleagues told me that he saw Gouzenko several times, but Gouzenko vehemently denied this, insisting that he was interviewed on behalf of British security only once by the man he later recognized as Hollis. It should also be appreciated that if Hollis was a Soviet agent when he was sent over to Canada he would have been under control and would have been advised on how to conduct the inquiry with minimum damage to the Russians and minimum risk to himself.

Hollis's first cabled report after seeing Gouzenko suggested that he did not believe that 'Elli' existed and that if he did he was not in MI5 but in some related organization. For no good reason he suggested that 'Elli' might be a member of the Double Cross Committee, the group chaired by the late Sir John Masterman and responsible for turning captured German agents into 'doubles' working under British instruction.[26]

A note of Hollis's dispatch, together with one about Peter Dwyer's original telegram about 'Elli', was recorded by Guy Liddell in his office diary, which he wrote up conscientiously each evening. The entry recorded Liddell's belief that there might indeed be a spy inside MI5 with speculation as to who 'Elli' might be.[27] The subsequent treatment of his collection of diaries, known by the code-name 'Wallflowers', will be seen to be of some significance.

Hollis spent much of his time in Canada assisting the Royal Commission inquiry and it was only after some interval that he lodged a more detailed report of his interrogation of Gouzenko in the MI5 files. The content of that report was later to intensify the suspicions concerning Hollis, as will be described in Chapter 52. Its immediate effect was to damage Gouzenko's credibility inside MI5 and to ensure that nothing of any consequence was done concerning the allegation about the existence of a spy called 'Elli'. This was exactly what the G.R.U. would have wanted. So if 'Elli' was sent out to resolve the 'Elli' problem in Moscow's and his own interests, he succeeded.

In contrast, Gouzenko greatly impressed the Canadian Royal Commission by the manner and certainty with which he gave his evidence and it had no reservations in accepting him as a completely truthful witness.[28] By establishing the extent of Soviet duplicity with documents which could not be refuted Gouzenko did supremely important service to the free world. He could have done more had proper notice been taken of all his information and especially of the lead about 'Elli'.

It has been suggested that Hollis could not possibly have misled MI5 headquarters over Gouzenko's evidence about 'Elli' because the conversations which Norman Robertson, the Canadian Foreign Affairs man, had with members of MI5 would have 'caught him out'.[29] I have established that Robertson did meet two members of MI5 on about 24 October and later was to become friendly with others, including Dick White. One of those members was almost certainly Hollis himself. As the main concern was Nunn May, the implications of the other identified spies and the need for tighter security in Canada, it is unlikely that the 'Elli' allegation would have been raised by Robertson. It was a British domestic matter and it would have been out of normal practice for Robertson to have raised it when Hollis was already supposed to be dealing with it. This view is supported by the fact that the 'Elli' allegation was omitted from the report of the Canadian Royal Commission on the Gouzenko revelations, though present in the secret evidence to it released in 1981.

It is convenient at this point to examine alternative candidates for 'Elli' who have been put forward by apologists for Hollis. Some have tried to suggest that 'Elli' was not in MI5 at all, but the facts refute this. According to original testimony, Gouzenko located 'Elli' as working in 'department 5 of MI' and in several conversations with me he made it clear that he meant MI5 and not Section 5 of MI6 or any other department.[30] This is supported by a recent statement by Mrs Gouzenko to me in which she said that her husband told her that 'in the same telegram with instructions for the transfer of a message, Elli was referred to as in MI5'.[31] A memorandum which Gouzenko submitted to the R.C.M.P. in May 1952, when there was no suspicion against Hollis and Gouzenko had never heard of him by name, is quite clear. It begins: 'Regarding your request for information about the person in British MI5 ...' Gouzenko provided the memorandum at the request of R.C.M.P. Superintendent George McLellan, who had been asked to secure it by the branch of MI5 making inquiries into the Philby and Blunt cases following the defection of Maclean and Burgess in the previous year. The memorandum is so revealing that it is reproduced in full in Appendix A.

In his original debriefing Gouzenko also claimed to have seen evidence of a leak to Moscow concerning a forthcoming visit to Ottawa by British counter-intelligence officers, referred to in G.R.U. coded parlance as 'the Greens'. This information had been sent to Gouzenko's chief, Colonel Zabotin, by the Moscow Centre in late 1944 or early 1945 and he had deciphered it for him. It warned Zabotin that 'the Greens' were to visit Ottawa to assist the R.C.M.P. in operations against Soviet agents.[32] This almost certainly referred to a secret visit paid in 1944 by Guy Liddell of MI5, making it likely that the leak originated from that agency.

After examining the numerous papers left by her husband, who died in July 1982 aged sixty-three, Mrs Gouzenko told me: 'Without any doubt "Elli" was in MI5.'[33]

The exposure of Anthony Blunt as a spy active inside MI5 has led some writers to assume that he must have been 'Elli', but Blunt and the rest of the Cambridge Ring were all recruited by the K.G.B. and worked exclusively for that organization throughout their espionage careers. 'Elli' was, beyond question, a G.R.U. spy whose reports were submitted by his G.R.U. controller to the G.R.U. Centre in Moscow where G.R.U. cipher clerks, like Gouzenko, dealt with them. The G.R.U. and the K.G.B. operated quite independently in 1942, as Gouzenko's detailed evidence to the Canadian Royal Commission clearly showed. They may have shared information once it had been received and processed but they did not share agents or raw intelligence, a fact confirmed to MI5 by several sources.

Further, Blunt was not able to bring out MI5 files about Soviet Intelligence officers serving in Britain. These files were located at Blenheim during the relevant period and Blunt was based in London, though he visited Blenheim on occasion. When Blunt was eventually interrogated in 1964 he said that his Soviet controller had specifically instructed him not to ask for files on Soviet Intelligence officers unless he needed to do so for his genuine MI5 duties, otherwise he risked drawing attention to himself.[34] The MI5 Registry records show that he obeyed this injunction.[35] Hollis, on the other hand, had daily reason for consulting such files as he was responsible for countering the activities of these Russians.

In 1945, when Gouzenko defected, Blunt was still attached to MI5 and was told about the 'Elli' allegation by his MI5 friend Guy Liddell. Blunt wondered if 'Elli' might be himself, as he had never been told his cryptonym, and later admitted that he had discussed the possibility with his Soviet controller, who was non-committal, not being prepared to discuss code-names with anybody. Blunt also speculated with Philby as to who 'Elli' might be since, as members of the Cambridge 'Ring of Five' they knew of each other's espionage activities, but if Philby suspected that Hollis was a spy he did not admit it to Blunt and it would have been his professional duty not to do so.[36]

During his long interrogations following his confession in 1964, Blunt became convinced, as did his interrogators, that he could not possibly have been 'Elli', and neither could Philby.[37]

In their efforts to dismiss the 'Elli' evidence Hollis's supporters have suggested that Gouzenko must have been referring to Philby or to another self-confessed spy called Charles 'Dick' Ellis, but both of these were in MI6. Ellis seems to have been put forward as a candidate for 'Elli' on the grounds that the names are so alike, but in 1942 and 1943 he was working in New York at British Security Co-ordination Headquarters and could not possibly fit the information detailed in Gouzenko's evidence.

Some have even suggested that 'Elli' was another MI5 officer called Graham Mitchell, whose case is considered in Chapter 33, simply on the grounds that 'ell' were the last three letters of his name! But Hollis also had three letters figuring in 'Elli', and Mitchell, who was concerned with overseeing fascist activities during the war, had no easy access to files, or to anything else of much interest to the Soviets.

There is no doubt in the minds of MI5 and MI6 officers who eventually investigated Hollis that he is the best fit for 'Elli', particularly given the G.R.U. connection, Sonia's presence in the Oxford area and 'Elli's' ability to bring out files and supply other information of vital interest to Soviet Intelligence.

In the last respect some new and recent information supplied by Svetlana Gouzenko would seem to be significant. Her late husband's papers recall the arrival of his replacement from Moscow, which was the reason for Gouzenko's decision to defect as he realized that he might never have another chance to live in

113

freedom. The new cipher clerk's name was Koulakov, and when he remarked to Gouzenko that his new job should be an easy post after Moscow, Gouzenko replied that he would soon find that the amount of information being supplied by the G.R.U. Canadian spy-ring was so staggering that there was enough to keep three cipher clerks busy. Koulakov then boasted that it was 'just a trickle' compared with the amount of material reaching G.R.U. headquarters from agents in Britain and America. 'They do not have a healthy spot left in their security agencies,' he said. 'Moscow has everything, including secret files of agents. I decoded these myself.'[38]

After reading her husband's notes on Koulakov's statements Mrs Gouzenko feels confident that the reference to 'secret files of agents' could have been, at least in part, files on Soviet agents operating in Britain. Clearly, these were being supplied to Moscow by G.R.U. agents in Britain, of whom 'Elli' was one.

In my opinion there can be little doubt that 'Elli' existed, that he was in MI5 and probably at Blenheim in 1942, and that inquiries into his identity which might have led to his exposure were smothered. The 'Elli' evidence alone goes far to dispose of the claim that no evidence against Hollis ever accrued from defectors and that the deficiency is a great weakness in the case against him. As will be seen, the evidence that 'Elli' could have been Hollis was to be strengthened years later when information from other defectors gave further evidence of the continuing existence of a Soviet agent at high level inside MI5.

Gouzenko's evidence and the ensuing prosecution of so many Soviet spies and agents in Canada, the U.S. and Britain gave a clear indication of the size of the G.R.U. espionage effort. In his book *This Was My Choice*, Gouzenko claimed that there were 'thousands of agents in Great Britain', and while this was probably an exaggeration the total was surely substantial. Few of them were ever detected because MI5 too readily assumed that the 'Red Orchestra' had been disbanded at the end of the war. Old hands had retired but new G.R.U. agents were being recruited and some old ones were kept in play with continuing advantage to Moscow, as the ensuing chapter shows.

The Potential Value of Oversight

If MI5 had known that its activities could be subject to independent examination by an oversight body its treatment of Gouzenko's information about 'Elli' might not have been so superficial and it might have been deterred from smothering of the information,

114

which undoubtedly occurred not only in 1946 but, as will be seen, in 1952. If the suppression had still been accomplished an alert oversight body would have required an explanation. Oversight could also have countered the complacency which prevented any serious attempt to discover whether there were active G.R.U. and K.G.B. rings in Britain. Gouzenko's evidence showed the existence of such rings operating quite independently in Canada and made it clear that they existed in other target countries. They had their own resident chiefs, their own case officers and agents, their own cipher machines, ciphers and cipher clerks. The K.G.B. and G.R.U. Centres were separately based in Moscow, as Gouzenko's evidence proved. While he was able to inform Canadian security about the G.R.U. in great detail, he knew nothing about K.G.B. arrangements and operations beyond their undoubted existence and the names of some K.G.B. personnel working under cover in the Embassy in Ottawa. MI5 should have assumed that such a situation must have existed in Britain and should have taken more effective steps to counter it. Effective oversight might have required them to do more in that direction than they did. As will be seen, their discoveries about the K.G.B. ring were the result of fortuitous events, and they learned virtually nothing about the G.R.U. ring. ring.

The arrest of Nunn May was to count as an MI5 success, though it derived entirely from Gouzenko's disclosures. As will be seen, MI5 was to depend for its further apparent successes on the evidence of defectors. Nevertheless, the same deprecating attitude to defectors which showed itself in Canada made itself felt in MI5 and still exists. Perceptive oversight might have detected this negative approach and done something to remedy it.

CHAPTER FIFTEEN

The Return of Klaus Fuchs

AFTER the final defeat of Germany in May 1945, the previous tenant of Avenue Cottage in Oxford required its return and Sonia had to find new accommodation. Some time in the summer of that year, after she and her children had attended the Victory street-party organized by Mrs Laski, she found an empty house in the Cotswold village of Great Rollright, near Chipping Norton.[1] The house, called The Firs, which still exists unchanged, is some thirteen miles from Blenheim Palace.

Sonia's husband was still serving in the army in Germany and was not to be demobilized until early in 1947. So it would seem that The Firs was stop-gap accommodation until Moscow decided what further work Sonia and, eventually, Len should undertake. Again, luck favoured Soviet Intelligence. Great Rollright was only about thirty-five miles from Harwell, the site of Britain's new nuclear research establishment, which Fuchs joined in June 1946.

Hollis was to tell the Washington Conference on Security Standards that when Fuchs was given his Harwell post as an established civil servant, MI5 gave special consideration to his case because 'he was not British-born of British parents'. This was probably incorrect. As I recollect events, which I was reporting actively at the time, the 'British-born of British parents' require-ment was the result of Fuchs's conviction in 1950. It is much more likely that MI5 was required to make a special investigation into Fuchs in 1946 because a list of espionage suspects had been sent to MI5 by the Royal Canadian Mounted Police as a result of the Gouzenko case and Fuchs's name was on it. This was confirmed to a Canadian Parliamentary committee in 1950 by Lester Pearson, the Canadian Foreign Secretary.

A Canadian professor, Israel Halperin, was among those arrested on Gouzenko's evidence in February 1946, though he was later acquitted. The police took possession of Halperin's pocket-book which contained many addresses, including that of Fuchs when he had lived in Edinburgh. Halperin, who knew Fuchs's sister, had sent him books and newspapers while he had been interned in Canada in 1940. The possible connection with Halperin, who was mentioned in Gouzenko's purloined documents as 'Bacon', was therefore available to MI5 before Fuchs returned to Britain.[2]

At Harwell Fuchs was the only scientist who was deeply involved in the design of the nuclear weapons which the British Government was developing following the collapse of the Anglo-American wartime collaboration. He was described as the 'one ubiquitous scientist at Harwell, on almost every committee'.[3] So he knew about the programmes to develop nuclear explosives as well as nuclear power, with project dates of the greatest interest to the Soviet Union. As will be seen, the special security checks applied by MI5 to this fount of secrets was incompetent in the extreme.

Before he had left the U.S. Fuchs had been given instructions for continuing his espionage in Britain, just as Sonia had told him how to contact Soviet Intelligence prior to his departure for America. 'Raymond' had told him that he was to present himself outside the entrance to the Mornington Crescent Underground station in London on the first Saturday of every month after his return. He was to be carrying five books bound with string and supported by two fingers on one hand, and was to have two books in the other hand.[1] Fuchs was to claim that he did not keep any of these meetings, saying that he had been ill and was having doubts about the wisdom of his actions. He also claimed that the Soviets made no effort to contact him or to renew the association in any other way.[5]

According to Alan Moorehead, Fuchs 'did not feel the need to pass information to the Russians until early 1947'.[6] In fact the date was late 1946 – so he did not waste much time.[7] As Sonia has recorded, she had quickly begun transmitting from her new address in Great Rollright in 1945 and from there could have continued to service a source in MI5, even if this had been Hollis, because he returned to Blenheim from London often enough. One of the few official documents known to have been released with his name on them shows that she still regarded Blenheim as his headquarters as late as September 1945.[8] Early in 1946, however, the Moscow Centre cut off communication with Sonia so that for some months she became inactive and stopped her transmissions. She suggests in her memoirs that 'something had happened in another country' of which she was told nothing. She was right, and it was an event which deeply involved Hollis. The Centre's precautionary action was due to the defection of Gouzenko in Canada and the resulting prosecution of Nunn May. The Centre would automatically have seen this as threatening Fuchs, whom Sonia had previously serviced, especially as she was in a G.R.U. network. As Fuchs himself was to admit, he was frightened by the ten-year sentence passed on Nunn May, only a month before he was due to return to Britain, though he felt confident that he would not come under suspicion.[9]

He had, in fact, become sufficiently suspect, as Hollis revealed to the Washington Security Standards Conference, for the Security Service to maintain 'for several months a very careful secret check on his activities' on his return to Harwell in 1946. Hollis explained that this had disclosed 'nothing derogatory' because it subsequently transpired that 'during this particular period, he was not engaged in any espionage activities'.

As Hollis had been so closely associated with the Gouzenko case and the subsequent prosecution of Nunn May he should have realized that other Soviet spies would have been ordered to become dormant until a safe interval, certainly lasting several months, had elapsed. It was right that MI5 should begin surveillance right away, in case Fuchs was foolish, but it should have been continued for more than several months. It is quite clear that it was not. Indeed it was ended just at the time when Fuchs was to be reactivated and if Hollis was responsible for this, as seems likely from his statements to the Washington Conference, then he was either grossly incompetent or worse. If Hollis was a spy he would have known from his controller that Fuchs had been deactivated on his arrival and also the date of his reactivation. Historians, no doubt, will be asked to believe that the ending of the surveillance when Fuchs was resuming his espionage was yet another coincidence.

During Fuchs's dormancy he would not have contacted his former German communist comrades; most of them had anyway already moved to East Germany, where their creed was being put into practice, and by the time he did re-establish contact the surveillance had been terminated. So, at the end of November 1947, when the Government wished to make Fuchs's post at Harwell permanent, MI5, which by that time was supposed to have its sights firmly on the threat from the U.S.S.R., reported that although an analysis of five previous inquiries into his background had suggested that he could be a sufficiently dedicated communist to leak information to the Soviet Union, the risk was slight.[10] Confirmation of his post therefore went ahead and he became head of the theoretical physics department, living in a boarding house in Abingdon for two and a half years before moving into quarters on the Harwell site.

Regarding the dormancy imposed on Sonia there was a factor, apart from her past association with Fuchs, which may have been more pressing. The Centre had also been told, by Philby if by nobody else, that Gouzenko had given a lead to an important spy inside MI5 with the code-name 'Elli'.

Contacts with Soviet spies and agents seem to have been disrupted in many parts of the world at that time and only when the Centre had reviewed the situation and had decided that Fuchs and, presumably, 'Elli' seemed to be safe did it resume contact with Sonia, who records that she was working again in the autumn of 1946. The speed with which full working contact was renewed suggests that the Centre had inside information about the lack of serious MI5 interest in Fuchs or 'Elli' and that any surveillance of the former had ceased.

The reactivation of Sonia by the Centre and Fuchs's alleged 'decision' to restart active espionage are unlikely to have been purely coincidental. It had long been stringent practice for Soviet agents to be very firmly instructed that if the Centre broke contact with them they must do nothing whatever to re-establish it until required to do so by the Centre, however long the delay might be.[11] So the odds are that Fuchs was positively reactivated in some way by the Centre. It is inconceivable that with Soviet interest in the H-bomb being so intense the Centre would have permitted its major source on that subject to lie fallow until it suited him to resume contact. The reality of the rather farcical defence put forward at Fuchs's trial that his mind was like a sieve which opened to let secrets out and then closed, only to reopen again, is probably that he was instructed to remain inactive and then informed that it was safe to restart the handing over of technical information. Yet both the court and MI5 appear to have accepted the explanation he offered.

If Fuchs's own account of his movements is to be believed, he tried to find his old friend and fellow-agent, Juergen Kuczynski, who by that time had left Britain for 'Berlin'. According to an F.B.I. document Fuchs claimed that he then contacted a woman 'whom he knew to be active in connection with the underground section of the German Communist Party' and with whom he would appear to have already been in touch.[12] She is named in the document as Johanna Klopstech and inquiries show that she was almost certainly the same woman as the Hanna Klopstoch named in the list of foreign communists considered dangerous that MI5 had supplied to the U.S. Embassy in December 1940. She was one of many Sudeten Germans from Czechoslovakia received into Britain after the Munich Agreement of 1938 because it was feared that they would be persecuted by the Nazis. She must still have been active in the German communist underground and was one of the pro-Soviet subversives for whom Hollis and his section were still responsible, as they had been throughout the war.

It is an ironic coincidence that just when Fuchs was resuming his spying, a report from the Chiefs of Staff warned ministers that a large number of communist scientists who had been recruited into secret defence establishments during the war were still in post.[13] The Cabinet Defence Committee, chaired by the Prime Minister, Clement Attlee, was told that the Soviet participation in the war had drawn people from the professional classes into the Communist Party and that some of them would feel it their duty to give the Soviets all the information they could. This and other evidence was to lead to a purge of defence scientists in some establishments but it did not touch Fuchs who had been effectively cleared by MI5 and remained so.

Fuchs claimed that he told Klopstech that he had 'lost contact' and asked her to let the Soviets know that he was keen to give them information. Within a week or so he was in touch with a Soviet Intelligence officer from the Embassy and, from then on, met him at intervals in London. Some indication of what he handed over is provided by a detailed report of long conversations between Fuchs and an intelligent fellow-prisoner, Donald Hume, a murderer. Hume's report, which came into my possession in March 1958 following his release from gaol, was vetted by MI5, to which I submitted it. Hume's notes are packed with information which could only have come from Fuchs during the many hours they talked together. Among it is Fuchs's statement that he started giving the Russians up-to-date information on the H-bomb in 1947. This included American data which he had learned while working in the Los Alamos laboratories, as well as post-war British deliberations on the problem.

While there is little doubt that Fuchs did meet Soviet Embassy Intelligence controllers in London on occasion, professional counter-espionage officers have assured me that it would have been Soviet practice to keep such dangerous contacts with a highly productive spy to a minimum and to have used a courier for more regular meetings and to service dead-letter boxes. Such a courier would not, normally, have been a Russian, particularly in view of the diplomatic repercussions of the very recent Gouzenko disclosures, but would have been an 'illegal' agent located more conveniently to Fuchs's home or place of work.

MI5 officers concerned with the case are in little doubt that this courier was Sonia, who not only had her own clandestine radio but was a safe person to use because she was then under no suspicion whatsoever. She had handled Fuchs expertly before his transfer to

America and was living within reasonable distance of Harwell. She had excellent cover, as a housewife and mother, and as both she and Fuchs had been German refugees who could have met socially, there was a reasonable explanation if they were ever seen together. There was the further social excuse, if necessary, that Fuchs had been friendly with her brother Juergen, who was still so far from being suspect that, before moving to an important post in East Germany in November 1945, he had worked in the U.S. Strategic Bombing Survey, with close connections with the American Office of Strategic Services (O.S.S.), the forerunner of the C.I.A.

On his posting to the U.S. Fuchs had been transferred from the G.R.U. to the K.G.B. While Sonia believed that she was still atttached to the Red Army (G.R.U.), the K.G.B. had gained such ascendancy over the G.R.U. by 1947, on Stalin's orders, that it would have been quite possible for Sonia to have been instructed to resume service as a courier for Fuchs. It is not inconceivable that Sonia herself had been transferred to the K.G.B. Juergen had, unquestionably, been sent to Britain as a G.R.U. agent, but by 1943, according to his own memoirs, he had become a close friend of Anatoli Gromov, the K.G.B. officer in the Soviet Embassy then controlling Philby, Maclean, Blunt and other members of the Cambridge Ring.[14]

Fuchs had quickly acquired a motor car on his return to Britain and was only half an hour's drive from Sonia. Further, when Sonia's husband Len was demobilized early in 1947 he bought a motorcycle which assisted them in keeping their assignations, including, according to witnesses, trips to Oxford and London.[15] It would, therefore, have been easy for Fuchs and Sonia to have met surreptitiously at some intermediate point, as they had previously met at Banbury.

It may be significant that while Fuchs was to tell his interrogators that on his return to England he met his controllers in London, one of the specific charges on which he was convicted related to an occurrence in Berkshire in 1947.

There is evidence, worthy of recording, if not completely reliable after such a long time-lapse, that Fuchs visited Sonia at Great Rollright. She was kept so busy with her three children and her espionage work that she had to get household help and the only way she could afford to do that was to take in a newly married couple, Mr and Mrs Tom Greathead, who assisted in the house in return for board and lodging. They moved in on 20 May 1949 and remained there until August 1950. They still live nearby and, when interviewed on my behalf, they described one fairly regular visitor whom they remembered as a well-mannered German who spoke good English in a quiet voice, had receding hair and wore spectacles. When shown photographs of Fuchs, without being told his name, they identified him as being like the German.[16]

Sonia remained busy in ways which aroused the suspicions of the Greatheads and their neighbours. The Greatheads recall that she was constantly typing in foreign languages and that she explained this by saying that she did a translation job for 'the Government'. They remember that nothing was ever left in a waste-paper basket and that every scrap of waste paper was burned daily in the garden.

Former members of the Home Guard, like Mr Jack Bufton, who remembers Sonia and Len well, wondered why she was in the habit of stringing up radio aerials, as did another surviving neighbour, Sister Hains.[17] When Mr Bufton delivered two sacks of potatoes to the landing of a flight of steps leading down to the small cellar, and some of them spilled down the stairs, he recalls how purposefully Sonia prevented him from going down to pick them up. Later he learned that the cellar contained a surprisingly large number of radio parts and components. So secretive was Sonia about the cellar that the Greatheads were astonished to learn, from my researcher, that there was one, though they had lived in the house for more than a year.

While Sonia did not invite her neighbours into her home there were many visitors from elsewhere and the Greatheads were told of several such people – likely to have had false names – who could use the house as they pleased if they arrived while Sonia was out or away. Sonia had much to say to her visitors, usually in German, but when she spoke to her neighbours, such as Sister Hains, or to the Greatheads, she never spoke about her past, and her children had been told to be equally tight-lipped on that subject.

In her memoirs Sonia tries to establish that after 1947 she ceased to function as a radio operator and contacted the Centre only through Russians whom she met clandestinely, usually in London, or through dead-letter boxes, but the evidence of living witnesses strongly suggests that she transmitted, at least occasionally, into 1949 and possibly until her departure in 1950. Whether her visitors included Fuchs or not, some of them are likely to have been co-conspirators and the fact that they felt safe in visiting her at her home is highly suggestive that, through the Centre, she knew that she was not under any surveillance. In view of the events described in Chapter 17 this was extraordinary, to say the least.

Sonia's continuing capability to transmit clandestinely from Great Rollright well into 1947, at least, is equally extraordinary. It must, surely, be presumed that the ban on the decipherment of Soviet radio traffic was removed soon after the end of the war when the U.S.S.R. was quickly recognized as a potential adversary. Responsibility for detecting her illegal transmissions had passed to G.C.H.Q. and I have been assured that if they had been detected they would have been the subject of discussions by the Counter-Clandestine Committee which had representatives from MI5 and MI6.[18] A plan of action for the location of the transmitter would have been formulated, but since no such action was taken it must be assumed either that her transmissions were never detected or that G.C.H.Q. was told to ignore them. It has been suggested that MI5 might have done that because Sonia had been turned and was serving as a double agent, but I can find no supporting evidence of that whatever and neither could the MI5 officers who were later to investigate Hollis and his possible connection with Sonia. This, of course, does not rule out the possibility that G.C.H.Q. was told to ignore Sonia's transmissions for another, more sinister purpose.

CHAPTER SIXTEEN

The 'Blowing' of Sonia

WHILE Hollis's Section F remained at Blenheim for the rest of the war he returned to London in February 1943 because the Director-General wanted all his section heads to be available quickly at headquarters in 57 St James's Street.[1] Hollis moved into 6 Campden Hill Square, W.8, a sizeable house in a fashionable part of London, close to Kensington High Street, where he was to remain until his retirement in 1965. The house must have been beyond his modest means and his colleagues believe that his wife paid for it.[2]

MI5 was working a six-day week throughout the war, and Hollis continued to visit his section at Blenheim about twice a week. So it would have been possible for Sonia to continue to service him there, and in London, which she was in the habit of visiting twice a month to see her brother. For several months, however, Hollis was in a sanatorium at Cirencester recovering from a recurrence of his tuberculosis.[3]

In the following year, 1944, Philby became his opposite number in MI6. They both served on the Joint Intelligence Sub-Committee which dealt with communist affairs and as Philby records, they were soon exchanging information about their investigations of Soviet and communist activities 'without reserve on either side'.[4] Colleagues of both men have told me that in such a partnership Philby would have been the dominant personality, being intellectually superior. If Hollis was a spy Philby may well never have known it. Nor is it likely that Hollis would have been told about Philby's true loyalty. If, however, they were each known to the other as a Soviet agent they would have formed a most formidable axis. In any case, the fact that it was Hollis who was responsible for countering Philby, among other Soviet spies, made their relationship either laughable or suggestive.

Few documents concerning Hollis's activities have been released but one, dated 10 September 1945, relates to a secret report forecasting the Soviet Union's aims for the part of Germany then occupied by its troops.[5] Hollis warned that the Soviets would set up an independent communist administration and Sovietize their zone. It has been suggested that this is *prima facie* evidence that he was loyal, but there is little else he could have said at the time because it was self-evident. The document confirms that Hollis's personal headquarters was still at Blenheim, with the telegraphic code-name of 'Snuffbox' and the address Box 500, G.P.O., Oxford.

With the ending of the war Hollis's standing suddenly improved. While the overseeing of communists and Soviet agents had been regarded as a relatively minor function during the war of national survival against Germany, Italy and Japan, it assumed great importance with the rapid emergence of the Soviet Union as the main adversary in what became the Cold War. Those of Hollis's former colleagues who explain his ensuing failures as due to incompetence have pointed out that these changed circumstances catapulted him into a position of responsibility for which he was not fitted, intellectually or temperamentally. Though he had never mentioned any knowledge of communists or communism when he had entered MI5 in 1938, he had become the accepted authority on international communism in the organization eight years later.

In May 1946 it became necessary to appoint a successor to the wartime Director-General of MI5, Sir David Petrie, who was sixty-six. Guy Liddell was the professional choice but the new Labour Prime Minister, Clement Attlee, was suspicious of the organization, perhaps with memories of the faked Zinoviev Letter, which had damaged the Labour Party in 1924, and his belief that the MI5 professionals could be guaranteed to be pro-Tory because of the way they were recruited. He therefore decided to appoint 'an honest copper' in the form of Sir Percy Sillitoe, a former Chief Constable, and told him that his prime task was to be the investigation and elimination of communist subversion, as it was becoming clearer by the day that the Soviet Union was determined to use its wartime position to extend its influence wherever it could.

This appointment of an outsider created hostility to Sillitoe from the beginning because it meant that several senior promotions were set back. Liddell, who was too old to succeed Sillitoe when his retirement came, was particularly bitter.

According to Sillitoe's biographer, A. W. Cockerill, the new chief instructed Hollis to brief him fully on communist subversion, but all Hollis did was to hand him a description of the state of the Communist Party, which he had already compiled.[6] Cockerill records that Sillitoe was deeply disappointed when Hollis produced so little evidence of communist subversion, especially as Attlee and his Cabinet, using their own resources, became convinced that communists were behind a series of crippling strikes.[7]

MI5's limited grasp of international communism was to be further illustrated when Alexander Foote, Sonia's former fellow-spy in Switzerland, defected from the G.R.U. to his native Britain in March 1947 and offered his services to MI5. He was interrogated by a counter-espionage specialist called Courtenay Young and told all he knew about the operations of the Lucy Ring, including Sonia's early role in it and how she had been involved in his recruitment and training. He alerted MI5 to Sonia's presence in Britain – the first they had heard of it, at least officially – and said that her husband, Len, who had also been a G.R.U. agent, had rejoined her.[8] If 'Elli' was still in MI5 when Foote arrived, as I believe he was, he must have been very frightened and would have taken all possible steps to nullify any information which threatened him.

It has been suggested that Foote was a double agent who had worked for the G.R.U. in Switzerland with Britain's knowledge and connivance, but my inquiries have satisfied me that this was not so. He did not supply any information to MI5 when he knew that Sonia was moving to Britain in 1940, nor did he mention Sonia's sister, Brigitte, who had been involved in his recruitment and was also in England. In fact, he supplied no information to Britain until he defected after a post-war visit to the Soviet Union where he had become disenchanted with the attitude to his own wartime sacrifices and to those of other members of the Lucy Ring, some of whom were given long sentences in Soviet prisons. After about eighteen months in the U.S.S.R. Foote had been sent back into the field to pose as a German, called Albert Mueller, and gain entry to the Argentine where he was to join a ring operating against the U.S. He was already ill apart from being disillusioned, and had therefore returned to Britain via Berlin.

When a man is a double agent he is in such a dangerous position that much of the material about him and his activities is held in MI5 on specially secret record. Foote's file in MI5 was an ordinary open file held in the General Registry, with no reference to secret volumes.[9]

Foote told MI5 of Sonia's claim, before she left Switzerland, that she was ending her allegiance to the Soviet Union because she had been so shattered by the Nazi-Soviet pact. In his book *Handbook for Spies*, published in 1949, Foote makes much of this disillusionment. Nevertheless, he told MI5 that a professional G.R.U. spy had moved to Britain in December 1940 and that she was a highly trained clandestine radio operator. Foote also added that while he had been told in Moscow that Sonia had been dormant in Britain during the war, he himself had been required to send her a message to contact a Soviet Military Attaché in London, who was almost certainly Kremer.

In June 1947 Sonia's 67-year-old mother, Berthe, died while staying at Great Rollright, and her father, René, who was mortally ill himself, remained with his daughter for a few months.[10] He was still there in late August when two MI5 officials and a local detective were dispatched to question Sonia about Foote's evidence. The C.I.D. man used her possibly bigamous marriage to Len as a pretext to gain entry to the house and open the proceedings.[11] From then on the behaviour of the MI5 men, and of their superiors at headquarters, was incredible.

As Sonia records in her memoirs, they told her – with her father in the room as a witness – that they knew she had been a Soviet agent. Then, over the tea which she provided, they assured her that they knew she had ceased to spy after being disillusioned by the Soviet Union's pact with Nazi Germany and that after her marriage to Len, whom they also knew to be a former agent, she had become a loyal British citizen. This made no sense, least of all to Sonia, her husband and her father, all of whom were spies, but she hastened to agree with them, finding the situation so comical that she found it difficult not to laugh.

In her memoirs Sonia claims to have been warned in the previous month about Foote's defection to MI5. Foote is supposed to have visited 'an Austrian comrade' in a trembling dishevelled state, muttered 'Sonia and Len! Great danger! Don't work! Destroy everything!' and then to have run away. This strange story could be disinformation concerning the true source, for the fact that she remained totally relaxed in what should have been a highly dangerous situation for her certainly points to her having been forewarned of the visit by someone. Both she and her husband, who by that time had a manual job with an aluminium company in Banbury, simply refused to answer questions.

Any memoirs written by a former Soviet spy and published behind the Iron Curtain are suspect. This applied particularly to those published while Andropov was still head of the K.G.B. as he was in 1977 when Sonia's memoirs appeared, because he encouraged the production of books which improved the image of the K.G.B. at the expense of the Western agencies. Sonia's account of the MI5 visit, however, has been confirmed to me by a prime source. The officers had been instructed only to confirm Foote's story that Sonia had retired from espionage before reaching Britain, and her memoirs record that they wanted to talk only about her activities in Switzerland. A desultory effort was made to induce her to become some sort of double agent, which could only mean that her legend of having been inactive since 1940 was not really believed in the higher levels of MI5. She indignantly refused, as did Len, and the officers went away without any search of the house, which might have revealed her transmitting equipment unless, being forewarned, she had hidden it.

That was the end of MI5's interest in the couple who had inflicted so much damage on the nation, until twenty years later when Hollis was to come under suspicion. I have established that no attempt was made to put her or her house under surveillance before she was approached or afterwards. Yet there is evidence that the very next day she and Len were scheduled to make an important rendezvous, possibly with Fuchs.[12] At that time he was shortly to make a visit to the U.S. for talks with American atomic scientists and could have been required to receive instructions about contacts there.

Sonia herself records that she and Len kept careful watch to ensure that they were not under surveillance, and they may have been assisted in this by professionals from the Soviet Embassy, but they soon satisfied themselves that nothing whatever was being done. Again, this could be disinformation to cover the fact that they had been told via an inside MI5 source that nothing was being done. She had, of course, immediately reported the episode to the Centre and claims that she became convinced that it would put an end to her use in Britain and that she and Len had already decided to emigrate to East Germany.

The only effect of MI5's visit was to warn the Beurtons that they were under suspicion, and it is difficult to interpret it other than as an exercise which had been necessitated by circumstances which could not be ignored but which was not seriously intended to yield anything. It would, therefore, be instructive to know who gave the visiting officers their orders and who briefed them. I have been advised that there would have been a meeting at MI5 headquarters, possibly with Sillitoe or his deputy present, but certainly attended by Hollis. Because of his special knowledge of communists and international communism and his responsibility for Soviet spies Hollis is likely to have been regarded as the best source of advice about how Sonia should be approached and treated and what, if anything, should be done about any follow-up. Regrettably, another officer likely to have been present at such a meeting, Courtenay Young, is dead, while his senior officer, who is still alive, cannot recall whether Sonia was interviewed or not.

Understandably, Foote came to believe that there were officers inside MI5 who had no intention of exposing the Beurtons. He went so far as to suggest that a committee of Privy Councillors should examine the reasons why no good use had been made of his information, but there was no sensible response.[13]

Foote had further reason for his concern which has only recently been made available to me. Because of his long experience in transmitting clandestine messages to Moscow, Foote was of the greatest interest to G.C.H.Q. He was therefore interviewed in depth by a G.C.H.Q. counter-intelligence officer called Ray Frawley who had a reputation as 'an intellectual tiger' determined to discover everything he could about Soviet methods of radio communication, codes and ciphers.[14] His interview with Foote was very comprehensive and provided a great deal of insight. A collateral interview with Sonia, who was far more experienced and closer to the G.R.U. Centre than Foote, should have been an essential requirement. I have established that no such interview was attempted. Why not? Was G.C.H.Q. not told about Sonia? I have been assured that Frawley would have made every effort to see her if it had been. Or was G.C.H.Q. given false information about Sonia by MI5? It seems inconceivable that Frawley could have interrogated Foote without learning about Sonia, unless Foote had been instructed by MI5 to avoid mentioning her.

The answer almost certainly lies in the MI5 legend that Sonia fled the country shortly after she had been visited by MI5 officers, a legend which has been repeated in several books. If Foote had been told that Sonia had fled by the time that Frawley was allowed to interview him, then G.C.H.Q.'s failure to see her is explicable; G.C.H.Q. would take MI5's word about Sonia's whereabouts. In fact, she was still living in Britain, at The Firs, and continued to do so until February 1950.[15]

It would be highly instructive to know who was responsible for the legend that Sonia fled in 1947, and the MI5 files should provide some clues if they have not been destroyed. I have established beyond question that Sonia's presence in Britain was not being kept secret because she was working as a double under MI5 control. Either MI5 was so incompetent that it believed that Sonia had fled, or someone in MI5 knew the truth and lied about it.

I have secured a highly professional opinion about MI5's attitude to the Sonia case and the view is that she survived because she was being protected by someone in a position to do so.

The MI5 legend about Sonia's flight is so firmly established that a very senior former officer concerned with counter-espionage at the time told me recently: 'When we did learn about her she bolted back to Germany, I think in 1947 or 1948.'[16] Her former lodgers, the Greatheads, can testify to her departure early in 1950, and this accords with Sonia's own account. Writers, including myself, have previously been led to believe that the Centre ordered her to move to the safety of East Germany as soon as arrangements could be made after the abortive MI5 visit. Although a precipitate flight might in fact have been judged imprudent because it would indicate her guilt and perhaps put her British sources at risk, the truth, as with so much that is on record about the Soviet Intelligence assault on the West, is very different – and much more intriguing.

Sonia records that the U.S. military authorities in Berlin refused to allow her to go there and that to expedite matters she visited Prague in January 1949 to meet her brother, Juergen, who had travelled from Berlin.[17] Again, this could be disinformation to account for the real truth – that Soviet Intelligence wanted her to continue her activities, possibly in servicing Fuchs and others, and that she had been assured that she could do this in complete safety until further notice.

In December 1949 her – and Hollis's – old Shanghai friend, the journalist and writer Agnes Smedley, visited Britain intending to move on to China. She stayed mainly in Wimbledon but also in Oxford where she was taken ill and died, aged fifty-eight, following an operation for an acute stomach condition.[18] In her memoirs Sonia says that though she heard that Agnes was close by she avoided seeing her because her own position was 'so critical and difficult'. It is more likely that if she did avoid a meeting, it was to protect her contacts because Miss Smedley might have been under surveillance – which she was not – or because she had another Shanghai connection in mind, in which case it would have been crucially important not to draw attention to it.

While Sonia's memoirs can be expected to contain some Soviet disinformation, I have crosschecked information which I have used. I carried out a similar exercise with the *Handbook for Spies*, published under Foote's name and regarded as something of a classic in the literature of espionage. It was in fact written by Foote's case officer, Courtenay Young, and it contains deliberate disinformation which will anger many serious researchers who have been misled by it.[19] It names Sonia's second husband, Len, as Bill Phillips, a name he never used, and her first as Alfred Schultz, which was fabricated by Young.[20] It also names Sonia's nanny as Lisa Brockel when her real name was Olga Muth. This 'muddying of the waters' was partly in keeping with MI5's practice of avoiding disclaimers by not mentioning the names of people who were still alive, but its main result was to make it difficult for any unwelcome investigator to find Sonia or either of her husbands. Such faking throws doubt on other aspects of the book which cannot be checked and gives cause to wonder whether Foote was really convinced that Sonia had ceased to be a spy when she left Switzerland. Perhaps Young, when ghosting Foote's account, exaggerated this conviction to help to excuse MI5's culpable negligence in failing to investigate Sonia. In that event it would be instructive to know who suggested that he should do so.

The publication of the *Handbook for Spies* in 1949 and the publicity it received presumably caused some concern to the G.R.U. Centre, and Sonia, who brands Foote as a traitor, may have suffered a few shudders, but the false names gave her some protection and she may have been made aware of the myth that she had already left the country. The fact that G.C.H.Q., which must have read the book with interest and may have been involved in its ghosting, did not demand to see Sonia supports the view that it, too, had swallowed the legend.

CHAPTER SEVENTEEN

The Rise of Roger Hollis

Sir Percy Sillitoe took time to work himself into the job before attempting the reorganization of MI5 which was necessary to deal with the post-war situation. With the retirement of the Deputy Director in 1947, Liddell was promoted to that post and Sillitoe had to rely heavily on him and on other professionals like Dick White for advice. In late 1947 or early 1948, though Hollis had not distinguished himself in any official capacity and letters confirm that he had been away ill for several months with a recurrence of his tuberculosis, he was promoted to be Director of C Branch.[1] This made him a member of MI5's governing directorate with access to much highly secret information outside his own department. An MI5 colleague who recalls the announcement of this promotion at an office party says it was received with astonishment and, on the part of several officers, with dismay, because other candidates were thought to have a stronger claim. It was normal practice in post-war MI5 for the directors to have a university degree, but for some unknown reason an exception was made of Hollis.[2]

The promotion was especially surprising because with the increased Soviet activity to penetrate British secrets, C Branch, which was responsible for security in general, would have enhanced importance.[3]

Apologists for Hollis have referred to his 'wartime achievements' as evidence of his loyalty, but if any exist they have proved extremely difficult to discover. While he had been responsible for overseeing the activities of Soviet agents and curbing their activities the following are known to have operated without hindrance from MI5, some of them on a catastrophic scale: Burgess, Maclean, Philby, Blunt, Cairncross, James Klugmann, Leo Long, Fuchs, Sonia, Juergen Kuczynski, René Kuczynski, Hans Kahle, Gerhart Eisler and many others, some of them Britons who are still sheltering behind the libel laws. I have in fact been unable to discover any Soviet agent whose wartime activities were curbed in any way by Hollis's counter-measures, with the possible exception of Springhall, who was mainly under routine surveillance by Special Branch.

In spite of Hollis's lack of achievement it was thought that he knew more about anti-Soviet counter-espionage than anyone else. As one of his contemporaries, working as a secretary, explained it recently, 'The trouble was that all the clever ones left MI5 as soon as they could when the war was over.'

In his new post Hollis was responsible for the prevention of espionage and leakages by methods which have been officially summarized by a later Director-General of MI5: 'Protective security is the body of regulations which regulate the behaviour, in relation to security information, of those who have access to it and it also regulates the selection of those who have access to it. It involves the processes of selection which are supposed to weed out those who may be unreliable and it embraces also their supervision once they have been taken on. It involves their education in security, in the things they should do and the things they should not do when they have charge of security information. It embraces an enormous range of rules for the handling of classified documents... It embraces the physical measures taken for the protection of information, such as locks and safes, guards on buildings and pass systems. Protective security also embraces the prevention of leakages... In support of counter-espionage the Director of the Protective Security Branch is very much concerned with it.'[4]

The last sentence is evidence enough that if Hollis was a spy his promotion put him in an excellent position to serve Soviet Intelligence for, in addition to being 'very much concerned' with counter-espionage, he attended the weekly directors' meeting where he learned about the activities of other departments. He was also superbly placed to receive rapid warning of any event which might threaten his safety, such as the arrival of a defector or the decipherment of a revealing Soviet intercept. It would also have been to his advantage that responsibility for counter-espionage against the Soviet Union had been passed to Dick White, who had become Director of Section B, for White had absolute confidence in Hollis, as shown by his support for his subsequent promotions.

Sillitoe soon found himself faced with a campaign of noncooperation and hostility on the part of the professionals, who were determined to get rid of him. Sillitoe's son, Tony, has recalled: 'The MI5 executives used to hold what they called the afternoon tea-club in the canteen. On one occasion I went to meet my father there. We were both chatting with Hollis and White when, suddenly, Hollis half turned his back on my father and switched into Latin, a language he was well aware my father didn't understand. I knew enough to know that they were talking in epigrams. I thought it was some joke but they carried on and on and it was evident that they were simply snubbing the man. My father called his chauffeur and stormed out of the building, white-faced. When we got in the car I asked, "What was that all about?" He said, "One word – bastards!" He would return home to the flat in Putney night after night and tell my mother, "Dolly, I can't get to grips with a brick wall."[5]

Former senior officers of MI5 have confirmed that Liddell, White, Hollis and others isolated Sillitoe. Tony Sillitoe names Hollis as being the officer most responsible for the campaign of hostility 'which alienated Sir Percy from his staff'.[6]

The attitude of Graham Mitchell, who succeeded Hollis as head of the section responsible for overseeing communists, is not known, but he certainly improved MI5's penetration of the British Communist Party, mainly through the recruitment of young girls prepared to pose as communists. One of these, Betty Gordon, has disclosed the details of her activities over ten years, one year being served, courageously, as a spy in East Berlin.[7]

Hollis, who picked up a ritual O.B.E. for his war work, continued with his open belief that the communists offered little threat to Britain. Lieutenant Colonel Noel Wild, who had been in charge of developing deception plans to cover the Normandy landings and was later concerned with intelligence operations in the Defence Ministry, has told me of an incident which worried him. When he and Hollis had been discussing a projected operation against extreme left-wing trade union leaders, Hollis had predicted, 'There will never be a threat from Communism to this country.'[8]

By 1947 MI5 was installed in new headquarters in Leconfield House in Curzon Street and in that year Hollis began a sexual liaison with his secretary, Val Hammond, which soon became the talk of the office, especially among the numerous girls in the Registry. His wife soon knew about it but they came to some arrangement whereby they continued to live together, a situation which attracted office criticism on the grounds that he was, to some extent, living on his wife's private income.[9]

Unlike her boss, Miss Hammond was a graduate of Oxford, having studied French and German at St Hilda's from 1939 to 1942, when she received her B.A., becoming an M.A. in 1946.[10] Her preference for remaining Hollis's secretary for about eighteen years when she was qualified for promotion to officer status surprised her contemporaries, especially as she was to accept such promotion as soon as he had retired.

From the time that he became Director of Security Hollis was forever stressing the importance of security in MI5 and the danger of sexual involvements, which might lay an officer open to blackmail.[11] This led to comments that he had one law for others and another for himself. He may have argued that he could never be blackmailed when so many knew about his affair but he could hardly have wanted it known in the higher echelons of Whitehall or Downing Street when, if ever, he came up for consideration for the top appointment which necessitated the Prime Minister's agreement.

Overt zeal for security was no certain mark of loyalty, as Henry Arnold, the chief security officer for Harwell, was wont to point out. Indeed it was Klaus Fuchs's excessive zeal for security which first made him suspect in Arnold's eyes.[12]

As early as 1948 one MI5 officer already suspected that Hollis was a Soviet agent and was warning others that he should not be trusted with information. He has told me: 'There were personal indications that this man was open to grave suspicions. I never made any secret of them within MI5 over a considerable number of years but I was a lone voice.'

In that same year the Anglo-American team deciphering intercepted K.G.B. radio traffic passing between Moscow and the K.G.B. out-station in the Soviet Embassy in Canberra secured information which proved that the Soviets were making a major espionage effort in Australia, which had been singled out by Stalin as ripe for political penetration. Communist-controlled unions had been very effectively penetrated and were taking orders from the K.G.B., using Soviet money, and were inflicting damage on the economy. In addition, the K.G.B. was undoubtedly securing secret information from the Department of External Affairs – the Australian Foreign Office. The Government infra-structure had also been penetrated at various levels.[13]

As a result of this discovery the U.S. security authorities opposed the sharing of any secrets with Britain in case some of them might be passed to Australia in the course of British-Australian defence projects, which were being intensified following post-war decisions to transfer a great deal of military research to the huge continent, which had space for missile, aircraft and atomic developments. Sir Percy Sillitoe was, therefore, sent to Australia with a staff delegation to appraise the Government there of its danger and to convince its Prime Minister, Ben Chifley, that he needed a counter-intelligence and security agency to combat the Soviet drive. Hollis was a key figure in the delegation and was selected to deliver the detailed information about the K.G.B. penetrations in Australia and the names involved. Because the breaking of the Soviet codes had to be kept secret he was required to present the information as though it had come from a spy.[14]

The K.G.B. traffic to and from Australia was almost unique at that time in that it could be deciphered easily and quickly and, while Hollis was still there, further code-breaks showed that the scale of Soviet penetration was even greater than thought. The identities of more spies and agents of influence were exposed.[15]

The chief civil servant in the External Affairs Department, Dr J.W. Burton, who disbelieved Hollis's allegations, suggested that to secure some evidence a big Soviet delegation visiting Melbourne should be carefully watched to ascertain any clandestine Australian contacts. This was done with totally negative results, which have since been ascribed to the clumsiness of the operation but could also have been the result of advance warning to the K.G.B.[16]

Shortly after Hollis returned to Britain the K.G.B. changed the code-pads it had been using and the routine decipherment of its secret messages to Australia was never possible again, though there were occasional successes. It was assumed that the Soviets had made the change as a regular security precaution but, later, the possibility that Hollis had betrayed the code-break was seriously considered. He would not have been able to warn the Soviets before his visit to Australia as he had been told nothing about it until immediately before his departure, not having needed to know it before then. Whatever the truth, the events constituted yet another coincidence in a list becoming too long for credence.
Intelligence Organization (A.S.I.O.) very much on the lines of MI5. Hollis had not only given basic advice about it but had helped to pick some of the key officers for it. With the setting up of A.S.I.O., the British hoped to convince the Americans that the Australians would be secure but, as events were soon to show, the penetration of security in Britain had been far more serious than in Australia.

Hollis was later to perform a similar service for New Zealand when that country set up a security organization in 1957. Of the original nineteen officers in the New Zealand Intelligence Service, seven were said to have been recommended by Hollis and were British.[17]

As already described, Hollis was MI5's chief representative at the tripartite Conference on Security Standards in Washington in June 1950 and if he was a Soviet agent his behaviour there was a futher indication of the advantage of being an important figure in a security service. He was able to smooth over his own deficiencies in the Fuchs case and even to evoke some sympathy. Further, he was able to employ a device which would give him an excuse if it could be shown, later, that he had misled his audience. Although the British delegation must almost certainly have decided before it left Britain that it would review the Fuchs case for the Conference and explain MI5's actions, Hollis chose to begin by claiming that he had not briefed himself from the records and would be speaking from memory.[18] As will be seen, Hollis was a master at leaving himself escape routes from criticism when events under his control went sour. This trait was more indicative of an innate shrewdness than of the bumbling ineptitude that some of his apologists have ascribed to him.

CHAPTER EIGHTEEN

A Highly Suspect Escape

SONIA'S eventual departure was precipitate. She had applied for a visa to visit East Germany and her request to live there had been secretly approved. Then, early in 1950, she announced to neighbours that she was going to fly to East Germany for a holiday and would be taking her two younger children with her. She was never to return. Len had been unable to accompany her, partly because his leg was still in plaster following a serious motorcycle accident, but mainly because he had to clear up the house once she had made her escape. The eldest son, Mischa, then eighteen, was also to stay behind temporarily to complete his education.[1]

Sonia was a British subject so her flight was the defection to a communist country of a most damaging traitor, yet MI5 did not even seem to know about it, at least officially.

Sonia records that Soviet Intelligence expected her to continue her espionage in another area but, having done twenty years, she claimed that she had done enough. She was made head of the Press Section of the Office of Information in East Berlin, her chief being another superannuated spy, Gerhardt Eisler, who had been a contemporary of hers in China.

According to the Greatheads, before joining his wife in East Berlin Len cleared out The Firs in late August 1950 and held a small sale, though the house had been so sparsely furnished that he could not have realized much. Other villagers and the subsequent tenants recall that Len burned every scrap of paper, save for bundles of communist literature, which were later found above a barn. His thoroughness was unnecessary. Nobody from MI5 displayed any interest.

Len was to work for twenty years in the East German News Service, a common enough cover for an intelligence agent and at the time of writing is still alive. His departure was also the defection of a traitor about which MI5 appeared to know nothing.

The fact that the Moscow Centre considered it safe for the Beurtons to remain for more than two years in Britain after the visit

138

by MI5 strongly suggests that it had solid reason for its confidence, based on assurances provided by someone in Britain who knew that no further action against them was likely. It seems certain, from the evidence of their neighbours and lodgers, that the Beurtons were usefully active for the Centre until Sonia's departure. What then was the event which caused her hasty flight? There can be little doubt that it was the fate of her friend and agent, Klaus Fuchs.

During the Second World War a mass of coded radio traffic passing between the Soviet Foreign Office and its embassies and between Soviet Intelligence centres and their out-stations had been intercepted by American radio security service operators. As tape-recording machines were not then available, the intercepted messages, mainly in morse, were taken down by hand on signal-pads, which were filed away because almost all the decoding effort had to be directed against the existing enemies, Germany, Japan and Italy. When the Soviet cipher clerk, Igor Gouzenko, defected from the Soviet Embassy in Ottawa in 1945 it became apparent, from the documentary evidence he brought with him, that though the Soviet Union had been a wartime ally, albeit relutantly, it had been plotting to undermine Canada, the U.S. and Britain by means of widespread subversion and espionage. An examination of the collected Soviet intercepts was therefore undertaken by American and British cryptanalysts to uncover any further evidence of clandestine activity. This unbelievably laborious operation, which was to take in post-war intercepts and would continue for many years, was code-named Operation Bride, later changed in the mid fifties for routine security reasons to Operation Drug, and then, in the early sixties, to Operation Venona, the last name leading to the term 'V-material' for the deciphered intercepts.[2] In the U.S., the main seat of the operation, the work was conducted by the Armed Forces Security Agency, which in October 1952 became the National Security Agency. In Britain G.C.H.Q. was responsible for such work.

The Soviet messages had been transmitted in the normally unbreakable one-time pad code system in which the person sending the message and the one receiving it each have a small identical pad, every page of which is covered with lines of letters or figures chosen at random. The encoder uses the letters or figures from one page to encipher a message and the decoder, who is told which page is being used, can easily decipher it. As each page is different the code is almost unbreakable, provided each page is used only once. During the war, however, they were used more than once. The wartime Soviet pads were produced at a single centre in Moscow and intense pressures caused by the German threat to the city meant that it had not been possible to turn out enough pads at one stage of the conflict, or to deliver them to agents. To fill the gap pairs of pads were copied out and re-used in the belief that it was extremely unlikely that any interceptors would ever discover this and so make use of it. In fact, though millions of messages had been recorded, the American cryptanalysts soon realized that there had been a double use and by ingenious techniques were able to decipher many of them. The code-breakers were greatly assisted in this mammoth endeavour by the chance acquisition of a half-burned Soviet code-book, which had been found on a battlefield in Finland and was made available to the U.S.[3]

In the summer of 1949 some of the decoded messages revealed that there had been a major leak of atomic bomb secrets from the Los Alamos laboratories and that the source was a scientist with the code-name 'Rest'. A later message from New York to Moscow revealed that 'Rest' had a sister studying at an American university. This pointed to Fuchs, and when it was found that information from a secret report which he had written also appeared in the deciphered traffic he became the prime suspect.[4] The information was passed to MI5, where the counter-espionage branch was then headed by Dick White, with Hollis responsible for security. The receipt of this information has been authoritatively dated as 5 September 1949.[5]

Arthur Martin, an MI5 officer who had made a big contribution to the analysis of the Bride information, was put in charge of the Fuchs case. He found that a written assurance that Fuchs was loyal and trustworthy had been given to the 'Manhattan District' – the American atomic bomb project – and that it had derived from Section F of MI5 when Hollis had headed it. He noted that following the Gouzenko revelations four years earlier an address book belonging to a suspect communist called Israel Halperin had contained Fuchs's name. He also discovered that when Hollis had still been in charge of Section F in 1946 he had declined to take any action on an analysis indicating that Fuchs might be a Soviet agent and had agreed to his appointment to Harwell.[6]

When Fuchs eventually confessed he claimed that he had been having such doubts about the Soviet system that he had broken off contact with Soviet Intelligence early in 1949.[7] This statement appears to have been accepted by the security authorities and by writers who have made much of the 'crisis of conscience' he must have suffered. It would seem far more likely, in view of the dates, that Fuchs was warned to break off further contact, probably without being told the full extent of his danger. It is certain that the K.G.B. avoided any further contact with him after he became suspect and, in view of their intense interest in H-bomb research, they must have had strong reason for doing so.

It has been assumed that the K.G.B. Centre was warned about the suspicion concerning Fuchs by Kim Philby, a long-serving K.G.B. 'mole' planted inside MI6, who had been posted to Washington as liaison man between MI6 and the C.I.A. and F.B.I. One of his functions was to oversee the interchange of information concerning the breaks achieved by Operation Bride. As soon as he learned of Fuchs's danger he alerted the K.G.B., as he hints in his memoirs.[8] The known dates, however, suggest that the first warning about Fuchs, which led to the ending of contact between him and the K.G.B., came from a different source. Philby did not leave Britain for the U.S. posting until late September 1949 and, according to official records, did not begin his new job until October.

Fuchs was put under some degree of surveillance, though it was by no means complete, from the time that he became deeply suspect by White early in September, in the hope that he might be caught meeting a Soviet contact. The lack of any success, then or later, suggests that the K.G.B. already knew of the danger, as they appear to have known with Nunn May and were to know with several other spies under surveillance.

The possibility that Fuchs was being given some advice emanating from the K.G.B., in spite of the absence of direct Soviet contact, is supported by his strange behaviour. In the middle of October, just when suspicion against him was so strong that his fingerprint card was being sent to the F.B.I., he approached the Harwell security officer, Henry Arnold, and said that he thought he ought perhaps to resign from the atomic project.[9] He said that his father had accepted a professorship of theology in Leipzig, in the Soviet zone, and that this might create security problems. This was interpreted as a crisis of conscience. Clearly Fuchs was in an appalling position, but it could also have been an excuse to sound out Arnold on the situation. If time allowed, Fuchs might have had it in mind to leave Harwell and join his father in East Germany, a move which the law might not have been able to prevent. Clandestine defection was ruled out by the K.G.B. because it would have indicated that the Centre knew of the suspicions, which would have seriously prejudiced Philby and the other source in MI5, if that had been implicated.

If Fuchs was receiving advice from the K.G.B. through a 'cut-out' and playing back information concerning his position, the likeliest person for that task would have been Sonia who was easily to hand and was a trusted friend. He was certainly to do all he

141

could to protect her, claiming, in his early confession, that all his contacts were 'completely unknown' to him.

At that stage the British and American security authorities had no knowledge that the Soviets had been made aware of their Bride breaks into the wartime codes, so the intercept evidence could not be used against Fuchs and, in any case, would have been inadmissible in a British court. The only way that Fuchs could be prosecuted was by inducing him to confess his treachery. This was achieved through the skill and patience of Arnold at Harwell and of Jim Skardon, an MI5 interrogator. Arnold originally suspected Fuchs from his observation that he was over-zealous about security, being perhaps too keen to create a good impression. Fuchs's information about his father's appointment in East Germany offered an opportunity for him to be questioned and he was interviewed by Skardon at Harwell on 21 December. He lied his way through several interrogations during which he was frankly accused of espionage and of being in contact with Soviet agents in New York. During the third week of January 1950 he was questioned again, and MI5 was about to abandon its effort, at least for a while, when Evelyn Grist, the woman who had listened in to Fuchs's replies to Skardon's questions and had transcribed them, remarked that she felt 'in her bones' that he was lying on four specific points. She urged Skardon to try again, concentrating on them.[10] He did so and on 24 January Fuchs decided to confess to having provided the Soviet Union with atomic weapons secrets over a period of seven years.

With hindsight it seems clear that Fuchs would have escaped prosecution had he obeyed the K.G.B. instruction to 'deny everything and admit nothing but keep talking to encourage the interrogators to reveal how much they know'. Perhaps the K.G.B. felt confident that he would do so. In the event he broke down, as Blake was to do later. Nothing is more corrosive of character than the practice of deception and only the most formidable characters can resist, for ever, the temptation to cleanse themselves through confession to somebody.

It is possible, as some MI5 officers believe, that after Fuchs had become so suspect that he could no longer continue in secret atomic research the K.G.B. felt it could afford to 'burn' him, that is to sacrifice him in the interests of preserving a more productive spy. It has been assumed that the spy in question was Philby, who was in Washington but, as already explained, it seems more likely to have been someone nearer home.

Fuchs was arrested on 2 February 1950 and was charged with espionage. There is evidence that MI5 was prepared to avoid prosecuting him and to try to use him as a 'double', presumably to feed some false nuclear information to the Soviets but also to avoid a national and international scandal.[11] I find it hard to believe that Sillitoe, 'the honest copper', would have readily agreed to this but in any case the situation was resolved by the unrelenting determination of J. Edgar Hoover, the F.B.I. chief, to ensure that the spy who had done so much damage to American interests should pay the proper penalty. I have been assured by a most senior authority that Fuchs was never 'turned'.

Fuchs's 76-year-old father moved from Frankfurt in the American zone of Germany to Leipzig in the Soviet zone, now East Germany, two weeks before his son's arrest.[12] This could have been coincidence or the result of a warning. His departure meant that he could not be questioned about his son either by Western security or by journalists. Indeed, in view of the father's age, it would seem that his move to the theological appointment in Leipzig had been contrived as part of an unsuccessful attempt to get Fuchs to eventual safety there.

Another associate of Fuchs who was in need of Iron Curtain safety, Sonia herself, was also on the move, as already described. She is imprecise in her memoirs about the day of her departure but she seems to have been in East Berlin in February. Whether this was before or shortly after Fuchs's arrest is not made clear. But it seems to have been close enough for the Moscow Centre to be sure that, at that stage, Fuchs had given no indication about her to his interrogators as he was still insisting that he did not know the identities of any of his contacts. The Centre could have known this from Philby who, from his vantage point in Washington, was kept informed of progress on the Fuchs case so that he could tell the F.B.I. Alternatively, the information could have derived from an MI5 source.

It would seem that the Centre either concluded or was informed that Sonia would no longer be safe once Fuchs had been convicted because he would be subjected to further interrogation in prison, where he would be so dejected that he might be induced to tell anything. Len was in no danger because he could deny ever having met Fuchs and he was never questioned by MI5 even after it learned that Sonia had been Fuchs's courier.

On 1 March 1950 Fuchs was sentenced to fourteen years' imprisonment in an Old Bailey trial which I attended. This was the maximum sentence for treason. He could not have been charged with high treason, which merited the death sentence, because that applies only to spying for an enemy. At the time of Fuchs's espionage the Soviet Union had been an ally.

The prosecutor, Sir Hartley Shawcross (now Lord), who was

143

then Attorney-General, told the court that investigations undertaken in 1940 and 1941 had failed to show 'any association whatever with British members of the Communist Party'. This evidence, which must have originated from the records of Hollis's wartime section, and about which Hollis may have been consulted, gave a false impression to the court. Foreign communists working 'underground' were always forbidden to belong to the Communist Party of the country in which they were living or to associate with its members. What was really relevant was Fuchs's association with members of the German Communist Party and there was evidence of that.

F.B.I. documents show that when Fuchs confessed, before his trial, he named Juergen Kuczynski as the communist who had introduced him to Soviet Intelligence in 1941, knowing that he had already left Britain for a permanent post in East Germany in November 1945.[13] An F.B.I. document dated 17 March 1950 states: 'By his own admission, Fuchs has implicated Juergen Kuczynski in this espionage case.' Yet Shawcross assured the court that the intermediary who had introduced Fuchs to the Soviets was 'not recognized by the British authorities as a person who would be a communist'. The statement clearly implies that the 'authorities' knew who the intermediary was, yet Kuczynski had never made any secret of being a fully committed communist and Hollis, in particular, knew that. Lord Shawcross has told me that what he said was 'on the explicit instructions of the Treasury Solicitor'.[14] Such instructions could only have been based on information originating in MI5. They induced Shawcross, unwittingly, to give false information to the court and it was information calculated to excuse MI5's apparent ignorance.

In spite of the considerable success in securing Fuchs's confession and his subsequent, though limited, assistance, the case was an MI5 disaster for he had done such irreparable damage that official assessments suggested that he had advanced the Soviet atomic weapons effort by between one and three years. The damage had accrued from the original clearance of Fuchs for work in Britain and the U.S. and later for further work at Harwell, Hollis's section being responsible for the information and advice which caused the clearances to be given. Yet, like prime ministers who were to succeed him, Clement Attlee was pressed into assuring Parliament that there were no grounds for casting 'the slightest slur on the security services'. On 6 March 1950 he also told Parliament that the information, which had come from the U.S. – the intercept without which MI5 would have known nothing about Fuchs's treachery – did not point to any individual.[15] That statement, which was calculated to make MI5's effort look even more impress-ive, was untrue and, like the brief for his original explanation to Parliament, must have originated from MI5. The capacity of MI5 for covering up its errors and securing political approval through prime ministerial statements has been of the greatest service to the K.G.B. and the G.R.U. in protecting their penetration agents.

Fuchs lied repeatedly during his original confession by insisting that he had no idea as to the identity of the woman courier who had collected secrets from him and given him instructions while he was at Birmingham University. Not long after he had been in prison, however, he learned from a visitor, whom I have not yet identified, that Sonia was safely in East Germany and he then told MI5 officers that his courier had been Kuczynski's sister. Because of the major American interest in the Fuchs case and all its devastating consequences MI5 should have informed the F.B.I. immediately, but it did not do so. Hoover's memorandum to the White House in June 1950 states: 'It is reported that the woman has not been identified by the British authorities to date.'[16]

This inaction by MI5, said to be due to dislike of Hoover's zeal for prosecuting spies, intensified the souring of Anglo-American relations on security and intelligence affairs. As will be seen, MI5 was to continue this short-sighted policy of reluctant co-operation, which was entirely opposed to the Labour Government's require-ment that everything possible should be done to improve the relationship regarding the interchange of secret information.

The F.B.I. had sent a distinguished officer, Robert Lamphere, to interview Fuchs in prison in late May 1950, and he has reviewed his records on my behalf. They show that Fuchs told him that he did not know the name of his woman courier, though Lamphere believed that MI5 did know it. Later, MI5 also withheld from the F.B.I. the fact that she had used the code-name Sonia and was the woman already described in *Handbook for Spies* as having been connected with the Swiss Lucy Ring, in which the F.B.I. had considerable interest. Lamphere told me, 'Your book, *Their Trade is Treachery*, contains more data on Sonia than I can recall having from MI5.'[17]

The F.B.I. document dated 17 March 1950 and another dated 22 March show that in spite of MI5's meagre assistance F.B.I. counter-espionage officers were already on Sonia's trail.[18] They knew that she was Juergen Kuczynski's sister and was a Soviet agent, having spied in China and Switzerland. They knew that she was married to Len Beurton, who had also been a spy, as had her previous husband Rolf Hamburger, and that she and Beurton were living in England. The documents show that their interest in her

145

was in connection with the Fuchs case but the one thing they did not know, because MI5 declined to tell them, was that Sonia had been his courier and probably his case officer.

It is difficult, therefore, to escape the conclusion that the MI5 management, which was already deeply embarrassed in American security circles and in Whitehall by the circumstances of the Fuchs case, deliberately withheld its previous knowledge of Sonia's existence in Britain because it did not dare admit that it had done so little to curb her activities after Foote denounced her, when she could still have been servicing Fuchs. Hoover, in particular, would have been appalled if he had learned how MI5 had handled the Sonia case and might well have suspected that someone was protecting her in their own interests. In that context it will be recalled that Hollis was the leading figure in the control of the Sonia case and had been deeply concerned with the Fuchs case.

Sonia's husband, Len, was still at Great Rollright when Fuchs named her as his courier but he was never interviewed by MI5 and the F.B.I. was not told that he was still in Britain. Either the legend that Sonia had fled in 1947 included Len or somebody in MI5 ensured that he was not disturbed.

The lies told by Fuchs cast doubt on parts of his confession and, in view of the way he was quickly incorporated into communist society in East Germany following his eventual release in 1959, his claims that he had become disenchanted with communism and service to the Soviet Union savour of disinformation. The uncritical acceptance of the lies and the claims by MI5 helped to build up a legend about Fuchs which, like that of Sonia, has been widely accepted as historic truth. Both legends would seem to have suited MI5 as a whole or an individual inside it. Fuchs's talks with his fellow-prisoner, Hume, support the belief that he had not wavered far in his dedication and had little, if any, genuine remorse. He was particularly scathing about MI5. When interviewed by a *Daily Express* reporter who had secured access to him in prison, he said, 'British security is symbolized by a very fine veneer on top and utter departmental confusion underneath.'[19] If Hollis, or somebody else in MI5, had been protecting him he would not have known about it. Soviet Intelligence would have restricted his knowledge to instructions as to what he should or should not do.

Though Sonia had been actively engaged in espionage in the Oxford area from 1941 until 1950, regularly transmitting to Moscow from several addresses, she did not fall under any official suspicion in that respect until Fuchs named her, when it was too late to interrogate her, had MI5 wished to do so. Even MI5's scant interest in her previous espionage for the Soviets had arisen only

146

because of the chance defection of Alexander Foote back to Britain. As was to happen repeatedly in the future with Soviet controllers and couriers, Sonia and her husband, who should both have been prosecuted, were warned of their danger and were able to reach the safety of communist territory. It was clearly in the interests of several people in Britain whom she had serviced that they should not be seriously interrogated.

When the security authorities belatedly had to admit to themselves that Sonia had been transmitting regularly from the Oxford area and had never been detected, there was a backtrack to discover the reasons for the failure, with all concerned making excuses. Some of her traffic had been recorded by a foreign country and it was among a lot of such material acquired by British Intelligence in the 1960s.[20] G.C.H.Q. and MI5, working together, succeeded in deciphering some of it, along with related material sent on Sonia's behalf by the Soviet Embassy in London. One message, early in 1941, told the G.R.U. Centre that she was having difficulty in making radio contact and referred to agents whom she was required to pay.

This modest deciphering success suggests that a great deal more could have been learned about Sonia if her traffic had been recorded and then deciphered after the wartime ban of decoding secret Soviet messages had been lifted. There can be little doubt that the Radio Security Service did record some of her messages and handed them to Hollis but little if any action was taken then and much of the recorded material is said to have been destroyed round the time of the hand-over of the R.S.S. to G.C.H.Q. at the end of the war. If this destruction can be verified the identities of those responsible for it could be instructive, for it would have been very much to the advantage of Soviet agents like Sonia and those British spies whom they serviced.

In view of what my son and I uncovered by inquiries in Great Rollright in January 1983 what might MI5 have learned in 1950 when Sonia's trail was still warm? The names of those who were to be given free run of her house, now forgotten by the Greatheads, might have provided leads to Soviet agents, some now known, others still unknown. Surveillance or inquiries in 1947 after the farcical MI5 interview might have led to Fuchs who, on his admission to Hume, did not give the U.S.S.R. details of the triggering mechanism for the H-bomb until the following year. But Sonia was never placed under any kind of surveillance. Nobody in the Great Rollright area can remember any inquiries having been made even after Fuchs had named her as his courier in 1950, and nobody questioned the Laski family about Sonia's activities at

Avenue Cottage, when she was actively servicing Fuchs and, almost certainly, 'Elli'.[21] Nor, apparently, have any security officials made any inquiries on the checkable admissions made by Sonia and her brother, Juergen, in their memoirs.

It seems inescapable that ever since MI5 learned, in 1947, that Sonia had been a Soviet spy, the security authorities have deliberately avoided any serious investigation of her activities and continue to do so. The Sonia case remains a major MI5 defeat which has been conveniently concealed, yet her activities were crucial to some of the most damaging Soviet espionage ever achieved.

While those MI5 officers involved in investigating Hollis realize that her importance was seriously underestimated and that proof of her relationship with Hollis would clinch the case against him, others, who would then be seen to have been derelict in duty, continue to denigrate her role. One of them tried to assure me that Sonia was no more than a 'magpie sending back everything she could pick up from relatives and friends, which could not have been important when Russia was an ally'.[22] The same source claimed that 'Foote knew all about Sonia', which he clearly did not, and that the 'Sonia connection had been gone into pretty thoroughly and been found wanting', which I believe to be the reverse of the truth.

There is, presumably, some mention of Sonia's activities in the official papers relating to the Fuchs case but the latter were all withheld when Cabinet and departmental papers for the year 1950 came up for release in 1981 under the thirty-year rule. They are to remain withheld for a further twenty years. I have been assured by competent authorities that there is nothing in those papers which could be of assistance to any foreign power and their suppression is to save embarrassment to people who are still alive. Some of these people are Labour politicians but others are civil servants and security officials.

In 1969 Sonia was decorated with a second Order of the Red Banner, the highest order of the Red Army, for her work in Britain.[23] This was the first Soviet admission that she had been a spy, her previous decoration having been kept secret, even inside the Soviet Union. The East German semi-official account *The Red Orchestra Against Hitler*, gives prominence to the fact that Sonia was among very few to be awarded even one Order of the Red Banner, the others being those who had operated in extreme danger inside Germany during the war and had been executed when caught.[24] To have received two Orders her services must have been outstanding.

The minor spies to whom she has been permitted to give clues in her memoirs could not have been the basis for the additional Order

148

of the Red Banner. She claims that she built up her own network, which included an unnamed R.A.F. officer who had been a welder in civilian life, her brother and her father, who died in London in November 1947. A lifelong political activist, Dr René Kuczynski had contacts with Labour politicians who supplied him with economic information which he passed to Sonia for transmission to Moscow. Such modest material would have been of insufficient value to warrant the posting to Britain of a G.R.U. officer of Sonia's capabilities and dedication, especially when, on her own statement, she had been promoted to full colonel for services already rendered. Both her father and brother had been successfully supplying information to Moscow before her arrival and had no need of her. Juergen says in his memoirs that he was able to get information out of Britain via Soviet supply ships, and through his friend Anatoli Gromov in the Soviet Embassy he could have used the Soviet diplomatic network rather than overburdening Sonia's transmitter.

Juergen Kuczynski, who is still alive at the time of writing, has made several visits to Britain since his departure for East Germany. He was in Cambridge during 1968, for instance.[25] There is no evidence that MI5 has ever tried to question him about his own espionage or about the wartime activities of Sonia. Indeed, the four members of the Kuczynski family known to have been active Soviet agents had a charmed life in Britain and, in the circumstances, it is reasonable to wonder why. If the connection between Sonia and Hollis can ever be proved the answer may emerge.

Though 'Fuchs' is a burned-out case still living in East Germany, Sonia was not allowed to mention him in her memoirs. Neither was Juergen Kuczynski, but in his more recent *Dialog mit meinem Urenkel* he revealed that when Fuchs was arrested he moved in a hurry from the American occupation zone of Berlin to the Soviet sector, leaving his wife to follow later. The instruction to move came from Walter Ulbricht, then Moscow's chief German representative and future East German head of state, who clearly feared that Kuczynski might be arrested as an accessory to Fuchs's treachery, as he should have been. Kuczynski gives no precise date and the warning may have reached him before Special Branch pounced on Fuchs.[26]

Sonia makes no mention of Hollis either, or of any other MI5 source, but she does admit in her preamble: 'In the writing of memoirs each author has difficulties: selecting, compromising and telling the truth. That was my way.' It was also the K.G.B.'s.

In 1977 when her memoirs were published it did not seem likely that there would ever be any publicity about Hollis as the MI5 case against him had been buried so long and his career had been too undistinguished to attract a biographer. Perhaps, in a later edition of her memoirs – she has already made a few additions to the original – she may respond to this book, especially as Hollis is now being mentioned, if only vaguely, in Soviet books on espionage, which are all vetted by the K.G.B. With respect to the details she has been permitted to reveal already, including facts about her days in China, many can be crosschecked with other sources, as I have done wherever possible.

In 1984 Sonia, the super-spy among women, is still alive, aged seventy-six, and has realized her literary ambitions by publishing several successful books, including novels, under the name Ruth Werner. She is held in such high regard in East Germany that she has been awarded the Order of Karl Marx and a television film of her contribution to the march of communism is reported to be in preparation, apparently by the Soviet authorities.

In the late 1970s the current inhabitant of The Firs, Mrs Davenport received a visit from Peter Beurton, Sonia's son by Len, who was visiting Britain in connection with scientific research. Then in his middle thirties, he recalled how he had been dragged away from Great Rollright, which he loved, ostensibly on a holiday, to discover that he had been deprived of all his toys which had been left behind. 'I was very bitter about it,' he said. 'Oddly enough, I still am.'[27] Later, in April 1983, Sonia's daughter Nina, by then a grandmother, making Sonia a great-grandmother, also turned up on Mrs Davenport's doorstep for a nostalgic and emotionally charged visit.[28] Efforts were made for her to be interviewed on my behalf and she agreed to a meeting in London but failed to keep it, presumably after taking advice.

Letters which I have sent to Sonia and to her brother have, so far, elicited no replies though there are indications that they caused considerable concern.

Government concern with the continuing danger from pro-Soviet communists crystallized in the summer of 1950 into specific fear that they intended to paralyse British industry by sabotaging power stations at the height of the Korean War, in which British forces were engaged. At Prime Minister Attlee's request MI5 undertook an inquiry and Hollis, as Director of Security, was in charge of it. At a meeting of a Cabinet Committee he was required to check on the activities of certain communists among power-station workers and to report on security precautions to prevent sabotage. A Cabinet minute, dated 17 August 1950, records that there was no reason to believe that any organized outbreak of sabotage was imminent. While this report was negative it is confirmation of Hollis's continuing close involvement with counter-Soviet subversion while serving as Director of Security.[29]

A couple of months later, the Government and MI5 were faced with a Soviet subversion effort on an embarrassingly successful scale – the defection of a leading Harwell nuclear scientist, Dr Bruno Pontecorvo, in mysterious circumstances guaranteed to generate maximum publicity. A specialist in the design and operation of heavy-water reactors, he had disappeared behind the Iron Curtain with his wife and family while ostensibly on holiday in Italy. The subsequent inquiries were to show that security procedures, especially vetting, had failed repeatedly in spite of damning information which was available had it been effectively sought and evaluated.

Pontecorvo was a distinguished Italian physicist who had fled from his homeland to France because he was Jewish and also because he had relatives high in the Italian Communist Party. He was gregarious and likeable, and popular with his colleagues. In Paris he worked with the overtly communist scientist Joliot-Curie. After the fall of France in 1940 Pontecorvo fled further, to the U.S., which gave him and his Swedish wife refuge.

At the beginning of 1943 he joined the British atomic team in Canada, eventually working at Chalk River in Ontario, where there was a large nuclear research project. Canadian officials assumed that he had been cleared for security in Britain, but he was never in Britain until January 1949 when, after being granted British citizenship in the previous year, at the age of thirty-five, he was transferred to Harwell. The Royal Canadian Mounted Police had in fact relied on a security clearance which had never taken place.[30]

Following the Fuchs case Pontecorvo was screened six times by the Harwell authorities assisted by MI5. He told friends and relatives that he had come through 'clean as a whistle'. The Harwell security officer, Henry Arnold, had heard rumours that Pontecorvo and his wife had 'communist sympathies' and had tackled him about it. Pontecorvo had simply denied the suggestion and the British authorities had no firm information, though the F.B.I. had secured documentary proof that he and his wife were active communists and intensely anti-American. Pontecorvo had retained his American home while he was working in Canada, hoping to secure post-war employment in the U.S., and the F.B.I., which was suspicious of him, had searched it. They found documents showing the Pontecorvos' dedication to pro-Soviet communism and sent the material to the British Embassy in Washington for forwarding to MI5. They fell into the hands of Philby, the liaison

151

man in the Embassy, who suppressed them. They were not found until Pontecorvo had defected.[31]

Philby would, undoubtedly, have told his Soviet controller in Washington about the F.B.I.'s information and this may well have led the Soviets to warn Pontecorvo of his predicament, whether he was already in touch with them or not. This would explain why Pontecorvo decided to leave Harwell and get himself out of a position where his communist affiliations were an embarrassment. After being at Harwell only a year, he accepted an academic post at Liverpool University, which meant that he would be severing his connections with secret work.

In July 1950 Harwell granted him leave of absence to take a holiday in Europe, including visiting Swiss scientists on business When he failed to pay the visit or to communicate with Harwell the security authorities began a search for him on 21 September. They discovered that he and his family had flown to Moscow via Stockholm and Helsinki on 2 September.[32] Whether he went for purely ideological reasons or because the K.G.B. was able to apply blackmail pressure has never been established.

Inquiries produced no proof that Pontecorvo had been an active spy during the investigations resulting from Gouzenko's defection, though there is a possibility that an unidentified agent, code-named 'Gini' and known to have been Jewish, may have been Pontecorvo. If he had been recruited by the K.G.B. neither his real name nor his code-name would have emerged from these inquiries because nothing has ever been discovered about the K.G.B. network that Gouzenko claimed existed in Canada.

Later inquiries connected with a damage assessment of Philby's activities confirmed that following Pontecorvo's decision to leave Harwell, which cut off his access to secrets, he was induced by the Soviets to defect because they urgently needed his expertise in connection with their drive to produce an H-bomb. He was one of the few scientists with working knowledge of the type of nuclear reactor needed to make an essential component of the H-bomb called lithium deuteride. His contribution, supplementing the details of H-bomb design supplied by Fuchs and other spies, may have accelerated the Soviet Union's acquisition of thermonuclear weapons by several years. Whether Pontecorvo, who became a Soviet citizen in 1952, was an active spy or not is therefore somewhat academic. Once in the Soviet Union he would have supplied the nuclear weapons scientists with every scrap of information in his possession.

While MI5 was only indirectly concerned with the case of Pontecorvo until his defection, it was another security disaster impinging on Hollis. In 1949, when Pontecorvo became of concern to Britain, Hollis was Director of Security responsible for advising Government departments not only about regulating the selection of those who were to have access to classified information, but on the supervision of those already with access. The case further disrupted Anglo-American relations on the exchange of nuclear secrets for, to quote Hollis's successor, Sir Martin Furnival Jones, 'It is a scandal that a man has got through the defences.'[33] That the American authorities considered the case scandalous is clear from the official report on Soviet atomic espionage published in Washington in 1951.

The Potential Value of Oversight

If any effective arrangements for the activities of the secret services to be overseen by an independent body had existed they would surely have been suspended during the war. Nevertheless it would seem to be a worthwhile exercise, in assessing the potential value of oversight, to consider what might have happened regarding the cases of Sonia and Fuchs if it had been in operation.

With hindsight it is clear that the decision to suspend the decipherment of clandestine Soviet radio traffic was extremely damaging to the counter-espionage effort against Soviet agents and their British spies. If oversight had existed the few members of the Y Board who made the decision might have been less precipitate and at least have taken steps to secure the agreement of the Prime Minister, Winston Churchill, which might not have been forthcoming. The existence of oversight might also have prevented the destruction of those records of the traffic which were made. As the results of Operation Bride quickly showed, that too had been a high-level blunder. Fuchs was caught only because the American records had been preserved.

The knowledge that decisions might be questioned might also have made MI5, and Hollis's section in particular, more cautious in its various reports which resulted in the repeated clearance of Fuchs for secret atomic research, though that would depend on the degree of access provided to the oversight body.

The point at which oversight could have been highly effective followed the defection of Alexander Foote to Britain and MI5's ritual visit to Sonia at Great Rollright in 1947. I greatly doubt that whoever was responsible for that appalling performance would have dared to perpetrate such a superficial operation, completely lacking in follow-up, had he known that his action, or lack of it, might be subject to independent inquiry. The perfunctory treatment of Foote's information about Sonia, like that of Gouzenko's warning about 'Elli', offers an excellent example of the potential of oversight to deter incompetence of such a degree that it might be contrived in the interests of treachery or, had it occurred, to detect it and investigate its causes. While Sonia was tough and determined, she was not necessarily unbreakable and enough evidence could have been adduced from witnesses for her to be held for questioning, which might have led to uncovering 'Elli' and other agents whom she now admits to have serviced. Instead, she was allowed to defect in a way which to an oversight body might have seemed contrived.

There can be little doubt that if Attlee and his advisers had had access to the full details of the way Fuchs had been repeatedly cleared of suspicion his attitude to MI5 would have been less forgiving. He would also have been angered by MI5's treatment of the F.B.I. at a time when the repair of relations was so important, particularly in the nuclear field. In this context it is to be hoped that an oversight body would have close liaison with its American counterpart and, in the knowledge that this was so, the British secret services might be less ready to offend the F.B.I. and C.I.A. than they have been in the past.

Detailed oversight of the Fuchs and Sonia cases might have raised concern about MI5's competence and even, perhaps, the suspicion that some matters had been so mismanaged that more than inefficiency was involved. As things stand in 1984, managers of the secret services can be assured that, barring a security commission inquiry or a leak to an investigative writer, 'legends', fabricated or promoted to cover inefficiency or worse, will survive indefinitely because the papers that might reveal the truth may never be released. A continuing oversight body might also find cause for wonder in the extent to which legends which suited MI5 and MI6 also suited the K.G.B.

CHAPTER NINETEEN

The Cambridge Conspiracy

Up to and including the 1950s – and continuing beyond – British governments of all colours treated the public, Parliament and the Press with disdain, almost amounting to contempt, concerning those operations of the Government machinery carried out in secret. Contrary to the situation prevailing in the U.S., where some public right to know is enshrined in the Constitution, British administrations took the view that there was never any requirement to tell their people anything which Whitehall regarded as its secret preserve. No announcements regarding secret matters should ever be made, even when the need for secrecy had totally evaporated. If such matters were ever to become public it should only be through historians riffling through papers released fifty, or even one hundred, years after the events concerned. Whitehall's extraordinary success in concealing its secrets is exemplified by a major military operation launched in November 1951.

The Tory Government, headed by Churchill, dispatched an assault force, including three aircraft carriers, from Portsmouth to capture the Egyptian port of Alexandria. Simultaneously, troops and light armour based in the Canal Zone and at Port Said were to join the attack, which was code-named 'Rodeo' and was intended to depose King Farouk and establish a British military government in Egypt. On the way to Cyprus, where the assault force was to pause, troops of the Royal Inniskilling Fusiliers embarked on the carrier *Triumph*, and those aboard other warships were briefed on their part in the operation. Before the force left Cyprus 'Rodeo' was suspended, apparently because it was believed there had been a security leak. H.M.S. *Triumph*, with many troops aboard, sailed for Port Said to await further orders. In the following January a new operation code-named 'Rodeo Flail' was set in motion to occupy Cairo and Alexandria, but it was pre-empted by an uprising in Cairo. As a result the British attempt to topple Farouk was abandoned, that purpose being achieved by a revolution in the following year which had British covert support.[1]

It now seems extraordinary that these operations, though never completed in anger, could have involved so many men and so many ships and have remained secret. But in the 1950s Whitehall was suprised only when such a secret did become public; there was complete confidence that no internal act of treachery could ever affect the super-secret departments like MI5 and MI6. It was unthinkable. Had it been thought about there would have been no doubt in the minds of the managements of those agencies that any such scandal could be safely concealed from the public because should investigative writers, for example, seek out such information they could always be threatened with prosecution under the Official Secrets Acts, which were passed to deter and to punish spies but have been monstrously misused to prevent the disclosure of official information of all kinds. Parliament, to its shame, has long been party to this conspiracy of silence. Supinely, it has accepted ministerial assurances that this and that information would be prejudicial to 'national security', 'the national interest', 'the public interest' and other political conveniences. Party Whips are required to induce M.P.s to desist from asking Parliamentary questions on security and intelligence matters and the various select committees have studiously avoided investigating them.

In 1946 the unmasking of Alan Nunn May, the Cambridge-educated British scientist working as a Soviet spy in the Canadian section of the atomic bomb project, dented a few Whitehall illusions and some consideration was given to suppressing the case 'in the national interest'.[2] Nunn May, however, was a scientist and scientists were known to be odd, especially concerning their belief that their discoveries belonged to the whole world. So his conviction and imprisonment did not raise any widespread fears that the Soviet Union might have recruited young men who might be in even more sensitive, non-scientific, employment. Four years later the case of Klaus Fuchs caused more widespread concern but, again, he was a scientist and a foreigner with no inborn loyalties to Britain. A closer watch on foreign-born scientists and a ruling that, in future, applicants for highly sensitive posts should be British-born of British parents were regarded as being sufficient in the way of extra safeguards.

The event which shattered this complacency and led to a new attitude to the conservation of secrets was the defection of two British-born Foreign Office officials, Donald Maclean and Guy Burgess, on 25 May 1951. The case caused a public furore, especially when Maclean's personal behaviour and Burgess's homosexuality and other excesses became known, but even those of us who were involved in investigating the circumstances had no

156

real conception of the consternation and astonished incredulity behind the scenes in Whitehall. The confusion and shame were so great that a new attitude to information about the event, and others like it which might arise, was quickly generated in the Foreign Office, Cabinet Office, and in the secret services. The truth had to be kept from the public by every means, from misinformation when total silence could no longer be maintained to blatant lies. That policy of cover-up concerning disasters which are embarrassing to politicians and their senior servants has continued to the present time.

While much has been written about the Maclean and Burgess affair – against every Government obstacle – there is so much that is unknown to the public, especially concerning the cover-up, that I shall deal with it at some length. It was a watershed in the art of news management in Whitehall, and on that score alone it demonstrates the need for Parliamentary oversight of departments operating in secrecy.

By late 1950 further progress with Operation Bride, the decoding of wartime Soviet radio messages, had produced evidence of serious penetration of British and French secret departments by the K.G.B.[3] The British were deeply involved in Operation Bride but the French were not. Without being told of the source of the information the French security authorities were warned of the infiltration and agreed to join a Tripartite Security Working Group, which held its first meeting in Washington in April 1951. The American representatives gave a presentation of their security procedures, which they hoped that the French would introduce, and the whole party then flew to London for a presentation by MI5 of the British methods of preventing penetration.[4] The party then moved to Paris where the procedures were to be incorporated in the French security system. These included the 'purge' procedure whereby the post-war Labour Government had hoped to remove and exclude communists from access to secret information.

The French talks had barely begun on Monday, 28 May, when the leader of the British delegation, Sir Robert Mackenzie, was called to the telephone to be told that a senior Foreign Office official named Donald Maclean had disappeared, along with a more junior official called Guy Burgess. The deeply embarrassed Mackenzie was also told that the Foreign Office was fairly sure that they had defected to the Soviet Union.[5]

A select number of people, who included Mackenzie, knew that Maclean had been under deep suspicion for many months because of a break in Operation Bride. The circumstances made it clear that Maclean had been warned of his danger and that somehow

Burgess had been involved in the escape. Neither the French nor the Americans at the Paris talks were told of the defections and in London every effort was made to keep them secret, though the atmosphere in a very few areas of Whitehall, and particularly in MI5, savoured of panic.

Anglo-American relations were already in severe disarray because of the Fuchs case and the Labour Government had been trying to improve them in the hope of re-establishing the interchange of nuclear information. Though the public was not to know it for many years, Maclean had previously been concerned with secret Anglo-American atomic affairs while based at the British Embassy in Washington.[6]

Not until 7 June did the public become aware of the disappearance of the two men. Following information secured in Paris, the *Daily Express*, which I then served as defence correspondent, was able to reveal that two Foreign Office employees had apparently defected to Moscow and might have taken important information with them. A statement naming the two men was made by the Foreign Office in such a way that it suggested that Maclean might not have recovered from a medical breakdown. As will be seen, this was deliberate misinformation because it was known that Maclean had defected to avoid interrogation by MI5 officers who were convinced that he was a long-term Soviet spy.

The Foreign Office was to take the brunt of the public and Parliamentary censure, but MI5 was largely responsible for the disaster, through either bungling or betrayal, or possibly both.

To appreciate the extraordinary circumstances of this defection, and of further highly suspect events involving Hollis, it is necessary to examine the case histories of four Soviet spies who were all recruited at Cambridge University – Maclean, Burgess, Harold (Kim) Philby and Anthony Blunt.

Donald Duart Maclean, who died in Moscow in 1983, was born in 1913, the son of a Liberal M.P. who, as Sir Donald Maclean, was to become President of the Board of Education. Tall, slim, rather good-looking, intense and humourless, he won a scholarship to read modern languages at Trinity Hall, Cambridge, in the autumn of 1931. There he met Guy Francis de Moncy Burgess, the son of a naval lieutenant, who was some two years older. Burgess, thick-set with blue eyes and wavy hair, was an aggressive homosexual who had preceded Maclean at Cambridge by a year. He was a highly intelligent youth who had quickly established himself as a 'character' of notable wit and outrageous habits. He had joined an exclusive Cambridge club called The Apostles which, at that stage, was a centre of both homosexuality and communism.

Burgess also made the acquaintance of Harold A. R. Philby, known to his friends as Kim, who had entered Trinity College in 1929, having won a scholarship from Westminster. Philby, then twenty-one, was not an Apostle nor was he known to have any homosexual tendencies. He was, however, deeply interested in radical politics, in communist ideals and ideology and, with other undergraduates, in the Marxist interpretation of the current world slump. The Marxist group was soon to be joined by Maclean and by James Klugmann, a Jewish schoolfriend of Maclean whose whole life was to be openly dedicated to the pro-Soviet communist cause and whose clandestine activities were to have historic consequences.[7]

So far as is known, Philby never carried a Communist Party card but he, too, was totally committed to the communist cause before he left Cambridge in 1933 with a good second-class degree in economics. With £50 provided by his father, a famous and eccentric Arabist, Philby went to Vienna, partly to improve his German but also to witness the struggle of communism against fascism, arriving there in the late summer. There he secured a room in the home of an Austrian girl, a militant communist named Alice Friedman who called herself Lizi, often misspelled Litzi, as she pronounced it. Soon they were living together and then married, apparently to give Lizi a British passport as a means of getting out of Austria because she was Jewish. The MI5 view is that Philby was recruited to Soviet Intelligence while in Vienna, his wife already being in the Soviet fold. Whoever recruited him it is certain that it was on behalf of what is now called the K.G.B., not the G.R.U.[8]

In view of what has been written about the 'climate of treason' which induced young undergraduates to become traitors, it should be appreciated that Philby, Burgess and most of their fellow-spies did not decide to assist the Soviet Union essentially as a reaction to the Spanish Civil War and Hitler's treatment of the Jews, as has been claimed by apologists for them. They did so because of their commitment to Marxism-Leninism and to the Communist Party which, at that time in Britain took the Moscow line in its entirety. Anti-fascism was much more of a hindsight excuse for their behaviour, which continued to be staunchly pro-Soviet even when Stalin made his non-aggression pact with Hitler. This was a patently cynical move which enabled the Nazis and the Soviets to partition Poland and ensured that many thousands of Polish Jews were made available to the S.S. who sent them to concentration camps and to the gas chambers. It was part of the pact that the Soviets would hand over to the Nazis German communists who had taken refuge in their share of Poland. Many of these, who were

159

also Jews, were handed over to the Gestapo by the Soviet forerunner of the K.G.B. at the Brest-Litovsk bridge on the new border.[9] How Jewish communists like Klugmann and the Kuczynskis, who were also of Polish origin, could condone this and live with their consciences is extraordinary. They did so because they were 'Moscow right or wrong' communists and put their dedication to the Party line of Stalin, as bloody a dictator as Hitler, before genuine concern for their own people. They were to continue to do so when the pact, which ensured supplies of petrol and food to Germany, allowed the Nazis to conquer France and the Low Countries and subject millions more Jews and anti-fascists to persecution. The undergraduate traitors behaved in a similarly callous and cold-blooded manner.

Once back in Britain Philby secured a job as a journalist for a magazine and set up a news agency with one of his wife's pro-Soviet friends, called Peter Smolka, who was himself a Soviet agent throughout the war and later.[10] In his book *My Silent War*, not all of which is to be believed as much of it is a K.G.B. disinformation exercise, Philby recalled how he was given instruction when he met his Soviet controller at regular intervals in open spaces in London. This controller, known as 'Theo' and almost certainly Theodore Maly, a former Hungarian priest who had become a Soviet citizen, was replaced early in 1937 by another 'illegal' controller known to his agents only as 'Otto' and believed to be a Czech. He has been described as a short man with no neck and swept-back, straight hair. MI5 has spent much time trying to establish 'Otto's' identity but without success. While Philby remained based in London, he returned to Cambridge frequently on Soviet business, a fact which, according to him, MI5 was unaware of when it interrogated him later.[11]

At that time promising recruits to Soviet Intelligence were advised to try to insinuate themselves into certain selected organizations, according to their qualifications and circumstances. In order of priority the list ran: MI5, the Secret Service(MI6), G.C.H.Q. (known during the war as the Government Code and Cipher School, based at Bletchley), *The Times*, the B.B.C., the Foreign Office and the Home Office, there being no Defence Ministry as such in those days.[12]

One of the first orders which Philby obeyed was to pretend to have given up his communist beliefs. To this end he was encouraged to associate himself with anti-communist and pro-fascist organizations. He joined the Anglo-German Fellowship, a useful move in itself because it meant that to some extent he infiltrated it. He even became acquainted with von Ribbentrop, the German

160

Ambassador in London, and visited Berlin frequently for talks at the Propaganda Ministry, passing all that he learned to the K.G.B.

Another Soviet requirement for recruits was assistance in the recruitment of others and among the first of those whom Philby brought in, probably in 1934, was Burgess. Having satisfied himself that Burgess was willing to serve as a clandestine agent, Philby introduced him to 'Theo' who gave him some tuition in conspiratorial practices and served as his controller until he was handed over to 'Otto'. It cannot be stressed too often that under the Soviet system, whether run by the K.G.B. or the G.R.U., agents are continuously under Soviet control. Spies are not recruited, told what to do and left on their own to do it. Each time a new situation arises there must be communication with the controller either direct or by dead-letter box and advice is then sought from Moscow before the agent is instructed further.[13]

In the K.G.B. messages which the controllers sent to Moscow Philby's contributions were referred to as from 'Stanley', while Burgess had the code-name 'Hicks'.[14]

Burgess had also become friendly with a fellow Apostle called Anthony Blunt, a homosexual with whom, according to MI5 informants, he had a sexual relationship, though Blunt was later to deny this. Blunt, who was born in September 1907 and was some four years older than Burgess, was the son of a parson, the vicar of Holy Trinity, Bournemouth, and later of St John's Church, Paddington. His family had impressive connections with landed gentry and his social relationships were to prove of value. After attending school at Marlborough Blunt won a scholarship to Trinity College, Cambridge, where he went in 1926 to study first mathematics and then French and English. After taking his B.A. degree he remained at Cambridge doing post-graduate work in his real love, the history of art. By the time he was twenty-five this tall, thin, rather drooping man, was elected a Fellow of his college and taken on to the permanent teaching staff. In an interview with *The Times* much later Blunt stated that he had become a communist and more particularly a Marxist in 1935 after a sabbatical year away from the university. 'When I came back, in October 1934, I found that all my friends ... had suddenly become Marxists under the impact of Hitler coming to power.'[15]

During his interrogation in 1964, Blunt described the insidious method whereby he and others had been recruited. One day when he and Burgess were discussing the international situation in late 1934 or early 1935, Burgess, who tried to recruit anybody whom he admired, said, 'Anthony, we must do something to counter the horrors of Nazism. We can't just sit here and talk about it. The

Government is pacifying Hitler so Marxism is the only solution. I am already committed to work secretly for peace. Are you prepared to help me?'[16]

This was the standard form of recruitment laid down by the Soviet controllers to be applied to committed communists who had been talent-spotted by existing recruits like Burgess. The first appeal was to be made in the cause of peace, a term which the communists used as a euphemism for subversion even at that early stage. When Blunt, or any other recruit, had agreed to work for 'peace', which was difficult to refuse, he was then informed that he would be working for 'peace' through the Comintern, the argument being that the installation of communist governments throughout the world would eliminate fascism and ensure peace and goodwill everywhere. This too was not difficult for naive young people to accept. The next step was for the Comintern recruit to be introduced to his controller who was, in fact, a professional Intelligence officer working not for the Comintern but for the K.G.B. One of the controller's first tasks was to secure some form of written commitment from the recruit through which he could be blackmailed later, if necessary. He was also required to induce the recruit to accept a small payment of money for expenses and sign a receipt for it.[17]

Cambridge was a particularly fruitful area for recruitment in the 1930s because there were several influential dons, like Maurice Dobb, who were openly inducing their students to join the Communist Party or, at least, to embrace Marxism.[18] I can find no hard evidence that these dons were in touch with Soviet Intelligence, but the K.G.B. was quick to latch on to the potentialities. The chain seems to have been recruitment to communism and Marxism through the influence of dons and fellow-undergraduates, recruitment to working for 'peace' through the Comintern by fellow-students already in the net, and commitment, unwitting at first, to service to Soviet Intelligence through contact with professional Soviet officers. The danger and excitement of clandestine work was stressed in this last stage and, apparently, had additional attraction for many ardent young men anxious to help 'the cause'.

This, assuredly, was the way that Blunt was recruited, though he could contribute little at first. He appeared in the K.G.B. traffic under the code-name 'Johnson'.[19] The recruits were never to know their code-names but those who had assisted in the recruitment of others knew that their conquests were spies – a situation unusual in conspiratorial practice where spy-masters prefer to run their agents separately so that one cannot betray another.

When Blunt was interrogated by MI5 he was able to describe how he had been involved in the recruitment of Maclean to the

K.G.B. Some time before the spring of 1935 Philby's controller, after reference to Moscow, gave him instructions to pass on to Burgess with the purpose of recruiting Maclean to Soviet Intelligence without delay. In March 1934 Maclean, an open communist playing a leading part in anti-Government marches, had written a letter to *Granta*, the university magazine, urging that something had to be done about 'the capitalist, dictatorial character of the University'.[20] This, together with Burgess's talent-spotting reports, demonstrated Maclean's susceptibility and the Russians may have become concerned that he was exposing his beliefs too forcefully for him to gain entry to a Whitehall establishment unless checked, as he could be if recruited. Burgess brought Blunt into the act by asking him to invite Maclean to stay with him, with Burgess being a chance fellow-guest. The recruitment, along the usual lines, went through without much difficulty and Maclean became the fourth member of a ring of spies all known to each other. When Blunt made a statement to *The Times* following his public exposure in 1979 he said that he did not learn that Philby and Maclean were spies until during the war. That was either a senile lapse of memory or, more likely, a lie.

The recruitment of Maclean bore fruit for the K.G.B. with remarkable rapidity. He sat the examination for the Diplomatic Service in 1935, no doubt on the advice of his Soviet controller or, at least, with his enthusiastic support. According to Foreign Office records Maclean was granted a certificate as a Third Secretary in October 1935.[21] Like all ministries the Foreign Office is responsible for its own security and for such vetting of entrants as it considers necessary. In those days no positive vetting system existed. While there must have been several people already in the Foreign Office who knew of Maclean's open communism at Cambridge, the fact that he was the son of a former Cabinet minister would have been sufficient qualification as regards reliability. In September 1938 Maclean was posted to the Embassy in Paris, no doubt also being assigned as a K.G.B. operative in that city. His eventual K.G.B. code-name was 'Homer', though he may have had a different cryptonym in his early days.[22]

The insertion of Maclean into the Foreign Office was a major step, though not necessarily the first, in a determined Soviet operation to penetrate the main British institutions. According to Michael Straight, a Cambridge contemporary of Maclean, students who were prepared to burrow in Moscow's interests in their places of professional work were already known as 'moles'.[23] Their purpose was not only to supply secrets but to influence policy and so undermine the foundations of capitalism in a process which, in communist circles, has become known as 'the long march through the institutions'. When it was realized in Moscow that communism would make little impact in Britain either through the ballot box or through revolution, the 'long march' through the Whitehall departments, the unions, education, the media and even the Church, was conceived and is still in progress.

The full extent to which the Cambridge spy-ring influenced policy is uncertain and should, one day, be the subject of academic investigation. There is a belief among certain former officers of MI5 that Maclean, Burgess and those who assisted them, like Dennis Proctor, carried some responsibility for the outbreak of the Second World War, or at least its timing, because of their influence on Stalin's decision to make a non-aggression pact with Hitler. When the pact was being signed British officials were still in Moscow hoping to conclude a triple alliance of Britain, the Soviet Union and France which should have effectively curbed Hitler in 1939 because he lacked the capability to fight on two fronts. It is suspected that the British spies in Whitehall assured Stalin, through their K.G.B. controllers, that the Foreign Office was not to be trusted and had no real intention of concluding an effective treaty and were playing for time to re-arm. Once the Soviet Union became an ally, in 1941, advice to the Foreign Office given by people like Philby, Blunt and especially Maclean may have carried considerable weight and assisted Stalin in his highly successful bid to win the peace.

On 10 June 1940 Maclean married Melinda Marling, a petite American four years younger than himself, who was already pregnant by him. They were married hurriedly in Paris and with other refugees escaped from the German advance into France, reaching Britain about three weeks later. There is no doubt that Donald and Melinda Maclean were a devoted couple and it is my belief that this mutual love and dependence was a much more important factor in the circumstances of the sensational defection than has hitherto been realized.

Meanwhile, there had been little that Burgess could do, apart from helping to recruit others. He had suffered a nervous breakdown in his third year at Cambridge and his degree examination had, in consequence, been disappointing.[21] Still an open communist, he returned to Cambridge as a post-graduate student in 1934 with the object of securing a fellowship. He was soon ordered to appear to turn against communism and to leave Cambridge to insinuate himself into some important organization. Though disappointed, Burgess accepted the instructions and moved to London where he started supplying MI6 with scraps of information about the Nazis on a freelance basis. This ingratiated him with secret service officers and through it he even managed to meet Winston Churchill. In 1936 he fulfilled a K.G.B. requirement by joining the B.B.C., remaining there until 1938 and working in the Talks Department, where he came to know many M.P.s who were keen to appear in a programme called *Week in Westminster*.

Two years later he graduated, in K.G.B. terms, by insinuating himself into Section D, a branch of the War Office set up for training saboteurs for the war with Germany which seemed inevitable. He achieved this through social contact with the man running it and thereby became an effective 'mole'.

Blunt, too, found his clandestine activities limited by his circumstances at Cambridge but following the departure of Burgess he took on the role of recruiter. Among those whom he drew into Soviet espionage were a rich young American called Michael Whitney Straight and Leo Long, a linguist of working-class origin. Both were members of The Apostles. In 1936 Blunt widened his interests by becoming art critic for the *Spectator* and, in the following year, left Cambridge to take up an art appointment with the Warburg Institute. He was then aged thirty.

Having steadily enhanced his reputation as an art historian and connoisseur, Blunt left the Warburg Institute in 1939 to become Reader in the History of Art at London University and Deputy Director of the Courtauld Institute of Art in Portman Square. He was allotted a room at the Institute and was able to use it in the interests of the K.G.B., as I shall relate.

At the outbreak of war Blunt volunteered for army service and was commissioned. He remained in touch with his Soviet controller who suggested that he should apply to attend a five-week military intelligence course at Minley Manor, Camberley, in Surrey. His application was accepted, for Blunt was fluent in German as well as in French and Italian, but the Commandant, Brigadier John Shearer, received information from the War Office that Blunt had a Marxist past and he was therefore judged to be a security risk. His application was rejected 'by the same post', as Blunt recalled it.[25] It has been assumed that the War Office's evidence about Blunt's link with communism was obtained from MI5 but I have been told by MI5 officers involved in investigations into Blunt that there was no such information on Blunt's file. So if the information ever existed there it was removed by some friend or fellow-spy. Alternatively, the War Office may have been better informed on that issue than MI5.

In spite of this experience Blunt gained entry to the Intelligence Corps and went with the British Expeditionary Force to France as a field security officer, eventually being evacuated from Dunkirk. According to Lady Llewelyn-Davies, Blunt was popular with his men. He saw all his troops safely aboard a ship bound for England and remained behind, sheltering under a railway wagon, while he destroyed secret papers. Apparently his sergeant was so concerned about him that he returned to France on a destroyer and brought Blunt out.[26]

Once back in Britain Blunt was put under pressure from his controller to secure entry to an intelligence organization of a more fruitful kind, preferably MI5. Such a target should have been impossible for a person with a communist background, but Blunt succeeded with the help of a friend in MI5. The man who was instrumental in getting Blunt in was a wealthy art dealer and artist called Tomas Harris, his name indicating his half-Spanish origin. Harris had been recruited to the Iberian section of MI5 because of his linguistic ability and wide knowledge of Spain and Portugal, which were both heavily infiltrated by German agents. While there is no firm evidence that Harris was a Soviet agent, and Blunt was later to insist that he was not, Harris was fully aware of Blunt's Marxist views and support for the Soviet Union, which was then a virtual ally of Hitler.[27]

Within only five years of being recruited to work for 'peace' Blunt had achieved the top priority target set for him by the K.G.B. – membership of MI5, the Security Service, as a trusted officer right inside headquarters, then at 57 St James's Street.

Philby's path to a similar position in the heart of the sister service, MI6, was to be different but equally rapid. The K.G.B. had decided to send him to Spain to infiltrate the Franco side of the Civil War there and to service other Soviet agents. After intelligence training in Paris he reached Spain early in 1937 under cover of being a freelance journalist and with instructions to get as close to the hub of the Franco administration as possible. The operation was, of course, financed by the K.G.B. To improve his cover, which was thin, Philby began sending articles to *The Times*. He hoped to become its accredited correspondent, which would provide a better explanation of how he was managing for money, if questioned; it would also fulfil one of the priority targets laid down by his controller and, with *The Times* cachet, greatly improve his status. *The Times* hired him and he quickly secured the confidence of some of the Nationalist commanders in Spain, and was thereby able to supply useful information to Moscow which had heavy stakes in the other side. He eventually left the country in August 1939 having, meanwhile, parted from his too overtly communist wife, Lizi, who went to live in Paris.[28]

Philby continued his career as a war correspondent for *The Times* in France and was evacuated from Dunkirk following the French collapse. His controller then instructed him to seek an opening in the intelligence or security services, which were still expanding. First, he applied for a post at the Government Code and Cipher School but was rejected.[29] He then decided to try the branch of the Secret Intelligence Service (MI6) which had been set up to conduct sabotage operations abroad and which already had Burgess on its staff. Burgess arranged an interview for Philby, for whom he vouched, and in June 1940 another dedicated Soviet spy was eased into the organization, for if any check was made with MI5 it came back with the negative 'N.R.A.' – Nothing Recorded Against. No attempt was made to check out his communist wife, Lizi, to whom he was still married, though separated.

When the sabotage organization was disbanded Burgess became redundant. Philby, who looked entirely reliable, moved to a new sabotage training establishment set up as part of the newly formed Special Operations Executive (S.O.E.) at Beaulieu where, given that he was a former journalist, he specialized in the preparation of propaganda.

Though Philby had done well to gain admission to any branch of the Secret Intelligence Service, number two on the K.G.B.'s priority list, he was in something of a backwater as far as secret information was concerned, so his controller urged him to secure a transfer to a department in or near headquarters. Once again Tomas Harris was the effective instrument. He introduced Philby to an officer in MI5 called Dick Brooman-White who was head of MI5's Iberian section. MI6, which was responsible for espionage and counter-intelligence operations abroad, also needed an Iberian section, and because of Philby's experience in Spain Harris suggested him as being highly suitable. By the autumn of 1941, with Brooman-White's support, Philby was taken on the strength of MI6 with little or no check on his background.

Soon after Burgess had been made redundant in the sabotage division of MI6 he was recruited as a wartime supernumerary by MI5, his well-known homosexuality being considered no bar.[30] One of Burgess's most valuable qualifications as an agent-runner and K.G.B. spy was his continuing access to men and women of distinction. It was through his friendship with Sir Joseph Ball, who was a Director of the Conservative Research Department and wielded influence behind the scenes in Whitehall, that MI5 recruited him in good faith. Ball had served in MI5 briefly after the First World War and was involved in the reorganization of it early in the Second World War. It so happened that the agent in MI5 who was to control Burgess was his old friend and fellow-spy Blunt.[31]

As will be described more fully in Chapter 36, the main MI5 target allotted to Burgess was penetration of the London embassies of the neutral countries such as Sweden and Switzerland with a view to discovering their intentions and activities. He was also required to recruit and run agents to penetrate the pro-Nazi embassies such as Spain's. This was clearly of assistance to Philby in his work, for both Britain and the Soviet Union in the Iberian section of MI6.

The wartime careers of the four original members of the Cambridge Ring, Philby, Burgess, Blunt and Maclean, testify to the extraordinary ability of Soviet Intelligence to select and train young spies who at the time had nothing but potential but who managed to obtain positions in the most secret departments of state where they secured information of the highest value. In this astonishing achievement – for, as will be seen, others were selected and manipulated with similar success – Soviet Intelligence was greatly assisted by an appalling degree of inefficiency on the part of those responsible for preventing penetration of the secret departments and for detecting the activities of any who might have slipped through the defences. MI6 and the Foreign Office respectively were mainly responsible for failing to counter the activities of Philby and Maclean, but Hollis's section of MI5, which was charged with countering all Soviet spies during the war, must carry some of the blame. It was totally to blame for failing to counter the depredations of Blunt and Burgess inside MI5. Hollis's section was also responsible for failing to take any action against the activities of Philby's wife, Lizi, who had returned to London in 1938, remaining there throughout the war and serving as an ardent agent of Soviet Intelligence. Between the departure of 'Otto' in 1938 and the arrival of a replacement from the Soviet Union in 1940, the Ring of Four and others were serviced by Lizi, another refugee who repaid Britain's hospitality with treachery.[32] She passed information, usually documents, to another courier called Edith Tudor Hart, who gave it to a Communist Party official who had overt reasons for visiting the Soviet Embassy where it reached the K.G.B. 'resident'.[33]

Philby and Hollis were closely associated in their counter-intelligence activities, being counterparts in the sister services. Hollis appeared to trust Philby, which suggests that he was insulated from the views of both the Director-General, Sir David Petrie, and his deputy, Guy Liddell. Sir John Masterman, who ran MI5's superbly successful Double Cross operation, has recorded that during the war he was warned by both of them to treat Philby with caution and release as little information to him as possible.[34]

In view of Hollis's association with Philby, he and his section were at fault for failing to discover that Philby had been married to a Soviet agent, unless a blind eye was turned. An indication that the information had been known but ignored came from MI5 early in 1946 when Philby, who had been cohabiting with a Miss Aileen Furse, who had borne him three children and was about to give birth to a fourth, decided that he should marry her. Having decided to remain in MI6 after the war to serve the K.G.B. there, Philby was keen to secure promotion, possibly even to the top job, and some degree of respectability might be helpful. As he explained to Blunt, he had delayed securing the necessary divorce from Lizi because this might alert the security authorities to the fact that he had been married to a hardened pro-Soviet communist whose activities could not stand serious investigation.[35] By that time Lizi had left Britain to live with a well-known communist in East Berlin, so Philby asked his MI6 chief for leave to discuss the divorce with her in neutral France.[36] Part of his purpose was to disarm his chief by a show of frankness while suggesting that his marriage to Lizi had been just a youthful folly.

After Philby had acknowledged that he had known of his wife's political leanings when he had married her a note was sent to MI5, as Philby had anticipated, asking for a 'trace' on Lizi. The reply blandly stated that MI5 knew that Lizi was a Soviet agent. This occurred early in 1946, before the post-war reorganization of MI5, while Hollis and his Section F were still responsible for counter-intelligence against Soviet spies. At that stage nothing was done either in MI5 or in MI6 as far as Philby was concerned. He was not questioned further about Lizi or what he knew of her activities during the war.[37]

As an established K.G.B. officer, Philby could make no important moves without first consulting the Moscow Centre through his controller. While the divorce from Lizi was desirable for a regular MI6 officer on grounds of respectability, it was not essential at that point and was clearly dangerous, had MI5 been zealous in pursuing leads. So why did the Centre agree to it? With Philby poised in such a sensitive position, with incredible access to the highest secrets, the Centre would have been extremely loath to take any unnecessary risks, even to the point of eliminating the need for a divorce by liquidating Lizi. It is reasonable to assume, therefore, that the Centre was confident that no steps would be taken to follow up the Lizi lead. This could have been due to the Centre's general contempt for MI5's inefficiency in Soviet counter-espionage or, more likely, to the receipt of clandestine assurance from an MI5 source who, at that date, could not have been Blunt.

The divorce went through, quietly and without consequence, and Philby married Miss Furse in September 1946, the witnesses being Tomas Harris, the art dealer who had facilitated his entry to MI6, and Flora Solomon, an employee of Marks and Spencer who had introduced Miss Furse to Philby, whom she had known since he was eleven years old, as she relates in her memoirs published in 1984.

Mrs Solomon's association with Philby was to precipitate his eventual defection to to the Soviet Union in 1963, as described in Chapter 32. Meanwhile it is relevant to record here that in the memoirs she states that Philby made an attempt to recruit her for 'important work for peace' in 1937, and that in the following year she realized that he was 'still associated with the Communist Party, the cause he had espoused at Cambridge'. She also reveals that she knew that Philby had worked in Intelligence during the war, because for a while he was in an office of a 'branch of Intelligence' which had taken over the top floor of Marks and Spencer's headquarters in Baker Street (S.O.E.). She admits that she was also aware that Philby's former wife, Lizi, had been a communist and was living in East Berlin. She also knew that after the war Philby was 'in the Foreign Office', but claims not to have realized that this was a cover for work in MI6.

CHAPTER TWENTY

The Great Defection Legend

By 1940, after the damage inflicted on the Soviet Intelligence services by Stalin's insane purge of experienced controllers like 'Otto' and 'Theo', who had worked courageously as 'illegals' without any protection if caught, the K.G.B. decided to supervise its agents by means of 'legal' controllers, that is professional intelligence officers operating under diplomatic cover. The man sent to London for this purpose was one of the most successful in the history of the K.G.B. He has been positively identified as Anatoli Gorski who was working in the Soviet Embassy as Anatoli Gromov, officially listed as an 'attaché' from 1940 to 1944.[1] Gromov was known to the British spies he controlled only by the code-name 'Henry' though one German communist spy, Juergen Kuczynski, knew him as Gromov.[2]

Maclean must have proved to be a very valuable source of Foreign Office information, for shortly after he was posted to the British Embassy in Washington on 2 May 1944, Gorski followed him there, still under the false name Gromov and posing as a First Secretary in the Soviet Embassy. There he continued to control Maclean and other Soviet agents who had been recruited in the U.S. and who knew him as 'Al'.[3]

It may be wondered why a K.G.B. officer servicing so many agents was never detected in the act of contacting them. The main difficulty, according to MI5, is that professional Soviet Intelligence officers are highly skilled at avoiding detection and employ watchers to ensure that they are not being followed before making a dangerous contact, the process being known as counter-surveillance. Further, during the war, most of the MI5 surveillance effort was directed at possible German spies. Nevertheless, as the Soviet control of the Cambridge Ring began well in advance of the outbreak of war, when the U.S.S.R. was hostile, their success does nothing for MI5's reputation.

In Washington Maclean was appointed First Secretary and then head of Chancery with access to the Embassy code-room and the

Ambassador's private cipher. This enabled him to learn much about the American and British deliberations previous to the summit meeting in Yalta, where Stalin played such a successful hand. In 1947 Maclean was nominated to serve as joint secretary of the Western Allies' Combined Policy Committee on atomic energy development. This gave him access to Anglo-American atomic secrets of the greatest interest to the Soviet Union, especially as he had a pass which permitted entry to the Atomic Energy Commission building without an escort, a privilege denied even to J. Edgar Hoover, the head of the F.B.I.[4] Through regular contact with 'Henry' Maclean passed on everything of interest to the Kremlin.

In November 1948, after a month's home leave, Maclean was posted to Cairo as Embassy Counsellor and is believed to have continued his espionage activities there.

In the autumn of 1949 another British spy arrived in Washington in the form of Philby, who was posted to the British Embassy there in the guise of Second Secretary but whose duties included serving as MI6 liaison officer with the C.I.A. and F.B.I. Dr Wilfrid Mann, who knew him there, described him as suave, self-possessed, charming and erudite in public but frequently drunk, helpless and sometimes in tears at home.

Philby formed firm frienships with some of the senior officials of the C.I.A. and F.B.I. whom he met through his liaison duties.[5] He also quickly established contact with a Soviet controller to whom he regularly passed all the information he could gather and from whom he received instructions and advice. Dr Mann has recorded that while working on Anglo-American intelligence concerning Soviet atomic weapons, all his secret messages for MI6 were given to Philby, whose office was down the same corridor in the small main Chancery.[6]

By that time U.S. Intelligence, aided by G.C.H.Q., was making major breaks in Operation Bride and these included the information that there had been a series of high-level leaks in Washington to Moscow about top-secret messages passing between Churchill and the American Presidents Roosevelt and Truman.[7] At first it was not certain whether the agent responsible was in the British Embassy or in the White House or some other American department.

MI5 first received news of this break in January 1949 from the F.B.I. officer, Robert Lamphere, who has kindly told me the facts as he remembers them.[8] Before Philby left London for Washington in October, he was briefed by his MI6 colleague, Maurice Oldfield (later Sir Maurice), about the suspected leakage from the British Embassy, and he may have guessed or have known that the culprit was Maclean. There can be no doubt that he would have alerted his Soviet controller in London and given further details to his new controller in Washington after he had been given further information there by Lamphere.

Philby had never been close to Maclean, as he had been to Burgess, but he knew that he was an active spy and was, therefore, extremely interested in any suspicions which might fall on him or on any other member of the Cambridge Ring, especially as the interrogation of Maclean might lead to his own exposure. MI5 officers concerned with Bride are convinced that as soon as Philby received news of the break Maclean was warned that, while there was no suspicion at that stage specifically against him, counter-intelligence was on his trail. The normal route for the delivery of this warning would have been from Philby to his Soviet controller in Washington then, via the K.G.B. Centre in Moscow, to Maclean's controller in Cairo. Its purpose would have been to warn Maclean to be careful and to watch for any signs that he might be under suspicion and to report them to his controller.

The American Bride cryptanalysts then discovered, by further decipherment of wartime K.G.B. radio traffic, that the unidentified spy had the K.G.B. code-name 'Homer'. This information was passed to Lamphere, who was the officer responsible for liaising with the British on the problem. His counterpart in Washington was the MI5 representative, Geoffrey Patterson, who transmitted the news to MI5 headquarters in London.[9]

It has been widely assumed that the C.I.A. was involved in the search for 'Homer', but Lamphere has assured me that it was not. The search was essentially an F.B.I.-MI5 concern and the C.I.A. knew nothing about it until a much later stage. Nevertheless, since Philby also liaised with the F.B.I. as well as the C.I.A., Lamphere told him about the 'Homer' find.

Meanwhile the London-based MI5 officer who was helping to interpret the Bride discoveries, Arthur Martin, had made extensive trips interviewing possible suspects and had become convinced that the leaks had originated in the British Embassy in Washington and that the traitor must have been one of the six First Secretaries who had been responsible for encoding and decoding the high-level messages.[10] Maclean had been one of them.

In researching the ensuing events, which culminated in the defection of Maclean and Burgess, writers, including myself, have made an assumption which has been assiduously fostered by Whitehall and which happens to be crucial in the search to discover the truth of what really occurred. This was the belief that, because of the intense Washington interest and because the Americans had produced the first leads, London was at pains to keep the U.S. authorities fully and immediately informed of any British progress.

In a series of letters Lamphere has assured me that this assumption was false and so are the interpretations which have been based on it. The stark truth, according to Lamphere who was the American officer in charge, is that the U.S. authorities were told nothing about the suspicions attaching to Maclean until after he had defected.

This new information, made available to me by Lamphere as recently as April 1984, changes the entire texture of the events leading to the joint defection, and especially of the part played by Philby, which can now be seen to have been another legend to which British ministers have contributed on advice given by MI5.

Lamphere, who has been re-examining the events for his own account to be published in the U.S., has told me categorically: 'We did not learn that Maclean was a suspect until after the disappearance of Burgess and Maclean. Patterson and Philby then came to see me, as Philby describes in his book, and I was then told, as was Assistant Director Ladd, that Maclean had been a suspect and had now flown.

'MI5 had always tried to impress me with their personal regard for me, some of which I feel was genuine, but there is no question but that they double-crossed me in this matter.'[11]

In another letter he states, 'I pressed Patterson over and over to find out why there had not been more progress by MI5 in developing a list of suspects who were in the British Embassy at the pertinent period. He would tell me that he would inquire, or that there was nothing new.'

As will be seen, Lamphere was to be told later by MI5 that the pressure to keep him in ignorance came from the Foreign Office. That could well be true as some of Maclean's senior colleagues would have been loath to let any outsiders know that he was suspect until he had been given a chance to clear himself. What remains in doubt is the extent to which Patterson and Philby were being kept informed of the British progress by their respective London headquarters. Were they given the information and instructed not to tell the Americans? Or were they, too, kept in some degree of ignorance? The latter would seem to be possible because there would have been little point in telling them when their main function was to pass it on to the F.B.I. Further, London would realize that once they knew the information there would always be the danger that it might leak to their American counterparts on a friendship basis - what is usually referred to in Whitehall as 'the old pals' net'.

During the eventual confession made my Maclean's Cambridge contemporary, Anthony Blunt, he said that Philby had told him that he had given Maclean a further warning when it became established that 'Homer' was a Briton.[12] That knowledge, which must have caused Maclean great anxiety, is believed to have been largely responsible for his frequent drunkenness and his general deterioration, which puzzled his friends and culminated in senseless violence, causing a colleague to fall and break a leg, and the wrecking of the flat of a girl working in the American Embassy in Cairo.

This breakdown was conveniently attributed to excessive work by Foreign Office officials and, early in May 1950, Maclean was recalled to London on sick leave which lasted six months. It was surprising that in such a condition, which frequently resulted in violence in Soho clubs during his treatment, Maclean was able to maintain his cover, though he sometimes came close to breaking it. While drunk on one occasion in mid-1950 he remarked unpleasantly to an acquaintance, Goronwy Rees, 'You used to be one of us but you ratted!'[13] This was a clear indication that Maclean was still a communist but Rees did not report it, as he realized later he should have done. According to Cyril Connolly, the writer and critic, Maclean told another friend that he was a communist agent and challenged him to report the fact, as though trying to secure release from intolerable pressures. The friend did not do so.[14]

Maclean, who had been formally cleared of unbecoming conduct, was eventually pronounced fit in the belief that he had been 'dried out', though he was drunk again at a party on the night before he took up his new appointment on 6 November 1950 as head of the American Department of the Foreign Office in London.[15] This was an appalling appointment given that he was one of the six suspect First Secretaries and that Attlee was anxious to improve relations with Washington after the Fuchs and Pontecorvo disasters. It might be thought that Maclean was given this prestigious post on the advice of MI5 to lull him into a sense of security while he was being watched, but I have established that this was not the case.[16] For MI5 to have done that would have meant informing more people in the Foreign Office about the suspicions surrounding Maclean and those in the know there, and in MI5, were opposed to that. It may well be that those in the Foreign Office responsible for the appointment knew nothing of the suspicions, but MI5 certainly did and the result of taking no action meant that for several more months Maclean was able to channel secrets of the highest political significance to the Kremlin.

Later it was to be suggested by Foreign Office spokesmen that the new post was not as important as it sounded with respect to access to secret information, and Lamphere has told me that, after the disappearance of Maclean, Arthur Martin of MI5 'strongly down played the importance of the American desk and Maclean's being posted to it'. After Maclean's death in Moscow in 1983, however, Soviet sources are said to have revealed that the defector's continuing espionage from his American desk had played a crucial role in determining the outcome of the Korean War.[17] Maclean was quoted as having boasted that he gave the Kremlin every significant decision on the progress and conduct of the war taken by President Truman. These included the forbidding of General MacArthur to bomb the bridges over the Yalu River, to engage Chinese aircraft in hot pursuit or to retaliate against Chinese cities with atomic or conventional bombs. This information was said to have been passed by Stalin to the Chinese leadership, which was thereby encouraged to increase its support for the North Korean communists.

These claims are exaggerated because the Chinese had already entered the war while Maclean was on sick leave, before he joined the American desk. However, he was there in time to provide information which could have encouraged the Chinese to launch their first major attack, which changed the nature of the war, on 25 November.[18] The secrets Maclean passed to his London controller may also have included an intriguing historic detail made known to me during my inquiries.

On 29 November Truman had inadvertently referred to the possible use of nuclear weapons at a press conference at a time when the U.N. forces under General MacArthur were in retreat. Following an anxious debate in Parliament, Attlee announced his intention to fly to Washington for talks with the U.S. President as there was a substantial British and Commonwealth commitment to the Korean War. It has been widely believed that during the talks between 4 and 7 December Attlee took the initiative, which ensured that MacArthur would not be given permission to use atomic bombs in the conflict. However he did so in a rather peculiar way, according to my informant, who witnessed what I am about to describe and whose word I have absolutely no reason to doubt.

On the day before Attlee was due in Washington, General Sir Neil Ritchie, commander of the British Army Staff in the American capital, was summoned by helicopter from a golf course to the White House, along with other military and diplomatic officials. There Truman explained that he needed the British Prime Minister's assistance to counter the effect of his remark about the possible use of nuclear weapons and MacArthur's insistence that he should be allowed to employ them. Truman therefore announced to the gathering that he proposed to telephone Attlee and ask him to make it clear, during their talks, that if MacArthur used nuclear weapons the British and Commonwealth forces would have to be withdrawn. In the presence of witnesses Truman made the call and Attlee readily agreed. Aides were then instructed by Truman to leak to the American Press that the British and Commonwealth forces would pull out of Korea if MacArthur was allowed to use atomic bombs. The joint communiqué, which favoured a negotiated peace, made it so clear that they would not be used that Churchill criticized it for depriving the U.N. forces of being able to make use of the bluff that they might be. The atomic factor was, therefore, public knowledge and there was no need for Maclean to leak it.

It has recently been alleged that Maclean, as head of the American Department, accompanied Attlee to Washington as part of the team, but he is not listed in either the British or American archives as a participant, though he might have been on hand for advice.[19] Whether he was present, or not there is little doubt that he leaked the secret results of the talks, helping the Chinese to inflict more British, American and Commonwealth casualties. Like several other traitors, Maclean is dead and apologists for them argue that it is wrong to accuse them when they cannot defend themselves. My response is to point out that their victims are also muted and were deprived of the means of defending themselves effectively when sent to their deaths.

The behaviour of Burgess, who had left the B.B.C. in June 1944 and joined the press department of the Foreign Office as a temporary, was even more reprehensible than Maclean's. Though his salary remained small, nobody questioned the extravagant life he led, with friends noticing the hundreds of banknotes which he kept in shoe-boxes in his flat. For years he wined and dined influential politicians, diplomats and businessmen at the Dorchester Hotel, securing interesting information for which the Soviets paid. As he tried to recruit some of his guests to the Soviet cause they, at least, must have suspected that he was an agent but kept his secret until interrogated themselves after the unmasking of Blunt.

In 1946 Burgess was invited by his socialist friend, Hector McNeil, to become his personal secretary after McNeil's appointment as Minister of State to Ernest Bevin in the post-war Labour Government. This put him near to the heart of the nation's foreign affairs, with access to documents of great interest to his Soviet controller. McNeil had been warned that Burgess was a communist but, understandably, took little notice when there were ministers

177

like John Strachey, who had been so openly associated with communism.

In 1947 Burgess applied for permanent status in the Foreign Office and, to his own surprise and the anger of some of his colleagues, he was accepted. A former Foreign Office man has described to me how Burgess would return to the office after a long lunch 'tight as a tick. He could get away with behaviour which would speedily have been fatal for the likes of myself.'[20] By the end of the year he was pushed into a newly formed department called I.R.D. (Information Research Department), a semi-intelligence organization for countering Soviet propaganda and waging a modest degree of psychological warfare. He was dismissed from it for general slovenliness after only two months' service but not before he had had time to reveal its purpose and methods to the Soviets. From there he was shunted to the Far Eastern department, where he specialized in Red Chinese affairs, even lecturing on the subject to a Foreign Office summer school attended by officers of MI5 and MI6. He too saw secret documents about the Korean War.

Late in 1949, during a holiday in North Africa, Burgess was reported for security breaches as a result of indiscreet talk about secret matters, but he was only reprimanded in spite of the fact that by that time, it was obvious to some colleagues that he was dependent on drugs as well as drink. He had also developed diabetes. Partly to get him away from headquarters but also to 'give him foreign experience' he was posted to the British Embassy in Washington as a Second Secretary, an extraordinary appointment in view of the importance of improving Anglo-American relations, for Burgess was well known to be virulently anti-American.

The posting to Washington is made all the more incredible by the fact, recently disclosed to me, that Burgess was under such deep suspicion before he went to Washington in August 1950, that someone was sent out from London to take up an appointment specially created to enable him to keep Burgess under some degree of surveillance and to report regularly on his behaviour. Confidentiality requirements forbid me to give as much detail of this operation as I would like, but there can be little doubt that it was organized by the security authorities, either MI5 or MI6, with Foreign Office security possibly being in receipt of the reports. The individual concerned, then a serving army officer, who did not want the task, was ordered to Washington and told that arrangements would be made to get him into the company of Burgess, to whom he was to be as friendly as possible. On being informed of Burgess's sexual habits the officer told his superiors that he was totally unwilling to accommodate any homosexual advances. He performed the unpleasant surveillance duty until very shortly before the eventual return of Burgess to London when the job ended. The post had put the army officer in touch with information which could have been of great value to the Soviets and it may have been hoped that, realizing this, Burgess would try to pump him. In the event Burgess behaved scrupulously whenever the observer was in his company.[21]

In spite of the precaution taken it was a gross folly to send to the Washington Embassy a man who had been reprimanded for breaches of security so soon after the Fuchs case and while a former Embassy official, Maclean, was under some degree of suspicion, if only slight at that stage. It may be that the security authorities who had set up the surveillance of Burgess were unwilling to tell the Foreign Office that he was suspect in their eyes. Whatever the reason behind the posting, it was to do such irreparable damage to Anglo-American relations that it could hardly have suited the Soviet purpose more admirably if it had been planned by the K.G.B.

Burgess arrived in Washington in August 1950 and was promptly reunited with his old friend Philby, who lodged him in his home against the better judgement of his wife who foresaw trouble and unpleasantness from such a guest. Philby and Burgess worked together closely in the small main Chancery of the Embassy.[22]

Philby's apparent folly in taking Burgess into his home may, in fact, have been the result of the security decision in London to put Burgess under surveillance. As a senior MI6 officer, completely trusted by his superiors, Philby may have been told in advance about it and found it safer to have his friend under his own eye as much as possible. In that event Philby would have warned Burgess which, in turn, would account for the fact that the army officer's surveillance produced nothing of significance. The fear generated in Burgess by the knowledge that he was under deeper suspicion than he had appreciated could also account, in part, for his appallingly drunken behaviour at parties, when the person detailed to keep an eye on him was not present.

As the Bride inquiry progressed in Britain, the deciphered traffic suggested that the Soviet authorities trusted 'Homer' absolutely, which implied that he was an ideological spy, probably with a left-wing background. On that score, and other grounds, the suspects had been narrowed to two by mid-April 1951, but the Americans were not told. Arthur Martin in London then advised the code-breakers to look for some administrative message added at the end of one of the K.G.B. dispatches, which might pinpoint the culprit.[23]

179

At the beginning of May code-breakers at G.C.H.Q. made the crucial break which revealed that 'Homer' had been able to meet a Soviet controller in New York twice a week on the pretext that he had to go there to visit his wife who was pregnant. Maclean was the only suspect who had a wife in that condition then and she happened to be staying with her American mother in New York at the time.[24] Again, the Americans were not told though the material which had been deciphered had been supplied by their National Security Agency.

When Maclean's treachery became known to those few Foreign Office men who had to be told of it, the consternation can be imagined. Like all ministries, the Foreign Office was, and still is, responsible for its own security and it had singularly failed to suspect Maclean in spite of the many signs of his instability and former communism. There seems to have been a disastrous in-built reluctance to consider the possibility that a British diplomat could be a traitor.

The reluctance of MI5 to inform the American authorities that 'Homer' was almost certainly Maclean may have been partly rooted in Foreign Office sensitivities. There was argument that it would be wrong to name a diplomat as a likely traitor, even under conditions of absolute secrecy, before there was firm proof. Lamphere told me that after Maclean's disappearance, MI5, in the form of Arthur Martin, claimed that the lack of liaison had been due to pressure from the Foreign Office.[25] There was, however, a much more potent reason for the British decision to keep the Americans in ignorance: there was no intention of prosecuting Maclean, whatever he might confess. After Hoover's determination to ensure that Fuchs was brought to justice, it was feared that he would demand the same treatment for Maclean. It was, therefore, considered essential that the F.B.I. should not be told, and in the interests of secrecy the C.I.A. had to be deprived of the information too.

I have been assured by former officers of MI5 and MI6 that the sole purpose of interrogating Maclean was to produce a confession so that a damage assessment could be made and any associates and controllers neutralized. Former Foreign Office officials have told me that the view inside that service was totally opposed to prosecution on the grounds of international damage and injury to Foreign Office morale and reputation. It remains a matter for wonder whether the Americans would have been told if Maclean had confessed and not been prosecuted.

Whoever was finally responsible for the failure to keep the F.B.I. informed was stupidly short-sighted, especially when Attlee was setting such store by the resumption of the nuclear secrets interchange. Lamphere had been waiting for months for MI5, through Patterson, to produce a list of suspects, but this was never done.[26] The defection of Maclean, which was bound to become public, forced MI5 to confess the truth to the F.B.I. as soon as it was established tht Maclean had flown. Patterson and Philby had the job of doing it and Lamphere and his colleagues, including Hoover, were very bitter at the way they had been treated. Lamphere told me: 'Patterson personally lost standing with us in the Maclean affair as he was forced to lie to me over quite a period and was a personal friend.'[27] It is, of course, possible that neither Patterson nor Philby had been kept fully in the picture by London as the list was narrowed down for, if they were forbidden to pass on the information, they had no need to know it. Philby certainly knew what was happening but he may have been kept informed by his K.G.B. controller who was receiving information originating from some quite different source in London.

Maclean was put under surveillance but for reasons which have never been satisfactorily explained this was restricted to central London. Watchers followed him to Charing Cross railway station, to which he commuted each working day from his home at Tatsfield in Surrey. Once he was on the train, he was left until the following morning when watchers were waiting for him to arrive at the same station.[28] This gave Maclean ample opportunity to meet surreptitiously with Soviet controllers or cut-outs, or to visit dead-letter boxes, either during breaks he made in the journey or at Tatsfield itself, which was well within the thirty-mile circle from London in which Soviet diplomats were allowed to travel without seeking special permission.

I have also established that until the later stages of the case his telephone at Tatsfield was not tapped. This may have been due to reluctance on the part of MI5 to secure the necessary warrants from the Home Office as this would have meant alerting the Home Secretary to the suspicion that a senior Foreign Office man was a Soviet spy. Even when the telephone was tapped it was not 'tapped live'. Conversations were simply recorded on tape and listened to the following day or later. The same was true of microphones surreptitiously installed in the house, so no quick action could have been taken had it become necessary. The case was under the control of the counter-espionage branch headed by Dick White, but Hollis, as Director of Security, was also involved.

It has been stated that once suspicion against Maclean was strong secret reports were withheld from him, which he may have noticed.[29] If that is true, the behaviour of the security authorities was unbelievably ham-fisted. Allegations that the watchers were

181

also so clumsy that a car carrying them almost bumped into Maclean's taxi are K.G.B. disinformation.[30]

The mechanics of what occurred when Philby, who was still in Washington, learned – from whatever source – that MI5 was nearly certain that the spy called 'Homer' was Maclean appear to have been as follows: Philby immediately arranged a meeting with his Soviet controller who alerted the Centre in Moscow which, after deliberations, sent back instructions to the controller and to the K.G.B. resident in London. The K.G.B.'s immediate task was to warn Maclean that the danger of exposure, of which he had been aware for more than a year, had suddenly intensified and that arrangements might have to be made to ensure his safety from interrogation. The K.G.B. realized, and had probably observed, that Maclean was under surveillance by MI5 watchers, whose purpose was to catch him in contact with a Soviet Intelligence officer, an event which would have provided sufficient reason for his immediate interrogation.

The K.G.B. might have learned from a source inside MI5 that Maclean was not under surveillance once he had left Charing Cross, but it could never be sure, with the case coming to a climax, that the restriction had not been lifted. So the normal channels of communication with Maclean could not be used. Indeed, Maclean's controller in London would have been instructed to cease contact with him as soon as the spy had been identified as 'Homer', if not before. Some totally trustworthy intermediary who could meet Maclean without arousing suspicion and pass the warning to him was urgently required. Of the very few who knew about Maclean's treachery the best fitted for the task was Burgess. The two were known to be friends.[31] Both were employed by the Foreign Office and could meet as colleagues. And to add to this Burgess, in spite of his occasional outrageous behaviour, was a highly capable agent with a long record of devotion to the Soviet cause.

In its forward planning on the Maclean case the K.G.B. would have examined all foreseeable contingencies and would have prepared for them, and there can be little doubt that it had been decided that Maclean would eventually have to defect to the Soviet Union. The Soviets had continuing insight regarding Maclean's mental condition through his controllers, and also had the judgements of Philby, Burgess and Blunt. All of these three, according to Blunt, who may well have been consulted by the K.G.B., believed that Maclean would crack easily under interrogation.[32] While Blunt paid Maclean the compliment of believing that he would try to protect his friends, he said that if subjected to hostile questioning

182

he could decide to be a martyr, bragging about his exploits to show his contempt for the Establishment.[33]

The K.G.B. could have resolved its problem by assassinating Maclean, but such action is never certain, since an attempt can fail and its perpetrators can be arrested. Even a successful attempt is counter-productive because of its effects on other spies. Further, there was great political advantage to be gained from a defection because of its obvious effects on Anglo-American relations.

It is known, from defector evidence, that K.G.B. officers conferred in Moscow to plan Maclean's escape, and they must have given deep thought to his likely reaction when ordered to leave Britain.[34] He had never been to the Soviet Union, could not speak the language, and the prospect of spending his life there in exile must have been not only cheerless, but extremely frightening. He knew what had happened to 'Theo', 'Otto' and other Soviet spies who had given loyal service to Stalin both before and since the war and, in 1951, Stalin was still alive and in full control. In Maclean's condition it was not impossible that he might prefer to face interrogation than to defect. The intermediary used to inform him, therefore, had to be someone who could explain the absolute necessity for his defection and assure him of his welfare once he reached the Soviet Union. He also had to be capable of convincing him that his wife, Melinda, on whom Maclean felt dependent, would be able to join him. Her condition greatly complicated the situation because she was due to have another baby in mid-June.

Burgess, who had recruited Maclean in the first place, was the obvious choice on all counts. There have been suggestions that the K.G.B. behaved unprofessionally in selecting Burgess to warn Maclean, because it put an end to Philby's career as a spy, but it had no safe alternative and, in the result, the choice proved to be justified. As will be seen, there was another compelling reason, which the K.G.B. had almost certainly foreseen, for the selection of Burgess.

As a Government White Paper was later to admit, the British security authorities had strong grounds for suspecting that Maclean was the traitor whom they were seeking in April, before Burgess left the U.S. MI5 wanted to search his house for evidence, such as one-time pads and photographic apparatus, but they had decided to delay that operation until June when Mrs Maclean was due to go into hospital to have her baby and a surreptitious entry would be safer. The evidence strongly suggests that Philby knew both these facts, which meant that there was no great urgency in dispatching Burgess to Britain. Burgess was able to return via the *Queen Mary* instead of racing back by air, after various contrived speeding offences had brought about his deliberate recall to London in disgrace. On arriving in Britain on 7 May, he behaved in a leisurely fashion which has previously defied explanation and has been attributed to his unreliability, a feature which he did not display in his highly successful espionage career.

It seems likely that Philby had been officially informed by London, perhaps via Patterson, about the suspicions concerning Maclean. According to information quoted by Andrew Boyle in *The Climate of Treason* Sir Robert Mackenzie, the regional security officer stationed at the Washington Embassy, looked into MI5 headquarters to see Guy Liddell only two days before Maclean disappeared and suggested that Maclean should be pulled in without further delay and given a hostile interrogation. That suggests that Mackenzie knew that Maclean was on the short list of two at least, and if he knew, then presumably Patterson and Philby in Washington also knew. It would also suggest, however, that Mackenzie did not know any details of MI5's timetable for investigating Maclean beyond the fact that they did not appear to be in any great rush. Nor does he seem to have been given any further details by MI5. Mackenzie had no need to know them, nor did Patterson or Philby in view of the ban on informing the Americans. While it seems clear that Patterson and Philby had been told officially of the early development of the short list of six and, possibly, of its reduction to two, Lamphere and other professional security officers see no need why they should have been given further details which would have contravened the 'need to know' rule. Yet the leisurely nature of Burgess's behaviour suggests that Philby *did* know. Who could have told him?

The information could have originated only in MI5 itself, and if the K.G.B. was being given a running commentary on the 'Homer' case by an agent inside MI5, as several former officers suspect, then Philby could have received it through his K.G.B. controller in Washington. Burgess remained relaxed during the fortnight after his return and this suggests that he had complete confidence that he and the K.G.B. controllers in London would be given adequate warning of any sudden intensification of Maclean's danger. Such a warning could come only from some inside source at high level in the Foreign Office or in MI5. The existence of such a source would explain virtually everything which appeared to be mysterious about the defection of Maclean, including the fact that Burgess accompanied him.

Burgess was personally out of touch with the new Cambridge Ring controller, Yuri Modin, but he knew how to re-establish contact in order to secure the K.G.B.'s instructions for Maclean's flight to the Soviet Union should this become necessary, as seemed likely. The day after his return he went to spend the weekend with Goronwy Rees, at the latter's country home.[35] He seemed much cleaner and spruce in his appearance and spoke of his plans for the future, indicating that he knew that he was finished at the Foreign Office. On returning to his flat in London, which had been occupied by a friend called Jack Hewitt, he telephoned Lady Maclean to find out how to get in touch with her son. Then, after contacting Maclean himself by telephone, he had a long call to the U.S., probably speaking either to Philby or to a Soviet controller or cut-out.[36]

Blunt has described how Burgess imparted the first news to Maclean, having, no doubt, been careful to avoid making any reference to his danger on the telephone. Though officially suspended from duty, he breezed into the Foreign Office and into Maclean's room. Either he guessed that the office was bugged or had been told so. Without saying anything he placed a written statement in front of Maclean, warning him that the net was tightening around him and giving the time and place for a rendezvous. As he shut the door of Maclean's office on his way out he noticed two men, who were MI5 watchers, in the corridor. One of them was unprofessional enough to follow him and at the earliest opportunity Burgess informed Maclean that he was under surveillance, though he must already have assumed that he was.[37] About a fortnight after Burgess's return the two spies lunched at the R.A.C. Club and then, or on some other occasion, Maclean learned that he was being required to defect, with details of how and when this could be accomplished, Burgess having been appraised of them by his K.G.B. contact in London. What the details were at that stage is uncertain, but the fact that MI5 was anxious to delay any action with regard to Maclean until mid-June offers a possible clue. If the K.G.B. knew of this date and ensured that MI5 would find nothing incriminating at Maclean's home, it might have planned to induce Maclean to use the birth of the child as an excuse for taking his wife and family for a recuperation holiday in Switzerland. The defection of the family as a whole from such a foreign country would have been easy, as Pontecorvo had proved in the previous year. At the stage when the K.G.B. might have been considering such a ploy, the firm evidence that 'Homer' was Maclean had not emerged – it did not do so until early in May – so, after drawing a blank at Maclean's home, MI5 would have little on which to base any interview and, astonishing as it may seem, the authorities would have had no legal power to stop him leaving the country, as the White Paper made clear.[38] The Macleans could even have remained in Switzerland because espionage is not an extraditable offence and, without a confession, there was no evidence that could have been brought to court. All that Maclean had to do was to decline to be interviewed until he returned from his holiday.

Such a defection plan would have been much more acceptable to Maclean than any other, and details of it, or something like it, may have been imparted to Maclean by Burgess on Modin's instructions. If the Macleans had been able to defect as a family, supporting each other in their alien surroundings, there would have been no reason for Burgess to accompany them and no suspicion would then have fallen on Philby. Further, if they had remained in Switzerland for a year or two, the whole case would almost certainly have been covered up, with 'recurrent health problems' being given as the official reason for Maclean's departure from the Foreign Office.

Any plan for a leisurely defection suddenly collapsed on the morning of Friday, 25 May, when Herbert Morrison, the Foreign Secretary, arrived at his office and was told of the case against Maclean. Morrison was later to tell Parliament that, while he had heard of suspicions against an unnamed Foreign Office official in the previous month, he did not receive any written minute about Maclean until that Friday.[39]

It has been assumed by most writers that when Morrison received the minute, which had almost certainly been drafted on the previous evening, there was a meeting at which he heard arguments from MI5 men, who wanted to postpone any interrogation until Mrs Maclean went into hospital, and from Foreign Office officials who wanted a quicker resolution. The head of Foreign Office Security, George Carey-Foster, is supposed to have been present, but in recent notes to me he has declared that 'there was no meeting with Morrison' and this has been confirmed by Lord Sherfield, formerly Sir Roger Makins, then Number 2 at the Foreign Office. The arguments seem to have been thrashed out at a previous lower-level meeting, perhaps on the Thursday afternoon or evening, and all that Morrison had to do was to sign a document giving his formal permission for MI5 to act.

Whatever the exact truth of what occurred – and the documents describing the event are never likely to be released – Morrison made that decision quite early on the Friday morning. As will be seen, the mechanics of the proceedings in the Foreign Secretary's room are important because of the time-factor.

Because it was Friday and MI5 needed to make certain dispositions, it was agreed that the confrontation would take place in Maclean's room at the Foreign Office on Monday morning,

28 May. The Foreign Office officials claimed to be completely confident that Maclean would be at his desk then.

At lunchtime, Friday, which happened to be Maclean's thirty-eighth birthday, it has been assumed that he did not know about the impending interview. Cyril Connolly was sure of this after meeting Maclean then, and has expressed this opinion both in print and to me personally.[41] But for some reason Maclean, who should have been on duty on the following Saturday morning, asked permission to absent himself and this was granted, as Lord Sherfield has also confirmed. This request may have been coincidental, but it might also have been the result of his knowledge that he would not be in Britain on Saturday morning and did not want any hue and cry then. Significantly, on the Friday afternoon he told Lord Sherfield, who knew the Maclean family, that his sister-in-law was staying at Tatsfield which may have been a false excuse for being absent on Saturday.

At 5.30 on the Friday evening, Maclean left his office in Whitehall and was followed by watchers to Charing Cross, where he caught his usual train. That was the last that MI5 was ever to see of him.

I have been told by officers that one of the reasons why Maclean was not followed to Tatsfield on that Friday evening was an assurance by Foreign Office men that he would certainly not defect, even if he got wind of the decision to question him, because his wife was so close to confinement. Someone in MI5 was responsible for accepting this ludicrous advice. Lord Sherfield believed that Maclean was under surveillance when outside London, and other Foreign Office officials may have been equally misled.

There have been suggestions that Burgess learned of the impending decision by Morrison on the previous evening, after the minute to the Foreign Secretary had been drafted, and that this information had come from Philby, perhaps by telephone.[42] For reasons already stated it is highly improbable that Philby had been officially informed of the meeting or that he would have dared to contact Burgess by telephone. Philby might conceivably have been told by a K.G.B. source, but it would seem far more probable that any warning to Burgess came from a source in London who knew of the minute to Morrison. Burgess seems to have been perfectly relaxed on Thursday evening and took no known actions, apparently still intending to take a weekend holiday in France with an American friend whom he had met on his voyage back to England on the *Queen Mary*.[43] This suggests that he did not know of any decision to advise Morrison to agree to the quick interrogation of Maclean. If the information came from an MI5 source, however,

Burgess may have been told that the intention was still not to interrogate Maclean until after the birth of his new child, which was several weeks away, since MI5 might have been reasonably confident that as the normally unchallengeable authority on security matters its view would prevail.

This interpretation of events is supported by the fact that on the morning of 25 May Burgess rose in his usual leisurely style, being still officially suspended on leave, drank his tea in bed and read *The Times*, as witnessed by his flat-mate, Jack Hewitt.[44]

It is known that shortly before 10 a.m. he was making social calls in connection with the weekend holiday. It would seem certain that by 10 a.m. he would have read his morning post, so there seems to have been nothing in that which excited him. Nor is there any evidence of the arrival of any cable. Shortly afterwards, however, he rushed out of the flat to secure a large cash sum, though he already had £300 in notes, buy clothes and a suitcase, and hire a motor car, while cancelling arrangements he had almost certainly expected to keep in the ensuing week.[45] At about 10.30 Burgess kept an appointment with his American friend and said that he would have to cancel their trip because 'A young friend in the Foreign Office is in serious trouble and I am the only one who can help him', a rash statement to have made to a near-stranger.[46]

Clearly, the news that Maclean was about to be interrogated had reached Burgess and he was reacting to it, probably in a way predetermined in some contingency plan. The K.G.B. would have considered the possibility that the inevitable interrogation of Maclean might be brought forward. But how did the precise information that the possibility had suddenly become fact reach Burgess between 10 a.m. and 10.30 on that Friday morning, within an hour of the Foreign Secretary's decision?

It has been generally assumed that Philby, who had given Maclean the general warning about his danger through Burgess, also gave Burgess the final warning about the exact date of the coming interrogation. As Prime Minister Mrs Thatcher even gave that explanation as a fact to Parliament when reading from an old brief on the Blunt affair prepared for the previous Labour Government.[47] Most investigators have believed that, immediately after Morrison's decision that Maclean should be interrogated, MI5 and MI6 had to communicate that information to Patterson and Philby in Washington so that the F.B.I. and the C.I.A. could be told about it. That was why Philby must have known of it and been in a position to give the final warning to Burgess. Lamphere's evidence shows this notion to have been false. As the Foreign Office and MI5 did not want the F.B.I. to know about the impending

188

interrogation, and as the C.I.A. was not involved at all, there was no need for any such message to be sent and certainly no requirement for any haste. Even if a message was sent, it was wildly improbable that Philby could have received it in time to warn Burgess. It would have been about 5 a.m. in Washington, and if Philby was awake then, he would not have been in his office.

Lamphere has assured me that even when Maclean had fled and the F.B.I. had to be told that he had been under suspicion, he was not informed about the proposed interrogation and was not told of it until 'long after' Patterson and Philby admitted to him that Maclean had vanished.[48] Further, there is no evidence in any of the records of MI5 or MI6 that Philby was ever told the date of the proposed interview.[49]

F.B.I., C.I.A. and MI5 sources privately maintain that the circumstances do not possibly allow for any information about the timing of the interrogation to have reached Burgess from Philby.[50]

It might be argued that Philby had been given notice of the timing of the interrogation on the Thursday on the grounds that the signing of the document by the Foreign Secretary was to be merely a formality agreed to but this, too, is unlikely in view of Lamphere's evidence. Even if the London authorities had belatedly decided to alert the F.B.I. through Philby or Patterson, it would not have been safe to do so until the Foreign Secretary had actually signed the document, for there was no certainty that he would sign it. He might have wished to consult the Prime Minister. If the Foreign Secretary had decided that the interrogation should be deferred, as MI5 advised, then the F.B.I. would have been misinformed by any earlier warning, an event which the British authorities would have been anxious to avoid.

The fact that Philby has already publicly taken credit for giving Burgess the final warning makes it even less likely that he did so. In *My Silent War*, published in 1968, he told a story of how he had sent a letter warning Burgess that if he failed to 'act at once' he would have to send the Lincoln car he had left behind to the scrap heap. This was supposed to be a veiled warning to get Maclean out without delay, but if Philby had really known the date of the interrogation all he had to do was to alert his Soviet controller in Washington, who could then have signalled Modin in London, on a safe line and with greater precision than any garbled communication by letter or cable.

Philby's car story and his claim that it was the final panic warning are almost certainly items of disinformation inserted by the K.G.B., with Philby's assistance, in the probable interest of protecting the true source. It is common practice that once a spy

189

has been blown, as Philby was by his own defection in 1963, use is made of him to cover other spies who are still active or vulnerable to interrogation by openly crediting him with operations in which he played no part. It is known that Andropov himself, when chief of the K.G.B., encouraged Philby to write *My Silent War*.

It seems much more likely, therefore, that the warning to Burgess in his flat in London originated from a source in London - from one of the few people who knew about the decision immediately after the Foreign Secretary had made it, or from someone who had been told about it very quickly by one of those people. At that stage, the leak could have come from a high-level friend in the Foreign Office and Burgess certainly had such friends. Or it could have come from MI5.[51] If there was no MI5 representative present when Morrison signed the document, then all that was needed was a quick telephone call to MI5 headquarters on the secure line to impart the news. If an MI5 officer was present it would seem certain that he would have returned to headquarters in Curzon Street without delay, a journey of fifteen minutes at the most.

Among those who needed to be told immediately of the decision were Arthur Martin, Maclean's case officer, and Hollis, the Director of Security. No suspicion has ever attached to Martin, and while Guy Liddell, who would also have been told the result, cannot be totally discounted because of his association with Blunt, those who knew him inside MI5 consider Hollis to be the likelier suspect.

If someone in MI5 was responsible, how did the information reach Burgess? The MI5 headquarters was only a few minutes' walk from Burgess's flat at 10 New Bond Street, so a note could have been delivered. It would seem more likely, however, that personal contact was used to ensure that Burgess received the information, and it is doubtful that any MI5 officer would have taken that risk. A telephone call would not normally have been safe, unless made through some prearranged code, but I have established that Burgess's telephone was not being tapped because he was not under sufficient suspicion, and an MI5 source might well have known that. Such a source who was a regular Soviet agent could have alerted his controller to the fact that Burgess's telephone was safe to use. He would also have been more inclined, under the existing conspiratorial rules, to have passed the information to the controller and to have left the action to him. The controller could then have contacted Burgess directly or used a cut-out to do so, though this would have put another link in the chain, making the short time-scale even more difficult to explain. Mrs Thatcher, reading a statement originating in MI5, told

190

Parliament in 1979 that Blunt had admitted to MI5 that in 1951 he used his old contacts with the Soviet Intelligence Service to assist in the arrangements for the defection.[52] But she also told the Commons that 'it was Philby who warned Maclean that he was about to be interrogated', which is almost certainly incorrect. Blunt has consistently maintained that his assistance in the defection was limited and did not involve delivering the final warning.[53] By publicly blaming Philby and Blunt, who were known spies, officials may, wittingly or unwittingly, have been covering a suspect who was unknown in 1979. Since then the chief suspect has been shown to be Hollis and it could be significant that in the brief concerning the Hollis case that was prepared for Mrs Thatcher to read in 1981, Philby and Blunt were named again as being probably responsible for events with which they could not possibly have been connected.[54]

Blunt had no direct access to secret information in 1951 and if he did deliver the warning it was because he had been deliberately informed of the imminent interrogation so that Burgess could be alerted. He had remained friendly with Liddell, whom he met regularly at the Travellers Club, and with Hollis.[55]

As it is now known, from Blunt, that Yuri Modin, the controller posing as an attaché in the Soviet Embassy, organized and oversaw the defection, he must have learned about the sudden need for it very quickly. Blunt's interrogators spent much time on many occasions discussing the circumstances of Burgess's flight with Maclean and were left in no doubt that Burgess went not only with full Soviet agreement but under strong K.G.B. pressure. His flight was not a last-minute whim, as has previously been assumed. Blunt made this clear publicly in a statement to *The Times* when, referring to a Soviet attempt to induce him to defect as well, he said, 'they might simply take me out as they took him out', meaning Burgess.[56]

When plans for the escape were being discussed in advance at the Moscow Centre two reasons for Burgess's defection would have been evident. While he might be a stronger reed than Maclean, he had become addicted to drugs as well as drink and so might crack if interrogated harshly, a possibility which had to be entertained. Since Operation Bride had uncovered that 'Homer' was Maclean, as the Centre knew from Philby's reports, it might also reveal that 'Hicks' was Burgess. The danger of permitting Burgess to be questioned by MI5 was also publicly stressed by Blunt in his *Times* interview when he declared that he 'was very nearly round the bend under the strain'. The second and much more pressing reason was Maclean's reluctance to leave Britain without his family, who

191

could not accompany him because of his wife's physical condition. Even if Maclean could be forced, by threats, to leave Britain alone there was no certainty that he would complete the frightening journey and he could well end up drunk and incapable in the hands of the police in France. He had to be accompanied and Burgess was not only on hand and a trusted agent, but could be spared, as he was out of contact with prime source material and unlikely to resume contact with it.

The exact time when Burgess first knew that he might have to go with Maclean is unknown. It is not impossible that he knew before he left Washington, for as a successful agent of long standing, he might have been at the meeting with Philby and the controller when it was decided to use him as the messenger to Maclean. Indeed Burgess's main purpose in returning to Britain may have been to accompany Maclean out of the country.

Philby's claim in *My Silent War* that he remarked to Burgess, 'Don't you go too', does not ring true in the circumstances and is probably a touch of disinformation to continue the fiction that Burgess was not a spy.

It must have been foreseen that the disappearance of Burgess would inevitably focus suspicion on Philby. That could be a major disaster for the K.G.B. because, while he could be relied upon to brazen his way through interrogation, it had been hoped that he would continue inside MI6 for many years, even, possibly, becoming its Director-General. Nevertheless the risk had to be accepted because Philby would probably be totally exposed if either Maclean or Burgess were subjected to hostile questioning. Philby's controller must have discussed the prospects with him, and if Philby knew that Burgess would be defecting before he himself left Washington, he had some time to prepare his position.

It was certainly realized by the Moscow Centre that the defection of Burgess would also throw suspicion on Blunt, his close friend, as will shortly be seen.

On receipt of the warning Burgess clearly knew exactly what to do and that it was his duty to flee with Maclean and see him to safety. It is possible that he had been lulled into believing that he could then return home but, as events showed, he was required to remain in the Soviet Union until the end of his short life. While defection was a huge sacrifice for Maclean, it was equally so for Burgess, who hoped and believed that the Soviet Union might convert Britain to a communist state but had no wish to live in Moscow. He, too, must have appreciated the risk of being killed or imprisoned by Stalin.

Nevertheless, he moved swiftly and not in panic. Wisely, he

made no effort to contact Maclean in London, where he knew he might be observed. He did, however, take a risk by telephoning the wife of Goronwy Rees from the Reform Club, and in the course of the twenty-minute conversation saying that he was about to do something that would 'shock many people'.[57] She thought that he was incoherent but Rees later recorded that when she told him about the call he surmised that Burgess had fled to Moscow.

Later in the day, using a hired car, Burgess drove out towards Maclean's home at Tatsfield, where he must have been confident that he would not be observed. Insufficient attention has been paid to this confidence. K.G.B. watchers keeping MI5's watchers under surveillance might have been able to inform Burgess and Maclean that the latter was not normally under surveillance once he had left Charing Cross station, but after the decision to interrogate Maclean had been taken, the K.G.B., in line with its own practice, should have assumed that this might no longer be the case. Yet Burgess must have been advised, presumably by Modin, that it was safe for him to visit Tatsfield. How would the K.G.B. have known this? The only plausible answer is that the K.G.B., or Burgess directly, had been assured that Friday that Maclean and his home were still free from MI5 surveillance. Again, the number who knew this was very small, and Hollis, as Director of Security, was one of them.

According to the flat-mate, Hewitt, Burgess received a telephone call from a person whom Hewitt later believed to have been Maclean. It could, however, have been from someone else with further information, including the assurance that it was safe to visit Maclean at Tatsfield.

The precise details of how and when Burgess arrived at Maclean's home and whether or not he first met up with Maclean earlier at the station, or elsewhere, are unknown. The most commonly recorded account, which derives mainly from the subsequent questioning of Mrs Maclean, alleges that Burgess arrived about half an hour after Maclean, at about 6.30 p.m., and introduced himself to her as 'Roger Styles', a colleague from the Foreign Office.[58]

Mrs Maclean is not supposed to have known who 'Styles' was or anything about the planned escape, beyond the fact that her husband had told her that 'Styles' was coming to dinner. In view of her later behaviour, culminating in her own surreptitious flight to Moscow, nothing she said should necessarily be believed. She was almost certainly fully aware of what was about to happen and of 'Styles's' identity and was acting on instructions to 'muddy the waters'.

Eventually, so her story went, Maclean left with 'Styles', simply telling his wife that they had a pressing engagement and that he would be taking an overnight bag in case he could not get back. Whatever the true circumstances, the evening must have been dramatic in the extreme. Even if Mrs Maclean had been told of the inevitability of eventual defection the shock of knowing that the time had now come and that she would be left alone must have been great. The conspirators said nothing within sound of any hidden microphones that gave any indication of their plans. In any case, their conversations would not have been processed until the following day.

Those officers in MI5 associated with the Maclean and Burgess case now believe that Mrs Maclean's account was a concoction and that she not only knew about the coming defection but had also been assured that she would be able to rejoin her husband after her baby had been born. One such officer has assured me that MI5 never really 'bought' her story suspecting, from the start, that she was a communist herself, probably having been converted by her husband. There is evidence to that effect in the form of a statement by Gordon Young, a highly reliable journalist, who was told by a former communist wartime internee that Maclean had told his controller, 'Theo', early in his espionage career that he had taken his wife into his confidence and that she was helping him in his work.[59]

I have been unable to discover any collateral evidence to support Mrs Maclean's story, which seems to be the sole basis for the belief that Burgess went to Tatsfield to pick up Maclean. They may, in fact, have met elsewhere. MI5 would appear to have accepted the story and possibly there was some evidence in support of it from the 'bugs' which had been planted in the house, though I have been told that they yielded nothing. The White Paper which MI5 subsequently prepared for the Government stated that it had been established that the two defectors left Tatsfield together by car.

The fact that Mrs Maclean did not report her husband's disappearance until 10 a.m. on Monday morning, by which time the defectors were safely out of reach, intensified MI5's suspicion. It would have been routine for the K.G.B. to have kept an eye on Mrs Maclean to ensure that she did not disobey instructions and alert the Foreign Office sooner.

Burgess and Maclean arrived at Southampton dock at 11.45 p.m. on Friday night just in time to rush aboard the midnight boat, *Falaise*, to St Malo. It would, of course, have been prudent for them to have arrived as late as possible to reduce the chances of their being recognized before the boat sailed. It has been accepted as an odd coincidence that two days previously Burgess happened to have booked two berths on the S.S. *Falaise* for that evening, ostensibly to take him and the American who he had met on the *Queen Mary*. Being suspicious of such coincidences, I would suggest a different explanation. It seems unlikely that the K.G.B. would have permitted Burgess to drift off to France, purely for a jaunt, at such a time. It is possible that he was being sent there for a purpose, the American providing his cover for the visit. Defector evidence was to reveal that the defection plans were being partly directed from France, so Burgess may have been required to go there to meet a contact.[60]

The two traitors left the ship at St Malo, abandoning suitcases and some of their clothing. It was reported, though never established, that they took a taxi to Rennes and thence a train to Paris, where they disappeared. (The K.G.B. defector Petrov was to say that they had reached the Soviet Union via Berne and Prague.)

Blunt then received an urgent message to meet the Soviet controller, Modin, and he did so in London, which is further evidence of his continuing close connection with the K.G.B. Blunt had already realized that because of his friendship with Burgess MI5 was bound to go through the motions of interrogating him. Modin told him that the Centre was so fearful that he might break and reveal the names of other agents that it had been decided that he should defect as well.[61]

Again, the K.G.B. must have realized that it might be only a short time before Operation Bride revealed that 'Johnson' was Blunt. The proposition also held certain advantages for the K.G.B. The defection of Burgess and Maclean was certain to disrupt Anglo-American relations regarding the exchange of intelligence and military secrets. With the added defection of Blunt, a former MI5 officer and trusted servant of the Royal Household, the consternation in Congress and in the American Press could have been catastrophic for the West.

Blunt was told that all the escape routes had been prepared and that there was no time for argument. Nevertheless, Blunt, true to character, did argue and demanded time to think. The last thing he wanted to do was to abandon his international career as an art critic, which looked so promising, professionally and financially. He had some familiarity with the Russian language, having studied it as a diversion during stints of fire-watching during the war, and had visited Leningrad and Moscow briefly, but the prospect of a Soviet-style apartment contrasted rather sharply with his Director's flat in the Courtauld Institute, where his personal art collection, including a large Poussin – 'Rebecca at the Well' –

which he had picked up in Paris for £100, was already very valuable. Later he told close friends that he so hated the thought of going to live in the Soviet Union that he would never have gone, whatever pressure the K.G.B. might have attempted to apply.[62]

Sensing the way MI5 was likely to respond to any suggestion that it had harboured a spy and aware that it had no hard evidence against him, Blunt felt confident that he could withstand any interrogation of the kind to which the Surveyor of the King's Pictures was likely to be subjected. This confidence might have been strengthened by his knowledge of a secret mission he had performed for the Royal Family and which might embarrass them if he revealed it.

Further, if Blunt was aware that the timely warning to Maclean had come from an on-going source in MI5 there seemed to be no reason to doubt that he, too, would receive similar protective treatment. He may even have been assured by a friend in MI5 that while a routine interrogation could not be avoided, it would not be hostile and could be successfully countered by bland denial.

In the event he told Modin, firmly, that he proposed to stay and to rely on the standard K.G.B. advice – admit nothing, deny everything but keep on talking to discover how much the interrogators know.[63] Again, the reasons behind Blunt's confidence when he was aware that Philby, who was sure to be questioned, and several others, including the American Michael Straight and Leo Long whom he had recruited, knew that he was a spy, do not seem to have been adequately investigated.

Modin must have been concerned about Moscow's reaction to his failure to induce Blunt to defect, but his success in handling the escape of Maclean and Burgess was to be sufficient for him to be given the responsibility of organizing the defection of Philby twelve years later.

On the Saturday morning MI5 watchers, who had been told that Maclean would be on duty at the Foreign Office, were waiting at Charing Cross to begin their shadowing duty. There was some anxiety when he did not appear, but inquiries at the Foreign Office revealed that he had been given the morning off and officials had forgotten to tell MI5! No inquiries were made at Tatsfield to ensure that he was really there.

Mrs Maclean was interviewed by Foreign Office security officials following a telephone call by her to the Foreign Office on the morning of Monday, 28 May, when she told the 'Styles' story and played the innocent so effectively that they claimed to be convinced that she had known nothing about the defection. At that stage it suited the Foreign Office to believe her and, while some MI5

196

officers thought that she must be lying, it was only later that the organization officially decided that she had misled them.

Later on the same Monday morning, Hewitt reported the disappearance of his flat-mate, Burgess, to Blunt, knowing that he was another close friend and had been in MI5. Blunt then reported the fact to MI5 headquarters and that, apparently, was its first news that Burgess had left with Maclean.[64]

It may be asked why, if the K.G.B. Centre had required Blunt to defect because he was bound to be suspected, the same did not apply to Hollis, had he been a spy responsible for the final warning to Maclean and other essential leaks to the K.G.B. Hollis was in no obvious danger as he was not, and never had been, associated with the Cambridge Ring in its treachery. If he was recruited in China it would have been on behalf of what quickly became the G.R.U. The Bride breaks which led to the exposure of Maclean and, later, to the code-names of Burgess, Blunt and Philby had been through intercepts of K.G.B. traffic. No G.R.U. traffic was being deciphered. If Hollis was transferred later to control by the K.G.B., as it increased its dominance over the G.R.U., his code-name and any details of his activities would not have appeared early enough for them to have been deciphered by Operation Bride, which was restricted to intercepts recorded over only a short period during the war, as the K.G.B. knew from Philby.

When the disappearance of Maclean and Burgess became public, Sillitoe, who was in France, was recalled to London and ordered by Attlee to fly to Washington to try to placate the American authorities and Hoover, the F.B.I. chief, in particular. Hoover had discovered that Maclean had been allowed unescorted access to the U.S. Atomic Energy Commission building and, as had been anticipated, he was furious that the spy had escaped retribution.

Sillitoe spent an evening being briefed on the case by his lieutenants. His son, Tony, recalled: 'When my father called for files relevant to the defection before flying to Washington to see Hoover, Hollis failed to produce them saying that they had 'gone missing' or were 'unavailable'. There was something about 'dear Roger', as my father called him, that disturbed his policeman's instincts.'[65]

Arthur Martin, the case officer for Maclean, accompanied Sillitoe to Washington and they flew out on 11 June 1951, Martin being disguised as a chauffeur, ludicrously as it turned out because they were photographed at London Airport.[66] The files they took with them had been doctored to remove the evidence that MI5 had known that Maclean was suspect for many weeks and had withheld the information from the F.B.I.[67] In a farcical attempt to delude the newspapers, airline officials were instructed to tell the Press that Sillitoe and Martin had cancelled their flight, which was untrue. It is possible that Sillitoe was not aware that the files which he showed Hoover and the C.I.A. chief, General Bedell Smith, were deliberately misleading but his efforts to explain why they had been kept in ignorance and his excuses for the failure to apprehend Maclean impressed nobody in Washington. As a result, the Anglo-American interchange of secrets was set back for several years and has never, in fact, been renewed so far as weapons are concerned.

Maclean's flight had, of course, convinced his would-be interrogators that he was guilty of treason but the embarrassment was so great that everything possible was done to maintain the fiction that he and Burgess were just two drunken dissolutes who had fled the country because their careers were in ruins. Publicly, Whitehall was to continue for four years to pretend that it did not know where they were and that it had no evidence of disloyalty by either of them.

Security officials still argue that they had to remain tight-lipped about their knowledge that Maclean had been a spy to avoid letting the Soviets learn how much they knew and particularly to protect the secrecy of Operation Bride, which was likely to produce more results. If this was so the silence served no purpose for the Soviet penetration of the British secret services was so deep that Philby had been providing Moscow with a running commentary on Bride from its inception.

Internally, the certainty of Maclean's guilt was sufficient for a damage assessment to be carried out by the Foreign Office.[68] It showed that Maclean had sat on several committees dealing with political information of extreme interest to the Kremlin. This included the Anglo-American exchanges about the North Atlantic Treaty and early meetings which resulted in the eventual creation of N.A.T.O. He had information about uranium requirements and ore availability. Perhaps most importantly, he had access to U.K. diplomatic codes and ciphers so that British diplomatic traffic must have been an open book to the Kremlin. Even after he was on the list of suspects, as head of the American Department, he had been the Kremlin's ear at meetings of interest to it and particularly on those concerning the Korean War.

The C.I.A. made its own analysis of MI5's handling of the case and concluded that it had been appallingly bungled. C.I.A. officers maintain that once it was known beyond doubt that Maclean was 'Homer' he should have been under constant surveillance to catch him with a Soviet controller or with a cut-out like Burgess.[69] Then, once it had been decided to interrogate him, it would have been normal practice to inform him of his coming ordeal to panic him into some damning reaction, which round-the-clock surveillance could have detected. According to C.I.A. standards the way the Maclean case was handled in its terminal stages was the least likely to succeed.[70] Curiosity therefore persists as to why the MI5 management was convinced that Soviet Intelligence officers and cut-outs would never attempt to contact Maclean outside central London. Was there some special reason for the lack of surveillance at Maclean's home and on his journeys there?

There remains the possibility that the defection of Maclean was deliberately made easy because it was the best available solution to official anxieties. This continues to be roundly denied by the security authorities but it is doubtful that the question will ever be answered satisfactorily as the documents concerning the case have been listed as MI5 papers which may not only be withheld indefinitely but will probably be 'weeded' or even destroyed 'in the public interest'.

Four months after Maclean's defection his wife told MI5 that she wanted to leave Britain to start a new life in Switzerland, away from prying newspapermen. There was no power to stop her going and she went to live in Geneva. Two years later, on 11 September 1953, in another K.G.B. operation, she left surreptitiously with her three children for Moscow where she lived for almost thirty years before returning to the United States. During that time she left her husband to cohabit with Philby, which must have been a bitter experience for Maclean.

MI5 appears to have taken no interest in her while she was in Switzerland. Shortly before she disappeared it had been intended to send two officers to see her but the story was put about in MI5 that one of them had been unable to find his passport and that as a result Mrs Maclean had flown before they could have arrived.[71]

MI5 interest was not aroused again until the defector, Vladimir Petrov, revealed that the K.G.B. had arranged her departure from Switzerland.[72] Plans to take her to Moscow had existed in 1952, and perhaps before that. Again it was 'embarrassing' for the MI5 management to admit, internally and in Whitehall, that for such a woman to take three young children to the U.S.S.R., where they would become Soviet citizens with no certainty that she or they would ever be able to leave, implied that she was a dedicated communist and probably had been so at the time of her husband's defection.

The justified fear of an incensed American reaction to the

defection of Maclean and Burgess forced the Government and Whitehall officials to go through rapid motions aimed at locking stable doors to prevent the bolting of further rogue horses and the entry of new ones. It was an exercise which was to be repeated with depressing regularity over the years.

Following the Gouzenko revelations and the conviction of Nunn May in 1946 there had been a reluctant realization in Whitehall that it had been too trusting regarding the loyalty of defence scientists and other civil servants with access to highly secret information. The Attlee Government set up the Cabinet Committee on Subversive Activities and in the spring of 1948 a loyalty programme was introduced to prevent known communists and others who might be security risks from working in posts where important secrets might be learned. It became known as the 'purge procedure' and was devised by Treasury officials working in liaison with MI5. As Director of Security, Hollis was the MI5 officer responsible, being assisted by Graham Mitchell, who was in charge of overseeing communists and fascists.[73] The procedure was negative in the sense that it depended for its application on the existence, in MI5 or police records, of evidence of communist connections and this was usually not available. As an indication of how half-baked the system devised by Hollis and the Treasury was, it was not to be applied to new recruits to secret posts until Attlee queried it.[74]

The weakness of the system became publicly evident by the conviction of Fuchs and the flight of Pontecorvo, who had been cleared for access to secrets several times. Privately it had ruined the Attlee Government's chance of renewing the interchange of atomic information with the U.S., a situation of benefit to the Soviet Union. With repeated British pleas for restoration of the interchange there was pressure from Washington for the introduction of a system of 'positive vetting', under which all people with access to information classified Top Secret would have to be questioned and their background and previous activities investigated. This was being resisted in Whitehall and, it seems, in certain quarters of MI5, as being an unwarranted invasion of civil liberty, though the country and the system against which the new measure was directed were intent on depriving the whole nation of its civil liberties.

When the guilt felt about the defection of Maclean and Burgess forced some action, the Labour Cabinet agreed to introduce positive vetting, but it lost the ensuing general election and it fell to the incoming Churchill administration to announce its introduction early in 1952. Hollis was, again, the main architect, and while the various departments were to be responsible for carrying out the positive vetting procedures and for supplying the necessary investigating officers, MI5 was to provide general advice and assist with difficult cases.[75]

Each person requiring access to Top Secret information for his work would have to agree to fill in a questionnaire which included questions about past or present communist connections. He would have to supply the names of two referees who could be consulted about his character, and investigating officers would be empowered to make limited inquiries about his background and activities. MI5 would be consulted if any suggestion of subversive activity by the candidate or his close relatives came to light.

As an official adviser to the House of Commons Defence Committee in its inquiry into positive vetting in 1983 I had access to full information about the system and how it worked. It became clear that the system had been introduced in a 'softly softly', piecemeal manner which could almost be guaranteed to be ineffective. The field investigations into individuals were either not carried out at all or were in the hands of people unqualified to make them. Character defects were not regarded as a bar to access to secrets until 1956, and the system has had to be patched up repeatedly after every major spy case. As a result, spies can still defeat it.

Incredibly, both MI5 and MI6 opted out of the general positive vetting system, maintaining that their circumstances were so special that they would have to make their own secret arrangements which they would run themselves.[76] The Government deferred to their view and left it to them to sort out their security problems. As Director of Security, Hollis must have been particularly influential in MI5's decision to exempt itself from positive vetting.

MI6 did not introduce positive vetting in full measure for its own staff until Maurice Oldfield, as MI6 Head of Security, did so in late 1963 and early 1964. Hollis did little concerning MI5, even when he became Director-General, claiming that his staff were above suspicion, though one former member and friend of his, Blunt, was deeply suspect by then. Positive vetting was not introduced in MI5 until immediately before Hollis's retirement late in 1965, even though Blunt had confessed to being a Soviet agent by that time.[77] Even then its introduction seems to have occurred only because an MI5 officer investigating Soviet penetrations had complained to Hollis that he was preventing the use of even elementary precautions. After some indignant argument, Hollis introduced positive vetting in the following week and the officer was among the first to be processed. Like all the officers in MI5 and MI6 he was vetted by one of his own colleagues. An MI6 officer has described to me how he was vetted by one of his closest friends, a performance which smacked of pantomime.

Hollis himself was never positively vetted before he retired, a matter of considerable regret for the team that was eventually to investigate him.

The Potential Value of Oversight

In May 1981 thirty years had elapsed since the great defection and documents concerning it should have become available to scholars and other interested parties under the usual rules. Instead, the Government decided that the papers should remain withheld and arrangements were made with the U.S. Government for the relevant Washington papers to be held back too – a requirement to which the American Administration had to agree under standing bilateral convention. Thus did the cover-up continue and is likely to continue, essentially to save face, not only for individuals but for Government departments.

This situation alone would justify the need for oversight into comparable cases. An independent group could assure Parliament and the public that information was being withheld in the genuine interests of the nation, if that were the case. If it were not, it could apply pressure for the release of the information.

In more urgent need of official consideration is the deterrent effect which the existence of an oversight body, independent of the Government and Whitehall, could have exerted on those in the Foreign Office and MI5 who were responsible for the succession of misjudgements which led to the fiasco. To what extent did these people take action, or avoid taking it because they were certain that their errors, however gross, could never be the subject of serious censure? Would they still have taken the decision to avoid watching Maclean once he had left London? And could they have continued to conceal the true extent of the catastrophe through misleading statements which an oversight body would have known to be fraudulent? I think not. If there was any deliberate desire to facilitate the defection, would that have been considered practicable if subject to oversight? Assuredly not.

More importantly, would not an independent oversight body have demanded a more thorough investigation into the circumstances that had enabled Maclean to receive the final warning which touched off his flight? The convenient excuse that it was all due to Philby, which continues to be upheld in the Cabinet Office

202

and which is almost certainly untrue, could well have enabled another and even more successful Soviet spy to remain in place and reach the pinnacle of office. Examination of the facts by independent minds untrammelled by prejudice and Fifth Estate tradition might have suggested, at some stage, that the final Philby tip-off was a legend that the K.G.B. could foster, as it eventually did through Philby's book and other media.

My experience as an adviser to the House of Commons Defence Committee strongly suggests that the positive vetting and other precautions taken to prevent penetration following the defections would have been more stringent and more rigorously applied had oversight existed. It would seem most unlikely that the Fifth Estate would have been allowed to regard itself as exempt from positive vetting had an oversight body known what was happening, or not happening, in those overly autonomous organizations.

Many officers of MI5 and MI6 oppose any form of oversight on the grounds that intelligence and counter-intelligence are risk-taking activities and that reasonable risks may not be taken if those responsible are subject to censure when operations fail. I can find no evidence to suggest that a properly constituted oversight body would fail to appreciate the necessity for some risk-taking. What remains in doubt is whether an oversight body would have considered the failure to keep Maclean under surveillance outside London and the failure of MI5 and MI6 to introduce positive vetting without undue delay to have been reasonable risks.

The outstanding virtue of an oversight body would be its capacity to ensure that lessons learned from previous security failures are applied. Had such a body learned about the peculiarities of the surveillance of Fuchs it might well have raised queries about the surveillance of Maclean. The major lesson provided by the Fuchs case was the need to avoid offending the American security authorities and Administration further when the British Government was laying such stress on improving relations. Yet, left to their own secret devices – as they still are – both MI5 and the Foreign Office took the narrow departmental view and withheld their information about Maclean to preserve secrecy and avoid embarrassment. They might not have done so had an oversight body existed and it seems most unlikely that they would have compounded their sins of omission by deliberately lying to the F.B.I. As Robert Lamphere's testimony shows, the results were damaging to the nation's interests.

In sum, I submit that the Maclean and Burgess cases offer fair evidence of the need for independent oversight of the secret departments of state.

CHAPTER TWENTY-ONE

Chief Liaison Officer – for the K.G.B.

THE defection of Burgess along with Maclean cast immediate suspicion on Philby who was still in Washington, serving as chief liaison officer between MI6 and the C.I.A. and F.B.I. Though he was safer than if Maclean had been interrogated, both he and his Soviet controller realized that his position was under considerable threat and contingency plans were made for his escape. It was felt, however, that there was no immediate need for action. In the Soviet Union a person in Philby's position would have been interrogated until he broke but, with Philby's guidance, the K.G.B. assumed that, provided he kept his nerve, he stood a strong chance of avoiding exposure and, with the help of influential friends, of even continuing in post. C.I.A. officers who realized that there were too many anomalies in Philby's career to be explained by coincidence persuaded their chief, General Bedell Smith, that he was most probably a Soviet agent. Though the evidence was circumstantial it was enough for the U.S. authorities to insist on Philby's immediate recall and swift action on his return to London.

In the meantime, certain officers in MI5 had come to the same conclusion. Arthur Martin, anxious to achieve something positive from the Burgess/Maclean fiasco, had back-checked on Philby's record which, by that time, showed his sudden conversion from communist leanings to membership of the Anglo-German Fellowship, his previous marriage to a known Soviet agent, a peculiar letter he had written to MI6 headquarters which seemed phrased to protect Maclean, another expressing uncharacteristic second thoughts about Burgess, and what looked like the deliberate fouling-up of what has become known as the Volkov Affair.[1]

On a beautiful summer day in August 1945 a Soviet citizen called Konstantin Volkov had walked into the British Consulate-General building in Istanbul, which housed the Turkish branch of MI6, and asked to see an official called John Read. Mr Read, who spoke Russian, having served in Moscow, has given me a first-hand account of the incident and its consequences.[2]

Believing that Read was in charge of what he called 'the anti-Soviet bureau', which did not exist, Volkov introduced himself as the local Soviet Consul-General and said that he and his wife wished to defect to Britain. As the conversation developed, Volkov said that he was involved in intelligence work but did not say whether it was for the K.G.B. or the G.R.U. and Read did not ask him, not then being aware of the separate identities of the two organizations. He offered to supply impressions of keys to filing cabinets in Moscow and the numbers of the cars used by Soviet Intelligence officers. He claimed to have been employed for several years in the 'British Department' of his intelligence agency and was, therefore, of particular interest to British counter-espionage. He said that he had deposited documents in a suitcase in a flat in Moscow and offered to provide the address and a key if the British authorities could let him have £27,000 – probably a round sum in roubles – and arrange for his safe defection.

A couple of days later, Volkov returned with a typewritten document in Russian, which was later to become known as his 'shopping list', and gave the British three weeks to decide whether his services would be needed.

Read sat up most of the night translating the document. It warned that there were two Soviet agents in the Foreign Office who were providing copies of telegrams. For this and other reasons the Russians were able to read the British diplomatic codes, so Volkov urged that his offer should not be sent by telegram but only in the diplomatic pouch. He also made other security stipulations which were observed. Volkov offered to provide information concerning the identities of hundreds of Soviet Intelligence officers serving overseas, and their agents, plus details of the organization of the Soviet Intelligence Service.[3]

As translated by Read, who was not a Russian scholar, the crucial passage in the typescript read, '...files and documents concerning very important Soviet agents in important establishments in London. Judging by the cryptonyms [the code-names in secret cables between London and Moscow] there are, at present, seven such agents, five in British Intelligence and two in the Foreign Office. I know, for instance, that one of these agents is fulfilling the duties of Head of a Department of British Counter-Intelligence.'[4]

Read reported this most interesting development to the Ambassador in Turkey, the late Sir Maurice Peterson, who, along with many other career diplomats, had a rooted objection to the Secret Intelligence Service and disliked the thought of having to house any of its officers under diplomatic cover. He seized on Volkov's reference to the 'anti-Soviet bureau' and declared that the rest of his information must be equally unreliable. He was the type of man, common enough in the Foreign Service then, who could not bring himself to entertain the possibility that any colleague could be a traitor. As a result, the report went to London without the Ambassador's backing, receiving little attention in the Foreign Office before being passed to MI6.[5] There it reached the desk of Philby who was gripped with fear as he identified the 'Head of a Department of British Counter-Intelligence' as himself.

Philby's first move was to contact his Soviet controller to alert Moscow to make every effort to prevent Volkov's defection. He then drew the attention of his chief, Sir Stewart Menzies, to Volkov's offer, suggesting that it was a promising development worthy of his personal attention. Menzies, who seems to have been unusually compliant in his dealings with Philby, agreed that Philby himself should be the man to travel to Istanbul to meet Volkov and make the arrangements for his departure to Britain.

To give the Soviets plenty of time to deal with Volkov, Philby delayed his arrival in Istanbul for more than a fortnight. Meanwhile, the hapless Russian, heavily bandaged on a stretcher, left by plane for Moscow where, it is believed, he was interrogated and executed. When Read asked Philby why he had taken so long to leave for Turkey, he stammered, 'It was a question of leave arrangements.'

As treachery was not in anybody's mind, apart from Philby's, Read attributed the failure to secure Volkov as nothing more than inefficiency. Since then, he has felt some guilt, not only at the loss of a defector who could have stopped British traitors before they did so much damage, but for Volkov's fate. Read's reminiscence in this respect is illuminating: 'At that time the official attitude was that we must, at all costs, accommodate the Russians and do nothing to precipitate East-West hostility. Indeed, any reference to ulterior Soviet intentions was likely to provoke the accusation of "fascist tendencies". It was a very unhappy time for anyone who had served in Moscow and shed any illusions.'

It would seem that the Foreign Office made no use whatever of the preliminary information which Volkov had given them. No notice was taken of his allegation that the Soviets were able to read diplomatic ciphers because of the incredibly complacent belief that no Briton with access to them could possibly betray them. Yet Donald Maclean had continuously done so, especially at the time of Volkov's disclosures, when he was serving in the British Embassy in Washington.

The MI6 inquest into the failure of Philby's mission seems to have been a perfunctory affair and must have strengthened Philby's belief that his risk of being caught in such an inefficient organization was small. He was even permitted to keep the Volkov 'shopping list' in his own safe instead of in the central Registry, thereby limiting the number of people who might see it and become suspicious.

Philby's handling of the Volkov case is an excellent example of the advantages a spy enjoys through being inside an organization which is responsible for detecting spies. It also illustrates the self-preservation syndrome – that espionage inside an intelligence or security agency is self-perpetuating in that it forces a spy to continue his treachery, whether he wishes to or not, when he gets wind of a potential defector. He has to supply the information to his alien masters with all speed, not just to satisfy their requirements but to protect himself.

All the members of the Cambridge Ring seem to have led charmed lives, but while they probably had more than their share of luck there were two other factors which helped to preserve them: appalling inefficiency, or worse, by MI5, and rigorous control by K.G.B. professionals. While Philby and some of the others, like Blunt, may appear to have been 'super-spies' they essentially did what they were told to do by their controllers who, in turn, received considered instructions from the Moscow Centre. The Volkov case is also an excellent example of control and co-operation by the Moscow Centre to resolve an emergency.

The news of the intended defection of Volkov in Istanbul had overlapped with the actual defection of Gouzenko in Ottawa. Though MI5 was not to realize it until much later, this was the reason why Philby had not dared to go to Canada and interrogate Gouzenko. His Soviet controller had advised him to remain in touch with the Volkov case, which appeared to threaten him more immediately, and as a consequence the Gouzenko case had been handed to Hollis.

After the MI6 chief, Sir Stewart Menzies, was informed of the joint suspicions in MI5 and in Washington, Philby was recalled to London for questioning by Menzies himself. At this brief meeting Philby took the initiative and, more or less, dismissed himself when Menzies asked him, 'Concerning your position, Kim. What would you do if you were in my place?'

'I should tell me that I had to leave, Philby replied.

'That is what I think,' Menzies said, relieved that the embarrassing situation, which of course was intended to remain secret for ever, had been so easily resolved.[6]

Within MI6 several of Philby's friends regarded this treatment as entirely unjustified, as had Maclean's friends in the Foreign Office, and as would the friends of Blunt and Hollis in MI5. It was pointed out that while Philby had been in Washington he had known the details of fourteen important cases, including that of Fuchs, which had been brought to a successful conclusion. But, as Philby was to reveal in his own book, he had forewarned his Soviet masters about them all. It was only for reasons advantageous to the K.G.B., including the protection of Philby himself, that no action had been taken by the Soviets.

Philby was out of the Secret Intelligence Service by July 1951 and after that he never had any official access to secret information, though at intervals over the following twelve years he was to meet with old colleagues who still believed in his innocence and from whom he almost surely gleaned professional gossip of interest to the K.G.B.

MI5 proceeded with its investigation into Philby and, to keep it as secret as possible from the staff, who might see documents, he was given the internal code-name 'Peach'.[7] Hollis must have been questioned at length about Philby because the two had worked so closely overseeing Soviet and communist operations. As Philby was to recall, 'We both served on the Joint Intelligence Sub-Committee and never failed to work out an agreed approach to present to the less well-informed representatives of the Service departments and the Foreign Office.'[8]

Whatever Hollis may have contributed, the inquiry made no substantial progress until the autumn of 1951 when MI5 was informed that a K.G.B. agent with the code-name 'Stanley' in the Bride traffic might be Philby. Against the wishes of MI6, which would have preferred to allow the Philby case to lie fallow following his removal from access to secrets, the MI5 management secured agreement for Philby to be subjected to interrogation in the hope that he might break down and confess his guilt. This interrogation, in November 1951, has been referred to as a 'secret trial', but it was a routine operation. Philby was told that a judicial inquiry into the Maclean and Burgess defections had been ordered and that he would be required to give evidence. He duly appeared, though he could have declined. Both he and the K.G.B. must have been keen to know just how much MI5 had discovered. Of course, if Hollis was a spy they would have already known details of the plans for the interrogation since he would have been privy to them, especially in view of his previous close involvement with the suspect.

The chief interrogating officer was Helenus 'Buster' Milmo (now Sir), a wartime member of MI5 who was to become a judge. He was assisted by Arthur Martin, who prepared the brief for the

208

interrogation and sat in on it. Some authors have given the impression that Milmo made a hash of it, trying to bully Philby into making admissions which he cleverly avoided doing. The tape-recordings of the interviews reveal a very different picture.[9] Milmo conducted it with great skill and soon had Philby making excessive use of his stammer to gain time to answer awkward questions, such as the source of his finances when he went to cover the Spanish Civil War as a freelance. Astonishingly, nothing was made of the fact that it had been firmly established that Philby's former wife, Lizi, was a Soviet agent. Perhaps this had been withheld from Milmo on the grounds that it would be too embarrassing to involve a former officer's wife.

Philby's performance nevertheless convinced both Milmo and Martin that he was guilty, but the interrogators lacked hard evidence or reliable witnesses and Philby knew that he was safe so long as he continued to deny everything and admit nothing.

Philby maintained this stone-walling when questioned by the MI5 interrogator Jim Skardon, but though he has been almost admired for his bland evasions his performance was poor compared with that of the fragile-looking Blunt, who was to withstand eleven interrogations far more persuasively.

What would have happened had Philby confessed? In view of the previous handling of Maclean and later events involving Blunt, Long and others, and eventually Philby himself, I very much doubt that he would have been prosecuted. This view is shared by former officers of both MI5 and MI6 who are in a better position to form a judgement. It is just possible that at that time American pressure for a prosecution might have been irresistible, but every argument would have been mounted against it, allegedly in the interests of securing the maximum information from Philby but really to minimize damage to the image of the Fifth Estate.

While Martin, White and others in MI5 were convinced that Philby was not only the Third Man, who had been involved in warning Maclean of his danger, but a long-standing Soviet agent, Hollis took a legalistic line when the case was discussed at a directors' meeting. 'Prove it,' he challenged, in support of his view that Philby should be given the benefit of the doubt unless and until hard evidence should emerge.[10] This view prevailed. Martin regarded the case as open to proof if actively pursued, but he was not permitted to spend money on it developing leads. This suited MI6, which did not formally accept that Philby had been disloyal. Not only were inquiries discontinued there but no damage assessment was made to establish the injuries which he might have inflicted.[11]

Meanwhile Philby, who had been given his commuted pension in a lump sum of £2,000 plus a further £2,000 to be paid in instalments, remained outwardly cool, nourished by the sympathy of his friends, both in MI6 and MI5, and the knowledge that the K.G.B. would contact him again when it was considered safe to do so.

Those officers in MI5 who were convinced of Philby's guilt included the Director-General Sir Percy Sillitoe, who told the C.I.A. that Philby's debits outnumbered his assets, meaning that while there was no proof the circumstantial evidence had persuaded him. This attitude was so unwelcome in MI6 that one of Philby's former friends there remembers asking him, late in 1951, why he did not leak the MI5 allegations to the newspapers so that when they were published he could deny them. Philby made a rather lame response.[12]

Early in 1952, as part of the inquiry into the identity of the Third Man, Dick White, then MI5's Director of Counter-Espionage, decided that another look should be taken at Gouzenko's allegation about the spy in MI5 with the code-name 'Elli'. On 6 May Superintendent George McClellan of the Security Branch of the Royal Canadian Mounted Police asked Gouzenko, on MI5's behalf, to submit a memorandum giving as much detail as he could remember of the circumstances in which he had heard about 'Elli'. Gouzenko produced the document to which I have already referred and which is reproduced in Appendix A. The memorandum was classified Secret, and while Gouzenko was adamant that the spy had existed in 1942/43, and probably still did, it led to no result, much to Gouzenko's disgust. He heard no more about it or about 'Elli' until 1972 – twenty-seven years after his original lead!

The memorandum became public only through a leak, through Gouzenko himself, to the *Toronto Telegram* in September 1970. Again, though given publicity then, and since, it led to no known result. Gouzenko, who had proved himself a completely reliable informant, was certain that 'Elli' had been in MI5 and therefore could not have been Philby, who had always worked in MI6. Further, as already pointed out, 'Elli' was unquestionably a G.R.U. spy in 1942/43, while Philby always operated for the K.G.B. Nevertheless, there seems to have been no serious effort to discover which MI5 officer might have been 'Elli' until 1972, in the strange circumstances described in Chapter 52. Until then it would seem that somebody at high level had decided that it was in MI5's interest, or possibly in the interest of some other agency, not necessarily British, to ignore the information.

During the early 1950s investigative reporters continued inquiries into the Burgess and Maclean defections; there was little doubt in my mind concerning Philby's implication. During a lunch with Cyril Connolly, who had known both defectors, he gave me the names of Philby and Blunt as prime suspects, but such are the British libel laws that no Fleet Street lawyer would permit speculation concerning either of them.

Meanwhile the K.G.B. was having doubts about Philby. The easy way he had been allowed to leave MI6 and the 'golden handshake' made the Soviets fear that he might have been successfully 'turned'. In July 1954, Dr Otto John, who had become head of the West German counterpart of MI5, was closely questioned by the K.G.B. after being abducted behind the Iron Curtain, according to his account. He has told me that the K.G.B's sole purpose was to discover from him whether Philby had become a double agent.[13] An old friend and fellow-spy of Philby, Peter Smolka, then living in Austria and whose loyalty to the Soviets was never in doubt, was also interrogated and was able to convince the K.G.B. that there was no danger that Philby would ever become a British 'plant'.[14] As a result the Soviets contacted Philby again in late 1954 or early 1955 by what Philby was to describe as 'the most ingenious of routes'. The probable nature of this route is described in Chapters 36 and 45.

The Potential Value of Oversight

There are many aspects of the Philby case, both before and after his departure from MI6, which suggest that the existence of oversight by an independent body could have been highly beneficial. Philby knew that the complacency inside MI6 was such that his lame excuse for taking so long to reach Istanbul to deal with Volkov would not be seriously questioned. Would he have been so confident had he known that he might be questioned by others likely to be less accommodating? It would seem unlikely that either MI6 or the Foreign Office would have been so cavalier in ignoring the leads given by Volkov in his 'shopping list' had they been subject to outside examination on the matter. The same applies to MI5's lack of action on Gouzenko's 1952 memorandum regarding the MI5 spy called 'Elli'. Indeed, my analysis of defector cases in general suggests that there is urgent need for independent oversight. While agencies may wish to deny it, there is an undoubted tendency on the part of some counter-intelligence officers to discount or decry the evidence of defectors when it exposes their past incompetence. Excessive denigration of a defector would be likely to be more apparent to an independent observer than to a superior, and the motive behind it might be questioned.

I suggest, too, that an oversight body might have been less likely than the MI6 management to accept the alacrity of Philby's agreement to virtual dismissal without wondering why he had not objected if he were innocent.

CHAPTER TWENTY-TWO

Second-in-Command

On 1 September 1953 Sir Percy Sillitoe was replaced by Dick White as Director-General of MI5. The Prime Minister, Winston Churchill, let it be known in Whitehall that he had been greatly displeased by the publicity which Sillitoe had attracted to himself, and Fleet Street editors were told in confidence of White's appointment and their co-operation was sought in keeping his identity secret.[1]

White immediately appointed Hollis as his deputy, a promotion which astonished the MI5 rank and file and was resented by many officers, though some were not surprised because the two men had been close ever since White had helped to bring Hollis into MI5 in 1938.

If Hollis was a spy the K.G.B. must have been delighted because, as Deputy Director-General, he suddenly achieved far greater influence and much wider access to information. His duties included responsibility for overseas security problems in such countries as Rhodesia, Kenya, Malaya and Cyprus, as well as for liaison with allied security organizations like those of the U.S., Canada and Australia. The post entailed much travel abroad – an ideal situation for safe meetings with Soviet controllers.

As a headquarters liaison man with the American F.B.I., and to some extent with the C.I.A., Hollis could hardly have been a happy choice, in view of his known anti-American attitude. What could be construed as evidence of Hollis's anti-Americanism frequently came my way during my long and close dealings with Rear-Admiral George Thomson, when he was Secretary of the D-Notice Committee. Whenever MI5 complained to the Admiral about security leaks in newspaper articles which I had written he almost invariably assured me that he had been told that I would hear nothing further provided I was prepared to say that the information had come from some American source, even when that was not so. At that time the Admiral dealt, through an intermediary, with Hollis, who may have been able to use the allegations to counter

213

F.B.I. complaints about the weakness of British security.[2]

One of Hollis's first routine visits was to the Canadian security organization which was then run by the Royal Canadian Mounted Police. A former officer in the R.C.M.P. Security Branch remembers a lecture given by Hollis and describes him as 'a dowdy little man – very unimpressive and disappointing'.[3] Photographs of Hollis taken in the early 1950s while on a visit to Germany support this description.[4] During his visits to Canada Hollis was treated to what the Solicitor-General, Robert Kaplan, was to describe as 'confidences of security'.[5] I shall present new and seemingly relevant information concerning MI5's dealings with the R.C.M.P. in Chapter 42.

An unexpected development in Australia resuscitated the Maclean/Burgess/Philby case which might, otherwise, have remained suppressed for many more years. As the former security adviser to the Australian Government and the existing chief liaison officer, Hollis became involved. On 13 April 1954 a K.G.B. officer called Vladimir Petrov, working under cover in the Soviet Embassy in Canberra, defected to the Australian Secret Intelligence Organization (A.S.I.O.) and was soon joined by his wife, who was also a professional K.G.B. officer. Among the material he provided was the fact that his assistant, Fillip Kislytsin, had previously been in charge of the section in Moscow which had processed the information and documents provided by Maclean and Burgess, whom he knew to have been long-term spies, recruited in their student days at Cambridge. Petrov further revealed that the defection of the British traitors had been planned in Moscow and directed by the K.G.B. in London, France and elsewhere. He said that the reason they had been forced to flee was that they knew they were being investigated by MI5. Kislytsin also told Petrov that the K.G.B. had been responsible for organizing the flight of Melinda Maclean from Geneva to Moscow.[6]

Hollis had a particular professional interest in the Petrov revelations, but according to one source then in G.C.H.Q., his interest was suspiciously greater than it should have been.[7] Petrov's defection came as no surprise to certain G.C.H.Q. specialists because they had heard of it in advance either through an intercept or through liaison with Australia's Defence Signals Bureau. Because Hollis was Deputy Director-General of MI5 he was informed by G.C.H.Q. that the defection of Petrov was confidently expected within a few days. He had, in fact, known of the impending event for some time, having been officially informed by A.S.I.O. through an intermediary, the circumstances of which are described in Chapter 45. A senior MI6 officer was also told by G.C.H.Q.

214

Otherwise the secret was thought to be tightly held.

When Petrov had successfully defected both Hollis and the MI6 officer asked how G.C.H.Q. had obtained the advance information. The G.C.H.Q. officer concerned declined to tell either of them on security grounds, pointing out that neither of them needed to know. The MI6 officer asked no further questions but Hollis repeatedly pressed for details and went over the G.C.H.Q. officer's head to his superior. The superior upheld his colleague's refusal and later told him that he 'deserved a bunch of red roses' for refusing to be badgered into an admission by Hollis, who had no right to the information or any official need for it.

From that moment onwards Hollis was suspect in the minds of at least two G.C.H.Q. officers; had they known certain details of the Petrov case, their suspicions would have been stronger. The Australian security officer in charge of the Petrov defection, Michael Thwaites, has told me that in view of the precautions taken in Australia it is extremely unlikely that the Russians became aware of it in advance through any leakage there. Yet it is certain that they were warned in advance, as the Australian Parliament has been told by a former Prime Minister, Sir William McMahon.[8] The Russians failed to seize Petrov only by a few hours, two strong-arm men having been dispatched from Moscow for the purpose.

If the leak reached Moscow from London then Hollis was one of the very few who could have been responsible, though, as explained in Chapter 45, Philby could have been the culprit. If Hollis feared that G.C.H.Q. had obtained the information through an intercept he would have been most anxious to determine whether any information which might concern his position was likely to follow Petrov's defection. That would explain his persistence in trying to uncover G.C.H.Q.'s source. MI5 officers have confirmed to me that, like Philby, Hollis had a reputation for nosiness about security and intelligence matters outside his province. The reason for Philby's behaviour in that respect is now fully established.

Because of Hollis's seniority the G.C.H.Q. officers did not dare to voice their suspicions outside their own organization, a reluctance which typified those who suspected Philby before the Burgess and Maclean defections and which indicated the increased protection that a spy enjoys through promotion. The G.C.H.Q. aspects of the Petrov defection, which have not previously been revealed, offer a further comparison with the Philby case. If the K.G.B. men had reached Canberra in time, as they did to apprehend Mrs Petrov, then Petrov himself could have ended up like Volkov. Hollis's suspicious behaviour has since raised questions concerning other apparent leaks to the Soviets over the period 1952–4. James Bennett, who was head of the General Search Section at G.C.H.Q., responsible for analysing intercepts of clandestine radio messages passing between Soviet agents and their headquarters, noticed that as soon as a Soviet cipher was broken the relevant agency, the K.G.B. or G.R.U., would switch to a new one. He and his assistant jointly reported their suspicions; their view was that the leak, if there was one, could only be from G.C.H.Q. or from MI6 or MI5, to which results were channelled. The only response was an instruction to them to drop further inquiries, the suggestion being that all was under control, though they felt sure that it was not.[9]

Regarding defections it is apposite to point out that during Hollis's time in MI5 the agency achieved very few defections. In several instances where probable defections were being arranged by field officers they had suddenly gone sour, with the would-be defector changing his mind or being forced to do so by K.G.B. pressure.

A possible reason for this had already been suggested by Gouzenko when he submitted his memorandum on 'Elli' in 1952, namely that 'Elli' was still in MI5 and had smothered the investigation. Shortly before Gouzenko died in 1982 he told me, in a telephone conversation, that he believed that if he had tried to defect to MI5 in 1945, instead of to the Canadians, he would have suffered a fate similar to Volkov's.[10]

More definite evidence to explain the diffidence of Soviets to defect to Britain emerged in 1954 but its significance was not to be appreciated until the late 1960s, when MI5 was conducting a specific investigation into Hollis. It was then realized that the Petrov case linked with a previous defection disaster.

Early in 1946 a Soviet Intelligence officer of the G.R.U. had approached a British naval attaché saying that he was prepared to provide secrets. He gave details of arrangements whereby he could be met in Moscow. Two reports about the agent reached MI5 where Hollis dealt with them, as he was still then acting head of Section F, dealing with Soviet espionage. He instructed a junior officer to start a special file about the agent and the two reports were placed in it and stored in the Registry pending further developments.[11]

No more was heard abut the agent until 1954, when another Soviet Intelligence officer called Yuri Rastvorov, the director of a Soviet espionage ring in Japan, walked out of the Soviet Embassy in Tokyo to defect to the West. He eventually made contact with the Australian authorities there. He refused to go to Britain or to any British-controlled territory because he was convinced that

British Intelligence was penetrated by the Russians and he was frightened that he might be betrayed and assassinated. He agreed to go to Australia but, while waiting for his flight at Tokyo Airport, he learned that he was going via Singapore, which was then a British colony. He fled from the airport and took refuge in the American Embassy from where he was flown to the U.S. When debriefed by the C.I.A. he explained that he knew that British Intelligence was penetrated because a G.R.U. officer who had been in the process of defecting a few years previously had been betrayed by a British source and had been caught and shot.[12]

When the C.I.A. passed this information to the British authorities it was assumed that Philby, deeply suspect in 1954, had been the source of the leakage, as in the case of the would-be defector Volkov. A very different explanation emerged, however, when a third Russian, from K.G.B. counter-intelligence, successfully defected to the C.I.A. He claimed to have been the case officer who had been concerned with countering the attempted defection of the G.R.U. man in 1946. He said that the K.G.B. had received copies of both of the reports originally sent from Japan to MI5 and that the details of the contact arrangements had enabled him and his colleagues to catch the would-be defector.[13]

The K.G.B. counter-intelligence officer was later shown the two documents in the MI5 Registry file and declared them to be identical with those he had seen in Moscow, where they had been stapled together in the same way. A search showed that only in MI5 had the documents been stapled together.[14] (A truly professional spy does not unstaple documents for ease of photography if he can possibly avoid it because an examination of documents to detect which and how many have been unstapled and rejoined can be revealing.)

It might be thought that Blunt had been responsible for purloining the documents, as he had been with so many others, so that the Soviets could photograph them, but by early 1946 he had ended his routine duties in MI5 and could not have had access to them. It is also unlikely that Philby, then in MI6 headquarters, could have taken them out of MI5 to photograph them. So, among known suspects, Hollis remains the likeliest culprit.

These episodes, centred on the Rastvorov defection, make further nonsense of claims by Hollis's supporters that there has been no defector evidence against him. Gouzenko's evidence had already pointed in his direction, and this was strengthened later, as described in Chapter 52. And, as will be seen, the would-be defector Volkov was probably referring to a spy in MI5 and not to Philby.

Perhaps the most extraordinary, and most disturbing, aspect of the Rastvorov episodes is the fact that nothing whatever of any consequence was done about information which should have rung alarm bells. Again, the comparison with Philby's activities is irresistible – somebody was able to smother it.

Coupled with the suspicious lack of K.G.B. or G.R.U. officers prepared to defect to Britain was the all too regular breakdown of efforts to recruit double agents to work against the Soviets in London. Occasionally the K.G.B. or G.R.U. tried to recruit a university student who would report the approach to MI5 and offer to accept while really working against the Soviet Union. Whenever this happened the Soviets found out so quickly that it seemed that they must have been in touch with someone with access to that very secret information and such a person must have been in MI5. The same happened to most businessmen who offered their services in a similar manner.

In the same, dismal vein, when MI5 secured advance information of a meeting between a Soviet Intelligence officer and one of his British agents, watchers would be carefully stationed but the meeting would not take place. As had happened with Nunn May, Cairncross and others, the Russians always seemed to have been forewarned.

The public had been led to believe that the arrest in 1952 of William Marshall, a Foreign Office radio operator who had been recruited to Soviet Intelligence while working as a cipher clerk in Moscow, had been a triumph for MI5 counter-espionage, but like other apparent successes it was an absolute fluke. An MI5 watcher, alighting from a bus while off duty, spotted a Soviet Intelligence officer, whom he happened to recognize as Pavel Kuznetsov, in earnest conversation with an Englishman. He kept an eye on them and followed the Englishman to his home in Southfields, N.W.4 and noted his address. He turned out to be Marshall; he was put under surveillance and eventually sentenced to five years' imprisonment for revealing secret information. There would have been no way that a spy inside MI5 could have interfered to save Marshall without making his existence too obvious – a risk the Moscow Centre would not have been prepared to take.

Retrospectively, MI5 investigators were later to examine more than fifty attempts by MI5 to penetrate the K.G.B. effort mounted against Britain and could not find one which had been run for more than a few weeks before collapsing. Some could have failed as a result of routine Soviet counter-measures; all could have failed through leaks.

The cause of the persistent 'case-deaths' and other failures seemed to be so obvious that the daughter of a retired MI5 officer, who was working in MI5, told her father that there must be a spy in it.[15] It was only the operations against the Soviet bloc which fell flat so regularly, those against other countries being reasonably successful.

The Potential Value of Oversight

If an oversight body had been alerted to take a special look at the circumstances surrounding defections, then the suspicions attaching to the British end of the Petrov case, as described in this chapter and in Chapter 45, might have been subjected to productive inquiry. The virtual absence of successful defections to MI5 and the peculiar behaviour of Rastvorov might also have raised queries requiring some official answers, especially when set alongside the long run of other case-deaths and failures. As will be seen, these raised grave anxiety in the minds of several middle-level officers of MI5, but this was dismissed by the top management as scare-mongering, and there was nobody else to whom the officers could appeal.

Oversight of Petrov's information and what was already known in MI5 could also have discouraged the Fifth Estate from misleading Parliament and the public on the Maclean/Burgess/ Philby issue, as the next chapter describes.

The 'Whitewash' Paper

IN the spring of 1954 the Foreign Secretary, then Sir Anthony Eden, was told of Petrov's disclosures about Maclean and Burgess. He made no statement to Parliament about it, and the advice from the secret services was that he should avoid saying anything for as long as possible.In September 1955, however, following newspaper publicity about Petrov's defection, the Government could no longer continue its pretence that it knew nothing about the missing diplomats and on 23 September 1955 it produced a White Paper entitled 'Report Concerning the Disappearance of Two Former Foreign Office Officials'.[1] MI6 was required to prepare the brief for it because of its close association with the Foreign Office, but it passed the requirement to MI5, which had been more closely involved and had been mainly responsible for the fiasco. Graham Mitchell, then head of counter-espionage, was assigned to the task under the close guidance of Hollis. Mitchell was instructed to 'take into account outside interests'. The result was bland, misleading and, in some parts, stupidly inaccurate.[2]

With the help of the Foreign Office and the Law Officers the brief was developed into the White Paper, which went through several drafts. In spite of that it contained elementary blunders, like the statement that Maclean had been at Trinity College, instead of Trinity Hall, and that Tatsfield was in Kent, when it is in Surrey. Its main features, however, were the limited information it supplied and the way it was presented to protect MI5 and the Foreign Office as much as was practicable – a transparent ploy which earned it the name of 'Whitewash' Paper in the Press.

The document, part of the official historic record of the case, suggested that proper action had been taken concerning the appalling drunken and violent behaviour of both Maclean and Burgess. This was manifestly untrue. It suggested that prior to mid-April 1951 there had been no grounds for doubting Maclean's loyalty. This was a lie because he had been on a short-list of six suspects for being 'Homer' for many months.

The document was so slapdash that while being deliberately worded to suggest that Maclean's post as head of the American Desk was not particularly sensitive, it stated that 'arrangements were made to ensure that information of exceptional secrecy and importance should not come into his hands'. The excuse made for the failure to maintain surveillance on Maclean was particularly feeble, as was pointed out by newspapers. Far too little attention was paid by the authors of the White Paper to its effects on Anglo-American relations, and it was badly received by the F.B.I., where Hoover knew that Hollis had had a major hand in preparing it.

The misrepresentations were compounded and extended by ministerial statements in the Parliamentary debate which followed on 7 November.[3] Harold Macmillan, who had become Foreign Secretary when Eden succeeded Churchill as Prime Minister in April, spoke for more than an hour and did his best to excuse his own department and MI5. To allay suspicions that a Third Man had warned Maclean of his danger, he even suggested that the arrest of Fuchs in February 1950 might have made Maclean suspicious. Macmillan told Parliament that there had been no firm starting point for an interview with Maclean, which was untrue because when the Bride intercepts had shown that 'Homer' had been in regular contact with officials of the Soviet Consulate in New York while visiting his pregnant wife there, suspicion had centred on Maclean. Pursuing an even more devious line to excuse Eden's failure to tell Parliament about the Petrov disclosures in the previous year, he said: 'Petrov let it be known that if, as soon as he said anything to the Australian Security and Intelligence Organization, it was to be given publicity in this country he would refuse to say any more at all. This is a most important point.' It was a point that had been invented for him by the department supplying the brief. I have checked with Michael Thwaites, the Australian officer in charge of the Petrov defection, and he has assured me that Petrov made no such threat, nor was he in any position to do so.[4] Macmillan could have made such a technical point only on professional advice which, in all probability, he believed. That advice could have originated only from MI5, the agency in touch with A.S.I.O.

The officials who prepared the speech also ensured that Macmillan would try to protect those who had been privy to Morrison's decision that Maclean should be interrogated. He said that Petrov's evidence suggested that the defections had been planned well before 25 May so that no suspicion could fall on those present at the meeting with Morrison. That completely evaded the issue, which was not the time of the general planning but the time of the interrogation.

The speeches of both Macmillan and Eden did all they could to excuse MI5. Eden pointed out, justifiably, that MI5's wartime record against the Germans had been superb and then added, 'I can't go into our record against Communist spies since the war but I think, on the whole, that the result will compare not unfavourably', a statement that was already untrue.[5] Macmillan told Parliament that positive vetting was operating in all Government departments having access to classified material; presumably he had not been informed that it was not being applied at all in MI5 or MI6.

While giving an account of Burgess's career he avoided mention of any connection with MI5, again probably because he had not been told about it. He said that until Burgess disappeared there were no grounds for suspicion against him, which must have been untrue in view of the arrangements made for keeping him under some degree of surveillance in Washington.

In a previous Parliamentary skirmish, a fortnight earlier, Marcus Lipton, a Labour back-bencher, had used the privilege protecting him from a possible slander suit to ask the Prime Minister if he had 'made up his mind to cover up at all costs the dubious Third Man activities of Harold Philby?'[6] Following this unexpected question Hollis interviewed Lipton in the lobby of the House of Commons in the hope of finding out what the M.P. really knew. Lipton declined to tell him but later told Patrick Seale, the writer, that he knew the name of an MI5 officer who had pointed out Philby to a journalist as the Third Man and that this had been his source.[7]

Hollis concluded that Lipton had no worthwhile evidence against Philby, which was confirmed when the M.P. eventually withdrew his allegation in Parliament. Possibly having been privately assured of this in advance, Philby agreed to a cross-examination by three old colleagues anxious to prove his innocence. The tape-recordings of this event show that Philby was permitted to parry questions until acceptable answers were put into his mouth.[8] The Law Officers then prepared a brief, based on the interviews, for the Foreign Secretary, Harold Macmillan, who was responsible for MI6. I discussed this brief with Mr Macmillan in his study at Birch Grove in 1981. He said: 'The Law Officers told me that they were certain that Philby was guilty but I had to answer the question asked by Lipton. If I had suggested that Philby was guilty, using the privilege of the House, he would immediately have said "Would you mind saying that outside?" and

222

I should have looked cowardly and stupid.'

Macmillan therefore used the opportunity of the White Paper debate to tell Parliament: 'No evidence has been found to show that he was responsible for warning Burgess or Maclean. While in Government service he carried out his duties ably and conscientiously. I have no reason to conclude that Mr Philby has, at any time, betrayed the interests of his country, or to identify him with the so-called Third Man, if indeed there was one.'

By 'evidence' Macmillan meant legal evidence which could have been used in a British court, and while this was true it was misleading because most M.P.s and members of the public construed it as meaning no evidence of any kind, when intelligence evidence certainly existed.

I have been told that Macmillan exceeded his brief but he remains unrepentant about it insisting that honour gave him no alternative. 'I regard that speech in defence of public liberties as one of my best,' he told me.[9] Its main effect, however, was to ensure the public liberty of one of the most treacherous and vicious of all traitors. One lesson to be learned from it is that no ministerial statement concerning a suspect spy, or any important security issue, is necessarily to be believed.

At the end of the debate Eden made an indirect admission of Whitehall's previous complacency by suggesting that the House of Commons should convene a small, informal Conference of Privy Councillors from both sides of the House to examine security procedures in the public service. This was done.

Philby called a press conference and, acting on MI6 advice, hid behind the Official Secrets Act to avoid being effectively questioned by journalists, as Blunt was to do nine years later. He even had the effrontery to claim that any publicity would damage MI6 and MI5! He said that he had not spoken to any known communist since 1934, though MI5 then knew that his wife, Lizi, from whom he did not part until 1936, was not only a communist but a Soviet agent.[10]

This clearance of Philby was badly received in Washington, where it reinforced the view that the British were averse to punishing spies. An effort was made to convince the American authorities that Philby was less likely to defect, having been cleared, and that as long as he remained in Britain MI5 could continue with inquiries. The subsequent behaviour of MI6, which ensured that Philby would go abroad, quickly showed how thin this excuse had been.

Sir Dick White, MI5's Director-General, made it clear that he was not impressed by the clearance. He wrote to his MI6 counterpart, then Sir John Sinclair, advising him that the evidence against

Philby still stood and that he should continue to be barred from access to secret information.[11] Some of his officers wanted to do a damage assessment on the basis of Philby's guilt but were unable to do so because access to the MI6 files was refused. Had the assessment been done it would have been obvious then – as it was to be later – that too many of Philby's cases had collapsed. Later, after Philby had defected in 1963, examination of MI6's files could no longer be denied and it was learned that the report on his performance as station chief in Turkey had stated: 'Philby was an outstanding head of station who had the misfortune that all his operation against the main target, Russia, had failed disastrously.'[12] A later head of MI6, Sir Maurice Oldfield, agreed that if this information had been known to the Law Officers, the brief they prepared for Macmillan might have been different.[13]

Early in 1956 Philby spent several months in Ireland – where he could easily have had access to K.G.B. representatives – assisting a former colleague to compile a history of a family business. His influential friends then prevailed upon the MI6 management to ignore the MI5 advice and to employ him as an agent-runner operating from Beirut, then a thriving city, to secure information about Near East affairs. To provide him with cover and additional income, the *Observer* newspaper and *The Economist* magazine were induced to employ him as a foreign correspondent. He was probably paid a retainer by MI6 plus a payment for each intelligence report, according to value. This move effectively put Philby beyond further action by British security because offences against the Official Secrets Act are not extraditable and, in that same year, 1956, assassination as an instrument of clandestine policy was ruled out for the Secret Intelligence Service.[14]

When Sir Dick White was switched, unexpectedly, from the leadership of MI5 to that of MI6 in 1956, he was furious when he discovered that Philby was being employed but he did not insist on any change, arguing, later, that as the new man in a difficult position, he had to tread warily. Nor, with his new-found loyalty, did he inform MI5 about what had happened – or if he did Hollis, who had replaced him as MI5 chief, never actually put it in the records.[15]

The extent to which Philby was able to continue to assist the K.G.B. following his arrival in Beirut has been greatly underestimated, as will be explained in the damage assessment on Philby in Chapter 32, and those who sent him there, believing in his innocence or simply to get him out of Britain, have much to answer for. There is no doubt that throughout his stay in the Middle East Philby was in regular touch with Soviet controllers and told them everything that he and his sub-agents were passing to British Intelligence. He also performed specific jobs for the K.G.B.

His journalistic dispatches were reasonably competent but he began to show the symptoms which had characterized Maclean and Burgess when they became convinced that eventual exposure was inevitable. He drank heavily and became rowdy and unreliable in his domestic and social life. Even his most forgiving friends found his attitude to others unacceptably callous, an attribute which he demonstrated, shockingly, when called to the telephone from a cocktail party in December 1957. Aileen, the mother of his four children, had been seriously ill in Britain and Philby returned to the throng with a wide smile to announce: 'You must all drink to my great news. Aileen's dead!'[16]

While Philby remained publicly 'cleared' his connections with communism which, like those of Maclean and Burgess, had been appreciated all too late, appear to have impressed the Conference of Privy Councillors set up by Parliament to examine security procedures. In March 1956 the Conference issued a report recognizing, rather late in the day, that 'defects of character, such as drunkenness and loose living, could make a man unreliable and expose him to blackmail or influence by foreign agents', but its main conclusion was that while the main risk to be guarded against had previously been espionage by foreign powers, the situation had changed and the chief risk was being presented by British communists and those subject to communist influence.[17] In reaching this opinion, which was soon shown to be manifestly wrong, the Privy Councillors had taken advice from MI5 witnesses, among whom Hollis, as the expert on international communism, was likely to have been influential. If the intention, and the result, was to concentrate counter-espionage attention on British communists rather than the professional agents of the K.G.B. and G.R.U. then Moscow must have been delighted.

The two prime communists whom the Privy Councillors had in mind, Maclean and Burgess, were in grave danger of being liquidated when they arrived in the Soviet Union because Stalin was still purging people he believed he could not trust. They were kept in Kuibyshev, an industrial city on the Volga, for two years while they were 'dried out' in a rest-home for alcoholics and their loyalty was investigated.[18] Only then were they allowed to go to Moscow where they were used as advisers to the Soviet Foreign Office.

The Soviet authorities, who had denied that Maclean and Burgess were even in Eastern Europe, much less in the U.S.S.R., ignored the Petrov disclosures and the consequent British White

Paper. Then, without warning, on 11 February 1956 British journalists in Moscow were summoned to a so-called press conference at the National Hotel. Few attended but those who did were astonished to find Maclean and Burgess on display. It was clear that Burgess, who handed out a statement, was regarded as the senior figure. The statement, which had clearly been drafted first in Russian, no doubt by the K.G.B., was largely dishonest. It claimed that while the two defectors had been communists, they had never been Soviet agents and had left Britain mainly because they had both realized, independently, that the Anglo-American policies being pursued by the Foreign Office would lead to war. As they had failed to influence these policies while in the West, they felt they could best serve the cause of peace by moving to the Soviet Union.

While the statement was too crude to carry conviction, it was obviously meant for overseas, rather than Soviet consumption. The K.G.B. knew that the British authorities, though not the British public, were aware of the real truth. So what was the purpose of producing the renegades in public?

The purpose appeared to be mainly political. Khrushchev and Bulganin, then the joint Soviet leaders, were to visit London within two months to talk to Eden and other British politicians about the pursuit of friendship between the two nations. They may have wanted to get the mystery of the defectors' whereabouts resolved before being questioned about them, though I greatly doubt that the British politicians or officials would have raised the subject. They might have thought that the views of two former diplomats about Foreign Office policy might carry some weight with the British public but, if so, they had been badly briefed. Was there some other reason?

To MI5 the production of the defectors seemed to be some kind of provocation to which the Politburo must have agreed. The K.G.B. must have been confident that MI5 would not produce evidence which could show that Maclean had certainly been a spy because that would prejudice Operation Bride, about which they had been informed by Philby. They may also have known that MI5 had no evidence of real consequence that Burgess had been a Soviet agent, for that was not to materialize until the interrogation of Blunt in 1964.

While it went largely unnoticed by the Press and public, the Moscow statement included a fact about Burgess which must have horrified MI5: 'Neither in the B.B.C., nor in the Foreign Office, nor during the period that he, Burgess, was associated with the secret service and *also MI5 itself* [my italics] did he make any secret from his friends or colleagues either of his views or the fact that he had been a Communist.'[19] The admission that he had worked for MI5 must have been received with great alarm for, while MI6 was under suspicion for having harboured a traitor in the form of Philby, no hint of treachery had then been ascribed to MI5. Parliament and the whole of Fleet Street, including myself, were gravely at fault for failing to follow up that admission.

Whatever the Soviet purpose behind the sudden appearance of the traitors, the MI5 management decided that it had to take some action to offset certain dangers posed by the unwelcome development. A decision was made to use my services as chief writer on intelligence affairs in the *Daily Express*, which then had a huge circulation. On the morning of 26 February Rear-Admiral Thomson as Secretary of the D-Notice Committee asked me to attend his office to meet Bernard Hill, head of MI5's legal department, who urgently needed my help. I was later informed that Hill had been instructed to see me by Hollis, then Deputy Director-General. Hill, who always seemed to wear a muffler, irrespective of the weather (and, one suspected, belt as well as braces) opened the conversation by declaring: 'I am now putting you under the Official Secrets Act,' which, of course, he had no power to do. He then said that in the fortnight since the theatrical production of Maclean and Burgess he and his colleagues had subjected their statements to minute analysis which had convinced them that it was the prelude to further statements by the two traitors, which would be calculated to sow the maximum distrust between Britain and America. In particular, prominent people, especially in the Foreign Office, would be discredited by being accused of sharing Maclean's and Burgess's views on America's foreign and defence policies.

Whoever had masterminded this interpretation – and Thomson assured me at the time that he had been told that it was Hollis – it was to prove hopelessly wide of the truth. The defectors were never used in that capacity.

The meeting concluded with a request that the *Daily Express* should publish a prominent article to warn the public that what the defectors had said was lies and whatever they might say in future would be K.G.B. 'disinformation'. The wily Hill, whom I had met before, tried to avoid telling me anything in return, but before I agreed to write the article I managed to induce him to admit that MI5 had evidence of Maclean's treachery stretching over many years, though not of a kind which could be brought into a British court. Regarding Burgess, he said that there was no certainty that he had been a spy, and while there was nothing legal to prevent his return to Britain, he thought that that was unlikely.

In fact, as Burgess had worked in MI5 and must have told the

K.G.B. all that he knew about that organization, he would undoubtedly have been in breach of the Official Secrets Act to an extent which would have provided *prima facie* evidence for his arrest. Stupidly, I did not appreciate that at the time, nor did I realize that Hill's main purpose was probably to convince M.P.s and other interested parties, including the Americans, that Burgess's claim to have worked for MI5 was false, when in fact it was one of the few things in the statement which was true. Further, having gone out of its way to mention MI5 in its statement, the K.G.B. might well go into greater detail in later announcements by Burgess and Maclean.

Since the issue made legitimate news and was straight out of MI5, the *Daily Express* obliged on the following morning with a front-page 'splash' headlined 'Beware the Diplomats!'.[20] MI5 was duly delighted.

Later events were to indicate that Hollis, and perhaps other members of the MI5 top management, had also been concerned to prevent any possible return to Britain by Burgess, an event which could have caused deep embarrassment in many quarters and might possibly have appealed to the Soviet political leadership, which had recently changed.

After Burgess's brief appearance at the National Hotel, Tom Driberg, who had known him well and was temporarily out of Parliament, went to Moscow to see him to write a book about his experiences, having first contacted him by letter, probably with back-door K.G.B. agreement. It was not known at the time the book, *Guy Burgess, a Portrait with a Background*, appeared in 1956 that Driberg was a long-serving agent of MI5 and that the project had MI5 agreement.[21] The book was not an MI5 initiative but the agency took advantage of the situation once Burgess had replied to Driberg's letter with his – and the K.G.B.'s – agreement to the project. MI5 knew that the book would inevitably be a K.G.B. disinformation exercise, containing plausible lies and other mis-statements, because Driberg had agreed to submit the proofs of the book to Burgess for vetting and, as MI5 also knew, Driberg was in touch with the K.G.B. in London, serving as something of a double agent.[22]

Driberg worked quickly on the book, which contained little real information, and visited Moscow again, where he was photo-graphed working on the proofs with Burgess. The proofs had, of course, already been seen and approved by MI5. The book enabled Burgess to insist, again, that he had never been a Soviet agent, and Driberg ended it by saying that he believed him. This was a monstrous lie but a lie which suited MI5.

In November 1956, by which time Hollis was Director-General, I was again approached by Admiral Thomson on behalf of Bernard Hill. I was informed that I – and the *Daily Express* – might be interested to know that Burgess had now committed an offence under the Official Secrets Act for which he could be charged if ever he returned to Britain! On his first visit to Moscow, Driberg had induced Burgess to recall some incidents and names concerning the brief time he had spent in the Special Operations Executive and these had been included in the proofs which Burgess – and the K.G.B. – vetted on Driberg's second visit to the Soviet capital. On his return, Driberg instructed his publishers, doubtless at MI5's request, to go through the motions of submitting the script to the security authorities for formal vetting, without telling them that they had already seen it. The publishers were then duly warned that unless they deleted the details and names about the S.O.E., they risked prosecution under the Official Secrets Act. These parts were duly removed and the book was published, whereupon Admiral Thomson told me that MI5 would be greatly obliged if, through the *Daily Express*, I would let Burgess and the world know that he was likely to be arrested and charged if he ever set foot on British soil. Having no knowledge then of Driberg's connivance, I was happy to do so with a news item headed 'Burgess burns his boats'.[23]

When I asked Thomson why MI5 had made so much of such a thin potential charge he told me that Hollis was determined to dissuade Burgess from ever returning to Britain, even if only for a short visit to see his mother, to whom he was devoted. No doubt the authorities would have looked foolish if Burgess had visited his old haunts in London, giving interviews to newspapers about the glories of life in the Soviet Union, but I have always suspected that there was more to Hollis's determination, for it was not his last effort to prevent the return of the two traitors. Though the next attempt did not occur until April 1962 it is convenient to deal with it now.

Through official channels defence and crime correspondents were told that a tip had been received from Dutch Intelligence that both Burgess and Maclean had been invited to attend a communist conference in Cuba and that the airliner carrying them would be touching down at Prestwick Airport in Scotland. By that time Martin and other MI5 officers had more solid evidence, especially against Maclean, and were keen to interrogate them so that the damage assessments of their treachery could be improved, but the MI5 management went out of its way to ensure that they would not have the opportunity. On the morning of 17 April the police applied to the Chief Metropolitan Magistrate for arrest warrants for Burgess and Maclean. This was followed later in the day by a statement from the Metropolitan Police Commissioner: 'There are grounds for supposing that Donald Maclean and Guy Burgess may be contemplating leaving or may have left the U.S.S.R. for some other territory.'

In fact, the defectors never moved out of Moscow and the newspapers were eventually told that the tip must have been false. In my belief the whole episode was an MI5 plan engineered to frighten the two men from ever trying to return. Several visitors to Moscow had reported seeing or meeting Burgess, who looked rather pathetic in his Old Etonian tie and red waistcoat and answered to the name Jim Andreyevitch Eliot. Whitney Straight, elder brother of Michael, went so far as to report that Burgess had 'retained his fundamental interest in England and loved the old country'.[24] By 1962 Burgess was severely ill with diabetes and its consequences and may have been hoping to return to die in Britain, but it is unlikely that by that time the K.G.B. had any intention of allowing him to leave.

The fear that Burgess might cause immense embarrassment by suddenly arriving in Britain seemed to persist in MI5 until September 1963 when it was announced that he had died of heart failure in a Moscow hospital, aged fifty-two.

The Government and its Whitehall machinery were unable to resist the temptation of using the White Paper and the ensuing debate as a means of excusing their incompetence in the secret battle with the K.G.B. This was so patent to the C.I.A. and other American authorities that it inflicted further damage on Anglo-American relations, to the continuing advantage of the Kremlin. There was particular bitterness in Washington about the effective clearance of Philby which had been quite unnecessary. Macmillan's statement could have been worded to leave the case open simply by saying that inquiries were continuing. Instead, the American authorities were led to believe that the British were opposed to pursuing the Philby case, which was correct as far as his former service, MI6, was concerned. The K.G.B. profited in the immediate future by having the continuing services of Philby, who had been made virtually free from newspaper criticism or inquiry. When Philby ultimately defected, eight years later, it scored again by showing the world that it had run rings round both MI5 and MI6. The K.G.B. was, and remains, particularly concerned to promote its reputation as an elite force and exert psychological ascendancy over its opponents.

In view of later events, the White Paper and the debate, which were both supposed to be historical records, damaged the Parliamentary process by proving to be misleading and to be evidence of the depressing fact that the veracity of ministers is only as dependable as that of the officials who prepare their briefs. Briefers from the closed communities of the secret services are more than usually prone to mislead, if only because they are remote from the moderating requirements of reality.

The Potential Value of Oversight

The existence of an oversight body could have exerted some restraint on those who prepared the White Paper and the ministerial briefs. Though it is possible that Philby was cleared because Macmillan exceeded his brief in an excess of zeal to demonstrate his championship of civil liberties, the secret services may have been initially responsible. If so, their zeal to protect their former colleague might have been dampened had they known that they might be quickly called to account.

Regarding the reappearance of the defectors in Moscow, an alert oversight body should have investigated the claim that Burgess had worked for MI5, and that could have led to a quicker assessment of his past role and the damage he had inflicted.

CHAPTER TWENTY-FOUR

Momentous Escapade

To understand why Hollis suddenly, and most unexpectedly, found himself promoted to Director-General of MI5 it is necessary to consider the sad case of Commander Lionel 'Buster' Crabb, the gallant frogman who lost his life in April 1956.

In that month the joint Soviet leaders, Bulganin and Khrushchev, were scheduled to arrive in Portsmouth aboard the cruiser *Ordzhonikidze* on a goodwill mission to Britain. The Prime Minister, Sir Anthony Eden, hoped that the visit would reduce East–West tensions and moderate the Cold War. He therefore issued a directive to all services, banning any intelligence operations against the cruiser because of the risk that they might be discovered and give the visitors cause for complaint. This directive was to be widely disobeyed as a challenge from a 'wet' Prime Minister who was ignoring the blatant efforts made by Soviet Intelligence whenever British warships visited Leningrad, when frogmen were used for inspection purposes almost contemptuously.

Officers from MI5 had already been operating in Claridge's Hotel, where the Soviet leaders were to stay, and had installed microphones in their rooms as well as surveillance devices on buildings nearby.[1]

Admiralty intelligence was particularly keen to discover whether the Soviet ship was fitted with an anti-sonar device, code-named Agouti, which decreased the cavitation effects produced by the screws and thereby reduced underwater noise.[2] This and other objectives could be achieved only by underwater examination of the hull and screws by a frogman, and the most experienced operator in the field was Crabb, who had made a fine reputation for professionalism and daring during the war, winning the George Medal. Then forty-six and retired from the Navy, he was operating as a freelance.

As the Admiralty was unable, or unwilling, to mount the operation itself, the Director of Naval Intelligence approached MI6, which then had a special naval section in a separate London station in Vauxhall Bridge Road. The head of the London station was Nicholas Elliott, the MI6 officer who was later to interrogate Philby. Crabb was approached and was enthusiastic for the task even though he appreciated that he was being used as an 'illegal' spy who could be disowned and even denounced.

MI5 was required to give minor support to the project and was approached by the liaison officer of the MI6 London station, John Henry. A meeting was held in the room of the MI5 Director-General, Sir Dick White, with his deputy, Hollis, present. Clearance was given for MI5 support, though it was noted that the approval of the Foreign Office had not been obtained [3]

In the previous year a major reconnaissance effort had been mounted against the *Ordzhonikidze*'s sister-ship, the cruiser *Sverdlov*, when it had visited Portsmouth. A technical section of MI10 had collaborated with the Admiralty to set up radar equipment hidden in galleries in the cliffs of Dover. The Navy also had a submerged submarine on the cruiser's route to record sound and pressure waves from the warship. Some of these activities were also repeated with the *Ordzhonikidze*. [4]

Soviet security for the whole event was known to be extremely tight. In March the K.G.B. chief himself, Ivan Serov, had visited London with a team of electronic 'sweepers' to check the hotel accommodation for hidden microphones, which they failed to detect. Because Serov's appalling record of savage suppression was so well known he was badly received by the British public and the newspapers made it plain that he would not be welcome when the Soviet leaders arrived on 18 April. He nevertheless accompanied them, but remained aboard the ship in charge of security there.

Crabb was confident that he could accomplish the task without detection and booked into a small hotel in Portsmouth accompanied by a secret service officer from the London station who had been detailed by Elliott to assist him. This officer signed the hotel register as 'Bernard Smith' and, rather stupidly, gave his occupation as 'attached Foreign Office', which was then the standard cover for MI6 operatives. There were no Americans involved, as has been claimed by some writers, but a local MI6 officer, Ted Davies, took part.

On the following day Davies suffered a mild heart attack but insisted on continuing and, early on the morning of 19 April, he accompanied Crabb to a jetty only a few hundred yards from the moored cruiser and its two attendant destroyers. Crabb returned after a few minutes in the water for an extra pound of ballast weight, took off and was never seen alive again by his colleague. [5]

There was consternation in MI6 and the Admiralty, and the help of MI5 was sought in an attempt to cover up the frogman's disappearance. In the hope that this might be successful ministers were told nothing. In the course of the day, however, the commander of the Soviet flotilla, Rear-Admiral V.F. Kotov, told the Chief of Staff of the Portsmouth base, Rear-Admiral Philip Burnett, that his sailors had seen a frogman on the surface near his ships and expected an explanation. Burnett, who knew nothing of the operation, rejected the complaint. That evening the First Lord of the Admiralty, James Thomas, was dining with some of the Soviet visitors, including the *Ordzhonikidze*'s captain who asked, 'What was that frogman doing off our bows this morning?' Thomas, who had no knowledge of what had happened, made inquiries but it is not known whether the Prime Minister was informed at that stage.[6]

MI5 then made a determined but ill-advised and clumsy attempt to remove all clues to the embarrassing gaffe by asking the head of the Portsmouth C.I.D. to visit the hotel where Crabb and his companion had stayed and to tear out the relevant pages from the hotel register. The detective did so and threatened the manager with the Official Secrets Act if he told anybody anything about what had occurred.

Hopes rose in Whitehall that Parliament and the public could be deceived because it seemed that the Soviets had decided against making any political capital out of the event. So on 29 April the Admiralty, with the connivance of MI5 and MI6, issued a false statement that Crabb was missing, presumed dead, after failing to return from 'a test-dive in connection with trials of certain underwater apparatus in Stokes Bay', three miles from Portsmouth. It must have been clear that the Soviets could not possibly accept the implied explanation that Crabb had strayed so far off course. So the statement was intended to fool Parliament, the public and, possibly, the Prime Minister, if he was still in the dark.

Journalists were not fooled and quickly discovered the removal of the pages from the hotel register and what had been in them. Speculation that Crabb had really been spying on the Soviet ships was rife and the Kremlin seized on this to make the truth public. It sent a private note to the Foreign Office requiring an explanation and the Government had no option but to admit that the frogman seen by the Soviets had been Crabb.

While Whitehall still remained silent publicly, hoping that the truth would remain private, the Kremlin released the texts of both the British and Soviet notes, revealing that the public and Parliament had been victims of an Admiralty and Whitehall cover-up and that deliberate lies had been told to spare ministers and officials embarrassment.

Eden was then required to answer questions, which he declined to do, and a debate was forced in which the Labour leader, Gaitskell, charged that there had been 'a grave lack of control and an unsatisfactory state of affairs' within MI6, which could not be denied.[7] Eden, however, declined to provide any more information beyond saying that what had been done had been without the knowledge of ministers and that disciplinary action was being taken against those responsible for the 'misconceived and inept operation'. This was evidence enough that the Admiralty statement about the testing of equipment in Stokes Bay had been a lie and that Crabb had been attempting to examine the hull of the cruiser. cruiser.

What had happened to Crabb? It was known that the *Ordzhonikidze* had a 'wet compartment' – a chamber below the waterline from which frogmen could operate – so it remains possible that Crabb was intercepted by Soviet frogmen and was either killed or captured. Several years later the K.G.B. defector, Anatoli Golitsin, volunteered information to the effect that G.R.U. naval intelligence had been forewarned of Crabb's mission and that waiting frogmen had captured him. The defector even cited the Crabb affair as evidence that either MI6, MI5 or the Admiralty was penetrated by Soviet Intelligence.[8]

The British authorities are nevertheless satisfied that Crabb died as a result of an accident. His closed-circuit oxygen apparatus and his suit were of good standard but, at forty-six and a heavy smoker and drinker, he was not fit. The MI6 men claim that they had been concerned about this but Crabb had been so enthusiastic and had so much experience that he had overborne their objections.

There is evidence that the K.G.B. disinformation department continued to exploit the Crabb affair by stimulating publicity from time to time with fake reports that he had joined the Red Navy, and this seems to have continued after the headless and handless body of a frogman was washed up at the mouth of Chichester Harbour in June 1957, miles from where Crabb had disappeared fourteen months previously.[9] What was left of the suit was identical to that worn by Crabb and, from this and other evidence, the coroner at the inquest concluded that the remains were those of the gallant diver who had perished in the service of his country. The Admiralty, which in those days was an arrogant law unto itself, then repeated its lie that Crabb had been testing underwater equipment in Stokes Bay, while journalists, stimulated it seems by K.G.B. disinformation, claimed that the body, which was probably not Crabb's, had been planted by a Soviet submarine.

The claim that Crabb was alive was to be supported a few years later by a Labour M.P., Bernard Floud, who claimed to have established through an MI6 contact that British naval officers had witnessed the capture of Crabb and had reported it but, as will be seen, Floud had been recruited earlier by Soviet Intelligence, and MI5 officers who investigated him believe that he was in contact with the K.G.B. at the time.[10]

Eden was so furious with MI6 that its chief, Sir John 'Sinbad' Sinclair, was removed. Eden chose the charming and intelligent head of MI5, Sir Dick White, to succeed Sinclair, perhaps being unaware of MI5's contribution to the fiasco. There could hardly have been greater dismay in MI6, which regarded the appointment of anybody from MI5 as the severest reprimand imaginable.

White's unexpected departure meant that his job suddenly became vacant. He recommended that his deputy and friend, Hollis, should fill it. In those days, such a recommendation was almost certain to be accepted by the Prime Minister and his advisers, as it was in this case. It was an unanticipated bonus for Hollis who, being a year older than his superior, would normally have retired first and could not have expected to succeed him. No doubt White felt that Hollis was the best candidate, but he would have been less than human had he not wished to leave behind a Director-General who was not only friendly but beholden to him in the almost inevitable event of future conflicts between MI6 and MI5.

Many of those who had witnessed Hollis's remarkable rise were puzzled to find themselves commanded by such a remote, withdrawn and unintellectual figure. One woman colleague, who does not believe that Hollis was disloyal, has commented: 'We were somewhat astonished when we heard that he had been made D.G. as we realised that he had been promoted above his capabilities and this always leads to trouble...' Still, it has been common enough in Whitehall, and even in Westminster, for nonentities to succeed to high office by being in the right place at the right time and having the right friends.

If Hollis was a spy Soviet Intelligence could never have foreseen that he would fly so high and if the leak about Crabb's mission, alleged by Golitsin, had come from him the result was piquant in the extreme.

The Potential Value of Oversight

The Crabb case provides an excellent example of how the existence of some degree of oversight by an independent body responsible to Parliament might have prevented damage to British interests, to secret services and to ministerial reputations.

The operation was conceived and conducted in the belief that ministers would never hear anything about it and that even a prime ministerial directive banning any such attempt could safely be ignored. It seems unlikely that MI6, MI5 or even the Admiralty would have taken such a chance had they known that an oversight body would be likely to learn of it. Had such a body been approached for prior collusion it would not have been obtained.

It is also unlikely that the Admiralty would have been prepared to lie so blatantly when subject to possible exposure. Nobody benefited from the lie, which simply cast doubt on anything further the Admiralty might ever have to say.

The argument that the secret services must take risks if they are to display initiative and achieve results, especially against an adversary like the K.G.B., which imposes no limitations, cannot be dismissed, but the Crabb affair shows that there are instances where the secret services might need to be saved from their own excess of zeal.

The case also raises the question of whether an independent oversight body should be involved in the inquests on security disasters. These continue to be carried out internally with assistance from the Security Commission but the activities of the latter are restricted to cases of espionage and leakages. It is unlikely that the Security Commission would be involved in a case comparable with the Crabb affair, since the odds are that there would be another attempted departmental cover-up with all its possible consequences.

CHAPTER TWENTY-FIVE

In Control

WHILE the appointment of Roger Hollis as Director-General did not surprise most MI5 officers who knew of his closeness to Sir Dick White, they were appalled by it, as were other more junior members of the staff. The extent of his responsibility and the power, for good or ill, which went with it, was to be stated publicly by his successor as 'the defence of the realm as a whole from external and internal dangers arising from attempts at espionage and sabotage, or from actions of persons and organisations, whether directed from within or without the country, which may be judged to be subversive of the security of the State'.[1] In 1956 such dangers were springing mainly from the ambitions of the Soviet Union, which was then believed to be 'flexing its muscles' for possible conflict, and Hollis was regarded as MI5's expert on communism and international communism. If MI5 agreed with the Conference of Privy Concillors' foolish belief that the main threat came from British communists rather than from professional K.G.B. and G.R.U. operators then he had a special qualification. To many of his colleagues, however, Hollis lacked the qualities of leadership required to direct a team responsible for such a remit. To one of them, who had no particular animosity towards him, he was 'absolutely without the panache a leader of such an organization should have. He was dull, shy and dreary.' A woman who worked with Hollis in the headquarters at Leconfield House described him to me as 'an appalling D.G. He moved like a wraith; looked through you. I could never understand how he got the job. It was a standing joke that everything would go wrong – and it did.' In a joint appreciation two other female former MI5 employees described Hollis as 'not very bright but dangerous because he looked as though he could be manipulated'.

Nor did Hollis show any signs of growing into the job as he grappled with the challenge, as some apparently mediocre men do. A later Attorney-General, who had reason to survey his record, was to describe him as a 'blundering buffoon'. This performance came as no surprise to those officers who had become aware of his previous failure to counter the communist and Soviet threat and, on that score alone, found his promotion both bewildering and frightening.

As Director-General Hollis's salary was substantially increased but remained modest considering the responsibility. Though not a civil servant, the D.G. was rated by the Treasury for salary purposes as a Deputy Permanent Secretary in Whitehall, entitled to some £3,250 a year.[2] This rank was maintained so that the D.G. was junior to the Permanent Secretary of the parent ministry, the Home Office. The increase must have helped with outgoings such as school fees for his son, Adrian, who was at Eton, though family money may have assisted there. The appointment inevitably involved more entertaining, especially of visiting security officials, for which a rather meagre expense allowance was provided. Perhaps not surprisingly, those who experienced the hospitality of the Hollis household recall it as 'austere – with very little to eat or drink'.[3]

According to visitors to the Campden Hill Square house it was dark, unwelcoming and very untidy. For some years, including the time when Hollis was D.G., the first Lady Hollis ran a second-hand clothing business from it to raise money for her charity, a club in Bermondsey. Her enthusiasm clearly overcame her house-pride for customers remember rooms being 'littered' with second-hand women's and children's clothes, the narrow hallway obstructed with old trunks. 'The sitting-room was awful,' one of them recalled, 'full of old clothes and there were people in the house trying things on. I don't see how you could have asked anybody there.'[4] The same person remembers that Lady Hollis told her that her husband had objected to the trunks but would have to put up with them. Lady Hollis was described as 'domineering and looking rather frigid', while a professional colleague recalls her as being 'mousey and someone to avoid being cornered with at an office cocktail party'. While this is probably unkind to the late lady, the picture does perhaps help to explain why Hollis sought solace with his secretary.

His illicit relationship with Val Hammond was widely assumed to be the reason for his habit of staying late in the office after other colleagues had left but there seem to have been many occasions when Miss Hammond too had departed and he remained until 8 p.m. or later. Case records show this to be a necessary habit of agents in place who need time and complete privacy for the removal, copying or photographing of documents.[5] As D.G., Hollis had right of access to any documents he wished and, having his own safe, could keep them overnight while other officers would be required to return them to the Registry.

If Hollis was a spy his high-level associations with officials from other Western security agencies would have been of the greatest benefit to Soviet Intelligence, as would his visits abroad to them. Hollis had appointed Graham Mitchell, an even more reserved and inscrutable character, to succeed him as Deputy Director-General and overbore him on most issues, including overseas travel, Mitchell doing relatively little of it. The advantage to any spy of opportunities for travel can hardly be exaggerated. As many cases show, Soviet Intelligence prefers to restrict meetings between controllers and important agents to overseas locations, when practicable, to reduce the risk of surveillance. As Director-General, Hollis's almost complete immunity to investigation and the aura attached to the position practically guaranteed his safety, especially as he required immediate notification of any defector or other eventuality which might threaten his position.

Hollis was already a member of the Reform Club in Pall Mall in 1956 when he joined the club next door, the Travellers' Club, which had long been the first choice of officers from the Fifth Estate, and still is. He was proposed by the former Deputy Director of MI5, Guy Liddell, and seconded by Walter Bell, an MI5 officer who had formerly worked in MI6. Bell had been in line to go to Washington as 'Security Adviser' in the British Embassy there, meaning MI5 liaison man with the C.I.A. and F.B.I., a post for which he was extremely well qualified, not only through experience but because he was married to the daughter of a senior American general. But Hollis had countermanded the posting and insisted that Bell should be his personal assistant in London. Membership of the Travellers Club enabled him to keep in social touch with White, who also joined in 1956, and with Blunt, who was a regular attender at the bar there, having been a member since 1948.

While Blunt and Hollis appeared to be poles apart in their general interests, they remained friendly. According to Derek Tangye, Hollis had not been a member of Blunt's 'clique' when at Blenheim, but Blunt was an occasional dinner guest at the Hollis home in London later in the war.[6] Such meetings were, presumably, the result of their professional association, for there is no evidence that Hollis had much interest in art or its history, and suggestions that he was a member of the Management Committee of the Courtauld Institute, as several of his Whitehall colleagues were, seem to be groundless. Blunt, however, had a reputation for being an interesting table guest on other counts and both were 'good bottle men'. When Blunt was questioned about Hollis in the

240

late 1960s he claimed that he had seen him only occasionally, 'mainly at public functions', after 1951, the date when Blunt had first become suspect. MI5 accepted this assurance but mutual friends of both men have told researchers, such as Dr Anthony Glees, that they continued to meet. A visitors' book for the Campden Hill Square house is said to exist and could be revealing.

There were other, more tenuous, connections. Hollis's son was taught by Blunt's elder brother, Wilfrid, a drawing master at Eton, and Hollis seems to have been friendly with Blunt's other brother, Christopher.

Hollis's long affair with his secretary, Val Hammond, made further inroads into a social life already limited by the restrictions of his calling and he had few other close friends when he became Director-General. It also decreased his popularity inside the organization where some employees recall his puritanical attitude to the danger of sexual liaisons with some bitterness. One officer has told me, 'He would lecture the staff on morality saying that all his officers had to be above suspicion,' while a secretary recalled, 'We all knew about his affair with Val Hammond yet if we had been in a similar position and he had known about it we would have been out, smartly.'

When one MI5 agent-runner had an affair with one of his female agents Hollis insisted that he should be dismissed and he was, in spite of pleading by the head of Personnel. One officer who was particularly incensed by this was Courtenay Young, the highly intelligent and experienced head of the Soviet counter-intelligence section from 1956 to 1960. One of Young's colleagues told me, 'Courtenay was not a strict person but what enraged him was that Hollis penalized other members of the staff for the offence he was committing.'

Hollis is also remembered for his parsimony with the money allotted to 'The Firm', as MI5 is sometimes called internally. He always liked to spend less than the Government had voted him so that he could return a sizeable sum at the end of the financial year. This meant that agents were not paid as much as they could have been, and in this context one officer recalls that a Rumanian woman agent whom he was running was improperly rewarded for the information she was providing at some risk. This man also said that he suspected that Hollis was a Soviet agent from the late 1940s so strongly that he would never reveal the names of his agents to him, for fear that it would lead to their betrayal.

He and other officers think that Hollis's cheeseparing was intended to ingratiate himself with the Treasury but it did the reverse because Treasury officials thought him foolish in that it enabled them to resist any further demand for an increase.

Another characteristic for which Hollis is remembered in his early days as Director-General was his occasional display of temper. At the time of the Suez crisis in 1956 one of his officers had developed four agents inside the Egyptian Embassy in London, one of them having access to ciphers. When Hollis discovered this he made him drop them all, angrily asserting that if the Egyptians found out and made it public, the Foreign Office would be embarrassed and he would then be held responsible.[7] Information from such sources could have been of the greatest value had the expedition to seize the Suez Canal not been abandoned, and it was Hollis's responsibility to obtain it if possible.

Several former officers whom I have consulted recall Hollis's preoccupation with avoiding any embarrassment to Government departments, at the expense of MI5's efficiency. This may have been behind his decision in the late 1950s to discourage his officers from keeping in contact with Professor R.V. Jones who had been Director of Scientific Intelligence in the Ministry of Defence from 1952 to 1953, when he was ousted as a result of petty in-fighting there.[8] As Professor Jones's outstanding wartime career testifies, maintaining a relationship with him could only have been to MI5's advantage, but Hollis appeared to prefer to avoid upsetting the anti-Jones faction then in charge in the Defence Ministry.

Such moves would, of course, also have been in the interest of the K.G.B. had Hollis been a Soviet agent, for negative action can be almost as effective as positive espionage in reducing the efficiency of a security or intelligence agency. Political embarrassment was used so often as a reason for inaction by Hollis that it began to look more like an excuse.

The first espionage case in Hollis's nine years' reign as Director-General resulted in another embarrassing defection behind the Iron Curtain and, but for circumstances outside his control, would have been written off as a total disaster. In March 1956, a 22-year-old R.A.F. Flying Officer called Anthony Wraight was seen visiting the Soviet Embassy by routine watchers, and when his letters were intercepted as a consequence he was seen to be in dangerously intimate communication with a G.R.U. officer called Solovei, who was working under cover of being a Soviet film representative at the Embassy. When questioned by MI5 and R.A.F. military police late in October, Wraight, a fighter pilot, claimed to know nothing about an R.A.F. rule requiring all personnel to report any contacts with Soviet officials, but it was found that he was lying. After being warned that he might be court-martialled, Wraight, who had virtually become a communist, flew to Berlin and defected early in December. He was thoroughly debriefed regarding all he knew about secret R.A.F. matters and was used in a propaganda broadcast. Nothing was then heard about him for three years, when he decided to return to Britain of his own volition. After admitting that he had been debriefed by Soviet bloc intelligence he was sentenced to three years' imprisonment.[9]

When one of Hollis's supporters was listing the MI5 triumphs under his leadership he included the Wraight case!

MI5's operations continued to fall apart, seemingly because the K.G.B. had advance information about them, and in that context there is no more dramatic example than the so-called 'Arago' affair. In the autumn of 1957 a cipher clerk in the Czech Embassy in Washington, called Frantisek Tisler, who had been recruited by the F.B.I., provided some information which was quickly passed to MI5. The clerk, who was given the code-name 'Arago', reported that while in Prague he had spoken with Colonel Oldrich Pribyl who was Czech Military Attaché in London, where he had already served for three years, and was on a visit to Intelligence headquarters in the Czech capital. Pribyl confided that Soviet Intelligence must have a spy inside MI5 who was a wonderful source and could be tapped at short notice. As evidence he described how he had needed to debrief one of the British traitors he had managed to recruit and, to avoid being watched or overheard, had talked to him while driving his car through London. He realized that he was being followed by what he suspected to be an MI5 car but managed to shake it off in the traffic.[10] Fearful that MI5 might have discovered the identity of his agent, Pribyl consulted the Soviet Military Attaché, a professional G.R.U. officer with whom he had regular contact. The Russian said that he could normally have found out quickly whether or not MI5 knew the name of Pribyl's agent but as the meeting was on the Friday of a Bank Holiday weekend it would take him a few days but that he expected to have an answer by Tuesday.

On that day the Russian contacted Pribyl and told him that while MI5 did not know the agent's identity, its watchers had indeed been following him but had decided that he was simply giving driving instruction to another Czech and so had broken off the surveillance.

There was deep concern in certain quarters of MI5 at this information from 'Arago' because it was entirely correct and could only mean that the Soviets had a source able to supply details of watcher operations.

'Arago' also revealed how the Soviet G.R.U. officer had warned

243

Pribyl about a change in the tactics of the MI5 men who followed cars used by intelligence officers of the Soviet bloc in London. Previously they had waited close by the communist embassies to detect cars with numberplates they knew to be used by known or suspected spies. Now they were to make themselves less conspicuous by waiting near certain Thames bridges that the spies were most likely to use. This ruse, which had been code-named 'Coverpoint', must have been betrayed to the Soviets almost immediately for none of their cars used the bridges and the project had to be abandoned within a fortnight.[11]

The assumption in MI5 was that someone in the Watcher Service was responsible for the leaks but, as Chapters 33 and 44 show, they could have originated from a higher source. Though the evidence of serious penetration of MI5 by the Soviets – and by the G.R.U. in particular – provided by 'Arago' was compelling, nothing effective appears to have been done about it.

At the time Pribyl spoke to 'Arago' the latter was high in Czech favour because the F.B.I. had provided him with some true 'chickenfeed' information to supply to Prague headquarters to improve his position in Czech Intelligence. This may explain why Pribyl spoke to him so freely. During their conversation Pribyl broke a golden rule and was indiscreet enough to name one of his British spies as Brian Linney, an electronics engineer, who was providing secret information about a new R.A.F. missile being produced at a factory at Shoreham, Sussex. Once again, through 'Arago', MI5 learned of the existence of a dangerous spy by pure chance from a double agent working for the F.B.I. who was, eventually, to defect to the U.S., taking a mass of documentary information with him.

Linney was placed under close surveillance and MI5 learned of a projected meeting with Pribyl, when it was intended that Special Branch officers should pounce and catch the spy in the act of handing over documents and information. Linney went to the rendezvous and was followed, but Pribyl never even left his London office, strongly suggesting that he had been warned by someone who, in view of 'Arago's' other information, was almost certainly in MI5.

Linney was eventually bluffed into confessing his treachery by a particularly persuasive interrogator, who taped his confession, and was sentenced to fourteen years' imprisonment.

It may be significant that 'Arago's' information to MI5 all derived from the G.R.U., via the Soviet Military Attaché or from the comparable Czech organization via Pribyl, which liaised closely with the G.R.U. The suspected source inside MI5 to which the

Soviets had access, either directly or through an intermediary, was therefore likely to have been recruited by the G.R.U. This clue would later be regarded as fitting Hollis rather than any other suspect.

Pribyl eventually returned to Prague, covered by his diplomatic immunity, but not before he had been involved in a monstrous act of treason by a Czech refugee enjoying freedom and hospitality in Britain. This treachery, which continued for several years without detection by MI5, resulted in the loss of more than 100 agents working overseas for MI6, some of whom were executed. It was perpetrated by Karel Zbytek, who had been in England during the war with the Free Czech Army. He had returned to his native land but defected to Britain while visiting Wales as a member of a choir in the early 1950s. Zbytek secured a job as a filing clerk with an organization based in London called the Czech Intelligence Office. Its purpose was to recruit Czech exiles in Britain and Europe to counter the communist regime which had seized power illegally in Czechoslovakia. MI6 financed it and was involved in planning its operations, which until 1956 were highly successful in penetrating areas of interest in Czechoslovakia. In the spring of that year Zbytek, who was greedy for money, wrote anonymously to Pribyl giving information about several MI6 agents operating at high level in Czechoslovakia and offering more for payment. The truth of his material was quickly established with the secret arrest of eight of the MI6 agents, two of whom were sentenced to death. Pribyl contacted Zbytek, who was given the code-name 'Light', and from then on the traitor met with controllers regularly in London, gradually revealing the entire British operation in Czechoslovakia and also receiving some £40,000 in the process.[12]

With the Czech Intelligence Office in disarray, Zbytek, who had acquired British citizenship and changed his name to Charles Charles, 'retired' and ran a boarding house in Folkestone, where he died from a heart attack in 1961. Nothing was known of the treachery of this Soviet bloc agent, later known as the 'Czech Philby', until 1969 when two defectors from Czech Intelligence revealed it to the C.I.A. and then to MI5.

My inquiries among former MI5 officers show that in the late 1950s and continuing into the 1960s there were many cases which collapsed because they had apparently been 'blown' while investigations were in progress. A Soviet spy in a factory in Luton had begun to confess to an MI5 case officer when the case was suddenly and unaccountably called off on instructions from the MI5 management.[13] The same officer claimed that inquiries into penetrations responsible for these collapses were 'swept under the carpet'.

Fears continued that leaks of most secret information were reaching the Russians at great speed from a source connected with the watchers. It seems that whenever the watchers were about to be staked out to carry out surveillance the Russians knew in advance and were able to avoid it.

As the watchers used radio to keep in touch with each other and with headquarters they varied the frequencies in the hope of avoiding being overheard by Soviet counter-surveillance men. The Russians retuned to the new frequencies so quickly that it was felt that they must have been informed of them in advance.

On one occasion the MI5 management had been deluded by ingenious K.G.B. disinformation into staging a major operation in the Midlands which involved switching most of the watchers out of London. On the day that they departed the Russians switched off the radio listening equipment on the roof of the Soviet Embassy and did not switch it on again until the watchers returned from their fool's errand. It was deduced that the purpose of the disinformation had been to remove the watchers from the London area so that Soviet Intelligence could have a free run in the capital for a few days to conduct an operation which was never discovered.[14]

Another operation which is believed to have collapsed owing to an MI5 betrayal involved the use of a new device called a probe microphone, which could be inserted into a party wall to overhear and record conversations. MI5 technicians were required to use it to tap a certain room in the Soviet Consulate in Bayswater Road. They bored a very narrow hole so that it came out behind a moulded leaf in a high frieze in the target room of the Consulate. The microphone operated for only a short time because the hole behind the leaf, though completely hidden and no wider than a pin, was plugged with plaster by the Russians.[15] If this was the result of another MI5 leak it is unlikely that it could have originated from the Watcher Service, suggesting that if the Russians had only one source, it was someone with wide and rapid access to a broad spectrum of secret information.

As Director-General Hollis was informed of these suspicious events as they happened but did not seem to be unduly disturbed, a feature of his character to which Sir Dick White was probably referring when he eventually wrote in Hollis's obituary notice in *The Times*: 'The hotter the climate of national security, the cooler he became.'[16]

Serious suspicion that the Director-General himself was a source of the leakages to the Russians did not arise until 1963, but there were some people, both inside and outside MI5, who were uneasy about him. One of those outside was a senior Southern Rhodesian security officer. While visiting London in the late 1950s Special Branch showed him disturbing evidence of Soviet interest in Southern Rhodesia (now Zimbabwe) and he asked why it had not been made available to Rhodesian security before. He was told that such information had to be channelled through MI5, which had declined to transfer it. The security officer then visited Hollis and suggested that a Rhodesian security official should be placed in Rhodesia House, in the Strand, to liaise with MI5 regarding information about Soviet activities with Z.A.N.U. and black insurgency movements. The officer records that Hollis rejected the suggestion with a show of temper. His department received no information from MI5 in its struggle against the insurgents and the officer never trusted Hollis again. Later, when Hollis was invited by the Southern Rhodesian Prime Minister, Sir Edgar Whitehead, to check the efficiency of the security service there, the official ensured that his access was limited to the minimum.[17]

In June 1960 Hollis provided his staff with further, and well remembered, evidence for their feeling that he demanded standards from them which he was not prepared to apply to himself. His son Adrian, then nineteen, was invited to take part in a chess tournament in Moscow. There was a long-standing rule that members of MI5 and their close relatives should not be allowed to travel behind the Iron Curtain for fear that they might be suborned by the K.G.B., and contemporaries of Hollis are convinced that if they had applied for permission for such a visit on behalf of a close relative he would have forbidden it on security grounds. In his own case he evaded the rule by writing to the Ambassador to the U.S.S.R., Sir Patrick Reilly, to ask if it was wise for his son to go. Reilly replied on 15 June: 'I can see no reason to advise against your son's visit. If the Russians take note of his parentage, it is, if anything, more likely to make them treat him with the extra respect due to the son of an important, if hidden, member of the Establishment.'

As Hollis must have appreciated, this was a specious reply. There could be no doubt that the Soviets had taken note of his parentage and there is no evidence that the K.G.B. has ever been impressed by rank in its subversive activities.

Hollis wanted to break the rule because it suited him, and the letter from Reilly, who could hardly have replied otherwise, was his cover if ever he was faced with any problem concerning the visit at some later date.

It has been suggested that had Hollis been a spy he would never have bothered to write for permission but simply allowed his son to go, knowing that he would be safe. On the contrary, he had his own colleagues to think about and needed an answer to any objections they, or even the Home Office, might make. To have broken the rule without a fall-back position could well have increased suspicions that he had special reason for being supremely confident that there was no possible danger.

During the early years of Hollis's rule the damage to Anglo-American relations caused by the Maclean/Burgess/Philby affair remained very severe. When Hollis took over, there was minimal liaison between MI5 and the F.B.I. and virtually none between MI5, or MI6, and the C.I.A. But in spite of his known anti-American attitude, relations did slowly begin to improve after Hoover invited Hollis to reopen liaison because the F.B.I. needed assistance on certain technical problems and an MI5 technical officer was sent to Washington.

The Potential Value of Oversight

Irregular sexual or marital relations are listed among the 'defects of character' which can be exposed when a candidate for access to top secret information is subjected to positive vetting. There is no evidence of which I am aware that Hollis's long affair with his secretary harmed British security interests but it was unfitting for a Director-General of MI5 and especially for one who objected to such liaisons by his staff. It would therefore seem to be doubtful that he would have continued to indulge himself in that respect had he known that his behaviour was likely to come to the notice of an oversight body.

Extra piquancy could have spiced the situation had independent observers responsible to Parliament appreciated that MI5 was compiling information about the sexual activities of M.P.s, including ministers, which was being supplied by inside sources such as Tom Driberg as well as by members of the public.

The degree to which oversight would be permissible would depend on the terms of reference given to the oversight body but if it covered operations, as I understand it does in the U.S., then much more might have been done about the quite dramatic information about the penetration of MI5 provided by 'Arago'. An oversight body could at least have satisfied itself, on the nation's behalf, that such leads were not being deliberately stifled in the interests of a well-placed spy. The other case-deaths and disasters might also have generated more concern than appears to have been the case inside MI5 itself until a few anxious officers could tolerate them no longer and demanded action, as will be seen.

The fact that some officers had begun to suspect Hollis and were unable to express their feelings suggests that an oversight body could serve some purpose in that respect. While such a system for reporting on superiors could be abused by disgruntled officers, security is of such supreme importance that there might be a case for it. Events to be described will show that with a person like Hollis in command, suggestions to the senior management about possible Soviet penetration served no purpose. The powers of patronage of any Director-General are so great that few subordinates are likely to challenge his actions, or lack of them, directly for fear of prejudicing their own positions.

CHAPTER TWENTY-SIX

A 'Pig' Called 'Lavinia'

HOLLIS received the routine knighthood for his appointment in 1960. The honour was to be followed by the exposure of a series of security disasters, which was to continue until his retirement.

Two years previously a high-ranking Polish Intelligence officer with close liaison links with the K.G.B. in Moscow had begun to write letters, in German, addressed to The C.I.A., c/o The U.S. Ambassador, Berne. They were signed with a word which translated as 'Sniper' or 'Sharpshooter' and gave the names of Polish agents operating against the West. In a total of fourteen letters, 'Sniper', whose name proved to be Michal Goleniewski, gave so many leads to K.G.B. operations that a perceptive C.I.A. officer correctly deduced that he was a member of the First Department of the U.B., the Polish Intelligence Service, which worked in such close collaboration with the K.G.B. that it was virtually an offshoot of it.[1]

Late in 1959 Goleniewski, who was given the MI5 code-name 'Lavinia', reported that the K.G.B. was running a highly productive spy in the British Admiralty. He described the spy as having first been recruited by Polish Intelligence while serving in the Naval Attaché's office in the British Embassy in Warsaw and having a name like 'Huton'. MI5 quickly identified him as Harry Houghton, a clerk in the Underwater Weapons Establishment at Portland, Dorset, where he had easy access to highly secret information about anti-submarine warfare and performance details of nuclear submarines. He had been spying there for years with the help of his mistress, Ethel Gee, a filing clerk, who also had access to secrets, handing over copies of documents and information to a Soviet Intelligence officer in return for money.

Once more, MI5, under Hollis's leadership, was to learn officially of the existence of two most damaging Soviet agents, who proved to be part of a ring, only because a chance Iron Curtain defector had warned the C.I.A.

A search of Admiralty records showed that Houghton's chief,

when he had been in Warsaw had submitted an adverse report about Houghton's reliability, but this had been ignored and the spy had been posted to one of the nation's most secret defence establishments. Houghton was placed under surveillance, particularly on the first Saturday of each month when he usually visited London by train accompanied by Miss Gee. In June 1960 he was seen handing a package to a man who, from the number of his car, was identified as Gordon Lonsdale, a Canadian who ran a business leasing jukeboxes to cafés, pubs and arcades.

A massive surveillance operation, said even to have included helicopters, was mounted by Jim Skardon, who was, by then, in charge of the Watcher Service. In August, Lonsdale, who soon proved to be a Soviet 'illegal' spy called Konon Molody operating under the name and passport of a dead Canadian, was seen to deposit a briefcase and an attaché case at a bank in Marylebone. Permission was secured by Special Branch to examine these and the attaché case was found to contain a cigarette lighter, the base of which was hollow and contained one-time pads of the type used by the K.G.B. and a schedule for radio contacts. MI5 officers photographed all the pads and returned the case to the bank.

Lonsdale's flat on the sixth floor of the White House, a residential block in Regent's Park which had been under sound-observation from the flat next door, was searched. A radio capable of receiving morse messages from Moscow and headphones for the purpose were found, but there was no transmitter, though as an 'illegal' Lonsdale would often need to radio material to the Moscow Centre, as Sonia had done. The surveillance was therefore continued to uncover the whereabouts of the transmitter and to reveal any other members of the group, which was to become known as the 'Navy Ring' or the 'Portland Spy-Ring'.

Lonsdale left Britain in September and there were doubts about whether he would return, but he did so in the following month when he was seen visiting the bank to pick up his belongings from the safe deposit. He was successfully shadowed through London crowds and on the Underground to a private house in Ruislip, occupied by two American citizens calling themselves Peter and Helen Kroger and posing as booksellers.

MI5 officers, using probe microphones in their observation flat in the White House, had been able to log the times when Lonsdale was listening to messages from Moscow. By entering his flat when he was out and opening the base of the cigarette lighter they were able to see which pads he had used to decipher the messages. G.C.H.Q. had records of the messages so they could be deciphered there. The results provided further confirmation that he was an active 'illegal' and must have access to a transmitter, which the security officers guessed must be in the Krogers' house in Ruislip.[2]

In January 1961, after patient surveillance, Houghton and Ethel Gee were arrested by Special Branch, having just passed secret material to Lonsdale, who was also arrested. The Krogers were then detained on suspicion and, after a difficult search, the Soviet-made transmitter was found, along with false passports and other incriminating evidence. The Krogers were soon identified as Morris and Lona Cohen, wanted by the F.B.I. for being accomplices of the Rosenbergs, who had been executed for espionage ten years previously. All five were convicted and sentenced to long terms of imprisonment.

The case appeared to show that while MI5 and the rest of the Whitehall security apparatus was slow to discover spies, it could work very professionally once it had been alerted. There was truth in that but MI5 officers concerned with the case, headed by Arthur Martin, harbour strong suspicions that, once again, they had been betrayed by some colleague, almost certainly at high level.

Because of the complexity of the Lonsdale-Kroger set-up and the K.G.B's long-term investment in it, the officers felt sure that they were servicing other agents apart from Houghton and Gee. During the trial Houghton, in the hope of being allowed to turn Queen's Evidence and secure a lighter sentence, had alleged that he knew of three other Russians serving as undercover case officers in Britain but his offer was not pursued, probably because it was felt that anyone so smoothly professional as Lonsdale would never have allowed Houghton to know any other members of the ring.

For technical reasons, which remain secret, the MI5 officers believed that the K.G.B. had been alerted to the fact that Lonsdale's one-time pads had been photographed. The radio traffic from Moscow to Lonsdale suddenly slackened and only messages concerning 'Shah' – Houghton's K.G.B. code-name – were sent to him. As one MI5 officer put it to me, 'There was definitely a leak to the Russians about the MI5 examination of Lonsdale's possessions.'

Hollis and a very few others in the top management knew that the investigators were keen to run the case for three months longer than they were eventually able to do in the hope of identifying other British members of the ring. If the K.G.B. had been made aware of this by an MI5 source monitoring the case for them, it would have felt that it had plenty of time to withdraw Lonsdale and the Krogers to safety, as they had withdrawn Maclean at the last minute. When Lonsdale was asked in prison, 'Were you taken by surprise when we arrested you?' he replied, 'We did not think you would do it so quickly' – a fair indication that he and the Centre knew that the ring was under suspicion.

A complete cessation of K.G.B. messages from Moscow to Lonsdale would have exposed the existence of the source of the warning, so a diminution, restricting the messages and their content to those already prejudiced, was in keeping with K.G.B. practice. From what the K.G.B. apparently knew, Houghton and Gee would be finished as spies anyway and, as they had worked only for money, there would have been no plans to withdraw them.

Lonsdale and the Krogers were arrested before they could have been spirited away because an unexpected event required MI5 to bring the operation to a premature close. In December 1960 Goleniewski, who had supplied the original lead, had suddenly alerted the C.I.A. to his urgent need to defect physically. On Christmas Day, when he was least likely to be missed, the 58-year-old 'Lavinia' arrived in West Berlin, complete with his mistress, and was quickly transferred to the safety of the U.S. He said that he had been driven to defect because someone in the West had warned the K.G.B. that there was a spy in the Polish U.B. acting for the C.I.A. He said that he believed that he was not under personal suspicion, at that stage, because the K.G.B. had asked him to seek out the spy, saying, 'We have evidence that there is a "pig" in your organization.' Goleniewski had been warned about the 'pig' – the K.G.B. jargon for a traitor – only a few weeks after the MI5 officers had identified Lonsdale.[3]

When MI5 was told of Goleniewski's defection it was argued that the K.G.B. would assume that he would blow Houghton and that the rest of the ring would then be at risk. It was therefore decided that Lonsdale and the Krogers must be arrested without further delay. The diminution of the radio messages from Moscow to Lonsdale had also convinced the investigators that any other agents in the ring had already been switched to some unknown Soviet controller.

An ingenious last-minute ruse to detect some of these agents was devised and involved an agreement with the police that the arrest of the five known spies should be kept secret for forty-eight hours. For some unknown reason the news leaked from Bow Street police station, to the fury of the Attorney-General. Lord Wigg, who was later to have close links with MI5, has described this misfortune: 'Information about Lonsdale's arrest was leaked and heaven knows how many members of the Soviet spy gang took the tip and got out of England.'[4]

In some way MI5 was able to discover that the K.G.B. 'resident' in London and his chief assistant knew of the arrest of the spies before it was made public. They were both watching television when the first news of the arrests was flashed on the screen and seemed quite unsurprised and unperturbed. They made no effort to contact the Embassy or anybody else, indicating that those who needed to know already did.

The investigating team was congratulated by Hollis, but when they reported their reservations and suspicions that the operation had been blown by a leak from inside MI5, soon after it had begun, he ridiculed the idea as totally absurd. Later evidence from the defector Golitsin was to support the belief that after MI5 had photographed Lonsdale's one-time pads, other spies under his control were transferred to another 'illegal' controller who has never been identified.[5]

In the biography which Lonsdale helped to write after his return to the Soviet Union and which was, apparently, ghosted by Philby on behalf of the K.G.B., it is claimed that he had immediately detected that the attaché case which he had left at the bank had been searched because he had 'laid a fairly simple trap for would-be snoopers'.[6] I suspect that this is K.G.B. disinformation to make what had been a leak from a most valuable source appear as MI5 incompetence. When the book was published in 1965 the leak-source was believed to be either Mitchell or Hollis, the latter being still in command. I know the precautions taken by the expert MI5 technicians who opened the attaché case and I find it hard to believe that they would have been deceived by any simple trap. The biography also claims that Lonsdale had agents in the Microbiological Research Establishment – the so-called Germ Warfare Station – at Porton on Salisbury Plain. This, too, may be disinformation to cause wasteful inquiries there and thereby help to protect real agents somewhere else. What is certain is that Houghton, who returned to Britain in 1952, following his recruitment in Warsaw, was handled by a previous controller, who passed him on to Lonsdale in 1956 and remains unknown.

MI5 might have learned more about the other spies involved with Lonsdale if they had paid more attention to claims made by Houghton, who stated in his own autobiography that 'they let the big fish get away'.[7] While his book was sensationalized to increase its sales, Houghton did have accurate information about his previous controller, whose code-name was 'Nikki', and about another, known to him as 'John'. He probably told MI5 some lies, after his offer to turn Queen's Evidence had been rejected, but all his information seems to have been dismissed far too readily suggesting, perhaps, that somebody in MI5 was not all that keen to expose the other Soviet controllers and any agents they might have been running.

The two Americans, Morris and Lona Cohen, who had disappeared from New York in 1950 and were wanted by the F.B.I. for questioning as communist associates of the Rosenbergs, had used false passports supplied in Paris by a New Zealand diplomat to enter Britain as the Krogers. They established a deep-cover legend as booksellers. The New Zealander, a Soviet agent called Paddy Costello, had also moved to Britain and became Professor of Russian at Manchester University. He was put under surveillance and was seen in contact with other Soviet agents, but firm evidence against him did not accrue until after the confession of Anthony Blunt, by which time Costello had died. The discovery of his complicity with the Krogers, however, led to inquiries in New Zealand where it was found that the K.G.B. had built up a network of informers after it had suspended operations in Australia following the Petrov defection, and two Soviet 'diplomats' were expelled.[8]

Lonsdale's biography contains one true statement, inserted to expose the falseness of a 'legend' leaked to the Press suggesting that MI5 had been alerted to Houghton's treachery by the discovery that he was spending more than he earned: 'The truth is quite different. MI5 were given the tip by a traitor who handed it over on a plate. Without that they would never have got me.' The traitor, of course, was Goleniewski.

The K.G.B. made great efforts to secure the release of Lonsdale, the first Soviet national to be convicted in Britain. They succeeded in April 1964 when he was exchanged for the Soviet-held British courier, Greville Wynne. The recent inclusion of Lonsdale's name in a Soviet publication about 'hero spies', along with those of Sorge, Rudolf Abel and Philby, suggests that he gave far more effective service than merely controlling Houghton and Gee.[9]

An analysis of how Goleniewski's espionage for the C.I.A. had leaked to the K.G.B. prior to his defection – the tip about the existence of a 'pig' '- was conducted separately by the C.I.A. and MI5. The MI5 analysis concluded that while there is strong evidence that Goleniewski eventually came under strong K.G.B. pressure in the U.S. and may have been forced into acting as a disinformation agent from 1963 onwards, he was genuine before the time of his defection and for some time afterwards, His main haul of information, in the form of hundreds of Minox camera films of secret Polish documents, had been hidden by him in a hollow tree which he had passed on his way home from his office in Warsaw. The C.I.A. was told of the tree's location as soon as Goleniewski reached the West and its man in Warsaw emptied it and sent the cache via the diplomatic bag to Washington, where it was seen to contain far more secrets than Soviet bloc intelligence would have been prepared to sacrifice to establish a false defector. It seemed that the Soviets had been made aware that there was a spy inside the Polish U.B. in the latter part of 1959 and were feeding doctored information into the U.B. as 'barium meals' to pinpoint the leaker. Some of this information was of a detailed kind, which could only have originated from a Western source inside an intelligence organization and under continuous K.G.B. control. Such a source could also have been responsible for the original warning to the K.G.B. of the existence of the 'pig'. The date of this warning coincided with the time when the C.I.A. had told MI5 the information which led to the detection of Houghton. Conforming with the usual requirements of security, the C.I.A. had not told MI5 anything about Goleniewski himself which, perhaps, saved him from arrest and execution. His flight may well have saved his life but it also put an end to his work in the most valuable of all espionage roles – that of an agent in place.

In anticipation of the inevitable onslaught from the Labour Opposition about the inadequacies of the security precautions which had enabled the Portland Ring to spy for so long, Macmillan set up an inquiry into all the circumstances, headed by Sir Charles Romer, a former appeal judge.[10] It discovered that Houghton had broken almost every rule in the spy's self-preservation code yet had operated for seven years under the noses of security men without being caught. He had been loud-mouthed and boastful and lived blatantly above his income, flashing wads of notes in pubs. He dropped enough hints to his wife to arouse her suspicions and she reported him to his superiors, who took no action. Four independent reports questioning his reliability had to be made before any effective action was taken. The circumstances revealed such appalling slackness that the Prime Minister declined to publish even an expurgated edition of the Romer report and restricted Parliament and the public to a brief summary.[11] This put the main blame on the Admiralty, but MI5 was criticized for failing to 'press an inquiry to a positive conclusion'. Hollis, who gave evidence to the Romer Committee, had taken over command of MI5 when the information casting doubt on Houghton's reliability had first reached it in 1956. He was held responsible by Macmillan for the slipshod lack of follow-up which had enabled Houghton to do so much damage over the ensuing years, as the Prime Minister indicated when he told Parliament that 'action had been taken to reduce to a minimum the chance of such a failure occurring again'.

Apart from that admission, Macmillan took the customary ministerial line of protecting his departments, and MI5 in particular, from admonishment in the House of Commons. He was also guilty of making a statement which he did not really believe. He told Parliament that there was no evidence to suggest that the information betrayed by the Portland spies had 'compromised more than a relatively limited sector of the whole field of British naval weapons'.[12] He said that he had every confidence that what the experts had told him was correct, but in his diary he wrote, 'Although I was assured by experts that no serious leakage had taken place...I had an uneasy feeling that either the Underwater Weapons Establishment served no very useful purpose or there were secrets of the highest possible importance.'[13] The latter hunch was correct. Years later Admiral Sir Ray Lygo, then Vice-Chief of the Naval Staff, told me that the leakages had been very severe and had taken years to rectify. Macmillan's statement was another example of the way ministers can be misled by officials over secret matters.

The Potential Value of Oversight

While the Romer Committee, an *ad hoc* body, produced a useful report which led to security improvements, it is reasonable to suppose that a standing oversight body with regular access to complex security and intelligence issues would have been more searching in its inquiries. From the Romer Committee's terms of reference it is unlikely that it concerned itself with the possibility that parts of the Lonsdale-Kroger network appeared to have escaped detection. An oversight body with on-going responsibilities, however, should have been active in that regard. The questioning of MI5 officers involved with the case would have revealed deep suspicion that it had been 'blown' and inquiries to discover the cause might have been productive at that stage.

The cavalier treatment of Houghton as a source might also have been thought worthy of examination, as might the circumstances of the leak from the police, which probably allowed other members of the K.G.B. network to escape.

G.C.H.Q.'s failure to detect and then locate the transmissions which the Krogers had been making for months, and possibly years, was, perhaps, worthy of deeper inquiry than it received, though the equipment they had used was of an advanced rapid-action type.

CHAPTER TWENTY-SEVEN

A 'Real Outsider'

BEFORE Goleniewski defected to America at Christmas 1959 he claimed that there was an active K.G.B. spy inside the British Secret Intelligence Service (MI6). The K.G.B. had told him that this spy had provided details of several agents being run by MI6 in Poland so that they could be neutralized. The spy had clearly worked for some time in MI6 headquarters because he had also provided the K.GB. with MI6's 'watch-list' for Poland, naming the known Polish Intelligence agents who should be kept under surveillance, in MI6's interests, if possible. The later defector, Golitsin, was to reveal that the spy's K.G.B. code-name was 'Diamond' but, as with Philby, MI6 could not bring itself to believe there was such a spy in its ranks and did nothing effective about the warning.

After Goleniewski had defected an MI6 officer was sent to interview him. The encounter was hilarious. The defector was so terrified that his interrogator might be 'Diamond' himself, sent to kill him on K.G.B. orders, that he insisted on being in one room while the MI6 man was in another, with an interpreter running between them. Goleniewski was contemptuous of the British failure to find 'Diamond' and ridiculed the suggestion that the MI6 documents he had seen and described had simply been filched from a safe in Brussels, as had been too readily and conveniently assumed. He then gave a further crucial clue to 'Diamond's' identity: he had operated for MI6 in Berlin.[1]

The evidence now pointed strongly to George Blake, an officer of Dutch-Egyptian origin who had joined the Secret Service in 1947, had taken a Russian-language course at Downing College, Cambridge, and had then been posted to Korea, where he had been captured and interned until April 1953. After recovery leave he had worked in the MI6 station in Berlin for four years, returning to London in 1959 to spend eighteen months at MI6 headquarters. At the time of his exposure he was attending an Arabic languages course at a Foreign Office school near Beirut.

At first the MI6 interrogators, still loath to accept that any of their colleagues could be a spy, believed that Blake had notched up too many apparent successes, ignoring the principle that the K.G.B. allows its agents to achieve some successes to maintain their credibility with their employers, but they could not escape the telling fact that the leakage of secrets had suddenly ceased when Blake had been posted to Beirut.

Blake was brought back to London on some pretext in April 1961 and after interrogation confessed to major acts of treachery, including the betrayal of more than forty MI6 agents and sub-agents, many of whom had probably been executed.[2]

He described how, as a Russian speaker, he had been involved in the planning of an Anglo-American operation, code-named 'Gold' by the Americans and 'Prince' by the British, to drive a 1,500-foot tunnel under the East-West boundary in Berlin to tap Red Army cables carrying signals and scrambled telephone conversations. The tunnel originated in the basement of a warehouse serving as a radar station and was fitted with highly sophisticated equipment to tape-record the communications so that they could be translated by a team in London. Blake confessed that he had warned the Soviets that the tunnel was to be built, at huge cost, before even a spit of soil had been dug. The enterprise cost about $25 million and produced nothing but a mass of carefully prepared misinformation, interspersed with some occasional accurate 'chickenfeed' to keep the operation going.

The Soviets permitted Operation Gold to continue for a year, partly to protect Blake, and then broke into the tunnel on 21 April 1956, making maximum propaganda use of this example of 'Western duplicity' just when the Soviet leaders, Bulganin and Khrushchev, were in London on their goodwill mission.

Blake admitted that he had betrayed everything he could about MI6, handing over documents to his controllers in the Soviet sector of Berlin, where he had permission to go in pursuit of his duties. He enabled the K.G.B. to kidnap prominent East Germans who had defected to the West. These included General Robert Bialek, a former East German security chief. His contempt for British security precautions in Berlin was demonstrated by his account of how he had photographed scores of secret documents. At lunchtime, when all offices containing secret papers had to be locked, he hid behind his desk to give the security guard the impression that the room was empty. He then had an hour and a half to do his photography without fear of interruption.

The internal inquiries following Blake's confession showed that he had damaged MI5's interests as well as those of MI6. For several months during his service in London he had acted as liaison man with MI5. One MI5 officer has told me how he was ordered by a senior man to tell Blake about a case he was running. He did so with great reluctance, and a most valuable incipient defector called Yudin, who had been a cipher clerk to the Soviet Military Attaché, was 'blown' with disastrous results, especially for Yudin. Blake was also able to give the Soviets the addresses of some of the 'safe houses' used by MI5 for operational and training purposes.

If there was a spy at high level in MI5 why did he fail to warn his Soviet controller that Blake had been detected and was to be arrested on his return to England? It would have been easy for the K.G.B. to have whisked Blake away from Beirut, as it was to do with Philby later. I asked the question and the answer given by MI5 officers was revealing, if only in a negative sense. The MI5 management was not told anything about the Blake case until shortly before his arrival in London, when it had to be involved to provide surveillance.[3] There had, therefore, been no time to warn the Soviets of Blake's position before he left Beirut.

Philby, who was working in Beirut, had no knowledge that Blake was a K.G.B. agent, nor did Blake betray Philby, as has been suggested, because the two spies had been recruited and operated by quite separate K.G.B. networks.

It was presumed that Blake would have consulted his Soviet contact in the Lebanon as a matter of routine before agreeing to return to London. If so, the Moscow Centre had no suspicions, or if they had they regarded it as safe for Blake to return in the belief that, provided he admitted nothing, he would be safe from prosecution, as was indeed the case. The Attorney-General at the time, Sir Reginald Manningham Buller, was to tell me later that there were fears that the prosecution of Blake might collapse if he suddenly withdrew his confession, claiming that it had been made under duress, because there were no effective witnesses who could have been brought to court.

Why Blake confessed remains a mystery. At first he denied the charges, and the menacing glances of his interrogator, Terence Lecky, at an imposing pile of files, seemingly full of evidence, had no effect. Then, at Lecky's last throw, he broke and admissions poured out of him. The case showed, as had that of Fuchs, that persistence can break down even the most unlikely suspect – a lesson which could and should have been applied to later cases, like those of Blunt and Long, had there ever been any real desire to prosecute them. No steps had been taken to secure the Attorney-General's agreement to offer Blake immunity in order to persuade him to retract his denials. Officers of both MI5 and MI6, who were his contemporaries, have told me that he was 'a real outsider, greatly disliked by his colleagues' and that this was the reason why there were no internal moves to save him from prosecution.

Steps bordering on the ludicrous were taken on behalf of the Secret Service to cover up the long-term presence of a most damaging Soviet spy inside it. A bare statement from Bow Street Court on 22 April that a Government official called George Blake had been committed for trial under the Official Secrets Act aroused only minor interest. My own interest was soon intensified, however, when Admiral Thomson, Secretary of the D-Notice Committee, sought my advice concerning a request from the Prime Minister, Macmillan, that he should write a confidential letter to all Fleet Street editors, news agencies and broadcasting services asking them to withhold certain information about the Blake case. It transpired that Macmillan wanted a security blanket on the fact that Blake had been an MI6 officer and on all details of the case, including any hint of links between MI6 and the Foreign Office. Thomson had been told that the purpose was to allow more time for MI6 to withdraw agents who had been jeopardized by Blake. I advised him that the argument was probably false and that Fleet Street would see it as a cover up device, for the 'blanket' was to be for all time, not just until the trial, almost all of which was to be in camera. He agreed but the Prime Minister, acting through MI5, insisted and the letter was sent. All it did was to stimulate newspaper interest and lead M.P.s to table questions about the attempted 'gag'.

Macmillan seemed unable to understand why the Press could not be silenced on the issue. He was to tell the Admiral, later, that the statement forced out of him in Parliament by a determined M.P. that the Secret Service was run by the Foreign Office was 'the most damaging admission' of his political career! Gentlemen and departments run by gentlemen cannot be associated with spies – at least not publicly.

There were public outcries at the unprecedented sentence of forty-two years' imprisonment imposed on Blake on 3 May 1961 but, by coincidence, it approximated to one year for each British agent whom he had betrayed.[4] It was deplored in MI5 as being unlikely to induce other traitors to confess but its main observable effect was in Parliament and in the newspapers where there were demands for an inquiry to explain what Blake could have done to have merited such a sentence, when Fuchs had received only fourteen years. When Macmillan refused an inquiry the Labour leader, Gaitskell, asked, 'How can we be sure that the plea for secrecy does not become a cloak to cover incompetence?'[5] Macmillan resolved the problem with the 'Privy Councillors' ploy' – an offer to give the facts to Gaitskell and any two Privy Councillors, under complete secrecy, so that they could reassure their side that the sentence had been deserved and the cover-up was justified. As a result the full disclosure made by Macmillan was passed on to me and made public in the *Daily Express*.

In spite of the savage sentence, Blake co-operated with MI5 while he was in prison. His sentence proved to be somewhat academic because after only six years he was 'sprung' from Wormwood Scrubs prison in 1966, reaching refuge in Moscow, where he still lives at the time of writing.

According to a former contemporary of Blake in prison, the spy was not subjected to any special security, my informant being a 'trusty' who often accompanied a warder outside the prison on various duties and so was able to take out letters for Blake. He also claimed to have supplied Blake with a radio and batteries.[6]

A former Home Office minister has told me of the amazement and chaos inside the department when news of Blake's escape was received. It was apparently the Home Office view that the escape had been planned by the K.G.B. which had made use of an Irish criminal to effect the break-out.[7] The escape had been so easy that MI6 was suspected of having rigged the circumstances but I can find no evidence to support this.

Neither is there any evidence whatever to sustain the theory that Blake was allowed to escape to Moscow because he had been 'turned' and had agreed to serve as a double agent for the British. He was very thoroughly investigated over many months on his arrival in the Soviet Union and the Kremlin's award of the Order of Lenin to him in 1970 seems to be evidence enough of the true focus of his loyalty.

The outcry in Parliament and the Press about the obvious security weaknesses which had enabled Lonsdale, Houghton, Gee and Blake to spy for so long until their existence was revealed by a chance defector forced the Government to take some public action. On 11 May 1961 it announced the appointment of an independent committee, headed by Lord Radcliffe, to review security procedures and practices with the object of improving them. The need for such a step was an indictment of those in charge of the existing security system and with the responsibility for maintaining its viability.

As part of yet another legend built up around Britain's known spies it has been generally assumed that Blake's story that he was converted to communism while being 'brainwashed' in a North Korean prison camp was true. In fact he told John Vassall, with whom he became friendly in prison, that 'in his early life he had thought of becoming a Roman Catholic priest but decided that the alternative course of the Communist world was the solution for him'. There is evidence that Blake's uncle, Henri Curiel, was involved in the founding of the Egyptian Communist Party and may have been a K.G.B. agent. So it seems that Blake was at least a dedicated pro-Soviet communist by the time he joined MI6 and there are suspicions in MI5 that he was recruited to Soviet espionage shortly afterwards, while attending the Russian-language course in Cambridge.

The Potential Value of Oversight

Had oversight existed in 1961 it might, conceivably, have spurred MI6 to take Goleniewski's information more seriously when first received. More positively, its existence might have deterred the Whitehall machine and the Prime Minister from making such futile and counter-productive efforts to hide the truth of the disaster from Parliament and the public when the facts were all known to the K.G.B. There are times when it is important to deny the adversary knowledge of how much a traitor has confessed but, after contact with this case for more than twenty years and with the benefit of discussions with officers close to it, I am satisfied that the prime purpose of the attempt to blanket the extent of Blake's treachery was to save face and embarrassment all round. It was no coinci-dence that while the security authorities encouraged widespread publicity for the Portland Spy-Ring case which, at face value, could be made to look a triumph for MI5, every effort was made to suppress the Blake case, which was an MI6/MI5 disaster.

CHAPTER TWENTY-EIGHT

A Defector in Place?

In April 1961 a Soviet Intelligence officer of the G.R.U., Colonel Oleg Penkovsky, approached MI6 through a British courier called Greville Wynne, who had commercial reasons for visiting Moscow and other Iron Curtain capitals. Though highly privileged himself, not only through his rank but through family contacts, Penkovsky claimed to be so disenchanted with the Soviet system that he had decided to undermine it by revealing all the military secrets he knew to the West. He had previously attempted to contact the C.I.A. and Canadian Intelligence but had been so blatantly obvious about it that he had been dismissed as a provocation agent – a plant whose purpose is to provide false information for some ulterior Soviet intention.[1]

It seems likely that the Canadians had reported Penkovsky's approach to MI6 and that, as a result, there had been an inquiry into his background. In any event, when MI6 became convinced that Penkovsky was probably genuine the C.I.A. decided to join forces in debriefing him and running him so that he became, effectively, a joint British-American agent from the start.

On 20 April 1961 Penkovsky, who had been given the MI6 code-name 'Alex', visited London as a member of a Soviet trade delegation. Under the G.R.U. cover of being Secretary of the Scientific Research Committee, his function was to build friendships with scientific and technical institutions which might prove of value to the Soviet Union. Instead, he submitted himself to a long and arduous debriefing session by an Anglo-American Intelligence team.

MI5 was involved, though only marginally, from the beginning because it was responsible for organizing the interrogation arrangements and the counter-surveillance precautions in the Mount Royal Hotel, where the Soviet delegation was staying.[2]

The main information supplied by Penkovsky in his early sessions concerned Soviet military missiles. He had brought with him some rocket training manuals and copies of training lectures.

He also gave the names of hundreds of G.R.U. Intelligence officers stationed in various parts of the world, though many of these were already known to MI6 and the C.I.A. Among them was that of Eugene Ivanov, the Assistant Naval Attaché at the Soviet Embassy in London, who was to become a central figure in the Profumo Affair.[3]

Penkovsky returned to London in July 1961 for a Soviet trade exhibition and was interrogated again at great length, as he was during a visit to Paris in September. He had been supplied with a camera to photograph documents, some of which he passed on to Wynne. In addition, the wife of an MI6 agent attached to the Soviet Embassy in Moscow, Mrs Rory Chisholm, agreed to serve as a courier and on fourteen occasions Penkovsky handed over films to her while pretending to speak to her children during walks in Moscow parks.

In October 1962, probably the 22nd, Penkovsky was secretly arrested by the K.G.B. in Moscow and Wynne was picked up while visiting Budapest on 2 November. Events quickly established that the K.G.B. had been aware of the activities of both men from a relatively early stage of the operation. By the beginning of 1962 both Penkovsky and Mrs Chisholm suspected that their meetings were under surveillance in Moscow, yet the spy continued to provide photographs and messages through dead-letter boxes. He even continued to pass material directly to Mrs Chisholm when they met at diplomatic parties, where he would also have been under K.G.B. surveillance. When Wynne was being grilled in the Lubyanka prison his interrogators played him a tape-recording of one of his conversations with Penkovsky. He recognized it as one of their talks in the Ukraina Hotel and it may not have been the first to have been recorded.

Had Penkovsky been 'blown'? The view of both C.I.A. and MI5 officers who reconstructed the case is that he had been.

It was judged unlikely that anyone in the C.I.A. or MI6 interrogation teams was either disloyal or indiscreet. When the MI5 involvement came to be examined it was found that when Hollis had learned of the requirement for MI5 to provide support of the case he had taken the unusual step of asking for the defector's real name and had been given it.

A defector in place anywhere behind the Iron Curtain is in such a dangerous position that only a very few people who need to know his real name are given it. Hollis had no need to know it, but he had insisted on being told it and nobody had felt able to withhold it from him. Later, when Hollis became suspect on other grounds, the fact that Penkovsky had belonged to the G.R.U. seemed significant, for a G.R.U. defector would pose a special threat to any British agent who had been recruited by the G.R.U. Whether Hollis was the culprit or not it is the view of senior C.I.A. officers, like James Angleton, that Penkovsky was betrayed by a British source, most probably in MI5.

There is, however, an alternative explanation for the leak. While people as senior as Angleton and Sir Dick White are convinced that Penkovsky was a genuine defector – White even told his staff that Penkovsky's information had staved off a nuclear war – there remains a fair possibility that he was a fake planted by the K.G.B., so that there was no need for anybody to betray him. His public trial and his execution in the Soviet Union, which may never have occurred, could have been part of a legend calculated to strengthen the belief of the Western intelligence services that what he had told them must be true – a necessity if Penkovsky had been part of a major disinformation exercise, as some analysts believe. The details of this alleged exercise are not relevant to this book, except in relation to the much later case of Geoffrey Prime, and have been described elsewhere.[4]

If Penkovsky was a K.G.B. plant then his over-confident carelessness, even when he knew he was under surveillance, is explicable. If he was a genuine defector, as most C.I.A. and MI6 officers concerned with the case still believe, then he may have been betrayed. It also remains possible, however, that his espionage was simply detected by the routine 'tradecraft' of the K.G.B., which ensures that it has enough watchers to keep all suspect foreigners under surveillance and may have followed Mrs Chisholm. It was later discovered, during further interviews in Wormwood Scrubs, that Blake had given her husband's name to the K.G.B. as a professional MI6 officer.[5]

Those who are convinced that Penkovsky was genuine rate him as the most productive Soviet Intelligence source of all time, and if they are correct the balance was firmly on the Western side, though the G.R.U. probably fed in some disinformation in the later stages of his activities. If he was a plant, however, the Kremlin reaped the major advantages on two counts. Firstly, his information seems to have furthered the Soviet objective of convincing the West that the Soviets were far behind the U.S. in nuclear missile technology, an exercise which has resulted in the recent American admission that they have achieved superiority, a situation which the U.S. is trying to remedy. Secondly, Penkovsky was involved in the Cuban missile crisis which appeared to have been a triumph of American firmness over Soviet threat but, in the longer term, has been more advantageous to the communists. In return for withdrawing Soviet nuclear missiles from Cuba in October 1962, the Kremlin received an undertaking from President Kennedy not to invade Cuba. Twenty-two years after that event Cuba is a client state of the Soviet Union, with Castro still in power, while the U.S. is under threat from intercontinental missiles based on submarines and in the Soviet Union.

The Potential Value of Oversight

The Penkovsky case raises an issue of principle concerning the extent to which oversight by a British body would be permissible in a joint operation with another ally. Presumably, the ally's permission would be necessary. Given the possibility of oversight on completion of the case, an independent body, assisted by its professional staff, might have been less determined to accept Penkovsky as genuine in view of the way he 'walked in' and his subsequent behaviour, which broke elementary conspiratorial rules. An MI6 officer has told me that after an interrogation in the Mount Royal Hotel in London Penkovsky demanded £1,000 in notes, claiming that the information he had already given was worth far more. When it was suggested that the colleagues with whom he had travelled to Britain would be suspicious if they saw him spending so much English money in London shops, his response was to ask, 'Whose neck will get it? Yours or mine?' He then spent all the money, chiefly on presents for senior officials and their wives.

The British and American officers involved in the case were so pleased with the information, documents and films they received from Penkovsky that the possibility that he might have been a fake was not considered until much later, by which time most of them were so committed to believing him to be genuine that their professional reputations would have suffered had they changed their minds or even expressed doubts. If Penkovsky's trial and execution was legend manufactured by the K.G.B.'s disinformation division, those British and American officers had a vested interest in preserving it. A detached oversight body with no personal commitments might have provided more balanced judgement, or at least have raised doubts, at an earlier date.

CHAPTER TWENTY-NINE

A Spy in the Labour Party

In 1961 information was received from a defector to the effect that Arthur Bax, who had been head of the Labour Party's Press Department for sixteen years, was in regular receipt of substantial sums of money from the Czech Embassy, which was extensively used by the K.G.B. as a surrogate agency for subversion and espionage. Bax was watched and it was noticed that he paid regular visits to the entrance hall of a block of flats where there were pigeon holes, for the occupants' letters. A Czech Intelligence officer was also in the habit of visiting the entrance hall and it was soon established that they were leaving envelopes for each other in pigeon holes allotted to flats which were empty.

Further surveillance established that Bax was part of a ring involving the New Zealander Paddy Costello who had provided the Portland Ring spies, Peter and Helen Kroger, with false New Zealand passports while he had been serving in the New Zealand Consulate in Paris in the 1950s.[1] Costello was also known to have provided an accommodation address for the wife of a Swedish diplomat known to be spying for the Soviet Union.

The evidence was put to Hollis, who opposed any attempted prosecution of Bax on the grounds that it would be difficult to prove that he had breached the Official Secrets Act and also because even an attempted prosecution would be extremely embarrassing to the Labour Party, which might soon be in power. Hollis also vetoed a suggestion that the Labour Party leaders, with whom Bax was on close terms of friendship, should be warned that he was passing on confidential information about them and their plans for the future. He argued that this would involve the organization in politics, to which he was averse.[2]

Bax was kept under some degree of surveillance: his telephone was tapped and his bank account was scrutinized at intervals. It was clear that he was continuing his paid contact with Czech Intelligence.

Nothing might have been done about Bax but for the fact that

George Brown (now Lord) wished to expose certain Labour M.P.s believed to be secret communists and sought my assistance in securing help from MI5. Hollis was unprepared to help for several reasons. He knew that the Prime Minister, Macmillan, would be opposed to it, if only on the grounds that it would not be in the interests of the Conservative Party for its opponents to appear to be cleansed of the communist taint. Neither he nor his colleagues were prepared to admit that MI5 had a list of secret communists because the surreptitious ways in which they obtained it and kept it up to date might become a matter for questions in Parliament, especially when some M.P.s and trade union leaders, who professed to have quit the Communist Party, were on it.[3] It also happened that some of the secret communists among the M.P.s whom Brown was after were valuable MI5 sources, providing information either directly or indirectly about the Labour Party and Labour M.P.s. Brown was therefore told that no information about M.P.s could be provided. However, at the suggestion of a case officer, he was fully informed about Bax. He was supplied with records of telephone conversations, bank statements and evidence of meetings between Bax and Czech agents. When confronted, Bax initially denied all the allegations but, fearing exposure, he then confessed to Brown that he had been passing information about internal Labour affairs for at least four years. He was allowed to resign on the grounds of ill health.[4] In this manner another case of treachery was covered up for many years to avoid political embarrassment.

Had Brown not approached MI5 it seems doubtful that Hollis would have taken any action even when Labour assumed office in October 1964, when Bax's access to information might have been of much greater value to Soviet bloc intelligence. Those of Hollis's former colleagues with whom I have discussed the Bax case believe that he would have continued to suppress it on the grounds he employed so frequently – that it was essential to avoid embarrassment, especially to ministers.

MI5 had been fortunate in learning about Bax's activities from a chance defector, but it had no such assistance regarding a much more important Soviet bloc agent who arrived in London in the late autumn of 1961 and was to spend four years there without raising any suspicions, while under the cover of completing a Ph.D. thesis at the London School of Economics. He was Hugh George Hambleton, a 39-year-old Canadian-born economist, who had been recruited to the K.G.B. in 1950 after meeting Victor Bourdine, an able 'Cultural Attaché' at the Soviet Embassy in Ottawa.[5] From 1956 until 1961 Hambleton had been a highly productive spy at N.A.T.O. headquarters, then in Paris, where he was cleared for access to 'Cosmic Top Secret' documents which he could claim he needed to consult for his work in the economic directorate. He photographed hundreds of them – some on specific orders from Moscow which had supplied him with the reference numbers of the documents – and passed them to K.G.B. controllers, either through dead-letter boxes or meetings held in Paris or abroad.[6] It would seem that Hambleton had one or more meetings with controllers in London because when he ultimately came to trial, in December 1982, one of the charges related to 21 December 1961.

Hambleton remained at the London School of Economics until 1964 when he returned, briefly, to Paris and then took an academic post at Laval University in Quebec. His later career, including a meeting with Yuri Andropov, then the K.G.B. chief, in Moscow will be described in Chapter 60.

CHAPTER THIRTY

The Numbers Game

LORD Radcliffe and the other four members of his committee set up to investigate existing security practices in 1961 after Blake was exposed produced their report, which was heavily expurgated, in April 1962.[1] As a witness to the committee I can testify to the intensity and depth of its inquiries. Its first conclusion overturned the main contention of the 1956 Privy Councillors' inquiry that British communists represented the biggest danger to security by stating that the main threat was posed by the professional intelligence services of the Soviet bloc. It also stressed the responsibility of MI5 by pointing out that counter-espionage against the activities of the Soviet bloc were all important. While it diluted its criticisms of MI5 and its Director-General, as all published reports almost invariably do, it clearly indicated that Hollis should have been more active in taking the initiative to improve security in Government departments, where it was weak.

What Hollis thought when he read the Radcliffe Committee's opinion that 'irregular sexual or marital relations' indicated a defect of character can only be imagined.

The committee's main recommendations, some of which remained secret, were to constitute the chief precautions against Soviet penetration for twenty years, but Lord Radcliffe's involvement in security affairs was far from finished, as will be seen.

There was one obvious and extremely important area of precaution which was omitted from the published report and if Radcliffe had made any recommendations in its respect they were ignored. I refer to the numbers of Soviet bloc intelligence officers posing as diplomats, trade delegates and other officials. Soon after the end of the Second World War the K.G.B. and G.R.U. decided to increase the number of their officers operating under diplomatic cover in the Western countries of major interest. This was to be achieved by the simple expedient of a steady growth in the number of accredited diplomats, trade delegates and other officials of whom fifty per cent or even more would be professionally trained agent-runners and

271

other subversives. Any comparable increase in the number of Western agents with diplomatic immunity in Moscow was to be resisted.

The purpose of the increase was two-fold. It would step up the espionage and subversion effort, and through sheer weight of numbers would saturate the Western counter-espionage defences. As up to twelve trained surveillance officers are needed to keep continuous watch on one suspected agent, even an increase of only three or four agents a year can exert a serious strain on an organization like MI5, which is kept as small as possible for political reasons.

The Soviet authorities were at pains to explain that the increases in the staffs of the embassies, consulates and trade delegations were essential because of the Kremlin's burning desire to improve general and cultural relations with Western countries and, though the real purpose was patently obvious, the ploy proved to be highly successful. In Britain, for example, the numbers steadily increased year by year with no effective opposition from the Foreign Office or any other Government department, even though spy trials and many unpublished incidents showed that scores of the so-called diplomats and trade officials were active agents doing all they could to undermine the nation. Why this was allowed to continue unchecked, which it was until 1971, has never been satisfactorily explained. Foreign Office officials feared 'reprisals' in Moscow, but the then Tory M.P. Anthony Courtney was probably correct when he claimed in Parliament and in public that the Kremlin seemed to have established some kind of moral ascendancy over the British Foreign Office.[2]

There is a story about a foreigner walking down Whitehall and asking an English passerby, 'Can you tell me on which side is the Foreign Office?' The answer was, 'On your side, you can be sure.' Diplomats, and especially ambassadors, tend to promote the interests of the country to which they are allotted, and this seems to have applied with special force to the Soviet Union.

The situation regarding the Soviet Union was exacerbated by the fact that while the Western embassies in Moscow had to employ Soviet civilians for various purposes, the Soviet embassies, consulates and other agencies in Western cities were staffed entirely by their own citizens, and even the doorman might be a K.G.B. officer.

I can find no evidence of any consistent complaint by MI5 to the Government about the steadily increasing burden, though it had to bear the brunt of it, with no proportionate increase in resources. MI5 officers complained to their departmental heads but the MI5 management, particularly under Hollis, seems to have been loath to complain to the Foreign Office or to the Home Office or Prime Minister, according to former officers whom I have questioned. This is made all the more peculiar by the fact that in 1958 Canada had given a lead which other Western governments should surely have followed. To its everlasting credit the security department of the Royal Canadian Mounted Police brought such pressure to bear on Canada's Foreign Department that the Russians were not only forced into accepting a ceiling figure for those with diplomatic immunity but were made to reduce the existing total.[3]

The man behind this salutary drive was James Bennett, the Welshman who had worked at G.C.H.Q. and was then running the R.C.M.P.'s Soviet counter-espionage desk. The number of R.C.M.P. officials available to counter the K.G.B. and G.R.U. agents among the fifty-eight Soviet 'diplomats' stationed in Canada was woefully small and the Russians were bent on improving their position by opening a consulate in Montreal. After putting up the customary resistance, based on the danger of offending the Kremlin, the Foreign Department gave way and the Russians were required to cut their diplomats to fifty-one, which was to be the ceiling figure. The Russians used every trick to avoid this action but the Canadians were resolute and applied ceiling arrangements to all the Soviet satellite countries, including Cuba. There was no effective retaliation in Moscow.

The R.C.M.P. informed the British and other close allies of this success but over the ensuing years there were no signs that any of them intended to follow the lead, to the continuing surprise of Bennett and his colleagues who quickly felt the benefit of their action. A former R.C.M.P. security officer has told me, 'There seemed to be a complete lack of will to reduce the expanding Soviet bloc establishments in the U.K. and this, I feel, was at the heart of their ineffectiveness because it gave the Soviet bloc Intelligence Service such freedom of action.'[4]

By 1962, when the Radcliffe Committee reported, the number of Soviet diplomats in London had risen to sixty-five compared with thirty-six British in Moscow, with a comparable imbalance in the number of Soviet trade delegates and other officials. Two years later there was to be a total of 218 Soviet diplomats and officials in London compared with 106 in Moscow.

I was not alone among journalists in drawing attention to this danger every time there was a spy case involving Soviet controllers who had posed as diplomats, though I was probably the most persistent. The Foreign Office was to take no action for a further nine years, by which time the number of K.G.B. and G.R.U. agents taking advantage of this unnecessary privilege had become so bloated that action became unavoidable. If it was right and necessary to reduce the numbers on security grounds in 1971 why had action not been taken sooner? Was it lack of pressure from the Director-General of MI5 which made it possible for the K.G.B. and G.R.U. not only to inflate its numbers but even to replace agents who had been expelled?

In the very month that the Radcliffe Committee reported, April 1962, Hollis received the first intimation, again from a chance defector to the C.I.A., of the existence of another Soviet spy, and possibly two, in the Admiralty. His reaction to this news, which he knew would be extremely unwelcome to the Government, is said to have been 'cool and calm'. What really went on in his mind will never be known.

CHAPTER THIRTY-ONE

A Defector Called 'Kago'

THE ever-present danger, which all Soviet spies fear most, is the possibility that someone who has worked in the Moscow headquarters and knows incriminating details about them may defect to the West. Such a person, able to provide leads to scores of Soviet spies and sub-agents in several countries, was Anatoli Golitsin, described to me by officers who debriefed him as short, squat and powerfully built with a round, heavy-jowled Slavic face and crew-cut hair. Like most defectors, he had a chip on his shoulder – the common belief that his talents were not being properly appreciated by the K.G.B. He had made himself unpopular by trying to put forward ideas to improve the service directly to Stalin. Though still only in his thirties he had decided to defect by the late 1950s.

Over the next few years he packed his undoubtedly outstanding memory with everything he believed could be of value to the West and made himself into a store of knowledge so vast that he was confident that he could not only sell it for huge sums but might even found an anti-Soviet intelligence organization, which he would run.

His opportunity to defect arrived in December 1961, shortly after he had been posted, as 'Major Klimov', to the K.G.B. station housed in the Soviet Embassy in Helsinki. He presented himself at the home of the C.I.A. station chief, handed over a batch of documents and announced, in reasonable English, that he wanted to defect with his wife and child. He explained that he had worked in the section of the K.G.B.'s First Chief Directorate that conducted intelligence operations against the U.S. and Britain. He had also served in the Information Department at K.G.B. headquarters – the Centre – collating intelligence for various Kremlin departments. More recently, he had specialized in processing reports from K.G.B. agents operating against N.A.T.O. headquarters.

Such 'walk-ins' are treated with great reserve because they can easily be false defectors or provocation agents, deliberately sent to create a diplomatic incident, but Golitsin poured out such a mass of highly sensitive secrets that the C.I.A. was quickly convinced that they were not 'chickenfeed', supplied to establish his good faith. He and his family were soon aboard an American ship. Because of the fear of assassination, his identity and whereabouts have been held stringently secret and no photograph of him seems to have been published.

In a 'safe house' in Maryland, not far from Washington, Golitsin proved his claims regarding his knowledge and the near-infallibility of his memory by picking out genuine secret N.A.T.O. documents, which he had seen in Moscow, from bogus reports interspersed among them.

News of the defection of such a valuable source was passed to MI5 and in April 1962 Arthur Martin was dispatched to the U.S. to debrief him on the issues of British interest. Golitsin, who was given the MI5 code-name 'Kago', was to reveal so much that his information is most easily digested if considered in the context of the exposures which resulted from it. The first was that of John Vassall, the homosexual spy in the Admiralty, who was sentenced to eighteen years' imprisonment in October 1962.

By the standard of Hollis's successor, Sir Martin Furnival Jones, that 'It is a scandal that a spy has got through the defences', the Vassall case was a scandal of appalling proportions.

Having met Vassall, I have to agree with Leo Abse, the M.P. who has made a study of the personalities of traitors, that 'he is as obvious a passive homosexual as ever I encountered. A few minutes' conversation with such a man and an awareness of his style of speech, manner and posture should have placed an alert security man on his guard.'[1] In spite of this, Vassall, then aged thirty, passed the positive vetting test before being sent to Moscow to work in the Naval Attaché's office in the British Embassy there in 1954. As Vassall was to write in his autobiography, 'The fact that an obvious homosexual should have been apointed to Moscow and allowed to remain there is a severe indictment of our Security Services and those responsible for them.'[2]

Desperately lonely, his plight and his susceptibility were quickly spotted by a K.G.B. agent called Mikhailski, who was among several Russians employed inside the Embassy. He arranged for Vassall to be shown the Moscow nightlife and he was soon deeply compromised at a drunken homosexual party, where photographs were surreptitiously taken and shown to him. Under threat of exposure he agreed to spy for Soviet Intelligence.

Vassall was positively vetted again after his return from Moscow in 1957, when he was transferred to the Naval Intelligence Division

Helping to rebuild East Berlin. Sonia as she was when she defected from Britain in 1950

Leon (Len) Beurton as he was when he married Sonia in Switzerland in 1940 to give her British nationality so that she could move to Oxford

Sonia in middle age, a successful author of political novels and memoirs, in which she admits much of her espionage, though muted by KGB security on most of it

Juergen Kuczynski, Sonia's brother, a major Soviet agent in Britain from 1936 to 1945. Among many other subversive activities he helped to recruit the atom spy Klaus Fuchs to spy for Russia

Above: MI5's Director of
Security, Roger Hollis (later
Sir) on a boat trip in West
Germany in 1951, wearing his
homburg hat, then a Whitehall
badge of seniority. His
noticeably hunched stance was
to be recalled by Gouzenko, the
defector whom he had
interviewed in Canada

Arthur Ewert, the dedicated
Moscow-trained communist
and Comintern official who
was friendly with Hollis and
Sonia in China
*(Institut für Marxismus-
Leninismus)*

Sir Roger Hollis, a studio portrait taken when he was Director General of MI5, the post he held for nine years
(Press Association)

The grave of Emily Browne in St Sepulchre's Cemetery, Oxford. It could have been one of the secret hiding places for messages used by Sonia when servicing the spy in MI5 code-named 'Elli'
(John Wolstenholme)

Igor Gouzenko, the Soviet GRU defector, and his wife, Svetlana, in 1975. He was so afraid of assassination by Russian revenge squads that the picture was not released until after his death in 1982. His eight children did not know his identity

HE WILL . . . HE WON'T . . . HE DOES
M.I.5 BOSS LEAVES FOR U.S.

Sir Percy Sillitoe, then head of MI5, and Arthur Martin, the MI5 case officer on the Maclean case, disguised as a chauffeur, at London Airport in June 1951 on their way to explain to the FBI and CIA how Maclean and Burgess had escaped to the Soviet Union *(London Express News Service and Weidenfeld & Nicolson Archives)*

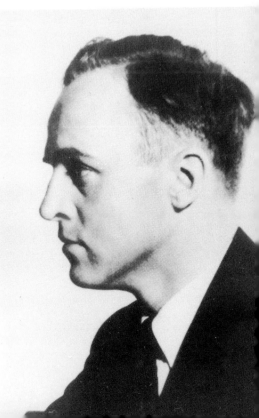

Michael Straight, the American who was recruited by Blunt at Cambridge to work for the Comintern and was to expose him as a traitor to the FBI, and later to MI5, in 1963

OPTIONAL FORM NO. 10
MAY 1962 EDITION
GSA GEN. REG. NO. 27

UNITED STATES G

Memorandum

TO : DIRECTOR, FBI (100-61929)   DATE: 7/17/63

Classified by

FROM : SAC, WFO (100-3644) (P) Declassification: OADR

SUBJECT: MICHAEL WHITNEY STRAIGHT

(OO:WFO)

ALL INFORMATION CONTAINED
HEREIN IS UNCLASSIFIED EXCEPT
WHERE SHOWN OTHERWISE.

The numerous references to STRAIGHT in WFO indices
have been reviewed. Nothing was found which could be described
as inconsistent or in conflict with the story related by STRAIGHT
and reported in referenced communications, nor was anything
observed which would make early reinterview of STRAIGHT necessary.

APPROPRIATE AGENCIES
AND FIELD OFFICES
ADVISED BY ROUTING
SLIP(S) OF

2 - Bureau
1 - Boston (Info) (RM)
2 - New York
1 - Richmond (100-3117) (Info) (RM)   100-61929-68
1 - WFO

REC-64   JUL 19 1963

JUL 23 1963

Typical page of an FBI document about Michael Straight released under the
US Freedom of Information Act. It shows the extent to which information is
blacked out, much of it at the request of British security, even though it had
only the low FBI classification 'Confidential'

Yuri Nosenko, the younger man on the right, photographed with a Soviet delegation in Geneva in 1964, after which he defected to the US. While some doubts persist, he was almost certainly a false defector – a KGB plant sent to the West to confuse the security authorities there and negate the information supplied by Golitsin and other true defectors *(Central Press)*

Charles Howard Ellis in old age after he had confessed to supplying secrets to the Germans while serving in MI6. He was also suspected of having been forced into spying for the Russians, but always denied it and nothing has yet been proved

James Bennett, the Welshman who became chief counter-espionage officer for the Royal Canadian Mounted Police and was later accused by some of his colleagues of being responsible for serious leaks to the KGB. He was cleared, and there is now official belief that the leaks could have originated in MI5

of the highest security classification to the offices of the First Lord of the Admiralty, the First Sea Lord and others. He was quickly in touch with a Soviet controller, Nikolai Korovin, the K.G.B. London 'resident' himself, passing a mass of information of the greatest interest to the Soviets. After a year in Naval Intelligence, Vassall was transferred to the office of the Civil Lord of the Admiralty, Thomas Galbraith, with whom Vassall became more friendly than his position would seem to have warranted.

Vassall had a flat in Dolphin Square, large enough for it to become the London residence of successive Directors of Defence Intelligence, took expensive holidays abroad and was clearly living beyond his means – on money supplied by the Soviets. Nobody in authority appeared to notice.

After two years in Galbraith's office, Vassall was transferred to the Military Branch of the Admiralty where the papers crossing his desk were of much greater interest to the K.G.B.

During the five years when Vassall was regularly passing copies of secret documents to the Soviets in London, MI5 suspected nothing. There is no reason to think that the security authorities, either in the Admiralty or MI5, would ever have been alerted to Vassall's massive treachery but for the defection of Golitsin, who was proving himself to be the most valuable source, to date, on K.G.B. activities in the West.

Golitsin gave Arthur Martin ten definitive allegations – known as 'serials' – about penetration of the British security and intelligence services by the K.G.B. One of them described the recruitment in 1955 of a man in the Naval Attaché's office in the British Embassy in Moscow. This recruitment had been made under the supervision of General Oleg Gribanov, who was responsible for internal intelligence operations in the Soviet Union. Golitsin said that Gribanov, whom he described as 'a ruthless little Napoleon', had insinuated an agent called Mikhailski into the British Embassy as an interpreter. This agent had been involved in the recruitment of a spy, whose name Golitsin did not know. During his service in Moscow the spy had kept the K.G.B. informed about documents passing through his office, as he was a competent photographer. Then, after returning to London, he had held a much more productive post in Naval Intelligence. Golitsin believed that the spy was still active, being run by K.G.B. agents posing as diplomats in the Soviet Embassy.[3]

The defector had not known that the spy had been recruited through homosexual blackmail but MI5 should, on the evidence given to them, have been able to pinpoint Vassall. Instead, the best MI5 could do at that stage was to put him on a short list of four possible suspects. One MI5 officer argued that he should be at the bottom of the list for investigation because he was known to be a devout Anglo-Catholic and seemed to be of high moral character. In fact, Vassall was a Roman Catholic. He had also been trained as a photographer while in the R.A.F. during the Second World War.

The second of Golitsin's 'serials' regarded as needing urgent attention related to another alleged naval spy, also recruited in Moscow but operating at a much higher level. He said that shortly before he had left K.G.B. headquarters in Moscow he had seen photocopies of three highly secret documents about naval plans. One, which was stamped Top Secret (Atomic), had dealt with the organization of a base in the Clyde for American Polaris missile submarines. Another concerned the disposition of N.A.T.O. warships in the Mediterranean, while the third was a report of a secret naval committee. The three original reports were withdrawn from the Admiralty files, interspersed at random among a pile of others and then shown to Golitsin. He picked out the correct ones without hesitation.[4]

A separate investigation was set up and the only suspect was a senior naval officer, now dead, who eventually became an admiral. The MI5 officers, led by Martin, wanted to interrogate him in the hope that he might confess, but Hollis refused to allow him to be approached. He argued that the evidence was too thin, that the suspect was then in a post where he could do little further damage and was within two years of retirement. He let it be known that a confession, followed by a court martial or civil prosecution of such a high-ranking officer would do great damage to the Navy and to American and N.A.T.O. relations. When Martin suggested that the Admiral might be offered immunity to prosecution Hollis remained adamant that he must be left alone.

As later developments were to indicate, the K.G.B. had realized that Golitsin knew enough to lead to the exposure of Vassall and assumed that he would have informed the C.I.A. abut the spy's existence. The arrest of the Portland Spy-Ring in January 1961 had also necessitated an interruption of Soviet espionage in London. Vassall had, therefore been instructed by his Soviet controller, Nikolai Karpekov, who had replaced Korovin, to cease spying until further order, and his camera had been taken away from him. As a result no progress was made with the case until June 1962 when MI5 was given another, more definite lead, by a further windfall – the defection of a K.G.B. officer called Yuri Nosenko.

While remaining at his post as a K.G.B. officer in Moscow and a member of the Soviet delegation on disarmament which occasionally visited Geneva, Nosenko began to feed information to the C.I.A., which passed relevant parts of it to MI5. Known to the British by the code-name 'Weary', Nosenko confirmed that the spy had been recruited under General Gribanov's personal supervision, and was 'a pederast and had been acquired by homosexual blackmail'.[5] He added that the spy 'had access to the highest level in the British Navy and gave us all N.A.T.O. secrets, including documents which had to do with a Lord'. By that time surveillance had revealed that Vassall was a practising and promiscuous homosexual, with various partners, including M.P.s, visiting his flat. As he also worked in the office of the Civil Lord of the Admiralty, he quickly became the prime suspect. He might still have escaped prosecution but for the fact that he had suddenly been instructed by his controller, Karpekov, to resume spying on an even bigger scale. He had been given back his special camera and told to produce as much secret material as possible, as Vassall has confirmed to me personally.[6]

While Vassall was in his office his flat was searched. Cameras for copying documents were found in a bureau and cassettes of exposed film were discovered in a secret compartment in a small bookcase, which the Russians had provided by leaving it in the luggage office at Victoria station and giving Vassall the ticket.[7] The film showed copies of more than 170 classified documents, and this was a single haul, which gives some indication of the extent of the haemorrhage of secrets during the seven years since Vassall had first turned traitor.

Vassall was arrested on 12 September 1962, confessed, and in the following month was sentenced to eighteen years' imprisonment, of which he was to serve ten.

When interrogated in prison Vassall was co-operative. He described how he had met his controllers in suburban avenues, having gone there by Underground railway, always taking several trains and doubling back on his tracks. He told how Karpekov had suddenly told him to stop spying, without any explanation, and had then just as precipitously reactivated him. He also convinced his interrogators – as he has since confirmed to me – that he had never seen two of the Top Secret N.A.T.O. documents mentioned by Nosenko. The documents had never, in fact, reached the office in which Vassall had been working at the time of their distribution. It therefore seems possible that Nosenko pointed the identifying finger at Vassall, who was already thought by the K.G.B. to have been heavily prejudiced by Golitsin's information, in order to protect the more valuable, higher-ranking naval spy. The near-simultaneous reactivation of Vassall by his controller, which ensured that he would be caught, was in keeping with the ruthlessness of the K.G.B. when a choice has to be made concerning the safety of its agents. The more expendable will always be 'burned' to protect the more productive. MI5 had certainly been induced, by Nosenko's information, to believe that Golitsin must have been mistaken and that all the treachery had been perpetrated by Vassall. The officers asked Hollis again for permission to interrogate the suspect naval officer but he refused and declared the case closed. In the interim he had ordered that all the papers referring to the case should be destroyed – a most unusual procedure.[8]

Though Karpekov remained listed on the roll of Soviet Embassy staff supplied to the Foreign Office until 1964 – a common type of Russian 'inaccuracy' – he had, in fact, left for Moscow shortly before Vassall was arrested, just as his predecessor, Korovin, had disappeared before the arrest of Houghton. Both men appear to have been warned in advance by some well-informed source.

Contrary to his behaviour with regard to the suspect naval officer and to other Establishment figures like Philby and Blunt, Hollis was strongly in favour of Vassall's prosecution. If Hollis was a Soviet agent why should this have been? In the first place, he had little option when the evidence became so firm and the C.I.A. knew all about the case, but a further explanation is offered by what has since become known about the defector, Nosenko. He has turned out to be, almost certainly, a K.G.B. plant sent to discredit the information supplied by Golitsin and used later to muddy the waters in other important areas, including the implication of the K.G.B. in the assassination of President Kennedy.[9]

Under hostile interrogation in the U.S., where he was held prisoner for many months, Nosenko admitted that he had lied about being a personal friend of Gribanov and about his rank in the K.G.B. and other matters. More significantly, he could give no acceptable explanation of how he knew the details about Vassall, as he had never served in a K.G.B. department that gave him access to such extremely secret knowledge. It has therefore been concluded by MI5 officers that before 'defecting' he had been instructed to identify Vassall. Karpekov, acting on instructions from the Centre, had then ensured that Vassall would be arrested and blamed for all the naval espionage. The prosecution and conviction of the Admiralty clerk suited the K.G.B.'s purposes by effectively ending the MI5 inquiry into the more important naval suspect.

Hollis's behaviour throughout the Vassall case was later to strengthen the suspicions of certain MI5 officers that he had been leaking information to the K.G.B. In May 1962, following Martin's return from America, Hollis had been told of the defector's allegation that there were two Admiralty spies and knew that MI5 inquiries were proceeding on those lines. In the following month Nosenko provided evidence 'out of the blue' which indicated that the Centre in Moscow knew that MI5 was conducting two separate investigations. Such information could have reached the K.G.B. only from a high-level source because very few people knew of the suspicions about the naval officer.

It is now almost certain that Nosenko's information, which caused the investigation into the naval officer to be halted – and, later, on Hollis's firm instructions, to be dropped – was false and had been deliberately supplied to him by the Centre for that purpose.

It could be significant that after the Vassall case was concluded Hollis made a point on at least two occasions of attributing its 'success' to Nosenko and not Golitsin. Yet Hollis knew that his investigating officers had serious misgivings about the integrity of Nosenko, whose prime function seemed to be the denigration of Golitsin, who had proved his genuineness by the unprecedented number of leads he had given which had been shown to be true. Hollis also knew that Nosenko was under deep suspicion as a fake in the C.I.A.

Almost at the same time that Nosenko offered his services to the C.I.A. in Geneva in 1962, another K.G.B. officer working under cover in the U.N. headquarters in New York volunteered to be a spy for the F.B.I. This man, an agent in place, was avidly accepted by Hoover, who felt starved of prime source information as most defectors went to the C.I.A. He was given the code-name 'Fedora' and, for more than ten years, fed the F.B.I. a mass of information which he claimed to have obtained surreptitiously from the K.G.B. when in fact he had been deliberately provided with it. 'Fedora's' disinformation was highly effective in undermining Golitsin's credibility and bolstering Nosenko's. It has recently been admitted by the F.B.I. that 'Fedora' was a fake and he is now safely back in the Soviet Union. It follows, almost automatically, that Nosenko was a false defector serving a similar purpose.

If Hollis was a spy he would have had a vested interest in supporting both Nosenko and 'Fedora', had he known them to be fakes. In the event of his becoming suspect while they were still in their K.G.B. jobs they could have been approached to try to secure information about him from K.G.B. records. The result would have been a firm negative.

There can be little doubt that once Vassall had been exposed by Golitsin and his confession became inevitable, the case proceeded in a way which suited the K.G.B. In spite of this, successive prime ministers, including Mrs Thatcher, have been induced to list it as an MI5 success. Vassall, who knows the extent and nature of the material he passed to the Soviets, says that Mrs Thatcher's description of his case as an MI5 success was 'fatuous'. 'It was a British security disaster,' he told me.[10]

Though the recommendations of the Radcliffe Report were barely being implemented Macmillan felt it necessary to allay public and Parliamentary concern over the Vassall case by setting up, on 23 October 1962, yet another investigative committee, headed by Sir Charles Cunningham.

Under pressure from the Labour Opposition, which attacked the Macmillan administration for the security failures which had permitted Vassall to operate for so long without check, the Government also agreed to an inquiry into the case, not because it conceded that any failures had occurred but to clear the names of two ministers, Lord Carrington, the First Lord of the Admiralty, and Thomas Galbraith, previously the Civil Lord, who had been accused of negligence by certain newspapers.

A three-man tribunal, headed by Lord Radcliffe, was set up to investigate the case – in public as far as possible. Hollis, as Director-General of MI5, was deeply concerned, not only because of aspects of the Vassall case which were still secret, but because of other secret factors. Golitsin was in Britain, Philby was in the process of being investigated in Beirut, partly on Golitsin's evidence, and MI5 was deep in the case which was to assume international importance as the Profumo Affair.

In a *Daily Express* article I had revealed that Vassall had been betrayed by a Soviet defector and, while the Tribunal could not avoid calling me as a witness, a deal was struck between Hollis and Radcliffe which ensured that I would not be pressed into revealing any more details about Golitsin while in the witness stand.[11] It was a sensitive situation which Radcliffe handled brilliantly, securing my evidence without forcing me into having to refuse to name sources, a situation in which other journalists found themselves and as a result of which two of them went to prison for contempt of court.

The Vassall Tribunal published its findings on 24 April 1963 and Parliament debated them on 7 May.[12] The security services and the Embassy staff in Moscow came in for severe criticism, which the Government and backbench M.P.s formerly associated with those services did their best to counter. The only constructive result was a suggestion by Macmillan which eventually resulted in the creation of the Security Commission. The gross inequality of the number of Russians stationed in London, which was 218, compared with the 106 British officials in Moscow was stressed, as was the strain it put on Britain's counter-espionage resources, but nothing was done about it.

The Vassall case, with all the additional publicity of the Tribunal, did not help the Tory cause in the run-up to the 1964 general election, especially when it was followed so smartly by the Profumo scandal. According to information given to me by Lord Carrington, Macmillan seemed to have a premonition that the Vassall case, which, through the Tribunal, alienated the Press when the two journalists were sent to prison, would be a political disaster. When Carrington first informed his Prime Minister, rather triumphantly, that Vassall had been arrested, Macmillan had reacted by declaring, 'Oh, that's bad news! Very bad news! You know, you should never catch a spy. Discover him and then control him but never catch him. A spy causes far more trouble when he's caught.'[13] He put this opinion on record in a different way by writing in his diary, no doubt with the Birch Grove pheasant shoot in mind, 'Unhappily, you can't bury him out of sight, as keepers do with foxes.' He might have added 'and as the K.G.B. does with spies'.[14]

These comments suggest that Macmillan, like the rest of the Whitehall-Westminster leadership, was in favour of granting immunity to spies to avoid the political and personal embarrassment of prosecutions. But while Hollis and others in the secret services limited this huge privilege to carefully selected traitors, Macmillan would, at least, have applied it to all as a matter of principle rather than of expediency.

Vassall has become the classic example of the spy who, while of lowly rank, can inflict enormous damage because of the excellence of his access to secret information. The severity of the damage assessment conducted by the Admiralty was to some extent mirrored in the length of Vassall's sentence but was largely concealed, partly on the usual security grounds but also to save face both in the Admiralty, where appalling security had enabled Vassall to take hundreds of documents to his flat to photograph, and in MI5, which carried overall responsibility for the failure to detect the massive leakage of secrets. The report of the Cunningham inquiry apportioned modest blame for the Vassall case among a few low-level officials while praising MI5![15]

After twenty years, and following discussions with officers concerned with the case, I am in no doubt that the recruitment and running of Vassall was a major triumph for the K.G.B. He provided information of the highest value to the Soviet defence chiefs in their successful drive to expand and modernize the Red Navy. It enabled the Soviets to develop early counter-measures to British and N.A.T.O. weapons advances, to which Vassall's documents alerted them. They were able to see the areas where the Royal Navy was taking chances, because of financial limitations, and to capitalize on them. This is one of the reasons why the Soviet Union has such a lead today in long-range anti-ship missiles, an advantage which has caused the British Sea Lords great concern. Through Vassall's activities alone the penetration of the Admiralty, regarded as among the most secret of all British institutions, was deep and severe, and if the second, more important, spy indicated by Golitsin existed, then it was devastating.

After any spy case a stable-door locking operation is performed in the hope of rectifying the weaknesses and errors which existed before. Following the reports of the Cunningham Committee and the Vassall Tribunal various improvements were supposed to have been made to the positive vetting procedures and to security in the British Embassy in Moscow but they were to prove to be of limited value. The Soviet homosexual who had suborned Vassall was sacked, but Soviet agents continued to pass through the vetting process with ease and the K.G.B. continued to intrude its agents among the Soviet staff employed in the Embassy. This was how a woman employed as a domestic servant seduced the Ambassador, Sir Geoffrey Harrison, in circumstances set up by the K.G.B. so that he could be photographed and compromised so deeply that he had to be withdrawn.[16]

The Potential Value of Oversight

While the existence of oversight would probably have exerted no effect on the Vassall case it might well have occasioned a more positive investigation of the alleged naval spy who, from the circumstances, would appear to have been more important to the K.G.B. than Vassall. Hollis might have been more diffident about preventing the interrogation of the naval officer. Though the evidence might have been thin, an interrogation was clearly demanded and, being under naval discipline, the officer could have been required to submit to it. Hollis's insistence that the case could be discarded because the officer was near retirement meant that no damage assessment was ever done. It is not impossible, had Hollis taken the same line in spite of the existence of an oversight group, that his own behaviour might have raised suspicion at an earlier stage than it did.

Where oversight could certainly have been beneficial would have been in ensuring that the lessons which should have been learned from the Vassall catastrophe were put into more positive effect.

CHAPTER THIRTY-TWO

Philby's Defection

HOLLIS's colleagues in MI5 were to describe 1963 as 'the year that the roof fell in'. Shortly before it began, the agency's reputation appeared to be enhanced when, in December 1962, Miss Barbara Fell, a civil servant of twenty-three years' standing, who was then Acting Controller of the Overseas Division of the Central Office of Information, was prosecuted for passing information from Government reports to the Press Counsellor at the Yugoslav Embassy. The Yugoslav had been her lover for several years and, on interrogation by MI5, she admitted her folly. As was made clear at the trial, the information was all of low classification – 'confidential' – and would eventually have been released to the foreign as well as the domestic Press. Further, she had been motivated not by ideology or money, but solely by affection. While she had subjected herself to the possibility of being photographed so that she might have been blackmailed into trying to secure more valuable information, this, apparently, had never happened.

The main evidence against her, apart from her admissions, consisted of monitored telephone conversations which may have been routine or instituted after a tip from a defector.[1]

In the circumstances many in Whitehall felt that dismissal, the loss of pension rights and the publicity would have been punishment enough but Miss Fell was sentenced to two years' imprisonment, the maximum for a 'misdemeanour' under the Official Secrets Act. Even in MI5, starved of success, some officers regarded this as unduly severe as there had been no damage to British security, but Hollis's view, given to an officer who asked him for it, was that he 'did not object to cases which showed that MI5 was on the ball'.[2] Not surprisingly, some MI5 officers still refer to the Barbara Fell case as the 'barbarous Fell case'.

It so happened that by the time Miss Fell was sentenced Hollis had taken highly secret steps to ensure that his old MI6 colleague, Kim Philby, a cold, calculating traitor who had betrayed masses of highly classified secrets during the war, should remain free from prosecution or public censure. Indeed, he would have been encouraged and assisted to pose as a loyal and much maligned public servant.

Following the 'whitewash' of Philby little had been done on his case. MI6 regarded it as conveniently closed and in MI5, Martin, the only figure who might have attempted to keep it alive, had been serving in Malaya. In April 1962, however, MI5 was forced to devote some effort and resources to it when Golitsin told Martin, then back in headquarters, about what the K.G.B. called the 'Ring of Five' – five British-born spies who had all been recruited at Cambridge before the war and had been insinuated into positions giving them access to secret information. He named Maclean and Burgess as two of the five and he knew that a third, who had been code-named 'Stanley', had first alerted the two to their danger. He was unable to identify Philby as 'Stanley' but he did reveal that certain K.G.B. operations against Arab states had involved 'Stanley' in the late 1950s. Until then MI5 had not appreciated Philby's role in the Middle East, nor did it know that he was back in MI6's employment.

When Martin returned to London, after interviewing Golitsin in the U.S., he suggested that Philby should be questioned again but Hollis insisted on having more evidence before he would move. Contrary to statements by apologists for Hollis that he pursued the Philby case with vigour, he did the reverse.[3] The K.G.B., on the other hand, moved with speed, as later inquiries were to show.

In May 1962 a K.G.B. officer of special significance travelled from Moscow to Beirut. He was Yuri Modin and it was the first time that he had moved out of the Soviet Union since his return there following his part in organizing the defection of Maclean and Burgess in 1951. There is little doubt in the minds of the MI5 officers who later learned of his visit that he saw Philby and warned him about Golitsin's statement. It is possible that the K.G.B. Centre had simply assumed that Golitsin would reveal what he knew about Philby and sent Modin over purely because of this, but as the visit took place so soon after the information had reached MI5 headquarters, a deliberate leak from that source to the K.G.B. would seem more likely, especially in view of what was to happen a few months later.

Failing another K.G.B. defector with knowledge of 'Stanley' it seemed unlikely that further progress could be made but, quite by chance again, more definite evidence emerged as a result of an event in Israel which had been concealed until the publication of *Their Trade is Treachery*. Later in 1962, Flora Solomon, Philby's old friend who was still living in London, was visiting the Weizmann

Institute, Israel's science research centre. Other people were present when, as she has since confirmed in her memoirs, she expressed anger at the way Philby was slanting his articles in *The Observer* against Israel and in favour of the most anti-Jewish Arabs.[4] Among the visitors who heard her outburst was Lord Rothschild, a wartime member of MI5 who retained contacts with the organization, as most former officers do. Mrs Solomon records that she exclaimed to Rothschild: 'How is it *The Observer* uses a man like Kim? Don't they know he's a communist? You must do something.' My informants, who were officers who had been involved with the Philby case, have assured me that she went further and said that Philby worked for the Russians. They already knew that he had been a communist. Rothschild urged her to repeat her statement to the British security authorities, and on her return to London, having been promised total confidentiality, she visited Lord Rothschild's flat where she was introduced to an MI5 officer. She was later questioned at length by Arthur Martin, during which she recalled that in 1937, during one of Philby's brief trips back to London while reporting the Spanish Civil War, he had confided to her that he was doing 'important work for peace' – the usual Comintern approach in an attempted recruitment – and urged her to join him. Mrs Solomon claims that she responded by saying that she had enough to do working for the persecuted Jews. My sources, however, insist that while she declined to commit herself she assured Philby that if ever he was desperate he could always come to her for help.

At that stage, as Mrs Solomon admits in her book, she knew that Philby had been a communist at Cambridge and had realized that he must still have been involved in 1938 when he told her that he was 'in great danger'. She told Martin that her suspicions had been strengthened in 1940 after the fall of France, when Philby had assured her that the fascists would never be beaten without Russia's help. She also knew that Philby had worked in Intelligence during the war and had moved to the Foreign Office, though she said she was unaware that he was in MI6.

Mrs Solomon excuses her failure to volunteer her knowledge about Philby earlier on the grounds that every public statement pointed to Philby's innocence. Yet no further evidence had accrued to her between the 'clearance' of Philby in Parliament in 1955 and her outburst in Israel in 1962. It is a sad commentary that, having enjoyed such a satisfying life and career in Britain, she did not attempt to expose Philby until he was seen to be acting against the interests of Israel. In view of the publicity given to the Philby case in 1955 and his press conference claim to have no connection with communism, Mrs Solomon could hardly have been unaware that he was lying.

Mrs Solomon reveals in her memoirs that she was also interviewed later by Mossad, the Israeli Intelligence Service, which was especially interested in any operations by Soviet agents like Philby to assist Arab subversive activities. She claims that, as a result, there was a leak to an Israeli newspaper which I observed and which was the source of my knowledge about her connection with Philby's exposure to MI5. Nothing could be further from the truth. The leak in the Israeli newspaper was the result of information which I gave to an Israeli journalist.

News of the windfall in the Philby case was given to Hollis. Whatever his immediate feelings might have been he did not betray them in any way, taking it with his usual deadpan calmness. He conceded that there was now hard evidence with which to confront Philby and, perhaps, to force a confession.[5] I have established from two of the people involved in the early deliberations that there was no intention in Hollis's mind, or in the minds of any of the few who knew of the development, of prosecuting Philby, no matter what crimes he might admit to. It was made clear to the officer who eventually confronted Philby that the purpose of the exercise was to induce him to reveal his past activities and his contacts so that a damage assessment could be made and possible 'repairs' effected. Philby could be far too dangerous to too many people in the witness box, and a trial, with all its publicity, would be too embarrassing for all concerned, especially in view of the 'clearance' given in Parliament by Macmillan, who was still in office as Prime Minister. Nor was there ever any suggestion that Philby might be kidnapped in Beirut and brought back to Britain forcibly, all use of violence by the secret services having been outlawed by that time.[6]

As Philby had been an MI6 officer, White was involved in all the decisions and it was agreed that following the sentence of forty-two years' imprisonment passed on George Blake after his confession, there was no likelihood that the wily Philby could be induced to return to London for initial interrogation, which would have to be done in Beirut. It was realized that Philby could simply refuse to be questioned, much less to confess, so it was decided to offer him the inducement of immunity to do so.

In this move, which then appears to have been unprecedented, Hollis was the effective motivating force, though it may have been first suggested by some other officer. The Attorney-General, the late Sir John Hobson, was formally approached and it was suggested that if Philby would provide checkable proof that he was prepared to co-operate fully with the security services he should be

Soviet controllers, Philby was asked if he could identify 'Otto'. He claimed that while 'Otto' had never revealed his true name to him he had learned that it was Arnold Deutsch, a Comintern agent, whom he had met in Vienna. Philby was lying again for, while it was known that Deutsch had moved to London in 1934, following Philby's return from Austria, he was definitely not 'Otto'.[12]

Philby offered to write a summary for Elliott to take back with him to London but declined to accept the immunity proposal, saying that he needed more time to think about it. What he usually meant when he asked for more time was time to consult his Soviet controller to find out what Moscow would like him to do.

It so happened that such a controller was present in Beirut and waiting to be consulted. Modin had returned to Beirut shortly before Elliott's arrival, presumably after being alerted about Flora Solomon's evidence and the decision to send Elliott out to question Philby about it. This evidence was, of course, a much more dangerous threat than the relatively vague information previously supplied by Golitsin. The K.G.B. would not have relied on its local station chief to warn Philby for that would have told him that there had been a leak to Moscow, probably from a source in London, and that source would then have been at further risk of exposure one day.

Modin was the obvious choice for the task and there is little doubt in MI5 that he had brought an escape plan for Philby with him and that he stayed on to supervise it.

The day after his 'confession' Philby gave Elliott a two-page typewritten statement and signed it but repeated that he needed a few more days before making up his mind about returning to Britain. With White's permission, Elliott then told the C.I.A. about the confession, speaking directly to James Angleton in Washington. Only then was the C.I.A. mission in Beirut told what had happened.[13] Elliott then left Beirut, taking the 'confession' and the tape-recordings with him. The MI6 station chief, Peter Lunn, took over responsibility for overseeing Philby's return if he agreed to take up the immunity offer.

Because the windows of the flat where Philby had been interviewed had been left wide open, the traffic noise seriously interfered with the tape-recordings. MI5 was, understandably, appalled by this, which it attributed to MI6 inexpertise. By processing the tapes it managed to secure about eighty-five per cent of the conversation.

The Prime Minister, Harold Macmillan, was informed about Philby's confession and wrote in his diary: 'We think we have at last solved the mystery of who "tipped off" Burgess and Maclean. It was a man, much suspected at the time, but against whom nothing could be proved — one Philby...In a drunken fit he confessed everything to one of our men...'[14]

Once again, a prime minister had been misinformed. Elliott has assured me that Philby was sober when he made his so-called confession. It would be instructive to know who passed on this misinformation to Macmillan, who was clearly uninformed about Philby's agent-running position with MI6 for he also wrote in his diary, when referring to Parliamentary and press questions: 'It was even insinuated that the Foreign Office were using Philby in the Middle East for secret work.' It was — through its agency MI6.

Although Philby had confessed to being a traitor, he and his third wife, Eleanor, were invited to dine at the home of the First Secretary of the British Embassy, Glen Balfour-Paul, who presumably had not been told of the confession and believed Philby innocent. The traitor's wife arrived but Philby did not.[15] He was on his way to Moscow, probably aboard a Soviet freighter, the *Dolmatovo*, registered in Odessa, which had been conveniently docked in Beirut. Modin may have been with him.

Macmillan wrote in his diary: 'He has now disappeared from Beirut, leaving £2,000 in cash for his wife. Whether he will appear in Russia or not we do not know. Anyway it means more trouble.'

It was decided to delay the trouble for as long as possible by keeping the defection secret.

An analysis of the events left little room for doubt that Philby had been warned of Elliott's impending visit and that Modin had been dispatched to prepare him for it. Elliott is convinced of it and Philby himself was to write, perhaps tongue in cheek, 'Maybe I was tipped off by a Fourth Man.'[16]

Recently, in 1983, statements were made in Soviet publications about spies, which can only have been written under K.G.B. control or guidance, that 'our Comrade Philby' was reluctantly pulled back to Moscow in 1963 because information was received that he was in danger.[17] According to a senior MI5 source, such admissions, which were formerly never made, stem from the influence of Yuri Andropov during his service in the K.G.B. in his effort to burnish the image and reputation of Soviet Intelligence, both at home and abroad. Andropov approved Philby's memoirs and also commissioned books to romanticize Sorge, Lonsdale and other spies.

Who had been responsible for the warning to Philby? It appeared most likely that the information had originated from one of the few Britons in MI6 and MI5 who had known about it. Of these the only two who were to come under serious suspicion were Hollis and his deputy, Mitchell, who was effectively cleared. Hollis had been one of the very few to be told, at an early stage, about Flora Solomon's information. He was also to become suspect as having been responsible for warning Maclean about his forthcoming interrogation.

What is absolutely certain is that Philby could not have warned himself nor could he have been warned by Blunt. I make this point at this juncture because another Prime Minister, Margaret Thatcher, misinformed by MI5, was to tell Parliament that the leads pointing to Hollis could be attributed to Philby or Blunt.[18]

It is unlikely that either Hollis or White expected Philby ever to return to Britain because it must have been obvious that the K.G.B. would not permit him to do so. The same factors which had made the Soviets insist on the defection of Maclean and Burgess applied to Philby. He had become drunken and unstable and, if allowed to return to Britain under complete immunity, he might provide all manner of dangerous leads. It would appear to be as certain as can ever be judged that Philby had no option but to defect and did so under firm K.G.B. orders and control, as Maclean had done and probably with the same degree of apprehension, for Philby, too, was a stranger to life in the Soviet Union, where reality is so terrifyingly different from the ideological dream.

If Philby was under K.G.B. control and about to defect why did he bother to confess anything? Why was he not just spirited away as Maclean had been? If he had defected before Elliott had interviewed him it would have been immediately obvious that he had been alerted. The K.G.B. had seen how their unavoidable withdrawal of Maclean, while he was pending interrogation, had led to the loss of Philby as an agent inside MI6. The sudden withdrawal of Philby would have put the source of their warning at risk. And he, too, was almost certainly an inside man, far too valuable to lose.

The best solution for the K.G.B. was for Philby to agree to make a limited confession which could be truthful about events and operations no longer of consequence, and to intersperse these with false or misleading information on important matters such as Blunt's involvement. As he could not be held against his will in Beirut, there was little danger that he would say too much, for he could consult with Modin each evening. So, having been offered immunity, which Philby may have known was to happen, he simply had to plead for time and then disappear, the ostensible reason for his defection then being that he did not trust the British assurance. The confession, which would have to be reported to the C.I.A., would have the additional advantage of souring relations between the British and American security authorities.

I have been told that when Philby's written confession was read in conjunction with the tape-recordings there was little doubt in MI5 that it was a K.G.B. concoction put together by Philby and Modin before Elliott arrived. It was concluded that the K.G.B. had been able to follow MI5's conduct of the Philby case at least from early 1962 onwards.

As Geoffrey McDermott, a long-serving diplomat, commented: 'Parts of Philby's confession could well have been bogus. He might have been protecting the real "third man" so that he could continue his activities among us.'[19]

On 29 March 1963 Edward Heath, speaking on behalf of the Foreign Office, announced the disappearance of Philby from the Lebanon. On the advice of the security authorities Heath was determined to conceal for as long as possible the truth that Philby had been a traitor, and he provided no further information.[20] Then on 1 July he was driven by publicity to admit that the security services were 'now aware, partly as a result of an admission made by Mr Philby himself, that he worked for the Soviet authorities before 1946 and that in 1951 he, in fact, warned Maclean through Burgess that the security services were about to take action against him'.[21] This brief, supplied by MI6 through MI5, was again deliberately misleading. The date of 1946 was pointless unless it was intended to conceal the fact that Philby had spied throughout the war and, as MI5 then knew, had been a Soviet agent for seventeen years. As the Soviets knew exactly what Philby had 'confessed' to Elliott there was no security purpose in keeping the public and Parliament in ignorance. The purpose was to try to diminish the fearful incompetence of the secret services throughout the entire Maclean/Burgess/Philby affair.

Labour M.P.s then tried to question the Prime Minister, Macmillan, on the issue but he effectively silenced them by using a device which remains standard practice. He offered to take the Labour leaders, Harold Wilson and George Brown, into his confidence, recording in his diary how they had responded 'nobly' by accepting his explanation and remaining silent about it. I can find nobody in MI5 or MI6 who can explain the 'one simple fact' – to quote Wilson – which convinced the Labour leaders that they should desist from further questioning[22] other than that it had nothing to do with the mishandling of the Philby case itself but was the startling fact that he had been tipped off and that investigations were already in progress into the possible disloyalty of the Deputy Director-General of MI5, Graham Mitchell.

Macmillan's private view of MI5 and MI6 at that time is

revealed by the diary entry he made on 11 July 1963 when he wrote: 'I had an hour with Harold Wilson and tried to explain to him how the so-called Security Services really worked.' Macmillan's public relations adviser and close friend, Sir Harold Evans, told me that the Prime Minister was deeply critical of the secret services at the time. While Macmillan was prepared to speak to me of Sir Dick White of MI6 with respect and affection he declined to discuss Hollis, affecting not to remember him although MI5 must have been etched on his heart as indelibly as Calais had been on Bloody Mary's.[23]

How much damage *did* Philby inflict as a result of the failure of the security authorities to detect him? The common description of him as a 'double agent' is misleading. A double agent is a person who begins to work for a secret agency of one side and then switches his allegiance to the other, ostensibly working for both and sometimes, when money is involved, actually doing so. Philby was a full-time, loyal Soviet agent deliberately intruded as a career officer into MI6, where he continued to work in the British interest only to the extent that it secured his continuing employment and promotion or also happened to serve the Soviet interest, as it did for part of the Second World War. There is no evidence whatever that he ever wavered in his total commitment to the Kremlin leadership and suggestions that he was expelled from MI6 as a device so that he could work against the K.G.B. and did so, even after his defection to the Soviet Union, are without foundation.

The damage assessment on Philby, begun so belatedly in 1963 and continuing to this day, comprises a staggering sequence of services to the K.G.B., which must have continued to astonish his masters as he fouled up the West's anti-Soviet operations and dispatched a mass of secret material to Moscow without raising any suspicion.

While his recruiting operations at Cambridge were to bear rich fruit and his clandestine activities in Spain were helpful to Stalin, he could not achieve his potential until he gained entry to the Secret Intelligence Service (MI6) in September 1941, after a limitedly useful year in the Special Operations Executive (S.O.E.). Over the next ten years he supplied a succession of internal telephone directories and other documents giving the 'order of battle' of MI6 – its divisions, personnel and functions. In the files of MI6 those officers and agents believed to be unknown to the adversary are designated 'Sovbloc Green'. While Philby was in MI6 every member was 'Sovbloc Red', though only the Soviets knew it.

Because Lisbon and Madrid, being ostensibly neutral, were places where British and German agents could meet, Philby, as head of the Iberian section, received early indication that certain German military chiefs, including Admiral Canaris, head of the *Abwehr* (Secret Service) were opposed to the way that Hitler was continuing the war and were open to an approach concerning possible ways of ending it. He did all he could to prevent the circulation of this information or any action on it because Moscow was totally opposed to any separate peace. Having secured the names of the Germans concerned he passed them to the K.G.B. for any action it cared to take.[24]

All information from Western agents operating in Spain and Portugal passed through his hands and he stifled it whenever it was inimical to Soviet interests. When Otto John supplied accurate information about the impending plot to kill Hitler, to be followed by a peace treaty, Philby suppressed it because by 1944 the Soviets were advancing into Europe and the last thing they wanted was peace until they had occupied as much territory as possible.[25]

Philby's duties brought him intimate knowledge of MI6's most secret department, the Government Code and Cipher School at Bletchley, where 'unbreakable' German codes were being deciphered by the ingenious process code-named Ultra. Dr R. V. Jones, who was in charge of scientific intelligence during the war, has assured me that Philby had 'complete details of decrypts of the intercepts of the Enigma signals sent by the *Abwehr*'.[26] He was also given Ultra intercepts concerning German secret agents operating in Spain. The greatest efforts were made to prevent the Soviets from knowing about Ultra because of the danger that it might leak back to the Germans but these were vitiated by Philby who told them everything.

Halfway through 1944 the MI6 management decided that with victory against Germany reasonably assured it should look to the future and start up a Soviet section, which would deal with all information of foreign origin concerning Soviet espionage, sabotage and subversion. Philby was urged by his controller to get himself transferred to this section and, as he records in his book, he turned to his friends in MI5 for help. By the autumn he had succeeded, not only in securing command of the Soviet section but in retaining his old Iberian section as well. Who were these friends? Brooman-White seems to have been the main one, but Hollis is a possibility, though their close association was to date from that time. As Hollis headed the counterpart MI5 section dealing with all information of domestic origin concerning Soviet espionage, sabotage and subversion, he liaised with Philby almost daily. So Philby learned a great deal about MI5 operations which he also funnelled to the K.G.B.

Philby and Hollis shared a mutual interest which may have brought them together, occasionally, in their off-duty time. Both were keen watchers of cricket and regular visitors to the Lords ground. Both were also substantial drinkers.

Philby's office was in the MI6 building in Ryder Street, off St James's, and as the same building housed the headquarters of the American O.S.S. he had ready access to information about U.S. operations, all of which he doubtless betrayed.

Philby had served the K.G.B. most usefully throughout the war, but it was after the German defeat in 1945 and the rapid emergence of the Soviet Union as the main adversary that he became really important and dangerous. While many of those recruited to MI6 during the war returned to their civilian professions, Philby elected to stay in the Service. By that time he was, almost certainly, a career K.G.B. officer with a rank and emoluments, as Sonia was, in the G.R.U. so he probably had no option but to remain in post there.[27]

It can reasonably be assumed that Philby gave the K.G.B. every item of information concerning British and American moves against Soviet espionage on which he could lay his hands, thereby nullifying them and assisting further K.G.B. penetration. He was able to warn the Soviets and give them play-back information on dangerous defections such as the Volkov and Gouzenko cases, providing details on the latter as quickly as they were relayed to MI6 headquarters from Ottawa. Whether by chance or by design, his hand-over of the Gouzenko case to Hollis effectively stifled any serious inquiry into the existence of a spy inside MI5 for seventeen years, by which time enormous damage would seem to have been done.

While still in charge of Soviet counter-espionage Philby stifled a major investigation carrying great potential danger for Soviet agents, including himself. The management of G.C.H.Q. wanted to make an early start on the decipherment of the many thousands of radio messages transmitted by Soviet Intelligence networks, which had been recorded, by hand, against the day when there might be time to try to decode them. As G.C.H.Q. was then still under MI6 control Philby was able to stop this British contribution to Operation Bride by arguing that any results could not be worth the enormous effort, which would be more profitably expended in other directions. In this view he was strongly supported by Hollis and Mitchell in MI5. Later, when Philby's written statement to G.C.H.Q. was discovered, following his defection, a drive to decipher the messages was mounted as part of Operation Bride, but by then many of them appear to have been destroyed, as already mentioned.

In 1946 Philby faced a serious situation respecting his divorce from Lizi but sailed through it unscathed. To what extent Hollis assisted him then is unknown but he was still in charge of the Soviet counter-espionage department, which knew that she was a spy, then living in East Berlin with a well-known communist.[28]

Philby was then posted to Istanbul as the chief MI6 officer in Turkey, under cover of being a First Secretary in the British Consulate. He was supposed to monitor Soviet activities and also to carry out counter-espionage against the Soviets. His operations collapsed with a regularity which should have generated suspicion but did not. During his stay he was also able to suppress valuable information about the G.R.U. supplied by a high-level defector from that organization called Ismail Akhmedov. In several interviews with Philby this defector, who had headed a technical intelligence section at G.R.U. headquarters in Moscow, gave so much information that it filled forty-two foolscap pages when Philby read it back to him. Philby sent only four pages to London, adding a comment which derided Akhmedov as a source. The full report, which has never been found, presumably went to the K.G.B. Akhmedov, who escaped being kidnapped, unlike Volkov, later gave evidence to the C.I.A., increasing doubts there about Philby's loyalty. After Philby's defection Akhmedov was interviewed by MI5 about G.R.U. penetration there and, in particular, to find out if he knew the identity of 'Elli', which he did not because another G.R.U. officer had handled agents operating in Britain.[29]

While Philby was in his MI6 post in Istanbul, and making trips to other parts of Turkey, a secret Whitehall group run by the Foreign Office and called the Russia Committee was examining ways of 'loosening the Soviet hold on the orbit countries and ultimately enabling them to regain their independence'. Assistance was therefore being given to Albanian refugees sheltering in Turkey and Greece who were planning to invade their homeland and free it from the harsh dictatorship of Enver Hoxha, who had been trained in Moscow. Philby was called in to assist and, using his MI6 facilities, he secured lists of Albanian anti-communists involved in carrying out raids across the Greek frontier and gave them to the K.G.B. so that many of them were ambushed and executed. Presumably by chance, though with Philby one always wonders, he was able to intensify his part in these treacherous massacres when he was transferred to Washington in the autumn of 1949.

By that time MI6 and the C.I.A. were jointly involved in training Albanian emigrés and intruding them by parachute and by sea, mainly in batches of four or five. As chief liaison officer between MI6 and the C.I.A., Philby was closely involved and by supplying details to the K.G.B., which transmitted them to Hoxha, about 200 agents are believed to have been lost. By March 1950 the casualties were so heavy that the operation was terminated. Lord Bethell, who has made a special study of it, suspects that there may have been up to 1,000 deaths and that Philby was responsible for many of them.[30]

In the subsequent MI6 'inquest' on the catastrophe Philby blamed 'the clumsy Americans', an excuse all too readily accepted. While it has been alleged that some C.I.A. officers suspected Philby at that stage, the American who had been operationally in charge, Frank Wisner, appears to have accepted much of the blame and later committed suicide.[31] The British records of the operation would be enlightening but when they became due for release under the thirty-year rule the Foreign Office declared them closed.

Only a few weeks before being forced to resign from MI6, Philby was able to continue his practice of sending Western agents to their death. Teams of parachutists were dropped into the Ukraine and eastern Poland on MI6 missions but none survived as Philby had betrayed them in advance.[32]

It has been recorded in Chapters 20 and 21 how Philby gave the K.G.B. a running commentary on the progress of the highly secret Operation Bride which assisted in the defection of Maclean and Burgess and could have enabled the Soviets to offset some of the disadvantages to them by feeding in disinformation. Chapter 18 relates how Philby had been involved in the defection of Pontecorvo, the atomic scientist, before the latter could be questioned about information which had reached the F.B.I.

It has perhaps been insufficiently appreciated that Philby was also the MI6 liaison officer with the Canadian security authorities during his tenure in Washington and that he inflicted damage there. He visited Ottawa several times a year for meetings with Canadian officials in which secret information was exchanged. Canadian security, which is still weak, as the recent Hambleton case showed, was even less adequate then and Philby would have been able to advise the K.G.B. on how best to penetrate it. It seems that he used this weakness himself when he needed a lengthy consultation with a controller which might have been too dangerous on American soil. An R.C.M.P. source has told me of one occasion when Philby drove from Washington to Ottawa in appalling winter weather for a discussion which was not particularly important and could have been delayed.[33]

Philby was also ideally placed as a feedback agent to keep the

K.G.B. continuously informed of the progress of its own counter-intelligence operations. This is one of the major functions of any penetration agent inside a secret service. Even more important to the Kremlin was Philby's capability to angle intelligence reports for submission to the Foreign Office – and eventually, when processed, to the Cabinet – so that they reflected the Soviet Union's interests. The most effective channel for misleading an adversary government is through its intelligence service on which it depends for information to guide its foreign policy decisions.

While the K.G.B. allowed Philby to lie fallow for a few years after his departure from MI6 the use it made of him once he had arrived in Beirut, his base for Middle East operations, has been under-estimated. He took part in major K.G.B. activities in Syria, Iraq, Jordan and North Yemen and contributed to Soviet subversion in general in those volatile areas.[34] For such damage as he then inflicted on Western interests those who organized his 'clearance' in 1955 bear heavy responsibility.

Philby's defection confirmed the long-standing suspicions in Washington that the British secret services had been responsible for enabling a K.G.B. spy to be privy to some of the C.I.A. and F.B.I.'s most sensitive secrets, all of which he had systematically betrayed. The effect on individuals who had trusted him, like James Angleton, was corrosive for future co-operation and the fears of those, like Hoover, who had always distrusted British security were shown to have been justified. This regeneration of suspicion damaged the Anglo-American relationship on intelligence and security that is so essential to the containment of the Soviet assault on Western freedom.

On arrival in the Soviet Union Philby was not welcomed as the hero he has since become there. Being rightly judged an alcoholic he had first to be 'dried out', as Maclean and Burgess had been, and was then held outside Moscow for many months while being thoroughly debriefed and while further inquiries were made to ensure that he was not a double agent.[35] Eventually he was given K.G.B. office work in Moscow under various cover guises, with no public references whatever to the fact that he was in the Soviet Union.

As the long debriefing of defectors from the K.G.B. has indicated, Philby's must have been of considerable value to the Soviets and he was on hand to help to interpret and analyse new intelligence being received from the West and especially against MI6 and MI5, knowing all the weaknesses there and, possibly, the names of officers and agents susceptible to recruitment.

With the growing emphasis on disinformation, forgeries, the

planting of 'scandals' and other K.G.B. 'dirty tricks' Philby's expertise must have been very welcome. He undoubtedly displayed it in his biography *My Silent War*, with many parts of the text angled or faked to protect spies like Blunt, and possibly Hollis,then still unexposed publicly. The book was worthwhile to the K.G.B. if only for the number of man-hours MI6 and MI5 spent trying to analyse its every nuance. Though fifteen years have passed since its publication various officers and former officers of MI6 still dread the next instalment, which Philby is alleged to have written. The new look at the Philby case, in progress at the time of writing, is believed to be connected with the preparation of a counter-document.

According to Philby's former wife Eleanor, he also ghosted the memoirs of the K.G.B. spy Gordon Lonsdale, published in 1965, which was certainly a mine of disinformation.

It is known that Andropov, when head of the K.G.B., encouraged Philby to write *My Silent War* as a way of projecting the organization as an elite force. British Intelligence also has reason to believe that Philby was influential with Andropov in improving the status of membership of the K.G.B. and the general sophistication of its officers, which has made them more acceptable in their efforts to penetrate foreign institutions and society when operating abroad.[36]

Philby has been allowed to meet the odd British visitor to Moscow, where he claims to be ideally happy, and he is permitted to correspond with selected old friends such as Graham Greene, who wrote the foreword to *My Silent War*. It has been reported that he has been allowed out of the Soviet Union to visit Cuba to advise Castro on espionage and propaganda but this is most unlikely to be true. Graham Greene has been prepared to meet Philby in Vienna, Prague or anywhere else convenient to him but such a meeting has never been permitted up to the time of writing.[37]

What would happen if Philby touched down in Britain on some flight to Cuba or for some other reason? The likelihood that he would be arrested and tried would seem to be remote. Even though he declined the offer of immunity, the fact that he was offered it might enable a good lawyer to insist that whatever he might have said in Beirut in 1963 had been under duress and was, therefore, inadmissible as evidence. Whenever I have discussed this alluring possibility with former secret service officers they have dismissed it as a nightmare which they prefer not to contemplate.

The Potential Value of Oversight

Of all the proven espionage cases Philby's demonstrates most forcefully how, in stage after stage of it, secrecy has been the enemy of genuine security. Secrecy for secrecy's sake has also been responsible for damaging the reputations of politicians who, sometimes knowingly and sometimes through being misinformed by officials, have misled Parliament and the public.

Hopefully an alert oversight body would have prevented those responsible for the Maclean and Burgess White Paper, which led to the first publicity about the Philby case, from deliberately including misinformation. Knowing that an independent body responsible to Parliament was aware of the true state of the circumstantial evidence against Philby might have prevented any prime minister from effectively clearing the traitor in 1955. The more one studies the record of statements to Parliament on security matters the more apparent becomes the need for oversight to prevent ministers from being misled by security officials.

The judgement of those in MI6 who strenuously protested that Philby was innocent, thereby enabling him to continue to serve the K.G.B. in Beirut, without MI5's knowledge that he was still operating for MI6, might have been subjected to more objective criticism, a matter of some importance, as some of them continued in important office. Others in high places might have been more reluctant to support Philby had they known that their views might lead to inquiry. One such was the late Sir Richard 'Otto' Clark, a Cambridge contemporary with considerable power and influence in Whitehall, who gave an assurance that Philby was 'a calm, dependable social democrat', when he almost certainly knew otherwise, having been an ardent left-winger himself, urging revolution to strip the privileged classes of their power.

It remains a matter for conjecture whether, with effective oversight, Hollis, White and the Attorney-General would so readily have taken the unprecedented step of granting Philby immunity to prosecution so that they could carry out a damage assessment of his crimes which should have been attempted years earlier, had not MI6 prevented it. They might have been aware that, to an independent oversight group, the secret services would look as though they were behaving like the mythical backwards-running tribe of Africa, which does not mind where it is going but likes to see where it has been. They might also have been more aware of the domestic political dangers of allowing a traitor and accessory to murders to remain 'respectable' into old age, rejoining his old clubs and posing as a patriot, unless tongues wagged audibly enough for some writer to expose him when, even then, he would be immune to penal punishment.

The handling of the final stage of the Philby case, as with that of Maclean, will continue to generate suspicion that its purpose may have been to encourage and secure defection as the most certain means of disposing of a situation embarrassing to the secret services and to ministers. An oversight body, without necessarily exposing details, could have reassured Parliament regarding that point.

It would seem that although the entire Philby case was disastrously handled nobody at any stage suffered any professional censure within the secret departments. An oversight body might have required some internal inquest so that lessons could be learned and individuals disciplined, as happened following the far less damaging but more public case of Commander Crabb.

CHAPTER THIRTY-THREE

The Mitchell Case

THOSE MI5 officers who had been apprehensive for some time about the probable penetration of the Service by Soviet agents were convinced by the circumstances of Philby's defection that there must still be an informer operating at high level. The two who had become most suspicious, working independently and without reference to each other, were Arthur Martin, then second-in-command of the counter-espionage section, and Peter Wright, who had been a scientific adviser, putting his major effort into the Soviet espionage problem.

Martin made a short-list of all those in MI5 who had known the secret of Elliott's visit. It comprised five people – four men, including Martin himself, and one woman who was Martin's assistant. A separate survey of all the penetration leads by another MI5 officer, Ronald Symonds, reduced the main suspects to two – Hollis and the deputy whom he had appointed, Graham Mitchell.[1]

Aware that Hollis was super-sensitive to any suggestion of disloyalty in his organization, Martin sought advice from his former chief, Sir Dick White, who could not bring himself to believe that Hollis, whom he had helped into MI5 and had consistently promoted, could possibly be guilty. Having no particular views on Mitchell he advised Martin to see Hollis and tell him of his fears about the Deputy Director. It was understood that White would say nothing to Hollis concerning Martin's suspicions about the Director-General himself.

On the evening when Martin told Hollis of his suspicions and that in his professional opinion Mitchell should be investigated as a start, Hollis seemed devastated and, without making any effort to defend Mitchell, suggested that they should continue the discussion without delay over dinner in the Travellers Club. Describing the experience to friends, later, Martin said that Hollis's behaviour was bizarre. Normally ice-cool, he was nervous, avoided talking about the issue they were supposed to be discussing and, in Martin's eyes, behaved 'like a broken man who had been found out'. At the end of the meal he declared that he would think about the Mitchell problem and let Martin know his views.

Shortly afterwards Wright was chatting in Martin's office about his fear that the agency was penetrated and suggested that it had to be Mitchell or Hollis. Martin then revealed that he had already seen Hollis about it and urged Wright to do the same. He did so and after Hollis had agreed to a limited investigation into Mitchell Wright was seconded for six months from his usual work to assist Martin with it. Both were told that nothing should be done that would enable anybody outside MI5 to hear about the inquiry.

Meanwhile, in March 1963, at the invitation of MI5 and with the promise of financial reward, the K.G.B. defector, Anatoli Golitsin, had come to Britain for an indefinite visit and possibly to settle in the country. In his debriefings he indicated the presence of a high-level spy in MI5 by claiming that, while in the British Department of the K.G.B. in Moscow, he had seen an index which had a section entitled 'Material from the British Security Service'. It was recent material, secured long after Blunt or any previously suspected spy had left MI5.[2]

Golitsin also said that there had been great excitement in the K.G.B. about a document describing British technical methods of intelligence which had been acquired from England. The document was almost certainly a paper produced by MI5 in 1960. He also revealed that the Soviet Embassy in London was almost unique in having no S.K. (Soviet Kolony) department, a group of security officers whose function is to ensure that there are no defections. Golitsin suggested that the Russians must have such an excellent source inside MI5 that they could be confident of being warned of any coming defection, so they could safely dispense with S.K. officers. To be so dependable an inside MI5 source would have to be at high level and in regular touch with a Soviet controller.

Defectors are very rarely able to give the true name of a Soviet agent, as identities are so closely guarded in Moscow, and are usually limited to providing leads and occasionally code-names. At no time did Golitsin point a finger specifically at Mitchell or at Hollis. This disposes of the specious claim that the suspicion against Mitchell and Hollis was the result of a 'mole-hunt' touched off by Golitsin who, his critics claim, was obsessed with the belief that Soviet agents had infiltrated every Western intelligence organization, including the C.I.A.[3] The suspicions were 'home-grown' and existed before Golitsin's evidence, being brought to a head by Philby's defection. Nevertheless, Golitsin's allegation of a high-level agent in MI5 helps to dispose of another claim, repeatedly made by

Hollis's supporters, that there was no defector evidence against him.

While Hollis may have been shattered by the suggestion that his deputy might be a spy, Martin felt sure that the Director-General himself was the culprit. He lost no time, therefore, in initiating the inquiry into Mitchell, which had to be completed before Hollis could be investigated.

To avoid damage to morale at lower levels of MI5, and to reduce the risk of tarnishing the reputation of the Service in other areas of Whitehall, the inquiry was kept as secret as possible and Mitchell was referred to only by the code-name 'Peters'. The case was to last several years and I shall report it in some detail because it illustrates MI5 methods of inquiry, demonstrates the belief inside MI5 that the agency was deeply penetrated and, as I shall show later, proves the falsity of an essential element of Margaret Thatcher's statement to Parliament in March 1981 – namely that the leads which pointed to Hollis could be attributed to Blunt, who severed connection with MI5 in 1946, or to Philby, who had no access to secrets after 1951.[1]

Beyond Mitchell's record of service there was little about him on file because few inquiries had been made when he had entered MI5 in 1939 and because Hollis had declined to introduce positive vetting, which would have required Mitchell to provide details of his past, while the routine private inquiries would have revealed more. Born in 1905, Mitchell had been a contemporary of Hollis at Oxford, though at a different college, Magdalen, where he read Politics, Philosophy and Economics. Unlike Hollis, Mitchell obtained a degree. He worked as a journalist on the *Illustrated London News* and then as a statistician in the research department of the Conservative Central Office, which was regarded by the K.G.B. as a useful jumping-off ground as it provided agents with a right-wing image.

Mitchell entered MI5 through the recommendation of Sir Joseph Ball, who later also assisted Burgess to enter as an agent-runner, and was assigned to the same section as Hollis, running the desk responsible for overseeing fascist subversion and other far-right activities in Britain. Remembered by colleagues as totally humourless and even more withdrawn than Hollis, he was evacuated to Blenheim in 1940 and spent most of the war there.[5] Some of his activities with respect to the British Union of Fascists, and Sir Oswald Mosley in particular, have recently become public with the release of wartime documents.

Since Mitchell was well established in MI5 by 1942, he was a possible candidate for the G.R.U. spy 'Elli', for while most of the known Soviet agents recruited at British universities were K.G.B., it is now certain that the G.R.U. also recruited there.[6] If he was 'Elli' he could have been serviced by Sonia and could have been the reason why she was posted to the Oxford area, but there is no known previous connection between Sonia and Mitchell, as there is believed to be between her and Hollis. Further, the information to which Mitchell had access throughout the war could hardly have been responsible for the excitement created by 'Elli's' reports at G.R.U. headquarters, as recorded by Gouzenko. The last three letters of Mitchell's name suggested a possible relationship with 'Elli', but Hollis also had three mutual letters, as did Guy Liddell and possibly others.

In the late 1940s, when Hollis was made Director of Security (Section C), Mitchell succeeded him as head of Section F, which was responsible for overseeing subversive activities in the U.K. So when positive vetting was introduced into other departments following the Fuchs, Burgess and Maclean cases, he was involved in much of the spade-work as he was responsible for overseeing communist activities, which had become much more significant. There is evidence that he suffered agonies of conscience when anyone who had previously been associated with communism was dismissed from the Civil Service or moved to non-secret work.[7]

Mitchell returned to London after the war and eyebrows were raised over some minor involvement in the Pontecorvo case. In 1953, however, under White's reorganization, Mitchell was made head of D Branch responsible for counter-espionage, in which position he would have been of great interest to the K.G.B., especially as he was concerned with the British investigations of the K.G.B. intercepts deciphered in Operation Bride which, by that time, was known as V-(for 'Venona') material. He displayed such little interest in these intercepts that he was in favour of shutting down G.C.H.Q.'s work on them as being wasteful of manpower, a suggestion which may have been based on a genuine belief that there were more pressing priorities but would certainly have had the whole-hearted approval of the K.G.B. Analysis of the V-material was, in fact, put on a care and maintenance basis only and was not restarted with vigour until Martin took charge of Soviet counter-espionage in 1959, after which it continued to yield results. Mitchell's behaviour in this respect, however, looked less suspicious later when it was discovered that Hollis had strongly supported Mitchell's recommendation and may have initiated it.

As I have described, Mitchell was involved in drafting the misleading MI5 brief for the 1955 White Paper on Maclean and Burgess. He also prepared the draft brief for Macmillan's state-

308

ment to Parliament which effectively cleared Philby.

In spite of this modest performance Mitchell was appointed Deputy Director-General when Hollis took over the top post in 1956. The Home Secretary almost invariably accepted the recommendation of the incoming Director-General so Mitchell was virtually appointed by Hollis. In his new post he became responsible for liaison with the security departments of Allied governments but, until he fell under suspicion, he seems to be little remembered by his foreign counterparts on whom he made scant impact, perhaps because Hollis did most of the travelling.

Former colleagues recall that in addition to being withdrawn, Mitchell had a habit of talking to himself, even when others were present, which gave him a reputation for being somewhat eccentric.

There was one factor which seemed to be in Mitchell's favour from the start of the inquiry into his loyalty. Before he had fallen under suspicion he had decided to retire prematurely on a reduced pension being, apparently, weary of the job after twenty-four years. Hollis had agreed that he should leave in September 1963, shortly before his fifty-eighth birthday, the normal retiring age being sixty. Those who suspected him realized that if the K.G.B. had an agent in such a superb position he would have been pressured into remaining there as long as possible.

The circumstances of Mitchell's premature retirement would seem to merit closer study than has been given to it. Long before he fell under any suspicion he was complaining that Hollis was making his life a misery by giving him too little to do, which implies that Hollis had taken responsibilities away from him, as the Deputy is normally busy. What were those responsibilities and why was Hollis fulfilling them himself? He could hardly have been restricting Mitchell on grounds of incompetence when they had been so close for so long.

While Hollis was most anxious to restrict all knowledge of the 'Peters' case to MI5, it was pointed out to him that this was impossible because Mitchell, being in charge of the MI5 watchers, knew them all and so they could not be used to keep him under surveillance. Reluctantly, Hollis agreed that watchers from MI6, who were unknown to Mitchell, should be called in. For this purpose Stephen de Mowbray, an able officer, who was in charge of the MI6 watchers, was seconded to MI5 to control the surveillance. The operation therefore became a joint MI5/MI6 exercise, which meant that Sir Dick White, as MI6 chief, was officially kept informed of developments.

By mid-June 1963 it was decided that to dispose of the case as quickly as possible Mitchell should be given the full technical treatment. Martin and Wright therefore needed the assistance of the head of Technical Operations and asked Hollis for permission to involve him. When Hollis refused, Martin felt that the investigation was being so prejudiced that he threatened to go over Hollis's head to the Prime Minister. To resolve the difficulty, Furnival Jones, who was in overall charge of the case, agreed that White should be consulted in the hope of obtaining his support. Martin and Wright met White by appointment at his residence, a house in Queen Anne's Gate which backed on to MI6 headquarters in Broadway and was connected to them by a passage. White had, meanwhile, learned that Nicholas Elliott was convinced that Philby had been forewarned of his visit to Beirut, probably by Mitchell or Hollis. So, after listening to Martin and Wright, White agreed to see Hollis the following day and, as a result, secured the immediate support of Technical Operations.

A mirror in Mitchell's office was removed and a see-through type substituted so that a television camera could be hidden behind it to allow watchers to see if the suspect was in the habit of copying secret documents.[8] A check was kept on his office telephone but when Hollis was asked to request the necessary Home Office warrant for Mitchell's home telephone to be tapped and bugged he refused on the grounds that this would mean informing the Home Secretary, Home Office officials and the Post Office. His objection could be interpreted as being due to the embarrassment of admitting to the Home Secretary that the man he had urged him to appoint as Deputy Director-General might be a Soviet spy. In that case, he was putting his personal considerations above the interests of the Service. With the aid of a Post Office team, the MI5 officers did, however, manage to insert a microphone into Mitchell's home, a procedure which did not need a warrant then but does now, so that they were able to listen to his part of any telephone conversations.

Meanwhile it was discovered that Mitchell, a chess enthusiast, was in the habit of playing correspondence games with chess masters behind the Iron Curtain, including some in the Soviet Union. The investigating officers wondered if the moves might be a method of communication and called in the British chess master, Hugh Alexander, who was working in G.C.H.Q. He examined the moves in intercepted letters to and from Mitchell but could discover nothing sinister. It was realized that this international chess interest might fit with Gouzenko's statement that the MI5 spy called 'Elli' had 'something Russian in his background' but, without asking Mitchell, it was not possible to discover if he had been playing with Soviet correspondents prior to 1942, when Gouzenko had learned the details about 'Elli'.

Harold Macmillan has told me how he was kept fully informed of the progress of the Mitchell case including the details of the one-way mirror.

A search of Mitchell's office carried out at night showed that there was one locked drawer in an antique desk which had been unused for years. Unlike the other drawers, the edges of which were dusty, the locked drawer had been in recent use. Mitchell's office connected by a door with that of Hollis, whose permission was sought by Peter Wright for the drawer to be opened on the following evening with a lock-pick after Mitchell had gone home. When the drawer was eased out it was empty but marks in the dust showed that some flat object with four button feet had been in the drawer on more than one occasion and had been hurriedly removed from it, probably within the previous twenty-four hours, because the scratch-marks in the dust were very fresh.

The marks were photographed and shown by Wright to Hollis who made no significant comment. It was thought that the marks could have been made by a battery-driven tape-recorder, the purpose of such a device being obvious. A weekly meeting was held in Mitchell's room to decide where MI5's limited number of watchers were to be used and a recording of it would be of the highest value to any Soviet Intelligence agent.

The only person who had known that the desk drawer was to be opened, apart from Peter Wright, was Hollis and nothing was ever put into the drawer again. Mitchell, almost certainly, had no knowledge of the suspicion against him at that stage. When Wright discussed the desk evidence with Martin they began to wonder if they had made an error in investigating Mitchell first.

Some false information was passed in routine documents to Mitchell to see if they would reach Moscow, which might then play back further instructions to the K.G.B. office in London indicating that they had received it.[9] G.C.H.Q. examined their deciphered K.G.B. traffic for telltale signs but never found anything of relevance.

The possibility that Mitchell might have warned the K.G.B. about the imminent interrogation of Maclean and Philby was carefully examined. It was decided that Mitchell had not had access to the Maclean information in time to betray it. He could have betrayed the information about Philby's interrogation, but if he was responsible for that then the investigators were dealing with two spies, not just one.

The 'candid' camera in Mitchell's office revealed that when he

311

was alone his face looked tortured, as though in despair. He talked to himself and, on one occasion, looked towards Hollis's door and muttered, 'Why are you doing this to me?'

He never copied any documents but the officer monitoring the camera was excited when he saw Mitchell drawing a crude map which he eventually tore up, putting the fragments in the paper liner of his wastebasket. Normally the liner would have been taken in the evening for burning or shredding but the investigators pieced the map together and found it was of an open area near his home at Chobham. There was a point on it which Mitchell had marked R.V., meaning rendezvous. The watchers staked out the area for several days but nobody ever arrived at the rendezvous.

The watchers reported that Mitchell was behaving as though he knew that he might be being followed. He wandered about in parks, repeatedly turning round, and would peer in shop windows as though looking at the reflections of passers-by.

The team decided that as Mitchell might have learned that he was under suspicion, possibly having spotted the watchers, they were unlikely to get any further without interrogating him. The torn-up map had given them a fair reason, so Hollis was approached for permission. Hollis told Martin that he had been to see the Prime Minister to secure his permission for the interrogation, which he was not required to do, and that this had been refused because Macmillan thought that Mitchell might defect, with terrible political consequences, especially as regards the exchange of secrets with the U.S. The MI5 officers suspected that Hollis was lying and my conversation with Macmillan on that subject suggests that they were probably right. While he was willing to go into details about the Mitchell case and remembered Sir Dick White in that connection, he seemed unable to recall Hollis. Further, he told me that he had always thought that Mitchell was only 'unbalanced' from the effects of being in MI5 too long and was not a spy. So it is most unlikely that he ever feared that he would defect.

In July, while Mitchell was under intensive investigation, he was involved in an episode concerning Golitsin which savoured of pantomime, had it not been so damaging to MI5's interests. Because of the real fear that Golitsin might be assassinated by the K.G.B. his presence in Britain was kept as secret as possible within MI5, yet in spite of this the editor of the *Daily Telegraph*, Colin Coote (later Sir Colin), learned that there was an important defector in Britain. Being determined to print an exclusive report, he demanded to know the defector's name but was given no official assistance by Whitehall. Coote managed to enlist the personal help of Lord

Home, then Foreign Secretary, and pressure was brought to bear on MI5 to give the *Telegraph* the name. As Hollis was absent from the office at the time it fell to Mitchell, as deputy, to ask Golitsin's case officer for the true name of the defector, whom Mitchell knew only by the MI5 code-name 'Kago'. The case officer, who happened, again, to be Arthur Martin, advised most strongly against releasing the name but Mitchell, who was not prepared to stand against the Foreign Secretary, insisted on knowing it. Martin wrote down the name as Anatoli Dolnytsin, which was the name of a Soviet diplomat who had served in Britain previously and, having K.G.B. connections, had been marginally involved in the Lonsdale case. Mitchell then arranged for this name to be given to Coote through the D-Notice Committee, which was the official link between MI5 and the newspapers. Instead of giving the name exclusively to Coote, the D-Notice Secretary, Colonel L. G. 'Sammy' Lohan, was instructed to release it over a news-agency tape so that every newspaper learned of it.[10] I was in the *Daily Express* office when the information surfaced on the tape-machine. While giving Dolnytsin's name it urged newspapers to avoid mentioning it, but it was obvious that with worldwide distribution of the tape some papers would ignore the request, and in fact most did so. Years later I was informed by the Chairman of the D-Notice Committee that this had been foreseen and the issue of the name was a ploy to deprive the *Daily Telegraph* of its scoop.[11]

The following day, when the name Dolnytsin appeared in the newspapers, Golitsin took fright and returned to the U.S. on the first available aircraft, thereby depriving MI5 of his further services.

Martin has since claimed that 'Dolnytsin' was a slip of the pen but I find it easier to believe that it was a deliberate ploy to protect Golitsin's real name from both Mitchell and Hollis.

The considerable loss of Golitsin's personal services was due to a dangerous leak by whoever it was who told Coote of the defector's presence in Britain. It is possible that the information was leaked to a *Daily Telegraph* reporter who told Coote. However, while once again coincidence could be at work, Coote was a golfing friend of Hollis, who was one of the very few who knew of the defector's presence yet did not know his name.[12] Coote had no connection with Mitchell.

It was in the interest of any spy inside MI5 that Golitsin should be frightened out of Britain before his debriefings, which, it was hoped, would be spread over several years, produced any more dangerous leads. Incidentally, Golitsin's precipitate flight back to the safety of the C.I.A. is evidence that he was not a K.G.B. plant, a false defector, as his detractors have claimed. Had he been under K.G.B control he would not have been in such fear of his life.

Mitchell retired from MI5 in September as planned, still unaware, so far as is known, that he was under suspicion of being a spy. Shortly before doing so he remarked to his old colleague, Colonel T. A. Robertson, that in retirement he would be 'playing about with his wireless sets'.[13] When Robertson, who knew of the suspicions, reported this there was immediate interest because the investigators had not known that Mitchell was knowledgeable about radio transmitters and receivers, a valuable attribute for an agent. The information was investigated but was found to be harmlessly connected with his interest in yachting.

A report to Hollis and to White, written by Martin, stated that though the interrogation of Mitchell had been forbidden, the suspicions against him remained so strong that under the Anglo-American agreements on security the C.I.A. and the F.B.I. would have to be informed because of the damage he might have done to their interests. At first Hollis insisted that the Americans should not be informed because the case was not proven, but when he was told that White would then have to consult the Prime Minister, because of the Anglo-American aspects, he suddenly announced, 'Right, I'll go and tell them myself.'

To Martin, who had expected to be chosen for the task, being at the right level to talk to his U.S. counterparts, this seemed like a panic decision by a desperate man determined to precede anybody who might suggest to the C.I.A. or the F.B.I. that Hollis himself might be the culprit. Hollis then reinforced this suspicion by announcing that he would be making the journey alone.

Normally, under such circumstances, the Director-General would have been accompanied by an officer who knew all the details of the case so that he could be on hand to brief him. So why was Hollis so determined to go to Washington alone? One possible answer was the urgent need for long discussions with a Soviet controller, which could not be safely conducted in Britain. By that time Hollis must almost certainly have been aware that Martin suspected him and, if he was a spy, he may have felt the need to seek guidance from Moscow about possible defection. It would not have been safe to meet a controller with Martin, or anyone else, by his side in the same Washington hotel. Alone there, he could be absolutely confident that whatever the suspicions in the minds of those like Martin, nobody would dare to arrange the surveillance of the Director-General of MI5.

Hollis flew to Washington and saw the F.B.I. chief, J. Edgar Hoover, and the head of the C.I.A., John McCone, thereby raising

314

what was a fairly thin case to a matter for discussion at the highest level. He also took the unusual step of explaining the purpose of his mission to the British Ambassador, Lord Harlech, thereby suggesting that MI5's case against Mitchell was stronger than it really was.

Hollis bluntly told Hoover and McCone that he had reason to suspect that one of his most senior officers, Graham Mitchell, was 'a long-term agent of the Soviet Union', but when the Americans asked for details he was unable to supply them, saying that Martin would be arriving with them later. They tended to disbelieve him and their feeling that he was exaggerating the case was strengthened when Martin eventually arrived, following Hollis's return to London, and told them that Mitchell had never been interrogated because Hollis would not allow it.

Having made something of a fool of himself, Hollis returned to London in a calmer and different frame of mind. He ordered a new analysis of the evidence of Soviet penetration by an officer junior to both Martin and Wright. He insisted that the officer must not consult either of the two previous investigators and indicated that he did not believe that MI5 had been penetrated by anyone.

What had changed Hollis's mind about the seriousness of the situation? Was it calming advice from the Moscow Centre that he had panicked unnecessarily and that in his position as Director-General he had the power to defuse the danger?

After several months the officer detailed by Hollis produced a report which exonerated Mitchell but, in view of all the circumstantial evidence, could not deny the possibility of penetration. Supporters of Hollis have claimed that by encouraging the exoneration of Mitchell he was fearlessly pointing the finger of suspicion at himself as the only other candidate, but they are probably unaware of his immediate response to the report. He drafted a letter to the heads of the F.B.I., C.I.A. and the Royal Canadian Mounted Police declaring that Mitchell had been found to be innocent and that there was no longer any evidence of any penetration of MI5.[14] Under intense pressure from his staff he deleted the second part about the penetration but insisted on sending the first, which Martin and others opposed because no suspect could be regarded as cleared until he had been interrogated.

At the final meeting on the Mitchell case, a few weeks before the October 1964 general election, Hollis declared that he was closing it because, even if Mitchell was guilty, he could do no more damage now that he was retired. He also said that the whole issue of the past penetration of MI5 was to be regarded as dead, the Blunt case having been disposed of secretly.

315

Later the investigating officers came to believe that Hollis took this course so that he would not have to inform the incoming government, whatever it might be, of the penetration issue. The new Prime Minister, or Home Secretary, might have wanted to know who was responsible for the obvious penetrations if Mitchell was innocent. George Wigg, who was appointed security overseer by Wilson as soon as Labour came into office, would certainly have wanted to know the whole story and would have informed Wilson, because it was his brief to do so, but he was told nothing. This belief is supported by the fact that in the following year, 1965, Hollis discussed Mitchell with the R.C.M.P. chiefs in terms suggesting that he did not think that he had been cleared.[15]

Martin was later to accuse Hollis of having destroyed material evidence concerning the Mitchell case, an accusation which Jonathan Aitken, the Tory M.P., mentioned in a letter he sent to Mrs Thatcher in 1980, warning her of the dangerous political implications of the Hollis affair.

The Mitchell case was to remain in its unresolved condition until after Hollis himself had retired, when it was reopened, as described in Chapter 41.

CHAPTER THIRTY-FOUR

The Profumo Affair

WHILE certain MI5 officers were weighing the eventual political consequences of the possible proof that either the Deputy Director-General or the Director-General himself was a spy they found themselves involved in an issue of immediate political importance – the so-called Profumo affair. After long study of this complicated case, close professional involvement at the time and discussions with well-placed witnesses, including MI5 officers, I am convinced that only blind reluctance to criticize the Security Service by the leading Establishment figures concerned enabled Hollis to escape severe public censure and even suspicion.

The official account of the Profumo affair is a long report by Lord Denning which has been hailed as a brilliant *tour de force* and a model of its kind in bringing to the general reader the intricacies of a complex case in an easily understandable way.[1] My inquiries, however, have satisfied me that it was one of the most misleading official documents ever foisted on the public. Lord Denning was repeatedly misled by witnesses and especially by the chief MI5 witness, Hollis.[2] To quote an MI5 officer who was involved in the case, 'Denning had wool pulled over his eyes'. As a result he made judgements which were flawed and excused officials who should have been censured.

For anyone interested in the activities of Soviet Intelligence against the West, and against Britain in particular, the Profumo affair offers illuminating insight into how the Moscow Centre seizes upon opportunities and exploits them.

The most contentious issue concerns a character whose activities Denning's witnesses and Denning himself were at pains to under-estimate. This was Eugene Ivanov, a Soviet naval officer who arrived in Britain on 27 March 1960 ostensibly for duties as Assistant Naval Attaché at the Soviet Embassy but, in reality, for intelligence operations because he was a professional G.R.U. official.

Ivanov took over contacts established by his predecessors but

317

was also required to establish his own through the diplomatic social network, which included journalists. Among the latter was Coote, editor of the *Daily Telegraph*, who was a patient of an osteopath called Stephen Ward, a strange character so sympathetic to communism and to the Soviet Union that some of his distinguished patients appear to have reported him to MI5 as an agent of influence. Ward was also a capable artist and had told Coote of his desire to visit Moscow to draw some of the Soviet leaders, including Khrushchev. Coote had offered to help and a little later, on 20 January 1961, hosted a lunch with Ward and Ivanov who said that he might be able to arrange a visit to Moscow. Following this lunch Ward and Ivanov became close friends.

The circumstances of this lunch, held at the Garrick Club, are odd. Fleet Street editors do not usually know Soviet defence attachés and there is evidence that Coote did not know Ivanov very well, if at all. He had invited his correspondent for communist affairs, David Floyd, to be present on the grounds that his knowledge of Russian would be useful but Floyd has told me that Ivanov's English was so good that he was no more than a spectator. A possible explanation for the lunch stems from Coote's friendship with Hollis, with whom he played golf. After being sounded out by Coote about the wisdom of putting Ward in touch with the Soviet Embassy, Hollis may have suggested the lunch with Ivanov for a highly irresponsible reason which will become apparent as the Profumo affair unfolds.

Ward was a sexual deviant and procured young women for friends and contacts of similar interest. Among these girls was nineteen-year-old Christine Keeler, then a hostess at a night club. She denies having been a prostitute but admits granting sexual favours in return for 'a good time'. Ward had the use of a weekend cottage on the Thames-side Cliveden estate belonging to Lord Astor, who was one of his patients and was also a sexual deviant, taking advantage of girls whom Ward provided. As a friend of Ward, Ivanov visited his London flat and the weekend cottage.

Ivanov may have been subjected to some degree of routine surveillance by MI5, which was alerted again to his true profession in April 1961 by the Soviet defector Oleg Penkovsky.[3] On 8 June 1961 an MI5 officer, who used the name 'Woods' but whose real name was Wagstaffe, warned Ward that Ivanov might use him to gain access to his high-level patients. Ward promised to be careful and to keep MI5 informed of any interesting developments. This response has been wrongly interpreted as meaning that Ward was recruited by MI5 and served as an agent. Nothing could be further from the truth. In fact 'Woods' noted that 'he is obviously not a person, we can make any use of', especially as his political ideas were 'exploitable by the Russians'.[4] From that first interview, if not before, MI5 knew that Ward was a committed communist sympathizer and probable agent of influence. The information was submitted to Arthur Martin, who was then in charge of the investigation section. At that stage Hollis may not have been informed because the situation had no particularly serious overtones.

As a result of Ward's occasional information MI5 became aware that Keeler had had sexual relations with Ivanov. The extent of these relations are of some significance and witnesses are at variance about them. Miss Keeler herself, with whom I have had recent conversations, claims that she had sexual intercourse, which she described as 'marvellous, passionate love', with Ivanov on only one occasion after he had driven her home from Cliveden.[5] This is not the recollection of an MI5 officer who has told me that he received information of a more regular relationship between Keeler and Ivanov from a woman who was a frequent informer on such matters. This officer reported that the woman who informed for patriotic motives, was concerned about the security aspects of Keeler's relationship with Ivanov and Ward. So the MI5 management was alerted to this from an early stage.

The MI5 officer's recall of events is supported by Michael Eddowes, a solicitor who interested himself in the case long before it became public.

Eddowes, who made contemporary notes which I have seen, claims that he was told by Keeler that she had been 'the lover' of Ivanov. He says that he received confirmation of this from Ward and from Keeler's associate, Mandy Rice-Davies.[6]

Eddowes, who gave evidence to Denning for two hours in the presence of his own lawyer, has assured me that he included this information which, on his own initiative, he supplied to the Special Branch police. His existing copy of his long statement to Special Branch confirms this, yet Lord Denning, in his report, went out of his way to state that while Ivanov may have had 'some kind of sexual relations' with Keeler on one occasion he was never 'her lover'.

The phrase 'some kind of sexual relations' would seem to be calculated to suggest that it was something short of intercourse, diminishing the importance of Ivanov in her life, which, on Keeler's evidence, is a false impression. The entire Denning Report, in fact, seems intent on minimizing Ivanov's significance, thereby softening the security aspects of the situation. In this process the influence on Denning of Hollis's evidence was crucial, as will become apparent. It was in the interests of MI5, as well as of the Government, that the direct link between Ivanov and Keeler should be made to appear as tenuous as possible to play down the security implications, which were far more dangerous politically than the moral aspects.

It has even been suggested, with gross naivety, that Ivanov's sexual relationship with Keeler was part of an operation organized by Ward on MI5's behalf to 'entrap' Ivanov and perhaps induce him to defect by the blackmail threat of revealing the fact to his Soviet superiors. The evidence would suggest that Ward did organize the relationship but to entrap somebody else on Moscow's behalf. The really serious security aspects arose from Keeler's simultaneous sexual involvement with John Profumo, who had become Secretary of State for War in July 1960.

On the evening of Saturday, 8 July 1961, Ward, Keeler and some other girls were bathing in the pool at Cliveden, which Lord Astor had given them permission to use. After Astor had finished dinner he took his guest, Mr Profumo, to the pool from which Keeler had emerged naked a few moments previously. She seized a towel and was reasonably decent by the time Lady Astor, Mrs Profumo and others arrived. It would seem that Astor knew that the girls were likely to be in the pool and took Profumo down for devilment. Keeler records that Ward had dared her to remove her bathing costume and he hid it behind a bush so that she would be discovered naked. It is therefore quite possible that Keeler was set up by Ward in this way to ensnare Profumo, as Keeler herself now suspects.[7]

Profumo responded to the sight of the half-naked Keeler by helping Astor to chase her round the pool and then showing her over the house so that he could flirt with her. As she remarks in her book, 'If it had rained during the weekend of 8 July 1961 many lives might have been different.'

Ivanov was not at Cliveden on that Saturday evening but on the afternoon of the next day there was a formal bathing party attended by the Astors and their guests, including Profumo, and by Ward and his guests, who then included Ivanov. Knowing that Profumo was there for the weekend Ward may well have summoned Ivanov down to take advantage of the situation. According to Keeler, Ward was serving as an intelligence agent for Ivanov. She witnessed the delivery of several bulky packages to the Soviet Embassy and records that Ward was in receipt of payments from Ivanov, albeit of small sums.[8]

During a convivial afternoon, during which Profumo and Ivanov swam races, the War Minister secured Keeler's telephone number from Ward who then encouraged Keeler to see him on the grounds that he was both distinguished and important.

A sexual liaison developed lasting, on and off, until the end of 1961. Keeler was later to tell various people that she would be in bed with Profumo and Ivanov on the same day, but she now insists that she had sexual intercourse with Ivanov only once, on the evening of Sunday, 9 July, when he drove her back to London. That was also the information she gave to Lord Denning when questioned by him.

Whatever the truth, and repeatedly in her book Keeler claims that her memory of the events is bad, it was in the Government's interests that the story about being in bed with the War Minister and a Soviet Intelligence agent on the same day should be branded as a lie, as it was by Denning.

During the period of Profumo's affair with Keeler, the U.S. Government was planning to arm the West German army with a medium-range ballistic missile known as Sergeant.[9] The nuclear warheads were to be kept under American control in West Germany until an emergency, when the German troops would be empowered to use them. This plan was common knowledge but the date when the missiles were to become operational was secret. For general intelligence reasons the Soviets would want to know this date because of the extreme sensitivity in Moscow to any access by the Germans to nuclear weapons. There were also more pressing reasons for Soviet interest in the date. Khrushchev had already taken the decision to build the Berlin wall and N.A.T.O. reaction could conceivably result in war. He had also decided to install medium-range nuclear missiles in Cuba which was certain to provoke angry American reaction. If Moscow could prove that the Americans were about to station nuclear missiles on the West German border the case for missiles in Cuba would seem more reasonable.

In such political contexts it is important to appreciate how Soviet Intelligence officers operate and Ivanov's career in Britain is an excellent example of how an apparently 'legal' defence attaché can be utilized in the Kremlin's interests. There can be little, if any, doubt that when Ivanov met Profumo at Cliveden he quickly reported the details to Moscow. Further, once he reported the establishment of Profumo's sexual liaison with Keeler, about which Ward informed him, there would have been high-level meetings in Moscow to consider how advantage could be taken of it. Ivanov was a G.R.U. officer but by 1961 the K.G.B. had secured control of the G.R.U. and would almost certainly have taken over the Profumo operation because of the political potentialities. There

321

was, in fact, quick evidence of Kremlin interest, including that of Khrushchev.[10]

From the evidence there can be no doubt that Ivanov was instructed to use his relationship with Ward and Keeler to discover the delivery date of the nuclear warheads to West Germany. It was a reasonable assumption that in view of the close operational relations between the German forces and Britain's Rhine Army, the War Minister might know the date, which turned out to be the following year, 1962', according to official German sources.[11] It has been suggested that a professional officer like Ivanov would not be permitted to prejudice his diplomatic position by trying to secure information, even indirectly, from a minister but the behaviour of other Iron Curtain attachés, before and since, shows this view to be ill-founded.

Keeler told several witnesses that she had been asked to discover the date from Profumo, though she had never done so. The most reliable of these, in my opinion, is Mr Eddowes, who interviewed Keeler for reasons of personal interest on 14 December 1962, two months after the Cuban missile crisis and, of course, long before she gave evidence to Denning. Eddowes' records show that Keeler told him that Ivanov had asked her directly to 'obtain from Profumo the date of delivery of nuclear warheads to West Germany'.[12]

Keeler has since insisted that it was Ward, acting on Ivanov's behalf, who asked her to secure the information and that it was done rather flippantly. But it is difficult to explain why Eddowes' notes show that it was Ivanov, which would make more sense because a professional intelligence officer would always prefer to state his requirements directly rather than through a third person and Keeler admits that she continued to see Ivanov at Ward's flat. Eddowes has assured me that he gave this information about Ivanov to Denning during their two-hour discussion, when he appeared as a witness.[13]

If I appear to labour the point about the nuclear weapons request there are two important reasons for doing so. Firstly, the Denning Report went out of its way to deny that Ivanov had made a direct appeal to Keeler, even suggesting that she may just have overheard a conversation between the two men. Secondly, the fact that, according to Eddowes' notes, Keeler used the term 'nuclear warheads' also suggests that she heard this technical expression, which was not then in common usage, from a technical man, namely Ivanov. The use of 'West Germany' also suggests a direct approach from Ivanov because a nineteen-year-old, fairly ignorant girl was unlikely to have known the difference between West and East Germany in those days.

Keeler now claims that Ward simply said, 'Why don't you ask Jack when the Americans are going to give the Germans the bomb?' but I find the existence of the phrase 'nuclear warheads' in Eddowes' contemporary notes most convincing because he is not a technical man and he had no knowledge from any other source that missiles, not bombs, were to be delivered to West Germany. He insists that his information originated only from Keeler who was repeating what Ivanov had asked her. Whether Ivanov or Ward did the asking is somewhat academic for the original request – to Ward or Keeler – must have come from Ivanov and, further back, probably from G.R.U. headquarters in Moscow.

It is important to appreciate that before Keeler gave evidence to Denning she was grilled in a hostile manner by men she believed to be from MI5 but were probably Special Branch or Metropolitan police. They questioned her repeatedly about her relations with Ivanov, with Ward and about the request for atomic information. She became very frightened of being involved in an Official Secrets Act prosecution and she would have been less than human, at the age of nineteen, had she not wanted to minimize the security aspects by claiming that the request had come from Ward more or less as a joke.[14]

In the several hours that Hollis spent as a witness with Denning he, too, did what he could to play down the security implications of the Ivanov-Profumo-Keeler relationship. As a result, Denning's report presented the evidence in a way which ridiculed the idea that the Russians would try to discover a military secret through a girl like Keeler. In fact it is common Soviet practice to use both women and men in this way to secure information. Even a Russian chambermaid was used to compromise a British ambassador.

As will be seen, the American security authorities were to take Ivanov's interest in their nuclear weapons most seriously and clearly thought it possible that his association with Keeler and hers with Profumo might have been used. Further, at that time Hollis must have known of the American concern because U.S. security officials were making specific inquiries about American servicemen who might have known Keeler not only at the N.A.T.O. base at Ruislip but at nuclear bases in Suffolk.[15]

The Denning Report also presented the evidence in such a way that, as the document progressed, the information sought by Ivanov ceased to be the date on which the West Germans would be receiving nuclear weapons and became 'atomic secrets'. As Profumo had no access to atomic secrets, a phrase which suggests technical know-how, this device enabled Denning to declare that the importance of the atomic episode had been 'greatly exaggerated'. It also enabled the Prime Minister, Harold Macmillan, in his memoirs to suggest that the idea of using Keeler as an intermediary was fatuous because Profumo knew no 'atomic secrets'.[16] He might well, however, have known the delivery date which Ivanov wanted. Whether intentional or not, this change of phrasing by Denning, which seems to owe much to the influence of Hollis's evidence, watered down the security implications to the advantage of MI5, and of Hollis in particular, when the part played by that organization came to be summarized in the report.

The information that Ivanov hoped to secure the delivery date was first given to MI5 by Ward in July 1961 shortly after the bathing party weekend at Cliveden. Hollis was later to tell Denning and others that he had been kept in the dark about it, but some of his officers insist that he was fully informed. I find it inconceivable, with the Secretary of State for War and atomic weapons involved and with a crisis situation in Berlin, that the MI5 investigating officers would have failed to warn the Director-General. Later Hollis told Denning that when he did learn about the atomic weapons request from Ivanov he was 'not greatly impressed with it'. Why ever not? The Security Service is deeply concerned with the preservation of military secrets and particularly those of an atomic nature.

Understandably, Denning knew nothing about the technical and strategic aspects of the nuclear situation and it would appear that nobody enlightened him in that request. If he depended on Hollis for such information it might have been a case of the blind leading the blind, though Hollis did have access to a technical department. Hollis would certainly not have consulted the Defence Ministry for advice because of his near-pathological objection to allowing anybody outside MI5 to know what was going on inside.

An action by Hollis on 9 August 1961 virtually confirms that he had been quickly informed about Ivanov's desire to secure the delivery date of the warheads via Profumo. Avoiding any direct contact with the War Minister, or any other, as was his wont, he went to see the Cabinet Secretary, Sir Norman Brook, and asked him to warn Profumo against confiding in Ward. He followed this with the outrageous suggestion that Profumo might help to induce Ivanov to defect to the West. This was most irresponsible because no minister of the Crown should ever be embroiled in such matters. When approached by Brook, Profumo wisely declined but, had he sounded out Ivanov, the Russian could have complained to his Ambassador and, had it suited the Kremlin, political capital could have been made of it.

The date when Hollis first decided to promote the idea that

Ivanov might be encouraged to defect is locked in the files of MI5, if such documentation still exists, but, in view of the lunch organized by Hollis's friend, Sir Colin Coote, it is not improbable that the first meeting between Ward and Ivanov was accomplished at Hollis's suggestion with that purpose in mind. From the data on Ivanov available to Hollis he must have realized that there was negligible chance that such a dedicated communist would defect. The suggestion might have originated at a lower level but it was Hollis who was instrumental in trying to involve Profumo in what seemed almost sure to be an abortive exercise. MI5 officers have confirmed to me that they knew that Ivanov was a totally committed communist with excellent career prospects, and Keeler is at some pains to confirm this in her book and in private conversation with me.[17]

Hollis assured Denning that when he went to see the Cabinet Secretary he had no knowledge of Profumo's affair with Keeler. Some MI5 officers whom I have consulted find this difficult to believe. In any event, Profumo thought that the warning he received from Brook did refer to his involvement with Keeler and he took action to end it. Ward would have told Ivanov that the affair was over by the end of 1961 and, after Keeler left Ward's flat to live elsewhere in March 1962, the Russian must have reported to the Moscow Centre that any hope of securing information via Profumo had vanished. Under normal circumstances the details would simply have been filed against the day when the War Minister's imprudence might, conceivably, have some value. But the circumstances were soon to be far from normal and Ivanov was also to be required to use his friendship with Ward in the Kremlin's interest in connection with the installation of Soviet missiles in Cuba.

In April 1962 Ward secured a meeting with the head of the Foreign Office, Sir Harold Caccia (now Lord), to promote Ivanov as a medium for discussing such Anglo-Soviet interests as Berlin and the Oder-Neisse Line. Such contacts eventually induced MI5 to see Foreign Office representatives and warn them that Ivanov was a G.R.U. Intelligence officer – a fact which MI5 had known for more than a year.[18] This was, presumably, done on Hollis's advice because he would have been involved with any moves concerning the Foreign Office.

On 16 October 1962 President Kennedy was given photographic evidence by the C.I.A. that the Russians were installing ballistic missile launching pads in Cuba. Six days later Kennedy broadcast this menacing development to the world and announced that a blockade of Cuba would be mounted by the U.S. Navy. There were justifiable fears that the situation could lead to war because if the Russians challenged the blockade the U.S. was prepared to bomb the Cuban missile sites before they could be completed. Ivanov, acting on instructions from the Soviet Ambassador, was active, with Ward, in trying to resolve the situation to the U.S.S.R.'s advantage through some British intervention. On 24 October Ward telephoned the Foreign Office and, using Lord Astor's name, suggested that Sir Harold Caccia should take some initiative in recommending a summit conference to resolve the Cuban crisis. The next day Ward induced the Tory M.P., Sir Godfrey Nicholson, to meet Ivanov who urged him to go to the Foreign Office and press for a summit conference. Ward also tried to use Lord Arran to reinforce this suggestion. Arran met Ivanov, who assured him that Khrushchev would accept the British invitation to take part in a summit conference with alacrity and, as a result, Britain would secure credit for breaking the deadlock.[19]

Ivanov, a naval captain, would not have dared to use Khrushchev's name in this way without specific permission from the Kremlin and these events demonstrate the level at which his game was being played, though nothing came of his efforts. On 27 October Khrushchev sent a letter to Kennedy offering to withdraw the missiles from Cuba if the U.S. would withdraw theirs from Turkey. This was highly significant in view of Ivanov's attempt to discover the date of the deployment of American missiles in Germany. If the Kremlin had secured that information, it might have included it in the Soviet price for withdrawing the Cuban missiles.

Kennedy agreed to Khrushchev's proposals in principle and to an additional, and far more important, Soviet demand, then secret, that the U.S. should give an undertaking not to invade Cuba.[20] The following day, 28 October, the U.S.S.R. agreed to withdraw its missiles and Soviet ships turned back from Cuba. It so happened that Astor gave another party at Cliveden on that day and Ward and Ivanov were present. Ivanov was extremely angry when news came through that the Russians had backed down but, with hindsight, he should have been delighted because while the Cuban crisis was hailed as a triumph for American resolution it was the Kremlin that reaped the reward. The U.S. was saddled with a promise not to invade Cuba and more than twenty years later Castro is still there undermining Central America and Africa in the Soviet interest. All that the Soviet Union lost was the part-built missile sites in Cuba which, within a few years, would have been of marginal value because the same American cities they could have threatened were soon covered by intercontinental missiles based in the Soviet Union and on submarines.

In these critical circumstances, with the Berlin wall and the Cuban missiles bringing the world to the brink of nuclear war, Hollis's continuing attitude to Ivanov's activities as being of no importance must be seen as a measure of his incompetence or worse.

A further false statement in the Denning Report deriving from information supplied by Hollis is the assurance that MI5 did not know that Profumo had been involved in sexual relations with Keeler until 29 January 1963 – the day that Ivanov skipped the country – though MI5 had been in regular touch with Ward and his set-up at Cliveden and elsewhere from 12 July 1961, immediately after Profumo first met Keeler. Hollis's statement to Denning on this count has been described to me by one MI5 officer as 'a brazen lie'. At a meeting in MI5 headquarters, before his encounter with Denning, Hollis had complained about being kept in ignorance of the sexual affair and had immediately been reminded of a six-page report about the relationship between Ward, Keeler, Profumo and Ivanov. The officer who submitted it had been informed of the Profumo-Keeler association by the patriotic *demi-monde* woman I have already mentioned. He had also heard of it through the general gossip among Ward's friends.[21] Ward could not keep a secret and Keeler records that he lost no time in retailing, with relish, how she had bedded both the War Minister and the Soviet Naval Attaché.

The next pro-Soviet move, which was to result in a personal tragedy for Profumo and a major shift to the left in British politics, seems to have been a mysterious telephone call, on 11 November 1962, to a prominent Labour Party backbench M.P. who interested himself in security matters, George Wigg, later Lord Wigg. Wigg described to me how he had received the call while lunching at the home of his party agent in his Dudley constituency, where very few people knew he was. In what appeared to be a deliberately muffled voice, the caller said, 'Forget about the Vassall case. You want to look at Profumo,' and then hung up.

There is evidence in the files of MI5 that the call was organized by the K.G.B., and it was almost a carbon copy of the event which triggered off the publicity about the defection of Maclean and Burgess in 1951. A *Daily Express* journalist, sitting in a restaurant in Paris, received a telephone call from someone who knew his name, alerted him to the story and then hung up.[22]

Wigg was immediately interested, having a political score to settle with Profumo, and set inquiries in train. On 14 December 1962 Keeler was shot at by a West Indian with whom she had been living. As a result she telephoned Eddowes, the solicitor, and in the course of their conversation told him of the liaison with Profumo and with Ivanov. Fate was also working against Profumo and in the Soviet interest when Keeler attended a party and met an M.P. in whom she confided details about her affair with Profumo and about the nuclear weapons request. This M.P. told Wigg, who appreciated the security implications and their political potential against the reigning Tory Government. The fact that Ivanov was still active in Britain while Wigg and others were making their inquiries increased this potential.

Events moved further when Keeler realized the financial possibilities of her position. On 22 January 1963 she signed a contract with a Sunday newspaper to tell her story and gave them a letter from Profumo in which she was addressed as 'Darling'. Profumo was soon alerted to the danger and asked Hollis to see him, apparently believing that MI5 might be able to stifle Press comment through the issue of a D-Notice. There was no way this could have been arranged and Hollis told him so. On that same day, 28 January, the Attorney-General, Sir John Hobson, heard about Keeler's allegation concerning Profumo from Ward's lawyer.

The fuse serving the bomb which was to destroy Profumo's career and bring the Government into disrepute, helping to end Macmillan's leadership, was well and truly lit and Hollis had consistently failed to warn the Prime Minister of the danger. Denning was to go out of his way to make excuses for Hollis but in the House of Commons debate on Profumo on 16 June Macmillan was to make his feelings clear. He told Parliament, 'The Security Services did not pass these reports to me. As things turned out I think, in the circumstances, it is very unfortunate that this information was not given to me. But the Head of the Security Service did not take these reports with great importance and after Ivanov had left the country he was satisfied that the indirect contact between Ivanov and Profumo did not involve any security. I strongly regret that this information, which came originally from the police, was not, through the files of the Security Service, passed to me.'[23]

Clearly Hollis should have 'failed safe' and warned the Prime Minister personally. Instead, there was an eleven-week delay before the police reports reached Macmillan, or any other minister, on 29 May 1963.

On 29 January Ivanov left Britain hurriedly, long before the time he was expected to do so. Denning was to state that this was the result of a 'tip-off'. He suggested that it might have come from Ward, but in view of the regularity with which Soviet agents in trouble were warned to decamp in the 1960s, Ivanov may have received his orders from the Moscow Centre as a result of information from a better informed source.

Events were moving fast because of the increasing interest by newspapers, both British and foreign, and on 1 February an executive of the *News of the World* called at the Prime Minister's office to inform him of the Ivanov implications and the fact that a rival newspaper had the 'Darling' letter.[24] This was to enable the leader of the Labour opposition, Harold Wilson, to allege, 'It would imply that the £60 millions spent on these services [MI5] under Mr Macmillan's premiership have been less productive than the security services of the *News of the World*.'[25]

On that same morning of 1 February Hollis had called a meeting of his senior officers and instructed them that 'until further notice no approach should be made to anyone in the Ward *galère* or to any other outside contact in respect of it. If we are approached we listen only.'[26] This astonished those officers who could see grave dangers ahead for the Government. One of them was so dismayed by this lack of action that he put his view in a memorandum to Hollis dated 4 February. It ran: 'If a scandal results from Mr Profumo's association with Christine Keeler there is likely to be a considerable rumpus...If, in any subsequent inquiries we were found to have been in possession of this information about Profumo and to have taken no action on it, we would, I am sure, be subject to much criticism for failing to bring it to light. I suggest that this information be passed to the Prime Minister and you might also like to consider whether or not, before doing so, we should interview Miss Keeler.'[27]

Hollis discussed the memo with his deputy, Graham Mitchell, whom he always overbore and who, at that time, was under active investigation as a suspected Soviet agent. Hollis decided to ignore the memo on the grounds that the issue was entirely political, not a security matter, and therefore outside MI5's concern. To underline this he issued another firm instruction against further inquiries.

Using his diaries Macmillan has recorded the extent of his meagre knowledge of the situation in the volume of his memoirs entitled *At the End of the Day*.

On 21 March 1963 George Wigg, who had received further evidence indirectly from Keeler, including the atomic weapons allegation, raised the matter in Parliament. From that moment a public scandal was assured. Hollis was still insisting that security was not an issue, especially as Ivanov had left the country, but without Ivanov's involvement the socialists could not have pursued the case. Wigg repeatedly told me that there were too many M.P.s with similar problems on his own front bench for it to have been practicable to try to censure Profumo on moral grounds.

Following Wigg's outburst the Tory Chief Whip was driven to consult Profumo and, with the help of four other senior ministers, a statement was drafted for Profumo to read in Parliament denying any intimacy with Keeler.[28] Many M.P.s and most of Fleet Street, including myself, were convinced that Profumo had lied. To fortify his claim Profumo sued two magazines for libel and won.

Through Ivanov, who, no doubt, was heavily debriefed in Moscow, the Soviets knew that Profumo was lying and from that moment he was open to blackmail by the K.G.B., though as Denning pointed out, and as I know myself from my acquaintance with Profumo, it is inconceivable that he would have submitted to such pressure.

With a political scandal about to explode, the Home Secretary, Henry Brooke, sent for Hollis on 27 March to be briefed on the background. Under the terms of his remit Hollis was directly responsible to the Home Secretary yet, though he himself had been kept informed of the situation day by day and was personally involved in the more important decisions, he had given no information whatever to Brooke. Indeed, until Brooke sent for him no Government minister had been told about Ivanov's interest in the atomic matter. Hollis kept that information from the Government for twenty-one months and presumably would have continued to do so had not Brooke summoned him. His behaviour in keeping both Brooke and Macmillan in ignorance is made all the more extraordinary by Brooke's statement to Parliament that after he had become Home Secretary in July 1962 he had had 'frequent, indeed constant, contacts' with Hollis and had met him 'from time to time in the company of Macmillan'.[29]

An MI5 officer involved in the case described Hollis's behaviour to me, in writing, as 'a grave dereliction of duty and responsibility – a default which could only have been intended to protect the prior interest of his other masters'.

Following this meeting with Brooke, another MI5 officer, Peter Wright, took issue with Hollis for his continuing failure to warn Macmillan. Hollis replied that he had done all that was necessary in informing the Home Secretary, who, in fact, also failed to warn Macmillan believing that Hollis had done so directly. Wright dissented in writing in a minute that is on file.

A further serious aspect of Hollis's failure to warn Macmillan has come to light. On 29 March 1963 Eddowes asked to see an officer of Special Branch, the Scotland Yard department that deals with security matters. An officer called Dickinson arrived at Eddowes' home and was given a long statement in the presence of Eddowes' lawyer. The statement, which I have examined, included details about Ivanov's request for the delivery date of nuclear weapons to West Germany. According to Eddowes, whom I believe, Dickinson remarked, 'This is a hot potato. It will be on the Prime Minister's desk in the morning.' That may have been no more than a conversational way of indicating that he thought it was important enough to be passed to the Prime Minister through the usual channels but when Eddowes telephoned Scotland Yard five days later to learn what had happened to his statement, Dickinson replied, 'It is out of my hands now.' Then he remarked, rather scathingly, according to Eddowes, 'Why don't you drop it?'

Special Branch did not pass the statement to the Prime Minister but, through the usual channels, it reached MI5 where Hollis prevented its further distribution. Nobody ever questioned Eddowes further until he eventually appeared as a witness before Lord Denning.[30]

On Monday, 27 May, Harold Wilson saw Macmillan to tell him the contents of a letter he had received from Ward and to urge him to take some action on the security issue. The Prime Minister's office sent a record of the conversation to MI5 as a routine procdure and asked for a re-examination of the security aspects of the case. On 29 May Hollis reported to Macmillan in person and told him about the request to Keeler to secure 'the date on which certain *atomic secrets* [my italics] were to be handed to West Germany by the Americans'. This, of course, was not strictly true and if the use of the phrase 'atomic secrets' was calculated to induce Macmillan to agree with Hollis that Ivanov's project was ridiculous because Profumo knew no atomic secrets, then it succeeded. When I discussed the matter with Mr Macmillan at his home at Birch Grove late in 1980 he asked rhetorically, 'What atomic secrets could Jack Profumo possibly have known?' As I pointed out then he could well have known the date, which was the only secret mentioned by Ivanov.

By the end of May it was clear to several ministers that Profumo had lied and that the truth would soon emerge. Macmillan asked the Lord Chancellor, Lord Dilhorne, to carry out a personal inquiry, which he began on 30 May. For reasons of conscience, and knowing that he would be interrogated by Dilhorne, Profumo decided to tell the truth, though he realized that his career and reputation would be ruined. On 5 June he resigned, leaving Macmillan to face a hostile debate, which I attended, not only from his Labour opponents but from several prominent Tories.[31] Macmillan's sorry plight was described by George Wigg: 'The Prime Minister's defence contained some amazing admissions...Three separate statements by Miss Keeler that she had been asked by Ward to obtain military information from Profumo had likewise never reached the Prime Minister – an admission that evoked the jibe "Nobody tells me anything!" '[32]

The Law Officers had a hand in preparing Macmillan's speech and for the security aspects they depended on a brief supplied by Hollis – a further indication of the power and influence wielded by a Director-General of MI5. It should surprise nobody, therefore, that the speech did its best to excuse Hollis's behaviour, though he had been heavily responsible for the Prime Minister's predicament. It gave the impression that there was nothing dangerous in the friendship between Ward and Ivanov, who was just an accredited diplomat. If Macmillan had been properly briefed he would have known that Ivanov was a professional G.R.U. officer. Macmillan assured the House that MI5 did not know of the relationship between Profumo and Keeler until January 1963 but he had only Hollis's word for that. Other MI5 officers believed that to be untrue but had no opportunity of saying so.

Macmillan said that Keeler had been asked to discover from Profumo 'certain atomic secrets', another misleading statement originating from Hollis. He went out of his way to discredit the evidence which Eddowes had submitted to the police. As in the Denning Report, a 1952 directive placing MI5 under the Home Secretary and outlining the Director-General's duties was exploited during the debate to excuse Hollis's lack of action.

It was suggested to Lord Denning that Ivanov's function was primarily to divide the United Kingdom from the United States by undermining American trust in British security. He certainly had some success in that respect for the whole Profumo affair made Britain a laughing stock worldwide, with American cabaret acts making the most of it.

By 13 June Lord Dilhorne had submitted his report to Macmillan who passed it to Denning on 21 June with a request to prepare a report of his own for publication. The Dilhorne report has never been published but Denning made much use of it, as Dilhorne, a close personal friend, made clear to me shortly before he died.[33] I know that Dilhorne believed Hollis to have been grossly at fault for keeping the Prime Minister and the Home Secretary in ignorance for so long but he was opposed to any public criticism of MI5 or its chief.

Like the Government, Denning appears to have accepted Hollis's statement that once Ivanov had left Britain the Profumo affair ceased to have any further security significance. It is, perhaps, understandable that Denning should have done so because Hollis was the expert to whom he had to defer on matters of professional opinion. In fact, Ivanov's precipitate flight was further evidence of the seriousness of his intelligence activities. He could not have been prosecuted because he held diplomatic immunity and, so far as is known, had sought information only about American weapons in Germany which was not an offence against the British Official Secrets Act. He could, however, have been held and questioned, and his controllers were clearly anxious to avoid that. For Hollis to suggest that Ivanov's departure should end MI5's interest in him or in his contacts transgressed all standard procedure. The normal practice is for inquiries to continue long after proven Soviet Intelligence officers have left the country. When Anthony Blunt confessed, MI5's interest centred on former Soviet controllers known to have been dead for many years. In Ivanov's case, as soon as he was out of Britain – and MI5, apparently, had a week's advanced knowledge that he would be leaving – Hollis made his departure an excuse for taking no further action on the whole affair and forbidding any of his officers from doing so. Those officers were convinced that in accordance with normal Soviet practice some other G.R.U. agent would immediately have taken on Ivanov's major commitments.

F.B.I. records, which have been made available to American researchers under the Freedom of Information Act, show that during June and July 1963, four months after Ivanov had fled, the security and intelligence authorities of the U.S. Army and U.S. Air Force became concerned about possible relationships between Keeler and American sergeants and officers which might have threatened nuclear secrets.[34] One document dated 17 July was headed 'Christine Keeler – Russia and Great Britain'. Three sergeants from a N.A.T.O. base at Ruislip were flown back to the U.S. for interrogation and a team of investigators visited Britain. As the F.B.I. was also involved it is inconceivable that Hollis was not made aware of this American interest in Ivanov but he seems to have avoided mentioning it to any Government minister or to Denning. It would have undermined his claim that security had ceased to be involved after Ivanov's departure. Nor can he have warned the F.B.I. of the request to Keeler concerning American nuclear warheads, otherwise U.S. security would have reacted more rapidly.

There are other, less important, aspects of the Denning Report which I know to be fallacious. On 15 March 1963, the *Daily Express* came out with a front-page report bearing the headline 'War Minister Shock' and suggesting that, for personal reasons, Profumo had offered to resign. On the right-hand side of the page was a picture of Christine Keeler headed 'Vanished Old Bailey Witness'. A representative from the *Daily Express*, Sir Tom Blackburn, told Denning that the juxtaposition of the two stories was entirely coincidental. That was completely untrue but Denning accepted it. I was privy to the talks preceding the setting up of the page and I know that it was intended to be the first break in the Fleet Street silence about the Profumo-Keeler affair. Sir Tom Blackburn had been selected because he had not been involved in the editorial decision and did not know the truth. This was, perhaps, a small detail but it shows that Denning could be misled.

It was Hollis who decided which of his officers, in addition to himself, should give evidence to Denning. One of them, whom Denning questioned about the surveillance of Ward, was Mitchell, who was under surveillance himself. To quote one of the less senior officers who had been involved in the case, 'The best informed, most reliable and personally disinterested witnesses were never called.' This particular officer realizes that he should have volunteered his evidence over Hollis's head but in those days – and probably even now – such action was unthinkable.

It is clear from the Denning Report that when Hollis was trying to explain his lack of action he made highly effective use of the guidelines which had been laid down by a previous Home Secretary to govern the activities of MI5. These stressed that no inquiries were to be pursued unless those in charge of MI5 were satisfied that an important public issue was at stake and bore directly on the defence of the realm. Can anyone doubt that the Profumo affair fulfilled these criteria? Yet Hollis appears to have convinced Denning that he was right in deciding that it did not.

Regarding the Security Service in general, Denning concluded, 'I find that they covered the security interest fully throughout and reported to those concerned...They took all reasonable steps to see that the interests of the country were defended...They kept the Foreign Office fully informed.' How Denning came to that conclusion would baffle anyone who studied his report, the ancillary evidence and the historic consequences. The overall effect of the Denning Report was to reduce the embarrassment factor in every possible way so that no Establishment figure was to blame. I am not saying that this was Denning's intention but it was certainly his achievement.

While the Profumo case was at its height I discussed it privately with Lord Beaverbrook who was extremely angry at the way events were moving. Shaking his fist he cried, 'Why in God's name should a great political party tear itself to rags and tatters just because a minister's fucked a woman?' Had I known then the details of

Hollis's handling of the case I might have been able to answer the question. Through Hollis's evidence to Lord Denning and his statements to Macmillan and others, another legend, which suited both the K.G.B. and his own interests, has been foisted on historians.

Historians may agree that the mishandling of the Profumo affair and the political capital which the Labour opposition were able to make out of it hastened the retirement of Harold Macmillan and the defeat of the Conservative Party at the general election in the following year. During the premiership of Harold Wilson, who had succeeded to the Labour leadership under the flag of representing its left wing, the Labour Party slid progressively to the left with trade union leaders who had been former communists exerting influence on policy. Labour ministers were permitted to support communist front organizations which had previously been proscribed and in the 1983 election the party's manifesto included commitments, such as unilateral nuclear disarmament and the elimination of American bases in Britain, which must have had the Kremlin's total support.

Harold Wilson also introduced severe restrictions on MI5's capacity to investigate M.P.s and peers who might be involved in treachery or subversion. Any form of surveillance was forbidden without the Prime Minister's agreement – a situation which still stands.

The ancillary documents of the Denning inquiry, including the testimony of witnesses, are unlikely to be released within fifty years and some may have been destroyed, but further light on the Profumo tragedy may be shed by the official biography of Harold Macmillan, now in preparation but to be withheld from publication during his lifetime.

The Potential Value of Oversight

The Profumo affair is surely an unquestionable example of how effective oversight of major MI5 activities, especially those with high political content, could have prevented the worst consequences. It is unlikely that Hollis would have behaved in the way he did had he known that his activities, or lack of them, could be subject to independent scrutiny. While he was able, effectively, to dispense justice in secret, as was to happen in the cases of Blunt and Long, he was also, through inaction, to cause injustice to Macmillan and his administration. These powers have recently been pruned, following the Long case, but as things stand it would still be possible for a Director-General of MI5 to behave as Hollis behaved over Profumo.

Because of the mystique still surrounding MI5, which itself is a reason for oversight, a clever director-general might still be able to mislead his questioners, especially by over-pleading the needs of operational secrecy. In any oversight arrangements there should be powers to call subordinate officers for questioning.

CHAPTER THIRTY-FIVE

A Clutch of Curious Incidents

EARLY in 1963 'Fedora', the fake double agent in New York, reported to the F.B.I. that Soviet Intelligence had managed to plant another valuable source of information inside one of the research establishments of the British Atomic Energy Authority.[1] He knew few details beyond the fact that the agent was ideological, meaning that he was a pro-Soviet communist, and had been inserted within the previous two years. Some MI5 officers were already half-convinced that 'Fedora' was a fake defector who might have planted the information for mischievous purposes, but there was such sensitivity about possible spies inside the atomic project following the Nunn May, Fuchs and Pontecorvo cases, that the tip could not be ignored.

The only person who fitted the indications was a 39-year-old Italian scientist called Dr Giuseppe Martelli, who was working for the Euratom organization at the Culham Laboratory in Oxfordshire, a few miles from the Harwell station. He had had no known access to nuclear secrets but inquiries revealed that he had been in contact with Russians believed to be intelligence officers. The police detained him after his arrival back in Britain from a holiday and when his house was searched the police found a set of one-time cipher pads for transmitting messages, along with other suspicious objects.

As Martelli had committed no known offence any prosecution would have to be under a section of the Official Secrets Act which makes it an offence to commit an act which is thought to be preparatory to espionage. The MI5 lawyers were doubtful about the wisdom of pursuing the case and Arthur Martin, in particular, among several MI5 officers, strongly advised against it. Hollis, however, who was supported by the suspect Mitchell, was very keen to press ahead with a prosecution, arguing that a conviction would help to establish the good faith of 'Fedora' for the F.B.I., which would improve relations with Hoover. Hollis knew that 'Fedora' was supporting Nosenko, in whom he claimed to have

337

faith, in contrast to those of his officers who suspected that Nosenko was also a fake, following the Vassall case. The strengthening of 'Fedora's' credibility as a source would, therefore, help to dispose of the suspicions that there was still a high-level naval spy, which Hollis chose not to believe.

As a result, Martelli was put on trial at the Old Bailey on 2 July 1963. The defence admitted contact with Soviet agents but pleaded that Martelli was being blackmailed by threats to his estranged wife, who had been educated in the Soviet Union and wished to return there with their two children. It also admitted the possession of espionage equipment but pointed out that that was not a crime and that Martelli had no access to secrets. Martelli admitted having met Karpekov, who became the K.G.B. 'resident' in London. He told the court that once, when they were about to lunch together at a pub, Karpekov produced a list of 'all the special cars used by MI5' so that he could check on the cars parked there. He said that Karpekov had boasted that Soviet Intelligence had 'very highly placed friends' in MI5, who, presumably, had provided the list.[2] This information cried out for rigorous examination, especially when taken in conjunction with all the previous evidence for the existence of one or more Soviet agents inside MI5. But I have been told that the claim was not pursued because there was no MI5 department with specific responsibility for doing so and that Hollis had no desire to create one.

On 15 July Martelli was acquitted on all charges, to the public and international humiliation of the police and of MI5, which had urged the prosecution. Whatever Hollis's motives might have been the result was in the K.G.B.'s favour for, among other debits, it exposed a weakness in British law which the K.G.B. could exploit in future. It must have seemed incredible to the Russians that a foreigner could be caught with the paraphernalia of spying, with admission to having been in contact with K.G.B. agents, and yet pay no penalty when he failed to report his position. The fiasco also exacerbated ill feeling between MI5 and the police, which had been involved in the prosecution on MI5's advice, and it did not go unnoticed in Washington. The F.B.I. considered that it had given MI5 accurate information and Hollis's outfit had made a hash of it. The proof in court that the information about Martelli's Soviet connections was accurate helped to establish the bona fides of 'Fedora' who was, in fact, a fake and had been given the information by the K.G.B. Centre for that purpose.

While the Martelli case was in progress 'Fedora' was active in another direction in an attempt to exacerbate the security aspects of the Profumo case. After returning to New York from a visit to

Moscow he told the F.B.I. that, by chance, he had met the Soviet Naval Attaché, Ivanov, and had had a long conversation with him. He claimed that Ivanov had boasted of having installed a microphone in Christine Keeler's bedroom and that the G.R.U. had secured valuable intelligence which Christine had, presumably, obtained from the War Minister. Hoover regarded this information as so important that he sent a copy of 'Fedora's' report personally to President Kennedy who declined to send it on to Macmillan, as Hoover had suggested, remarking that the British Prime Minister was in enough trouble already.[3]

When the report eventually reached MI5, officers who had examined Keeler's bedroom decided that it was 'unbuggable' and that the statement was further disinformation from 'Fedora', though it was possible that Ivanov had made the claim as a boast.

'Fedora' did not stop there. In an effort to persuade the F.B.I. that the K.G.B. had not engineered the Profumo scandal he said that he had discovered that it had been planned by French Intelligence, which made no sense to anybody, though the K.G.B. was keen to worsen relations between Britain and de Gaulle. 'Fedora' also claimed that there was a Soviet spy inside the establishment at Aldermaston, Berkshire, where nuclear weapons are designed. This turned out to be false but wasted much time and scarce security resources.

While the Profumo and Mitchell cases were at their height, an opportunity to improve the public image of MI5 was offered to Hollis in 1963, as it had been two years previously, by Sir John Masterman. He had been deeply involved in the highly successful MI5 Double Cross operation during the war, which turned German spies against the Nazis so as to feed them with a mass of misleading information and was a major contribution to the Allied victory.[4] Masterman, an MI5 'amateur' who was keen to return to Oxford as soon as the war was over, remained in the Service for a few weeks to write the official history of the triumph for MI5's records. In 1961 he had suggested that his report should be published because it would benefit MI5's reputation, which had been tarnished by post-war spy cases, but Hollis firmly declined. In 1963, after Sir Alec Douglas-Home, who was Prime Minister at the time, agreed with Masterman that publication would improve MI5's image, which by then had been further blemished by the Vassall case, Masterman approached Hollis again. Once more he rejected the proposal, assuring Sir Alec that he had the backing of his legal advisers.[5]

As a result, Masterman had to wait until 1972, after Hollis had retired, when he took matters into his own hands and avoided the problem of official agreement by publishing his book in the U.S. It was then republished in Britain and gives credit to MI5's wartime effort against the Germans.

It is possible that Hollis was motivated by a passion for total secrecy, especially in the middle of 1963 when so much was going wrong, but the fact remains that publicity for those sections of MI5 that had functioned with such brilliance against German agents would have underscored the abject failure of his wartime section against agents of the Soviet Union.

Masterman's personal views about the competence of Hollis are unknown to me but the book which Hollis suppressed was critical of his performance in counter-espionage against the Russians and particularly of his failure to recruit double agents.

Round about 1963 evidence became available that a former Conservative minister, who is now dead, might have been subjected to blackmail by Soviet agents and, as he had been in a sensitive post at the time, the MI5 officer who produced the information suggested an investigation. Hollis forbade any inquiries saying that the implications were potentially far too embarrassing to the Government, as they undoubtedly were. Later, when further independent evidence became available, an interrogation of the suspect was suggested but Hollis again forbade it. The Government was not told of the development and the suspect eventually received a high honour for his past services.[6]

Knowing the identity of the former minister, it seems most unlikely to me that the Government would have taken any action against him as the circumstances would have been particularly difficult for the Prime Minister, Harold Macmillan, but it was Hollis's duty to inform the Home Secretary of the situation in case it suddenly became public and caught the Government unprepared. Instead he preferred to remain silent, probably because he did not wish to be the bearer of what would have been extremely frightening news.

Other promising MI5 investigations continued to founder in ways which the frustrated case officers could attribute only to internal leakages from high level. One case, which is well remembered by these officers, concerned Mr Reuben Falber, a prominent member of the Communist Party who is still alive at the time of writing.

It had been known for decades that the Communist Party of Great Britain was supported with Soviet money. Because the Kremlin wanted to continue its pretence that it was not involved the money was always provided surreptitiously by the Soviet Embassy to paymasters, such as the late Bob Stewart, who received

340

it, often through cut-outs, in wads of notes, usually in shoe-boxes.

Since the receipt of such money was no crime under British law, MI5 could not attempt to interrogate any of the paymasters to find out details of the sums involved and what happened to them and whether any was funnelled to agents for espionage or subversion. It was assumed, however, that the Communist Party would keep ledgers, which would provide the answers if they could be examined.

In the early 1960s MI5 suspected, wrongly perhaps, that the man who might have the ledgers in his possession was Mr Falber who lived in a two-storey house divided into two single-floor flats. When it was noticed that he was advertising for a tenant for the lower flat MI5 secured it through an agency and installed a woman collaborator, known in the jargon as a 'granny', though she was quite young. She used the name 'Miss Taylor'.

Soon afterwards, at Christmas, Falber spent a couple of days in the country with Lord Milford, the communist peer (formerly Wogan Philipps), so MI5 decided to search his flat. The 'granny' had organized a Christmas party for 'friends and relatives' and various vans supplying food and drink were parked outside. Under this cover some of the friends and relatives were about to break into the flat when a radio message from watchers staked round Milford's house told them that Falber had left suddenly by car and might be returning to London. The search was therefore called off, unnecessarily as it transpired, because Falber, having been lost by the watchers, returned to Milford's house.

As soon as Falber did return home, after Boxing Day, he gave the 'granny' a week's notice without any reason. The MI5 management, including Hollis, had been informed of the proposed operation only two days in advance of it because approval had to be obtained before the flat could be entered. The officers suspected that Falber had been told the true nature of the 'granny' and her 'friends'. When I spoke to Mr Falber recently he commented, 'I soon sussed out Miss Taylor.' When I asked who 'Miss Taylor' was he replied, 'You'd better ask your 'friends.'

CHAPTER THIRTY-SIX

The 'Blunden' File

In the autumn of 1963, with the public scandal of the Profumo affair still fresh and the Mitchell case unresolved, Hollis was suddenly faced with evidence he could not ignore that his old colleague and friend, Sir Anthony Blunt had been a Soviet agent during the whole of his five years' service inside MI5 and possibly afterwards. The situation was exacerbated by Blunt's position in the Royal Household as Surveyor of the Queen's Pictures. Before Hollis's treatment of this case and of the chief investigator concerned with it can be dealt with, a brief survey of Blunt's activities inside MI5, where he came under no suspicion while he remained there, is necessary.

In Chapter 19 I have described how Blunt was recruited to Soviet Intelligence at Cambridge by Burgess and how he, in turn, had recruited others before being appointed Deputy Director of the Courtauld Institute of Art in London. In 1940 Blunt managed to insinuate himself on to the wartime staff of MI5 where he employed Burgess as an agent-runner in penetrating the embassies of neutral countries. Blunt operated for the K.G.B. under the code-name 'Johnson' and his Soviet controller when he joined MI5 was the highly professional 'Henry', the K.G.B. officer posing as a diplomat in the Soviet Embassy in London, where he was listed as Anatoli Gromov though his real name was Anatoli Gorski.[1]

Blunt had long discussions with 'Henry' about the organization of MI5 to decide where he should try to secure a permanent position. After talks with the Moscow Centre, 'Henry' told Blunt to avoid F Branch, which handled Soviet espionage and the activities of communists in Britain and was headed by Hollis. Blunt was later to agree that 'Henry's' instruction was odd and suggested that it implied that the Soviets already had a source there.

Blunt began his MI5 service in the Military Liaison Division, as he was still in army uniform, but he soon secured a transfer to B Division, which was responsible for security, intelligence and counter-espionage operations of the greatest interest to the Soviets.

For part of his time he was personal assistant to the Director of B Division, Guy Liddell, and was also in the MI5 Secretariat, assisting the Director-General, Sir David Petrie. Documents of the highest importance and secrecy crossed his desk and he never failed to report their contents to the K.G.B., usually taking them out of the office by the caseful so that the Soviets could photograph them. Pressure of work could always be claimed as an excuse for taking secret documents home, especially when bombing was causing extra difficulties, but there can be no escaping the fact that in MI5, as in MI6, internal security was appallingly ineffective.

By the time Blunt was installed in MI5 one of the Apostles whom he had recruited at Cambridge, Leo Long, a fluent German-speaker, was working in MI14. This was a separate section set up in May 1940 to provide a running estimate of the strengths of various Germany army groups and continuous assessments of future German actions.[2] Long had access to information supplied by Bletchley and must have known of the existence of Ultra. It follows that Blunt must also have known about it, even if he had not discovered its existence from his own sources, and that the Russians were informed about it from an early stage. MI14, which was renamed the Military Intelligence Research Section in 1943, also had access to U.S. Army Intelligence.[3]

When Long joined MI14 the Soviet Union was not in the war and was virtually an ally of the Nazis, being keen to see the defeat of Britain and the enforced dissolution of the British Empire, yet, when Blunt told Long that he must supply him with all the secret information he could for onward passage to the Russians, Long obliged. When eventually exposed, Long indicated that Blunt did not ask him for information until the Soviet Union was Britain's ally, but that proved to be false. Long was providing secret information for the Russians before they were forced into the war and there is every possibility that, with Stalin anxious to pacify Hitler and keen on the defeat of Britain, the K.G.B. passed some of it to German Intelligence, though they would not have revealed its source.

Blunt passed all of Long's information to 'Henry' and so served as Long's controller as well as being a spy in his own right. There is no evidence that Long was in direct contact with Russians during the war. K.G.B. orders for Long were transmitted by Blunt, who worked his friend hard. Over the three years when Long was based in London he met Blunt about once a fortnight, usually in pubs, to pass him detailed information which crossed his desk from agents operating in Europe. Blunt pressed him repeatedly to ensure that he was handing over everything of possible value to the Russians.[4]

'Henry' specifically told Blunt not to try to recruit anybody from inside the MI5 office as this would be too risky. Anybody in the office whom he considered recruitable would have to be weighed up by the K.G.B. Centre and possibly approached through different channels. It seems possible, however, that 'Henry' introduced Blunt to another Soviet agent operating in London throughout the war – Juergen Kuczynski, Sonia's brother. Kuczynski records in his memoirs having been on terms of close and open friendship with 'Henry', whom he visited at the Soviet Embassy.[5]

Another German refugee who might have provided a link between Blunt and the Kuczynskis, had MI5 been minded to question him, was Baron Wolfgang zu Putlitz, a homosexual who was also a close friend of Burgess, whom he had known at Cambridge. Between 1934 and 1938 zu Putlitz was a First Secretary in the German Embassy in London and had access to secret information of great interest to both MI5 and MI6. Klop Ustinov, the German father of Peter, the actor, was a friend of his and, being opposed to Hitler, he contacted the well-known anti-Nazi Robert Vansittart and offered to work for Britain. As evidence of his value and good faith he said that he could bring zu Putlitz with him. The offer was accepted and the Baron worked as a British spy both during his time in London and later when posted to the German Embassy in Holland. He was extracted from Holland with great difficulty when he fell under suspicion and then spent some time in New York.[6] In his memoirs he claims that he heard of the formation of a National Committee of Free Germany and wrote to Moscow, wishing it all success.[7] As a result he was approached by the Soviet Consul in New York, the predecessor of the notorious Anatoli Yakovlev, the spymaster for Fuchs and other Soviet agents operating in the U.S. Zu Putlitz was already communist-inclined and may well have been recruited as a Soviet agent, as his subsequent behaviour was to indicate. He returned to Britain, probably on K.G.B. instructions, and secured a job with the secret 'Black Propaganda' team headed by Sefton Delmer at Woburn Abbey.[8] It would seem most unlikely that zu Putlitz would have failed to contact the Free German Movement in the U.K., in which case he would have met Kuczynski. He certainly made contact with Blunt, for in the preface to his memoirs he pays tribute to that traitor's 'kindness and understanding', while making no reference to him in the body of the book.

Zu Putlitz went back to Germany in 1946 and Blunt is said to have accompanied him but he was not allowed to go to Berlin.[9] After returning to London zu Putlitz renewed his friendship with Burgess and attended the party which the latter gave before leaving for Washington in 1950.[10] In 1952 the Baron crossed into East Germany, where the family estates were located, and became an East German citizen.[11]

In the early part of the war Lord Rothschild, a distinguished Cambridge scientist who had joined MI5 and specialized in the study and dismantling of German booby traps, had rented part of a house at 5 Bentinck Street, where he lived with his wife. They offered accommodation to two former Cambridge friends, Patricia Parry (later Lady Llewelyn-Davies) and Tessa Mayor (later the second Lady Rothschild). When Lord Rothschild was posted out of London he wished to dispose of the lease and offered it to the two girls.[12] They could not afford the rent so it was agreed, as the accommodation was on three floors, that they could sublet to friends. One of these friends, well known to Lord Rothschild and then entirely above suspicion, was Anthony Blunt. He suggested that the fourth occupant should be Guy Burgess. Number 5, therefore, came to house two Soviet spies though this was unknown to the other occupants or to Rothschild.

Various members of MI5, such as Liddell, and of MI6 are said to have visited the Bentinck Street establishment. It is unlikely that Hollis did so but he is believed to have been a social friend of Blunt during the war and afterwards at least until 1951, when, according to Blunt's 'confessions', they ceased to meet except casually at places like the Travellers Club.

It has been said that the Bentinck Street house became notorious as a drinking den and a scene of riotous orgies but the two ladies, who lived quite separately from Blunt and Burgess, have no recollection of such activities. Naturally they saw both men but neither gave any indication that they were working for MI5, Blunt being particularly circumspect about his work.[13] Rothschild himself, who has been criticized for giving house-room to two spies, was remote from the scene. Innuendoes about his loyalty are completely groundless as his part in the exposure of Philby alone showed. He was awarded the George Medal for gallantry in dismantling booby traps, and Tessa Mayor, who became his assistant in MI5, and later his wife, received the Military M.B.E. for similar dangerous operations.

While Blunt betrayed the name and function of every MI5 officer, he could not easily discover the identities of agents run by some of the officers but he did his best to do so. One such agent was known inside MI5 headquarters only as 'M8' because he was being run by Maxwell Knight, whose code-initial was M.[14] 'M8' was the code-name for Tom Driberg, a journalist on the *Daily Express*, who had been recruited by Knight to penetrate the Young Communist

League and, eventually, the headquarters of the Communist Party. One of 'M8's' reports, which Blunt happened to see, concerned information about a secret aeroplane and revealed that the Communist Party knew about it. Blunt gave a copy of the report to 'Henry' who asked him to discover 'M8's' identity. Blunt tried for six months but failed. 'Henry' then told him that he had discovered it was Driberg. The K.G.B. made the error of informing the British Communist Party leadership headed by Harry Pollitt, who summarily expelled Driberg from the Party. This action angered Blunt because he was subjected to questioning about the leak but managed to lie persuasively yet again.

Since Knight's reports were regularly fed to Hollis it has been suggested that the latter's failure to 'blow' Driberg to the Russians is evidence of his innocence. My inquiries show that Knight, who operated independently from MI5 headquarters from an office in Dolphin Square, did not reveal the names of his agents to Hollis or to anybody else outside his unit.[15]

The eventual interrogation of Blunt by MI5 revealed that another of the most secret documents which he saw resulted in the loss of probably the only senior Soviet official ever to operate on Britain's behalf inside the Kremlin. Before the war MI5 had employed an officer called Harold 'Gibby' Gibson, who had the advantage of speaking Russian fluently because he had been brought up in Russia and had been at school there prior to the revolution. Among his former Russian schoolfriends was a Soviet citizen whom he met later in life and who had become disenchanted with communism and the way it was being manipulated in the interests of pathological power-seekers. At that time he was in the private office of Anastas Mikoyan, the small, moustached Politburo member once aptly described as having a face like 'an agonized parrot'.[16] Gibson's Russian friend agreed to help the West by supplying information on as regular a basis as possible concerning the Politburo's intentions, the hardest of all intelligence to acquire. Blunt handed a copy of one of the agent's reports to 'Henry' who told him, a few weeks later, that the source had been eliminated, which probably meant executed. What is certain is that no further reports were received from him.

For several months Blunt was the officer in charge of the Watcher Service, the men and women who carried out the surveillance of foreign agents and suspected spies. Not only was he responsible for allotting their tasks to them each week but he knew details of every case in which they were involved. This, of course, was invaluable information to the Russians because it enabled their controllers to avoid meetings which might be dangerous. When interrogated, Blunt recalled how, at one stage, he was giving 'Henry' such detailed information that he was warned against overdoing it because it could arouse suspicion in any alert organization. In MI5 it did not do so.

It is known that Blunt was able to warn the K.G.B that Communist Party headquarters in London had been bugged by MI5 and that Party matters were being monitored. He had done this within a week of the installation of the microphones and gave the Russians details of the secret techniques being used. The K.G.B. again foolishly warned the Party and a frantic search was made of the building in King Street, Covent Garden, to find the microphones, not all of which were discovered. When the MI5 men listening to the microphones overheard the search there was an immediate inquiry to discover the source of the leak and Blunt was among those questioned. He lied convincingly.

It might be asked why, if Hollis was a spy, the Communist Party had not already been informed because it was his department, Section F, that had been responsible for the operation. The answer could be that if Hollis was an active spy he was an agent of the G.R.U. which, in the early 1940s, was more experienced than the K.G.B. and too sophisticated to prejudice a spy's position simply to assist a local Communist Party.

I have mentioned how Philby kept the K.G.B. up to date on the 'order of battle' of MI6 by giving his controller internal telephone directories and other information about changes of personnel and duties. Blunt did the same with respect to MI5 and, as Gouzenko's evidence indicated, the G.R.U. was receiving similar information from another source.

For much of his time in MI5 Blunt was in charge of a sub-section concerned with penetrating the embassies of neutral countries such as Sweden, Switzerland, Spain and Portugal and even, where possible, examining their diplomatic pouches, to which MI5 had access during the war. His chief outside agent in this work was Guy Burgess who joined MI5 as a supernumerary in 1940.[17] As Blunt and Burgess were known to be old friends, their regular meetings in Blunt's room at the Courtauld Institute and elsewhere aroused no suspicions. Twice a week Blunt took out an attaché case of selected secret documents ostensibly as homework. Burgess added his own reports and the case was handed over to a K.G.B. officer at some pre-arranged point. They were photographed at the Soviet Embassy and returned to Blunt in time to be taken back to MI5 the following morning. They contributed so much that a later K.G.B. defector, Vladimir Petrov, was eventually to reveal that they created a considerable problem for K.G.B. headquarters in processing the

347

material.[18] The Russians also became concerned that Blunt might be caught carrying documents which he was not entitled to remove from the office, especially after a frightening experience when he was stopped by a policeman who demanded to see inside his case in the black-out. 'Henry' therefore provided the two spies with cameras so that they could photograph the documents in miniature and hand over the films. They did this for a time but became so short of sleep that they handed back the cameras and reverted to the old system. They were never caught.

Blunt also knew about many American operations because of the close contact between MI5 and the U.S. Office of Strategic Services in London from 1942 onwards and there is no doubt that he could have prejudiced some of them by informing the Russians.

Early in 1944 it was decided to set up a cover and deception unit under General Eisenhower at S.H.A.E.F. (Supreme Headquarters Allied Expeditionary Force) to support the coming Normandy landings. Under its new head, Lieutenant-Colonel Noel Wild, who had been switched from the Middle East where he had been engaged in similar work, the unit was divided into two sections – Operations and Intelligence. The latter involved close liaison with MI5 so a link was formed with the appointment to the unit of Anthony Blunt, who moved to Norfolk House, the headquarters of the D-Day deception planners. Looking back with hindsight Wild finds it fantastic that after being rejected from an intelligence course on security grounds, Blunt should have been attached to the invasion organization where he was to see the most secret documents and attend the most secret meetings.[19] Who recommended him? Wild asks with some justification but with no official answer.

Blunt gave the Russians all the details of 'Fortitude', the operation to deceive the Germans into believing that the main Allied invasion would be in the Pas de Calais area. As he then had to have access to the Ultra intelligence produced by the breakers of the German codes at Bletchley Park he was a further source of leakage to the Russians about that most secret operation, along with Philby, Long, and Cairncross. According to Professor Michael Howard, who has examined a lot of Blunt's work on 'Fortitude', he functioned efficiently but this was, of course, as much in the Soviet Union's interests as in Britain's, the U.S.S.R. by that time being in the war.[20]

Soviet supporters and apologists for wartime Soviet spies continue to try to excuse the treachery of traitors like Blunt, Philby, Maclean and, possibly, Hollis, by claiming that they were only funnelling secrets to a hard-pressed ally. As already mentioned, the truth is that this was accidental because they had been recruited long before the Soviet

Union was an ally and were passing secret information while that country was bound to Nazi Germany by a non-aggression pact. Stalin's desire to placate Hitler was then so great that he not only supplied Germany with food, leather for jackboots and petrol for tanks and bombers but also ensured that help was given to the German secret service, the *Abwehr*.[21] There can be little doubt that the traitors would have continued to assist the Soviet Union had that country managed to remain a pro-German neutral, as Stalin had hoped.

Colonel Wild suspects that information about Allied moves in France may have been fed back to the Germans by the K.G.B. in order to delay the British-American advance while Soviet troops moved westwards in the hope of securing more territory to communize or, at least, to bargain with at the peace conferences.[22]

When Blunt was asked, later, about his treachery while the U.S.S.R. was assisting Hitler all he could offer was a lame comment that he and Burgess had 'felt better about things' once the Soviet Union had been forced into the war.

On 1 April 1945 Blunt succeeded Sir Kenneth Clark in the unpaid post of Surveyor of the King's Pictures, which gave him responsibility for all the Royal collections of paintings.[23] As this date shows, he remained an active Soviet spy while in service to the Palace, for he did not leave MI5 for seven more months. According to close friends of Blunt he told them that he quickly became on good terms with Queen Mary, who was interested in old paintings and other antiques. He also professed to be on friendly terms with Queen Elizabeth, wife of King George VI. During his long term of office as Surveyor he is said to have acquired great merit by discovering some Holbein drawings and other priceless pictures hung in obscure places and not previously recognized as important.[24]

Some time in 1945, or possibly in 1946, Blunt carried out a secret mission to Germany on behalf of the Royal Family.[25] MI5 had been asked to provide a totally trustworthy and discreet officer for the purpose and Blunt was selected since he spoke and read German and already had a connection with the Palace. Nobody else was told the precise nature of the task and Blunt, who died in 1983, kept the secret, though he may have revealed it in papers not yet made public. It has been suggested that the purpose was to seize family letters written by Queen Victoria which were the property of the Hesse family held in a castle near Frankfurt. My inquiries, however, show that this correspondence was of small importance and hardly warranted a special mission.

Another explanation suggested to me concerns an alleged move by some of Queen Victoria's German relatives, including the

349

Emperor, to induce her to abdicate in the interests of all concerned. Following Prince Albert's death the Queen became very unpopular and, while perhaps it was not realistic, there was talk of revolution. Fearing a 'domino effect' on their own positions should the Queen be deposed, the German Emperor and ruling Princes are alleged to have prepared a round robin urging her to abdicate in favour of her son. It is said that while the missive was never sent, it was housed in some German archives and that Blunt was sent to extract it.[26]

Blunt's former colleagues in MI5 suspect that his mission was concerned with more recent history – the retrieval of captured German documents recording the Duke of Windsor's dubious connections with prominent Nazis. It is known that when the Duke was staying in Austria immediately after his abdication his lengthy telephone calls to his brother, King George VI had been tapped by German Intelligence. In October 1937 the Duke had spent two weeks in Germany visiting various cities to see the Nazis' economic achievements and meeting von Ribbentrop, Goering, Hess and Hitler, the Duke being fluent in German.[27] While many documents of the former German Foreign Office have been made available, any recording the Duke's conversations with Hitler and other leaders are said to have disappeared. The interest of MI5 and the Palace would have been more likely to reside, however, in the official German records of the Duke's clandestine conversations with German diplomats, intelligence chiefs and others in Madrid and Lisbon, to which he fled in June 1940, following the fall of France.[28] These records have been described as 'tainted', but they were secret reports to the Berlin Foreign Office never intended for publication and are likely to be accurate. They show that the Nazi leadership made a determined effort to induce the Duke to side with them in their bid to secure a separate peace with Britain and that he flirted with the idea. There is evidence that in the process he met two notorious Nazi secret police chiefs – Walter Schellenberg and Reinhard Heydrich, and, possibly, Rudolf Hess.[29]

Many of the German records have become available for study and are listed in Peter Allen's *The Crown and the Swastika* but some, which may have been highly embarrassing to Whitehall and to the Palace had they fallen into Soviet hands, have not been released if, in fact, they still exist. Documents are available under the U.S. Freedom of Information Act which include letters from the Foreign Office to American authorities requesting them to return or destroy their microfilmed copies of German papers relating to the Windsors' stay in Spain and Portugal during June and July 1940. The documents, about which the Foreign Office was expressing urgency shortly after the end of the war, had been discovered in Marburg

Castle, in the American zone of Germany.[30] The castle had been used as a storehouse for captured German papers, said to have comprised about 400 tons, and it is possible that Blunt visited it.

Some of Blunt's friends have claimed that the material that he recovered filled two or three packing cases. An official source has suggested to me that the bulk was taken up by valuable books which he also retrieved.[31]

While the object of Blunt's visit remains something of a mystery, the Royal Family seems to have been grateful for his services. In 1947 he was rewarded with the Palace decoration of Commander of the Royal Victorian Order and appears to have remained in fair odour in Royal circles even after his private exposure as a spy in 1964, though his personal contacts with the Queen were rare.

Soon after Blunt's Royal appointment he told his Soviet controller, then Boris Krotov, that he wanted to leave MI5 to devote all his time to art work. His request was referred to Moscow and, to his surprise, it was granted. When Blunt was interrogated after his eventual confession he admitted that the K.G.B. could have forced him to remain to continue his espionage under threat of exposure. He said that he would not have been too dismayed if this had happened because, in view of the modest intellectual competition from his colleagues, he had every prospect of becoming Director-General and could have continued with his art interests. He agreed with his interrogators that the K.G.B.'s permission to leave might well imply that they could spare him because they had at least one other productive source inside MI5. The K.G.B. Centre may also have thought that there might be some value in having an agent closely connected with the Royal Household where, at least, he might hear gossip of interest to the all-embracing analysts in Moscow.

Blunt ceased to work full time for MI5 in November 1945, at which point he remarked to a colleague, Colonel T. A. Robertson, 'Well it's given me great pleasure to pass on the names of every MI5 officer to the Russians.'[32] Robertson, who knew that Blunt made no secret of being a communist, passed the information to those who should have reacted to it but nothing was entered on Blunt's file. Hollis was still in charge of the anti-communist and anti-Soviet section and was close to Robertson, who was godfather to his son.

While handing over various projects to successors Blunt was in and out of the MI5 office for a further six months and, according to former colleagues, did further services on request for MI5 after that date.

Meanwhile Leo Long had moved from MI14 in London to the

Control Commission for Germany, later becoming deputy head of British Intelligence there, with a rank equivalent to major-general. In 1946 Blunt saw him on a visit to Germany and asked him if he would like to be recommended for a full-time senior post inside MI5 in London, almost certainly having first discussed the project with his K.G.B. controller. Long was then only thirty and the post would have taken him to retirement, giving him thirty years inside the secret agency which was going to be mainly concerned with countering Soviet spies operating in Britain. Long agreed and Blunt, who was still under no suspicion, proposed him for entry to MI5. Long was interviewed by the MI5 Selection Board but was turned down by a narrow margin as not being of high enough calibre, though one very senior MI5 officer supported his application.[33]

This information, which I believe to have been withheld from Mrs Thatcher when she made her Parliamentary statement on Blunt and Long, throws a different light on both traitors. Blunt did not go to see Long at MI5's request but on the instructions of his K.G.B. controller. Clearly the K.G.B. wanted Long inside MI5 and he must have known that if he succeeded in gaining entry he would be required to go on spying whether he wanted to or not, for the K.G.B. could always have threatened him with exposure. Further, the odds are that as Blunt had served as Long's controller and cut-out, passing on his information to the Russians, he would have been required to continue in that capacity, with his Palace position providing superb cover. Blunt, too, would have had no option but to do the Russians' bidding. His confident belief that he could intrude Long into MI5 as a replacement helps to explain why the K.G.B. permitted him to leave MI5.

Long has claimed publicly that after he lost contact with Blunt in 1946 he ceased spying but it seems inevitable that Blunt would have given the name of such an excellent and willing source to the Russians and it is most unlikely that they would have left him alone. In fact, Long told a different story to the MI5 officers who were eventually to interrogate him. He said that the defection of Burgess and Maclean was a factor in inducing him to get out of his Soviet entanglement and that did not happen until 1951. He also told his questioners that his marriage, also in 1951, was another factor. What is, perhaps, significant, is that his contract with the Control Commission expired in 1952 and he then ceased to have access to any information of value to the Russians.

Professor Sidney Hook has recently recalled that when he was in Germany in 1948 and in early 1950 he was told, several times, that many men and women in East Germany who had been informing

352

the West about what was happening in their area had been arrested and had disappeared.[34] It would seem more than likely that they could have been traced from material supplied by Long, whose department was responsible for processing it.

Meanwhile, in 1947 Blunt had been promoted to be Director of the Courtauld Institute, which took up more of his time, but he remained in close touch with many of his MI5 friends, especially Guy Liddell and Burgess, and including Hollis, occasionally dining at the latter's home in Campden Hill Square, as he had during the war.[35] He met Burgess frequently, mainly at the Reform Club, to which they both belonged, as did Hollis. He also performed conspiratorial services for Burgess, one of which he was to describe in detail during his subsequent confessions to his MI5 interrogators. A wad of banknotes and a message had been left for Burgess in a hiding place under a tree on a common in the East End of London and, as Burgess was indisposed, Blunt collected them for him. Those who find it impossible to believe that Hollis could leave his office in Curzon Street to impart secrets furtively to some Soviet officer in Hyde Park might find it helpful to picture the Surveyor of the Queen's Pictures and Professor of the History of Art leaving the Courtauld Institute or Buckingham Palace and travelling, by a circuitous route, to grope around some tree in the darkness on a muddy common. Such are the exigencies of dedicated service to the Soviet Union.

While the K.G.B. Centre had been correct in its appreciation that Blunt would come under suspicion following Burgess's defection, Blunt himself had been accurate in his prediction that MI5 would treat him so gently that he would be able to handle the situation. Again, the circumstances in MI5 were such that any fiction writer would reject them as too incredible.

When trying to recruit his friend Goronwy Rees, an academic who served in wartime military intelligence, Burgess had revealed that he was a Soviet agent and intimated that Blunt was another.[36] Rees kept the secret until Burgess's defection when he asked to be put in touch with MI5. When Blunt heard of this he tried hard to talk Rees out of making any statement but failed. Guy Liddell, then Deputy Director of MI5, invited Rees to lunch to hear his information and who should he bring with him but Blunt! Both Liddell and Blunt attempted to persuade Rees against making any formal statement about Burgess, indicating that it would be unwelcome. Liddell even threatened Rees, pointing out that his failure to report Burgess sooner could make him suspect. Nevertheless, Rees insisted on a formal interview with Liddell and White, then Director of Counter-Espionage, and both were clearly displeased. Writing twenty years later, Rees indicated that he suspected the presence of other Soviet agents inside MI5 who would cover up for anybody, like Burgess and Maclean, who might be unmasked: 'it seemed highly probable that if Guy [Burgess] and Maclean had been recruited as spies, so had others... but who? I had the uneasy feeling that the likeliest place to look was in the ranks of the security services themselves.'[37]

The next development was to savour of farce, had it not been so serious for national security.

MI5 needed to search Burgess's flat with minimum delay. Since Blunt had a set of keys to it he was asked to accompany two officers as this would avoid the necessity of securing a search warrant and forcing an entry. As a former MI5 colleague he offered to assist in the search and did so. The untidy, three-roomed flat contained scores of letters, some in a desk, others in old shoe-boxes, which Burgess had also used to stack the banknotes he received at intervals from his Soviet paymasters. The letters were to give leads to some of his homosexual friends, who were to curse him when eventually visited by MI5 officers.[38]

None of the letters removed to MI5 headquarters for study was to give any lead about the defectors but, as Blunt was to confess some thirteen years later, there had been one letter of great significance, which the MI5 officers had missed as a result of their stupidity in allowing Blunt to assist in the search. Burgess was an insatiable reader and his flat was full of books, each of which had to be shaken for possible hidden documents. While shaking one book, Blunt found and pocketed a letter to Burgess from Philby which told him that if ever he was in great difficulties he could be assured of help from Mrs Flora Solomon of the Marks and Spencer organization. Mrs Solomon, who published her memoirs in 1984, knew that Philby was a communist and a possible Soviet agent because he had tried to recruit her, as described in Chapter 32. Had she been interrogated then, as she would have been had the letter been found by the MI5 men, the remaining members of the Ring of Five and their associates might have been rounded up in 1951.

When Mrs Thatcher made her statement about Blunt to Parliament in 1979 she said that he had originally been questioned as a result of a belated statement (by Rees) that Burgess had named Blunt as a secret Comintern agent.[39] In fact the prime reason for the investigation of Blunt was his close association with Burgess inside MI5 during the war, a situation still being concealed by the security authorities.

An MI5 file was begun on Blunt, under the code-name 'Blunden', but Arthur Martin, the case officer assigned to the inquiry, did not interview him formally until 1952 when he became suspicious of his guilt, though he was unable to get much out of him. Ten further sessions of questioning were what Blunt himself has described as 'comfortable conversations' usually beginning, 'Anthony, we are still investigating Maclean and Burgess leads...' As Philby had done during his interrogations, Blunt kept talking in a way which convinced his questioners that he was trying to discover how much was known about him. As the questioners knew – and as Blunt was to admit years later – this was done on the advice given to him by his Soviet controller. This insistence on talking, rather than treating the questions with anger or contempt, convinced Martin and White that Blunt was an agent. Another officer, Courtenay Young, who had sat opposite Blunt in the MI5 office, was so sure that Blunt had been a spy that he said so to friends of mine, but no action could be taken.

After Philby had been forced to resign from MI6 in 1951 the K.G.B. ignored him, partly in his own interests but also to satisfy themselves that he had not been 'turned' by British Intelligence. Blunt, however, continued to see him and they discussed their chances of surviving exposure. In 1954, by which time the K.G.B. had satisfied itself of Philby's loyalty, it wished to contact him again and used Blunt to do so. Blunt was delivering a lecture on art and after he had finished speaking a group clustered round him to ask questions. Among them he was surprised to see his old controller 'Peter' – Yuri Modin – who had organized the defection of Burgess and Maclean and had then returned to Moscow. Modin handed him a postcard of a painting and asked his opinion of it. Written in a semi-circle, in handwriting which Blunt recognized as being Guy Burgess's, was the instruction, 'Meet me at 8 o'clock tomorrow night. Angel, Caledonian Road.' When Blunt attended only Modin was there to ask him to set up a meeting with Philby, which was soon accomplished.[40]

In 1961 Blunt saw Philby, though apparently by chance, while visiting Beirut. As he was eventually to tell his interrogators, Philby had remarked, 'I have been asked by our friends to make contact with you, Anthony, but I told them that you were not in a position to do anything useful.' Blunt says that he had answered, 'That is so, Kim.'[41] If true, this indicates that Blunt was out of touch with Soviet Intelligence at that time but the K.G.B. had its methods of making contact if necessary, as the previous experience with Modin in 1954 showed.

Blunt's confidence that he would go to his grave with his reputation unsullied must have strengthened as the years sped by and but for a completely chance event in 1963 his belief would, most probably, have been justified. I have mentioned how, early in 1937, Blunt had recruited a rich young American called Michael Whitney Straight who was a contemporary at Cambridge. Both had been members of The Apostles and when Straight was emotionally devastated by the death of a communist friend in the Spanish Civil War Blunt had recruited him to the Soviet cause.[42] Straight has told me that he tried to buy himself out of his commitment before returning to the U.S. but Blunt told him that the Kremlin had rejected his plea. When he became a speech-writer for President Roosevelt he was soon approached by a K.G.B. officer in Washington who demanded reports. Straight claims that during the eighteen months while he remained in touch with the officer, who called himself 'Michael Green', he gave him only information that would not damage American interests.[43]

On two occasions when 'Green' was otherwise engaged the K.G.B. behaved in its usual way and sent couriers to see Straight, having first telephoned him. One of these appeared to be a Jewish student from the New York region while the other could have been a Czech. Straight insists that he told them nothing.[44]

According to an F.B.I. report, recently declassified, Straight attempted to warn the British Embassy in Washington in 1948 that both Burgess and Blunt were members of the 'Russian International' but if the information reached anyone of consequence it was ignored.[45] He also told the F.B.I. that he warned Burgess in 1951 that he would expose him unless he resigned. As he confirms in his memoirs he failed to take advantage of other opportunities to expose Blunt, Burgess and Long, which could have prevented damage to British and American interests, but when called to the White House in June 1963 to discuss a possible appointment as the Presidential Adviser on the arts he was told that he would be subjected to a security check. He decided to reject the post but to confess his communist past to the F.B.I. Straight, then aged forty-seven, provided William Sullivan, the F.B.I. officer responsible for espionage cases, with a full account of his connections with the K.G.B., revealing that he had been recruited by Blunt, whom he knew to have been a Soviet agent. During many days of interrogation in June 1963 Straight told the F.B.I. that he knew that Blunt had been in MI5 during the war and that he realized that he must have been an active spy there. In 1949 he had attended the annual dinner of The Apostles in London and, following arguments that evening, had been admonished by Blunt and Burgess for deserting the Soviet cause – further evidence that Blunt, who was then fully installed in the Royal Household, was still at least an active agent of influence. When asked by Sullivan, in July, if he would repeat his allegations to MI5 Straight agreed to do so. At that time Blunt was performing another sensitive service for the Royal Family. Stephen Ward, of the Profumo case, had been committed for trial on what looked like a trumped-up charge of living on the earnings of prostitution and arranged for a sale of his drawings to raise money for his defence. The exhibition included portraits of members of the Royal Family and Blunt appeared at the gallery and bought them all.[46]

CHAPTER THIRTY-SEVEN

The Fixing of Blunt's Immunity

WHILE Straight was still being occasionally debriefed in August 1963 Blunt was in the U.S. at Pennsylvania University. It is not known whether the F.B.I. had Blunt under surveillance. What is known is that while he was there he tried to get a Slavonic girl on to the Courtauld Institute staff on the false pretext that the Russian section of the library needed reorganization.[1]

It was normal practice for the F.B.I. to carry out some inquiries into Straight and his American contacts at Cambridge, as its records show, but there should not have been an untimely delay before alerting MI5 to its discovery about Blunt. An MI5 liaison man was on hand in Washington, but officers involved in the Blunt case claim that the F.B.I.'s information about him did not reach London until November – a gap of five months – when John Minnick, the Legal Attaché at the U.S. Embassy who was also the resident F.B.I. officer, delivered a letter to Hollis marked 'Personal to the D.G.'.[2] It will be remembered that Hollis had been in Washington two months previously, in September, to see the F.B.I. chief, Hoover, among others, about the suspicions surrounding Graham Mitchell. Why was he not told about Straight's evidence then?

Having heard of the suspicions about Mitchell, Hoover may have been so appalled that he was loath to pass on the information, fearing that Blunt might be warned. Another possible reason for Hoover's long delay in informing MI5 may lie in his faith in the double agent 'Fedora'. He might have asked 'Fedora' to check out some questions about Straight and Blunt during one of his periodic visits to Moscow headquarters. As 'Fedora' was, in fact, a fake double agent, the Moscow Centre would have been informed of Blunt's exposure and would have delayed any answers until a decision had been taken about the K.G.B. action concerning Blunt. This would almost certainly have involved a warning to Blunt with instructions about the reaction he should make when eventually confronted by MI5. The F.B.I. files on the Blunt/Straight case would be informative but many of them cannot be released without British permission, which is unlikely to be given. Straight has been given copies of a few F.B.I. documents concerning his own case – with various sections blanked out – but others have been refused on the grounds that they might infringe the civil rights of 'Michael Green', Straight's K.G.B. officer![3]

Of course, it remains possible that Hollis was told about Blunt by Hoover when they met in September and kept the information to himself while he made private dispositions, possibly including a warning to his friend Blunt so that requisite action could be taken to prevent publicity. This could have been done surreptitiously or in conjunction with other very senior British officials equally anxious to keep the Blunt exposure secret.

Whatever the extent and reasons for the long time-gap, Hollis decided to introduce a further delay. He allotted the case to Arthur Martin who was already in Washington pursuing the Mitchell inquiries and could easily have seen the F.B.I. about Blunt. Hollis, however, told Martin nothing, insisting that he must first return to London for discussions before either the F.B.I. or Straight could be approached.

As was his wont, Hollis seemed to be playing for time before having to reveal the catastrophe to anybody in the Government or in Buckingham Palace or, possibly, while consulting someone else surreptitiously. Once again, he was faced with a major Soviet spy who had been exposed only because of information from an American source and the fluke circumstance that Straight felt he needed to clear himself. And, once again, the spy had been active for several years and this time was a friend of Hollis from inside MI5 itself.

If it is MI5's duty to prevent the penetration of the secret services by foreign spies and to detect them promptly when they do breach the defences then, in the Blunt case, it had failed abysmally. As Director-General for seven years and Deputy Director for three and, before that, a long association with operations against Soviet spies in particular, Hollis bore a major responsibility.

He knew that he could not suppress the Blunt case completely because of the Royal connection. The Palace would have to be told that it had a dangerous traitor on its staff. Otherwise, Hollis might well have secured internal support for stifling the case from other senior MI5 managers on the grounds that any exposure would be 'bad for the Service', 'against the national interest', or would 'embarrass ministers'. MI5 officers have repeatedly told me that it was regular practice for cases to be brought to an abrupt conclusion to avoid embarrassment to the Service or to ministers.

Correspondence between Straight and Martin in 1982 has established that Martin was not permitted to see Straight until early January 1964 – after a further two months' delay – when he visited Washington again.[4] The reasons for these delays have been insufficiently researched in the past and could be essential to establishing the truth about the handling of the Blunt case. Straight has recorded that he heard no more about the suggestion that he should talk to MI5 until William Sullivan telephoned him in January 1964 saying that a friend was flying to Washington from London and that Straight could be introduced to him at the Mayflower Hotel, which was duly done.[5] As Martin recalled the situation to an informant recently – relying on memory and with no access to documents – he had not been told of the Blunt issue when sent to Washington and was approached about it by Sullivan while there for another purpose. He seems to believe that the information he then received from Straight, in January 1964, was the first that MI5 had ever heard about it, implying that the F.B.I. had delayed for almost eight months before sharing its knowledge. This does not accord with my information from other MI5 sources.

It is, apparently, believed by Martin that Hoover hated MI5 so much that he was not prepared to tell the British about Blunt's treachery, but that is hardly in keeping with Hoover's nature. The F.B.I. chief took some delight in pointing out the deficiencies of British security, and the Blunt discovery offered him such an opportunity. Though no doubt appalled at the suspicion still attaching to Mitchell and with bitter memories of the Maclean case, he was friendly enough with Hollis around that time to send him a signed photograph and a set of golfing irons.[6] Further, though Sullivan eventually broke with Hoover in 1971 it is unlikely that he would have gone over the head of such an irascible chief in 1964 by telling Martin about Blunt surreptitiously, when Hoover was bound to hear that he had done so.

It is more likely that there was a previous arrangement between Hollis and Hoover whereby Martin would be given the information casually by Sullivan, the meeting with Straight having been set up in advance, as Straight's evidence shows that it was. Martin's return in triumph with the information would cover the fact that Hollis had known about it at least since the previous November, as I have been assured he did. This behaviour would be in keeping with Hollis's reputation for playing serious cases 'close to the chest'.

Having introduced Martin to Straight, Sullivan left them to talk alone, though there can be little doubt that the F.B.I. had 'bugged' the hotel room in which they spoke. Straight confirmed all that he had told the F.B.I. and gave further details of his association with Blunt. He said that he was prepared to face Blunt in a British court. He has since told me that he heard no more of this offer. When asked for the names of other Cambridge undergraduates who might have been recruited by Blunt he mentioned Leo Long. Straight told me that Martin's only response at hearing this was 'a low groan', an expression which could be of some significance.[7]

When Martin returned to London the results of his mission were immediately discussed with Hollis and other senior members of MI5. In a statement to Parliament, many years later, Mrs Thatcher was to say, speaking from a brief supplied by MI5, that the information which implicated Blunt was received 'early in 1964'.[8] That was the time when Martin brought it back but Hollis had apparently known about it from the previous November and possibly earlier. In a later statement, also prepared from an MI5 brief, Mrs Thatcher was to tell Parliament that MI5 had not known about Long's treachery until the same date; this, too, may have been incorrect.[9]

An F.B.I. document dated 25 June 1963 shows that Straight named Long as being a member of the secret Cambridge communist cell during his earliest interrogations by the F.B.I.[10] Straight and I have examined F.B.I. papers relating to a further interview he had with F.B.I. officers in June 1966. Though some names have been blanked out, in deference to British requirements, we are agreed that the documents indicate that when Straight first talked to the F.B.I. in 1963 he also appears to have named Long as a person who might have been recruited to Soviet Intelligence by Blunt. Long's name, therefore, would presumably have been in the statement sent to Hollis personally by Hoover in November 1963 and Hollis would have known of the implication of Long some two months before Martin's 'low groan'.

His groan suggests that there had been discussion about Long before Martin left MI5 headquarters for his trip to Washington. Otherwise I can see no reason why he should ever have heard of him. Long's name might have arisen marginally during inquiries by Martin into the Cambridge backgrounds of Maclean, Burgess and Philby but it is more likely that the groan was a reaction to the confirmation of suspicions already attaching to Long after an MI5 follow-up of the F.B.I.'s information and Martin's appreciation of the horrific consequences.

I have been assured that as soon as MI5 formally received the information about Blunt from the F.B.I. he was placed under continuous telephone and letter check. His flat at the Courtauld Institute was surreptitiously 'miked', but it was appreciated from the start that as a former security officer instructed in 'conspiratorial' practices he was unlikely to make elementary errors such as communicating with the Russians by telephone or by letter. For the same reason he was not put under physical surveillance, the argument being that having once been in charge of the MI5 watchers he would be knowledgeable about their methods. It is unlikely, then, that any part of the delay was due to genuine hope that he might betray himself by a foolish move. Nor does the alleged fear that he might defect if he was told or learned of Straight's accusation carry much conviction because he was never put under surveillance during his visits to the Continent on art affairs when, of course, he could so easily have contacted K.G.B. controllers.

After consulting the in-house legal experts, the MI5 management, led by Hollis, quickly decided, with some relief, that Straight's evidence as it stood could not be made the basis of a successful prosecution. Blunt's recruitment of him and his failure to declare that he was a communist when he entered MI5 in 1940 were not statutory crimes. While Martin reported Straight's willingness to confront Blunt and challenge him with being a spy throughout the war, on the basis of what he had heard at The Apostles' dinner, nothing was done about it. Blunt was not to be confronted by Straight until he was safe from prosecution.[11]

As I hope to convince the reader, a far more telling witness to Blunt's treachery was on hand in London in the form of Leo Long, who could have proved to the satisfaction of any jury that Blunt had been his controller. Hollis and his colleagues, however, were determined to ensure that Blunt would never be prosecuted. A trial would be far too embarrassing to too many people and positively dangerous to some, for there was no knowing who Blunt might take down with him. Hollis therefore ensured that Long was not questioned at that stage and no effort was ever made to induce him to serve as a witness against Blunt either in private or in public. With the full approval of other members of the MI5 management, steps were taken to ensure that Long could never give such evidence. The full dimension of the scandalous way in which immunity was granted to Blunt and, effectively, to Long has not previously been appreciated. MI5 is not, primarily, a law-enforcement agency but neither should it be used to make the application of the law impossible.

The management had plenty of time to question Long before approaching Blunt. Its records showed that Blunt had tried hard to get Long into MI5. Further, there were two security allegations against Long on file. While Long had still been in Germany an MI5 officer had visited Herford to interrogate captured *Abwehr* staff and had noticed Long riffling through files which did not concern him. The officer had reported Long as being possibly untrustworthy.[12] Later, in the mid-1950s, a Polish woman, who had previously shared an apartment with Long in Düsseldorf, made a full confession of espionage for the Russians. The same MI5 officer submitted a minute suggesting that Long should be interviewed. The response was that while Long's former communism was known, he was considered to be reliable.[13]

The reason given by some MI5 officers for the failure to tackle Long before confronting Blunt seems specious – that he was then only forty-seven, with good career prospects in the film industry and would not be foolish enough to admit anything. Such reservations had not prevented MI5 from questioning Blunt in 1951 when he was only forty-four and with superlative career prospects. Long might, at least, have been induced to turn Queen's evidence against Blunt who was, by far, the more damaging traitor. The reasons for failing to question Long or to use Straight to break Blunt savour more of excuses to avoid scandals damaging to MI5 or to save two dangerous and damaging traitors from retribution.

While several MI5 officers were in favour of granting Blunt immediate immunity from prosecution to get quick information about his past activities and contacts, the leading executive advocate of this course was the Director-General, Hollis. While some officers opposed it, the old argument that publicity about the case might have adverse effects on the interchange of intelligence secrets with the U.S. carried weight. The F.B.I. and the C.I.A. knew about Blunt but Congress and the American people did not.

Later, when Hollis was under active investigation, it occurred to the team involved that in favouring immunity for Blunt, as he had for Philby, Hollis could have been keen to create precedents in case he was ever exposed himself.

It was agreed inside MI5 that the Attorney-General should be induced to offer Blunt total immunity against prosecution or any other personal disadvantage, without any effort being made to break him unconditionally, on the verbal understanding that he would admit his treachery and subject himself to lengthy interrogation. This was an unprecedented decision. In the previous year Philby had been offered formal immunity in Beirut but only on the grounds that there was no other way of inducing him to return to London for debriefing. Blunt was on the spot and had never shown any inclination to leave Britain.

Because of Philby's defection some consideration was given to the possibility that Blunt might do likewise, once he had been approached. It was decided, however, to quote one of Blunt's

363

friends, that 'while Anthony liked to run with the communist hare', he much preferred to hunt with the Establishment hounds.[14] MI5 did not know, until Blunt told them, that he had declined to defect when ordered to do so in 1951.

Hollis's determination to avoid any prosecution of Blunt prevented the possibility that Blunt could ever be cross-examined by the Attorney-General or any other delving lawyer, or by anyone outside the secret confines of MI5. As I will show, Hollis's action also meant that Long could never be prosecuted either, thereby ensuring the freedom and prosperity of two known Soviet spies.

Neither Parliament nor the public has appreciated that when immunity was offered to Blunt it automatically meant effective immunity for Long and for any others whom Blunt had recruited or run as a spymaster. These people could not possibly be brought into court without revealing Blunt's complicity and that was barred under the immunity deal.

It has been suggested that granting immunity to Blunt was in line with the practice of granting immunity to other criminals who turn Queen's evidence, but, in the latter case, the action invariably leads to the prosecution of others. In Blunt's case the immunity assured the protection of all concerned. It caused great offence to some of the older MI5 officers when they learned of it.

The next firm date in this strange story is 2 March 1964 when, according to Mrs Thatcher, Hollis met the Home Secretary, Henry Brooke, whom he had served so badly over the Profumo affair.[15] Hollis is said to have told Brooke about Straight's information. It would be instructive to know how much Hollis told Brooke and, in particular, whether he mentioned the arguments at The Apostles' dinner, which would have enabled Straight to accuse Blunt of being a spy throughout his time in MI5. Hollis said that he would be discussing with the Director of Public Prosecutions how to conduct the interview with Blunt 'bearing in mind MI5's needs to get as much intelligence as possible about Soviet penetration'.[16]

It would also be instructive to know whether or not Hollis specifically told the Home Secretary about his plan to secure immunity. Statements made by Mrs Thatcher in the Blunt debate, from a carefully worded brief, suggest that he did not. To clarify what should occur in future in any comparable situation Mrs Thatcher said, '...if the Attorney-General is asked to authorise a grant of immunity from prosecution, in a case involving national security, he should satisfy himself that the Home Secretary is aware that the request has been made'.[17] It is hard to see why that entirely new principle should have been introduced as a result of the Blunt immunity if it had already been observed in that case.

On MI5's advice Mrs Thatcher was to tell Parliament that there was no reason to think that Blunt would do anything but maintain his stubborn denial if questioned without the prior offer of immunity.[18] But why should this assumption have been made? For the first time MI5 had two witnesses, Straight and Long, with whom to confront Blunt who was then fifty-six. He might well have broken down, for all Hollis and his managers knew. Mrs Thatcher also passed on the thin MI5 excuse that confronting Blunt with Straight's evidence might have alerted him to warn others. But what reason was there to suppose that he would not do that anyway before telling MI5 anything about any of his collaborators?

I have been assured by experienced officers of MI5 that the first principle of interrogation, and of the security procedures leading up to it, is to obtain an unconditional confession. It seems inescapable that the MI5 management did not want to risk a situation where Blunt might be forced into such a confession and the Attorney-General and Director of Public Prosecutions (D.P.P.) might feel bound to insist on a prosecution, as had happened with Fuchs and Blake.

Mrs Thatcher was to assure the House that Hollis had 'indicated' to the Home Secretary that he would be discussing the matter of Blunt's immunity with the D.P.P., but there is now doubt that he did so.[19]

The then Deputy Director of Public Prosecutions, Mr Maurice Crump, has assured me and has stated publicly that he dealt with the Blunt case and took the decision that the evidence supplied to him by MI5 was insufficient to warrant a prosecution.[20] Mr Crump cannot remember why he was required to handle the case but has suggested that the D.P.P. was either ill or away and remembers that the Attorney-General, Sir John Hobson, was ill at the time. 'I am quite sure I handled the case and I did not deal directly with Hollis,' he told me. 'Officials were sent to see me and I was entirely dependent on what they told me. I could not crawl around looking for clues. Because of the lack of evidence I had no hesitation in going along with the proposal to grant immunity which, I was told, should result in important intelligence from Blunt.'

Mr Crump confirmed his part in the affair in a letter to *The Times* on 19 April 1984. Since then he has told me that he cannot recall any mention by MI5 of the existence of Long as a possible witness.

Acting on Hollis's instructions, the MI5 officials assured Mr Crump that if immunity could be granted to Blunt a great deal of information should be obtained.[21] But how could MI5 be sure of this, especially when past experience had proved Blunt to be an inveterate liar? It was inevitable that given the authority and prestige of MI5 the D.P.P.'s office and the Attorney-General would defer to its advice, as it had done with the offer of immunity made to Philby. So, by preventing the prosecution of Blunt, Hollis and his managers were, in a sense, dispensing justice.

Whether the Attorney-General, Sir John Hobson, was seen by Hollis or by some intermediary is unclear but he was certainly approached because, having some misgiving, probably about the possible political repercussions, he imposed an important condition. He said that before immunity could be granted Blunt would have to give an assurance that he had ceased to spy after 1945, when the wartime alliance with the Soviet Union had ended.[22] Hobson had recently been involved, with much hostile publicity, in the case of John Vassall, who had been sentenced to eighteen years' imprisonment for spying for the Soviet Union in the 1950s and 1960s. He realized that if news of Blunt's immunity leaked it would look less damaging, politically, if it could be argued that he had been spying for a wartime ally.

Hollis told Hobson nothing whatever about Long, as has been made clear to Parliament by Mrs Thatcher. Had the Attorney-General or the D.P.P.'s office been informed about this potential witness they might have insisted that he should be approached first.

It is unclear whether either Hobson or Crump realized that their agreement to Hollis's proposal meant that the immunity would extend to others whom Blunt might expose. As Mr Crump recalls the case, 'I treated it like one of 10,000 criminal cases I must have handled.'

As Hollis was likely to have been aware, the avoidance of any prosecutions suited the Government in view of Blunt's position in the Palace.

Once Hobson and Crump had agreed to the immunity offer there remained the question of how much the Palace advisers and the Queen should be told. In April the Queen's private secretary, Sir Michael Adeane, now Lord Adeane, was invited to a meeting with Hollis and the chief civil servant at the Home Office, Sir Charles Cunningham.[23] When told that Blunt was to be questioned, under conditions of immunity if he accepted it, Adeane asked what action the Queen was being advised to take if Blunt did confess. He was told that, in Hollis's view, the Queen should take no action because otherwise the Russians might learn what had happened. Further, Hollis argued, his dismissal from the Palace, even if covered on the grounds of 'ill health', might alert some of the other traitors and collaborators to whom Blunt might point and so deprive MI5 of the element of surprise in approaching them.

It is not known whether the question of Blunt's secret mission to Germany on behalf of the Royal Family was ever raised at this meeting, or at any other. Hollis may not have known about it and Adeane would have been unlikely to mention it if, in fact, it had been of any significance to the situation. The suppression of the scandalous fact that there had been a K.G.B. agent of such distinction inside MI5 throughout the war, plus the inevitability that his public exposure would resurrect the Burgess/Maclean/ Philby scandals, could have been sufficient motivation for Hollis's action. If that was so, then the Queen was being used as an accessory to protect the reputation of MI5 and its Director-General.

Adeane alerted the Queen to the circumstances and to Hollis's plan to use Blunt as a source of intelligence.[24] The Queen is understood to have agreed to take the official advice in the national interest and when this decision was transmitted to Hollis it removed the last obstacle to a formal approach to Blunt. Again, the circumstances of Blunt's confrontation by Martin would be rejected by an author of spy fiction as too wildly improbable a scenario. It was held in Blunt's flat on 23 April 1964, six months after MI5 had first heard that he had been a Soviet agent.

The recording shows how Martin opened the proceedings: 'I saw Michael Straight the other day and he told me all about his relations with you and the Russians ...' Then, as Sir Michael Havers, a later Attorney-General, told Parliament, Blunt 'maintained his denial. He was offered immunity from prosecution. He sat in silence for a while. He got up, looked out of the window, poured himself a drink and, after a few minutes, confessed.'[25]

This makes it clear that Martin made no attempt to bluff Blunt into believing that his evidence was stronger than it really was. Normally, an interrogator would have returned to the charge time and time again without telling the subject the full extent of the evidence. But Martin had been instructed to be gentle with Blunt and to offer the immunity right away. In the haste, or because of instructions, Martin did not ask Blunt when he had ceased spying. Nevertheless, subsequent statements by Havers have made it clear that, from the moment Blunt accepted the immunity offer, no action of any kind could be taken against him, whatever he might confess and even if he had been an active agent inside the Royal Household in the immediate past.[26] Further, he could decline to answer questions which might incriminate his friends, as he repeatedly did in the years ahead.

When Havers made his statement on Blunt to Parliament, in November 1979, he gave the firm impression that Blunt had been

367

given two separate promises.[27] The first was a promise that his confession would not be used as evidence against him. The second, given in return for his co-operation and the provision of information useful to the Security Service, was that he would never be prosecuted for his previous spying activities. I can find no evidence to support the contention that two separate promises were made and those I have questioned say that Blunt would never have committed himself on the first promise alone. All the evidence made available to me indicates that full immunity was offered right away and was accepted.

I have been assured that Blunt made no inquiries about the precise nature of the immunity, which was offered verbally. Blunt was never given anything in writing and did not ask for anything. Martin specified that there was to be no publicity and Blunt did not inquire further on that sensitive score. Since the MI5 management felt that a leak about the immunity granted to such a prestigious former member could be disastrous to the Service, especially when lesser spies were being sentenced to long terms of imprisonment, Blunt was urged, from the beginning, to do all he could to prevent any leaks himself and to report immediately to MI5 if he heard any murmurs.

Too little attention has been paid by researchers, including myself, to the publicity aspect of the immunity deal. Blunt should have been the last person to draw public notice to what occurred yet I have been recently told that there was a persistent fear inside MI5 that he might do so, with calamitous consequences all round. The officers who interrogated him received strict instructions from a succession of Director-Generals, beginning with Hollis, to take Blunt gently and to do nothing which might provoke him to make a public statement.

While Blunt was to make much of his conscience, when publicly exposed in 1979, it is hard to believe that it could ever have pricked him into making a martyr of himself. Yet he must have remained under heavy mental pressure from fear of exposure, and possibly from continuing K.G.B. prodding, and may have experienced periods in which public confession offered the only road to release. Indeed, when Blunt eventually met Straight in London after his exposure to the F.B.I. and MI5 he thanked him for his service.[28] Possibly MI5 heard of threats by Blunt to reveal his own treachery from those of his intimate friends who were interviewed after his exposure by Straight and who already knew about it.

The fear in MI5 must have been intensified by the obvious consequences to the MI5 management of the outcry from Parliament and the public if they became aware that such a villain had been given such protection. On the other hand, it might be construed as supporting evidence for the belief that Blunt had an additional secret which had to be preserved. As will be seen, later events suggest that if this secret existed it might have had some connection with the Royal Family. In any case, the fear that Blunt might 'go public' unless handled gingerly gave him an advantage which he seemed to exploit for the rest of his life and which helps to explain many peculiar incidents.

In the original interview with Martin, which lasted only about twenty-five minutes, Blunt did little more than admit that he had been recruited by Soviet Intelligence at Cambridge and had spied for the K.G.B. throughout his service in MI5. When questioned about Long he confirmed that he had recruited him and had run him during the war. Though the Attorney-General's condition that Blunt should give an assurance that he had ceased to spy for the Russians after 1945 was not imposed, Blunt volunteered a statement to that effect, which later turned out to be false.

The interview was overtly recorded on tape by Martin and was played back to Blunt for his verbal agreement that it was true and accurate. As Blunt no doubt realized, if he had not already been told so, such a record was then inadmissible as evidence in any British court.

It was left to Blunt to decide whether he should engineer some excuse to resign from his Royal post. He suggested that if he did so the Russians might deduce what had happened. Martin agreed, knowing that Hollis had already secured the Queen's agreement that the traitor should stay on because MI5 wanted him to do so. He was to remain in the Royal appointment until his retirement in 1972 when, amazingly, he was given another which lasted until 1978.[29]

Why did Blunt confess within minutes of being offered immunity? That remains an intriguing mystery, especially as Blunt was not supposed to know that MI5 had already found out about his accomplice, Long. The explanation favoured by some sources is that he was fully informed about his position by surreptitious means before the formal approach to him was made.

Their suspicions that this had happened were first aroused when they realized that Blunt had been quick to fulfil the condition that he had ceased to spy after 1945, though no mention of this had been made to him officially. Further, as his own account of the meeting with Modin to discuss his defection indicates, it would have been more in keeping with his cautious character had he required a day or so to consider his position. On professional grounds, had he really been taken by surprise, he should have stalled to give himself time to take K.G.B. advice, as Philby had done so recently in a similar circumstance. It was also out of character for such a methodical and pernickety man to refrain from asking for a written guarantee covering all the details of the deal.

Some of his confidence could conceivably have stemmed from a belief that his secret mission for the Royal Family gave him an edge over his interrogator if, in truth, the mission had been that sensitive, but the fact that he confessed so readily on a verbal promise strongly suggests that he already knew the details of the arrangement and of Whitehall's determination to honour it and to conceal it in its own interests. He could have learned of them through the K.G.B. or through some surreptitious meeting with Hollis.

One of the people closest to Blunt in his later years believes that the circumstances of the immunity deal, which he has studied, conform with the probability that he had been given advance notice of it.[30]

Nobody at the Courtauld Institute seems to have been questioned about Blunt's visitors, who had included Philby and Burgess. This may have been a necessary omission because of the immunity guarantee and the requirement to keep it secret from the staff there but it might also have been required by Hollis to conceal a connection with Blunt which might have raised suspicions at that point.

Martin, who had no knowledge of any advance arrangements with Blunt, expressed surprise at how easily and quickly Blunt had been 'broken', or appeared to have been. There is also the odd fact that it had been so readily assumed that Blunt would accept the immunity offer that no thought had been given to the attitude which should be adopted if he rejected it. Yet acceptance was contrary to all his previous behaviour. Later, an MI5 analysis of what he had said and not said at that first interview concluded that he had probably been warned of the confrontation and advised what to do about it.

If Blunt was warned and advised who was responsible? As I have indicated in Chapter 20 the person most strongly suspected of having warned Philby, through the medium of K.G.B. controllers, was Hollis. If he was responsible for that warning in the Soviet interest then he would almost certainly have warned his controllers about Blunt, being one of the few who knew the relevant information.

It has not been possible to establish with absolute certainty that Hollis was still on friendly terms with Blunt in 1963. They were likely to have been meeting on occasion at the Travellers Club and, possibly, at the Courtauld Institute. A warning from Hollis could conceivably have been direct or could have been accomplished through a Soviet controllers. Since the decision had been taken in MI5 that Blunt should not be placed under physical surveillance no clandestine meeting would have been detected. Blunt assured a close confidant that he did not know whether Hollis was a spy or not and that if he was Hollis would have been under instructions not to reveal it to anyone else. But if Blunt really did know that Hollis was a spy he is most unlikely to have admitted it, just as he did all he could to protect his other friends who were in prominent positions.

If Hollis had alerted Soviet Intelligence about Blunt he would have done so soon after hearing about Straight's confession to the F.B.I. in the autumn of 1963. The K.G.B. would then have wanted time to consider its requirements and dispositions and this could account for some of the delay in MI5's action on the case. Any trips which Blunt made abroad at this stage could be significant.

It is not impossible that the K.G.B. learned of Straight's statement through its own resources or even that Blunt was told directly about it by some source. In the latter case Hollis might have learned of the development from Blunt! Inquiries into that possibility were never made by MI5 but some are in progress at the time of writing.

After the interview at which Blunt's confession was secured and immunity granted, Martin was determined to subject him to long and penetrating debriefing. As there seemed to be some reluctance on the part of his immediate superiors to provide the resources and back-up for the action he proposed, Martin saw Hollis, who also took the view that there was no need for haste and that Blunt should be handled gently. An argument ensued and Hollis responded with the unusual step of suspending Martin from duty for two weeks.[31] Martin suggested that if the Director-General did not want to see his face at headquarters he could, nevertheless, go ahead with the interrogations at Blunt's flat. Hollis told him that his suspension was total and that he should leave Blunt alone.

As a result Blunt, who must have expected to be qestioned without delay unless someone had surreptitiously told him otherwise, was left free without surveillance for a fortnight during which he could have sought advice from his Soviet friends or anybody else. He could also have warned friends who might be at risk, thereby nullifying Hollis's claim that an approach to Blunt without immunity would deprive MI5 of the element of surprise when investigating other people he might name.

When Martin returned to duty he prepared a very short brief of

Blunt's confession for the Queen's private secretary. In 1979 Mrs Thatcher was to tell Parliament that 'The Palace duly followed the advice which had already been given.'[32] There can be little doubt that in this instance the Palace was the Queen. I have established to my satisfaction that the Queen was told and asked if she still wished to follow the earlier official advice. Perhaps with some natural reluctance she did so. Blunt told a close associate that he did not know whether the Queen was told or not and that he was never able to discern any difference in their relationship.[33]

The ploy proposed at the highest level by Hollis and executed so as to conceal Blunt's treachery, and that of anybody whom he might expose, looked like succeeding totally in 1964 when any leakage of a matter so secret seemed extremely remote.

On Hollis's instructions the highest degree of secrecy was imposed inside MI5 so that, for many years, very few officers knew about Blunt's proven treachery and those who did were forbidden to discuss it with anyone else. This was reasonable security practice but Hollis probably appreciated that some of his officers would be appalled when they discovered that a colleague who had betrayed them and disgraced the Service had been virtually excused. 'I must belong to a different school,' was how one officer expressed his disgust to Hollis when, eventually, he did hear of it. Not unnaturally, some officers recalled that Vassall, the lowly clerk, was serving an eighteen-year prison sentence while Barbara Fell, who had been little more than stupidly indiscreet, was still in prison when the decision to 'immunize' Blunt had been taken. Hollis's critics feared that the concept of offering immunity to traitors would flout the law and inevitably lead to the charge that the secret services were prepared to support its full application to those outside while giving total protection to those inside. While Blake, an MI6 officer, had admittedly been prosecuted, he was a foreigner, half-Jewish and not a Fifth Estate figure like Blunt or Philby.

It can be argued that inequitable as the Blunt case may seem when compared with the treatment of other offenders, the course of action over which Hollis presided was in the national interest. The counter-argument can be developed by asking which course of action better suited the K.G.B. – the prosecution of Blunt and his collaborators or secret immunity?

The supporters of MI5's action claim that Blunt gave greater co-operation when he knew he was safe than he would have done had he been imprisoned for many years, but this is by no means certain. Fuchs, Vassall and Blake all gave confessions as reliable as Blunt's without being offered immunity and continued to oblige while in prison. So, more recently, did Prime. As the reader will see, when Blunt knew that nothing could happen to him once he had been granted immunity he became highly selective about what he was prepared to tell and his interrogators believe that he lied to them on many issues.

Michael Straight visited London in September 1964 and with Hollis's consent confronted Blunt, having been ignored by MI5 during a visit in the previous November.[34] Straight says that the meeting, held in Blunt's flat after a previous discussion with Martin, was cordial. Having just been told that Blunt had confessed there was little he could do in the way of accusation. Blunt claimed to be grateful but he was a consummate dissimulator. The few questions he asked may have been to satisfy his Soviet friends as much as his own curiosity.

On 17 June 1964, two months after Blunt had been granted immunity and had confessed, Hollis informed his political chief, the Home Secretary Henry Brooke, what had happened, saying nothing whatever about Long.[35] Brooke failed to tell the Prime Minister, Sir Alec Douglas-Home, as did Hollis, who had the right of direct access to him. This omission mystified some MI5 officers when they learned of it and one of them, who had been involved in the Blunt interrogations, was so concerned that he dissented in writing in a minute which, presumably, is still in the MI5 files. Hollis responded to the minute verbally, claiming that 'he had done all that was necessary in alerting Brooke.' It was suspected that Hollis had presented the facts to Brooke in such a way that he would consider it unnecessary or inadvisable to tell the Prime Minister, in spite of the involvement of the Queen. It could be more than coincidental that, after discussions with Hollis, Brooke had not warned the previous Prime Minister, Macmillan, about the security aspects of the Profumo affair. Such is the mystique attaching to the office of Director-General of MI5 that a pliant Home Secretary or Attorney-General may be induced to take advice he would reject from anyone else.

There was a further factor which might have affected Hollis's and Brooke's behaviour: in January 1964, while Martin was in Washington securing first-hand information about Blunt, Sir Alec Douglas-Home had announced the establishment of a Standing Security Commission, headed by a judge, to carry out independent studies into breaches of security with a view to recommending improvements in security precautions and, if necessary, to apportion blame for the breaches.[36] If Sir Alec had been informed of the immunity proposal it is not impossible that, being the kind of man he is, he might have felt it incumbent on himself to refer the case to the Security Commission, which opposition M.P.s would surely have demanded had they known about the case. In that event Hollis's plans for immunity would have been torpedoed because the opposition leader, Harold Wilson, would have had to be informed under the rules of the Security Commission, and some report to Parliament would have been required. To a man as secretive as Hollis the establishment of a Security Commission, with powers to obtain information from himself and other MI5 officers must have been anathema.

When the Labour Government was installed in October 1964 Hollis should have taken steps to ensure that the new Home Secretary or the new Attorney-General was informed about the sensitive Blunt situation which, still being recent, might leak with particular embarrassment to ministers who had ridiculed Macmillan for being ignorant of the Profumo affair. Again he remained silent. George Wigg, the security 'watchdog' appointed precisely to prevent such ignorance, was also uninformed and so, as a result, was the Prime Minister, Harold Wilson.[37]

While the full truth behind these omissions may never be known, one thing is certain: another extremely sensitive situation involving a Soviet spy, fraught with political considerations and dominated by Hollis, never reached the ears of any prime minister so long as Hollis remained Director-General of MI5. Was the similarity to the Profumo affair due only to the ham-fisted way Hollis handled such issues? Or was it due to the direction of Hollis's behaviour, in both cases, by an outside Soviet influence?

CHAPTER THIRTY-EIGHT

The Interrogation of Leo Long

THE precise date when Long was approached by MI5 after Blunt had confirmed Straight's statement that he had been a Soviet agent has not been revealed officially. It must presumably have been after the fortnight during which Martin was suspended from duty and may have been weeks later. If it was deliberately delayed by Hollis it could have been for the purpose of enabling him to see the Home Secretary, as he did in June, without the necessity of telling him about Long, who had not then been given the chance to confess. All that Parliament and the public have been told is that he was approached after Blunt had been granted immunity.[1] The circumstances of the approach, which are known, are extraordinary even by the standards of the secret world. The first that Long is supposed to have known about his exposure was a telephone call from Blunt who said, 'Something has come up', meaning Straight's statement, and that he should make his way to Blunt's flat for a drink and a chat. Martin, who had arranged the visit with Blunt, was not present when Long arrived. The sitting room was 'miked' but it would seem likely that the co-conspirators would have talked briefly somewhere else off the record. According to the tape-recording, Blunt told Long what had happened and, without mentioning that he had told MI5 that his own work for Soviet Intelligence had ceased at the end of the war, he urged him to agree to see the security authorities and, as he put it, 'come clean'. With Martin's previous agreement Blunt then assured his former agent that if he agreed to co-operate it was very unlikely that he would be prosecuted.[2] In fact it was absolutely certain that, whatever he might confess, no action would be taken against him.

Blunt then telephoned Martin saying that Long was ready to talk and the MI5 man, who had been awaiting the call, went round to the flat. The master-spy remained in the room, sipping his gin, while Martin conducted his first interview with the pupil-agent in the comfortable atmosphere provided by the Professor of the History of Art and Surveyor of the Queen's Pictures.

375

According to Mrs Thatcher's eventual statement to Parliament about Long, seventeen years later, Long asked Martin for immunity from prosecution in return for information. 'This was refused,' Mrs Thatcher said, giving the impression that the authorities had taken a tough line with this traitor.[3] In fact, the real reason why immunity was refused was that only the Attorney-General could have granted it and Hollis had not told the Attorney-General, then Sir John Hobson, anything about Long. Nor did he ever do so.

Hollis may have been motivated by the disgrace of having to admit that there had been yet another Soviet spy in British Military Intelligence throughout the war, when it had been his responsibility to detect and counter such people. But he could also have been concerned about Hobson's likely reaction to the revelation that a possible witness against Blunt had been to hand and had been concealed from him. As will be seen, Mrs Thatcher had only just been made aware of this – in November 1981 – when she made her statement on the Long case. The information had been withheld from her when she had made her statement about Blunt two years earlier.

Being unable to offer Long official immunity, Martin did the next best thing and confirmed Blunt's assurance that he was unlikely to be prosecuted if he co-operated. The possibility that Martin might be required to give this assurance, which would be binding in British law because it was an inducement, must have been discussed previously by MI5's legal department and agreed to by Hollis. In any case, as already mentioned, Blunt's immunity would automatically cover Long because any prosecution of Long would inevitably lead to the exposure of Blunt and the fact that he had been exempted from prosecution himself.

Hollis's argument for giving the assurance to Long, which was supported by some of his senior colleagues, was revealed by Mrs Thatcher when, following a brief supplied by MI5, she told Parliament, 'Mr Long could not have been expected to co-operate in the Security Service's inquiries if he believed that he was likely to be prosecuted if he did so.'[4] What a way to treat a dangerous criminal! Long was later to admit that his wartime activities had been 'frankly treasonable'.

In approving the assurance to Long, Hollis had been in breach not only of Government requirements but of MI5 practice. To quote a former long-serving MI5 officer, 'It is not in the gift of any official or officer of the Government, other than the Attorney-General, to distribute bonanzas among malefactors.'

Long has insisted that when he was first questioned by Martin he did not know about Blunt's immunity but, as they were together in

376

private, this seems most unlikely for Long would surely have asked Blunt about his position. Had he not known about Blunt's position it is doubtful that he would have requested immunity because he would not have known that Hollis had changed the rules regarding the treatment of Secret Service traitors.

From his first meeting with Martin, and during several more interrogations, Long was to admit that his conduct had been treasonable.[5] Like Blunt, he insisted at first that he had ceased to spy for the Soviet Union in 1945 after his controller had left MI5. Yet he had remained in touch with secret information of the greatest interest to the U.S.S.R. until his intelligence post in Germany ended in 1952. Blunt must have told the Russians about Long during the six years when he was passing on his information because they would have demanded to know the source to be confident of its credibility. Is it conceivable that the Russians would have left Long alone between 1945 and 1952 when they had such a hold over him? Blunt's attempt to get Long on to the staff of MI5 in 1946 was certainly carried out under Soviet instructions, for no such initiatives were permitted without the approval of the Moscow Centre. So Long's spontaneous insistence that he had ceased to spy after 1945 raised the suspicion that he, too, had been informed surreptitiously of the Attorney-General's similar condition concerning Blunt, which had not been imposed. It could, of course, have been Blunt who advised him how much to admit before they began their 'bugged' conversation or even on some previous occasion. Or Long could have been advised by somebody else.

The interrogation of Long, which continued over several sessions, produced a lead which enabled MI5 to identify another Cambridge recruit to Soviet Intelligence who was then working in Australia and had previous access to secret information. Steps were taken to ensure that this man had no further access to secret information.

MI5 applied the same restrictions of extreme secrecy to the Long case as it did to Blunt's in order to protect Blunt's immunity deal and its own reputation since the failure to prosecute Long would have caused intense embarrassment. Nothing was heard about it until the publication of *Their Trade is Treachery* which contained the following paragraph: 'Blunt was more forthcoming about a man he had recruited himself in the 1930s, volunteering his name and some details of what he had done. This man held a position which gave him access to valuable secrets during the war, but now works for a commercial company. When faced with Blunt's evidence and following a personal encounter with him, he admitted to having

377

been a spy but managed to convince MI5 that he had ceased to help the Russians when he had married, realizing the danger to his family. No action was taken against him.' Long's name was in the typescript of the book but the publisher's lawyers deleted it for libel reasons. I therefore gave it to various newspapers in the hope that, with their more buccaneering approach to the libel laws, they would follow up the lead. None did so.

Long was eventually exposed publicly by the *Sunday Times* in November 1981 and Mrs Thatcher made a statement to Parliament confirming his treachery.[6] He then appeared on television saying how much he regretted his actions.

CHAPTER THIRTY-NINE

The Interrogation of Sir Anthony Blunt

WHEN Blunt confessed to having been a Soviet agent after his acceptance of immunity in April 1964 he did not then produce a flood of revelations, as MI5 had hoped. On the contrary, disclosures and leads had to be dragged out of him in a long succession of interviews which stretched into 1972. When Martin was permitted by Hollis to begin the serious interrogation of Blunt, after his extraordinary two-week suspension, he was assisted by his technical colleague, Peter Wright. The questioning was carried out mainly in Blunt's flat, which had been wired and miked, and was timed to his professional convenience. As the interviews progressed Blunt appeared, increasingly, to appreciate the strength of his position. Martin recalled to an informant that Blunt seemed to be 'gently amused' by the whole procedure. He became more and more reluctant to incriminate close or highly placed friends. He was, however, prepared to be helpful about his Soviet controllers whose operations dated back thirty years. MI5 was to rate the information he gave about them as among the most important results of the Blunt interrogations, which counters suggestions by Mrs Thatcher and others that such old events are no longer of consequence.

Blunt's descriptions of his first controller, whom he knew only as 'Otto', did not lead to a firm identification but there was no doubt that the next, whom he knew only as 'Henry', was the Soviet 'diplomat' and highly successful K.G.B. agent-runner listed in London as Anatoli Gromov and whose real name was Anatoli Gorski. Claims that 'Henry' was a Soviet journalist writing under the name Ernst Henry are incorrect.[1] It was to Gromov that Blunt handed his most damaging material – the MI5 'order of battle', the tip that there was a British agent in the Kremlin and the masses of documents abstracted by himself and by Burgess.

Among the first leads to other British traitors given by Blunt was information about his Cambridge associate John Cairncross, whom he did not like and whose treachery proved to be very serious and is dealt with separately in Chapter 40. Blunt was then asked about

379

others who might have been recruited and responded by saying, 'If you are looking for other people who might have been recruited by Burgess, then pay attention to those he praised lavishly, because he always tried to recruit them.' Among those who were investigated following this remark was Alister Watson, a scientist who figures in the famous picture of a group of Apostles, taken while he was at Cambridge, and who had, indeed, been admired by Burgess.

This was by no means the first lead which MI5 had been given pointing to Watson. Ten years previously a highly trusted former MI5 officer, who had been at Cambridge at the relevant time, warned his old office that Watson was an ardent communist and should be investigated. No notice was taken of that lead. Later, when Michael Straight was questioned by MI5 in 1964 he named Watson as 'a member of the King's College Communist cell in 1936'.[2] Evidence suggested that Watson had been a major proponent of Marxism at Cambridge and had helped to convert Blunt to that creed. When asked if Watson had ever been recruited to Soviet Intelligence Blunt denied it saying tersely, 'Watson is not relevant.'

Watson had been regarded as an outstanding theoretical physicist at Cambridge but he wrote a thesis which contained an elementary error and this wrecked his prospects as a don. Inquiries showed that he had openly rejected communism, to the great surprise of his friends, and had then joined the Admiralty as a research scientist in 1939. He worked in the highly secret Signals and Radar Establishment until 1953, when he was posted to the Admiralty Research Laboratory at Teddington, Middlesex, where he eventually headed a group working on the detection of submarines, achieving the rank of Senior Principal Technical Officer.

A small MI5 team was allocated to the case. They tapped his home telephone, installed hidden microphones and subjected him to surveillance. He was never observed in contact with Soviet Intelligence officers but it was proved that he was still a committed communist. The investigators proposed that they should confront Watson because he had made a false statement on his positive vetting form declaring that he had no connections with communism or communists but Hollis declined to give the case the necessary priority and no interrogation was possible until after he retired from MI5 at the end of 1965.

In 1967 the Admiralty wanted special clearance for Watson to enable him to visit the U.S. to see a secret underwater anti-submarine array. So, with the agreement of Hollis's successor, he was pulled in for hostile interrogation spread over six weeks. Watson admitted that he was still a committed communist and always had been and had therefore breached the Civil Service security rules by failing to admit this when positively vetted. He admitted having been Blunt's mentor in communism and to having met 'Otto', the early Soviet controller of the Cambridge Ring. He agreed that he had abandoned overt communism in order to secure a post in a Government defence establishment but he denied ever having been recruited as a spy, specifically stating that Burgess had never attempted to recruit him.

When shown a spread of photographs of Soviet bloc intelligence officers he picked out three men whom he had met, admitting that he had breached Admiralty security regulations by failing to report such contact, even though they might have been innocent. One of the Russians was Yuri Modin, who had supervised the defection of Burgess and Maclean and had controlled Blunt. Another was Sergei Kondrashev, a senior K.G.B. officer. Four years previously, the K.G.B. defector, Golitsin, had alleged that Kondrashev had been sent to Britain to control two particularly important communists. One of these had been George Blake, and he believed that the other had naval connections. Golitsin had recalled how this British communist had quarrelled with Kondrashev because he thought him 'too bourgeois' to be a good Soviet communist. When Watson saw Kondrashev's picture he cried, 'I hated that man. He was so bourgeois and had a pet poodle.' The third Russian picked out by Watson was Nikolai Karpekov, who had controlled the Admiralty spy, Vassall.

To the MI5 officers it seemed highly unlikely that Watson would have met three spymasters on purely social grounds and he became suspect as probably the fifth man of the Cambridge Ring.

In a final attempt to induce Watson to commit himself he was confronted by his old friend Blunt in Brown's Hotel off Piccadilly, with MI5 men sitting in, a situation described by Blunt as Kafkaesque. During the prolonged session, which lasted past midnight, the officers turned the conversation to Yuri Modin and they noticed that Watson, who had drunk a lot of sherry, referred to him once by the K.G.B. code-name 'Peter', which he was unlikely to have known had he met him only socially.

The use of Blunt in this way made it certain that Watson would not be prosecuted, even if hard evidence came to light or he confessed, and it is a fair assumption that Blunt had been assured of this before he agreed to confront his old friend. MI5 officers have told me that there was never any intention to stage a prosecution and that their purpose was solely to discover what damage Watson might have done and who his contacts had been. As a last-ditch effort to secure a confession, Watson was offered immunity from prosecution – the precedent set by Hollis being continued by his successor – but he ignored the proposal as though he had not heard it.

Watson had been positively vetted three times and had repeatedly failed to admit his involvement with communism so, in view of the extreme secrecy of his work, he could have been dismissed. There were fears, however, both in MI5 and in the Admiralty, that he would fight any dismissal through his union, the Institution of Professional Civil Servants, with consequent publicity. This might have revealed the Blunt case and would, undoubtedly, have inflicted further damage on Anglo-American relations. So action was limited to his removal from secret work. The security authorities withdrew his P.V. clearance, barring him from access to Top Secret information, and in November 1967 he was transferred to totally non-secret work at the National Institute of Oceanography, a move which he and his union accepted without a battle as he was not far from retirement.

As with the cases of Long, Blunt and other instances embarrassing to MI5 and Whitehall generally, the suspicions concerning Watson were kept as secret as possible and his Admiralty colleagues were never questioned about him. Nothing had been heard of the case until the appearance of *Their Trade is Treachery* in 1981, by which time Watson had retired on full pension. He died in 1983.

Following my disclosure of his name to the *Observer* he was interviewed and continued to proclaim his innocence while admitting that MI5 had good reason to suspect him.[3] He accused MI5 of pressing him to such an extent that, at one stage, he became confused and asked to see a psychiatrist because he feared that he was saying things that he did not mean to say.[4]

After Long had effectively been given immunity from prosecution, Blunt provided information about his activities which led to a Soviet agent, whose identity remains concealed. This man, another Cambridge contemporary who is well known academically, had been recruited by the G.R.U. and tried to recruit Long for that espionage organization. When he told Blunt of this effort there was consternation because Long was already working for the K.G.B. and Blunt had to ask his controller, 'Henry', to sort out the matter. This information confirmed MI5 suspicions that the G.R.U. had also been active in recruiting at Cambridge.

Blunt admitted that he learned about the G.R.U. attempt to recruit Long because he was having a homosexual affair with the man who had made it. It had been assumed that Blunt had always been a very discreet homosexual with steady, almost marital, relationships but MI5's inquiries and his own admissions revealed that he was, in fact, openly promiscuous, haunting public lavatories and 'gay' bars and even picking up sailors.[5] Blunt said that he was ashamed of this side of his life and realized its dangers, but had been unable to control it, even when in the service of the Palace.

Blunt was also forthcoming, ungallantly in the circumstances, about a woman colleague at the Courtauld Institute, Phoebe Pool, with whom he had collaborated on a book about Picasso. Miss Pool was an unfortunate figure, described by a contemporary as 'rather tall, gangling with glasses, a longish bob and very deaf, being required to wear a bulky hearing aid'.[6] Blunt induced her to act as a courier for agents who had been recruited for communist and Soviet work. Without indicating that he had confessed, he tried to jog her memory about her activities on behalf of himself and others so that he could pass on her recollections to MI5 before she herself was interviewed. She recalled meetings with 'a sinister little Russian in Kew Gardens', who was almost cetainly 'Otto', and named two men whom she thought Blunt should warn if MI5 was looking into communist undergraduates who might have been recruited by Soviet Intelligence. One of these was Sir Andrew Cohen, a former member of the Apostles who became a senior diplomat, while the other was an Oxford graduate who then held a high-level post in the Home Office and whose name would later be put forward, unsuccessfully as it happened, for a top position in MI5! Miss Pool also named a Labour M.P. called Bernard Floud as a crypto-communist and possible Soviet agent, claiming that in 1936 he had recruited for underground communist work a young Oxford undergraduate called Jenifer Fischer-Williams, who had then secured highly sensitive work in the Home Office.[7]

Miss Pool was never questioned by the MI5 officers because, shortly after Blunt had quizzed her, she threw herself under a train. Whether Blunt felt any responsibility for her suicide will never be known but his interrogators did not notice any sign of remorse about any of his actions though, publicly, he was to go through the motions later of expressing regret for his treason. Sir Andrew Cohen also died, of a heart attack, before he could be questioned.

Miss Fischer-Williams, who by that time was Mrs Jenifer Hart, married to Professor Herbert Hart, a distinguished lawyer and philosopher who was to become Principal of Brasenose College, Oxford, was interviewed by MI5, as she has recently confirmed in a television broadcast. She said that she had joined the Communist Party in 1935 and when it was known that she intended to join the Civil Service she was instructed to become a secret member, carrying no Party card and disassociating herself publicly from other communists. She named Floud as her first mentor. She did well in the Civil Service examinations and entered the Home Office, when she was introduced to a more professional controller, a middle European whose name she claimed to be unable to remember but who was, almost certainly, 'Otto', then also serving as controller for Burgess, Maclean and Philby.

Whether by luck or by design, Miss Fischer-Williams was soon in the department responsible for handling the written requests from MI5 for official Home Office permission to tap the telephones of suspects. As she confirmed later in the television interview she 'saw a lot of the MI5 people'. In fact she took the signed warrants from the Home Office to MI5 and became friendly with Brigadier A.W. 'Jasper' Harker, a very senior MI5 officer. She was even asked to recommend friends who might want to join MI5. In 1941 she married Herbert Hart who was then working in MI5.

Mrs Hart told her interrogators that she had become disenchanted with communism after the Nazi-Soviet pact in 1939 and that 'Otto' had specifically told her to do nothing for ten years. As she recalled in her T.V. interview, in 1983, the MI5 officers did not believe her, to her lasting annoyance. Such an instruction was certainly out of character for 'Otto' or any other Soviet controller when a recruit was in such a position. Mrs Hart, however, insists that she was never aware that she was recruited for Soviet Intelligence but only to serve the Communist Party and that, in the event, she did not even do that because she was not required to do so.

The MI5 officers were unable to interview and question Bernard Floud because he was an M.P. and the Labour Prime Minister, Harold Wilson, had ruled that M.P.s and peers were to be exempt from investigation by the security authorities unless he gave special permission. It was also forbidden to tap their telephones and put them under any kind of surveillance without special leave. An opportunity to take action arose, however, in 1967 when Wilson was thinking about making Floud, M.P. for Acton, a junior minister. As a matter of routine the Prime Minister's office needed an assurance from MI5 that it had nothing on record to his detriment. Wilson was told that Floud, who had been an open communist at Oxford, had been recruited to the Soviet cause by James Klugmann, had recruited others and had retained his ideological commitment while serving in the Intelligence Corps during the Second World War. Wilson then gave permission for Floud to be interviewed and he was interrogated for two weeks, during which he admitted his former communism but denied any connection with Soviet Intelligence. The MI5 officers suspected that he was, in fact, still in touch with the K.G.B. and said that if he confessed and could convince them that he had ended his relationship with the Russians some time ago they might not object to his ministerial appointment.

After further unproductive sessions, Floud, who was suffering from depression exacerbated by his wife's recent death, went home and committed suicide. The extent to which the interrogations contributed to his death will never be known.

When Jenifer Hart was being questioned about Floud she was asked about other convinced Marxists she had known and she named Sir Dennis Proctor, then Permanent Secretary, the top civil servant, in the Ministry of Power. A check with the MI5 files showed that Flora Solomon, the woman who had exposed Philby, had named Proctor as a communist but there had been no follow-up because she had been convinced that he lacked the courage to be a spy. Blunt, who had been deliberately misleading about his old friend Watson, took a similar line about Proctor but the MI5 officers decided to make further inquiries. They showed that he had been a close friend of Burgess who, as Blunt had pointed out, tried to recruit people whom he admired. When Burgess had been actively spying before the war, handing over every scrap of political, economic and strategic information to his Soviet controller, Proctor had held secretarial posts to Stanley Baldwin and other senior politicians, which gave him access to information of the greatest interest to the Kremlin. It was established that Proctor had also been friendly with Blunt. Proctor had become an Apostle while at Cambridge in 1927 and had met Blunt later through functions of that secret society and also through a mutual interest in art, Proctor being chairman of the Tate Gallery in the 1950s. When Blunt was again asked if Proctor had assisted Burgess or any other member of the Cambridge Ring in their work for the Soviet Union he denied any such connection. 'He was never in the game,' he replied curtly.

The MI5 officers were particularly suspicious of a peculiar move which Proctor had made in 1950 when he resigned from his promising career in the Civil Service to take a post with a shipping company in Copenhagen. In 1953 he had returned and re-entered the Civil Service. This was interpreted as possibly implying that he had taken fright in 1950, having heard, perhaps from a Soviet controller, that Maclean's code-name had come to light in deciphered K.G.B. radio traffic and that his own might therefore be revealed. His departure abroad had put him outside the jurisdiction of the Official Secrets Act. Then in 1953, when Maclean was safely away and the furore had died down, it was surmised that he had considered it safe to return, again perhaps on Soviet advice.

The investigating officers sought Hollis's permission to interview Proctor but Hollis refused on the grounds that the suspect was close to retirement. So, until Hollis himself retired, nothing could be done.

By the time that Hollis's successor agreed that the case should be pursued, in 1966, Proctor was living in Provence. He was visited by Peter Wright who was armed with a copy of a letter which Burgess had written to his old friend from Washington. In a long and rather bibulous discussion, lasting far into the night, Proctor admitted having been a Marxist at Cambridge and having been so friendly with Burgess that he had held no secrets from him but denied that he had ever given any information of value to the K.G.B. because he had none to give. Wright reminded him that it appeared certain that Burgess had supplied the Kremlin with secret information indicating that Britain was not serious about coming to any mutual assistance agreement against Germany and that when Stalin learned this it had contributed to his decision to make a non-aggression pact with Hitler, which had initiated the Second World War.

Proctor admitted that following the defection of Maclean and Burgess he should have reported receiving the letter from Burgess in 1950, since it could have been of value to the security authorities. Then when suddenly asked at 3 a.m. why he thought Burgess had not tried to recruit him he replied, 'He didn't need to. I held no secrets from him.' He reaffirmed that he had never known that Burgess was a spy and totally rejected MI5's interpretation of his move to Denmark and his return to Britain. When Wright went over his modest admissions on the following day Proctor became angry and tried to retract them.

On being told the results of the interview Blunt smiled and said 'I can now tell you that Dennis was the best source Guy ever had for the Russians.'

Proctor was interviewed again after further inquiries but he persisted in his denials. No further action was taken and the case was regarded as unresolved but steps were taken to ensure that Proctor could not serve on any Whitehall committees giving him access to secrets, as former permanent secretaries frequently do.

Following the first disclosure of the Proctor case in *Their Trade is Treachery*, Sir Dennis, then seventy-six, was interviewed by journalists to whom I had given his name.[8] He admitted having been interviewed twice by MI5 and said, 'I suppose the security people had good reasons for their suspicions but I was not a spy...It is true, as was said in Chapman Pincher's book, that I was not interviewed until after I had retired. Don't ask me why. I don't know.' He roundly denied that he could possibly have been the best source Burgess ever had.

Another lead from Blunt concerning an academic whom Burgess had admired led to an interrogation in which the suspect admitted that Burgess had tried to recruit him to service in the Comintern but claimed that he had failed. The investigators were not satisfied and this man was also barred from work on secret Government committees.

Through a Blunt lead it proved possible to identify the New Zealander, Paddy Costello, who had become Professor of Russian at Manchester University, as an active Soviet agent, as already mentioned in Chapter 26. Costello died in 1964 but one of his New Zealand friends was still an active secret communist and MI5 was able to prevent his appointment to a very important position where he could have wielded damaging influence.

Blunt was also helpful in confirming the recruitment to Soviet Intelligence of a Canadian student at Cambridge, called Herbert Norman, whose case I record in Chapter 42. When told of the evidence against Norman, who had committed suicide in 1957, Blunt said, reluctantly, 'Herb was one of us,' meaning a recruit to Soviet Intelligence and not just a homosexual, which he also was.

On several occasions Blunt's interrogators had reason to suspect that he was being given a play-back account of the results of the consequent inquiries. While the talks were usually 'comfortable', to use Blunt's own description, it was decided to mount a sudden hostile assault by announcing, as though new evidence had come to light, 'You realize that people have died and been tortured as a result of what you have done, so come on! Who else is there?' Blunt lost his composure only momentarily and, with apparent confidence that no new evidence was in the interrogators' possession, replied firmly, 'There was nobody else', an answer which like many others was to prove untrue.

On another occasion a tape-recorder went wrong and it was quickly repaired by Wright, who was highly qualified technically, though Blunt was not supposed to be aware of that. The two had not been contemporaries in MI5 and everything had been done to keep Wright's identity and expertise secret. Nevertheless, as the machine began to roll again Blunt commented, 'How marvellous to see a real expert technician at work.'

Until his retirement Hollis was kept informed of the continuing interrogation of Blunt because he insisted on being consulted before anybody of consequence was approached as a result of Blunt's leads. Martin repeatedly complained to his immediate superiors about Hollis's limitations on inquiries into these leads and his feelings were relayed to the Director-General, who made them an excuse, in 1965, for getting rid of his most able investigating officer. After consulting Sir Dick White, Hollis called a meeting of his directors and told them that Martin was the ringleader of a 'Gestapo' which was threatening MI5 morale and that he proposed to face him with the choice of a compulsory transfer to MI6 or dismissal with no pension. I have been told that Hollis's original intention was simply to dismiss Martin but that White, who admired the officer's investigating skills, was keen to acquire him.

As Martin was too aggressively active for the taste of most of the members of MI5's top management, and as they would be disinclined to disagree with the man whose recommendations would have considerable influence on their own careers, they concurred. Martin had little option but to accept the transfer because MI5 officers are not permitted to belong to any union which might fight for them. He was convinced – and still is – that Hollis got rid of him because he had 'rumbled him' as a spy.

Whether this was true or not Hollis's action is a further example of the power that any director-general who is a spy can wield in order to protect himself. It can, of course, be argued that with Hollis near to retirement an officer like Martin, who was zealous to expose more examples of MI5's incompetence, was like a messenger who brings bad news and was merely treated as such. Whatever the reason for Hollis's action Martin's close colleagues regarded the dismissal of such an experienced counter-intelligence officer as a positive victory for the K.G.B., and some suspected that it could have resulted from a Soviet suggestion, especially as the use of the word 'Gestapo' was common in Soviet propaganda.

Hollis may have hoped that Martin, who was nothing if not proud, would accept the dismissal. Instead, he found that with White's agreement Martin remained a member of the MI5/MI6 team which was to investigate Hollis himself. The continuing interrogation of Blunt was left mainly to Wright and to an able woman researcher.

Blunt was prepared to volunteer information about several of the Cambridge Ring's associates and helpers who were dead. One of them was a homosexual friend of Burgess, called Tom Wylie, who had been a resident duty officer in the War Office and had a flat there. Burgess was in the habit of dropping in there for a drink in the evenings and Wylie allowed him to browse through any available papers. MI5 intended to question Wylie but before they could do so he died from a sudden heart attack.

A journalist who had been talent-spotted by Burgess was interviewed and while his story was not entirely believed he gave a genuine lead to a wartime colleague of Klugmann who had almost certainly been an active Soviet agent. Another Cambridge associate of the Ring who had already been named by Michael Straight as likely to have been recruited, a view with which Blunt agreed, was also seen but would admit nothing. A similar negative result was obtained with three further Cambridge associates, two of whom were eminent doctors, the third being Richard Llewlyn-Davies, who had been an Apostle and subsequently became a Labour life peer.

Blunt was questioned closely about the figure who fits most uncertainly into the jig-saw of suspects, the half-Spanish art dealer and artist, Tomas Harris. He was a master of deception, as Ewan Montagu expresses in the dedication to his book, *Beyond Top Secret U*, but most of the MI5 and MI6 officers I have questioned do not believe that he was an active Soviet spy or even a dedicated communist.[9] Born of a Spanish mother and an English father, who ran the Spanish Art Gallery in London, he eventually studied painting in Rome where, it has been alleged but with little evidence, that he was recruited to the service of the K.G.B. by an Italian art dealer who was an underground communist. A good-looking, gregarious and amusing man, with wealth enough to run a fine house in Mayfair, he entertained lavishly and provided a meeting place for many involved in security and intelligence work, as well as for many who were working primarily for the K.G.B. Philby, Burgess, Blunt and Liddell went there regularly. He began his own professional association with British secret work as a 'glorified housekeeper' at the S.O.E. training school at Brickendonbury Hall. Because he spoke Spanish and had such excellent contacts in Spain he was brought into the Iberian section of MI5 by Liddell, where he performed outstandingly.

On the other hand, he strongly supported moves to get Philby into the corresponding section in MI6 and remained such a close friend that he was a witness at the traitor's wedding in 1946. There is no doubt, either, that Harris was involved in the recruitment of Blunt into MI5.[10] He is supposed to have helped Philby financially after his enforced resignation from MI6 in 1951. Two years later he may also have assisted in the escape of Melinda Maclean to Switzerland, so it is possible that he served as a paymaster for the Russians.[11]

Blunt, however, remained his closest friend, and questions in the Canadian Parliament have revealed that after the war they operated in the art business together. In 1955 the National Gallery of Canada bought a picture by Poussin, called 'Augustus and

Cleopatra', which was certified as original by Blunt and purchased from Harris's gallery.[12]

In 1963 Flora Solomon, who knew Harris well, had named him as having assisted Philby as a courier during the Spanish Civil War, but as Harris was then living in Majorca, nothing was done to follow up the information. Then because of the long delay in acting on Straight's information about Blunt it was too late to interrogate Harris about his part in Blunt's entry into MI5 and other matters. Three months before Blunt confessed, Harris was killed in a rather mysterious car crash. While driving in Majorca his car, which was new, ran off the road and struck a tree. Mrs Harris, who survived, could not understand why this happened as Harris was not driving fast and no other car was involved. Flora Solomon seemed convinced that he had been murdered and his death remains suspect to many MI5 officers. The date could be significant. It was 27 January 1964, shortly after Martin had returned to London with the information that was bound to lead to the interrogation of Blunt and then to Harris. Moscow could have been alerted by a high-level MI5 source and Harris's car could have been tampered with to prevent his interrogation. An accident would seem to be the likeliest explanation but it was convenient for the K.G.B. and is certainly another strange coincidence.

Before the disclosure that Straight had been responsible for exposing Blunt it was widely assumed that it was Harris's death that led Blunt to say, publicly, that he had confessed because an incident in 1964 had freed him from loyalty to his friends, a specious statement which had the full support of MI5.[13]

Harris bequeathed a large collection of Goya prints to the British Museum. It would seem unlikely that an avowed enemy of Britain would have done so unless, perhaps, he did it as penance for sins regretted.

Altogether more than twenty suspects were interviewed or approached in the process of Blunt's admissions but, apart from Long and Cairncross, none was positively identified as a full-blown spy and nobody was prosecuted.

The implications of the Blunt case for the investigations being mounted about Hollis were noted as they arose. His suspension and then dismissal of Martin strengthened suspicions against him. So did his actions in delaying any interrogation of Watson and Proctor. Hollis had been responsible for overseeing the activities of communists when many of those brought to light by Blunt's leads had been active but, from the MI5 records, it would seem that he had been unaware of any of them or had ignored them. The same was true of the secret communists identified as a result of the interrogations of Long and Cairncross.

Blunt's interrogation lasted, spasmodically, from 1964 until 1972. The amount of valuable information he might have provided under really hostile interrogation and the shock of imprisonment will never be known.

While the K.G.B. would have gained some immediate advantage from Blunt's trial and conviction, through the damage it would have inflicted on Anglo-American relations, it always prefers that its agents should not be prosecuted if this can reasonably be avoided. A long gaol sentence for a K.G.B. agent does not encourage others to offer their services and, callous though the managers of Soviet Intelligence may have to be on occasion, they have preferred, since Stalin's death, to see their long-term aides rewarded rather than punished. In addition, with Blunt at liberty and still in his prestigious post at the Palace the possibility remained that he might be reactivated some day for he could easily be contacted during his many trips abroad on art business, as Philby's approach in Beirut in 1961 indicates. Knowing the extent to which every scrap of gossip concerning high-level personalities is referred back to Moscow from K.G.B. agents operating in London, I am convinced that there would have been continuing interest in anything that Blunt could provide from his position in the Royal Household, when attending private dinners and other functions, and when speaking with Household staff who, of course, did not know of his connection with Soviet Intelligence. I also find it hard to believe that the K.G.B. failed to try to impose pressure upon him to continue his services, at least as a talent scout. If anything, the immunity, which was probably known to the Russians even before it was granted, intensified the blackmail pressure which could be applied to Blunt. Indeed, the requirement for keeping the whole affair secret was so great that it is doubtful that the authorities would have dared to take any open action had Blunt been caught acting for the Russians after 1964. Evidence to this effect is presented in Chapter 55 when the first real fear of damaging publicity about the cover-up of Blunt's treachery was generated in the Cabinet Office.

The Kremlin, which tends to continue the pantomime pretence that only the perfidious West indulges in espionage, is extremely sensitive to the exposure of K.G.B. activities in any way which affects relations with other countries. So while Hollis's solution to the Blunt problem may have saved MI5, the Palace and Government ministers from deep embarrassment, it also saved face for the K.G.B. and suited Moscow in other ways. It is my belief that if the directors of Soviet Intelligence had been asked how they would like

MI5 to play the Blunt affair they would have opted for the solution selected by Hollis. And if there was a Soviet penetration agent at high level in MI5 at the time, as seems certain, then the Soviet view would, assuredly, have been sought.

The same comments and consideration apply to the case of Leo Long, though there the responsibility resides entirely with Hollis. The K.G.B. must have been delighted with the treatment of Long if only because it would have given comfort to any other Soviet spies inside the secret services, who could feel confident that they, too, would be safe from prosecution and exposure, if caught. Indeed, any who knew about the secret immunity given to Blunt and Long and offered to Philby could have used the threat of exposing it as a means of securing similar favour for themselves. In particular, if Hollis was a spy, he was introducing, as routine, a practice which he could be virtually certain would be applied to himself.

Not until 1966, after a further general election and after Hollis's retirement, did MI5 acquaint Harold Wilson and his Home Secretary about the Blunt affair. As will be seen, the investigation into Hollis himself was under way at that time, and perhaps the possibility that he too might have to be offered immunity in the foreseeable future helped to induce the new MI5 management to inform the Labour Government about the 'highly productive precedent' set by the Blunt and Long cases.

The Potential Value of Oversight

When James Callaghan learned of Blunt's treachery during his Prime Ministership he was appalled that such a man should have been allowed to continue in freedom and respect, though he had been fully briefed on the beneficial results of the immunity claimed by MI5.[14] My inquiries have shown that a similar view is held by many other politicians and public figures who have the interests of the secret services at heart. The circumstances show that because of the virtually indisputable authority of the Director-General of MI5 prevailing in 1964 on security issues, Hollis was able to overbear the Attorney-General, the Director of Public Prosecutions and his deputy, and Palace officials to agree to a course of action which, to many, seems reprehensible, in spite of gallant efforts by Mrs Thatcher to excuse them. It would seem, therefore, that the Blunt case is another excellent example of a serious security issue on which the advice and judgement of a panel of experienced Parliamentarians or Privy Councillors would have been valuable in countering the weight of Hollis's *ex officio* authority and in contributing sounder judgement than was available in a man of Hollis's limited capabilities.

Callaghan was not informed of the Long case. Had he been he would probably have been even more incensed, for in the Long case Hollis was effectively dispensing justice without reference to any of the Law Officers. This power in the hands of the Director-General of MI5 to award effective immunity by offering inducements continued until the public exposure of Long in November 1981. On learning about it, Mrs Thatcher took steps to end it, though with careful avoidance of any criticism of Hollis for having wielded it. Inducements may now no longer be offered without reference to the Attorney-General.[15] It would seem to be fair to deduce that had MI5 been subject to oversight and accountability in 1964 the pernicious practices applied to both Long and Blunt would have been ended then. It can rightly be argued that law enforcement is not the prime purpose of the secret services, but the cases of Blunt, Long, Philby and others show that, while the law has been enforced for what might be termed second-class spies, there has been a blatant reluctance to apply it to traitors who have been connected with the secret services. MI5 has also been having its cake and eating it in another respect when circumstances suited. While insisting that law enforcement is not its prime purpose, it has taken a legal attitude to the admissibility of evidence when this has suited its management. In fact, what is inadmissible in court is often perfectly admissible in an espionage inquiry.

CHAPTER FORTY

Big Fish Escapes as Small Fry

WHEN MI5 officers searched Burgess's flat following his disappearance in May 1951 they found some handwritten notes concerning affairs in the Treasury. There were also pen-portraits of various officials, some giving details of alleged character weaknesses and other features which might be exploited, indicating that they had been written by a pro-Soviet talent scout. Sir John Colville, who later became secretary to Winston Churchill, has told me that he was one of twenty-five people mentioned.

The papers, which dated from the early 1940s, were unsigned and their author might never have been discovered but for a fluke occurrence. They had been passed to Arthur Martin who happened to have a sharp-eyed secretary. She recognized the handwriting as that of a Treasury official called John Cairncross. A check of his record showed that he had been at Cambridge at the same time as Burgess, Maclean, Klugmann and others and that, like them, he had been an overt communist. This was regarded as understandable as he had been a scholarship boy from a poor home in Glasgow.

Cairncross was placed under letter and telephone check and this revealed that he was being urgently summoned to an emergency meeting with a K.G.B. officer in a wood in Surrey in connection with the Burgess and Maclean defections. He was already under surveillance and a most careful trap was set up in the wood. Cairncross duly attended but the Russian never appeared. Nor did later surveillance ever catch Cairncross in touch with his controller suggesting that, once again, Soviet Intelligence had been given a warning which could only have originated inside MI5.

When it became clear that surveillance was producing no result Cairncross was interviewed by Martin in 1952. He quickly admitted that he had written the notes which had contained information of value to the Russians in 1940, when they had been virtual allies of the Nazis, though it had not been highly classified. He denied being a spy or any kind of Soviet agent and said that he did not believe that Burgess was a Soviet agent either. His offer of resignation was accepted and he soon obtained a post abroad, first in Canada, then in America, finally joining the Food and Agriculture Organization of the United Nations in Rome in about 1958.[1] The reason for his departure from Whitehall was not revealed and no further interest was taken in his case.

The way in which Cairncross was dismissed as 'small fry' in 1952 is a dreadful indictment of MI5's handling of the case and this is a view not conditioned by hindsight. His insistence that he had not known that Burgess was a Soviet agent was accepted far too readily. His assignation with the known K.G.B. officer was proof of his K.G.B. connection and fair evidence of Burgess's. The MI5 management was probably only too pleased to hear him deny Burgess's guilt but its dismissal of the case against Cairncross at that stage failed to expose a much more serious act of treason. Cairncross's full service record was easily available and, had it been properly examined, loud alarm bells should have sounded. In 1942 he had used his fluency in German to get himself on to the staff of the most secret and most sensitive of all establishments, the Government Code and Cipher School at Bletchley Park, where he worked as an editor dealing with Air Intelligence.[2] In 1944 he had moved to the headquarters of MI6 itself.[3] So, either it did not occur to MI5 that he might have continued his activities on behalf of the K.G.B. in both establishments or the managements of MI5 and MI6, which had run Bletchley, were so embarrassed by the discovery of a potential agent there that they simply wanted to be rid of the Cairncross case and ensured its total suppression. His departure abroad meant that he could not be prosecuted as extradition is not possible under the Official Secrets Act.

During Blunt's long but spasmodic interrogation he continued to protect his high-level friends whom he admired but, being an arch snob, had no compunction about naming associate spies of humble origin whom he disliked, especially when he knew that they were no longer of any value to the K.G.B. Among the first he named was Cairncross, admitting that he had reported him to his Soviet controller as a potential spy while teaching him at Cambridge and that the next stage in the recruitment had been achieved by the other communist Cambridge contemporary, James Klugmann. MI5 had no option but to take some action and in 1964 Martin travelled to Rome to interrogate Cairncross who could, of course, have simply refused to be interviewed.

When told about Blunt's admissions, Cairncross, knowing that he was beyond the reach of the law, a legal fact which Martin may have confirmed to him, made what MI5 considered to be a full and contrite confession. He claimed that he had embraced Soviet-style communism as the only way of securing social justice. He confirmed that it had been Klugmann who had introduced him to his first Soviet controller, the ubiquitous 'Otto', during a visit to Regent's Park, where the K.G.B. man was waiting for them. 'Otto' had instructed him to reject his open communism, go 'underground' and get into the Foreign Office instead of pursuing an academic career, as he would have preferred. Cairncross officially quit the Communist Party late in 1936 and competed for entry to the Foreign Office, passing top of his list. For two years he worked in the German Department, where Maclean was a colleague.

Cairncross explained that after 'Otto' had been recalled in the 1938 purge he gave his material to Burgess, which was how some of it came to be in the defector's flat. Burgess, whom he knew to be a Comintern agent, had passed most of it to Philby's estranged wife Lizi who was working in London as a full-time Soviet courier, also servicing Maclean and others.

Before 'Otto' left Britain he suggested that Cairncross should apply for transfer to the Treasury, presumably because Maclean was already giving the K.G.B. sufficient coverage in the German Department. Cairncross was successful, demonstrating again the extraordinary facility with which the K.G.B. was able to recruit unknown people with uncertain futures and intrude them into secret departments of its choice. From the Treasury the K.G.B. was able to move Cairncross to a position of far greater potential.

From Philby, and probably from Long and Blunt too, the K.G.B. already knew that Bletchley was breaking the German Enigma-machine codes by the ingenious processes known by the code-name 'Ultra'. Cairncross described how, having managed to get himself on to the Bletchley staff on Soviet instructions, he had copied secret documents and took them to London at weekends to give them to his new controller, 'Henry' (Anatoli Gorski). He said that to facilitate this service the Russians had given him money to buy a cheap car and run it. The traitor took some pride in recalling that he had received special commendation from Moscow for one particular batch of documents which contained details of Luftwaffe dispositions before the crucial battle of Kursk, in which the Germans were defeated. He described another endeavour which, he said, had enabled the Russians to destroy hundreds of German aircraft on the ground.

While trying to claim extenuating circumstances on the grounds that the Soviet Union was an ally, Cairncross admitted that he had spied for the K.G.B. against the interests of his own country while Stalin was assisting Hitler to defeat France.

As Martin listened to this monstrous recital of treason in war, a capital offence then, he must have realized how ineptly the case had been handled in 1952. The information that Britain was breaking the German codes could easily have leaked from the Russians to Germany, especially as it has been established that the K.G.B. was in close touch with senior German Intelligence officers who were taking out personal insurance against the possibility of a Nazi defeat.

After the war Sir Winston Churchill praised the staff at Bletchley as 'the geese who laid the golden eggs and never cackled'.[4] Cairncross had cackled directly to the Russians during two crucial years, as had others.

When Cairncross switched to the headquarters of MI6 in 1944, a move facilitated by the fact that Bletchley was run by that department, he worked first in German counter-intelligence and then moved to Yugoslav affairs. He was in the section run by David Footman, who remembered him as 'an odd person with a chip on his shoulder'.[5] One of Cairncross's most important field officers was the man who had recruited him, James Klugmann, then a major based in the Italian port of Bari. Between them they provided the K.G.B. with a continuous reading of Allied plans concerning Yugoslavia, and Klugmann helped to change them in Moscow's interests.

Through his linguistic ability Klugmann had insinuated himself into Special Operations Executive (S.O.E.) and had been on the staff of the Balkans Division based in Cairo. His open membership of the Communist Party was known but because he spoke Serbo-Croat and was a skilled wireless operator his desk dealt with all radio messages between Cairo and the British and American officers attached to the partisan forces of General Mihailovich fighting the Germans in the mountains of Yugoslavia. Both in Cairo and later in Bari, Klugmann did all he could to induce S.O.E. headquarters in London to dump Mihailovich, who was anti-communist, and switch all support to Tito, a partisan leader who wanted a communist Yugoslavia after the war. He saw to it that pleas for food, weapons and other supplies from Mihailovich's forces were suppressed or, if any action was taken, that the supplies were diverted to Tito. News of Mihailovich's successes were withheld from the B.B.C., which reserved its propaganda for Tito.[6] Klugmann even manufactured a false signal purporting to have originated from General Sir Henry 'Jumbo' Maitland Wilson, the Commander-in-Chief, Middle East, to Churchill stating that the former diplomat Brigadier Fitzroy Maclean was unsuitable for an assignment in Yugoslavia.[7] Wilson never sent such a message. The Russians feared that Brigadier Maclean would encourage Tito to break with Stalin and become independent – as he did, though

Klugmann, and Cairncross who assisted him, tried hard to prevent it.

Cairncross remained in MI6 until the end of the war and then returned to the Treasury where he had access to high policy documents and assessments of the U.K. economy which, he admitted to Martin, he continued to pass to the Russians. After the war he continued to meet his Soviet controller about once a month and he confirmed that immediately after the defection of Maclean and Burgess he had been called to an emergency meeting in a wood in Surrey which the Russians failed to attend. That was the meeting of which MI5 had secured advance warning. Cairncross assured Martin that the K.G.B. lost interest in him once he left Britain in 1952, a move with which the Russians had agreed in the belief that MI5 was bound to dig into his wartime activities at Bletchley and in MI6 headquarters which, in fact, it failed to do.

All this was duly reported to Hollis who is remembered as having taken little personal interest in the case.[8] So long as Cairncross remained abroad Hollis could avoid taking action and he did not inform any ministers about the confession and all that it implied concerning wartime security in MI6 and Bletchley in particular.

Cairncross's evidence about Klugmann's part in his recruitment could not be ignored, however, for it was the first hard information about that traitor's treachery. Klugmann was openly pursuing his ardent support of Soviet communism in Britain, so when Martin and others urged that Cairncross should be used to try to break Klugmann Hollis was in no position to raise objections, had he wanted to do so. There was urgent need to discover any others whom Klugmann, who operated at Oxford as well as Cambridge, might have recruited, and it transpired that these included Bernard Floud, the Labour M.P., and his brother Peter, and a man who had become an important civil servant.

Cairncross was told that he could return to Britain for a limited period without fear of arrest if he would agree to confront Klugmann – a dispensation to which Hollis agreed without securing the permission of either the Attorney-General or the Director of Public Prosecutions. It would have been routine practice for Hollis to have taken the advice of MI5's in-house legal advisers and, if they interpreted the law as Sir Michael Havers was to do in 1981, Hollis would have been told that the offer to Cairncross could be construed as an inducement, which would prohibit future prosecution if he accepted it. Whether or not this was made clear to Cairncross remains secret.

Displaying some courage, Cairncross saw Klugmann and threatened to expose him, with inevitable damage to the Communist Party, unless he too agreed to co-operate with MI5. Klugmann angrily and contemptuously rejected the offer and, because he resolutely refused to be interviewed by anyone from MI5, Cairncross's effort came to nothing. No attempt was made to induce Cairncross to accuse Klugmann publicly for that would have exposed MI5's deal with him, a proven spy, and, perhaps, the deal with Blunt. It would also have exposed MI5's ineptitude in 1952.

Cairncross gave leads to several other Britons who had served the interests of the K.G.B., naming some of them as spies.[9] One of them, another communist who had served inside the Treasury, the Cabinet Office and other Whitehall departments of great interest to the K.G.B., had been openly communist at Cambridge. He received high honours and a lucrative capitalist directorship on his retirement in a company of particular interest to the K.G.B. Another, also recruited at Cambridge, was a highly placed civil servant when Cairncross exposed him and continued his career until normal retirement on full pension, though some effort was made to restrict his access to secrets. Both men simply refused to be interviewed by MI5 and nothing could be done about them. From information supplied by Cairncross MI5 was also able to secure the removal of two highly suspect people from G.C.H.Q.

The only substantial result of Cairncross's visit to Britain, therefore, was to make him immune to prosecution, though he was given to understand that he could be prosecuted if he returned after going back to Rome and may have believed this. He preferred to live in Italy and this suited the MI5 management who did not want him loose in Britain, knowing as much as he did about Blunt. He remains there and in 1981 was sent to prison, briefly, for a currency smuggling offence.[10]

Owing to the tight security formerly obtaining in MI5 there was no publicity whatever about Cairncross's treachery until after Blunt's public exposure in 1979 when some information about his interogation and statement in 1952 became known. On this evidence Cairncross was, understandably, dismissed as 'small fry' by the media and that remained the common view until the full story of his activities, given to me from MI5 sources, was published in March 1981. Those newspapers that had previously dismissed him as unimportant ignored the evidence, as did Parliament. It would have been reasonable to think, at least, that the myth that Bletchley had never been penetrated would no longer be allowed to persist, but little has been made of Cairncross's treachery there, probably because reputations are at stake.

Until the publication of *Their Trade is Treachery*, Cairncross continued to deny that he had ever been a spy. He has not done so since: he simply points out that he has never admitted having been a spy.

Was Cairncross the Fifth Man of the original Ring of Five mentioned by the defector Golitsin? He was certainly controlled by 'Otto' and 'Henry', who were assigned to the Ring of Five, but the original five were friends who were all known to each other as spies. Cairncross could never be described as having been a friend of the other four, a fact underscored by Blunt's readiness to expose him. MI5 officers who have studied the Ring believe that the fifth member was someone who was more in the social style of the other four and was, in fact, a member of The Apostles.

The identity of the fifth person to be recruited to the Cambridge Ring remains of interest but is somewhat academic in view of the eventual extent of the pro-Soviet network which developed from it. It might be more profitable, even at this late stage, for counter-espionage resources to be applied to uncovering the second, third, fourth and fifth *rings*.

The Potential Value of Oversight

The discreditable details of the Cairncross case would seem to be further evidence of the need for oversight to deter inefficiency and cavalier decisions. It would seem unlikely that with the possibility of oversight queries the wartime activities of Cairncross would have been totally ignored, as they were following his departure from Britain in 1952. And the strong indication that the K.G.B. had been warned against attending the clandestine meeting with Cairncross in 1951 might well have led to a more vigorous attempt within MI5 to discover the source of the leak.

The statements made by Attorney-General Havers in Parliament in 1981 make it clear that Hollis overstepped his rights in granting Cairncross effective immunity from prosecution, and steps have been taken to ensure that this cannot happen again.[11] This kind of excess within MI5 might well have been prevented many years earlier if some degree of oversight had existed in 1964.

More importantly, perhaps, the whole standard of competence inside MI5 might have been improved had an independent oversight body been able to judge, from the details of the Cairncross case, how dangerously poor it had been and still was. It was a scandal that Cairncross should have been able to spy undetected from 1936 to 1952. It was a scandal that no full inquiry into his activities should then have been made. It was a scandal that when the full extent of his treachery became known the case was completely concealed in the belief that it would remain hidden forever. MI5 was more than content to allow Parliament and the public to swallow the legend that Cairncross had been 'small fry'. With effective oversight in 1952, or even later, the circumstances might have been less damaging to the nation and to the reputation of MI5.

Greater attention might also have been paid to Klugmann whose activities have never been fully investigated because MI5 found it convenient to avoid 'wasting further resources' on his case once he had refused to be interviewed. Klugmann, a candidate for the title of Fifth Man of the Cambridge Ring, merits a full-scale damage assessment.

CHAPTER FORTY-ONE

A Committee Called 'Fluency'

THE shock to those in the secret services who knew of the suspicions against Mitchell and the confessions of Soviet penetration agents like Blunt, Long, Cairncross and others was suddenly intensified by a body-blow which could have been fatal to morale had it proved to be as vicious as first suspected. The MI5 management was informed that the Polish defector, Goleniewski, had told the C.I.A. that there was an extremely well placed K.G.B. agent still inside MI5 headquarters in London. He gave such precise details that they could apply to only one man – Michael Hanley (now Sir Michael), then the 45-year-old Director of Protective Security, the branch mainly concerned with preventing the penetration of secret departments by Soviet spies and which had once been run by Hollis.[1]

No suspicion had ever attached to Hanley, who had given excellent service, was well liked by his colleagues and was clearly heading for further promotion, but Goleniewski had previously been so reliable with his leads that his information had to be taken seriously. Though Mitchell had already retired the investigations about him were still in progress, so there were immediate fears that the inquiries might have been concentrating on the wrong man – unless there had been more than one 'mole' in MI5.

To keep the inquiry into Hanley as secret as possible he was given the internal code-name 'Harriet', which was used in all the relevant documents and conversations.

It was soon obvious that Hanley did not fit most of the crucial evidence of treachery inside MI5, such as the advance warnings to Maclean, Cairncross and Philby. Nor had he been involved in many of the cases which had mysteriously collapsed. The investigators could therefore make no further progress until Hanley was subjected to questioning. When Hollis was approached for permission to do this he refused and insisted that on no account should Hanley be informed that there was any suspicion against him. Nothing further could be done until after Hollis had retired at the end of 1965. By that time, as will be seen, a special committee had been set up to investigate the whole series of security disasters described in this book.

Over many hours of interrogation Hanley, who was completely co-operative, was able to account for every relevant action in his professional life and was forthcoming about his reasons for entering MI5 and about his youth, details of which had been known to Goleniewski. By the end of 1967 he had cleared himself to everyone's satisfaction and to that of the C.I.A. chiefs who had been informed of the position since they knew of the defector's allegations. Five years later, Hanley was to become Director General of MI5, a post he held under three prime ministers, and with no major disasters, until his retirement in 1978.

Since then MI5 officers of a special investigating section, called K7, have carried out an inquiry into the origin of what was, undoubtedly, false information. They are now satisfied that it had been cleverly fed by the K.G.B. to Goleniewski who accepted it unwittingly or may have been under pressure to accept it.[2] It was regarded as extremely odd, from the start, that the defector had never mentioned such an important matter before, especially when he seemed to have recalled it in such detail. There was also C.I.A. evidence that the information had reached Goleniewski after his arrival in the U.S. at the beginning of 1960.[3]

The K.G.B. stood to gain from the disinformation on three counts. The existence of yet another 'mole' at senior level in MI5 threatened Anglo-American Intelligence relations yet again. It might have led to the removal of Hanley, who was a most able officer who later strengthened the counter-espionage branch. And it could have thrown the MI5 investigators off the trail of the real 'mole' for several years, as to some extent it did. As Mitchell had already left MI5 and would have been of no further use to the K.G.B., had he been a spy, it seemed unlikely that the move had been made to protect him. The protection of Hollis would have made sense as he still had two years to run in the prime position.

An even more intriguing puzzle was the origin of the details about Hanley which, it was concluded, could only have been supplied by someone with access to his record of service, tightly held inside MI5. Only two officers had right of access to it, Hollis and another who has never been under suspicion. Mitchell had not been privileged to such access and while, at one stage, Blunt was suspected of having supplied the information, there were details of Hanley's later career which he could not possibly have known.

What is certain is that by forbidding any resolution of the Hanley case, whether for an ulterior purpose or not, Hollis ensured that the suspicion against his colleague would remain until he himself was safely in retirement.

Hollis's attempt to terminate all inquiries into the past penetration of MI5, following his disposal of the Mitchell case, was thwarted by a few of his officers who were determined to intensify them. One of them went to see the new Deputy Director-General, Furnival Jones, to complain, with some force, that unless an inquiry into the very substantial evidence of penetration was carried out properly, he would have to resign, with perhaps the unspoken implication that if he did so other ways of ensuring action might be taken. Furnival Jones agreed that a proper inquiry was called for and that, to widen its scope, it should also apply to evidence of penetration of the sister service, MI6.

To this end a meeting was sought, over Hollis's head, with the MI6 chief, Sir Dick White.[4] Meanwhile Arthur Martin had seen White privately and horrified him with his remark, 'I'm sure it's Roger!'

It was a symptom of the complacency of the time that, in spite of the Blake and Philby cases, there was still no department, either in MI5 or MI6, for investigating possible penetrations. It so happened that the MI6 security department was under new and more energetic management, and the concept of a body with special responsibility for inquiring into suspicious events suggesting Soviet penetration received strong support for the first time. There was, therefore, eventual agreement from Hollis that a joint MI5/MI6 committee should be established for that purpose and that it should operate in the highest secrecy under the code-name 'Fluency', which happened to be the next name on a current list. The chairmanship should rotate every six months between MI6 and MI5. Its terms of reference were to collate and investigate all the allegations of penetration of the Security Service and the Secret Intelligence Service, and to make recommendations as to what further inquiries were necessary.

This sounded workmanlike, but the lack of any sense of urgency on the part of the MI5 and MI6 managements was indicated by the requirement that all members of the Fluency Committee should continue with their normal work as well. This made the inquiries into a dangerous degree of penetration by Soviet agents, which was believed by the Committee members to exist, almost into a spare-time effort and meant that the financial and technical resources allotted to them would be limited.

Apologists for Hollis have asserted that he authorized a full internal inquiry into possible penetrations of MI5 with enthusiasm, insisting that he himself should not be exempt from it. Officers involved in the eventual inquiry have denied this to me as 'rubbish'. The 'freelance' investigators, Martin and Wright, had compiled a list of about forty instances strongly suggesting that MI5 had been, and might still be, seriously penetrated. When they showed the list to Hollis, he was adamant that no members of his staff should be investigated, saying that the idea of setting up a special internal team to check on leaks was 'intolerable and would break morale'. The Fluency Committee was forced on him and he never approved of its activities Indeed, when trying to get rid of Arthur Martin, he spoke of a 'Gestapo'.

It has also been falsely suggested that the Fluency Committee was specifically set up to investigate allegations made by the defector Golitsin before Hollis ever became suspect. The facts are as I have described them. If any single factor was responsible for the formation of the Fluency Committee, it was the circumstances of Philby's defection.

There were three members from MI5 on the Committee and three from MI6, plus a chairman. In addition, specialists were called in to assist when relevant. One such was Evelyn McBarnett, an outstanding research officer. She had carried out an investigation, in conjunction with another woman researcher, into the possible penetration of MI5 in 1949, and their notebook was made available to the Committee. It suggested, even at that early date, that if there was a spy inside MI5 it was either Hollis or Mitchell! Among those who served on the Committee over the years were Arthur Martin, Peter Wright, Geoffrey Hinton – a Director of Counter-Intelligence from MI6 – Terence Lecky – who had broken Blake – Christopher Phillpotts of MI6, and Stephen de Mowbray – an able officer who had been involved in the Mitchell case.[5]

With the Mitchell case in abeyance when the Committee began its work, it soon found itself concentrating on Hollis who, to limit knowledge of the suspicions against him as tightly as possible, was given a code-name. The next name on the approved list was 'Drat' and that name was used throughout. It chanced to look like a typical example of British understatement. Before dealing with the 'Drat' case further it is convenient to dispose of the Mitchell case.

At the end of 1967, two years after Hollis had retired from all contact with MI5, the new Director-General, Sir Martin Furnival Jones, agreed to the demand of the Fluency Committee that Mitchell should be subjected to the long-overdue interrogation. No new evidence had accrued so the decision marked a reversal of Hollis's view that the evidence had been too thin to warrant an interrogation and disposed of his claim that it had been necessary to secure the agreement of the Prime Minister, for Wilson, who had

405

succeeded to the premiership, was certainly not approached.[6]

On request, Mitchell presented himself at headquarters and after due explanation was taken to a 'safe house' which was wired for tape-recording, where he was interrogated by John Day, a former Marines officer.

Mitchell appeared to have no difficulty in answering every question and his memory of events was good. There were no peculiarities about his recruitment to MI5, as there had been with Hollis. Concerning his eccentric behaviour he explained that, because of the nature of his work, he had always taken precautions against being followed. So far as his miserable demeanour when alone in his office was concerned, that had been due to the fact that Hollis had treated him badly, refusing to delegate his proper work to him, even before he had fallen under suspicion, and insisting on dealing with certain files himself. Mitchell did not admit that this might have led him to suspect that he was under suspicion and that this might have been at the root of his anxiety.

When questioned about the torn-up map marked with a rendezvous he said that it was part of a game in which one of his grandchildren was taking part on Chobham Common. The fact that he had placed the torn-up fragments in the wastepaper basket, an act which would not have been typical of a spy who had evaded suspicion for so long, was greatly in his favour.

He denied ever having tape-recorded any meetings. He admitted having known about the intention to interrogate Maclean in May 1951 and Philby in January 1963 but denied having told anybody about them. Due consideration was given to Mitchell's decision to retire early, which would have been against Soviet interests had he been a spy. It was also appreciated that he had stepped up the penetration of the British Communist Party after he succeeded Hollis as head of Section F.

As a result of the interrogation the Fluency Committee decided that Mitchell was, almost certainly, not their man. A former Director-General of MI5 has told me in writing that the case against him collapsed 'like a house of cards'.[7] There were, however, some dissenters among the Committee, as there still are at the time of writing.

In 1972, when Furnival Jones retired, there was a farewell party and Mitchell attended, looking rather forlorn. He has recently publicly denied all the charges against him, as he did to me in a letter he sent shortly after I revealed the case against him in March 1981.[8]

The details of the Mitchell case prove the absurdity of suggestions that Hollis was as anxious as anybody to solve the penetration problem, if there was one. In that context a statement by one of the officers closely involved in the inquiries is relevant: 'The investigation of Mitchell was a continuous fight with Hollis to get proper resources and it ended with a blank refusal by him to allow an interrogation to clear the case up. Of course, if Hollis was a spy, it would have been in his interests, in more ways than one, to leave the case unresolved.'

I have established to my satisfaction that, whatever might have been proved, Mitchell would never have been prosecuted. The object of the MI5 inquiries was to find the source of the leakages, plug it, and then assess the damage with a view to repairing as much of it as possible. The scandal and embarrassment to the Service would have been so great, had a prosecution resulted, that it was never in the minds of those so assiduous in the investigations.

As the bulk of the evidence indicates, firmly in my view, that Mitchell was not a Soviet agent, then the only damage inflicted by his case was to morale among those members of MI5 who knew that he was under suspicion. The Mitchell case marked the beginning of a 'mole-hunt' which has continued even since the convenient disposal of the Hollis case and which, in the process, has done great damage to morale, involving accusations against officers who were totally loyal and culminating in the walk-out resignation of at least one of these in angry protest.[9]

It has been suggested that the mole-hunt in MI5, like that conducted in the C.I.A., resulted from deliberate disinformation concocted by the K.G.B. and planted by its agents, of whom Golitsin may have been one. The 'Harriet' case apart, the actual events and the record and character of those officers responsible for initiating and conducting the mole-hunt in MI5 make such an explanation quite impossible. The impetus for the hunt for Soviet penetration agents arose from events and circumstances originating from action or inaction inside MI5 itself.

The Potential Value of Oversight

The Mitchell case demonstrates how a determined Director-General of MI5, with similar implications for MI6, can limit and even terminate inquiries into the possibility that his own organization has been penetrated by foreign agents. Whether this is done for reasons of professional embarrassment, genuine concern for the Service or for some treacherous purpose, it remains dangerous to national security. Would Hollis have behaved in the cavalier way that he undoubtedly did had he known that an oversight body might hear of it? And might not an oversight body have required

407

more attention to be paid to the strange circumstances surrounding Hollis's lone flight to Washington in connection with the Mitchell case and his complete change of mind following his return? There is nobody in MI5 who can question the Director-General about his motives in such a situation but, presumably, an oversight body could do so.

The manner of Golitsin's sudden return to the U.S. and the whole, farcical Dolnytsin affair should surely have been a matter for independent inquiry, particularly as to the source of the leak to the editor of the *Daily Telegraph*, Sir Colin Coote. A suggestion that the C.I.A. had arranged it because it wanted Golitsin back in the U.S. was altogether too glibly accepted. An oversight body with fewer inhibitions might have been less easily satisfied.

Another matter for concern was the way Hollis repeatedly protected suspects from interrogation on the grounds that, being close to retirement they could do little or no further damage. An effective oversight panel should have seen this practice as a transgression of the normal rules of security and required some explanation, especially in a case as potentially serious as that of Mitchell.

Mitchell's complaint that Hollis had taken work away from him might also have aroused the curiosity of an oversight body. It was Hollis who had recommended his promotion to Deputy Director-General so he might, reasonably, have been asked to explain his behaviour which, it so happened, gave him earlier and more detailed access to information about Soviet defectors in Canada, Australia and other countries with which MI5 maintained close liaison.

The main benefit from oversight would have been independent scrutiny of the horrifying fact that the Deputy Director was under deep suspicion of being a Soviet spy because so much had gone wrong – a situation which the Director-General was doing his best to conceal.

CHAPTER FORTY-TWO

The Canadian Dimension

As pre-war Canadian governments had not concerned themselves with the gathering of foreign intelligence and had devoted little attention to counter-espionage operations at home, it was understandable that when the Gouzenko affair alerted the post-war Government to the security dangers posed by Soviet Intelligence reliance on advice from MI5 and MI6 would be heavy. It was decided that a counter-espionage branch should be formed inside the Royal Canadian Mounted Police (R.C.M.P.) and that promising people should be recruited to it. Inevitably the chief adviser on many aspects of this new Canadian development was MI5's Director of Security, then Roger Hollis, who made several visits to Canada in that connection. Former R.C.M.P. officers have been kind enough to brief me on their professional associations with Hollis.[1]

MI6 already had an officer accredited to Washington for liaison with the C.I.A. and automatically he and his successors, including Philby, were also accredited to Ottawa for liaison with R.C.M.P. security. After the Gouzenko case an MI5 man was also accredited to Washington and Ottawa. The R.C.M.P. had had a liaison man in London for many years but his activities had been restricted to criminal and immigration matters. An R.C.M.P. security officer called Terry Guernsey was the first to be stationed in London as MI5/MI6 liaison officer soon after the end of the war and underwent some training in counter-intelligence

When backtracking into the evidence provided by Gouzenko, Guernsey realized that the R.C.M.P. had not exploited it as exhaustively as they should have done, having virtually ignored the warning that there was a K.G.B. network in operation in Canada. He therefore proposed the setting up of a permanent on-going inquiry into Soviet subversive activities and particularly into the penetration of Government departments, including the R.C.M.P. itself. With the Maclean and Burgess case in mind, he suggested a compilation of the names of all Canadians known to have been communists and claiming to have turned against the creed with a view to finding out how many had entered Government service, where they might be operating as 'moles'. The R.C.M.P. management rejected the proposal at first and for several years the operation was no more than a file kept by Guernsey and marked with the code-name 'Featherbed'.[2] In the early 1960s, however, with a new R.C.M.P. leadership and the exposure of more Soviet spies in Britain and elsewhere, Featherbed was converted into a separate secret section with its own full-time staff.

On Guernsey's advice MI5 officers were invited to lecture to the R.C.M.P. security branch. They included Jim Skardon, who instructed on interrogation and watcher techniques, and Hollis, who spoke on his specialities. From then on visits by MI5 specialists, including technical experts like Peter Wright, became regular.[3] At first the flow of advice and know-how was all one way – from London to Ottawa – but, as will be described, important Canadian innovations were to be adopted by MI5. There was one field, however, in which the flow of information remained almost entirely one way – information about current operations. The R.C.M.P. told MI5 almost everything about cases they had in hand or contemplated but, except for the Mitchell case and later the Hollis case, MI5 told the R.C.M.P. nothing about its operations. The original reason for this was based on the need-to-know principle. The Canadians did not need to know about British cases but the R.C.M.P. often required advice on handling its cases and for that purpose details had to be supplied to the British liaison officers with Ottawa, who usually resided in Washington. These officers were not only of high calibre but were personally popular with the R.C.M.P. and, as a result, learned almost everything of significance concerning Canadian counter-espionage operations and duly passed it to MI5 headquarters in London.

Among the men recruited to R.C.M.P.'s counter-espionage department was the Welshman, James Bennett, to whom I have already referred and whose contributions were to have a major impact on the agency. After joining the British Army in 1940, at the age of twenty, Bennett worked in Signals Intelligence, including brief service at the interception and decoding centre at Bletchley. On demobilization he joined G.C.H.Q., serving in Austria, Turkey, Australia, Hong Kong and finally at Cheltenham. During his time in Turkey he met Philby. Much was to be made of this later, but the meeting had been brief and their paths never crossed again in any other country.[4]

After marrying an Australian girl, who disliked living in England, he agreed to emigrate to Canada and resigned from

410

G.C.H.Q. in March 1954. After trying other jobs in Ottawa he joined the security and intelligence department of the R.C.M.P. where his previous G.C.H.Q. experience would obviously be of value. He soon became deeply involved in counter-espionage against the Soviet bloc. As liaison officer with the Canadian equivalent of G.C.H.Q. and through membership of secret committees he became privy to the most sensitive secrets.

While the R.C.M.P. security service continued to rely heavily on MI5's technical expertise, the advantage was not all one way, largely because of the innovative capability of Bennett. In the late 1950s he conceived the idea of what has become known as Movements Analysis – the regular check on the daily movements of members of the Soviet Embassy and its satellite embassies, consulates and associated bodies, such as trade delegations, Aeroflot and T.A.S.S. Those diplomats, delegates and officials who were genuinely what they claimed to be would have a routine, spending most of their working day in their offices, while those who were really intelligence officers would spend little time at their desks, having to be about their business of agent-running, recruitment and other subversive activities. While surveillance could not be applied to all suspects, because of manpower limitation, a watch on the comings and goings at the embassies and other buildings should supply sufficient evidence, over a period of time, for a list of the intelligence officers to be established. It would also provide insight into the seniority and professional status of the proven intelligence officers – which of them were in various teams and which ones were involved in counter-surveillance not only of the R.C.M.P. officers but of their own staff.

Bennett improved the system with an 'on-line cipher link' which ensured that the latest information was quickly available to the watchers, but it remained only modestly effective until all the information could be computerized. MI5, which had snapped up Bennett's idea, achieved this in the late 1960s and it was to produce a sensational result. By 1971, Movements Analysis, followed by more detailed surveillance of suspects, had shown that more than 300 Russians resident in Britain were actively involved in espionage and subversion. MI5 selected 105 of the most blatant for expulsion by the Foreign Office – which was duly achieved – and the Soviet Ambassador was warned that if Moscow retaliated a further 200 would follow.[5] At that time Movements Analysis was so secret that it was deliberately attributed to a K.G.B. defector, Oleg Lyalin, and it was still secret in 1981, as I indicated in *Their Trade is Treachery*. Since then, however, the system has been 'blown' by a Canadian writer who secured his information from the R.C.M.P.[6]

Bennett also devised the Vehicle Sighting Programme which monitors the movements of cars driven by Soviet bloc officials. Originally it was not effective in London because of apparent leaks from MI5 to Soviet Intelligence, as already explained.[7]

The R.C.M.P. achieved some successes against the determined subversion and espionage effort being mounted by both the K.G.B. and the G.R.U. but, as in Britain, operations began to collapse in ways which were unaccountable unless they were through betrayal.

The first important Canadian case to 'die' in a way which strongly suggested that there had been a deliberate leakage of secret information to Moscow was called Operation Keystone. This was an attempt to turn an 'illegal' Soviet agent into a double working primarily for the R.C.M.P. The agent, whose R.C.M.P. code-name was 'Gideon', had landed at Halifax with a false American passport in the autumn of 1952 and spent many months doing no more than establishing himself as a native Canadian and reporting his progress through messages left in dead-letter boxes. His long-term objective was to secure a genuine Canadian passport and other documents which would enable him to move into the U.S., where he could service other K.G.B. agents, but his courage failed him and the K.G.B. Centre gave him permission to stay in Canada, where his job would be to run other agents with whom he would be put in contact.

In November 1953, having begun to enjoy life in Canada and having acquired a mistress, he decided to defect from the K.G.B. and contacted the R.C.M.P. in Ottawa. He was hired as a double agent to provide the R.C.M.P. with first-hand knowledge of K.G.B. techniques and leads to other agents. Early in 1954 an R.C.M.P. officer went to London to brief MI5 about Keystone and to secure advice. James Bennett, who was then still working in G.C.H.Q. at Cheltenham, was asked to check 'Gideon's' methods of contacting the Moscow Centre to make sure that they were authentic.[8] Soon afterwards Bennett emigrated to Canada and, after joining the R.C.M.P. security service in July 1954, became involved with the case there.

'Gideon' led the R.C.M.P. to a Canadian spy in an aircraft factory and, to allay K.G.B. suspicions, he was given some genuine information as 'chickenfeed' to transmit to Moscow. In 1955, however, 'Gideon' was required to return to Moscow for routine leave for debriefing and further training, and to see his wife and family. The R.C.M.P. made an arrangement with MI5 and MI6 so that British agents in Moscow could assist 'Gideon' to escape if the K.G.B. established that he was a Canadian agent while on holiday there.

It soon became apparent that 'Gideon' was under surveillance by the K.G.B. in Moscow, and he never returned to Canada. Other indications left no doubt that Operation Keystone had been 'blown' soon after its inception and that the K.G.B. had then mounted a cleverly contrived deception to protect the source of the warning to them. The inquest on Keystone showed that the source had to be in Canada, in the R.C.M.P., or in Britain, in MI5, MI6 or G.C.H.Q. Early in 1984 a former Mountie, James Morrison, was to be prosecuted for betraying 'Gideon' to the Soviets shortly before the defector's return to Moscow, but Morrison was granted a permanent stay of prosecution because the authorities had waited too long – more than twenty-five years – in bringing the charges.[9] A former senior R.C.M.P. official has assured me, however, that there are strong indications that the case had been betrayed before any action by Morrison by some other source who had known many more details than the Mountie.

On New Year's Day 1956 the Soviet Embassy in Ottawa, a three-storey mansion, was destroyed by fire. While the fire was still raging, Mounties dressed as firemen had been able to confirm that the intelligence set-up was exactly as described by Gouzenko when he had defected from the building ten years previously, though the Mounties had been unable to check the secret rooms because Embassy staff had barred their entry while anything of interest remained in them. As the rebuilding had to be done by Canadian contractors, the R.C.M.P. security service decided to seize the chance of installing listening devices in what it thought would be the new secret areas. The operation was code-named Dew Worm and MI5 was asked to supply eavesdropping 'bugs' which would be difficult for the Soviets to detect plus expert advice on how and where to install them.[10] The MI5 officer seconded for the purpose was Peter Wright.[11]

Examination of the plans suggested that the new secret rooms would be in the north-east corner of the second floor and cables to service the hidden microphones were laid in that area. Each night, as the walls rose, Mounties, using various subterfuges, pulled the cable a little higher. When the windows were almost ready for installation eight microphones were hidden in the stonework surrounds. But a building disaster almost wrecked the operation. While part of the wall was being rebuilt a worker who did not know about the cable went through it with a drill but, by ingenious improvisation, six of the eight microphones were properly connected to the cable.

When the building was almost complete the Soviet Ambassador was recalled to Moscow and a team of electronic 'sweepers' moved in and searched the area where the 'bugs' had been installed. It was clear that the Russians knew the area had been 'bugged' because the live microphones relayed the noise they made when they were trying to locate them. The secret communications and cipher rooms were moved to the centre of the building and though the Russians were short of space they never occupied the 'bugged' area until more sophisticated sweeping techniques had enabled them to find the microphones and remove them several years later. During that time odd snippets of information appear to have been fed over the microphones to induce the R.C.M.P. to continue to waste resources listening to them.

Both the Canadian security authorities and MI5 were in no doubt that the Centre in Moscow had been told about the bugging of the building and the rough location of the microphones. I have established that most of the details about Operation Dew Worm had been sent back to MI5 and were on record there for examination by anyone with access to them.[12] At the time, however, no serious consideration was given to the possibility that there could be a spy inside MI5 so the assumption was that the leak had occurred in Ottawa.

Soon after the loss of 'Gideon' the R.C.M.P. received overtures from a G.R.U. agent called Nikolai Ranov who was posing as a Commercial Attaché in the Soviet Embassy in Ottawa. Claiming to be disenchanted with life in the U.S.S.R., Ranov was recruited as a double agent, but although he was in a position to supply some information its value was less than the genuine material that the R.C.M.P. had to give him to feed back to the G.R.U. Centre to assure it that he was still busily at work in its interests. The R.C.M.P. therefore decided to end the exchange and to arrest him the next time he was scheduled to receive a batch of chickenfeed. He would then be offered the chance of defecting to a good life in Canada with ensuing publicity, which would embarrass the Russians and increase the prestige of the R.C.M.P. or, if he declined, he would be declared *persona non grata* and deported, an act which would improve the R.C.M.P.'s image at home. But Ranov failed to attend any further meetings with the R.C.M.P.'s courier, indicating that the G.R.U. had been warned of the danger and so deprived the R.C.M.P. of its coup. There can be little doubt that Ranov was a plant from the start because after being withdrawn by the G.R.U. from Ottawa he appeared as an official of the Soviet airline Aeroflot in Cyprus from which he was eventually expelled for spying. As with the R.C.M.P.'s previous operations, MI5 had been informed of its intentions, so the leakage could have occurred in either Canada or Britain.

In 1959 the R.C.M.P. received information from the C.I.A. that another G.R.U. agent had insinuated himself into Canada and was setting up a small business in Vancouver to serve as a cover. The effort made to unmask this agent was code-named Operation Apple Cider and eventually led to a recent immigrant calling himself Rudolph Kneschke, an unobtrusive bachelor who had established a small radio and T.V. repair business. Surveillance revealed that he was almost certainly the clandestine radio operator for some other agent or agents. As soon as this had been established Kneschke let it be known that he was going to Europe for a holiday and, like 'Gideon', he never returned. The R C M P had little doubt that Moscow had been warned that the spy's cover had been broken. The warning could have originated from inside the R.C.M.P., the C.I.A., the Swiss security service, which had first informed the C.I.A., or from inside MI5, which had been fully briefed on the case because its help was sought in monitoring Kneschke's movements when receiving transmissions from Moscow.

The next counter-espionage operation to go sour centred on a communist Canadian who was assisting Soviet Intelligence by photographing pipelines and other installations which would be sabotage targets for the Russians in the event of war. In an operation code-named Moby Dick, the communist was put under heavy surveillance and he was 'bugged' wherever he stayed but though he never seemed to detect that he was being followed the K.G.B. ended their interest in him in 1963 in a way suggesting that they had been told that his treachery was known to the R.C.M.P. Again MI5 had been briefed about the case as it had progressed.

Following a lead from the defector Golitsin, the R.C.M.P., and Bennett in particular, became involved in a case of considerable consequence for MI5 and all Western counter-espionage agencies. It exposed the level at which the K.G.B. was prepared to strike, showing that nobody was off limits as a target, however exalted his position. It was also to cause Western agencies to soften interrogation techniques with elderly suspects who might have medical problems, for the subject died from a heart attack during interrogation. This experience was to limit the hostility of interrogation techniques applied to British suspects, including Hollis.

MI5 officers who had debriefed Golitsin in the U.S. visited Ottawa to tell the R.C.M.P. that he had indicated that a former Canadian Ambassador to Moscow had been the victim of a K.G.B. blackmail operation after agents had exploited his homosexuality. The operation to identify him, code-named Rock Bottom, was given firmer evidence in the autumn of 1963 when a Soviet film-script writer called Yuri Krotkov defected to MI5 while visiting London with a group of Soviet writers and artists.[13] Krotkov, who was exceptionally handsome, confessed that he had been used by the K.G.B. to set up blackmail operations to entrap foreign diplomats. His information indicated that the Canadian Ambassador for whom the R.C.M.P. was searching was John Watkins, who had served in Moscow from 1954 to 1956 and had returned to a high-level post in Ottawa, where he had had access to intelligence of the highest grade. Confirmation that the suspect was Watkins came in 1964 from the defector Nosenko, who told the C.I.A. that Watkins had been so well known for his homosexuality that Khrushchev had mocked him at a drunken dinner party given for visiting Canadian dignitaries.[14] It was decided to interrogate Watkins, who had retired to Paris after a further foreign posting as Ambassador to Denmark.

Watkins, then aged sixty-two, was interviewed in Paris by Bennett, who induced him to continue the talks in London away from the curiosity of French security. Watkins confessed his homosexuality and the K.G.B. attempt to involve him in treachery but denied any disloyalty. Through a friendship with a Soviet Foreign Office official he knew as Oleg Gorbunov, but who was really General Oleg Gribanov, the K.G.B. officer in charge of internal intelligence operations in the Soviet Union, he was given access to areas of the U.S.S.R. normally barred to foreigners and on one of these trips became involved with a Soviet poet and a labourer. It also transpired that Watkins had been friendly with a Professor Nikitin, of the Moscow Institute of History, who was none other than Anatoli Gorski, the K.G.B. controller whom the Ring of Five had known as 'Henry'!

Bennett prevailed upon the suspect to return to Canada for further questioning and the interrogation continued in a suite at the Holiday Inn in Montreal.

Watkins confessed that shortly before he was due to return to his influential post in Ottawa, 'Gorbunov', still pretending to be friendly, warned him that the K.G.B. had a file about his homosexual exploits, complete with incriminating photographs, but that all would be well if the Ambassador was prepared to be helpful once he was in Canada. It was suggested that he should do this by being specially friendly to the Soviet Ambassador in Ottawa and by 'liberalizing' procedures for Soviet citizens resident in Canada, meaning spies and subversives, especially those using Canada as a point of entry to the U.S.

The records showed that Watkins did not serve as an agent of influence and had actually been party to reducing facilities which assisted the K.G.B.[15] He had also carefully avoided meeting the

Soviet Ambassador. After twenty-six days of interrogation Bennett and his co-interrogator, Harry Brandeis, were convinced of his innocence. Arrangements were made for Watkins to return to Paris, and he agreed to submit to a further short session of questioning before he left. While talking in a seemingly relaxed way about his career he fell dead in his chair.[16]

The Montreal police were induced to hush up the circumstances of the tragedy and details have emerged only recently following inquiries and a long-delayed inquest which appeared to be, at least partly, consequential to the publication of *Their Trade is Treachery*.[17] Bennett submitted a 325 page report on the case which was cut to eighty pages on the instructions of the R.C.M.P. Commissioner who feared that the interrogation would otherwise seem to have been too long and too tough. The pathologist who signed Watkins' death certificate was unaware that he had been under interrogation and claimed that, had she known the circumstances, she would have performed an autopsy.[18]

Brandeis, who became chief of R.C.M.P. counter-intelligence in 1980, claimed that the exact circumstances of Watkins' death had been covered up 'for reasons of national security and to protect Watkins' reputation'. It would seem more likely, however, that it was to cover up the fact that in 1954 the Canadian Foreign Office had appointed a homosexual, who later admitted to 'cruising' round Ottawa to pick up partners, as Ambassador to Moscow, where the K.G.B. had compromised him. Further, the R.C.M.P., which was already suffering from the publicity about the suicide of another Canadian ambassador, Herbert Norman, had known that Watkins had a heart condition though Bennett, fully aware of this had treated him as gently as possible.[19]

Anthony Blunt reluctantly admitted, during his interrogation in 1964, that one of his former Cambridge associates, a Canadian called Herbert Norman, had been a member of a communist cell and had been recruited to Soviet Intelligence. On learning this the R.C.M.P. renewed its inquiries into Norman who was a known homosexual.[20] Norman had first raised doubts in the minds of Western counter-intelligence officers through his friendship with a Japanese Marxist who lived in Washington. After this man had been hurriedly deported, following the attack on Pearl Harbor, Norman had tried to gain access to his apartment claiming, falsely, that he was there on Canadian business. When the flat was searched by the F.B.I. secret reports about American defence production were discovered. Later, at the end of the war, an American called Elizabeth Bentley confessed to the F.B.I. that she had served as a courier for Soviet agents and she named Norman,

417

who became publicly identified with communism in 1951 during American hearings which were conveniently branded as witch-hunting.[21]

Norman escaped serious investigation mainly because he was protected by his friend Lester Pearson, a Canadian Foreign Office official who became Foreign Secretary and later Prime Minister.[22] Norman was sent to Japan as Ambassador, was later High Commissioner to New Zealand and, in 1956, Ambassador to Egypt. There seems to be little doubt that he worked for the K.G.B. in all three postings. One recent biographer, for example, is convinced that his K.G.B. activities while serving in Tokyo in 1950, 'went far to contribute to Moscow's decision to give the North Koreans the green light to invade South Korea in June 1950'.[23]

Following increasing suspicions, Norman was recalled to Ottawa in 1957 for 'discussions', but prior to his departure, which had been arranged on a pretext, a C.I.A. man in Cairo imprudently encouraged him to speak of his links with the Russians. Norman is then said to have remarked, 'I can't go back to Ottawa because, if I did, I would have to betray too many people.' That night he jumped from the roof of the apartment block where he had a flat and killed himself. Either he had guessed the purpose of his recall or he had been surreptitiously told of it.

The Norman case was one of the first to be analysed in detail by the Featherbed team which concluded that he had been a long-serving Soviet spy who had faked his break with communism to gain entry to the diplomatic service as a 'mole'. New evidence to be published soon will confirm this.[24]

In the early 1960s Golitsin also gave a lead to the R.C.M.P. that strongly indicated the existence of a K.G.B. agent able to penetrate the Canadian Foreign Office and under the control of the Soviet agent-runner, Victor Bourdine.[25] This is now believed to have been Hugh Hambleton, since convicted of spying, but no progress was made with the case at the time.[26]

From 1964 onwards the R.C.M.P. security service became increasingly disinclined to reveal details of its cases to MI5. There were two reasons for this. There was growing realization that Canada's security interests were more closely bound with those of the U.S. than with Britain's and liaison with the C.I.A. and F.B.I. was becoming more intimate. More importantly, there was a growing fear that MI5 had been penetrated at high level by Soviet Intelligence agents. This fear had originated from indiscretions by MI5 liaison officers either attached to the R.C.M.P. or visiting Ottawa from London. At first only hints had been dropped concerning the alarming number of cases and double-agent operations which had gone sour in London, but Mitchell and Hollis were soon named as the prime suspects. Then, when the Mitchell case was still active, Hollis himself briefed the R.C.M.P Commissioner about the suspicions concerning his Deputy, as he had previously briefed the chiefs of the C.I.A. and the F.B.I.[27] The Fluency Committee was under the strictest instructions not to mention the case against Hollis to anybody, but Bennett and a very few other senior R.C.M.P. officers were told that the inquiries were being concentrated on the Director-General, who would soon be visiting Ottawa on a leg of his farewell tour before retirement. This knowledge made the dinner given in his honour in Ottawa, in 1965, so embarrassing for those who knew the facts that one of them was to describe the atmosphere as 'hellishly awkward'.[28]

The fears concerning Hollis had become so strong inside MI5 by 1969 that senior R.C.M.P. officers were told about them more forcibly, but still unofficially. This led to a further embarrassing incident when John Starnes, a civil servant who was about to be appointed Director-General of the R.C.M.P. security service, was indiscreet enough to tell Maurice Oldfield of MI6 that he knew of the suspicions against Hollis. It must be assumed that Oldfield reported this to his London headquarters but the information was to remain unconfirmed officially until the mid-1970s.[29] By that time R.C.M.P. liaison with the C.I.A. had become closer still, at some expense to MI5.

Once the R.C.M.P. had reduced the flow of information about their cases to MI5 more of them succeeded. There were examples of such successes in Hollis's time when MI5 had been given details only after the operations had been completed. They resulted in the expulsion of Soviet Intelligence officers either quietly or, when the R.C.M.P. wanted it, with publicity.

When Hollis was visiting Ottawa in 1965, James Bennett asked him to explain MI5's failure to follow the R.C.M.P.'s lead in inducing the Government to impose a ceiling on the number of Soviet 'diplomats' and other officials posted to the country – a move which the Canadians had made seven years previously and which had been effective in limiting K.G.B. and G.R.U. operations. Although the question was posed in a friendly manner during a drive to a convivial lunch, Hollis reacted by bridling, losing his temper and dismissing it without explanation.[30] As recorded elsewhere, the number of Soviet Intelligence officers under diplomatic privilege and other guises in London was to go on mounting, saturating the counter-espionage resources.

One of the R.C.M.P. officers who witnessed Hollis's behaviour on that occasion told me, 'He was a grey man, rarely animated and under a high degree of personal control but, on that day, he lost his cool. I wonder why.'

The eventual interrogation of Hollis as a suspected Soviet agent was to offer a possible explanation. It was to be followed by an event almost as traumatic to the R.C.M.P. as the Hollis affair was to MI5 – the interrogation of Bennett as a suspect 'mole'.[31]

CHAPTER FORTY-THREE

Hollis's Last Cases

THE perturbing pattern of events in which damaging British traitors were detected only through chance leads provided by foreign security agencies continued into Hollis's last year as chief of MI5. Late in 1964 a Soviet source told the American F.B.I. that information concerning British naval missiles had leaked to Moscow and the news was passed to MI5. At first it was feared that another Admiralty spy might be involved, with consequent embarrassment for that department, but the details supplied by the Soviet source indicated that the culprit was an officer called Frank Bossard who worked in the Guided Weapons Branch of the Aviation Ministry.[1] Examination of Bossard's record showed that thirty years previously the tall, tubby and well-dressed officer, who affected to have had a public school education, had served six months in prison for buying watches with worthless cheques and selling them in pawn shops. After joining the R.A.F. in 1940, then aged twenty-seven, he had falsified his educational record to secure a commission, which had been granted. Leaving as a flight-lieutenant in March 1946, he had joined the Ministry of Civil Aviation, and had then been seconded to the War Office as an intelligence officer. In 1956 he had been transferred to a branch of the Joint Intelligence Bureau at the Bonn Embassy in West Germany, his main task there being the interrogation of East German scientists who had defected to the West. He had been positively vetted in 1954 since his intelligence work had involved access to Top Secret information. He failed to mention his criminal record and, when this was discovered, the vetters accepted his excuse that he had forgotten about it because it was so old. In 1958 he returned to London to an important intelligence assignment in the Defence Ministry and in January 1960 he transferred to the Naval Guided Weapons Branch of the Aviation Ministry, becoming a project officer on the air side in July 1964. Though his job enabled him to witness highly secret missile tests off the Welsh coast, he was not subjected to any further positive vetting because the documents to which he had access were only classified Secret or less. And because the Aviation Ministry did not need to know of his criminal record it was not told of it.[2]

Bossard had almost certainly been talent-spotted by the Russians while working in Bonn where he had demonstrated enjoyment of an extravagant lifestyle. On his return to London, where his allowances were drastically reduced and his enjoyment thereby curtailed, he was approached by a Soviet recruiter in a public house on the pretext that he shared his interest in coins. Bossard was to date this approach as taking place in 1961 but suspicion remains that he had accepted money from the K.G.B. and was working for the agency before that. Bossard was a completely mercenary spy, having no communist ideals or connections. His record showed that, by nature, he was unable to resist easy money to the extent that he was not deterred by the heavy sentences imposed, with much publicity, on spies like Blake and Vassall, though it may well be that he was already firmly in the Soviet net then with no chance of escape.

Until 1964 Bossard had used his interest in numismatics as a cover, having a small room near his office said to belong to the Coin and Medal Association. There he had carried out his illicit photography of secret documents in safety. Later, he hired nearby hotel rooms for the day, under false names, keeping his photographic equipment in the left-luggage office at Waterloo Station and taking it out only when required.

He was kept under surveillance for several months in the hope that he might be seen meeting with some other member of a spy-ring or a controller, but he proved to be a lone operator, communicating with the K.G.B. through dead-letter boxes, such as drainpipes and hollow trees, located for the most part near his home at Stoke D'Abernon in Surrey. There he left his rolls of film and picked up his reward, on one occasion £2,000 in notes.[3]

One essential part of his communication system was discovered by MI5 when his suitcase was inspected after he had re-deposited it at Waterloo Station. It contained five gramophone records of popular Russian tunes, such as 'Moscow Nights' and the 'Volga Boatmen', which all spelled a different message to him when he listened for them being broadcast from Moscow at prearranged times. A combined effort by G.C.H.Q. and surveillance officers confirmed that Bossard was tuned in when the broadcasts were made.[4]

On 12 March 1965 Bossard was followed during his lunch-hour, first to Waterloo Station where he withdrew his suitcase, then to the Ivanhoe Hotel, where he had hired a room for the day. Special

Branch officers burst in as he was in the act of photographing the contents of four secret files. He pleaded guilty at his trial in May when, then aged fifty-two, he was sentenced to twenty-one years in gaol. The judge stated that had he not been co-operative with the security authorities after his arrest he would have received more. That a traitor with access to only secret data can still do enough damage to warrant such a severe penalty suggests that the positive vetting system is inadequate in applying only to those with Top Secret clearance.

The Security Commission's report on the Bossard case revealed serious failures of security procedures in the War Office and Aviation Ministry but went out of its way, yet again, to exonerate MI5 from any blame whatever.[5] Admittedly, Bossard had been a difficult spy to detect because he had carefully carried out K.G.B. instructions. Appreciating his limitations more astutely than the British authorities, his Soviet controllers had forbidden him to secure any files to which he was not properly entitled or to pump colleagues for information outside his field. He had not lived obviously above his means and had banked his reward money in different accounts. Nevertheless, he had met with a Soviet controller on at least two occasions without any surveillance of those controllers by MI5 and the positive vetting procedure laid down by MI5 did not stipulate that anybody with a criminal record should be denied access even to secret material, as it does now. Further, Bossard had spied on a regular basis for at least four years without raising any suspicion.

Although Bossard would almost certainly have gone on spying successfully but for the tip from the U.S., Hollis must have regarded the case as an MI5 triumph because he took his son, Adrian, then twenty-five, to witness the trial at the Old Bailey.[6]

Because of the American source of the initial information and the heavy involvement of Aviation Ministry officials, there was no way that any Soviet agent inside MI5 could have seriously interfered with the Bossard case. He was, in fact, such an expendable spy that the K.G.B. would never have prejudiced an inside MI5 agent in order to protect him. The Soviet bloc has never made much effort to safeguard purely mercenary spies once they have become suspect, preferring to reserve its strenuous care for those who are ideologically committed.

The Security Commission's report on the Bossard case was unprecedented in naming certain civil servants whom it considered as deserving of criticism for departmental failures to prevent the espionage, and the Whitehall mandarins – the so-called Permanent Secretaries Club – reacted with alacrity. An independent inquiry under a former mandarin, Sir Henry Wilson Smith, exonerated the civil servants and overruled the Commission, Smith's findings being quickly published as a White Paper.[7]

The Potential Value of Oversight

The Bossard case gave the Security Commission its first major chance to show its value and it exposed many weaknesses and inefficiencies in the security screen. These were rectified in what was another stable-door-locking operation. The Security Commission is limited by the fact that it is called into action only when an event, such as a serious spy case, indicates the existence of yet more deficiencies. An effective oversight body, such as that currently operating in the U.S., would have the advantage of being in continuous touch with security issues and should therefore have greater opportunity to detect weaknesses before they cause so much damage. My experience as adviser to the House of Commons Select Committee on Defence while it was dealing with positive vetting showed that Whitehall departments have come to lean on the Security Commission, awaiting its recommendations before making changes in security procedures. This means that little tends to be done in the way of improvements until there has been another security disaster requiring the Security Commission's attention.

Almost coincidental with the Bossard case was that of Army Staff Sergeant Percy Allen, which had no direct Soviet connections.[8] Allen, who worked in the War Office, had access to intelligence documents concerning British interests in the Middle East. Being in financial difficulties he tried to sell some of them to Iraqi and Egyptian diplomats in London but was so foolhardy that he made telephone calls from a Whitehall telephone box which was almost continuously monitored. As a result he was arrested while attempting to hand over classified papers to an Iraqi and was sentenced to ten years' imprisonment. The case was so straightforward and so uncontroversial that MI5 simply handed it over to Special Branch for action. The post-mortem on the case revealed more unfortunate breaches and weaknesses in security procedures.[9] Allen, too, had an early criminal record which had not come to light when he had been positively vetted.

The last prosecution of Hollis's reign, in February 1965, was as humiliating for MI5 as the ill-fated Martelli trial and acquittal had been. Two employees of the Kodak company were accused of selling commercial secrets about photographic processes to a Belgian who said he was passing them on to an East German firm.

424

The Belgian, who had been working for East German Intelligence, had turned informer for the Belgian security service, which warned MI5 of the position. No genuine security considerations were involved but because of the clandestine way in which the information was being imparted, and as one of the Kodak employees was a communist, the MI5 management decided to involve the agency, supplying watchers for the surveillance of the suspects. This might have been justified but the management should not have involved itself in the prosecution of the Kodak men because this had to be brought under the Prevention of Corruption Act, as no official secrecy had been breached. When the defence counsel was able to riddle the credibility of the Belgian informer the case was dismissed and what was hoped would be a 'triumph' for MI5 ended in ignominy.[10] Hollis must have been aware of the decision to support the prosecution and it would be reasonable to believe that he approved this bad misjudgement. Nor was it to his or MI5's credit that an undercover inquiry was then made into the background and possible political affiliations of the successful defending counsel. Its completely negative results underlined the spite that initiated it.

Hollis had acceded to the Director-Generalship of MI5 as a result of an ignominious security fiasco, the Crabb affair. He relinquished it in the wake of another, the Kodak affair. While his predecessor, Sir Dick White, had introduced substantial improvements to the organization of MI5 during his three years as D.G., Hollis left no noticeable mark after his nine years. The impression his reign left upon most of those of his staff whom I have been able to question is that 'almost everything went wrong and we were not surprised'.

The Kodak case ran for almost a year and Hollis must have been party to MI5's involvement, which was outside the agency's remit. Though he was due to retire, the quality of his judgement would have remained highly significant with respect to one crucial issue – the choice of his successor. In the past the retiring Director-General had usually been very influential in this regard and an oversight body would assuredly have interested itself closely in the choice. Had it been aware of Hollis's powers of judgement, as evidenced by the Profumo, Martelli and Kodak affairs alone, it might have advised the Prime Minister of the day against paying undue attention to his advice. The Prime Minister was Harold Wilson and, initially, he was determined to override Hollis's advice and appoint an outsider – another 'honest copper' in the shape of Sir Eric St Johnston, whom he knew personally and admired. Sir Eric, then Chief Constable of Lancashire, had been helpful to Wilson, who had held the Lancashire seat of Huyton.[11]

The fact that Hollis survived for a year as Director-General following Wilson's general election victory in October 1964 is remarkable, in view of the castigation he received from the Labour leader in the Parliamentary debate on Profumo's resignation held on 17 June 1963. Wilson clearly blamed Hollis for the failure to warn Macmillan of the security issues and, being anxious to avoid being served in that way himself, he wanted someone from outside whom he could trust. Sir Eric has told me that he would have been unable to resist the offer. In the event the approach was never made because of the intervention of George Wigg, Labour's Paymaster-General.

Wigg's main function was to serve as personal watchdog over security affairs so that Wilson would not be kept in ignorance of security problems, as Macmillan had been. He confided to me that after listening to 'professional advice' inside MI5 he had been convinced that the previous 'honest copper', Sir Percy Sillitoe, had almost wrecked MI5 by introducing police methods and attitudes. He had also, incidentally, set back everybody's promotion prospects for several years, as would St Johnston, who was only fifty-three. Much of the professional advice came from Hollis to whom Wigg had access, so when Wilson agreed to the appointment of Hollis's deputy, Furnival Jones, it was, indirectly, on Hollis's recommendation. Wigg, who knew nothing of the suspicions against either Hollis or Mitchell, told me that he had been assured that some of MI5's apparent failures in the past had really been due to Whitehall delays in acting on its warnings. I have been unable to find any foundation to this explanation, which was passed on to Wilson, and was, I suspect, MI5 disinformation.

While Furnival Jones was regarded by colleagues as rather dour and uncommunicative, it is generally conceded that he was a big improvement on Hollis and there was no cataract of case-deaths during his tenure. Perhaps an oversight body would have favoured the appointment of Furnival Jones but it might have been for reasons other than those which secured it.

During much of 1965 Hollis, who was due to retire at the end of November of that year, a few days short of his sixtieth birthday, was abroad on the customary farewell visits to Allied security organizations. His deputy, Furnival Jones, was therefore in command and he refused to allow anybody outside MI5 or MI6 to know about the suspicions concerning Hollis which, when first told of them, he regarded as 'grotesque'. This greatly hampered the

Fluency inquiries because it meant that no official help could be sought from the C.I.A., the F.B.I. or the security departments of Canada, Australia and New Zealand, with which Hollis had close associations and which might have furnished evidence. Furnival Jones's attitude was understandable. He was in an extremely embarrassing position as Hollis's likely successor and claimed to be fearful of a leak back to the Russians, who might require Hollis to defect if, by an incredible chance, he was a Soviet agent.

No minister and no other Government official was told of the 'Drat' inquiry and the need for absolute secrecy was constantly underlined to those few involved in it. The restriction meant that neither Hollis's wife nor his mistress could be questioned and friends were also ruled out because they might have warned him.

As the Home Secretary's permission would have been required to tap Hollis's telephone that, too, was prohibited and he was not placed under physical surveillance because too many in the Watcher Service would have known of the situation.

As much new secret information as practicable was kept from Hollis, as a precaution, during his last year of office. He was not told, for example, the reason for a visit to London by William Sullivan, deputy head of the F.B.I., who came to warn MI5 that 'Fedora', who had allegedly been serving the F.B.I. as a double agent, was almost certainly a K.G.B. plant and should not be trusted. The difficulties of withholding much information from the Director-General were, naturally, enormous if his suspicions were not to be aroused, and he saw most of the important material

The Fluency Committee officers had good reason to believe that their precautions had failed and that Hollis was not only aware of his position but did not care if they knew it. Shortly before he retired he called the Committee chairman, Peter Wright, into his office and staggered him by asking, 'Tell me, why do you think I am a spy?'

Seizing his opportunity, after his initial shock, Wright gave his reasons and added, 'Do you dispute these undoubted facts?'

Hollis shrugged and responded, 'All I can say is that I am not a spy.'

'But is there any evidence to swing the balance your way?' Peter Wright persisted.

'No,' Hollis replied. 'You think you have the manacles on me, don't you?'

He might have detected that certain papers were being withheld from him, in which case it was odd that he never queried the fact. He may also have been warned of his predicament during his farewell trip to Ottawa. Against the advice of the Fluency Commit-

427

tee, Hollis had previously told Canadian security officials that Mitchell had been cleared whereupon a member of the Committee had advised the Canadians that the evidence of high-level penetration of MI5 still stood unexplained, with Hollis himself being the alternative candidate for investigation. I have established from former members of R.C.M.P. security that this was so and that it is not impossible that some R.C.M.P. official warned Hollis. Alternatively, he may have been told of his position by a friend in MI5.

If Hollis was a spy he would have reported his situation to a Soviet controller who would have sought advice on his behalf from the Moscow Centre. In that event, Hollis's initiative with Peter Wright would have been in keeping with the Centre's requirement to discover how much was really known against him in the confident belief that, whatever might be proved, he would never be prosecuted or subjected to public censure.

Hollis had retained the diaries of Guy Liddell, which had been code-named 'Wallflowers', in his private safe and shortly before his retirement he removed them and ordered his secretary to destroy them. Peter Wright managed to intercept them and preserved them until Hollis had left when they were returned to the archives. As the diaries contained information about the MI5 spy called 'Elli' and speculation about his identity, this attempt to destroy records would also have been in keeping with advice from the Centre, as was to be appreciated by the Fluency Committee when they were informed of it.

Hollis was given a farewell dinner in London by his six directors but I have been told that nobody else was present. When he finally left the office he irritated those who disliked him by buying a lot of whisky in the MI5 canteen at substantially reduced prices.

There is, clearly, no truth in rumours that Hollis was forced to retire early because of his handling of the Profumo case. Nor, as has been stated, was he 'roasted' by Macmillan.[12] The Denning Report had saved him from both indignities.

At the time of his retirement he was drawing a salary of about £5,800 a year giving him take-home pay of about £76 a week after tax – ludicrous reward, even in those days, for anyone with such responsibilities.[13] His salary fixed his pension at about £50 a week after tax.

In the 1966 New Year Honours Hollis was given the additional award of a K.B.E. This has been interpreted by some as proof that there could not have been much, if any, evidence against him but those involved in making the recommendation to the Queen were in complete ignorance of the suspicions and no attempt was made to interfere with the award, though it caused some rueful comments in MI5. An even grander award, the G.C.M.G., was to be given two years later to Sir Geoffrey Harrison, Britain's former Ambassador to Moscow, after he had confessed to having prejudiced his position through sexual indulgence with a Soviet domestic servant who was really a tool of the K.G.B. Again, those involved in the recommendation were ignorant of the events, and in such ways the honours system extends the process of cover-up, for there were many in the Foreign Office and in MI5 who could have intervened.

There is evidence that Hollis and his wife, who had long been aware of his liaison with his secretary, hoped to restore their old relationship in his retirement when he would be out of daily contact with his mistress, and she accompanied him on his routine farewell tour to say goodbye to Commonwealth security agencies.[14] On their return the reconciliation prospects collapsed and Hollis resumed his affair, as quickly became known to the MI5 staff because Miss Hammond, who had been promoted to officer rank, spoke openly about it.[15]

In February 1968 Lady Hollis, who according to friends was 'broken up' by her husband's desertion and was living in London while he was in Wells, brought an action for divorce on the grounds of his adultery with Miss Edith Valentine Hammond.[16] Shortly afterwards Hollis married his former mistress and they went to live in a cottage in the Somerset village of Catcott, where he took part in the community life, becoming a rural district councillor. He continued to play golf, becoming captain of the Burnham-Berrow Club and president of the Somerset Golfing Union.[17] He remained a member of the Travellers Club until 1969 and then resigned, presumably because his visits to London were so rare.

It may be asked why, if Hollis was a dedicated Soviet agent, he quietly retired to Somerset. What else could he do? The K.G.B. would have had no further interest in him once he had ceased to have access to secret information and to have required his defection would have revealed his treachery, which the K.G.B., most assuredly, would not have wished to do. If Hollis was a spy his retirement to a cottage in Somerset, his home county, was no more surprising than Blunt's retirement to a flat in London.

Hollis retained contact with a few old friends but while most retired senior officers of the Security and Intelligence Services continue to meet in London at special gatherings he did not attend them. On one occasion, at a dinner for a very senior Whitehall official, all the surviving chiefs of MI5 and MI6 were invited except Hollis. When someone remarked on his absence, Sir 'Joe' Hooper, who had organized the dinner, said, 'We didn't invite him.'[18] Hooper, who had been Director of G.C.H.Q., had known of the

429

suspicions against Hollis.

It was also customary for former heads of the secret services to be offered paid part-time appointments on Whitehall committees and panels. Hollis did not receive any and appears never to have been consulted about anything, apart from his own possible disloyalty, about which he was questioned in 1970.

CHAPTER FORTY-FOUR

The 'Drat' Inquiry

EARLY in 1966 the Fluency Committee formally recommended to the new Director-General, Martin Furnival Jones, that Hollis should be given the full investigative treatment but Furnival Jones continued to regard the possibility that the man who had promoted him was a Soviet agent as 'grotesque' and the Committee remained limited in its endeavours. Recourse to Hollis's file in MI5 provided meagre information. Little had been recorded concerning his entry in 1938 and as he had never been positively vetted there was no evidence on that score. His reluctance to introduce positive vetting into his own organization seemed suspicious in itself, especially when he had finally done so only when it was too late for him to be subjected to it, so that he had never been asked about any connections with communists or communism.

Because of his unsuccessful attempt to enter the Secret Intelligence Service (MI6) there should have been a file on him there but, if it had ever existed, it had been removed. It was known that he had served in China, and the Fluency Committee realized that he might have been recruited there but access to any records still existing in the country was impossible in the middle 1960s because of the poor relations with the Chinese Government. In fact there was a rich potential source in the form of the detailed records of the former Shanghai Municipal Police which had been removed to Washington and were in storage there.

While Hollis had been in Shanghai in the 1930s he lived, like most British residents, in the International Settlement, which had its own police and security force manned mainly by Britons and other English-speaking officers. Because of the danger from Chinese communism, which was heavily supported by the Soviet Union, the force was ruthlessly efficient, particularly with regard to its records of all those under the slightest suspicion. Mr Jack Tilton, the former member of the Shanghai Municipal Police, to whom I have already referred, has assured me that if Hollis was acquainted with communists as active as Agnes Smedley and

Arthur Ewert, as he certainly was, then his name would have been in the police files.[1]

My inquiries concerning the fate of these files produced the following statement from the National Archives and Record Service in Washington: 'The Shanghai Municipal Police files were seized by the Japanese during World War 2. They excised all records of Japanese personalities but, otherwise, kept the files in good order. After the end of hostilities the Chinese Nationalists assumed custody of the files and kept them until about February 1949, when the C.I.A. assumed custody of them because of the imminent Chinese Communist take-over of the area.

'In March or April 1949 the files were loaded on a tank-landing ship for shipment to Japan. Because the arrival of the Chinese Communists was so close the loading had to be done hurriedly and, in the haste, some of the boxes fell into the water and were not recovered. Some of the files were further damaged during a typhoon on the journey to Japan. Eventually some fifty-five cubic feet of the original files arrived in Washington, the bulk of the collection spanning the period from 1929 to 1944...

'There are many dossiers relating to Communist subversion. Some of them have not yet been processed to see whether information they contain should still be withheld on security grounds.'[2]

I can find no evidence that any attempt was made by the Fluency Committee to consult these files in the late 1960s though it should have been aware of their existence because they had been given wide publicity in 1952, when Major-General Charles Willoughby, Chief of Intelligence to General MacArthur, published a book called *The Shanghai Conspiracy*.[3] In it he confessed how he had secured many of the Shanghai Municipal Police records and particularly those of Agnes Smedley, Richard Sorge and others who happened to have been contemporary with Hollis, though Willoughby was unaware of Hollis's existence.

The official reason given to me for MI5's failure to search these archives in Washington is that it could not have been done without informing the C.I.A. and the F.B.I. and that the management of MI5 would not have permitted this because of the embarrassment of having to admit that Hollis was under suspicion. This may be an excuse, however, for I have established that some of the officers on the Fluency Committee did not know that the files existed and this may have applied to all of them.

On the authority of a professional intelligence officer and an historian who examined the Shanghai Municipal Police files, I can say that they have been very thoroughly 'weeded' twice. The first weeding is believed to have taken place in the Soviet interest while the files were still held in Shanghai. The second seems to have been made in the British interest during the storage of the documents in Washington.[4] Apart from the crates which were lost at sea, about ten per cent of the files are missing and the removals seem to relate exclusively to individuals in whom Soviet Intelligence had high interest. Thus, while Sonia has confessed to being an active Red Army agent and an assistant to Sorge in Shanghai and to have operated her own network there later, there are no available papers about her.[5] If any still exist they would be withheld simply because she was still alive when the inquiries were made and, as she had never been convicted, they could infringe her 'civil rights' if released. Though Hollis has been dead since 1973, any papers referring to him could not be released under the American Freedom of Information Act without British permission, the British Government having secured general assurance in this respect.[6] The chances that anything which the U.S. authorities might have about the Hollis case will ever be released seem to be negligible in view of action taken by the British Lord Chancellor, Lord Gardiner, in 1967. A new rule requiring the release of British official documents after an interval of thirty years instead of fifty years, as formerly, was introduced but on the initiative of the legal section of MI5, all the internal files of MI5, MI6 and G.C.H.Q. were exempted from the rule and are to be withheld indefinitely. I have been told officially that this indefinite ban will apply to any related documents held by the U.S. security and intelligence authorities, unless there is joint agreement to release them.

The date of the weeding of the Shanghai files in the British interest is in doubt but probably occurred after the introduction of the U.S. Freedom of Information Act in 1966 and possibly not until the amendments to the Act in 1974 permitted wider access.

Several important contemporaries of Hollis in China were alive and available for interview when the Fluency Committee was active but, except for the army officer who gave the lead to Hollis's connection with Ewert, the Comintern leader, no attempt seems to have been made to question them.[7]

Some of the Fluency Committee members had taken the opportunity to question Hollis about his days in China when they happened to encounter him socially in the office canteen or at the Travellers Club but, never forthcoming about his past, he proved to be particularly reticent about China, especially about his journalistic activities there. In any case, they had no knowledge then of his past association with Ewert or of the significance of Sonia or, it would seem, of Hollis's possible connection with proven spies like Sorge through his friendship with Agnes Smedley.

433

In 1967 Golitsin was invited by MI5 to visit Britain again and came as a consultant on two trips, each of about two months' duration, being paid about £10,000 a month.[8] In connection with the inquiries into the penetration of the secret services he was shown a number of secret files in which real names had been blanked out and, without prior briefing, was asked to suggest which suspect was the most likely spy in MI5. His answer was that 'Drat' was the likeliest, though he had no idea who 'Drat' was. This event, which was no more than a judgement based on limited evidence, is the likely explanation of American claims, originating in the C.I.A., that Golitsin 'had put the finger on Hollis'.

The investigators then made a search for any evidence from defectors indicating the presence of penetration agents in the secret services. Having decided to examine all the evidence with as few preconceived notions as possible, the Committee arranged for a re-translation of the 'shopping list' which had been handed in to British Intelligence by the would-be defector Konstantin Volkov in Istanbul in 1945, as described in Chapter 21. It was accomplished by a G.C.H.Q. officer who had been concerned with decoding K.G.B. traffic and knew the terms and jargon then in use. His translation of a passage referring to agents planted in secret British departments seemed particularly significant: 'I know, for instance, that one of these agents is Acting Head of a Department of the British Counter-Intelligence Directorate.' Previously this statement had been translated 'Head of a Department of British Counter-Intelligence' and had been interpreted as referring to Philby, which is how Philby himself had interpreted it. Philby had been in MI6, but the re-translation could only refer to someone in MI5. Philby had never been 'Acting Head' of anything, but MI5's Section F, responsible in 1945 for counter-intelligence against the Soviet Union, had an acting head in the form of Roger Hollis.

Igor Gouzenko, who had still been working as a Soviet cipher clerk in 1945, was also asked to translate the passage and produced the same result. So did the K.G.B. defectors Vladimir Petrov in Australia and Golitsin in the U.S.

The tentative conclusion that Volkov had been referring to Hollis had one misleading consequence. It was known that Volkov had been a K.G.B. officer and it was therefore assumed that if Hollis was a spy he, too, had been recruited by the K.G.B., just as Maclean, Philby, Blunt and the rest were known to have been. There was even a hunch that he might be 'Johnson' of the decoded K.G.B. traffic, though it is now certain that Blunt was the spy with that code-name. It is equally certain that if Hollis was a spy he was recruited by the G.R.U. and the failure to realize this early meant that the Fluency Committee did not appreciate his possible connection with Sonia, who, by that time, because of the Fuchs case, was known to have been a G.R.U. courier and controller.

Looked at with hindsight this is surprising because in 1967, when the Fluency Committee was active, the decoders made their first break into the mass of messages which Sonia had transmitted to Moscow from Oxford or which had been sent on her behalf. In a separate operation code-named 'Farouche' thousands of messages sent by 'illegal' Soviet agents during the war were dredged up from various sources which had recorded but not decoded them. Some of these sources were foreign and proved to be rewarding. They revealed that prominent men among the wartime Free French based in Britain, politicians such as André Labarthe and Pierre Cot, and forces chiefs like Admiral Muselier, were regarded by Moscow as Soviet agents. They disclosed the existence of two Britons working as spies for the Soviet Union in Sweden, one of them being a former agent of MI6. They contained the K.G.B. code-name of a West German who is still active in politics. They also contained a message from a G.R.U. officer in the Soviet Embassy in London informing the G.R.U. Centre that Sonia had been unable to contact them through some fault in her radio and that she had paid her agents various sums of money for expenses. This was the first time that Ursula Beurton's code-name had been deciphered and it proved that she continued to use the same code-name which had been given to her during her China days and which she employed during her service in Switzerland in the Lucy Ring.[9]

As Volkov was a K.G.B. officer how would he have known anything about Hollis, a suspected G.R.U. spy? As I have explained, the K.G.B., under the direction of Stalin who feared any espionage organization under Red Army control, had begun to take over the G.R.U.'s more important assets and the spy inside MI5 could well have been one of them.

Extending their researches into the Gouzenko evidence, the Fluency Committee discovered the allegation of the existence of a spy inside MI5, code-named 'Elli', which until then had been virtually ignored. Various candidates were considered, including Mitchell, but, again, too little attention was paid to Hollis at that stage because it was certain that 'Elli' had been a G.R.U. spy and the Committee was working on the assumption that, if Hollis was a spy, he had been recruited by the K.G.B. This is further evidence that MI5 did not concern itself very seriously with the British branch of the Soviet 'Red Orchestra', which was essentially a G.R.U. operation. It had undoubtedly existed in Britain, as

435

evidence from Krivitsky and others indicated. MI5 would seem to have assumed that as the 'Red Orchestra' was concentrated against the Germans, there was no necessity to look into it during the war, when in fact the British branch, as evidenced by Sonia and her agents, was working against British interests, just as the G.R.U. was in Canada.[10]

Former members of the Fluency Committee ruefully admit that they did not pay enough attention either to Sonia or to 'Elli'. It is astonishing that even though finances for the investigations were limited, nobody from the Fluency Committee went out to question Gouzenko, who insisted to me that he was never seen again by a British representative until 1972, as will be described in Chapter 52.[11] The information he gave then and in the following year was to heighten the suspicion against Hollis and strengthen the evidence that he was the best fit for 'Elli', but in the late 1960s the significance of the 'Elli' information was missed.

While the code-names of Philby, Burgess, Blunt and Maclean have been established from deciphered wartime radio traffic, 'Elli' has never been firmly attributed to Hollis or to anyone else. The reason for this is that all the breaks secured in Operation Bride, later renamed Venona, came from K.G.B. traffic because it was that organization which failed to maintain full code security. The G.R.U. traffic in which 'Elli' would have appeared was not broken and if, by 1945, 'Elli' had been taken over by the K.G.B., he would have been given a different code-name. Several cryptonyms from the K.G.B. traffic such as 'David' and 'Simpson' were deciphered but it has never been established to whom these referred.

In its search for defector evidence against Hollis the Fluency Committee looked at that provided by Yuri Rastvorov and Ismail Akhmedov. When the 'Elli' material came to be properly appreciated later it was seen that there was more defector evidence pointing towards Hollis than there had been to many spies who were induced to confess by interrogation. Regrettably, because of the ban on the interrogation of Hollis, he was not to be confronted with the evidence until five years after his retirement when, being ill, he pleaded impaired memory.

The Fluency Committee also took note of the fact that there had been a marked absence of defectors to MI5 during the time that Hollis had been there and that some of those who defected to the U.S. indicated that they had been fearful of defecting to Britain because of Soviet penetrations there. As already mentioned, Gouzenko told me, 'If I had defected in England instead of in Canada I do not think I would have been allowed to survive.'[12]

The Committee's re-examination of the Burgess and Maclean

defection satisfied them that there was an alternative explanation to the belief that the last-minute warning had come from Philby, which had been accepted too readily. It could have originated from a source inside MI5.

Hollis's strange behaviour during the Mitchell inquiries culminating in his insistence that he must fly to Washington alone to convey the news of the suspicions personally to the heads of the C.I.A. and F.B.I. came under critical scrutiny. It was seen as possibly the panic reaction of a man anxious to demonstrate that he could hardly be a spy when so anxious to expose another. The episode reminded the Committee of Philby's behaviour when he feared that the suspicion against Maclean might extend to himself. He had taken action to remind his superiors of the evidence of Krivitsky concerning a possible spy in the Foreign Office, a move which, like Hollis's was later to create suspicion rather than avert it.

The Committee considered it possible that Hollis's visit to Washington might have been occasioned by his urgent need to meet a Soviet contact to secure advice, and even, perhaps, to discuss defection. He would not have attempted the meeting in London, where he might have been under surveillance. It was common for important meetings between Soviet Intelligence officers and key agents to be held in a third country and Hollis could have been confident that he would not be under surveillance in the U.S. because the American authorities would not have been informed, officially, of any suspicions against the MI5 Director-General at that stage.

It was also appreciated that Hollis's adamant refusal to allow Mitchell to be interrogated and his technical limitation on inquiries into his behaviour could have been a device to divert attention from himself. In retirement Mitchell would remain under deep suspicion which might never be resolved and the possibility that there could have been two Soviet agents in the form of the Director-General and his deputy would seem even more 'grotesque'.

The record showed that Hollis had developed a habit of finding excuses for preventing the interrogation of possible suspects. There was the admiral who could have betrayed important N.A.T.O. secrets, as indicated by Golitsin and Alister Watson, the Admiralty scientist; there was Sir Dennis Proctor, and there were others arising out of the leads provided by Blunt.

The clue of the locked drawer of the antique desk in Mitchell's room, which might have contained a hidden tape-recorder, as described in Chapter 33, was seen as also being meaningful to the Hollis case. As Director-General he did not attend the weekly meetings when the watchers were allotted to the various operations in progress, 'bids' being made by the case officers for use of the limited resources. His office, however, had a connecting door with Mitchell's and as the key to the drawer was missing Hollis may have had it. He had been approached for permission to open the drawer and because of his habit of working late when others had left he had had ample opportunity to remove the recorder, if that is what the locked drawer had contained.

A weekly record, in advance, of what the watchers were to do and their locations would have been of inestimable value to Soviet agents operating in London and could go far to explain MI5's long lack of success against them. Only Hollis and Peter Wright, the Fluency Committee officer, who investigated the desk, knew of the intention to open the drawer and it would seem that something had been removed from it shortly before. Wright had shown the fresh marks to Hollis and photographed them. The key of the drawer was never found.

The suspicions received support from Hollis's habit of remaining in his office until about 8 p.m. Colleagues have told me that they assumed his purpose was to be alone with his mistress but it had been a characteristic of known spies. His preference for walking home across Hyde Park instead of using the chauffeured car at his disposal was also in keeping with clandestine appointments or visits to dead-letter boxes.

The Committee also found that Hollis had something of a reputation for destroying records, including the original tapes and full transcripts of Blunt's interrogations. The peculiar way in which he had sent Liddell's 'Wallflowers' diaries to be destroyed was also marked against him, especially when it was found that they contained interesting speculation about the identity of 'Elli' as well as other matters relevant to the Hollis case.

The unprecedented removal of Martin from MI5 by Hollis, which slowed down inquiries into the penetration of the Service, was also seen as a symptom of the Director-General's fear that he might be about to be exposed.

The recent 'Harriet' case in which Michael Hanley had been falsely accused as a result of K.G.B. disinformation, which had included a detailed description of Hanley, was re-examined and the Committee noted that Hollis, who might have had an interest in red herrings to absorb MI5's limited investigative resources, had been one of only two officials with access to Hanley's record of service.

The Committee then prepared a chart of MI5 operations that had collapsed, either totally or in part, and included known Soviet

Intelligence operations which had gone undetected until long after they had succeeded, Sonia's part in the Fuchs case being one of them. When compared with the records of various case officers, it was apparent that Hollis's activities, or lack of them, dominated the chart to an extent too excessive to be accounted for by coincidence. (See Chapter 48.) His earliest possible involvement concerned a continuous operation, during five years in the late 1930s, when British counter-intelligence had been decoding radio traffic between Moscow and Comintern agents in Europe. Items of interest to MI5 were passed to various selected officers who needed them. Soon after Hollis started work in MI5 the traffic ceased abruptly, the last message being a curt announcement that other means would be employed for future communication. This occurred before Blunt was recruited to MI5 and before Philby entered MI6. The salient points on the chart covered almost every case from the activities of the Ring of Five to the Mitchell case, which was still current in the eyes of the Fluency Committee.

Discreet and carefully worded inquiries were made among former MI5 employees who had worked closely with Hollis.

One member of the Fluency Committee was so perturbed by the weight of evidence pointing towards Hollis that he went to the trouble of consulting a psychiatrist for reassurance that he was not deluding himself into believing that the chief of the agency to which he had devoted his professional life might be a traitor. Such was the state of morale inside MI5 created by the Mitchell and Hollis affairs.

In its first formal report, in 1967, the Fluency Committee concluded that the evidence indicated that MI5 had been penetrated by one or more Soviet agents over many years since the departure of the only proven MI5 spy, Anthony Blunt. Totting up what it called 'debits' and 'assets' it named Sir Roger Hollis and Graham Mitchell as the likeliest suspects and, because so many suspicious incidents were attributable to Hollis, the Committee believed that the Hollis case should be developed without delay by interrogating him but, knowing Furnival Jones's antipathy to such a step, it recommended that Mitchell should be interrogated first. Furnival Jones agreed and the interrogation was carried out with results which cleared Mitchell to the Committee's satisfaction, as already described.

Sir Dick White, as head of MI6, received a copy of the Fluency Committee's report but nobody else outside MI5 did so and knowledge of the Committee's existence and its findings was restricted to the minimum number of people inside MI5.

CHAPTER FORTY-FIVE

The Ellis Case

AMONG the unsolved suspected cases of penetration of the secret services taken off the shelf by the Fluency Committee for re-examination was that of Colonel Charles Howard Ellis, a senior MI6 officer known to his friends as 'Dick'. The case had caused deep concern in MI5 at the end of the Second World War, when evidence had indicated that he might have been spying for the Germans, and again in the early 1950s following the Philby case. On both occasions MI6 had refused to consider the possibility, rejecting it as absurd, and when the Fluency Committee approached Hollis about reopening the case he, too, was dismayed. He warned the chairman that it would make MI5 very unpopular with the MI6 management but Hollis's deputy, Furnival Jones, said that he would deal with any objections from MI6, which he eventually did.

The files showed that Ellis, who was born in Sydney in 1895, had been an outstanding student of modern languages, had served in the Middlesex Regiment during the First World War and had then taken part in British operations in Transcaspia against the Bolsheviks, when he had learned some Russian.[1] He had continued his studies at Oxford, arriving there in 1920, and had then spent some time in Paris, at the Sorbonne, perfecting his French. While there he also improved his Russian, becoming almost bilingual, by marrying a White Russian from an émigré family called Zilenski. His qualifications had enabled him to work for the British Foreign Office in junior diplomatic posts and he had then moved into MI6 as an agent in 1924 in Berlin, where his cover was his appointment as an officer in the British Passport Control Office, and in Paris where he worked among the Russian émigrés. The White Russian community in Paris was known to include spies who were working for both German and Soviet Intelligence to earn money, and Ellis's task there was to make use of them wherever possible and transmit his findings to London. He worked as a journalist to provide extra cover and had managed to recruit several promising agents, including his young brother-in-law, Alexander Zilenski, whom he was later to blame for his own known treachery.[2]

Alexander proved useful to him because he had access to a White Russian, Waldemar von Petrov, who was influential in the movement to overthrow the Soviet régime, then centred in Paris. Von Petrov was friendly with two leading generals in this anti-Bolshevik group, who were really Soviet spies – Nikolai Skobline and Prince Turkul. General Skobline was to become notorious in 1937 as being responsible for the kidnapping by the Russians of General Eugene Miller, a former Czarist staff chief, who was almost certainly executed.[3] Turkul, who was later to take part in a major Soviet deception exercise against the Germans when the Soviet Union was forced into the war, had succeeded in gaining the trust of Himmler, the Gestapo chief, and Alfred Rosenberg, who were both close to Hiltler.[4] Through such sources Ellis was able to provide a lot of information about the internal affairs of the Nazi Party but much of it proved to be false, either because it had been faked by informants or dreamed up by Ellis himself to improve his standing at headquarters. When questioned, Ellis blamed the sources, and Zilenski in particular, but he was distrusted for a long time, recalled to London and barred from headquarters, though not dismissed.

With MI6's rapid expansion in 1938 due to the imminence of war, Ellis, who had divorced his Russian wife and married an English woman, had been taken back and by August 1940 was sufficiently re-established to be sent to New York to become deputy head of British Security Co-ordination (B.S.C.) with the rank of Colonel.[5] This organization had been set up on Churchill's initiative to collect intelligence about clandestine German activities in America and to secure every type of assistance from the U.S. Government for the Allies. Its chief was William Stephenson, later knighted, a rich Canadian inventor and businessman, who had selected Ellis, having been impressed by him in London. When the U.S. entered the war, after Pearl Harbor, in December 1941, B.S.C. became much more important with a staff eventually numbering 1,000. When its story was eventually told, Stephenson became famous as 'Intrepid', the code-name he had adopted for his communications with London.[6]

American documents released under the Freedom of Information Act indicate that the U.S. State Department was misled over Ellis's true function. He was officially listed as 'His Britannic Majesty's Consul in New York', which gave him diplomatic immunity in the event of any clandestine activities to which the U.S. Government would have objected.[7] The F.B.I. knew the truth, however, as is

441

made clear by Dusko Popov, the wartime double agent being run by the British Double Cross Committee to feed false information to the Germans.[8] There is also F.B.I. evidence that Ellis acted clandestinely in the U.S. using the alias 'Howard.'[9]

Ellis's relations with the F.B.I. might repay critical study by historians because he could, possibly, have been responsible for Hoover's decison to ignore a clear warning from Popov about the forthcoming attack on Pearl Harbor. Ellis might have given a bad report on Popov to Hoover, who became aggressively unpleasant to the agent and disinclined to believe anything he said. On the other hand, if Ellis had still been assisting the German intelligence authorities he would have told them what he knew about the Double Cross operation and there is no evidence that they learned anything about it.

Ellis returned to MI6 headquarters in London in 1944, eventually being awarded the U.S. Legion of Merit to add to the C.M.G., C.B.E. and O.B.E. he had received from Britain. In 1946 he was promoted to be MI6 Controller responsible for South-East Asia and the Far East, based in Singapore. Following discussions in London he was sent to Australia in 1950 to give advice about the new Australian Secret Intelligence Service (A.S.I.S.). He also became MI6 Controller of North and South American Affairs, which meant that for several years he was in charge of MI6's activities in almost half the world and was, effectively, number three in the hierarchy.

Until 1951 there had been no suspicion concerning Ellis's loyalty, apart from the occasion when he was thought to have manufactured intelligence, which had been explained away as the exuberance of youth. But evidence of his treachery then emerged by accident, as it so often does in intelligence affairs.

MI5 officers who were convinced that Philby had betrayed their case against Maclean began to examine old documents for clues, including statements made by Krivitsky, the Soviet defector who had been based in Holland, from which certain Soviet spies operating in Britain had been controlled. When he had been debriefed in London in 1940, Krivitsky had said that a White Russian called von Petrov had been an important G.R.U. agent and had valuable sources of secret information in Britain.[10] One source, in particular, had supplied highly secret details about the British Secret Intelligence Service itself. When investigators examined the old file on von Petrov they found that according to the testimony of an *Abwehr* (German Secret Service) officer who had been interrogated after the Nazi defeat, the White Russian had also been a source of intelligence about Britain for the Germans. This

442

officer had also named Zilenski as having a good source inside British Intelligence. The file contained the evidence of a German naval officer in the *Abwehr* who had known the source's name as Captain Ellis. He had also stated that Ellis was an Australian and had a Russian wife. He claimed that Ellis had provided the *Abwehr* with documents giving MI6 the 'order of battle' – its organization and personnel, including their specific duties.

The *Abwehr* officers' evidence also recorded that this Captain Ellis had warned the Germans, before the war, that the British were listening in to secret telephone links set up between von Ribbentrop, the German Ambassador in London, and Hitler in Berlin and that the conversations had, therefore, been ended.

The MI5 officers could not understand why no action had been taken to track down Captain Ellis and question him at the time and the reason was not to emerge until much later: because of the White Russian connection the information had been passed to the MI6 head of Soviet counter-espionage for action. That official was Philby, who had written on the report, 'Who is this man Ellis? N.F.A.' N.F.A. meant No Further Action and the document was duly filed and forgotten. At that time Ellis was working in an office in MI6 headquarters a few doors down from Philby.

The operation against the German telephone link had been conducted by MI6, so in 1953, when the MI5 officers had progressed as far as they could, they asked MI6 to look at their old records of it, not having any right of access to them themselves. The first reaction from MI6 was that nobody there could recall any such operation and that the *Abwehr* information in the MI5 files must have been 'disinformation'. Under pressure, however, the records were found, and while agreeing that somebody must have warned the Germans that the line was being tapped MI6 denied that Ellis had ever been involved in the operation or had any access to information about it. There is no doubt now that in 1953, incensed at MI5's suspicions against Philby, which his colleagues believed to be unwarranted, MI6 was totally opposed to supporting any suspicions against another MI6 officer as senior as Ellis then was.

Undeterred, the MI5 men re-examined an event which had made international headlines – the 'Venlo Incident' when, in November 1939, the *Abwehr* had laid a successful trap for the two chief MI6 officers operating in Holland, which was then still neutral. *Abwehr* agents posing as anti-Nazis had induced these two officers, Major H.R. Stevens and Captain Payne Best, to attend a meeting at Venlo, near the Dutch-German border. They were driven across the border, seized, and interrogated over many months.[11] A German document secured after the war showed that under duress the officers had supplied detailed information about MI6 and other intelligence and security departments, but on their return to Britain, as released prisoners, they described how they had done little more than confirm what the Germans already knew, saying that they had been astonished by the detailed questions they were asked.[12] The MI5 officers who debriefed them were convinced that the *Abwehr* had indeed been in possession of a mass of highly secret information which could only have come from a source inside MI6. This conclusion was endorsed when they were able to question the *Abwehr* officers who had grilled Stevens and Best. To their horror, the MI5 men learned that it was a British Intelligence source that had advised the *Abwehr* on how to lay hands on the two Britons.

Ellis had been in a position to supply the information so MI5 again asked for permisson to examine the relevant MI6 files. Again this was refused. The MI6 management argued that the White Russians with whom Ellis had been in contact before the war had proved to be double-crossers and fabricators of 'intelligence', so von Petrov and the rest must have convinced the *Abwehr* that Ellis had been their agent when, in fact, they had been his. This argument did not explain how the MI6 secrets had leaked, so the MI5 officers suggested that the best way to resolve the problem was to interrogate Ellis. They asked their chief, Sir Dick White, to request the co-operation of MI6 in this venture but White, who had just succeeded to the Director-Generalship of MI5, was anxious to avoid exacerbating the ill will between the two services generated by MI5's continuing insistence that Philby was the 'Third Man'. After being told in 1953 that Ellis had decided to retire, spontaneously and at his own request, White agreed to shelve the case. In short, at the top level of both MI5 and MI6 there was agreement that the Ellis scandal should be covered up for ever 'in the national interest'.

In pursuance of this cover-up the American F.B.I. was told nothing officially of the strong suspicions against Ellis though they should have been because of Ellis's service in the U.S. from 1940 to 1944. Recently, however, F.B.I. papers available under the Freedom of Information Act have revealed that as early as January 1953 the F.B.I. was making espionage inquiries into Ellis and that these continued through 1956.[13] Almost all the information about Ellis in the papers, which are memoranda from the F.B.I. office in New York to headquarters in Washington, has been blanked out for security reasons. Expert examination of the various numbers and initials still remaining suggest that the blanking out was done

444

prior to declassification at the request of the C.I.A. acting on behalf of MI6.

It is possible that the F.B.I. had been warned about Ellis unofficially by an MI5 officer but the documents suggest that it was following its own leads from a special informer who may have been a Soviet defector. One of the F.B.I. officials listed in the documents as having special interest in the case was head of the Russian Section.[14] In any event, the information was considered to be so important that it was channelled directly to the F.B.I. chief, Hoover.

During the Fluency Committee's inquiries into Ellis he had been referred to in documents by the code-name 'Emerton'. This was a standard precaution to reduce the number of people in MI5 and MI6 who could learn about the suspicions and to prevent Ellis himself from hearing about them.

In the middle of 1953 Ellis left MI6, two years before the usual retiring age which was then sixty, claiming that he had been advised to do so on health grounds as his doctors had diagnosed heart trouble. He said that he had decided to return to Australia, where he could take things easy and where the climate would be more suitable. He travelled alone, by sea, having already divorced his second wife, and nine days after his arrival, despite his alleged heart trouble, he signed a two-year contract to work for A.S.I.S., which he had helped to establish. A.S.I.S. had been told nothing about the suspicions against Ellis and, understandably, made no security check with MI5 which, as a result, did not know of his A.S.I.S. appointment.

After only two months Ellis broke his contract saying that he had decided to return to England to remarry. He booked a sea passage, as he disliked travelling by air, and arrived back early in 1954. Ellis's supporters have seen nothing strange in this behaviour and what almost certainly lay behind it was not to become apparent until the defection of Kim Philby from Beirut in January 1963. The setting up of the Fluency Committee soon after that event gave MI5 right of access to MI6 files and those on Ellis revealed how Philby had ensured that no action would be taken against him.

Philby's action in covering up the evidence against Ellis seemed strange because the Russians were keen to bring retribution to anyone who had assisted the Nazis and Philby would, undoubtedly, have consulted his Soviet controller about the case, but the Fluency Committee put forward a possible explanation. As it was certain by then that von Petrov had been primarily a G.R.U. agent Moscow would have known about Ellis's espionage activities the Germans. It seemed likely that von Petrov would have been

445

required to recruit Ellis for Soviet Intelligence, using the blackmail threat if necessary. Whether this had happened or not the Fluency Committee regarded it as inconceivable that once Philby had alerted the K.G.B. to Ellis's position, the Russians would have failed to try to exploit it. The need to find out everything possible about Ellis's activities was therefore greatly increased and the Committee had to move beyond examining the record of a man who might have spied for Germany before and during the early part of the war.

Its first move, however, was to establish whether Ellis could have been involved in the betrayal of MI6's tap on the telephone line between von Ribbentrop and Hitler which had been secretly installed when the German Embassy had been renovated. No record of the personalities involved could be found in the MI6 archives because the tapping operation had been carried out by the security department of the Post Office. A research officer was sent to delve into old Post Office records and subsequently found a file which included a list of the six translators of German who had been involved. The top name on the list was that of Captain C.H. Ellis.

The Fluency Committee then examined his career inside B.S.C. in New York where he could have done great damage had he still been working for the Germans. Various serious leakages could have occurred there, though Sir William Stephenson is understandably loath to admit this.[15] The recent release of American secret documents shows that a verbatim minute of a British War Cabinet discussion dated 31 July 1940 had leaked to the Germans. Because it concerned the possibility of a Japanese intervention against America in the Far East the minute had almost certainly been passed to the B.S.C. office in New York where Ellis was installed.[16] It has since transpired, however, that this leak was due to the capture of a British merchant ship by a German raider when it was taking documents and codes to the British Commander Far East.[17]

The Fluency Committee knew that decipherment of some of the Bride traffic, the K.G.B. messages transmitted from New York to Moscow, had shown the existence of at least twelve Soviet sympathizers inside B.S.C. A few, like Cedric Belfrage, a former member of the British Communist Party, were identified but most of them remain known only by the code-names used in the traffic. The Committee therefore concentrated on the possibility that Ellis was one of the unknown agents having, perhaps, been pressed into K.G.B. service, through blackmail or money, after 1940.[18] It was recalled that Ellis's services had been made available to Colonel William Donovan to assist him in setting up the American

446

Intelligence agency which became the Office of Strategic Services (O.S.S.).[19] Ellis was said to have selected some of the staff including a White Russian who was chief of the espionage section. So, if Ellis had been working for the K.G.B. many of the O.S.S. failures could be attributable to his activities. It was known by then, through decipherment of the Bride traffic, that the O.S.S. had been deeply penetrated by Soviet agents.

Ellis's sudden departure for Australia on the grounds of non-existent heart trouble in 1953 immediately appeared to have an explanation. Ellis knew, from his position in MI6, that the MI5 inquiries into Philby were gathering momentum and he may have feared that he would come under suspicion or he may even have been warned to get out of the country by a Soviet controller, who had been tipped off by a pro-Soviet source inside MI5. Once in Australia, Ellis would be safe from prosecution or interrogation because a suspected spy cannot be extradited for offences under the Official Secrets Act. But why had he returned to Britain so precipitately? The possible answer supported the suspicion that Ellis had been a K.G.B. agent.

Soon after his arrival in Australia he had called on Sir Charles Spry, the Director-General of the Australian Security Intelligence Organization (A.S.I.O.), at his headquarters in Melbourne. Spry had every reason to believe that he could trust Ellis, and in return for information about the Philby case told him that an important member of the Soviet Embassy in Canberra, who was a K.G.B. agent, might be about to defect. The K.G.B. man's name was Vladimir Petrov and Spry said it was hoped that he would bring out documents and other information about K.G.B. agents operating in Australia, Britain and other countries.

The Fluency Committee realized that Ellis had decided on his quick return to Britain only a few days after he learnt about the Petrov case. Petrov, who turned out to be the head of the K.G.B. in Australia and had worked in headquarters in Moscow, might well have known of Ellis's involvement had he been a Soviet spy. In that case Australia would have been a more dangerous place to be in than Britain, from which defection to the Soviet Union, if it became necessary, would be much easier. Further, by signing his contract with A.S.I.S., Ellis had put himself under Australian law. It was also appreciated that Ellis might have thought that Petrov was none other than Waldemar von Petrov, who had first-hand knowledge of his previous espionage activities.

When Ellis informed A.S.I.S. that he was returning to Britain he was asked by A.S.I.O. to brief the top management of both MI5 and MI6 on the latest situation regarding Petrov as this seemed to be a secure way of achieving that. At that stage A.S.I.O. expected that Petrov would defect in April and Ellis arrived back in Britain in March, taking with him the motor car he had bought on his arrival in Australia – further evidence that he had intended to remain there. He is on record in documents as having briefed both the MI5 and MI6 leadership on the Petrov operation. In return, and probably because he made inquiries about it, Ellis was briefed on the state of the Philby case by Maurice Oldfield, an old friend in MI6. Oldfield put this briefing on record together with his instruction to Ellis that he should not see or speak with Philby, who had been out of MI6 for three years.

In fact, Ellis was found to have taken immediate steps to contact Philby, leaving a note on Travellers Club paper for him at the nearby Athenaeum, which Philby still used. Philby did not pick up the message for more than a week but then telephoned Ellis to fix an appointment. This is known because Philby was under telephone surveillance but, as he was not being watched, it is not known what transpired when the two met for lunch.

What is known is that on that same afternoon Philby telephoned his current girlfriend and told her that he had received some good news over lunch. He then added, 'The clouds are parting', a significant remark in view of what he was to write in *My Silent War* in a chapter entitled 'The Clouds Part'. He recorded how, after the K.G.B. had remained out of touch with him for two years following his dismissal from MI6, he received 'through the most ingenious of routes a message from my Soviet friends conjuring me to be of good cheer and presaging an early resumption of relations. It was therefore with refreshed spirit that I watched the next storm gather. It began with the defection of Petrov in Australia...'

Confirmation that Philby had advance information about the Petrov defection eventually came from Blunt in his confessions. The Fluency Committee therefore inferred that Ellis had not only warned Philby about the coming defection, which could incriminate them both, but also put him back in touch with the Russians.

If Philby and Ellis had known about Petrov in advance why did the Russians fail to prevent the defection? The answer is that they did take steps to prevent it and bungled them. The Russians expected Petrov to defect several days later than he actually did, being convinced that he would not flee the Embassy without his wife, another K.G.B. officer, to whom he was known to be devoted and was still under Soviet control in Canberra while her husband was visiting Sydney. According to Golitsin two strong-arm men were sent from Moscow to Canberra to take the Petrovs back by force if necessary and were penalized on their return for their

448

failure, though they very nearly managed to abduct Mrs Petrov. Sir William McMahon, a former Prime Minister of Australia, has told the Australian Parliament that he knew that the Russians had been tipped off about Petrov's impending defection.[20] Petrov himself knew that a safe, in which he kept some documents, had been searched by the Soviet Ambassador who was looking for evidence against him, this being the event which precipitated his early flight.[21]

Ellis always claimed to be short of money and after he had hurriedly returned to Britain his old firm, MI6, helped him to live on his pension by taking him back on the payroll, part time. He was employed 'weeding' the MI6 archives, that is the removal and destruction of files considered by the weeder as being of no further value. Ellis's supporters have insisted that this appointment was proof of his innocence, for MI6 would never have used him had serious MI5 suspicions really existed. The fact is that they did employ him in that sensitive capacity just as they were to employ Philby as an agent-runner in the Middle East when MI5 was certain that he had been the Third Man. If Ellis was a Soviet spy at the time he might have had opportunities to destroy documentary evidence of his own misdemeanours and those of others whom he knew or thought to be Soviet agents or sympathizers. Fortunately there were documents which never reached him.

As I have recorded, the F.B.I. was still conducting its own inquiries into Ellis in 1956, when he was busy 'weeding', but no action was taken on either side of the Atlantic until the Fluency Committee's researches produced leads, early in 1966, indicating that Ellis might have spied for the Soviet Union. It then sought evidence of Soviet control both before and during the war. The investigators questioned a former Pole called Elisabeth Poretsky whose husband, also known as Ignace Reiss and by the code-name 'Ludwik', had been a Soviet Intelligence officer for the G.R.U. and later for the N.K.V.D., the precursor of the K.G.B. She had already revealed that while her husband had been in charge of intelligence against Britain, operating from a base in Holland in 1928 and 1929, he had managed to place an agent inside British Intelligence, meaning MI6.[22] Interviewed in Paris, Mrs Poretsky assured an investigator that the MI6 officer controlled by her husband had not been Philby. She said that when 'Ludwik' had run the spy from Amsterdam, Philby had been a schoolboy. She declined to be very helpful but when shown a spread of photographs she picked out those she knew and also selected Ellis, though saying no more than that he looked familiar. On her advice the MI5 officer went to interview the widow of a Dutchman called

Henri Pieck who had run spies in England. She also picked out Ellis's photograph but refused to supply any details.

MI5 knew that Richard Sorge, the Soviet agent who operated so successfully in China and Japan, had previously visited London briefly in the late 1920s to meet a very important agent, so an officer was sent to question his widow, Christiane, who was living in the U.S. She recalled her husband's mission to London, which she described as 'very dangerous', and said that he had taken her to the rendezvous, which was on a street. When shown Ellis's photograph she said that he could have been the agent but she was not sure.

After analysing all the evidence in 1966 the Fluency Committee was convinced that Ellis had been a paid agent for the Germans before the war and in its early phases up to May 1940. It was regarded as possible that he had managed to remain free of German control while in New York but that it was most unlikely that the Russians would have failed to blackmail him into spying for them from 1945 onwards. They suspected that his espionage work for the Soviet Union could have extended back into the late 1920s and that he could have been the spy run by 'Ludwik'. It was therefore decided that Ellis should be subjected to hostile interrogation. Though he was retired he could be required to attend at Room 055 in the War Office because he was in receipt of an MI6 pension. The MI6 Director of Security, Christopher Phillpotts, agreed.

Ellis was then seventy-one but he was fit enough to have found himself a job with a European freelance intelligence agency called the International Documentary Centre (Interdoc), being its British representative with an office in London.[23] Nevertheless, because of his alleged frailty, it was decided to interview him for only a few hours a day. He was put under surveillance by Special Branch to ensure, as far as possible, that he could not defect, and as an additional precaution his telephone was tapped without the formality of a Home Office warrant. The Post Office agreed on the understanding that the warrant would be applied for later when the interrogation was over, as duly happened.

During the interrogations, which were tape-recorded, MI5 arranged electronic coverage of Ellis's office and discovered that he was in the habit of muttering to himself such remarks as, 'They did not know about... They can't possibly know about...'

The interrogators decided to concentrate first on his pre-war activities after he had been told that there was serious evidence impugning his loyalty. The first day, a Monday, was spent going through his life-history and establishing the accuracy, or otherwise, of the MI5 record of his career. The following day he was confronted with the report of the *Abwehr* officer who had named him as a spy. He maintained that the document must be a forgery, probably concocted by the White Russians and handed to the Germans. He insisted that he had never heard of the secret telephone link between Hitler and von Ribbentrop and that he would never have told Zilenski, or anyone else, about the MI6 'order of battle'. On the third day the interrogators took him through the whole matter again and ended by showing him the Post Office list with his name at the top of the translators involved in the tapping operation. He was clearly shaken but claimed that he had no recollection of it, pleading lapse of memory, though he appeared to remember events clearly when it suited him. He was sent home to give the issues further thought and was given to understand that MI5 had more documentary evidence against him.

On the Thursday the ground was covered again but in a more hostile manner. Ellis continued to maintain his innocence complaining that he was too old to defend himself. He blamed all the suspicions on his former colleagues in MI6, denigrating them one by one. When he was sent home at the end of the day he was warned that if he failed to tell the truth he would be confronted with the German officer and that the case would be handed over to Special Branch, the arresting arm of MI5. That, in fact, was a bluff because MI5 did not know whether the officer was still alive and the management had no intention of staging a prosecution, whatever Ellis might confess. The policy of non-prosecution of intelligence and security officers found to be spies, which had been introduced by Hollis, was being continued.

On the Friday morning the interrogation remained deadlocked but, after lunch, Ellis returned with a document which was an attempted apologia for his behaviour. It alleged that after he had begun working for MI6 in 1925 he had been sent into the field in Europe without adequate training or proper briefing to collect intelligence about the Soviet Union as well as about Germany. This complaint was regarded as justified because, at that time, training in MI6 had been minimal all round. The document stated that the intelligence about the Soviet Union that he had produced had been gratefully received in London but headquarters had given him insufficent money to pay his agents. He had therefore started giving them trivial information about British affairs so that they could feed it to the Russians who paid them for it. The Fluency Committee regarded this limited admission as establishing an early connection with Soviet Intelligence.

The document went on to state that he had been hard pressed

financially and had had to borrow money from an agent, who suggested that the easiest way out of his problem was for him to povide more information about MI6 which he could sell to the Germans and Russians. Ellis claimed that he realized that he was becoming dangerously involved and therefore insisted that he could supply no more secret information. This was met by a threat to expose him to MI6 unless he continued to supply more and better intelligence for his customers. Ellis said that he needed the money badly because his wife was ill, but the Fluency Committee eventually concluded that he had taken the easy way out through weakness of character.

Ellis's apologia was regarded as being an abject admission of spying not only for the Germans but for the Russians because at least one of his agents was trading with both and Ellis had known that. He was then asked four questions: 'Did you hand over detailed charts of MI6 organization just prior to the war which could have been used by the Germans in the interrogations of Steven and Best after their capture in the Venlo incident?' He admitted that he had done so. When asked, 'Did you betray our breaking of the von Ribbentrop-Hitler telephone link?' he answered, 'I must have been mad.' To the question, 'When you were providing the secret material, to whom did you think it was going?' he replied, 'I don't know – the Germans, I suppose.' Finally, when asked when he was last in contact with Zilenski or his associates he answered, 'In about December 1939. I sent them an envelope via an MI6 officer who was going to Paris. He brought back a sealed package of money for me.' This misuse of a brother officer, who had no knowledge of the contents of the packages, was regarded as particularly treacherous.

Ellis was told that he had committed treason in war and that if it had been discovered at the time he would have been hanged for communicating secretly with the enemy. He was told to present himself for further questioning on the following Monday.

When he arrived at 10 a.m. he was asked to give details of his secret dealings with Soviet Intelligence. He denied any direct dealings, claiming that he had always been anti-communist and had published books which proved that. He was told that there was indisputable evidence that the White Russians, with whom he had dealt, had been recruited as agents of the Soviet G.R.U. His response was to describe the White Russians as 'a double-crossing lot of bastards who would sell intelligence to whoever would pay them.'

On the following day the interrogators concentrated on Ellis's post-war activities. He claimed that he had hardly known Philby, which was false. When he was asked why he had taken a full-time post with A.S.I.S. after resigning from MI6 on health grounds he had no answer but insisted that his decision to return to Britain had no connection with the Petrov case. He claimed that he had decided to marry a woman whom he had met in England and had to return to do so. When asked for her name he gave it, and an address. Overnight MI5 traced the girl and found that she had married an American serviceman two years before Ellis's departure for Australia and was living, happily, with her husband in America. When interviewed she said that she had known Ellis but had never had any intention of marrying him. When faced with this Ellis said that he had been so upset by the accusations that he had given the wrong name and then gave another. When this girl was traced it was learned that she too had married before Ellis had left for Australia. Later in 1954 Ellis had, in fact, married a Mrs Alexandra Wood, he did not give her name to his questioners.

Ellis then proceeded to strengthen the suspicions against him with a succession of lies. He denied having met Philby or that Maurice Oldfield had warned him against doing so.

After being questioned repeatedly over several weeks to induce him to admit a connection with Soviet Intelligence he appeared to sense that there was no documentary evidence in that regard. Fearing that he might collapse under the strain, as John Watkins, the Canadian diplomat had done two years earlier, it was decided to ask the Attorney-General to agree to an offer of immunity to prosecution in return for a full confession and co-operation in further inquiries. The Attorney-General agreed, not having been told by MI5 that Ellis had already admitted to spying for the Germans. Appearing to distrust the offer, Ellis maintained his position so far as the Soviet Union was concerned.

After lengthy consideration of the case the Fluency Committee concluded that the circumstantial evidence suggested that Ellis could have been a conscious agent of the Soviet Union for almost thirty years, being first with the G.R.U. and then, after 1945, with the K.G.B. when Philby had alerted his controller about him. While he had spied for the Germans for money, any assistance he had given the Russians had probably been through fear of exposure, though some payment may have been forthcoming.

Both A.S.I.S. and A.S.I.O. were informed of the outcome of the Ellis case in November 1967 because of their close ties with MI6 and they carried out assessments of the damage he might have done to their interests. To maintain secrecy as far as possible the F.B.I. and C.I.A. were not told. Because of the impact of the publicity generated by the Philby affair MI6 was determined to conceal the Ellis case from everyone who did not need to know.

As has recently been explained in Parliament a self-confessed spy can be deprived of his pension rights only if he is prosecuted and convicted.[24] Ellis continued in honourable retirement on full pension in Eastbourne. As I did not discover his treachery before he died in 1975 he was never subjected to any public censure in his lifetime. The secret of his confession had also been successfully held from most of his MI6 colleagues, his friends and relatives. Understandably, most of them continue to disbelieve that he was ever even suspect.

A few of Ellis's former MI6 colleagues have congratulated me on the exposure, though they would never have made it themselves. Further independent confirmation of Ellis's treachery came from an international authority on intelligence affairs who had been involved in setting up the International Documentary Centre. He was approached by an MI6 officer who was trying to find out how Ellis, a self-confessed traitor, had managed to secure a post inside an organization which would give him access to information that was at least confidential if not secret. It was the first that my informant had heard of Ellis's treachery and he had not been concerned in recommending him for the post as the MI6 man had believed. Later it transpired that the recommendation had been made by a former head of MI6 who had known all about Ellis's confession! Further, Ellis was allowed to continue in his post with Interdoc because MI6 was adverse to informing his employers. In such ways do members of the secret services help to conceal the crimes of their erring colleagues. Much was made by Ellis's supporters of the fact that Sir Maurice Oldfield remained in friendly touch with Ellis in the latter's old age but, being a fervent Christian, Sir Maurice, who briefly discussed the Ellis case with me on his deathbed, was very forgiving. I also sensed that, as with others among Ellis's colleagues in that precarious profession, there was a feeling that 'There but for the grace of God go I...'

When Margaret Thatcher commented on *Their Trade is Treachery* in 1981 she avoided any mention of the Ellis case though she had been informed of his guilt. She declined to clear his name when written to by relatives but took the opportunity to suggest that I was at fault in exposing Ellis when, being dead, he could not defend himself. He had been given every opportunity to defend himself in his long interrogations and, so far as the espionage for the Nazis was concerned, had been unable to do so effectively. The Prime Minister had been advised to avoid the Ellis case because the details were so accurate that confirmation of it would have made it difficult for her Parliamentary statement to cast any doubt on my sources concerning the case of Sir Roger Hollis.

Some three months later, in July 1981, F.B.I. documents concerning the American inquiries into Ellis were declassified.[25] As already mentioned, almost everything in them was blanked out in the interests of a 'third party' which was, almost certainly, the British Government. American informants have told me that there is a strong belief in the C.I.A. that Ellis had functioned as a Soviet agent during his wartime sojourn in the U.S. and that backtrack inquiries in that respect are in train.

The Potential Value of Oversight

It would seem unlikely that any workable oversight scheme could have such access to detail that Philby's action in stifling the hard evidence against Ellis in 1951 would have been detected. On the other hand, with even the remote possibility that it might do so, Philby might have been less confident in taking such a cavalier attitude. With hindsight, it is scandalous that Krivitsky's specific information was not pursued. The MI6 management, as a whole, might also have been less self-righteous in its attitude to the possibilty that it might harbour spies, and an oversight body might have ensured that MI5 had access to MI6's files, when this was necessary in particular counter-espionage operations.

It is astonishing that, following the debriefing of the two MI6 officers captured in the Venlo incident and released after the war, no effort seems to have been made to trace the source of the leakages to which they pointed. An oversight body should have wanted to know why.

As happened with several of the cases controlled by Hollis, a convenience was made of Ellis's premature retirement to avoid the embarrassment of an interrogation. Oversight might have stopped this practice which was more in the interests of the secret service managements than in the nation's.

An oversight body would surely have queried the employment of Ellis in 'weeding' secret files, had it been aware of the evidence on file against him. Finally, it seems doubtful that, in the knowledge that the action would become known to the oversight body, a decision to cover up Ellis's treachery and permit him to retire honourably on full pension – which would be index-linked today – would have been taken. It has been established by a statement in the House of Lords that, as the law stands, public service pensions can not be withheld in the case of traitors and other serious offenders under the Official Secrets Act unless the individuals

455

concerned have been convicted of the offences.

In sum, the Ellis case speaks eloquently of the value of oversight in the interests of the efficiency of the secret services themselves.

CHAPTER FORTY-SIX

The American Secret Behind the D-Notice Affair

No incident has more blatantly demonstrated the determination of Whitehall officials and politicians to mislead Parliament and the public on security and intelligence matters than the so-called D-Notice affair of 1967. Only now has it become possible to divulge that the real reason for their extreme sensitivity on that occasion was that the whole Anglo-American relationship on secret intelligence matters had been put in jeopardy, along with the political reputation of President Lyndon Johnson and the professional survival of some of his chief officials.

On 21 February 1967 I published a front-page report in the London *Daily Express* disclosing that copies of all the private cables being processed by the Post Office and private cable companies were being made available for scrutiny by the intelligence services. It later emerged that all telex messages were being treated the same way. The practice had been in operation for several years – I did not know how long – and I felt that because of its massive and continuous nature it was an invasion of privacy which should not be countenanced in a free society.

While I had been making inquiries, the Defence Ministry, MI5 and the Foreign Office had been alerted and a plan to induce me and my editor to suppress the information was hatched at the highest levels involving the Foreign Secretary, then George Brown. As a first gambit the Secretary of the D-Notice Committee, Colonel L. G. 'Sammy' Lohan, was instructed to warn me that the report would infringe a D-Notice – a certain advisory note requesting the Press to avoid mentioning any secret methods used by the intelligence authorities. When this failed, because it could be shown that the vetting of cables was not effectively covered by any D-Notice, the editor was asked to suppress the information on Lohan's assurance that it was an important security matter. When this plea was rejected, after searching discussions, the Foreign Secretary put pressure on the newspaper's proprietor, which also failed.[1]

The usual Whitehall reaction to such a report, once it had

appeared in print, would have been to decline to comment and to rely on more pressing news to obliterate further media interest. Instead, the Prime Minister Harold Wilson decided, against strong advice from officials, including his Cabinet Secretary Sir Burke Trend, to secure some revenge against me and the *Daily Express*, though this would inevitably provoke more publicity.[2] Whether he had been told of the American dimension at that stage remains in doubt. In Parliament he accused me and the *Daily Express* of deliberately breaching a D-Notice and inflicting great damage on national security and as a result he set up a committee of three Privy Councillors to investigate the circumstances and to report its findings to him.[3] The committee was headed by Lord Radcliffe who had wide experience of dealing with security issues.

MI5 had already put heavy pressure on the Chief Press Officer of the Defence Ministry to make a false statement to the newspapers telling them that there was no truth in the cable-vetting report. An operation calculated to ensure that the Radcliffe Committee would be given false testimony by certain Government witnesses whom it might call was then organized by Christopher Ewart-Biggs, who was head of the Foreign Office department liaising with G.C.H.Q., which controlled the cable-intercept operation.

The *Daily Express* inquiries had shown that there was nothing illegal about the scrutiny of private cables under British law. It had, in fact, been authorized under the Official Secrets Act of 1920 and, though I had not known it when I wrote my report, it had been in secret operation since that date. What has only recently become apparent is that under an Anglo-American pact dating from 1945 – the U.K.U.S.A. agreement on the interchange of intelligence – the British cables and telex messages were also made available to the American counterpart of G.C.H.Q., the National Security Agency (N.S.A.) so that it could examine them for intelligence of special American interest.[4] This could have caused a sizeable furore in the British Parliament had M.P.s realized what was happening when the D-Notice affair was running or at any time previously or since. But that, alone, was insufficient to account for the monumental efforts made to suppress the cable-vetting story and, when they failed, to ridicule it as false. The main danger lay in the fact that the U.S. Intelligence authorities had been doing exactly the same with private American cables for twenty-two years, unknown to Congress or the public, in spite of the fact that it was completely illegal under U.S. law. Because of the utmost need for secrecy, the American cable-vetting operation was given the code-name 'Shamrock'.[5]

The forerunner of the N.S.A. had made a secret deal with the three major American cable companies, which undertook to supply the cables daily in the national interest, though with much reluctance because it was illegal. Ordinary copies of the messages had been supplied at first, then as technology advanced the information was handed over in the form of microfilm, then punched tapes, and finally on magnetic tapes which could be processed rapidly through computers, programmed to respond to certain names, organizations and activities of interest to the American security and intelligence authorities. While the original purpose had been to search for information about subversive and espionage activities, the system was being used in the U.S. to collect information about dissidents and people involved in drugs traffic. So while the British Government was in the clear legally, it was aiding and abetting the U.S. Government in an operation which was highly illegal.

When the executives of the American cable companies became fearful of being prosecuted if the secret ever leaked, President Eisenhower was induced to give the scheme his backing, and it is possible that Presidents Kennedy and Johnson were also informed. The concern in Washington when the *Daily Express* cable-vetting story appeared can therefore be imagined. American reporters might well have launched inquiries to discover whether anything comparable was in progress in the U.S. and might easily have unearthed the truth.

Under pressure from Ewart-Biggs and Defence Ministry officials, Colonel Lohan was induced to change the statement he had made about his previous discussions with me and my editor and to give false information to the committee when he appeared before it.[6] Officials also instructed the Director of Public Relations (D.P.R.) at the Post Office, who had privately confirmed the existence of the cable-vetting process to me, to submit a statement to the committee which was contrary to the truth, and they made it clear to him that he was expected to support his statement when questioned by the committee. As the report of the Radcliffe Committee was to reveal, other more senior Foreign Office officials were party to what can only be described as a conspiracy to conceal the truth.

Lohan duly made false statements, both verbally and in writing, misinforming the Committee about crucially important timings of telephone calls; he even altered the dates on some documents.[7] He also mentioned G.C.H.Q. but was immediately silenced by Lord Radcliffe, an event which should have aroused my curiosity. To the consternation of Whitehall, however, the Post Office public relations chief and some other witnesses told the truth under cross-

459

examination and, as a result, the Committee completely exonerated me and the *Daily Express*.[8] The Prime Minister, who had expected the reverse, then declined to accept the findings and insisted on producing a counter-document in the form of a White Paper claiming that my disclosure had been 'a matter of the utmost gravity' and that 'the effect on national security had been to cause damage, potentially grave, the consequences of which could not be fully assessed'.[9] Perhaps, by that time if not before, he had been fully informed of the possible American reaction to what Washington might construe as a breach of security which threatened the U.K.U.S.A. agreement.

The White Paper was inevitably followed by a Parliamentary debate resulting in a *Hansard* report of the proceedings containing many inaccurate statements by Labour M.P.s in support of Wilson, which still stand in the historical record.[10]

Whitehall's revenge on those who had failed to carry out its requirements successfully was swift and merciless. Lohan was removed from his post under ignominious circumstances while the Post Office D.P.R. who had told the truth was prematurely retired. Wilson was to find that his handling of the affair was to become his worst self-inflicted wound, as he was to describe it in his memoirs.[11] His rejection of the findings of the Committee, which he himself had established, and his too obvious attack on the *Daily Express*, on myself and on Lohan, who had many friends in Fleet Street, alienated the media for many months. Ten years later he was to apologize to me and claim that his real purpose in pursuing the D-Notice affair was to rid Whitehall of Lohan.[12] He had been trying to do that for several months without success after being told that Lohan had been supplying Conservative back-benchers with material to use in Parliamentary questions to embarrass the Labour Government. Unfortunately for Lohan, one of those back-benchers was serving as a spy inside the Tory Party for Wilson and informed on him. Lohan's handling of the D-Notice affair and the 'discrepancies' in his evidence to the Radcliffe Committee, which had been forced upon him, offered an excuse for enforcing his resignation.

No American reporter investigated Operation Shamrock until July 1975, when an article in the New York *Daily News* claimed that the N.S.A. had monitored commercial cable traffic to and from the U.S.[13] Two months previously, perhaps after being alerted to the newspaper inquiries, the U.S. Secretary of State for Defense had ordered the termination of Shamrock with every provision for the continuing secrecy of its past endeavours.[14] Following the publicity, the Senate Committee on Intelligence and a Congressional sub-committee began an investigation, involving the questioning of witnesses from the American cable companies. President Ford exerted all his powers to prevent any disclosures and, while some of the witnesses nevertheless gave evidence, the full facts were never revealed in any published report, and the prosecution of N.S.A. officials was avoided by legalistic manoeuvres.[15] Who knows what might have happened if the facts had been prised out following the D-Notice affair in 1967.

While no effective damage to Anglo-American relations resulted from the D-Notice affair, because the American aspects of the issue did not become public, MI5 maintained that it had damaged British interests on two counts. Firstly, it had always been the British Government's policy to deny that it condoned the interception of foreign communications in peacetime, even though the Official Secrets Act had legalized it. Secondly, the cable-vetting had been providing useful information about the smaller foreign nations whose London embassies were using the cable facilities for intelligence communications. The main damage, however, was to the relationship between the media and Downing Street, which is believed to be important to the democratic process. Harold Wilson's petulant response alienated the entire Press for many months, and the lack of trust and mutual suspicion lingered for years. In so far as Britain's political adversaries relish any damage to her interests, the advantage went to them. There was a further long-term disadvantage to the truth – which is supposed to be one on the planks of democracy's foundations – the concocted White Paper and the Parliamentary Debate on the D-Notice affair. These misleading statements, which had been deliberately contrived and were made by back-bench M.P.s as well as Ministers, remain as the historic record and no official attempt has been made to correct them.

Cable-vetting has not been resumed in the U.S. but has continued unabated in Britain, with the British cables and telex messages remaining available for American scrutiny. Lohan and Ewart-Biggs are dead, the latter having been assassinated by the I.R.A. The published report of the Radcliffe Committee and its secret annexe remain as permanent records of how security issues are rarely what officials say they are.

The Potential Value of Oversight

While the efforts to suppress the cable-vetting report were understandable, in view of Whitehall's pathological concern for the secrecy surrounding G.C.H.Q. and because of the American dimension, it would seem unlikely that the security officials would have stooped to lies and other excesses had they known that their

461

activities might be subject to scrutiny at some later date by an independent oversight body. The officials, who included MI5's legal adviser, Bernard Hill, were convinced that nobody outside a small circle would ever know what they had done and were horrified when Lord Radcliffe, assisted by George Wigg, insisted on publishing the evidence.

Suppression could have been achieved in the national interest by a more honest approach to me or to my editor and, while no oversight body might have been capable of influencing the Prime Minister, who was determined to proceed in his own way, it would, at least, have been able to recommend against any such conspiracy of lies and subterfuge in the future. There is no evidence, in spite of the disastrous results they produced, that officials apportioned any blame to themselves or that the experience deterred them in any way from similar action in the future. It would also be reasonable to assume that senior civil servants would have been less merciless in their hounding of Colonel Lohan, at the behest of the Prime Minister, had they known that their actions, which were all taken in private, might be subject to independent criticism and even censure.

CHAPTER FORTY-SEVEN

Presents from Prague

LORD Wigg was to claim that his active personal oversight of the security situation 'built up the status and quality of MI5' and halted the serious run of security failures.[1] He may have had some effect, though MI5 officers resented what they called his 'interference', but he ignored what may have been a major factor in the sudden improvement – the fact that Hollis had retired. Such spy cases as did arise after he had left were almost all the result of treachery that had occurred, without impediment from the counter espionage efforts of MI5, during Hollis's reign.

The first case to come to public notice under Furnival Jones's leadership was in 1968 when an R.A.F. chief technician called Douglas Britten was seen by routine watchers delivering a message to the Soviet Consulate in London. He had been recruited by a Soviet Intelligence officer in London six years previously through his interest in 'ham' radio and had done most of his spying in Cyprus, where the damage he inflicted earned him a prison sentence of twenty-one years. Apart from being an important R.A.F. base, Cyprus housed one of Britain's main intercept and listening stations. Britten was a purely mercenary spy and when he tried to extricate himself he was blackmailed into continuing his treachery by being shown a photograph of himself receiving money from a recognizable Russian.

The severity of the sentence testified to the seriousness of the military damage caused by six years of continuous espionage without incurring suspicion. While Britten co-operated to the extent of revealing his Soviet sources and their methods, there was no opportunity to use him to feed disinformation to the Russians.

The Security Commission, which investigated Britten's case, called him an accomplished liar and raised doubts about the date of his recruitment, which might have been earlier.[2] Its report made no recommendations and no indictments. While the Security Commission is a standing body, it remains passive until required to act following a security breach. An on-going oversight body, with

463

accumulating expertise, might have paid more attention to the situation in the Soviet Embassy where, in 1968, the number of alleged career diplomats had risen to an all-time high of eighty, compared with thirty-seven accredited British diplomats in Moscow. One of these 'diplomats' who returned to Moscow a few days after Britten was arrested, was Alexander Borisenko. He had been listed as 'First Secretary in the Cultural Department' and had been the spy's controller after his return from Cyprus in 1966, though it is unlikely that Britten was his only source. Nothing was to be done about this blatant abuse of the diplomatic privilege for a further three years.

While it had long been known that several Members of Parliament had been recruited to the Soviet service, at least as agents of influence, none had been prosecuted, usually for lack of evidence which could be brought into court but mainly because of the reluctance of governments to tarnish the reputation of Parliament. The capability of M.P.s to serve as Soviet agents had been greatly enhanced in 1964 when, shortly after becoming Prime Minister, Harold Wilson introduced measures which made it almost impossible for the security authorities to produce any evidence against them. According to information supplied to me by the late Lord Wigg, both he and Wilson were convinced that Tories, who were enraged about their part in the Profumo case, would do all they could to exact revenge, preferably by finding a security case involving a Labour minister or M.P. Wigg was appointed Paymaster-General, a sinecure post, and was given the special task of liaising with MI5 and other security departments, ostensibly to strengthen security measures. He was, in fact, a one-man oversight body, but only for the Prime Minister, and his main function was to give Wilson the earliest possible warning of any imminent security scandals so that they could be eliminated, if possible. Failing that, the Prime Minister would be able to assure Parliament that he had not been ignorant of the position, as Macmillan had been with Profumo.

As an additional safeguard, Wilson, who had been shocked by MI5's treatment of the War Minister, called Hollis in to see him and told him that he must seek his personal approval before making any investigations involving any member of either the Commons or the Lords. Hollis was told that this meant that MI5 was forbidden to carry out any form of surveillance of any M.P. or peer without his permission. This included telephone tapping, the opening of letters, examination of bank accounts and the other routine procedures applied to suspects. Wilson also told Hollis that he would be unlikely to accept the evidence of defectors as a basis for any investigations of M.P.s and peers. These restrictions, which were partly conditioned by Wilson's belief that MI5 was anti-Labour and over-zealous to identify any left-wing Labour Parliamentarian as pro-communist, were confirmed to Hollis in writing and made known to the MI5 staff. Parliament, however, was not told about them until 1966 when Labour M.P.s who suspected that their telephones were being tapped were told, by the Prime Minister, about their immunity to such surveillance. Tory M.P.s objected on the grounds that no citizen who might become suspect should enjoy such protection, but the situation remains unchanged.[3]

There was considerable surprise, therefore, in April 1970 when a long-serving Labour M.P. called Will Owen was charged under the Official Secrets Act of betraying defence secrets to Soviet bloc intelligence, especially when it became known that the information about him had come from yet another chance defector to the U.S.[4]

Owen, then aged sixty-nine, had been Labour M.P. for Morpeth since 1954 and had been recruited by Czech Intelligence in 1957, being given the code-name 'Lee'. He was a mercenary spy, being paid £500 a month as a retainer with additional payments for special information and free holidays in Czechoslovakia, which he justified through his position as secretary of an East-West trade committee. According to Josef Frolik, a senior Czech Intelligence officer who defected to the C.I.A. in July 1969, Owen had met his Czech controller in London parks almost weekly for thirteen years without detection. It was MI5's responsibility to counter Soviet bloc agents, such as Owen's controllers, and it had failed before M.P.s were given special protection. During that time Hollis had been Director-General but his successors also failed to detect Owen's treachery until alerted to it by Frolik, who had served on the British desk at Czech Intelligence headquarters in Prague from 1960 to 1964 and then in London itself until 1966.

Frolik alleged that Owen had provided secret information especially after February 1960 when he had become a member of the House of Commons Defence Estimates Committee. The Prime Minister therefore gave permission for Owen to be questioned. He denied having received any money from the Czechs. When examination of his bank accounts showed that he had received large sums which he had never declared for tax he admitted lying and resigned from Parliament. At his trial, however, it could not be proved that he had transmitted actual defence secrets, especially as Frolik's evidence was hearsay and therefore inadmissible, the files to which he referred being in Prague. Owen was therefore acquitted, to his great surprise and to the anger of the MI5 management who had been involved in yet another failed prosecution.

The MI5 investigators found that Owen had received much more money than he had admitted and were anxious to interrogate him further. He agreed to help them provided the Labour M.P., Leo Abse, could be present to safeguard him from further prosecution. Abse has since recorded how MI5 assured him of Owen's further immunity and how he listened while the former M.P. confessed to treachery for which he should have been imprisoned. As Abse, a psychologist, put it, 'Owen certainly did his best to rape his motherland.'[5]

Because of the acquittal M.P.s have since been required to withdraw Parliamentary statements that Owen was a spy, which he undoubtedly was.

Owen died, in only marginal dishonour, in 1980, aged eighty.

The Owen case was another scandalous instance of a spy who had operated unchecked for many years and was eventually detected only because of a chance defection to the U.S. His admissions, following his acquittal, established that he had inflicted considerable damage on the defence interests of Britain and N.A.T.O. and had talent-spotted other M.P.s with possible character weaknesses. His prosecution further blunted MI5's defences because it made them even more reluctant to press charges against any M.P. and it strengthened Wilson's claim that defector evidence was unreliable. In fact, Frolik's evidence proved to be entirely true, and the court's rejection of it, while proper under British law, infuriated him. He had been brought over from the U.S. for debriefing by MI5 prior to the case and when this collapsed he declined to be of further assistance for some time. He had told his debriefer that MI5 had almost certainly been penetrated in the 1960s and he undertook to say more about it later but changed his mind after the Owen débâcle.[6]

In the eyes of Soviet bloc intelligence the Owen case encouraged the view that Britain was soft on spies and that retribution need not follow exposure, as cases like those of Blunt and Long had already shown. Whether Owen would have been prosecuted had he been a minister remains a matter for wonder.

Oversight of the Owen case might have led to constructive inquiries about MI5's facilities and resources for keeping watch on Soviet bloc controllers who, in the Owen case, had as usual been professional intelligence officers posing as 'diplomats' in the Czech Embassy. MI5's likely excuse that its resources were overstretched could then have led to an effective examination of the numbers of

Soviet bloc intelligence officers in London, which were already too high under the Tories and had reached grotesque proportions under the six years of Labour Government.

Owen's behaviour should certainly have led to some examination of the fitness of backbench M.P.s to serve on Parliamentary committees with access to classified information but I can find no evidence that it did so.[7] The tendency was to regard Owen as a solitary rogue, but Frolik named several other M.P.s as Czech sources. They included Sir Barnet Stross, the former Labour M.P. for Stoke-on-Trent, code-named 'Gustav', who provided information about Labour Party policies while it was in opposition and about defence matters when it was in power. Others were Tom Driberg and John Stonehouse, a minister.

Inquiry by an oversight body into the circumstances which caused Wilson to agree to the investigation of Owen would have focused attention on the immunities to surveillance enjoyed by M.P.s and could, possibly, have led to their suspension on the grounds that they are inequitable and unsafe. Such immunities still exist being, to use a Whitehall phrase, 'set in concrete'.

MI5 had more success with the next spy exposed by Frolik, though again the circumstances were to cast further doubt on the efficiency of the counter-spy agency during Hollis's direction of it. In 1959 Czech Intelligence had recruited a thirty-year-old R.A.F. technician called Nicholas Prager during a visit he had made to Prague, where he had been born in 1928. He was the son of a Czech clerk who, after working for many years in the British Consulate there, had managed to acquire British citizenship and retired to Britain in 1948. According to Frolik's evidence, the father had worked for Czech Intelligence inside the Consulate and his son was also prepared to betray the country of his adoption, for he claimed British nationality through his father, joining him in England in 1949 and entering the R.A.F. Nicholas Prager, who was a committed communist but also spied for money, was highly productive because he was knowledgeable about the V-bomber force, which was Britain's main nuclear deterrent, and in particular had access to highly secret research on radar-jamming devices, which he passed to the Czechs, inflicting serious and expensive damage on Britain's defences. Since British defence chiefs were unaware that the Russians knew the technicalities of the V-bomber force's anti-jamming devices, Britain's power to deter a Soviet attack was correspondingly reduced at critical times, such as the Cuban missile crisis, when the V-force was readied for action. After leaving the R.A.F. in 1961 Prager joined English Electric, which was working on secret defence projects.[8]

For more than ten years Prager worked for the Czechs, meeting controllers regularly in London at Underground stations and elsewhere. He was never detected, even when he visited the Czech Embassy itself with a briefcase full of photographs of two secret devices known as Blue Diver and Red Steer, which he had taken with a polaroid camera provided by the Czechs. It is unlikely that he would ever have been exposed but for information provided by Frolik and another Czech defector, Frantisek August, who had been one of his London controllers, posing as the 'visa officer' at the Embassy from 1961 to 1963.[9]

When Prager's home was searched early in 1971 one-time cipher pads were discovered but all the charges related to the late 1950s and early 1960s. He was sentenced to twelve years' imprisonment and died in 1981 when attention was drawn to the disparity of his treatment and that accorded to Blunt and Long who had committed far graver offences. After serving his sentence, Prager was under continuous threat of deportation.[10]

The Prager case provided further evidence that, at least during Hollis's reign as Director-General, MI5 had been ineffective in curbing the activities of Soviet bloc controllers and recruiters, who operated freely in London. As already pointed out, MI5's watcher operations were being continuously thwarted in circumstances strongly suggesting that Soviet bloc intelligence in London was being informed of their programme from some traitorous source. An oversight body could have satisfied itself that enough was being done inside MI5 to rectify these serious problems.

The details of the case revealed appalling inadequacies in the vetting process. Prager had lied on his application form to join the R.A.F., claiming that he had been born in Britain and that his father was also British-born. These lies had been transcribed without check onto his positive vetting form. No inquiries were made into his Czech-born wife, who in fact was an ardent communist.[11]

An oversight body would surely have added the case to its list of those in which traitors had been detected only because of information provided to MI5 by a defector to the U.S., underlining the lack of such defectors to MI5, which could have been a matter for constructive concern. As stated, Frolik claimed that he believed MI5 to be penetrated, but little seems to have been done to follow up that most serious suggestion.

Frolik also gave a lead to a Labour M.P. who had been working for

468

Czech Intelligence and was known to him only by the code-name 'Crocodile'. He turned out to be Tom Driberg, the former MI5 agent inside the Communist Party who had moved increasingly to the left and become a double agent. When shown a spread of photographs by MI5, Frolik picked out Driberg and recalled that the Czech Intelligence mission in London had been censured by the K.G.B. for dealing with him because he was 'their man'. When questioned, Driberg admitted that he had sold the Czechs information about internal Labour Party matters, including details of the private lives of M.P.s who might be suborned. He said that he had known his Czech controller only as 'Vaclav'.[12]

Driberg had been dropped as an MI5 agent some time previously but was taken up again following Frolik's information in the hope of using him to supply disinformation to the Czechs.[13]

Driberg's triple act in spying for MI5, the K.G.B. and Czech Intelligence is so complex, with much of it still secret, that it is difficult to know which side had the advantage. He was undoubtedly valuable in his pre-war and wartime activities as 'M8' but appears to have moved towards the K.G.B. after his visit to Moscow in 1956 to see Burgess. He reported then to MI5 that the Russians had offered to pay him well for information about the Labour Party's internal proceedings and plans and, with Labour in opposition, the MI5 management, then led by Hollis, had no objection, provided he showed all his gleanings to them first. The K.G.B. provided him with two identical briefcases, bought in Britain, and when he handed one with his reports to his Soviet controller he was given the other containing his payment. MI5 had stipulated that the Soviet money should all be handed in but Driberg is believed to have kept a lot of it.[14]

An assessment made after the death of Driberg (then Lord Bradwell) in 1976 convinced MI5 that, since the war, the balance of advantage concerning his services almost certainly lay with the Soviet bloc.

It can reasonably be assumed that an oversight body, and particularly one with any Parliamentary representation, would have been astonished, and probably perturbed, to discover that an M.P. was being used as an active agent to spy on his own party and, with MI5 connivance, to pass information about it to the K.G.B., especially when it might be used to suborn other M.P.s. It might also be assumed that such a body would have required action to put an end to the situation, action which, surely, would have been in the public interest. The judgement of a Director-General who permitted such an arrangement might also have been called into question.

469

If and when an oversight body is established, some consideration might be given to an arrangement whereby the committee which scrutinizes candidates being proposed for honours could have access to it. The award of a peerage to Driberg, a half-traitor and haunter of public lavatories, was a mockery of the honours system and an affront to the Lords.[15] Others who were later ennobled might also have been vetoed on security grounds.

The most provocative name of an alleged Czech agent among British M.P.s supplied by the two Czech defectors, Frolik and August, was that of John Stonehouse, a former Labour minister in the Aviation and Technology Ministries and, later, Postmaster-General and Minister of Posts and Telecommunications. It was claimed that Stonehouse had been recruited by sexual entrapment and subsequent blackmail threats while visiting Czechoslovakia. In return he was alleged to have supplied Soviet bloc intelligence not only with aviation secrets but counter-intelligence material.[16]

No suspicion whatever had attached to Stonehouse, who entered Parliament in 1957, until the debriefing of the defectors, of whom August claimed to be the most important witness. MI5 had been reading G.C.H.Q. intercepts of Czech Intelligence messages and the presence of code-names indicated the existence of British agents working for it but efforts to link Stonehouse with any of them failed and neither Frolik nor August was able to supply hard evidence which, they claimed, existed in documents in the Czech secret service archives in Prague. No further action could be taken against Stonehouse, who was still Minister of Posts and Telecommunications, because of the Wilson ban on surveillance of M.P.s. Wilson was horrified when told of the suspicions, and being sceptical of statements by defectors, who might manufacture material to improve their value, MI5 was forbidden to carry out a hostile interrogation of the suspect. Instead, Wilson called Stonehouse to Number .10 Downing Street and in his presence the suspect was questioned by an MI5 officer. Stonehouse vigorously denied the allegations. In the absence of hard evidence from MI5, Wilson accepted Stonehouse's word and the matter was kept secret until 1974. By that time Stonehouse had faked his death by suicide to escape from serious business problems and Frolik's evidence against him was published in American newspapers as being, possibly, behind the disappearance. Wilson therefore decided to make a statement to Parliament.[17] On 17 December 1974 he announced that MI5 had advised him that there was no evidence to support the defectors' allegations.

470

Stonehouse later reappeared under an assumed name in Australia and was repatriated to Britain where he was sentenced to seven years' imprisonment in 1976 on theft and fraud charges.

Since his release he has begun a new career as a novelist and when I lunched with him in 1983 he suggested that we should write a joint book after interviewing Frolik in the U.S.!

Statements made by August and Frolik to official committees in the U.S. and published there did further harm to American trust in British security, especially when coupled with Stonehouse's reappearance and disgrace. Doubts created in the minds of Parliament and the public, in spite of Wilson's clearance of the former minister, further damaged the image and integrity of Parliament.

When M.P.s urged the Prime Minister to request the security Commission to investigate the Stonehouse affair and report to Parliament, nothing was done. Examination of the incident by an oversight body could have reassured Parliament while at the same time taking a critical look at the extent to which the limitations on inquiries into M.P.s had affected it. Both Frolik and August were to express their anger at the way their information had been treated. An oversight body could have satisfied itself on the extent to which Wilson's statement that there was no evidence referred to evidence that could be brought into a court, as opposed to intelligence evidence.

During his debriefings by the C.I.A. and by MI5 Frolik named several British trade union leaders as having been helpful to Soviet bloc intelligence and later went into some detail about these on a tape-recording, of which I possess a copy.[18] On this and other evidence, Stephen Hastings, then Tory M.P. for Mid-Bedfordshire, raised the matter in Parliament in December 1977 and mentioned certain names. He called for an inquiry, preferably in public, but again the attempt came to nothing.

The penetration of the British trade unions by communists and Soviet bloc intelligence is an integral part of the 'long march through the institutions' to secure communist control in Britain in the absence of any possibility of achieving that by democratic means. MI5 was not allowed to develop Frolik's evidence concerning the subversion of trade union leaders, actual and attempted, because of the embarrassment factor. An oversight body might have caused a more robust action to be taken or at least seen to it that the leads were properly pursued and the results made known to successive prime ministers.

It was Frolik and August who revealed the treachery of Karel Zbytek, the filing clerk who betrayed the operations of the MI6-financed Czech Intelligence Office in London, which is covered in

Chapter 25. They revealed a great deal more about the extent to which Czech espionage and subversion had continued, virtually unchecked, during the late 1950s and early 1960s. Some of it is on record in U.S. Senate and Congressional hearings, such as August's statement that during the recurring Berlin crises he assisted in preparing a list of British counter-intelligence facilities and individuals to be liquidated in the event of an invasion of Britain. Much of it was deleted from the published American reports, however, to spare Whitehall and Westminster embarrassment. The deletions included a clear lead to a former Board of Trade official alleged to have supplied the Russians with information which enabled them to secure better deals to the detriment of Britain's interests. This man later achieved a most important position in Whitehall and was subjected to investigations which came to no conclusion.[19]

After withholding information for a while because he was angered by the dismissal of his evidence against Owen and Stonehouse as 'hearsay', Frolik did eventually give MI5 the evidence for his firm belief that that agency was penetrated by a Soviet agent. In October 1965, a Soviet bloc intelligence officer, a Hungarian called Major Lazlo Szabo who was posing as a diplomat in the London Embassy, had defected.[20] Though he defected in London he chose to go to the C.I.A., which he achieved by walking into the American Embassy. MI5 was given the opportunity to debrief him, once he was safely out of Britain, because he said that he had been specially trained in Moscow to penetrate a British department, which has not been named. Frolik claimed that 'within days of Szabo's debriefing by MI5, the K.G.B. had a full account of it', the inference being that it could only have come from an MI5 source.[21] The incident had occurred during the last month of Hollis's tenure of office, so, if he was the source of the leak, it would have been his last service to Soviet Intelligence.

Successive governments have responded to Parliamentary requests for inquiries into the extent of Czech penetrations by attempting to undermine the credibility of the defectors' evidence and in this they have been assisted by the 'liberal' Press. In all Western countries there seems to be an ingrained dislike of defectors, who are traitors to their own countries, and this hostile attitude has been reinforced by the writings of left-wing journalists who deplore their disservice to the Soviet Union. Gouzenko, for instance, has been accused in Canada of being partly responsible for the Cold War, when all the aggression in that respect had come from the G.R.U. activities which he exposed. My researches suggest that much of the dislike

472

and disparagement originates in the security and intelligence services which have to deal with the consequences of defections. Their disclosures inevitably rebound to the discredit of the Service when a defector gives leads to spies who should have been detected years previously. Gouzenko, for instance, has not been forgiven by the R.C.M.P. for providing evidence about twenty Canadian spies.[22] Frolik's naming of British Labour M.P.s and trade union leaders was derided by Labour governments for reasons which are obvious.[23] By a similar token, Golitsin's lead to Philby was not welcome to the Conservative Government, which had cleared him in Parliament. In the mid-1960s Golitsin also became unpopular, and even suspect in the U.S., for reasons which had originated in MI5 in a way which has not, I believe, been explained before.

MI5 had been so impressed with the information and advice it had received from Golitsin that it paid him $100,000, then worth about £50,000, for his services up to and including his visit to London.[24] Before his unfortunate flight, MI5 officers had sounded him out on a number of minor mysteries to see if he could help solve them. The first, and most intriguing, of these concerned the death of Hugh Gaitskell, the right-wing Labour Party leader who was succeeded by Harold Wilson, who was then believed to be of the left.

On 4 December 1962 Gaitskell, then aged fifty-six, returned to London from Paris where he had made a speech about Britain's entry into the Common Market. He felt unwell, complaining of rheumatic pains, but worked on until the 14th when he was admitted to the Manor House Hospital in Hampstead and found to be suffering from virus pneumonia. He was discharged, after treatment, on 23 December and his doctor pronounced him fit enough to accept an invitation from Khrushchev to visit Moscow.[25] To obtain his visa Gaitskell had been required to visit the Soviet Consulate and, though he had gone there by appointment, he had been kept waiting for half an hour and had been given coffee and biscuits. That same evening he suffered what appeared to be a relapse.

On 4 January he entered the Middlesex Hospital and died there on the 18th. The cause of death was given on his death certificate as pulmonary oedema (fluid in the lungs), carditis (inflammation of the heart), and renal failure (failure of the kidneys). The disease responsible for these fatal symptoms was diagnosed as being, not virus pneumonia, but a condition called systemic lupus erythematosus, a rare complaint caused by the victim's own antibodies.

One of the doctors who treated him was so puzzled by the fact that the disease is not only comparatively rare in temperate zones but is particularly so in males over forty, that he contacted MI5. It transpired that Gaitskell himself may have had suspicions because he had told the doctor about the coffee and biscuits. Accordingly a scientific security officer was sent down to the Microbiological Research Establishment and then to the Chemical Defence Establishment, which are both at Porton on Salisbury Plain. The visits were negative because nobody could offer any information suggesting that the Russians knew how to induce the disease.

When Golitsin was presented with this information for comment he said that he remembered something very relevant. Shortly before defecting he had heard from the chief of the Northern European section of the K.G.B. that the organization was planning to murder a leader of an opposition party in his area. The MI5 officers did not take this too seriously, suspecting that Golitsin might be stretching the truth to enhance his status and his earnings.

On his arrival back in the U.S. Golitsin gave this same information to Angleton, as though it was something he had just remembered, and it seemed so far-fetched that it was to cast doubt in the minds of other C.I.A. officers concerning his general credibility. Angleton, however, took the information seriously and commissioned a thorough search of all the published medical literature on systemic lupus erythematosus and came up with the intriguing information that Soviet medical researchers had published three academic papers describing how they had produced a chemical substance which, when administered to animals, produced the fatal symptoms of the disease.[26] As Angleton, Golitsin and the MI5 officers were quick to realize, the demise of Gaitskell was the prime cause of the Labour Party's shift to the left and to moves which enabled communists to penetrate the party more deeply and more openly. Khrushchev's particular hatred of Gaitskell was to be recorded by the Polish defector, Major-General Jan Sejna, who wrote that the Soviet leader 'pronounced the name with disgust', remarking, 'If Communism were to triumph tomorrow Gaitskell would be the first to be shot outside the House of Parliament as a traitor to the working class.'[27]

Hollis showed no serious interest in the inquiries about Gaitskell but the view remaining in MI5 and in MI6 is that his death remains a mystery and that the possibility of K.G.B. involvement cannot be excluded.

The doubts about Golitsin's credibility following his return from Britain were intensified by a further development which had also arisen out of talks with MI5 officers. The decipherment of some wartime K.G.B. radio traffic had revealed the existence of a spy referred to as 'Agent 19', who had been present at some highly secret talks, code-named 'Trident', which had been held in Washington between British and American delegations led, respectively, by Churchill and Roosevelt. An MI5 officer had suggested to Golitsin, rather imprudently, that 'Agent 19' could be the distinguished American diplomat and former Governor of New York, Averill Harriman, who had also been U.S. Ambassador to Moscow. Golitsin gave this 'information' to the C.I.A. as though he had recalled it. As a result the C.I.A. mounted an operation, code-named 'Dinosaur', to investigate the 'suspect' and it was quickly shown that Harriman did not fit the details alleged by Golitsin.[20] The 'Dinosaur' farce did much to increase the influence of those in the C.I.A. who were beginning to be convinced that Golitsin was a fake defector.

Golitsin had already caused deep concern in the C.I.A. by alleging that a K.G.B. 'mole' had penetrated one of the agency's most sensitive departments – the Directorate for Plans. He was able to describe the American officer, knew the contents of some of the reports he claimed he had betrayed, and also knew that he had visited London on a certain date. A full inquiry produced no further evidence apart from confirming the London visit and this gave rise to a fear that Golitsin had been sent deliberately to spread suspicion in the agency, especially when, later, he alleged the existence of other C.I.A. 'moles'. Nevertheless, the C.I.A. management decided that so long as there was a doubt the benefit of it had to be given to the agency. The suspect officer was quietly dismissed.[29]

In a discursive way Golitsin's debriefers in London had discussed with him the possibility that the political split between the Soviet Union and China was a fake – part of a massive disinformation exercise to lull the West into believing that the enmity was real but which would be seen to be false when it suited the two communist powers to combine for an assault on the West. Golitsin also peddled this speculation as a concept of his own when he returned to Washington, attempting to back it up with evidence that he knew of K.G.B. officers still assisting China. He has since promoted this and other controversial theories in a book.[30]

Such follies were to lead to the formation of anti- and pro-Golitsin factions inside the C.I.A. with serious consequences for morale, which were to be reflected, later, in MI5 when supporters of Hollis took refuge in the false belief that the suspicions against him had been generated by Golitsin. An objective study of Golitsin's record, however, shows that, with respect to the evidence of his own experience inside the K.G.B., the 'assets' he yielded greatly outnumber the 'debits', which were due to later exaggerations and fantasies arising from his desire to prove that his information was not exhausted. Discussing Golitsin and other defectors over a dinner to mark his retirement as head of MI6, the late Sir Maurice Oldfield, a wine connoisseur, remarked to me that the first pressings from any defector almost always have the most body, while the third are always suspect.

It is the view of those MI5 officers who dealt with Golitsin, as it is of James Angleton and others of the C.I.A., that he was easily the most important defector since Gouzenko in alerting the Western powers to the scale of the effort being mounted against them by the K.G.B.[31] Unfortunately for Golitsin, as for Frolik and August, much of his information was unwelcome to those officers of security and intelligence agencies whose inefficiency or treachery it exposed.

I have been unable to establish whether or not the MI5 officers who had been unwittingly responsible for the fantasies which Golitsin took back to Washington have ever explained the truth about his 'debits'. The evidence suggests that they preferred to remain silent rather than admit to the C.I.A. that they had been the fount.

CHAPTER FORTY-EIGHT

The Interrogation of Sir Roger Hollis

By 1970 the activities of the Fluency Committee had swept several suspects out of MI6 following a re-examination of the Philby case. One of these was an officer who had had an affair with Lizi Philby and had failed to report it when Philby had defected. A senior member of the diplomatic service was also found to have been involved sexually with Lizi, and had also been very friendly with Philby himself, but he survived the suspicions and went on to become an ambassador. An MI6 agent who was a British subject resident in Sweden was also found to be a spy for the K.G.B., as already recorded, but nothing, beyond a damage assessment, could be done because under British law, he could not be extradited.[1]

Strong suspicion attached to a quite senior MI6 officer who waited until he retired and had received his retirement honour and then announced, with some gusto, that he had long been a practising homosexual and had denied being so when positively vetted. He taunted the security officials about their failure to discover his secret which should have been obvious from the man's lifestyle.[2]

Peculiarities in the professional behaviour of a quite senior MI5 officer of foreign origin led to his interrogation by a Fluency Committee member as a possible Soviet agent. Nothing could be proved but as he could not be positively cleared he was forcibly retired. When his full background was investigated it was realized that he should never have been recruited to MI5 because he had relatives behind the Iron Curtain who occasionally visited him in London.[3]

The removal of suspects from MI6 was unpopular with the remaining officers, even with Maurice Oldfield, the future chief, who believed it to be 'disruptive to the Service'.[4] Nevertheless it was decided in 1970 that the Fluency Committee's efforts warranted the setting up of a small but permanent section inside MI5, to be called K7, with the full-time function of investigating and analysing possible penetrations of MI5, MI6 and G.C.H.Q. It was not, however, *tasked* with the responsibility for preventing them through anti-penetration operations and moved only when leads were passed to it. Unless there has been a very recent change that is still the situation.[5] Under the new arrangements MI6 and G.C.H.Q. were to remain responsible for their own security but MI5 was to have right of access to MI6 files for the first time.

The chairman of the Fluency Committee recommended that no former members of the Committee should be included on the staff of K7 who would then be able to re-examine the evidence of past penetrations without prejudice and with new eyes. He was particularly keen to counter internal criticisms that some of the investigators had become 'too emotional' about penetrations.

From its inception it was also agreed that K7 should work on the principle that the benefit of any grave doubt should always be given to the interest of the Service concerned and not to the individual under suspicion. If a case against an individual could not be proved but, nevertheless, looked black, he should be removed as a safeguard by some contrived means such as premature retirement or transfer to employment depriving him of access to sensitive information.

On re-examining the evidence compiled by the Fluency Committee, the small group of K7 officers was quickly convinced that there had been substantial penetration. It could be argued that there had been a succession of different spies but that seemed unlikely. After all possible allowances had been made for the activities of the known spies, like Blunt, Philby and Blake, there was a mass of evidence of penetrations which could not possibly be attributed to them, for the leakages and the case-deaths had continued long after they had ceased to have access to secrets. The officers found it hard to avoid the belief that, throughout those damaging events, there had been a single guiding hand. To whom did it belong?

They re-examined the Mitchell case, listening to the tapes of his interrogation, and agreed with the clearance given by the majority of the Fluency Committee. They then turned to the Hollis case and it was soon agreed that it was strong enough for a hostile interrogation of the former Director-General, especially as the penetrations appeared to have ceased after his retirement. For this it was necessary to secure the agreement of the new Director-General, Sir Martin Furnival Jones. As expected, he hated the thought of dragging from retirement in Somerset the man who had recommended him as his successor, especially when he knew that there was no intention, anywhere in MI5, of pressing for the prosecution of Hollis, whatever he might confess. Even the most forceful members of the Fluency Committee had convinced them-

THE TOO INCREDIBLE ARM OF COINCIDENCE

In the early 1930s Hollis and Sonia were in Shangai and other Chinese cities simultaneously and had mutual communist friends.

Sonia was ordered to move from Switzerland to Oxford at exactly the time that Hollis was due to go there when MI5 was evacuated from London.

She secured lodgings close to where Hollis worked at Blenheim and then close to where he lived in Oxford.

Sonia's father, who was one of her agents, also secured an address and occasional lodging in Oxford.

In the autumn of 1942 Sonia moved nearer to Hollis's address in Oxford.

Any of Sonia's messages that were intercepted were passed to Hollis in MI5, where he held responsibility for ordering the location of her transmitter. It was never located.

Sonia was a G.R.U. officer sent to service a G.R.U. spy. If Hollis had been recruited in China it would have been on behalf of the G.R.U.

Sonia's brother was omitted from an MI5 list of communists considered dangerous and prepared by Hollis's department. He was allowed to operate as a spy and communist activist unhampered. Hollis was responsible for overseeing the subversive activities of such communists.

Serious mistakes by MI5 over the clearance of Fuchs enabled him to pass crucial atomic bomb secrets to Russia. Hollis's department was responsible for most of them.

The defector Gouzenko was interrogated in a most unsatisfactory manner by Hollis who did all he could to discredit his claim that there was a G.R.U. spy in MI5 called 'Elli'. The best fit for 'Elli' was Hollis.

Sonia's cover was blown by the defector, Foote, yet MI5's attempt to interrogate her was farcical. She was not put under surveillance and no attempt was made to interfere with her continuing espionage activities. Hollis was involved in the decisions.

When Hollis was sent to Australia, following code-breaks of K.G.B traffic to and from that country, the K.G.B. quickly changed the codes.

The Cambridge Ring of spies operated throughout the war without hindrance. Hollis was responsible for countering such agents.

The leak that Maclean was to be interrogated on the morning of 28 May 1951 almost certainly originated from an MI5 source in London. Hollis was one of the few who knew it.

While Hollis was Director-General cases fell apart with suspicious regularity and clear leads to traitors were never properly investigated.

The defector Golitsin gave a lead to a high-level Soviet agent in the Navy. Hollis frustrated all attempts to pursue it.

Philby was almost certainly forewarned that he was to be approached and interrogated in Beirut in January 1963. Hollis was one of the few who knew about it.

The way the Profumo affair was handled inflicted great damage on Britain's reputation and that of the Tory Government. Next to Profumo himself, Hollis was the key figure in the mis-management.

Blunt and Long were Soviet agents. Hollis did all he could to ensure that they could never be prosecuted and their immunity extended to anybody else they named as agents or assistants.

Blunt seems to have been warned about his exposure and the coming offer of immunity. Hollis is a possible source of that leak.

When there was strong suspicion that MI5's Deputy Director-General, Graham Mitchell, might be a Soviet agent Hollis would not allow him to be interrogated when he could have cleared himself.

Suspicions against Michael Hanley, a senior MI5 officer, were almost certainly planted by the K.G.B., which must have received details of his career from an inside MI5 source. Hollis was one of the only two with access to them.

Many Canadian cases against Soviet penetration collapsed because they seemed to have been betrayed. The culprit could have been in MI5 and Hollis had knowledge of almost all of them.

selves that the results of such a prosecution would be disastrous both for the Government and for the Service and would discourage others from confessing. At that stage, of course, there had been no publicity about the immunity offered to Philby and Ellis and granted to Blunt. 'The last thing we were after was retribution,' a member of the Fluency Committee has told me. 'We wanted a confession so that we could make a damage assessment and we would have pressed for immunity to prosecution had we thought it would help.'

Furnival Jones could not reject the urgent requirement of the independent section which he himself had created and, after accepting it, he called a meeting to discuss arrangements for it. He proposed to invite his old chief to headquarters at Leconfield House to talk to him privately before handing him over to John Day, head of the K7 inquiry, who was to do the interrogating. While appreciating Furnival Jones's embarrassment, K7 opposed his proposal on the grounds that the invitation to attend would be a warning to Hollis to take advice on what to do if, in fact, he was guilty. The investigating officers wanted to pick Hollis up from his home without warning and subject him to interrogation without delay. This view was supported by Michael Hanley, who had organized the setting up of K7 and who attended the meeting.

When Furnival Jones insisted that he must see Hollis first privately the officers suggested that as soon as Hollis had received the request to attend headquarters he should be placed under surveillance, with telephone and letter checks because, though he would, almost certainly, be out of touch with any Soviet controller after nearly five years' severance from secrets, he might still be able to re-establish contact and might then be caught doing so. The Director-General, understandably, was horrified at the suggestion because it would mean that so many more people, such as watchers, Post Office officials, bugging technicians, as well as the Home Secretary, would have to be told of the suspicions. He forbade surveillance of any kind. As a result, the K7 officers felt that the best opportunity for proving the 'Drat' case – panic contact with a Soviet controller – had been denied to them and, with so much warning, a professional with as much experience as Hollis would be very unlikely to confess. Their dissent from the Director-General's requirements was recorded in the 'Drat' file.

Furnival Jones wrote to Hollis asking him to attend MI5 headquarters on a day convenient to him. Several days later he received him in a friendly way in the privacy of his office saying that there were certain allegations which needed to be cleared up and which, he was confident, Hollis would easily do. This conversation was not recorded and no written report of it was provided to K7.

Hollis's agreement to submit to interrogation rather surprised the investigators because, in his position, he could have treated the request with contempt, as some of his supporters believe he should. They remembered, however, the standard advice of Soviet Intelligence under such circumstances – to admit nothing, deny everything but to keep talking to discover how much the interrogators know. It was thought that if Hollis was guilty he would realize that he might have been identified by some recent defector. In short, his readiness to undergo interrogation was not necessarily evidence of his innocence, as some apologists have contended, any more than it was in the case of Fuchs and Blake.

In a safe microphoned house in South Audley Street, John Day, whose suspicions that Hollis had been a long-term spy were very strong, led his subject first into the details of his early life and especially about his friendships with left-wingers like Maurice Richardson, Claud Cockburn and Tom Driberg, while Wright listened in through headphones. Hollis claimed to have had no political interests at Oxford and said that he must simply have forgotten to put a note about his friendship with Cockburn in the office files. As he had not been positively vetted there were no previous answers to statements about communist connections which they could check. It was noted that this situation appeared to have been contrived by Hollis through his failure to introduce positive vetting until immediately before his retirement.

When asked why he had left Oxford without taking a degree and why he had been so determined to go to China, Hollis explained that it was 'to get away from the Church and from the family'. While admitting that he had first earned his living in China by journalism he was not forthcoming about his work in that field, though quite keen to talk about his later employment with the British American Tobacco Company. He said that his friends and associates in China had been mainly journalists and others in the Press world, diplomats, members of B.A.T. and golfing enthusiasts.

He did not hold back on his known friendship with Agnes Smedley and admitted that he knew she was an ardent communist but denied that she or anyone else had tried to recruit him. When asked about Sorge, who was a journalist, he said he thought it probable that he had met him at various functions but could not remember him. He did not volunteer information about his friendship with Arthur Ewert, the senior communist revolutionary, and was not asked about it because his interrogators were not aware of it. It would seem unlikely that at the age of sixty-four, as he then was, Hollis would have forgotten such an outstanding character as Ewert and the MI5 officer's failure to follow up the Ewert lead, as already recorded, or leave mention of it in the records deprived the interrogator of a formidable weapon.

Similar deficiencies applied to Hollis's possible association with Sonia. Though Sonia's activities in the Oxford area, in connection with Fuchs and others, were on file, though virtually ignored, it appears that any link between her and Hollis through China, and Agnes Smedley in particular, was not appreciated at all. I can find no evidence that he was ever questioned about her, though I and others have previously assumed, or have been told, that he was and had denied knowing her.

The implications of Sonia's presence so near Woodstock, the location of MI5's wartime out-station, and later in Oxford, close by, were not appreciated either. So Hollis was never questioned about this remarkable coincidence or about any other part he might have played in ensuring that her transmitter was never located and in the ludicrous confrontation with her in 1947 when some action had become unavoidable. As a professional counter-intelligence officer who has studied the case put it to me, 'The gut issue of the Hollis case is the possible relationship with Sonia and the interrogators were not properly aware of it.' Had they been so, Hollis's interrogation would have been more searching and probably more hostile.

The failure to interrogate Hollis on the peculiar facts of the Sonia case meant that he was not questioned about her brother, Juergen, who has also escaped serious attention. This in turn meant that certain suggestive aspects of the Fuchs case were neglected as well.

According to a high-level C.I.A. source Hollis was friendly, while in Shanghai, with a 'particularly brutal recruiter for Soviet Intelligence', implying a person prepared to use threats and blackmail. An MI5 officer was also to refer to this 'brutal recruiter' though he might have heard of him from the same C.I.A. source. If this person existed, Hollis made no mention of him during his interrogation.

He was closely questioned about the visit he had made to Moscow on the Trans-Siberian Railway while serving in China and which he had occasionally mentioned to colleagues. The K7 interrogators, and others who have listened to the Hollis tapes and read the transcripts, feel certain that he told them that he had made this visit in 1936 on his final journey home from China, as this was the quickest way when he was ill. It has since transpired from letters, however, that he paid a visit to Moscow in the early autumn of 1934 on his way back to China after leave in Britain and that he made the final journey home via Canada.[6] The truth can be determined by those with current access to the MI5 records of his interrogation. If Hollis did say that he visited Moscow on his way home it could have been a device to cover his journey while in the middle of his stay in China, which intelligence officers might have interpreted as being more suspicious.

It is possible, though I have not been able to establish it, that a search of the Shanghai Municipal Police records had been made before the 1970 interrogation. If so, then it would seem that nothing against Hollis was found and this has been held as proving that he could not have been actively associated with communists. As I have stated, however, the records had, by that time, been thoroughly weeded.

Hollis was particularly reticent about his residence in Switzerland for treatment at a tuberculosis sanatorium, being so reluctant to speak of it that his son recently believed that his father had never been treated there.[7] In fact, there is little doubt that he was, though the place and date remain in question. As Sonia spent at least two years in Switzerland, and may have visited the country previously, that connection may possibly have been responsible for the reticence.

He was vague, claiming poor memory, about the whole period of his life soon after his return from China. There were letters and diaries which could have clarified the situation but he did not mention them. As he was in reasonable health his interrogators were puzzled by his inability to recall the address of the first house in London where he had lived after his first marriage. Inquiries showed that a former Oxford friend, called Archie Lyall, who had worked in MI6 and was well known in intelligence circles, had lived only four doors away. Yet Hollis denied that he had ever known that Lyall was a neighbour. Being a huge man, fat, flamboyant, moustachioed and very amiable, Lyall would have been difficult to miss. He had been a close friend of Burgess, and the interrogator felt Hollis was lying about Lyall – who had died in 1964, to the great sadness of his friends – in order to avoid a possible connection with Burgess.[8]

Hollis was particularly obscure about his reasons for being so determined to find employment in MI5 or, failing that, in MI6. He agreed that MI5 was the prime target for a Briton recruited by Soviet Intelligence but, rather lamely, suggested that he must have wanted to join because he thought the work would be interesting. The interrogators were working on the supposition that Hollis had been contacted by a Soviet controller on his return to London and had not only been given instructions but had been directed towards people who might help him. Without being told the names of people in MI5, or associated with it, Hollis would not have known who to cultivate, as he cultivated the major at the tennis club. It has been suggested that Hollis's wife had a relative in a secretarial capacity in MI5 but no such person was involved in the account of his recruitment to MI5 given to me by an MI5 officer intimately concerned with it and who claims to remember the details well.[9]

MI5's ignorance of Sonia's close conspiratorial links with Richard Sorge and other proven G.R.U. agents in China meant that Hollis was not questioned about 'Elli', the MI5 spy named by Gouzenko, in the context that he himself might have been that spy. Because of the certain knowledge that the Cambridge 'Ring of Five' had been recruited by the K.G.B., the K7 investigators had continued to work on the supposition that if Hollis was a spy he, too, had been operating for that agency. Hollis was simply asked why he had treated the 'Elli' allegations so dismissively in his report of his interview with Gouzenko. He replied that he could not recall the details and had simply taken the view that such a penetration of MI5 was impossible, an attitude, he pointed out, which had been taken by everybody else in the Service until the Blunt case.

As Chapter 52 will show, the investigators missed a major opportunity to grill Hollis deeply about highly suspicious discrepancies in his report on his Gouzenko interview because they had failed to take the precaution of consulting Gouzenko first. He was readily available in Canada, his memory was excellent and he had notes available for reference but no attempt had been made by MI5 to talk to him since Hollis's brief interview in 1946. My inquiries suggest that Hollis had told senior colleagues that he had seen Gouzenko several times, but Gouzenko denied this to me personally, as does Mrs Gouzenko today.[10]

Hollis was questioned about his relationship with Philby, especially in the light of remarks which Philby had made in his book *My Silent War*, published two years previously. He agreed with Philby's statement that the two of them had exchanged information about their investigations of Soviet and communist affairs 'without reserve on either side' but insisted that it was his duty to do just that with his MI6 colleague responsible for Soviet counter-espionage outside Britain. He assured his interrogators that, at that stage, he, like everyone else, had no suspicion that Philby was a Soviet spy and that Philby never gave him any indications to that effect.

Hollis could offer no explanations for the long series of case-deaths, the way the Russians always seemed to have been given advance warnings when their officers or agents were in trouble, or for the lack of successful defections to MI5. He was not questioned about similar events in the Canadian security service because any connection had not then been appreciated.

When asked about the marks in the locked drawer of the antique desk in Mitchell's office, which appeared to have contained a tape-recorder, Hollis admitted that only he and the investigating officer who opened the drawer knew of the intention to do so and, while agreeing that the photographs which had been taken of the marks in the dust suggested that something had been recently and hurriedly removed, he disclaimed all knowledge of any explanation.

Questioned about his dismissal of Martin from MI5 he claimed that he had been the ringleader of a 'Gestapo' intent on investigating every failure. This did not impress his chief interrogator, Day, who knew that it had been Martin who had been most consistently suspicious of Philby and Blunt and had been proved right in both cases.

Hollis was not asked to explain his nosiness about G.C.H.Q.'s secret information concerning the Petrov defection because the investigators did not know about it.

Hollis returned to Somerset after the first session of interrogation. Following further inquiries he was brought back to London for more questions but he never broke or showed any signs of doing so.

If he was guilty he would have been aware of his unassailability so long as he kept his nerve and declined to confess. As with Fuchs, Philby, Blake and Long the law was powerless without a confession and he, above all, would appreciate the stupidity of confessing anything.

He may have been assured that nobody outside a small circle in MI5 and MI6 was being informed of his position and, in any case, he could be confident that no government would put a former Director-General of MI5 on trial because it would be deemed to be 'against the national interest'. The effects on the continuing interchange of information with the U.S. could always be pleaded as an overriding consideration.

The possibility of offering Hollis immunity to prosecution in return for a confession, as had happened with Philby and Blunt, was not open to the interrogators. While they would have liked the option it would have meant an application to the Attorney-General and Director of Public Prosecutions for permission and Furnival Jones had insisted that nobody outside the secret departments was to be informed of the case. The interrogators were denied that weapon, and another which could have been applied in the Blunt case – threat of publicity. Hollis must have been aware of the total disinclination on the part of the MI5 management, and even of the hostile investigating officers, to take any action against him that would lead to publicity affecting the Service so seriously.

The total interrogation time was about ten hours – a short time for a case of such potential significance. The sessions were all recorded with other MI5 officers listening in to them and making notes of hesitancies and discrepancies.

Section K7 then began a detailed study of Hollis's responses, and lack of them, especially for the period 1936-8 when he might have been reactivated, and undertook various additional inquiries before making a formal report on the case to the MI5 management. Various witnesses were questioned including Hollis's first wife, who was asked about his early life and other personal matters, an inquiry which produced small result. I understand that Hollis's second wife was not questioned.

It would be easier for an MI5 officer to spy for a foreign power without his wife realizing it than for any other professional man. The sudden telephone call or assignation can always be attributed to line of duty as can the sealed lips about any peculiar event. Even a meeting with a Russian could be explained away as a duty contact with an agent or an attempt to secure a defection.[11]

In 1971, while K7's further deliberations were in progress, the possible danger of Hollis's illicit relationship while he had been in office was made public. One of his former friends, Commander Anthony Courtney, who had been defamed and professionally ruined by the K.G.B. exposure of a casual sexual adventure, claimed that Hollis had laid himself open to the possibility of K.G.B. blackmail.[12] My previous inquiries indicated that the blackmail danger was reduced because Hollis's mistress was a member of MI5 and because so many in high office knew of the relationship but Courtney's argument had some strength because ministers did not know of it and some of them might have considered it a cause for resignation had they been told of it, as might some M.P.s and members of the public.

The Potential Value of Oversight

It might be presumed that an effective oversight body might have been informed, or would have learned, of the suspicions against Hollis and of his interrogation. In that case, such an independent body might, reasonably, have been critical of the limitations imposed on the circumstances of the first interview. Indeed, such

486

limitations might not have been imposed at all had oversight been a possibility.

Hollis's lapses of memory, at the age of sixty-four, might have occasioned more curiosity than they appeared to do in the minds of the MI5 management and it might be imagined that his failure to introduce positive vetting would have called for more comment. It would also seem likely that an independent oversight body would have been less enthusiastic about shelving the case. If the great value of granting immunity to Blunt lay in the disclosures he was expected to make about his past activities and especially about his Soviet contacts, as successive governments have accepted, then it was even more important to pursue the Hollis case more resolutely because the suspicions attaching to him were more recent and, potentially, far more consequential. On the basis that the benefit of any doubt should be given to the Service, an oversight body might reasonably have required a thorough investigation into those officers whom Hollis might have recruited personally or whose entry he had supported.

CHAPTER FORTY-NINE

A Belated Purge

By 1970 the number of Soviet spies and subversive agents operating in and from London had reached such alarming proportions that the Foreign Secretary, Sir Alec Douglas-Home, and the Prime Minister, Edward Heath, were determined that it should be substantially reduced.[1] Over the preceding years the operation called Movements Analysis, which had been invented by James Bennett in Canada and imported and improved by MI5, had proved that more than 300 of the so-called diplomats, trade officials, cultural delegates and journalists sent to London by Moscow were active professional intelligence agents of the K.G.B. and G.R.U. This had been brought to the attention of the previous Prime Minister, Harold Wilson, by MI5's Director-General Furnival Jones, but no action had been taken. The Labour leaders were loath to take any steps which would disturb Anglo-Soviet relations and were supported by some Foreign Office officials and, to some extent, by MI6, which feared reprisals against the much smaller number of its agents making use of diplomatic immunity in Moscow.

Heath and Douglas-Home also wanted to avoid any public disturbance of Anglo-Soviet relations so the Soviet Foreign Secretary, Andrei Gromyko, was approached by Douglas-Home on a number of occasions and asked to take some action which would avoid damaging publicity.[2] Possibly Gromyko tried to secure some amelioration of the situation but nothing was done, his influence being far less than that of the K.G.B. chief, Yuri Andropov.

In the spring of 1970 MI5 recruited a K.G.B. officer who was to become its most important defector since the war. His name was Oleg Lyalin, a 34-year-old 'trade delegate' in the Soviet mission in Highgate and really a member of the K.G.B. assassination and subversion branch formerly known as Smersh.[3] A ban had been imposed on the use of sex by MI5 to recruit possible defectors but in Lyalin's case it had been ignored, without reference to the Home Office, as his potential was so great. MI5 had been watching

Lyalin's weaknesses and was in touch with his Soviet secretary, Irina Teplyakova, with whom he was having an affair, their respective spouses being in the U.S.S.R. Under her influence Lyalin had been recruited as that most important of all spies – an agent in place inside the adversary's intelligence service. He had been due to return to the Soviet Union and said that he was prepared to continue to serve MI5 there provided arrangements were made for the defection of himself and Irina, should he believe he had fallen under suspicion.

For six months he supplied most valuable information about K.G.B. operations in Britain to his MI5 case officer. He was able to confirm many of the names of the agents which had been deduced from Movements Analysis. It was his knowledge of what some of them were doing which spurred Douglas-Home and Heath into action. He confirmed the existence of subversion units in Britain tasked to commit sabotage in the event of a surprise attack by the Soviet Union. This included flooding the London Underground, blowing up the missile early-warning station at Fylingdales, North Yorkshire, V-bombers on quick-reaction pads and other military targets.[4] Then in the early hours of 31 August, Lyalin was picked up drunkenly driving his car. After being kept in a cell, following his refusal to undergo an alcohol test, he induced the police to alert MI5 and he and his girlfriend were taken to safety.[5] His usefulness as an agent in place therefore ended since he would be recalled to Moscow and probably dismissed from K.G.B. service. There was nothing, therefore, standing in the way of a public expulsion of the most dangerous of the agents on MI5's list and, as the Russians had not responded to Douglas-Home's warning, the Soviet Ambassador was called to see him at the Foreign Office. He was told that ninety Russians were to be declared *persona non grata* and that a further fifteen, who were out of Britain, mainly on leave in the Soviet Union, would not be permitted to return. In addition, the Kremlin would not be allowed to replace those being expelled.[6]

Furnival Jones had supplied the Foreign Secretary with details of the illegal activities of all 105, so that if the Ambassador questioned the expulsion of any of them reasons could immediately be supplied. The Ambassador was warned that if there were reprisals in Moscow Douglas-Home had a list of more Soviet agents who could be expelled. MI5 had provided him with more than 200 who could form a 'second strike'. Staggered by the unprecedented British action, the Kremlin's reprisals were minimal.

Lyalin was unable to name British traitors who had been recruited to the subversion units as he did not know them. Nor was he able to give any lead to the G.R.U. network which he knew to exist.[7] His leads led to the arrest of three of his agents, whose names he did know – two Greek Cypriots, sent to England by the K.G.B. and working under the cover of being tailors, and a civil servant, of Malayan origin, who was a clerk in the Greater London Council's motor licensing department. The clerk had access to the numbers of the surveillance vehicles used by MI5 and Special Branch. This had enabled the K.G.B. to detect counter-espionage operations.

Lyalin also told MI5 that one of Harold Wilson's personal friends, Lord Kagan, was on close terms with a senior K.G.B. officer, Richardas Vaygauskas, who was among those expelled. MI5 put Kagan under surveillance and witnessed meetings with Vaygauskas. In an interview with me Kagan confirmed his friendship with Vaygauskas but claimed that it was purely social. He agreed that Vaygauskas probably cultivated his friendship in the hope that he might use him as a source of information from Wilson but claims that the Russian never reached the point of suggesting that he should question the Prime Minister.[8]

Lyalin was not brought to trial for drunken driving because of the assassination danger. He underwent plastic surgery to change his features, insisted on earning his living – he spoke excellent English – and is believed to have settled to life in Britain.[9]

The fact that Lyalin served as an agent in place for six months and then successfully defected is excellent evidence that there was no spy at high level in MI5 in 1970–1. Several former MI5 officers are convinced that had he been contacted during Hollis's time he would never have survived.

The success with Lyalin was to lead to the long-overdue establishment of a properly organized defector programme to encourage Iron Curtain defections, especially of intelligence officers, something which Gouzenko had been advocating for more than twenty years.[10] Hollis's reluctance to encourage defectors as an active part of the counter-espionage effort was understandable if he was a spy. Defectors who might know about his activities or those of any other Soviet agent could hardly have been less welcome.

The Potential Value of Oversight

The mass expulsion was the most salutary action ever taken by the British Government – or possibly any other – against Soviet Intelligence. It reduced the number of spies and subversives at a stroke to a level with which MI5 could cope more readily. It showed the world the extent of the Soviet treachery at a time when the Kremlin was preaching détente. The size of the problem also publicized the extent to which it had been allowed to grow under both Labour and Tory administrations. The agents who were expelled, and many before them, had inflicted severe damage, much of which might have been prevented had their numbers been kept at a more reasonable level. The Heath Government was also tough enough to make it clear to the Kremlin that any more Russians expelled for spying could not be replaced, and this has enabled the total to be reduced still further, for the K.G.B. and G.R.U. have not lessened their total effort.[11]

An oversight body might have thought it prudent to find out exactly why the Russians had been allowed to play the 'numbers game' so effectively for so long, if only to ensure that it could not be repeated. They might have found that MI5 had made insufficient complaint during Hollis's time because he was so averse to causing embarrassment to the Foreign Secretary. A weak Director-General could always be a danger in such respects and a properly constituted oversight body might prevent damaging delays. An oversight body could also satisfy itself as to the extent to which warnings from MI5 had been ignored or side-tracked by Whitehall officials. If properly constituted, its own on-going records would assist it in such inquiries.

CHAPTER FIFTY

Operation Gridiron

THE collapse of so many Canadian operations against Soviet bloc espionage and subversion, coupled with the MI5 investigations of Mitchell and Hollis, induced the R.C.M.P officers involved with the Featherbed inquiries into Soviet subversion to fear that there might be a traitor within the R.C.M.P.'s own ranks. A special review of the files showed that one man in particular had been involved with the cases which had 'died' – James Bennett, the Welshman and former G.C.H.Q. officer who had been responsible for R.C.M.P. operations against both the K.G.B. and G.R.U. The top management agreed to a thorough investigation into Bennett but, first, he had to be moved out of counter-espionage work in a way which would not arouse his suspicions. This was achieved by promoting him to head the biggest section of the whole security organization.[1]

The search for the R.C.M.P. 'mole', with Bennett as prime suspect, was called Operation Gridiron and was to continue until 1972. The Featherbed team found that because of Bennett's previous employment with G.C.H.Q. there had been no real check on his background when he joined the R.C.M.P. When the British authorities were asked to supply details there was nothing on file either in G.C.H.Q. or MI5. To induce Bennett to give his own account of his early life, and possible communist connections, the R.C.M.P management decided to introduce positive vetting for everyone in the security service.[2] Just as Hollis had avoided the introduction of positive vetting into MI5 while insisting that other secret departments must be subject to it, so the R.C.M.P. chiefs had resisted it for themselves and their staff, in spite of recommendations by Bennett himself that it was essential.

Bennett was among the first to be positively vetted. He was forthcoming about his early life and working-class origins in Wales. Nothing incriminating was found. He identified a communist whom he had met while in the army in Egypt and it was on record that when he had learned that this man had become a major

492

involved with secret signals regiments he had reported him to MI5.

Meanwhile, at the R.C.M.P.'s request, MI5 had undertaken a backtrack into Bennett's early life and had reported that it could find no evidence of attraction to communism or any other factor which might have induced him to become a Soviet agent. His work at G.C.H.Q. had given no grounds for suspicion. Section K7 of MI5 had examined the possibility that Bennett might have been responsible for some of the British case-deaths but found that he had never been told anything about them while they were active. The flow of information about current counter-espionage cases had all been one way – from Ottawa to London. MI5 had always considered that the R.C.M.P. had not needed to know about British cases which had no Canadian interest but was always keen to know about Canadian cases in the hope that it might be able to assist.

The suspicion against Bennett caused concern in MI5 because he had been told about a new development in the analysis of foreign radio traffic and an investigation suggested that information about it might have leaked to Moscow, though, if so, it could have happened from MI5. If there had been a leak it had occurred while Hollis was Director-General.

Clearly Bennett, through his knowledge, could have betrayed some or all of the Canadian cases that collapsed but surveillance, the tapping of his telephone, the bugging of his house and the installation of a T.V. camera in his office produced no evidence of any treacherous activity. As there were no other major suspects the management would almost certainly have insisted on his being interrogated to round off the inquiry, but a contrived event made this imperative. As what is known in the jargon as a 'litmus test', Bennett had been told that the counter-espionage branch was arranging to meet a new Soviet defector in Montreal and had been shown a fake document to that effect. The area where the meeting was supposed to take place was covered by R.C.M.P. watchers on the look-out for any K.G.B. officer who might pass through in the hope of seeing the defector, who did not really exist. In the event, an official from the Soviet Consulate did pass through the area, suggesting that the Russians had been given information which could only have come from Bennett.

It was soon appreciated, however, that the plan to trap Bennett had been bungled. Russians were frequently passing through the centre of Montreal, where the defector had been supposed to appear, because there was a sizeable consulate there. The trap should have been set in some other city, like Toronto, to which any Russian would have had to make a special journey. Further, if

Bennett had been a Soviet agent the K.G.B. would have been so keen to protect him that it would never have sent a recognizable Russian into an area which was, clearly, going to be under surveillance if a defector had really been about to appear. At fifty-two Bennett seemed set for thirteen more years of service, with some advancement inside the R.C.M.P. provided his health, which was causing him some concern in the hard winters, did not deteriorate.

Nevertheless, it was decided that an interrogation of Bennett was necessary and this was begun on 13 March 1972 when the suspect was told that there were doubts about his loyalty. Bennett seemed genuinely amazed that he could be suspect but offered to co-operate fully and even insisted on being subjected to the polygraph, the so-called lie detector. He admitted to indiscretions in telling other members of the staff some matters which should have been withheld from them and had to correct some errors of memory but no evidence emerged supporting the suspicion that he had deliberately betrayed any cases.

Close surveillance over a long period had produced no evidence of any contact with Soviet Intelligence officers, communists or cut-outs. Nor had there been any suspicious movements suggesting visits to dead-letter boxes or any other means of clandestine communication. On the credit side there were events which argued overwhelmingly against the suspicion of Bennett. His move from G.C.H.Q. to Canada indicated that he could not have been a Soviet agent at that stage, in 1954. Moscow would never have allowed a spy in such a prime position to leave with no certainty of comparable employment in Canada. Throughout his career in the R.C.M.P. Bennett had warned, to the point of boredom, about the danger that the organization could be penetrated by Soviet bloc intelligence. He had pressed, repeatedly, for the introduction of positive vetting. He had been an important innovator, having invented Movements Analysis which, in the year previous to his interrogation, had resulted in the expulsion of 105 Soviet intelligence officers from Britain. Even more convincingly, he had been responsible for 'restraint procedures' such as the limitation of the number of Soviet diplomats in Canada, with the possibility that other countries might follow suit. He had secured closer liaison between the counter-espionage and counter-subversion branches of the R.C.M.P., with the introduction of on-going records of all contacts between Communist Party members and Soviet bloc officials, believing, quite rightly as it transpired, that the Russians were exploiting Canadian Communist Party officials. All this must have infuriated the K.G.B. and the G.R.U.

Further, no defector in any country had produced any evidence pointing to Bennett. Even Anatoli Golitsin, to whom Bennett had access in Washington and then in Ottawa, had not suggested that the K.G.B. had any source inside the R.C.M.P., though his leads to the extensive penetration of other secret services gave some impetus to the belief that there might be a 'mole' in the R.C.M.P. as well.

With the balance weighted so decidedly on Bennett's side it was concluded that he had not been an agent of Soviet Intelligence and he was told so by his chief interrogator. Nevertheless, the circumstances made it impossible for him to continue in R.C.M.P. employment. Too many of his colleagues had become aware of the suspicions against him. MI5, the C.I.A. and the F.B.I. had been told about Gridiron and, though eventually informed of the result, could not be expected to continue to exchange information as freely as before. Bennett had found the experience so searing that he decided to resolve the problem himself. After eighteen years of unstinting service he applied for a medical discharge on the genuine grounds that the Canadian winters had been proving increasingly inimical to his health. This was granted by a board that knew nothing about the security investigation. I have established to my satisfaction that this medical discharge and the modest pension which accompanied it were not in any way rigged as a means of hushing up the Bennett case. It was, in fact, concealed as much in Bennett's interest as in the R.C.M.P.'s but eventually leaked in ways which caused some people to believe that he had in fact been guilty. In 1977 the Canadian Parliament was assured that the R.C.M.P. was satisfied that there was 'no evidence that Mr Bennett was not a loyal and dedicated Canadian public servant'.[3] This, however, was so similar to the statement which had been given in the British Parliament on Philby's behalf that it did not carry conviction. As a result, Bennett, understandably, feels aggrieved, especially as the media interest in his case has pursued him to Australia, where he moved for health reasons and to be near his daughters. He has appealed to the British Prime Minister, Mrs Thatcher, to take a personal public statement attesting to his loyalty during his service with the British secret organizations, including G.C.H.Q., following adverse comments in the British media but without result.

Having examined the meagre evidence against Bennett produced both by the R.C.M.P. and by MI5 I am in no doubt that he was wrongly accused.

If Bennett was not the 'mole' who had betrayed the Canadian cases, who was? Nobody else inside the R.C.M.P. at that time fits the requirements. Details of all the cases had been made available

495

to MI5 on a regular basis by the liaison officers and through the frequent visits of officers like Peter Wright. Some had been given to MI6 and G.C.H.Q. but, at the relevant times, nobody in either agency who had access to the Canadian information ever fell under suspicion. Before the mid-1960s such information had not been given to the C.I.A. or F.B.I. so the leakages could not have originated there. MI5 therefore presents the likeliest location for the 'mole'. As already recorded, once Hollis had briefed the R.C.M.P. about the suspicions concerning Graham Mitchell, James Bennett had sent MI5 a list of Canadian case-deaths asking whether they could be attributed to that suspect. An investigation in MI5 then confirmed that the suspected leaks to Moscow could indeed have originated in MI5 and at high level. The possibility conformed to the fact that the source presumably did not know all the details of the cases concerned because the Russians did not seem to know them. Bennett, on the other hand, did know all the details.

When Mitchell was cleared the only remaining suspect in MI5 was Hollis but, by that time, the Fluency Committee had convinced itself that Bennett must be the culprit so far as the Canadian leaks were concerned. So no effort was made to link Hollis with the betrayals though through his long and close association with the R.C.M.P. he could, clearly, have been responsible. Hollis was not questioned about them at all during his interrogation.

When being interrogated Bennett did not suggest that Hollis or any other MI5 officer might have been the source of the Canadian leakages, which is much to his credit because he knew of the suspicions concerning both the former Director-General and his deputy, Mitchell. It is unlikely that the idea did not occur to him because the pattern of the probable betrayals in Ottawa was so similar to that in London, though on a smaller scale. If Hollis was a Soviet agent he would certainly have reported on Commonwealth cases to his controller when information came his way, especially if it concerned a defector who might endanger his own position. This has been appreciated in later examinations of the Canadian case-deaths. It has been realized that Hollis could have compromised Operations Keystone, Dew Worm, Apple Cider, Moby Dick and the Ranov case. Regarding Moby Dick, the Canadian investigator, John Sawatsky, who had had access to a great deal of R.C.M.P. information, has actually suggested that the operation could have been betrayed by Hollis or some other Soviet source inside MI5.[4] A prime R.C.M.P. source, who has assisted me, agrees with that possibility, insisting that, as the suspicions against Hollis remain unresolved, they cannot be ignored when the collapse of any Canadian case of which he had knowledge is being considered. He also appreciated that the R.C.M.P. should have paid closer attention to Gouzenko's allegation about the spy inside MI5 called 'Elli' and should have required some account from MI5 concerning the lack of action about it.

The details of a modest R.C.M.P. success in August 1961 support the suspicion that the leakages to Moscow about Canadian operations originated in London rather than in Ottawa. A distinguished Soviet scientist called Dr Mikhail Klochko, who was a member of a Soviet delegation, indicated that he wanted to defect and needed R.C.M.P. assistance because he feared that Soviet officials would forcibly restrain him if they heard of his intention. The decision and action which resulted in Klochko's successful defection had to be accomplished within a few hours, but there was time for a high-level 'mole' in the R.C.M.P. to have warned the Soviet Embassy but nobody did so. A 'mole' in London could not have received the information in time to take any action.

The collapse of an R.C.M.P. operation code-named Gold Dust, which did not start until after Hollis had retired, might suggest that the suspicions against him concerning previous Canadian cases were unwarranted, but a prime R.C.M.P. source is in no doubt that the case died because of an honest failure by the R.C.M.P. watchers. A G.R.U. agent-runner from the Soviet Embassy had suborned a young Canadian civil servant with access to Canada's mineral resources. The Russians dropped their contact suddenly in a way suggesting that they realized that the R.C.M.P. were aware of the situation, but the odds are that they had detected the surveillance team.

In Operation Deep Root, which began in 1968, the R.C.M.P. tried to secure the defection of a Soviet diplomat's wife who had been having a love affair with a Canadian. She was told that compromising photographs of her and her lover had been taken, with the hint that they might be shown to the Russians. After declining to be a traitor to her country she was put on a plane for Moscow under escort, indicating that the Soviet Embassy had discovered what had happened. As she had an eight-year-old daughter in Moscow and had no wish to live in the West, it seems probable that she confessed her indiscretion and that there had been no leak to the K.G.B.

A brief comparison of the Bennett and Hollis cases is instructive. No untoward evidence of communist association concerning Bennett has been found. Hollis had highly persuasive communist friends when he was in China. While Bennett joined G.C.H.Q. as a natural continuation of his war service, which had fortuitously brought him into contact with Signals Intelligence, Hollis sought entry to MI5 with no previous experience or overt reason, apart from the fact that he was unemployed.

There was no defector evidence against Bennett. At least four defectors, Gouzenko in particular, supplied information which pointed to Hollis. No Soviet agent-runner who might have served Bennett was ever found. The circumstantial evidence that Sonia may have served Hollis is very strong. Bennett repeatedly pressed for the introduction of positive vetting into the R.C.M.P., while Hollis delayed its introduction into MI5 until his own retirement.

As a matter of routine security, Bennett consistently warned that the R.C.M.P. might be penetrated by Soviet agents and strongly supported the Featherbed investigation into possible leakages. Hollis, on the other hand, ridiculed the concept of the penetration of MI5 and, until his hand was forced, prevented internal inquiries on the grounds that they would damage morale.

While Hollis repeatedly prevented the interrogation of suspects, Bennett was in favour of it.

Bennett was the innovator of several ingenious counter-espionage methods which were adopted by MI5 and other agencies, inflicting great damage on Soviet bloc intelligence. Hollis did nothing comparable.

Bennett campaigned effectively against the bloated size of the Soviet Embassy, Consulate and other agencies abused by Soviet Intelligence. Hollis did not.

When Bennett was under suspicion he was given the full treatment – physical surveillance, telephone and letter checks and electronic eavesdropping. Hollis, by contrast, was immunized from such precautions by his position.

Bennett's interrogation was sudden, extensive and hostile. Hollis was gently warned of his position and his interrogation was brief and relatively comfortable.

Finally, while the British Prime Minister went out of her way to give the impression that Hollis had been cleared, when his case became public, no comparable high-level effort was made by the Canadian authorities on Bennett's behalf. The R.C.M.P. seems to be treating the Bennett case in the same way that MI5 continues to treat the case against Hollis – it prefers to ignore any new evidence rather than resurrect an episode fraught with embarrassment both for the agency and the Government.

The investigation and interrogation of James Bennett resulted in the removal of a most able counter-espionage officer with no consequent advantages to Western security. The benefit to the K.G.B. and the G.R.U. would seem to have been so substantial that it has been suggested that the suspicions against him were the result of a deliberate K.G.B. operation to discredit him. I can find no evidence to support this, however, beyond the undoubted fact that Soviet Intelligence was, and still is, active in the use of any kind of smear to discredit Western Intelligence services and their officers, especially those of senior grade. In this context it has been widely suggested, but again without any evidence whatsoever, that the suspicions against Hollis were also planted by Soviet Intelligence. The origins of the case against Hollis, as presented in this book from prime source information, were internal, within both MI5 and, later, MI6, and could be Soviet disinformation only if one or more of the officers concerned had been a Soviet agent. There is no evidence giving cause to question the integrity of any of those officers.

The Potential Value of Oversight

MI5 took such an interest in the investigation into Bennett that an officer was detailed to assist with it. As a result a running account of their progress was available to MI5. Had the reports been available to scrutiny by an oversight body their relevance to the case against Hollis might have been appreciated. Though the MI5 officers had realized that the Canadian case-deaths might be applicable to the Mitchell case, they appear to have become so convinced of Bennett's guilt by the time the Hollis case was at its height that they failed to see their applicability there. Independent minds might have taken a different view.

CHAPTER FIFTY-ONE

The First K7 Report

In its manifesto for the general election of 1970, the Conservative Party promised to eliminate unnecessary secrecy and to review the operation of the Official Secrets Act. A high-powered committee under Lord Franks was therefore set up in April 1971 to fulfil that undertaking, with particular respect to Section 2 of the Act which, to quote the Franks Report, 'catches people who have no thought of harming their country', Section 1 being specifically aimed at spies. The Franks Committee worked hard and conscientiously, taking evidence from many witnesses, including myself, and reported to the Home Secretary; its report was published in four volumes in September 1972.[1]

Throughout its hearings the Whitehall establishment, including the Director-General of MI5, Furnival Jones, the Attorney-General, and many high-level civil servants strove to prevent any change to the Act, while journalists and others outside Whitehall urged the abandonment of Section 2, which a judge had recently described as being in need of being 'pensioned off'.[2] The Franks Committee decided that there was 'an overwhelming case for change' and suggested that Section 1 should be renamed the Espionage Act, while Section 2 should be replaced by an Information Act, under which it would no longer be a crime for an unauthorized person to be merely in possession of official information.

I spoke to several senior civil servants who assured me that Whitehall could be trusted to defeat the Franks Report on the 'Kick-it-around-until-you-lose-it' principle. They were right. More than eleven years have passed since the Franks Committee reported and, while successive governments have promised action, nothing whatever has been done. The blanket Section 2 remains in force, and while governments have also paid lip service to the need for less secrecy and more open government, little has been accomplished in that direction either.

When Furnival Jones was making his strenuous plea for the continuation of penalties against unofficial people who reveal secrets regarded as official by officials, K7 was completing its first formal report on the Hollis case and submitted it early in 1972. It supported the Fluency Committee's finding that MI5 had almost certainly been seriously penetrated during the 1950s and early 1960s. It clearly stated that Hollis was the main suspect and, as with the Fluency Committee's conclusion, this was not a minority view, as has been suggested. The report also stated that there was no evidence of serious penetration since Hollis had retired. The success of the operation resulting in the 105 expulsions, coupled with the fact that a defector of Lyalin's importance had remained in place for six months, convinced the K7 officers that no mole could have been functioning inside MI5 during the relevant time because Soviet Intelligence would then have been forewarned.

Listing the credits and debits attributable to Hollis during his career produced a balance sheet firmly on the debit side. Even the alleged successes, such as the Vassall and Lonsdale cases, had important aspects suggesting a measure of control in the Soviet interest. Hollis had repeatedly avoided or actively prevented inquiries and interrogations which could have been damaging to Soviet Intelligence, particularly in connection with the possible Soviet penetration of British secret services. The officers asked themselves what harm had accrued to Soviet Intelligence as a result of any action which Hollis had not been forced to take by pressure of circumstances. The answer seemed to be 'Very little'. The pattern of his behaviour seemed to mirror that of Philby in MI6 in that when he could not prevent damage to the Soviet cause he minimized it.

It was the view of the Director-General, Furnival Jones, that it was 'a scandal' when any spy got through the defences and by that criterion MI5's record during Hollis's tenure of the leadership had been 'scandalous' indeed.

The major weakness of the K7 report, like that of the Fluency Committee's, was the failure to find any firm link between Hollis and communism before he had joined MI5, apart from his admitted friendship with Agnes Smedley. It was still not certain, as it is now, that Smedley had been a Soviet agent and recruiter. The friendship between Hollis and Ewert was unknown and, while appreciation of the possible connection with Sonia appears to have increased, MI5 research into it had been superficial. Inadequate investigations in the Oxford area had led MI5 officers to the false belief that Sonia's father had been based there because of his transfer to an Oxford college, which was erroneous. As a result the fact that she must have been posted to Oxford deliberately for some other purpose went unnoticed. The dates and circumstances

501

convinced the investigators that she had definitely not been sent to service Fuchs, who was an additional windfall for her, but at that stage they did not connect her posting with MI5's presence at Blenheim. A former MI5 Director-General has assured me that 'the Sonia case was investigated and found wanting', but in fact it has never been properly investigated and witnesses whose memories were then fairly fresh were never questioned.

The report was considered at length by the MI5 management, and by Furnival Jones and his deputy Anthony Simkins in particular. They declared themselves unimpressed by the criticisms of Hollis's report on Gouzenko concerning the allegations about 'Elli'. They took the charitable view that in 1945/46 the idea that MI5 had been penetrated was so inconceivable that Hollis was merely doing what he could to discredit Gouzenko's evidence because it was so outrageous. It was argued that Hollis had done nothing more devious than look for some other interpretation of the evidence. This was a repeat performance of the attitude of the MI6 management to the evidence against Philby in the period from 1951, when he was first suspected of being the 'Third Man'.

Wherever possible undeniable leakages, case-deaths and other failures were attributed to Philby, Blunt and Blake which reduced the need to acknowledge the existence of a further spy in the secret services. Blunt and Philby had ceased to have access to secrets or to influence operations in 1946 and 1951 respectively and the K7 evidence clearly indicated serious leakages and case-deaths in the 1950s and 1960s. If no spy existed in MI5 after the departure of Blunt then the K.G.B. must have been staggered by its run of fortuitous successes.

While the weight of the circumstantial evidence against Hollis was far greater than that mounted against Philby, K7's report was received with some relief by the MI5 management. In the absence of any firm evidence of communist connection, the management took the legalistic view that as none of the evidence would have been admissible in a British court of law Hollis should be given the benefit of all doubt, though his innocence could not be proved. Officially, the 'Drat' file was left open, since no unresolved case is ever formally closed, but the management decreed 'No more active investigation', so the case was shelved indefinitely for all practical purposes, with no further resources being allotted to it. In the minds of the management Hollis was judged not to have been a Soviet agent or to have been disloyal in any way. That was not the view taken by most of the officers who had been involved in the 'Drat' inquiries. To them the management seemed to be in breach of the K7 principle that the benefit of any doubt should be given to the Service and not to the individual. The breach was academic in the sense that Hollis was beyond any retribution because, in 1971, he had suffered a stroke. He made a good recovery from it, but with the fate of John Watkins, the Canadian Ambassador who died under interrogation, in their minds MI5 officers knew that they could not press for another round of questioning.

It was, perhaps, no coincidence that both Furnival Jones and Simkins had been trained as lawyers and in that context the words of R.H.S. Crossman, the Labour politician who had been involved with wartime security, are apposite: 'The essence of security is to make up one's mind without the evidence because if one waits for the evidence it is too late. Lawyers, because of their great regard for evidence, are not necessarily the right people to form opinions about spies...'[3] On that score they may not be the right people to run a security agency. In October 1981 Furnival Jones and Simkins were to go on record in *The Times* as claiming that 'there was not a shred of evidence that Sir Roger Hollis had been disloyal at any time or in any way'.[4] In fact, the circumstantial evidence was very weighty indeed and is far greater now. Would a former Director-General of MI5 have been recalled from retirement to undergo interrogation had there been not a shred of evidence?

This then was the extent of the 'clearance' of Hollis by MI5 to which Mrs Thatcher was to refer in Parliament on the advice supplied by MI5. The K7 officers and the members of the Fluency Committee were never formally told that Hollis had been 'cleared'. The view today of one of the most important officers concerned is, 'He was investigated, interrogated and he was not cleared.'

I can find no evidence that any K7 officer ever saw anything in writing to the effect that Hollis had been told that he had been 'cleared', but it must be assumed that he was. He could hardly have been left wondering for the rest of his brief life. Perhaps he was told verbally, for if any document exists it is surprising that the Hollis family have not produced it.

The MI5 management was determined that the Government and senior civil servants should never learn that Hollis had ever been under suspicion. Harold Wilson, the Prime Minister when the investigations were at their height, was told nothing. Neither was his MI5 watchdog, George Wigg. Edward Heath, who was premier when K7 reported its findings, was kept in ignorance. Wilson learned the facts on becoming Prime Minister again in 1974 only because of a fluke circumstance which I shall describe shortly.

Peter Wright and Arthur Martin have gone on public record as believing that the MI5 management made a serious error in closing the Hollis case and ending the search for the high-level spy who undoubtedly existed. I am now sufficiently convinced by the additional evidence presented in this book that Hollis was a Soviet agent to believe that MI5 is gambling with the nation's security in assuming that he was not. However reticent the Government may remain, MI5 should now operate on the principle that Hollis was a spy throughout his twenty-seven years in the Service, and take action on two main counts. First, whatever the cost in resources, it should examine the security and counter-intelligence foundations to find out how they might have been affected in the Soviet interest, especially during Hollis's nine years as Director-General and three years as Deputy. Second, it should take a close look at the background and behaviour of every officer whose recruitment was facilitated by Hollis, or was wholly due to him. In view of MI5's reluctance to admit its faults, even to itself, Parliament should require an assurance that these precautions are being put into effect.

The Potential Value of Oversight

The treatment of the K7 report by the MI5 management would seem to offer an excellent example of the value to security interests themselves of independent oversight of MI5's activities. As a former Director-General of MI5 has indicated in a document which is currently confidential but should eventually be published, there was a pronounced difference of opinion on the Hollis case inside MI5 and an oversight body might have required more convincing reasons for the effective shelving of it. A well-informed body would certainly have questioned the facile attribution of leakages and case-deaths to Philby and Blunt, with which Mrs Thatcher was later to be saddled.

CHAPTER FIFTY-TWO

The Second K7 Report

WHEN Sir Martin Furnival Jones retired at the end of April 1972 he had fair reason for believing that the Hollis case had been laid to eternal rest within MI5's most secret archives. His successor took a different view.

Furnival Jones's imminent retirement gave the Whitehall mandarins an opportunity to secure the post for one of its number, a move which would create a 'slot' for other Civil Service promotions. They proposed a candidate from the Home Office and when he proved to be unsuitable they put forward another who, for various reasons, was even less acceptable. Furnival Jones was recommending his deputy, Michael Hanley, but he had been in that appointment for only a few months and the mandarins were making the most of his lack of experience in that direction. But a former member of MI5, who had access to the Prime Minister Edward Heath, ensured Hanley's appointment by revealing that the Whitehall candidate had been a friend of both Maclean and Burgess, a situation holding the possibility of grave embarrassment if the newspapers found out about it.

Hanley, being more uncertain of Hollis's innocence than Furnival Jones, agreed that active investigation by K7 should be reactivated.

A re-examination of the evidence, with new material which had emerged from the further decoding of intercepts in Operations Bride and Farouche, drew closer attention to the significance of the apparent connection between Sonia and Hollis and, for the first time, it was realized that if Hollis had been recruited in China before the war, he would have been an agent of the G.R.U., not of the K.G.B., as previously assumed. In that light he seemed to be incomparably the best fit for 'Elli', so it was decided that Gouzenko should be questioned again concerning his recollection of his interrogation by Hollis, early in 1946.

Gouzenko told me that the British security man who came to see him by appointment at the Royal York Hotel in Toronto in the

505

summer of 1972 gave his name as Stewart, but it could have been Stuart.[1] There was an MI5 officer of that name serving in Washington and it was from that city that Gouzenko's visitor said he had travelled. 'Stewart' read from a report which, Gouzenko was told, was from the British security files and which purported to record what the defector had said when first interrogated by the British late in 1945 and early in 1946. Gouzenko was astonished to find that the report consisted of several closely typed pages when his interrogator had asked him so little. His amazement increased as 'Stewart' continued to read. As Gouzenko explained to me, 'The report was full of nonsense and lies. It is what we called in Russian "an old grey mare". For instance, he reported me as having told him that I knew, in 1945, that there was a spy working for Britain in a high-level Government office in the Kremlin. I knew no such thing and had said nothing like that. It was clear to me that the report had been faked to destroy my credibility so that my information about the spy in MI5 called "Elli" could be ignored. I also realized that what Stewart was doing was part of an investigation into whoever it was who had written that report. If the report was written by Hollis then there is no doubt that he was a spy. I suspect that Hollis himself was "Elli".'[2]

There is no doubt that it was Hollis who wrote the report and an MI5 officer who read it has told me that its contents were 'nonsense'. Further confirmation that the report which Hollis submitted to MI5 was very different from what he had been told has come from a former security officer of the R.C.M.P.

Continuing his account of the 'Stewart' interview, the occurrence of which has been confirmed to me by Mrs Gouzenko, who was present, and by an independent Canadian source, Gouzenko said, 'Every time I commented, "That's nonsense!" about some paragraph or other, Stewart said, "I'm glad to hear you say so." So he must have suspected that it was nonsense too.' This most significant statement has been confirmed by Mrs Gouzenko who recalls, 'My husband denied the report's validity, stating that it was a total fabrication.'[3]

One former MI5 officer has suggested that K7 was trying to determine how much of the report had come from Hollis's own interrogation of Gouzenko and how much he had included from information supplied to him by the Mounties who had questioned the defector. Others, less charitable, suspect that the report was a fabrication, like Philby's report on Volkov, prepared with assistance from a Soviet controller. In that case opportunity would have been taken to insert disinformation, not only to prevent full investigation of the 'Elli' allegation but for other purposes. In the context of that possibility, Hollis's false statement that Gouzenko had said that he knew that Britain had a high-level spy in the Kremlin could be of deep significance.

As stated in Chapter 39, Blunt had been instrumental in eliminating a senior Soviet official who had been operating on Britain's behalf in the Kremlin and was later to admit this in his confession. In early 1946 MI5 did not know how this loss had come about and was still interested in resolving it. It would therefore have been in the Soviet interest for MI5 to have been told by a prime source like Gouzenko that Soviet Intelligence knew about the existence of the spy at a date earlier than Blunt, or any other spy in MI5, could have known about him and been responsible for exposing him. Gouzenko could have learned about such a spy only while working in G.R.U. headquarters in Moscow between April 1942, when he arrived there, and June 1943 when he moved to Canada. This could have pre-dated the exposure of the Kremlin agent by Blunt.

The report read to Gouzenko by 'Stewart' could, therefore, have been a 'legend' worked out by the Moscow Centre and passed to Hollis as a draft. Hollis would simply have been instructed to insert this legend into the MI5 files. He would not necessarily have been told why and would almost certainly have been told nothing about Blunt.

In the following year, 1973, 'Stewart' returned to Toronto on an assignment even more puzzling to Gouzenko.[4] After explaining that he was visiting Canada on leave from Washington with his wife and child, he showed Gouzenko a spread of six photographs and asked him to pick out the person who had interrogated him. As some twenty-seven years had elapsed since his very brief encounter with Hollis, Gouzenko did not find this easy. He selected two possible photographs, which was the best he could do. This visit seemed to imply that the MI5 records in London were lacking in information as to the identity of the man responsible for the false report. When confirming this to me Gouzenko said, 'It seemed that the British were trying to establish the identity of the person who had interviewed me – as though they had no record of it. Perhaps someone had destroyed the record. It was all very odd and Stewart offered no explanation.'[5] In view of further developments concerning documents involving the Gouzenko defection this may not be as surprising as it seems.

When Canadian interest in the Gouzenko affair was resuscitated by the appearance of *Their Trade is Treachery* in March 1981, it became known that Canadian documents dealing with his interrogation and other matters were missing. Extensive searches failed to find records of a high-level committee set up to examine the ramifications of Gouzenko's revelations. The former Prime Minister, Mackenzie King, had kept scores of diaries during his lifetime and these had all been preserved in boxes. Only one was missing, and still is at the time of writing – the very volume dealing with his account of Gouzenko's interrogation by the R.C.M.P. and British Intelligence, the crucial period from 10 November to 31 December 1945. As Mr J. W. Pickersgill, a literary executor of the Mackenzie King estate, remarked, 'If there is one volume on which the Soviets would have liked to get their hands it is the missing volume.' Professor Jack Granatstein, the distinguished Canadian historian, has stated, 'It is pretty clear that someone has gone through a wide variety of files and removed much of the material.'[6]

When K7 summed up the results of 'Stewart's' interviews it seemed that Hollis had done all he could to prevent any action on Gouzenko's allegation about the spy called 'Elli' and had been highly successful. They did not, however, grasp the possible significance of the false statement that Gouzenko had claimed to know about a British spy in the Kremlin.

While the significance of Sonia to the Hollis case was appreciated for the first time, little, if any, effort was made to develop the lead. No field inquiries were made in the places where she had lived and nobody of consequence among her former neighbours was interviewed about her activities. Of course, much more has come to light about Sonia which was not then available to K7 but the possible association with Hollis in Shanghai should have rung much louder alarm bells than it did.

Nevertheless, the second report by K7 on the Hollis case was much stronger than the first and the question it posed was: if Hollis was not the culprit, who was? While it was a non-proven verdict it convinced most of the K7 officers and the former Fluency Committee of the folly of failing to pursue the case. At no stage did the Director-General, Sir Michael Hanley, indicate to anyone that Hollis had been cleared and the case was still a subject of discussion in 1976.

On 26 October 1973, just a little short of his sixty-eighth birthday, Hollis suffered a further stroke, which proved fatal. According to the death certificate he had been under treatment for high blood pressure.[7]

With consistent respect for security his widow listed his occupation as 'Civil servant – Executive Officer (retired)'.

His obituary notice in *The Times* was written by Sir Dick White, his old friend who had helped him to enter MI5, had consistently promoted him and had then been placed in the embarrassing

508

position of having to agree to his investigation. He recorded that Hollis had joined MI5 in 1936, but this was a mis-statement or a misprint for 1938. The obituary recorded that 'the hotter the climate of national security, the cooler he became'.[8]

There appears to have been no memorial service for Hollis, either in London or in Wells, though his funeral was well attended by former colleagues who continued to regard him as innocent or who, at that stage, had no knowledge of the suspicions against him.

His published will showed that he left £40,000 net, a sum considerable enough in 1974 to warrant a newspaper headline 'Spy Boss Left a Fortune'.[9] His salary had never been high and his pension was not inflation-proof in those days. He had been required to pay alimony to his first wife, who died in 1980.

The Potential Value of Oversight

While Hanley was more robust in his treatment of the Hollis case, the second K7 report remained in limbo, so that the decision by the previous management appeared to be endorsed, so far as most of those who knew of the case were concerned. An oversight body might well have been curious to discover the truth behind the alleged fabrication of Gouzenko's evidence, which seemed to have been contrived to undermine his credibility. As with so many important leads in the Hollis affair, Gouzenko's later evidence would seem to have been filed without really serious follow-up and oversight might have produced some firmer action.

Nevertheless, Sir Michael Hanley was to be instrumental in furthering official doubts about Hollis by action so secret that it was confidently believed that nobody outside a very charmed circle would ever hear of it.

CHAPTER FIFTY-THREE

An Ultra-Secret Warning

FOLLOWING the close co-operation between the security services of Britain, Canada, Australia and New Zealand, established mainly through the agency of MI5, with Hollis acting as the main adviser, Commonwealth Security Conferences became customary. They tended to be held at the same time as the Commonwealth Prime Ministers' conferences and in the same locations, secret matters of mutual security and counter-intelligence being discussed.[1] In addition, at the end of the 1960s, when fears that British and American security and intelligence establishments had been penetrated by Soviet 'moles' were at their height, regular conferences of the 'White Commonwealth' security and intelligence agencies and those of the United States were initiated.[2] These Limited Conferences, the existence of which was held secret, were much more specialized both as to the subjects under discussion and as to participants. They derived from the U.K.U.S.A. agreement, which involves Canada, Australia and New Zealand, and the interchange of information of mutual interest is so intimate that representatives of all the member countries sit in regularly on certain meetings of the Joint Intelligence Committee in Whitehall.[3] Delegates to the Limited Conferences had to be high level and their major purpose was the protection of the agencies' lifeblood – their secret sources. This was to be achieved through stringently restricted access within the agencies to knowledge about sources, by the prevention of penetration of the agencies by spies, and by the rooting out of any who might be already there. Because the information discussed at the Limited Conferences was so extremely sensitive, the record of their deliberations was seen by very few people, other than those present, and any actions within the agencies were introduced in ways which could be made to appear to have arisen for other, more mundane, reasons. An initiative taken by MI5 in the ultra-secrecy of one of these Limited Conferences code-named CAZAB is of the utmost importance to a true understanding of the Hollis case.

Because of the extreme secrecy of these meetings and the

reluctance of the participating countries even to admit that they occur, it has not been possible to establish, officially, the date of the conference, but it was held in Britain between 8 and 10 May 1974. Present were the head of MI6, Sir Maurice Oldfield, his Director of Security and staff, senior members of MI5 headed by the Director-General Sir Michael Hanley, assisted by Peter Wright, the C.I.A.'s Operational Chief of Counter-Intelligence James Angleton, with several of his staff, the F.B.I.'s head of Domestic Intelligence and head of the Russian Desk, the Director-General of the Australian Security Intelligence Organization and staff, the R.C.M.P. Commissioner, the head of the R.C.M.P. security service and officers, and the Director-General of the New Zealand Secret Intelligence Service and officers.

As Wright publicly confirmed on British television on 16 July 1984, Hanley gave the delegates an account of the investigations into Hollis, who had died in the previous year, with no definite conclusions as to his innocence or guilt. His purpose in supplying the information, which had been officially withheld from them in the past but which had leaked to some of them unofficially, was to enable all the agencies represented to consider the consequences to themselves if in fact Hollis had been a long-term Soviet agent. It was made clear that they were being given the information because of Hollis's past associations with their services and his long access to information which they had supplied to MI5 over the years. It would help them to make assessments of any damage he might have done to them through his knowledge of their organizations and of their cases and then to take any remedial action which they might regard as still being worth while.

Both officially and unofficially the information was restricted to those agencies which might have been affected, N.A.T.O. Intelligence and the N.A.T.O. Security Committee were not told because of the risk of a leakage there.[4] Even the Defence Ministry's Director of Defence Intelligence was kept in ignorance because it was felt that he did not need to know.[5]

It was a bold step by Hanley to issue the warning and it cannot be claimed that it was done at the behest of any MI5 'Gestapo' or 'Young Turks', as the more determined members of the Fluency Committee have been called by supporters of Hollis. It was the second K7 report that had convinced Hanley that the case was unproven and no Fluency Committee members had been involved in its preparation.

As the visiting security and intelligence chiefs were given the information on a strictly inter-service need-to-know basis it was understood that it was not to be released to anyone outside without

MI5's permission. The meeting was recorded and minuted, with copies of the minutes being eventually provided to each representative of the countries attending. As with the minutes of all such highly secret meetings they have been very tightly held ever since. Retired Director-Generals like Sir Martin Furnival Jones were not even told that the meeting had taken place. Nevertheless, the existence of this warning in the minutes has been officially confirmed by a representative of one of the participants, the R.C.M.P.

Following the publication of *Their Trade is Treachery* there were many questions in Canada, both inside and outside Parliament, concerning damage which Hollis might have inflicted on Canadian interests. As a result, the then Solicitor-General, Mr Robert Kaplan, made a statement to the Press on 26 March 1981 declaring that 'in the mid-1970s' the R.C.M.P. security service was warned that Sir Roger Hollis may have been a Soviet agent. He said that security officials had 'governed themselves accordingly' after receiving the information that Hollis was suspect, meaning, as he explained, that action was taken to counter any possible damage to security.[6]

When questions about this statement were raised in the Canadian Parliament by Allan Lawrence, a previous Solicitor-General, Kaplan declined to give further information beyond saying that the warning had not come directly from the British Prime Minister, Harold Wilson, to the Canadian Prime Minister, Pierre Trudeau.[7] Trudeau later said that there could have been 'an official briefing'. In fact Kaplan had been given the information from the R.C.M.P.'s minutes of the meeting in London which I have described.

Mr Kaplan has not been prepared to confirm the precise date of the warning. Under the terms of the original arrangement he would have been required to consult MI5 first and, from correspondence I have had with him, I have reason to think that he did so and that permission was refused. It is my information that the current MI5 management and the British Government are annoyed with him for going so far as to admit that the R.C.M.P. was warned 'in the mid-1970s'.

These events make nonsense of claims that the inquiry into Hollis was merely a routine affair to clear him off a list of suspects and that there was not 'a shred of evidence against him'. Hanley and the other senior officers who agreed to the issue of the warning must have believed that considerable doubt still existed. I have been assured by several former MI5 and MI6 officers that unless the doubt had been really serious the matter would not have been raised, particularly when such an effort had been made by Hanley's predecessor to prevent any outsider from hearing about the suspicions. The efforts to repair damage which might have been inflicted by Hollis that were carried out by Canada and, I believe, the U.S., Australia and New Zealand, were expensive and time-consuming. These allies would not have been put to such cost and trouble without good cause. A senior R.C.M.P. source has told me that Hollis was 'so fully indoctrinated into Canadian operations and had such insight into R.C.M.P. counter-espionage and counter-subversion "philosophy" that it would be unrealistic to assume anything other than total compromise of everything during the relevant years'

Hanley's approval of the warning also vitiates the argument that he and succeeding Director-Generals of MI5 must have been satisfied with the clearance of Hollis. I have established that in 1976 Hanley was still discussing with colleagues the probability that Hollis might have been a spy. In 1977 MI5 asked the American Intelligence authorities to review their deciphered Bride (Venona) traffic concerning a wartime Soviet agent in London because of the possibility that it might have been Hollis.

What remedial action did MI5 itself take against the damage that Hollis might have inflicted on British interest? I have been told, authoritatively, that it was quickly decided that if Hollis had been a spy from the moment of his arrival in MI5, then the damage would have been so immense and far-reaching that no assessment of it was possible. To quote a prime counter-intelligence expert who is familiar with the case, 'with almost unlimited access, he could have compromised not only the national security of the United Kingdom but of all Commonwealth nations. He would have known about the operations and products of the U.S. National Security Agency as well as of G.C.H.Q., and could have had major impact on C.I.A. counter-intelligence and on the F.B.I. British collaboration with European security services would also have to be considered in any damage assessment. The effort to remedy any damage would be prohibitive.'[8]

It remains a matter for conjecture whether MI5's failure to warn the C.I.A. and F.B.I. much earlier than 1974 constituted a breach of the conditions of the Anglo-American interchange of security and intelligence.

The British warning and its consequences for America's interests remain indelibly imprinted in the mind of at least one senior C.I.A. officer who has been active in prompting the exposure of the Hollis affair.

513

The Potential Value of Oversight

It is my belief, and that of my professional advisers, that if prime ministers, from Harold Wilson onwards, had known of the issue of this warning they would have been less inclined to accept the internal MI5 view that Hollis had been cleared of suspicion and that the need to investigate evidence of Soviet penetration since the departure of Blunt and Philby had disappeared. Presumably an oversight body would have been aware of the secret meeting and its broad results, and in that case it would be reasonable to assume that prime ministers would not have been kept in ignorance, as they undoubtedly were. As will be seen, this would have spared Mrs Thatcher, in particular, from making a statement which was quickly shown to be inaccurate by the disclosure which followed from the Canadian Solicitor-General.

MI5's continuing disinclination to carry out a damage assessment on the assumption that Hollis might have been a spy could have called for comment from an oversight body. As occurred with Philby, all too belatedly, it would have shown that too many of Hollis's cases had collapsed for the suspicions to be abandoned.

CHAPTER FIFTY-FOUR

A Secret Verdict of 'Not Out!'

IN spite of MI5's continuing doubts about Hollis and the warning to Allied security organizations, the odds are that the case would have died of inanition but for the action of one man who felt that it should remain under scrutiny in MI5's own interests. This was Stephen de Mowbray, the MI6 officer who had been on the Fluency Committee and, like most of his colleagues, believed that the mystery of the recurrent penetrations of MI5 by Soviet Intelligence had to be resolved.

De Mowbray, a man of intellectual standing who had been recommended for recruitment to MI6 by his Oxford tutor, Isaiah Berlin, had been resolute in helping to clear out suspected traitors and proven security risks from MI6. After being seconded to MI5 for surveillance duties in connection with the Mitchell case he had served with enthusiasm on the Fluency Committee. All this had made him unpopular with the friends of those suspects who were removed, so he had been posted to Malta. On his return he discovered what had happened – or what had not happened – concerning the Hollis case. He found that he was not alone in suspecting that the case was being shelved for political convenience. John Day, the K7 officer who had interrogated Hollis and had been unimpressed by the results, agreed with him that the decision to close the case should be challenged. Others like Arthur Martin and Peter Wright, the former Fluency Committee officer, then serving as special consultant to the Director-General, were equally in favour of further action, though perhaps less vocal inside the closed circle of security/intelligence colleagues. While Martin could be accused – wrongly in my opinion – of promoting inquiries into the Hollis affair out of revenge on the man who had, effectively, fired him, no such charge could be laid against de Mowbray.

I have been unable to establish whether de Mowbray had learned about the warning concerning Hollis issued to the Allied security agencies early in May 1974, but shortly after that date he presented himself, a spokesman for the group, at the door of

Number 10 Downing Street and asked to see the Prime Minister, then Harold Wilson.[1] Normally such chance callers see nobody of importance but de Mowbray is a tall, distinguished-looking figure and, once he had established his credentials, he was shown to the office of the most important civil servant in Whitehall, the Secretary of the Cabinet, Sir John Hunt, now Lord Hunt of Tanworth. De Mowbray alleged that there had been a dangerous cover-up and that Hollis might have introduced other agents because, had he been a spy, he would have been under Soviet pressure to do so. Hunt made further inquiries and found that de Mowbray's former colleagues had been astonished at the way he had managed to do his daily work while still devoting so much time to the Hollis issue. Then, after a further discussion with de Mowbray and without committing himself to him, Hunt decided that he would recommend an independent inquiry and quickly secured Wilson's agreement to it. It was either at this meeting with Hunt, when Wilson first heard of the Hollis case, or a little later when discussing his knowledge of it with the Director-General of MI5, Sir Michael Hanley, that Wilson made the remark which his political secretary at the time, Marcia Williams, later Lady Falkender, recalls: 'Now I've heard everything! I've just been told that the head of MI5 himself may have been a double agent.'[2]

De Mowbray had expressed his particular concern about the danger of the established practice whereby each retiring Director-General of MI5 and MI6 attempted to appoint his successor by recommending him to the Prime Minister, and often succeeded.[3] Because of the danger that an outgoing Director-General might have been a foreign agent, he believed that the chain should be broken from time to time by the appointment of somebody from outside the organizations. Wilson, who remembered his effort to break the chain after the retirement of Hollis by bringing in the ex-Chief Constable Sir Eric St Johnston, agreed that the proposal merited serious consideration. He had been greatly unimpressed by Hollis's performance over the Profumo case in keeping his penultimate predecessor, Macmillan, in ignorance of facts which had helped to bring about his downfall.

It is possible that both Hunt and Wilson feared that if they did nothing de Mowbray might, in desperation, seek the aid of newspaper publicity but I have been assured that he would never have done so.

With the requirement to keep the Hollis case as secret as possible the problem was to find an independent group to carry out the new inquiry, for it would have to have access not only to witnesses from the secret services but to the top secret 'Drat' files inside MI5. A suitable body seemed to be to hand – the Security Commission, the standing body set up in 1964 for the precise purpose of making independent inquiries into security cases. Headed by a judge, and with members from the Services and Civil Service with knowledge and experience of security matters, it seemed highly suitable, but there was one overriding problem which ruled out its use. Under its constitution the Security Commission could not be put into action without prior consultation with the leader of the opposition and when its deliberations were complete the leader of the opposition had to be briefed about the findings, to some degree. The reigning Establishment in Downing Street had no intention of allowing any other politician or, indeed, anyone outside a tiny circle to know anything about the Hollis affair.

When the setting up of a Security Commission was first mooted by Macmillan following the Vassall Tribunal, it was intended that there should also be a small standing group of Privy Councillors who would be told the Commission's findings and could reassure Parliament about them when secrecy forbade their publication. This idea was shelved but during the premiership of Edward Heath efforts had been made to establish such a body – a very limited kind of oversight body – to which extremely sensitive issues could be referred, though the Privy Councillors were not to be serving politicians. In the result, to reduce the security risk, the number of Privy Councillors selected for this task was reduced to one – Lord Trend who, as Sir Burke Trend, had been Hunt's predecessor as Secretary of the Cabinet. Lord Trend, then sixty and Rector of Lincoln College, Oxford, was able to afford the time for the inquiry and began work on it in July 1974. Until asked to undertake it he had not been told anything officially about the case though he may have heard something about it on 'the old boys' network'.

It is doubtful that de Mowbray and the others were told that Lord Trend was undertaking the inquiry which they had suggested. Had they been so they would have been displeased on three counts, as they were to declare when eventually told about it in the following year. A part-time inquiry by only one man, however distinguished, would have been judged inadequate for such an important issue and, if it had to be restricted to one man, Lord Trend was a bad choice. Nobody would question the integrity of Lord Trend but he was the epitome of the Establishment figure, zealous to keep the image of Whitehall as clean and as bright as possible. His remit, according to the statement made by Margaret Thatcher seven years later, was to do no more than review the MI5 investigations in detail, to say whether they had been done in a proper and thorough manner, and whether, in his view, the conclusions reached were justified.[4] Another authority, much closer to the situation at the time, has described his task as 'being called in to adjudicate between two conflicting views'.[5]

Though it is not generally known, the Cabinet Secretary is the chief accounting officer for the secret services. Trend had held that responsibility for ten years (1963–73), two of them during Hollis's tenure as Director-General of MI5 when the suspicions against him were mounting. He would have been less than human had he had no natural desire to repudiate any suggestion that MI5's efforts had been nullified for almost thirty years so far as the Soviet Union was concerned. The weakness in appointing any person of Trend's training and experience to inquire into an intelligence and security situation which throws doubt on the integrity of the Establishment is that he is conditioned to defend it. This weakness must be exacerbated when the suspect and the MI5 management responsible for clearing him are old Establishment colleagues.

To maintain the tightest security Trend was given no investigative staff and his inquiry was very much a one-man effort. From the start, therefore, he thought it unlikely that he could take the allegations concerning high-level penetration of MI5 any further than the inquiries conducted by the Fluency Committee and K7. He interviewed all the available members of the two groups including de Mowbray, Martin, Wright and Day, the chief interrogator of Hollis and Mitchell. The only person he failed to interview was someone who was then serving overseas. He questioned the officers at length about the long delay between 1966, when the Fluency Committee had formally recommended that Hollis should be thoroughly investigated, and 1970 when the task, including his interrogation, had been finally undertaken by K7. He found that MI5's only defence for the delay, which wasted valuable years, was the inherent difficulty for a Director-General like Furnival Jones to come to terms with the possibility that his predecessor might have been a spy. Trend also questioned them concerning their dissent from Furnival Jones's insistence on seeing Hollis before K7 officers were allowed to question him.

All these men left Trend's office believing that he was impressed by the weight of evidence that there had been a high-level spy in MI5 over many years and that he agreed with them that it pointed to Hollis.[6] This evidence extended from the entry of Hollis into MI5 right through to his retirement at the end of 1965.

Trend then spent two days a week for several months browsing among the 'Drat' and 'Peters' (Mitchell) files at MI5 headquarters in Curzon Street. He looked carefully into the 'Peters' case and, though he did not interview him, he decided that the Fluency

Committee and K7 had been right in deciding that he was not the culprit, if there was one. He consulted former security chiefs who pointed out that some decision on the case had been logistically desirable because MI5 had limited resources to pursue it and the chance that further evidence might accrue was remote. They advocated their past opinion that the evidence was not strong enough definitely to incriminate Hollis, though his innocence could not be proved either. They laid much stress on what they called 'the absence of clinching evidence', pointing out that while it had taken a long time to clinch the cases of Philby and Blunt they had been clinched in the end, though this, admittedly, had happened purely because of the chance fact that two unexpected informers, Flora Solomon and Michael Straight, had supplied new information.

I can find no evidence that Trend was told about the warning given to the American and White Commonwealth security agencies. The existence of these joint meetings was then so secret that it may well have been withheld from him.

Much was made to Trend by Hollis's supporters of the fact that no Soviet defector had pointed a finger at the suspect, with the possible exception of Gouzenko and his 'Elli' allegation but no effort was made to question him, though he was easily available in Toronto and was then only fifty-four.[7] As I have shown, other defectors had provided evidence applicable to Hollis. Further, no Soviet defector ever pointed a firm finger at Maclean, Burgess or Cairncross, and Golitsin's information regarding Philby was by no means definitive.

The absence of any 'spoor' indicating past connection between Hollis and communists, which had been found in the case of Philby, Maclean and the rest of the Cambridge Ring, was also stressed. Trend may not have been aware of the paucity of the effort to find any and he certainly did not know of Hollis's friendship with Arthur Ewert.

It was also stressed by Hollis's defenders that no Bride intercept traffic had incriminated him as it had Maclean, Philby and, almost certainly, Burgess and Blunt. But there was no Bride traffic between the U.S. and Moscow that was likely to involve Hollis and very little of the corresponding traffic between London and Moscow was ever deciphered.

It was further argued in Hollis's defence that, because of his position, many more cases would have collapsed had he been informing the Russians of MI5's activities. The cases of Vassall, Lonsdale, Houghton and the Krogers were cited as examples. This argument had been used effectively in defence of Philby by his old colleagues who pointed out that he had known in advance of the suspicions against Fuchs, the Rosenbergs and others who were brought to trial. It is now certain that Philby did, in fact, betray those cases in time for the Russians to attempt to rescue some or all of them but they decided against any action and allowed them to be convicted and, in the case of the Rosenbergs, executed.[8] The spies in question were finished so far as their value to the Soviet Union was concerned, while Philby showed promise of further achievement. To have rescued Fuchs and the others would have revealed the existence of another spy with access to information about them so the Russians preferred to 'burn' them to preserve Philby. The same interpretation could apply to the few successes notched up by MI5 when Hollis was in command, though all these were limited, as has been explained.

As Trend's remit was restricted to examining the existing evidence he made no effort to consult evidence which might exist among the old Shanghai Municipal Police documents held by the C.I.A. in Washington, though there was no longer any reason to worry about a leakage about the Hollis case by having to explain the purpose of the search to the C.I.A., as that agency had been officially told about it.

I have been able to consult several people who have read the highly secret report which Trend eventually submitted to the Prime Minister, Harold Wilson, in the early summer of 1975.[9] They have confirmed that no new evidence reached him and no independent inquiries were made on his behalf. This means that many of the details indicating a possible connection between Sonia and Hollis and other communist associations were not available to him. In sum, then, in view of what is known now the evidence available to Trend was inadequate for the formation of a *final* judgement.

As the several authorities who read the Trend Report have confirmed to me, all that Trend was able to do at the end of his inquiries, which lasted almost a year, was to make a value judgement. While agreeing that Hollis's innocence could not be proved, there could be no certainty that he had been a spy. He therefore elected to support the official MI5 view and to give him the benefit of the doubt. Unless further evidence emerged, which was considered to be unlikely, the security departments could continue to assume that Hollis had not been an agent of the Soviet Union. While it was argued that some of the wartime evidence of Soviet penetration could be ascribed to Blunt, who was in MI5, and to Philby, who was in MI6, no explanation was offered for the mass of evidence relating to the years after Blunt had left in 1946 and Philby in 1951.[10]

In his report Trend said that there was no truth in de Mowbray's charge that the clearance of Hollis by the MI5 management was in any way a 'cover-up'. This was the response of a former Whitehall mandarin to whom 'cover-up' means something different from what it means to most people. The details of the Hollis case presented in this book show that from its inception it had been characterized by secrecy of such a special category that ministers, including prime ministers, the most senior civil servants and Britain's chief allies in the intelligence world had been kept in ignorance of it. But for the action of de Mowbray it is doubtful whether Wilson or Callaghan would have heard of it while they were in office, though potentially it could have suddenly become public, as it did in March 1981.

So far as Parliament and the public were concerned the Trend Report continued the cover-up, for very few people knew of its existence and it was never expected that such a highly secret document would ever leak, as evidenced by the fact that no protective statement had been prepared to deal with sudden publicity, as happened with the Blunt affair. The treatment of the Hollis case continued a long-running cover-up of security and intelligence scandals dating back to the Maclean and Burgess defections, with one misleading statement being issued after another. The security authorities who prepare the briefs on which such statements are based can always claim that their intention is to avoid giving unnecessary information to the adversary, but my advice, from inside sources, is that the prime purpose is always to avoid 'damage', meaning embarrassment to the Service and to the Government responsible for it.

In 1975 de Mowbray was invited back to Number 10 Downing Street to see Sir John Hunt who briefed him on the findings of the Trend inquiry. He was not allowed to see the report and when he was told how the inquiry had been conducted the declined to accept its findings, arguing that Trend had done no more than replay the MI5 management's scrutiny of the evidence, following the same convenient line.

De Mowbray and others, like Peter Wright, still believe that the facts of the Hollis case are explicable only on the basis that he had been a Soviet agent. To them, as to me, it would seem that, in cricket parlance, all that Trend had been able to do was to give an umpire's verdict on an appeal by a hostile bowling side, and he had decided that Hollis's was 'Not out'. As *The Times* was to put it later, '...there were serious professional suspicions about Sir Roger Hollis which do not seem to have been dispelled but merely disposed of, as it were, by majority verdict'.[11]

521

The new information about Hollis's communist connections and the additional circumstantial evidence concerning Sonia may fortify those views.

I can find no evidence that the Canadians, Australians, Americans or others were ever informed that Hollis had been cleared by a further inquiry carried out by Lord Trend. Had the Canadians been told, for example, the Canadian Solicitor-General, Robert Kaplan, would surely have mentioned it in his statement in 1981 revealing the warning about him which had been sent to the R.C.M.P. The Director-General of MI5 at the time of the Trend Report was still Sir Michael Hanley and, presumably, he was not prepared to commit himself further to Britain's chief allies on the Hollis case. Former colleagues of Hanley have told me that he still egards the case as unproven, accepting the strength of the circumstantial evidence of penetration of MI5 from 1946, after Blunt had left, until the mid-1960s and regarding Hollis as the suspect who best fits the evidence.

The Potential Value of Oversight

If effective oversight had existed during the early 1970s there might have been no need for the Trend inquiry as the MI5 management might not have been permitted to dispose of the Hollis case and the whole question of Soviet penetration so easily. If, in fact, an oversight body had been satisfied with MI5's handling of the case, then the Cabinet Secretary, and through him the dissident security and intelligence officers, could have been reassured, perhaps more acceptably than by an *ad hoc* inquiry by one man. Had the Trend inquiry, or something like it, nevertheless gone ahead, an oversight body's knowledge of the warning about Hollis to the American and white Commonwealth agencies would have raised legitimate doubts about Trend's conclusions. In that event the Hollis case would not perhaps have been permitted to mortify from inanition. Riddles which still exist might have been resolved and succeeding governments spared embarrassment.

Shortly after Harold Wilson resigned the premiership in March 1976 he committed the unprecedented act of making what amounted to a public attack on on the efficiency and the impartiality of MI5. In interviews with two journalists, who eventually reported their experiences in a book, Wilson revealed that senior MI5 officers had been suspected of being Soviet spies and that he believed in the existence of a 'Gestapo' inside MI5 which had been trying to undermine the Labour Government and his own position in particular.[12] It is now clear that Wilson's suspicions regarding the presence of Soviet spies in MI5 had been raised by the Trend Report, which revealed to him the extent of the evidence which had been adduced inside MI5 against both Hollis and Mitchell. The mere fact that both the Director-General and his deputy had been investigated and interrogated as possible Soviet agents would have shocked any Prime Minister and, because of his knowledge of their part in the Profumo affair, Wilson was especially sensitive. As an interview with I.T.N. was to show, he has never been entirely satisfied with the clearance of Hollis.[13]

Wilson also told the reporters that there were some MI5 officers who regarded him as a security risk and later he was to tell me that he had asked Sir Michael Hanley, then the Director-General, if that was the case and was informed that it was, though only a few of the officers held that view.[14] My inquiries showed that the officers concerned were more disturbed about some of the ministers appointed by Wilson, but they had received adverse information about the Prime Minister from C.I.A. counter-intelligence. This had occurred in 1965, while Hollis was still Director-General, and he had seen the Cabinet Secretary, then Burke Trend, about it. The evidence was so thin, however, that no action was taken and I do not believe that Wilson was told anything about it. If he did learn of it the knowledge would have increased his bitterness, especially when he became aware of the suspicions attaching to Hollis.

MI5's attitude to Wilson had not been helped by his response to the expulsion of the 105 Soviet agents by the Heath Government. While in opposition he had suggested that the move was merely a political ploy with no reasonable foundation and, when Labour was re-elected, he had made overtures to the Kremlin to 'make amends' for the expulsions which had soured Anglo-Soviet relations.[15] As a result of a trade deal, which he negotiated in Moscow early in 1975, the Russians were allowed to instal an unlimited number of inspectors in British factories supplying the Soviet Union with industrial equipment and MI5 had no doubt that both the K.G.B. and the G.R.U. would take advantage of this to intrude agents among them.[16]

Wilson's allegations shocked Whitehall and Westminster when they became public and, in the minds of many people, his motives have never been adequately explained. It may simply have been that he felt so strongly about the situation inside MI5 that he took the opportunity to draw public attention to it. In the result it had no noticeable effect and the Hollis and Mitchell cases were to remain covered up until the appearance of *Their Trade is Treachery* five years later.

Wilson's allegations caused dismay inside MI5 where there were meetings to discuss their origins and purpose. There was concern in the Cabinet Office that they might lead to exposure of the Hollis and Mitchell cases and, according to one of the journalists to whom Wilson confided, it could easily have done so.[17] Following a newspaper report, which I wrote, that Wilson had been correct in believing that he had been under electronic surveillance, Callaghan called in the chiefs of MI5 and MI6 for a rundown on the general security position during which Wilson's fears and statements were discussed.[18] Parliament was left in ignorance, however, and to this day M.P.s wonder about Wilson's strange behaviour and his motives. An oversight body might have been able to resolve the situation to its satisfaction and to have reassured M.P.s or to have undertaken any inquiries thought necessary.

In 1978 Sir Michael Hanley became due for retirement and as the Deputy Director-General, John Jones, was regarded as being too young, it was decided to bring in an outsider to provide a fresh approach, which the Home Secretary, Merlyn Rees, considered to be desirable from time to time, and also to 'break the chain' of one professional succeeding another. The man chosen was Sir Howard Smith who was serving as Ambassador in Moscow. This choice raised many eyebrows because it had been standard practice for several years to avoid recruiting any official who had served in the Soviet Union because of the possibility, however remote, that he might have been compromised. The case of John Watkins, the Canadian Ambassador, had alerted MI5 to the fact that rank was no protection from the attentions of the K.G.B. when a weakness could be spotted, and more recently, in 1968, one of Smith's own predecessors, Sir Geoffrey Harrison, had fallen victim to sexual entrapment by the K.G.B. Nevertheless, as there was no evidence whatsoever to impugn the integrity of Sir Howard Smith and as the alternative candidates did not impress the panel which considered them, he was appointed.[19]

Smith was to remain Director-General of MI5 until 1981 when he was succeeded by Jones, now Sir John Jones, so any 'breaking of the chain' had been short-lived. At the time of the appointment of Smith and of the new head of MI6, Sir Arthur Franks, the Prime Minister, James Callaghan, had written to media editors requesting that their names should not be published because of the terrorist threat, which was very real. Both names were released, however, by anti-Establishment magazines and Jones's name was published by the Labour Party.[20] It was also widely published in connection with the Bettaney case.

James Callaghan, who succeeded Wilson, appeared to continue the policy of 'making amends', a move which also pacified the left wing of his party whose support he needed. A further attempt by MI5 to secure the expulsion of more Soviet 'diplomats' was rejected and when two Hungarian intelligence officers, spying for the Soviet bloc, were caught taking photographs outside the nuclear weapons maintenance factory at Burghfield, Reading, the incident was played down by the Government.[21] Even the assassination of a Bulgarian dissident, Georgi Markov, on a London street by the insertion of a poison capsule into his body, apparently by means of a trick umbrella, provoked scant reaction from the Foreign Office.[22]

CHAPTER FIFTY-FIVE

The Public Exposure of Sir Anthony Blunt

FOLLOWING a penetrating analysis of the results of Blunt's inter-rogations by the woman who had been the research officer in the case, it was decided, in 1972, to cease further questioning unless some specific lead accrued from a defector or other source. It was concluded that while Blunt had given some valuable leads, he had avoided implicating some of his former friends who had been helpful to the Soviet cause and were still in important posts. The case officers agreed that he had not changed ideologically, had expressed no remorse and was still rather proud of his achieve-ments for the Russians. They strongly suspected – and still do – that he had lied about the extent of his contacts with Soviet Intelligence after the war during his service in the Royal House-hold.

It is unlikely that the case would have raised further interest in Whitehall but for an event, late in 1972, when shortly after his retirement as Surveyor of the Queen's Pictures a crisis in Blunt's health threw the Cabinet Office into near-panic. Through one of Blunt's former friends who had Cabinet Office connections, the Cabinet Secretary, then Sir Burke Trend, learned that Blunt was to undergo emergency surgery for cancer and was talking about leaving a testament of his activities for posthumous publication. The reaction in Whitehall was evidence of the concern that had previously shown itself in MI5. The Attorney-General, Sir Peter Rawlinson, was asked to re-examine the records of the case and confirmed that, if Blunt survived, there was no way of threatening him with prosecution to keep him quiet because the immunity was firm and permanent. Nor could any action be taken against him if, feeling that he had only a few months to live if he survived the surgery, he decided to cleanse his conscience with a public confession – the consequences of which would be extremely menacing.[1]

After meetings between the Attorney-General, the Cabinet Secretary and MI5, the Prime Minister, Edward Heath, was informed about the Blunt case and its dangerous implications for the first time in February 1973.[2] A document was prepared, with Palace approval, to counter embarrassing incidents which the traitor might expose. Meanwhile, in late 1972 several of Blunt's homosexual friends had been interviewed by Special Branch officers, apparently at the request of MI5 and presumably to acquire damaging material which might deter Blunt, or his executors, from publishing anything, or at least reduce its impact.[3] When Blunt survived the operation and made a remarkable recovery the counter-document remained in the Cabinet Office, bearing the title 'If Blunt Dies'.

In spite of this new threat Blunt was permitted to continue his prestigious connection with the Palace, having been appointed Adviser for the Queen's Pictures and Drawings in 1972 on relinquishing his previous position. This post gave him continuing access to the Royal collections and archives, which was of great value in his lucrative work as an art expert. It was terminated in 1978 only because his public exposure seemed to be imminent. This astonishing appointment could be further evidence of some Royal indebtedness to Blunt or it could have been an inducement to him to maintain his silence. My inquiries suggest that the appointment was made on the advice of the relevant authorities, who had been kept in ignorance of his treachery, and to have rejected it would have required explanation. On the other hand, one feels that it could have been rejected on the grounds of age or perhaps on some other pretext which the Queen would not have needed to specify.

In the result, Blunt continued to live as an honoured and privileged person, being in demand as a lecturer, writer and professional connoisseur in establishing the authenticity of paintings, especially those of the French artist Poussin. He lived in a London flat with a man to whom he was devoted. In 1975 he sold one of his own Poussin paintings to the Montreal Museum of Fine Arts for £100,000, certifying its authenticity himself. Having bought it for £20,000 in 1964, the year in which he had been granted immunity, he made a fair profit.[4]

In 1978 the security authorities and the Labour Government of the day became aware that the author Andrew Boyle had been told that Blunt had confessed to having been a traitor and had been granted immunity. Expecting publication at any time and also fearing that Goronwy Rees, the former friend of Burgess and Blunt, might expose the truth, as he was near death, the Cabinet Office counter-document was brought up to date at the behest of Merlyn Rees, the Home Secretary, so that the Prime Minister, James

Callaghan, could read it to Parliament if the Blunt affair became public. The Queen was asked to approve it and did so.[5]

Blunt's exposure did not occur until the following year, when Boyle's book, *The Climate of Treason*, appeared.[6] Boyle's wife has told me that when her husband set out to write his book it was to be no more than a study of the political and emotional climate in which certain young undergraduates had become ideological communists and had then been recruited as active agents for Soviet Intelligence. In the process of his researches, however, Boyle had learned two facts which were entirely new to the public and to Parliament – that Blunt had been a Soviet spy throughout his wartime service in MI5 and, having confessed, had been granted immunity to prosecution, with the result that the entire affair had been suppressed. His information was confirmed and extended by the other man who, it was feared in Whitehall, might expose the truth – Goronwy Rees, the former friend of both Burgess and Blunt. Boyle had managed to interview Rees on his deathbed.

Boyle did not name Blunt in his book but gave sufficient indications that the 'Fourth Man' of the Cambridge Ring was the former Surveyor of the Queen's Pictures to enable other publications to name him, which led to a question in Parliament. It was decided that Mrs Thatcher should make a confirmatory statement and when this was completed the Cabinet Secretary, Sir Robert Armstrong, telephoned Blunt's solicitor and called him to the Cabinet Office to see it in advance. This was later explained as being in fairness to Blunt, but it was done at the suggestion of MI5, which had other reasons. The immediate purpose was to warn Blunt to take refuge with some friend so that he could not be besieged by the media. Understandably, MI5 was totally averse to any interviews of Blunt which it could not control, indicating that there were still many things it was determined to suppress. The advance warning, which may not have been the first, was also calculated to reduce the provocation which might anger Blunt into saying more than he should.

In answering a written question from Edward Leadbitter, a Labour M.P., on 15 November, Mrs Thatcher confirmed that Blunt had indeed been a Soviet agent and had been granted immunity in return for a confession. In giving what appeared to be a remarkably frank account of Blunt's activities, the Prime Minister drew almost entirely on the statement prepared by the previous Government, as described. Later it fell to Merlyn Rees to remain silent while Tory M.P.s praised their leader for the statement which, they alleged, Labour would never have had the courage to make.[7] The unwritten rule that politicians who know the secret facts of security disasters must not make political use of them is an integral part of the established system of cover-up. Neither has Mrs Thatcher declined the praise poured on her then and since for so courageously exposing Blunt when, in fact, the statement, the decision to make it and the Palace approval of it all derived from the previous administration.

Immediately after the Prime Minister's statement Buckingham Palace announced that Blunt would be stripped of his knighthood, the first time that had happened since the execution of Sir Roger Casement for treason in 1916. This additional disgrace, which also involved the loss of Blunt's C.V.O., must have caused some concern in MI5, in view of the previous fears that Blunt might be provoked into making a statement, but it was unavoidable. I have been informed by a close friend of Blunt that the traitor fully appreciated that the Queen had no option and that he did not feel bitter about the removal of his honour. He may have been given advance warning of the move in view of the Cabinet Secretary's concern to advise him about the Prime Minister's statement.

On 20 November, after further consultations with MI5, Blunt was permitted to give a limited interview to *The Times* in a bid to end further media harassment and reduce the risk of further disclosures. It proved to be a blatant example of Whitehall news management. Blunt told deliberate lies and evaded difficult questions by hiding behind the Official Secrets Act, indicating that while his conscience had induced him to give all the secrets he knew to the Russians he could not reveal them to the British public. He claimed that he became aware that Philby was a Soviet agent only during the war, which was completely false.

Though Boyle and his publishers had avoided any contact with the security authorities, MI5 had managed to secure a copy of the book in advance and had advised Blunt on how to react when exposed. As a result, Parliament and the public were further misled about Blunt's activities, and newspapers drew many false conclusions, much to MI5's satisfaction. In particular, Blunt had been told not to name Straight as the man who had exposed him to MI5 and he did not do so.

On 21 November the Blunt affair was debated in the Commons and, when opening the discussion, the Prime Minister took the opportunity to expand on her original statement.[8] She said that while the spy's activities had seriously damaged Britain's interests it was unlikely that British military operations or British lives were put at risk. Yet for all Blunt knew, the detailed information about the D-Day deception plans and the material passed to him by Leo Long, all of which Blunt transferred to the Russians, might well have put both at risk. The specific reference to British lives was also misleading because there was no doubt that Blunt had threatened, and probably ended, the lives of agents who were serving Britain, though they were not British nationals, the agent in the Kremlin being just one example.

Mrs Thatcher said that the Government did not know exactly what information Blunt had passed on. Unless MI5 had failed to tell the Government of Blunt's confessed activities that was not true either. The statement had the effect of deterring specific questions about those activities and this may have been its intention. At that point the MI5 officers who had been involved in drafting the Prime Minister's brief were confident that details of Blunt's confession, such as were revealed two years later in *Their Trade is Treachery*, were never likely to be made public.

Mrs Thatcher's brief also caused her to say that 'it was Philby who warned Burgess to tell Maclean that he was about to be interrogated'. As I have pointed out, this was most unlikely to have been true and I suspect that MI5 knew it. One possibly intentional result of landing Philby with that particular act of treachery was to divert suspicion from another spy, perhaps in MI5.

As I have explained in Chapter 37, the information given to Mrs Thatcher regarding MI5's failure to interrogate Blunt without an offer of immunity in 1964 does not stand serious examination. She told Parliament, 'Blunt had persisted in his denial at eleven interviews [between 1951 and 1959]; the security authorities had no reason to suppose that he would do otherwise at a twelfth.' In fact there was every reason to suppose that he might do otherwise because the whole situation had changed with Straight's evidence that Blunt was a Soviet agent and his offer to confront the spy in London. Further, Long could have been questioned and could have provided hard evidence. Mrs Thatcher's brief compounded this misleading comment by stating, 'To this day there is no evidence which could be used as a basis for prosecution against Blunt.' This was true only because the possibility of using Long's evidence had been vitiated by the immunity deal for both spies, initiated by Hollis.

Every effort was made in Parliament by Mrs Thatcher, Heath and others to support Hollis's decision to press for Blunt's immunity, but M.P.s knew nothing about Long and it seems most likely that the Prime Minister and Heath were ignorant of it at that stage. Politicians are very sensitive to the term 'cover-up' but the highly significant facts about the Long case were certainly covered up in the Blunt debate.

The brief read by Mrs Thatcher went out of its way to stress that

530

'The Director-General of the Security Service followed scrupulously the procedures that had been laid down.' This diversion seemed somewhat gratuitous but the D.G. concerned was, of course, Sir Roger Hollis, and MI5 and a few senior people in Whitehall were aware that the case against him might break one day. The Prime Minister's statement did what it could to show him up in as good a light as possible if ever it did break. All that Hollis had done scrupulously was to ensure that he did not lay himself open to censure by failing to obey the rules when it suited him to obey them. I suspect that Mrs Thatcher had not been told of his unprecedented suspension of Blunt's case officer, Arthur Martin, for the crucial fortnight after Blunt's first confession, and I have established that the Attorney-General, Sir Michael Havers, had certainly not been told of it before he made his statement in the Blunt debate.

Mrs Thatcher went on to say, 'In the light of these events I see no need to change the principles governing the relationship between the Security Service and Ministers.'[9] She changed her mind after she had been told, belatedly, how Hollis had handled the Long case. In a separate statement on Long on 9 November 1981 she assured Parliament that she had instituted changes so that never again could a Director-General of MI5 make effective immunity arrangements, as Hollis had done with Long, without first consulting the Attorney-General through the Director of Public Prosecutions.[10] Clearly, at that stage, she thought that Hollis's conduct had been reprehensible but care was taken not to refer to him by name.

The most revealing statements in the Blunt debate concerning MI5 were made by James Callaghan who had wider experience of security and intelligence affairs than anyone else in the Commons. As Home Secretary he had been responsible for MI5, as Foreign Secretary for MI6 and G.C.H.Q. and, as Prime Minister, he had made it his business to be close to all three. He told Parliament that Blunt was 'merely one part of a highly complicated case that the Security Service has spent many years and many man-hours seeking to unravel to find the truth'. This was probably a general reference to the Ring of Five and their associates but he went further when he said that 'the morale of the Security Service has suffered greatly as a result of what took place when there was deep penetration during the 1930s and 1940s'.[11] Callaghan was well acquainted with the difference between the Security Service (MI5) and the Secret Intelligence Service (MI6) but to make sure I wrote to him asking if by Security Service he had meant MI5. He made an excuse to avoid answering the question so I wrote again pointing

531

out that I would assume that he had known what he was saying and had meant what he had said. This produced no disclaimer so it may be reasonably assumed that the former Prime Minister was telling Parliament that not only had MI5 been deeply penetrated in the 1940s, which could be taken as referring to Blunt, but also in the 1930s before Blunt joined. The only MI5 officers recruited in the 1930s who have fallen under serious and sustained suspicion were Graham Mitchell, who was cleared, and Roger Hollis, who remains suspect.

Callaghan added, 'The matter has never been fully cleared up and may never be....The truth of the matter will only be known in the deepest recesses of the Kremlin.'[12] He had been told all about the Hollis and Mitchell cases while still Prime Minister when he had called the heads of MI5 and MI6 to Number 10 Downing Street to brief him fully on outstanding problems, following a newspaper article of mine in the summer of 1977. He then went on to suggest that, on his information, MI5 was probably still penetrated in 1979 – 'because of the effluxion of time those concerned in that penetration of the Service have passed or *are passing* [my italics] out of active service because of age, ill health or death'. He further admitted, with first-hand knowledge, that in spite of the attempted defence of MI5 by ministers 'those concerned in the Security Service are in some ways deeply ashamed at what has happened'.[13] In saying that Callaghan was probably reflecting the views of the MI5 chief who had briefed him, Sir Michael Hanley, who has never been convinced of Hollis's innocence. And, taking his statement in the Blunt debate as a whole, it would seem that having taken the trouble to be thoroughly briefed on the Hollis case he was not satisfied by the so-called clearance given to the former Director-General either by the MI5 management in 1972 or by Lord Trend in 1974. Nor did he seem to approve of Hollis's action in pressing for immunity for his former colleague. 'Would Mr Blunt have had the same treatment if he had been a humble corporal in the R.A.F.?' he asked.[14]

My inquiries suggest that it was, partly, the doubts concerning Hollis that led to a decision by Callaghan and Merlyn Rees to bring in an outsider when a new Director-General of MI5 had to be appointed in 1978. Though there was no specific doubt attaching to the retiring D.G., Hanley, or to his deputy who might have expected to succeed him though he was young for the job, it was decided, as already mentioned, to 'break the chain' whereby the retiring D.G. recommends his successor who, customarily, is appointed.

Various back-benchers contributed to the Blunt debate, Mr

Leadbitter pointing out that Blunt had been deprived of his knighthood only after his public exposure, leading the country to believe that the 'immunity and the privileges he enjoyed were all right provided the public did not know'.

Many M.P.s wanted a Parliamentary inquiry into the Blunt affair and, with accountability to Parliament in mind, Merlyn Rees, who had recent experience of dealing with MI5, advised 'an inquiry into the procedures and control to reassure the community as a whole'. The Government, however, was opposed to any inquiry and got its way. Later I was informed that Mrs Thatcher had been 'within a hair's breadth of ordering an inquiry and had been talked out of it'.[15] At the time I did not know why she had changed her mind when she was so anxious to clear away the old problems, hopefully once and for all. Only later did it become clear that any deep independent probe into the Blunt case could have exposed the Hollis case, and MI5 and the Cabinet Office were opposed to taking that risk.

Having adapted to his situation, which involved the loss of academic honours such as his Honorary Fellowship of Trinity College, Cambridge, awarded in 1967, Blunt toyed with the idea of writing his own account of his experiences but changed his mind, claiming that he was 'getting too old' to write it and 'remained afraid of the Official Secrets Act', which had not deterred him when he was younger.[16] As he continued to write abstruse art books it seems more likely that MI5, having convinced itself that it could safely take a tougher line with Blunt, made it clear that he would have to submit any book for vetting and this would have left little beyond his attempt to justify his behaviour. He may have completed some manuscripts or notes which may, one day, be made into a book but MI5 will continue to insist on vetting the product.

Nothing further about Blunt's activities might have emerged for many years, if ever, but for the publication in March 1981 of *Their Trade is Treachery*, which contained the major parts of his confessions, secured from MI5 sources.

Blunt died suddenly from a heart attack on 26 March 1983. His estate of £858,121 was said to have included the valuation of £500,000 put upon his favourite Poussin painting 'Rebecca at the Well', which was offered to the nation in lieu of tax. Most of the remainder was willed to his close companion for thirty years, William Gaskin, a former Irish Guardsman.[17]

CHAPTER FIFTY-SIX

An Aladdin's Cave

DURING thirty-three years of active investigation in Whitehall and its out-stations I learned many sensitive secrets and was able to publish most of them but very few related to the work of MI5 or MI6 and almost all of those that did were given to me deliberately by officers of those organizations because they had been instructed to do so. These were rare occasions when MI5 or MI6 wanted publicity for their own purposes and I have described most of them in a previous book called *Inside Story*. Otherwise, security in MI5 and MI6 was so tight and so effective that it was virtually impossible to discover anything definite about its operations, past or present. Security and intelligence officers would rarely talk to journalists, or to anyone else, about their work and when I left Fleet Street in March 1979 my penetration of the secret services had been meagre, whereas at times my penetration of the Defence Ministry had been deep and highly productive. I had heard whispers of the Hollis case, and one former MI6 officer confirmed the suspicions about him, as I recounted, briefly, in *Inside Story*, but neither I nor anybody else was able to secure any details, so tightly were they held. It did not seem likely that, once out of the mainstream, information about the secret services would come my way when it had eluded me for so long, but through circumstances which I will never be able to reveal a mass of official information, some of it in the greatest detail, was suddenly made available to me. To someone as obsessively curious about the secret services as I am it was like being led into Aladdin's cave with nuggets and jewels sparkling everywhere.

It so happened that certain American Intelligence sources, who were deeply concerned about the British position because of the to a Government committee that ninety per cent of what had been written about his organization was false.[1] I also realized that much of my previous confidence in the efficiency of MI5 had been misplaced.

The Aladdin's cave was opened to me because, for the first time

534

in the history of MI5 and MI6, certain former officers had become convinced that the public should be informed of the appalling extent to which those services had been penetrated by agents working for Soviet Intelligence. They believed that only when Parliament, the public and the media were told the truth of Britain's poor record against the continuing assault of the K.G.B. and the G.R.U. would measures be forced upon the secret services to improve their performance in a technological age when security and intelligence have never been more important. As will be seen, their action forced the Government into mounting the first independent inquiry for twenty years into the efficacy of the measures being taken to prevent penetration by enemy agents.

It so happened that certain American Intelligence sources, who were deeply concerned about the British position because of the Anglo-U.S. interchange of intelligence and security secrets, were also agitating for some action. Their information happened to come my way at about the same time, entirely through a fluke circumstance. Through these various, prime, authoritative sources I learned most of the details of the case against Hollis and others. It became clear that the sources were partly motivated by fear that these high-level suspects might have brought in others before their retirement and that action was essential to discover whether such 'moles' existed and, if so, to root them out.

Having spent some months obtaining and digesting the mass of information and checking, where possible, on its authenticity, I faced the major problem of how to project it publicly when every item technically breached the Official Secrets Act. My resolve to produce as much of the information as possible in a book was fortified by my discovery that a Tory M.P., Jonathan Aitken, had been given details of the Hollis case by a former MI5 officer who had been associated with it and had passed it on to the Prime Minister, Mrs Thatcher, to warn her of the potentially explosive situation. Aitken and the MI5 man had collaborated in writing a five-page letter, which was a remarkably concise account of the case against Hollis.[2] Aitken also submitted a handwritten note. After about a month the Prime Minister replied indicating that she had heard of the allegations but saying no more.

I advised my publisher that, after consulting various authorities, it was my belief that provided the material could be published without the prior knowledge of the security authorities they would take no action but if the material were submitted for clearance or fell into their hands in any way they would be almost certain to threaten prosecution in such a way that publication would be impossible. While several names and some material were elimin-

535

ated on legal advice, because of the libel risk, nothing was removed in deference to the Official Secrets Act after I had been given professional assurance that no current or future operations could be prejudiced.

Precautions unprecedented in the publishing trade were taken to keep the existence of the book, *Their Trade is Treachery*, and its contents secret until newspaper serialization began a few days before the publication date, 26 March. No books were sent to booksellers until that day and none went out to reviewers.[3] As there had never been such a release of information about MI5 and MI6 before it was, of course, also necessary to preserve secrecy to prevent the media from 'milking' the book in advance. In spite of these precautions I was to discover, weeks later, that the security authorities had obtained proofs of the book several weeks before publication. This was not achieved as a result of any Whitehall initiative, though my inquiries had given MI5 plenty of warning that the book was in preparation.

The proofs went first to MI6, then to MI5. Copies were run off and distributed in secrecy to former and current senior managers of the secret services and Whitehall figures who were, or had been, involved. Meetings were held to discuss the reaction, first internally in MI5 and MI6 and then jointly with the Cabinet Office and Law Officers. The first reaction – as I have been told by one of those involved – was relief that I had not discovered facts unknown to the security authorities, an omission I feel I have rectified in this book. After much argument it was decided to advise against any ban on the book for two main reasons. Firstly a ban would appear to confirm the contents. Secondly, Jonathan Aitken had alerted the Prime Minister and the Cabinet Office, in his letter, to the fact that other journalists were actively investigating the suspicions which had arisen in MI5 concerning both Hollis and Mitchell. As some of these were deeply distrusted, as regards their motives, it was decided that if the information was to be exposed it was preferable that I should be allowed to do it.

A suggestion that parts of the book should be suppressed under threat of prosecution under the Official Secrets Act was considered but rejected on the grounds that, if properly applied, little of the script would remain. It was also appreciated, with some pleasure, that there were certain inaccuracies concerning the Trend Report which Government spokesmen could use to cast doubt on the whole.

It was realized that having seen the book in advance and failing to suppress it the security authorities would be unable to stage a prosecution, however strong the Parliamentary demand for one might be, because the prime purpose of the Act is to prevent the exposure of secrets, not to exact revenge. I have been informed that it was unanimously agreed that a prosecution would cause a sensation which MI5 would rather avoid as they would be required to admit the truth of parts of the book in court and it was assumed that I would have a high-level counsel who might try to force them to make admissions they regarded as damaging.

As there had never been such a haemorrhage of accurate information about MI5 or MI6 before, a senior MI5 officer, whose identity is known to me, was detailed to investigate the origin of the disclosures which, it was clear, could only have originated from current or former members of MI5 and MI6. Various officers were quickly interviewed and one of them, who had not been a direct source, remarked, 'It's all out of the files!'

After comments had been received from those allowed to read the proofs a brief was prepared for the Prime Minister, so that she could cast doubt on the entire Hollis disclosures by concentrating on a few real and alleged errors in my account of the Trend Report, which had been held so secretly that nobody outside a small circle had heard about it, much less seen it. The statement was to stress that all the episodes were part of a poisoned past which should be forgotten in the interests of concentrating security resources on the present and future.

The imminent exposure of the Hollis case meant that the one objection to the far-ranging inquiry which the Prime Minister had wanted at the time of the Blunt affair would be removed. When briefed on the position, Mrs Thatcher decided that the contents of *Their Trade is Treachery*, which could not be disputed, made a Parliamentary demand for an inquiry inevitable. She therefore decided to take the initiative and announce an inquiry, a move which was also calculated to forestall further questions which M.P.s might try to ask, as they could be told to wait until the inquiry had reported its findings. It was known that most M.P.s would have preferred a Parliamentary inquiry to be carried out by selected Privy Councillors reporting to the House, but the Prime Minister was urged by the security authorities to avoid this. In the event it was agreed that the inquiry would be undertaken by the Security Commission, which reports to the Prime Minister.

Mrs Thatcher's brief, of which there were several drafts, was accompanied by a more detailed verbal account of the background provided by various people, including Lord Trend, but I have reason to believe that she was not told, at that stage, about the warning issued to the American and Commonwealth authorities indicating that Hollis might have been a spy. As I hope to convince

537

the reader, the Prime Minister was poorly served in other ways with respect to her brief.

Serialization of the book began in the *Daily Mail* on Monday, 23 March 1981, to be followed a day later by the same material in *The Times*.[4] The reaction to the exposure of the Hollis case was so great that Downing Street indicated that the Prime Minister would be dealing with the matter in Parliament. This put the Cabinet Office in an embarrassing position. It did not wish to reveal that it had acquired the book in advance, presumably to protect the source of it, and therefore had to go through a pantomime exercise of acquiring a copy in a straightforward manner. This was accomplished by the Cabinet Secretary, Sir Robert Armstrong, who telephoned the managing director of my publisher, Sidgwick and Jackson, claiming that the Prime Minister needed a copy of the book so that she could be in a position to make a statement about it with the least possible delay, if pressed to do so in Parliament. Sir Robert said that he thought such pressure was likely, when, in fact, he knew that the Prime Minister had already made a firm decision to make a statement, including the announcement of the inquiry.

I suggested that a copy should be provided only if Sir Robert undertook, in writing, not to prevent or to delay publication, believing that, as a civil servant, he would not be able to do this without Government permission. In fact Sir Robert sent round a letter by hand, dated 23 March, assuring the publisher that no attempt would be made to prevent or delay publication. He also gave an assurance that the book would not go outside his office or the Prime Minister's before publication. He had been able to give these assurances because the political decisions had already been taken and photocopies of the text had been widely distributed. Sir Robert could, no doubt, argue that a final copy of the book was still required to ensure that there had been no changes but the reasons he gave for securing it from the publisher were questionable, though described by one former mandarin as 'No more than par for the course'.

The first clue that the security authorities had wind of the contents of the book came on the eve of the serialization with the disappearance of Lady Hollis from her cottage at Catcott in Somerset.[5] Her former office, MI5, had organized her removal to a 'safe house' for an indefinite period so that she could not be questioned by reporters. This was followed by prime source information that several former senior members of MI5 and at least one former Cabinet Secretary had read the book in the preceding weeks.

The Press reaction to the book, both nationally and internationally, was unprecedented and it soon headed the bestseller lists. As I was warned, by Whitehall friends, Downing Street quickly leaked the fact that the Prime Minister would be doing her best to defend Hollis and MI5 as a whole. That this was a chore she did not relish was indicated to me by someone who attended a Downing Street dinner shortly before she had to make her statement. When another guest was commiserating with her about various problems which beset her she had remarked, ruefully, 'And now I've got Chapman Pincher to contend with.'

CHAPTER FIFTY-SEVEN

A Flawed Announcement

IN the afternoon of 26 March 1981 the Prime Minister made literary history by delivering the first review of *Their Trade is Treachery* from the Dispatch Box in the House of Commons.[1] The text of her speech is given in Appendix B. The first third of it was devoted to the Hollis case, the many other cases in the book being ignored. While admitting that Hollis had been the subject of an internal inquiry, the main thrust of the first part of the statement was to tell Parliament that it had been concluded that he had not been an agent of the Soviet Intelligence Service. Mrs Thatcher then also confirmed that, as this view had been challenged, Lord Trend had been asked to review the investigations. As a result, he, too, had concluded that Hollis had not been an agent of the Soviet Intelligence Service, though it had been impossible to prove his innocence. While conveniently declining to comment on most of the facts – and they were facts – the Prime Minister's brief did its best to denigrate them by referring to 'allegations' and 'insinuations'. It then picked on certain views which I had attributed to Lord Trend, having based them on statements he had made to some of the witnesses he had questioned and who still believe them to be true. The remarks were calculated to cast the maximum discredit on my account of the whole Hollis affair. Case-deaths and other disasters which the MI5 investigators had attributed to Hollis, as the likeliest culprit, were laid at the door of Blunt or Philby, though the dates made no sense.

Having suggested that the book served no purpose, since it contained nothing that was new to the security authorities – which was hardly surprising as most of it had come from that source – the Prime Minister then went on to announce that she was setting up the first independent inquiry for twenty years into the safeguards against any future penetration of the secret departments. It was her first U-turn, as she had resisted the loud Parliamentary clamour for such an inquiry sixteen months previously after the exposure of Blunt. Any doubt that the inquiry was the direct result of the security disasters revealed in the book was later to be dispelled by the official report of the inquiry which, as Mrs Thatcher was to tell the House, resulted from 'the publication of a book which dealt with a number of cases of proven or suspected disclosure of sensitive information to Soviet bloc intelligence services'.[2] There can be little doubt that the Prime Minister and her advisers changed their minds because the danger that an inquiry into the security situation following the Blunt affair would inevitably uncover the Hollis case disappeared with the publication of my book.

Many M.P.s were immediately disappointed to learn that the inquiry was to be undertaken by the Security Commission, then headed by Lord Diplock, a 73-year-old judge. Mrs Thatcher promised Parliament that she would make the Commission's findings known in due course to an extent consistent with national security.[3]

As is customary with the Security Commission's inquiries, the leader of the opposition, Michael Foot, then rose to speak, having necessarily been called in to be told the substance of the Prime Minister's statement in advance. He had reason to be grateful to Mrs Thatcher for the decision, in her brief, to avoid any reference to the late Lord Bradwell (formerly Tom Driberg M.P.), for the book had shown him to have been a double agent for MI5 and the K.G.B. while serving in Parliament, even while Chairman of the Labour Party.[4] Foot had been a close personal friend of Driberg, and had written a postscript to the latter's autobiography, *Ruling Passions*.[5] Had the Prime Minister confirmed my disclosures about Driberg, which have been confirmed since, Foot's position and that of other Labour left-wingers could have been uncomfortable. Instead, Foot was able to imply that such references were among the 'inaccuracies' and 'distortions' mentioned by the Prime Minister.[6] At that moment it suited the Labour leader to accept the clearance of Hollis but in March 1983 a document published by a Labour Party study group, of which he was a member, was to state that 'a former Director-General of MI5, Sir Roger Hollis, had been inconclusively investigated as a suspected K.G.B. double agent' and that 'the investigation was entirely covered up – despite devastating implications for British security as far as foreign powers are concerned'.[7]

Sir Harold Wilson, the former Prime Minister, then rose to make a statement which was extraordinary in view of what he had said to me, in the presence of Lady Falkender, a few months previously while my book had still been in preparation. Over lunch at the Café Royal, where they were my guests, I had raised the Hollis affair and Wilson's knowledge that a former Director-General of MI5 might have been a Soviet agent. I asked Wilson, 'Was it Hollis to whom you were referring?' Wilson looked me in the eye and answered, 'I do not remember that man's name in that connection.' Yet, in Parliament, he rose to claim public credit for having set up the Trend inquiry. He said, 'Will the Right Honourable Lady confirm that, although Sir Roger Hollis operated during seven premierships, including my own, I was the first to set up an independent inquiry?'[8] This the Prime Minister duly did though in fact it had been Sir John Hunt, the Cabinet Secretary, who had really been responsible, Wilson having done little but initial Hunt's suggestion.

As the serialization of the book had been running for four days in the *Daily Mail* and for three in *The Times*, with unprecedented coverage in other papers, radio and television, many M.P.s wished to question the Prime Minister on specific points and rose from their seats to do so. The Speaker called only three backbenchers from each side of the House, all of them guaranteed not to ask controversial questions. The Speaker failed to call Dennis Canavan, who had asked the original question which had given the Prime Minister the opportunity to make her statement. He also declined to call Jonathan Aitken, who had first alerted the Prime Minister to the Hollis affair and who knew from different sources that my information was correct. I do not know if the Speaker was approached beforehand but I have been assured that under such circumstances he can be asked to limit questioners from the floor in the national interest and exclude any who might be contentious. One of the questioners called even suggested that I had been the victim of a K.G.B. disinformation exercise but, as I subsequently pointed out in *The Times*, if that had been so, then many of my distinguished informants, both inside and outside the secret services, must have been working for the Russians.[9]

In her answers to the few innocuous questions Mrs Thatcher was able to refer to the successes of the security services in Hollis's time, like the cases involving Lonsdale, Houghton, Ethel Gee, the Krogers, Vassall and Blake, all of which, as I have shown, were appalling security disasters and were never detected by MI5 or MI6 until they had been alerted by chance defectors. The only true success which she mentioned was the expulsion of 105 spies from the Soviet organizations in Britain in 1971 and, as I had pointed out in the book, that had happened after Hollis had retired. In a later statement, which Mrs Thatcher was to make in the case of Leo Long, she referred to 'the Hollis debate', but no such debate had ever taken place because none was permitted.[10]

Though Mrs Thatcher had done her best for Hollis she had 'damned him with no praise', as one politician remarked. There was no suggestion that he had been an able public servant whose reputation was being traduced. In private, ministers have expressed the opinion that Hollis's behaviour was incompetent rather than treacherous and one Law Officer has been reported to me as saying that Hollis was 'indecisive, ineffectual and bumbling'. It would seem extremely unlikely, however, that a professional as discerning as Sir Dick White would have recommended a bumbling incompetent to be his deputy or his successor. One of the MI5 officers who investigated Hollis declared him to be 'extremely shrewd'. When incompetence benefits an adversary on such a scale, deliberate action presents a more acceptable explanation.

The reaction to the Prime Minister's statement by some former members of the Fluency Committee and K7 was to conclude that she had been grossly misled into giving the impression that Hollis had been cleared and that no suspicion concerning him remained. As they knew that no MI5 case is ever closed until resolved they carried out an analysis of the statement and found at least six areas where it was grossly at variance with the facts as they knew them. The statement was worded to give the impression that all the events I described in the book were very old when, in fact, Hollis was not interrogated until 1970 and was still being investigated in 1975, two years after his death. It indicated that the inquiries leading to the suspicions of Hollis arose from routine investigations following the defection of Burgess and Maclean in 1951. In fact their inception had no direct connection with the Burgess and Maclean case. They were undertaken because so many MI5 operations in the 1950s and 1960s went so seriously wrong that they could be explained only if there was a high-level spy still in the organization.

Mrs Thatcher's statement compounded this misleading suggestion by saying that the case against Hollis was based 'on certain leads that suggested, but did not prove, that there had been a Russian Intelligence service agent at a relatively senior level in British counter-intelligence *in the last years of the war* [my italics]'. This innuendo that the only leads pointing to Hollis dated from 1945 and before was so opposed to the evidence that I wrote to Lord Trend because I knew that he had examined leads which had arisen in the 1960s. His reply indicated that he was not prepared to be associated with the restriction of them to 'the last years of the war'.[11]

Mrs Thatcher's brief also stated that each of the leads pointing to Hollis 'could also be taken as pointing to Philby or Blunt'. Blunt left MI5 in 1945/46 and Philby left MI6 in 1951. So this was clearly an attempt by the officials who prepared the speech to lumber Blunt and Philby with penetrations achieved by the K.G.B. long after they had ceased to have access to secret information. It was calculated to support the misleading contention that the penetrations which had led to the Hollis investigations were all part of the 'poisoned past' and could safely be ignored. The MI5 investigators and others associated with the Hollis inquiries had no hesitation in calling that part of the statement a fabrication, as did a former very senior Whitehall official who told me that it was not Trend's conclusion and that he could not understand why Mrs Thatcher had been induced to indicate that it was.

The falseness of the claim is also proved by the facts of the Mitchell case which resulted from an attempt to discover the perpetrator of serious leakages up to and including the defection of Philby in 1963. Mitchell was subjected to an interrogation which covered the whole of his career, from 1939 to 1963 and, as the Hollis investigations and his eventual interrogation were undertaken for precisely the same purpose, they also covered the whole span of his career from 1938 until the end of 1965. In neither case were the inquiries restricted to the war years or to the immediate post-war years ending with Philby's dismissal in 1951. It is inconceivable that if the Russians had managed to recruit Hollis before or during the war they would have left him alone when he became Deputy Director-General and then Director-General.

The suggestion that Hollis's behaviour after the end of the war was not the subject of searching inquiry by the security authorities is so false as to throw doubt on the rest of the statement. The serious penetration problems did not disappear after Blunt and Philby left but did appear to cease when Hollis retired. In the interests of the historic record the Prime Minister should be required to correct her statement with regard to the time of the leads pointing to Hollis.

Former MI5 and MI6 officers also took exception to the Prime Minister's claim that none of the leads pointed specifically in his direction. Several of the leads were unattributable to anyone else, once Mitchell had been cleared as Peter Wright stated publicly in his television interview in July 1984.

Parliament and the public were further misled by the suggestion that the investigation into Hollis had been little more than a routine procedure to eliminate him from a list of suspects. For those few people who knew about the Hollis affair it was one of the most traumatic episodes in the history of Whitehall, as one former Director-General of MI5 has confirmed to me. Mrs Thatcher's statement that the fact that somebody has been the subject of investigation does not mean that he has been positively suspected could not possibly be applied to Hollis, though Parliament was clearly intended to assume that it did. If he had not been positively suspected would he have been subjected to the indignity of interrogation? The avoidance of any mention of the interrogation would not seem to have been by chance.

The officers who analysed the statement, and Peter Wright independently, were adamant that its crucial claim that the internal investigations had concluded that Hollis had not been an agent of the Soviet Union was incorrect. In their clear recollection the case had been left unproven.

The Prime Minister's brief stated that the internal clearance was challenged by 'a very few of those concerned'. While few may have gone through the motions of challenging it, many disagreed with it. The Fluency Committee consisted of seven experienced officers. Its replacement, the MI5 section K7, involved several more. Independently they recommended that Hollis should be interrogated in the belief that he might break down and confess. So it was not a minority view that Hollis might have been a spy. It was the decision that Hollis should be given an umpire's verdict of 'Not out' that was taken by a very few of those concerned. Further, those few had acted contrary to the principle that the benefit of any doubt should always be given to the Service rather than a suspect individual. In Hollis's case the individual was dead and could do no more damage, but a formal clearance meant that the implications of his guilt for the Service, including the possibility that he might have brought in other potential agents, could thenceforth be ignored.

Mrs Thatcher was at pains to claim that in the Hollis case nothing had been covered up. Until my disclosures nothing had been heard of the Hollis case or the Trend inquiry. The scandal that MI5's affairs had been in such disarray that the Director-General had ended up being interrogated as a possible Soviet spy had been totally concealed, not just from Parliament but, for several years, from the Government. I am not suggesting that such matters should be made public but when they are, ministers should not deny that they have been concealed. It is reasonable to ask what would happen if clinching evidence disputing Trend's verdict should arrive via a defector, an intercept or some other windfall. I suspect that it would be withheld and that the statement given by Mrs Thatcher to Parliament would be allowed to stand as the historic record, unless some investigative writer with prime sources chanced to uncover the truth.

The brief on Hollis prepared for Mrs Thatcher was altogether too reminiscent of the White Paper on the Maclean and Burgess defection and Macmillan's statement to Parliament on Philby. Her assurance that no evidence had been found that 'incriminated' Hollis was also true of Fuchs, Blake, Maclean, Philby, Blunt and Long against whom all the evidence was circumstantial or so secret that it could not be used in court unless legitimized by a voluntary confession. Considering that the various officials had had several weeks in which to prepare the brief it was a poor effort and politically dangerous for the Prime Minister. No doubt they convinced themselves that they were acting in the best interests of Whitehall, the Government and the nation, but all they needed to have said was that Hollis had been suspected, had been investigated and that the case remained unproven either way. Instead, Mrs Thatcher was induced to go out on a limb which could be sawn off any day. As I have indicated, proof that Hollis had been in contact with Sonia in China, Oxford, or both, might be sufficient.

Mrs Thatcher might have been more cautious had she accepted a first-hand run down on the Hollis case by a senior member of the Fluency Committee when this was offered to her in a letter from Jonathan Aitken early in 1980.[12] She declined this on the advice of officials, who preferred that she should put her faith in the Trend report. Like the Prime Minister, I was trained in a scientific discipline. Had I needed to know the nature and results of an investigation I would have consulted those who conducted it. I would not have put my faith in the views of the Dean of the Science Faculty.

One member of the Fluency Committee described the Prime Minister's statement as 'a standard denial normally given when espionage cases do not end in prosecution', but others were less charitable, calling it 'an Establishment concoction intended to bury the Hollis affair', as Wright also did in his television interview.

When the former MI5 and MI6 officers made their analysis of the statement, and concluded that Mrs Thatcher had been grossly misled, they were not aware of the warning to the American and Commonwealth security authorities in May 1974 that Hollis might have been a spy. Had they known that, their criticisms might have been much stronger, especially as it seems certain that Mrs Thatcher had not been told about it until the Canadian Solicitor-General publicly referred to it shortly after her statement.

It is instructive to compare the statement prepared by officials for Mrs Thatcher with that given, on his own initiative, by Mr Callaghan during the Blunt debate, a year and a half earlier. While her brief gave Parliament the firm impression that Hollis had been satisfactorily cleared so that the case could be forgotten, Callaghan told the House that the shameful matter of Soviet penetration had not been cleared up and might never be. Yet in those eighteen months no new information of any consequence had accrued and the only explanation for the discrepancy seems to lie in the determination of officials to urge the Prime Minister to try to put an end to allegations about further penetration of the secret services after the era of the Cambridge Ring once and for all.

The Potential Value of Oversight

The Prime Minister's statement on the Hollis affair provides some of the most compelling evidence to date for the urgent need for some degree of Parliamentary oversight of intelligence and security matters. In the first place I feel confident that if those who drafted it had known that an independent Parliamentary body might question those secret service officers who disagreed with it, various assurances, which were clearly incorrect, would have been omitted. I refer, in particular, to the claim that each of the leads pointing to Hollis could also be taken as pointing to Philby or Blunt and that they dated from 1945 and before. Those who drafted the brief might also have been less confident in believing that they could assure Parliament and the public that Hollis had been completely cleared when, in fact, the case was unproven. As things stand, intelligence and security issues can be so managed in Parliament by the Government in office that the drafters of statements can be virtually certain that errors and omissions will not be effectively challenged. Such a situation, vividly exemplified by the Prime Minister's statement on the Hollis affair, is not conducive to the establishment of the truth, either at the time or historically, because of reliance on *Hansard* reports. As a subsequent report by a Labour Party study group was to show,[13] the involvement of the leader of the opposition is no adequate safeguard.

It would seem unlikely that an oversight body would have been satisfied with the statement, and the questioning of James Callaghan alone would have raised grave doubts about it, in view of what he had said previously.

The existence of an oversight body would, I believe, also induce ministers, including prime ministers, to question their briefers more thoroughly and to require confirmation of every important point. This is as much in the interests of ministers as of Parliament and the public. In the past ministers have too often been used as a mouthpiece for misleading information prepared by officials.

An oversight body may have prevented the convenient closure of the Hollis case, which meant the penetrations would remain unexplained.

CHAPTER FIFTY-EIGHT

Aftermath

As had happened with previous books and articles of mine drawing attention to K.G.B. activities in Britain and the fact that Labour M.P.s had been recruited to the Soviet cause, a Labour left-winger asked the Prime Minister to arrange for an investigation of my sources.[1] Mrs Thatcher replied that one was already in progress and that any relevant evidence would be submitted to the Attorney-General, presumably with the possible intention of a prosecution. A modest inquiry had, in fact, begun as soon as MI5 had access to the typescript of *Their Trade is Treachery* and the Prime Minister was not responsible for it. I can find no evidence of any further Parliamentary interest in the inquiry though on the previous occasions there had been follow-up questions to the Attorney-General until he was driven to announce that no prosecution was intended.

Checks were made on travels I had made overseas to see whom I might have visited but I was never consulted myself. I had made it clear that I would be of no assistance to anyone in any effort to discover my sources and, while I suspect that my telephone was tapped and letters opened during the inquiry, I heard no more and no action was taken against those who had assisted me or against anyone else. Nor, as far as I know, was any action threatened.

In November 1982 the MI5 Director of Establishments sent a letter to retired MI5 officers, which began somewhat ominously, 'Dear Pensioner...' warning them of their obligations under the Official Secrets Act and urging them to report any approaches by writers, but that was mainly the result of the imprudent activities of another author.

While ministers and even retired civil servants have continued to pay lip service to the need for more open government most of the executive action has been in the direction of preserving official secrecy. Investigations into leaks have been intensified with the unprecedented use of the police in that connection. Searches of C.I.A. and F.B.I. documents made on my behalf have produced evidence of the recent weeding, and even clawing back, in the British interest of files previously released under the U.S. Freedom of Information Act. One researcher found some papers in the C.I.A. archives which referred to Guy Liddell by name and asked for photocopies but when he went to pick them up three weeks later the pages concerning Liddell had been removed and there was a card in their place stating that they had been withdrawn at the request of British Intelligence.[2] There are many other instances of documents being withheld or 'sanitized' by blanking out in the British interest. F.B.I. documents covering the interviews with Michael Straight in 1963 and 1966 have been heavily blanked out and professional examination of the various code-marks on them show that most of the censorship has been in the British interest. Canadian documents have also been withheld. In such ways does the 'embarrassment factor' reach far beyond the confines of Whitehall and, whether by coincidence or not, much of the censorship has occurred since the publication of *Their Trade is Treachery*.

One particular event has revealed the lengths to which Whitehall departments will go to prevent any disclosure by American officials of information which the security authorities wish to keep secret. A U.S. State Department official, who is a personal friend and had access to information of relevance to the Hollis affair, wanted to see me while on a visit to London. It is standard practice that such an official wishing to speak to a foreign journalist or writer must consult the U.S. Embassy for permission, and my friend did so. After Embassy inquiries at the Foreign Office he was told that the British authorities were opposed to any conversations with me because I had 'given away important information about signals intelligence'. As I had done no such thing the Embassy made further inquiries at the Foreign Office and were told that, regrettably, my name had been confused with somebody else's but that a meeting with me was still undesirable. Not only did we not meet on that occasion, I was not even aware of his presence in London because of the Foreign Office action, which appeared to involve a deliberate lie.

If the Prime Minister's statement on *Their Trade is Treachery* was a disinformation exercise, engineered not to misinform the Soviet adversary but the British Parliament and public, it succeeded because most newspapers and the other media accepted the view that Hollis had been effectively cleared. As I had anticipated, after so many years in Fleet Street, those newspapers which had been 'scooped' through the exclusivity purchased by the *Daily Mail* took every opportunity provided by the statement to suggest that none of the information was correct or new, even, to further the

549

circulation war, castigating the *Daily Mail* for publishing the extracts. Some papers preferred a personal attack, accusing me of inaccuracies which they soon had to withdraw – though with extreme reluctance – as independent confirmation rolled in from other sources. The television programmes, in particular, persisted in saying that I had accused Hollis of being a spy when what I had really done was to disclose that the Director-General of MI5 had been suspected of being a spy, a statement which the Prime Minister had amply confirmed.

The generally favourable nature of the media reaction to Mrs Thatcher's statement was, to some extent, pre-conditioned by the reputation she had established for courage and honesty in exposing Blunt but, as I have pointed out, all she had done on that occasion was to read out a statement prepared for her predecessor, James Callaghan, who had taken the courageous decision. As it had seemed that the Prime Minister had told the full truth about Blunt it was assumed that she must be doing the same about Hollis. It is hardly to the credit of the media that, with few exceptions, it accepted the MI5 and Cabinet Office 'clearances' of Hollis without further inquiry, even though the previous Parliamentary 'clearance' of Philby was fresh in recollection.

In retrospect, the reluctance of the media to follow up major disclosures, like the fact that Philby, who was known to have sent many people to their deaths, had been offered immunity to prosecution, was astonishing, being matched only by the silence from back-benchers in Parliament.

The Labour M.P. Leo Abse proved to be a notable exception in print. In an article entitled 'The Judas Syndrome', he pointed out that the Prime Minister had not really dismissed the charge against Hollis but only insisted that the charge was not proven. 'Why should Hollis be retrospectively exempted from the criteria the Security Service insists must apply to all other civil servants?' he asked. He was referring to the practice of positive vetting which works on the principle that, for the safety of the state, a person with access to Top Secret information who is suspect on reasonable grounds should be judged guilty until proved innocent.[3]

As I had predicted in the book, I was heavily criticized for impugning the integrity of a dead man who could not defend himself. Regrettably, I did not discover the facts about the investigations of Hollis until after his death but, had he been alive, he would not have been allowed to defend himself, as already mentioned, because of the requirements of the Official Secrets Act, and the public would still have had to depend on a ministerial statement prepared on his behalf by the same agencies responsible for the statement read out by Mrs Thatcher. Knowing Fleet Street as well as I do, I am in no doubt whatever that those newspapers who claimed that it was wrong to reveal the truth about Hollis after his death would have had no hesitation in doing so themselves if the information had come their way. The fact that he was dead would have been regarded as an advantage because it would have disposed of any libel risks. In any case, it is utter humbug to suggest that dead people who were important in the public service should not be criticized. All honest biographers are required to record details which the dead person and his relatives may prefer to keep suppressed.

Senior officers of MI5 and MI6, both current and retired, who saw advance copies of *Their Trade is Treachery* gave considerable thought to possible reaction by the K.G.B. when the book was published. Some suspected that the K.G.B. would try to capitalize on the disclosures, particularly those about Hollis, with items planted in the foreign Press, and especially in the U.S., to denigrate British security and so weaken the confidence of allied nations in any interchange of intelligence material. Others, who believed Hollis to be guilty or thought he might be, predicted that the Russians would remain silent, as they had in the past even about self-confessed spies like Fuchs, Blunt and even Maclean, until his death.

The Soviet people are told little, if anything, about the K.G.B.'s activities abroad and are given the impression that only the West indulges in the 'dirty game' of espionage. Even Richard Sorge, who did so much to save Moscow from German occupation, at the eventual cost of his life, received public recognition in the Soviet Union only relatively recently, when his head appeared on a Soviet stamp. Still, some response for foreign consumption seemed likely and when none came those who were convinced that there had been a spy in MI5 at high level over many years regarded the silence in Moscow as further evidence in support of their belief. As one very experienced counter-espionage officer put it to me, 'Moscow would want to ensure the continuing protection of an agent of that calibre, even after his death, to keep MI5 guessing and to protect any residual agents recruited through his activities.' This officer then went on to predict, 'But I would expect the K.G.B. to keep the issue alive by a little judicious prodding from time to time.'

What would seem to be an example of this prodding appeared in a little book published in Moscow in the Russian language early in 1983.[4] Entitled *The Chekists Explain*, the book is one of a series intended for mass readership, with the propaganda objective of showing the K.G.B. and its much feared predecessor, the Cheka, as heroic organizations forced to stoop to unpleasant measures to protect the Soviet state against ruthless enemies, such as Britain. One chapter, called 'A Drop of Blood', by Nikolai Pekelnik, almost certainly a pseudonym, relates what is projected as a true story of a Briton who sold secrets to the Soviet Union in the 1930s and later, betraying his own country for money. This villain was called Sir Edward Pelham Hollis.

I have had this chapter translated and, while it is full of detail and conversations between Sir Edward and the Soviet agents who ran him, inquiries show that it is entirely fictional, though presented as fact. This Hollis is supposed to have been a senior Foreign Office diplomat but no such person has ever worked for the Foreign Office.

All the authorities whom I have consulted insist that such a book could not be published without the agreement and control of the K.G.B. and that it was almost certainly written at the instigation of the K.G.B. The choice of the name Hollis is therefore intriguing to say the least. I have asked several intelligence officers for their interpretation and the consensus is that it is a crude piece of disinformation to provoke reaction and wonder about what might be coming next. Nobody suggested that the choice of the name Hollis was a coincidence.

Over the past three years, through direct contacts and indirectly through what might be described as 'cut-outs', I have been able to discover the attitude of present and former members of MI5, MI6 and G.C.H.Q. to the Hollis case. The relatively few who are completely convinced of his innocence mainly comprise those responsible for promoting Hollis, like Sir Dick White, and those who owed their promotion to Hollis, like Sir Martin Furnival Jones. In view of the unprecedented furore inside the secret departments created by *Their Trade is Treachery*, public support from the pro-Hollis faction has been surprisingly small. A brief letter in *The Times* signed by Furnival Jones and Anthony Simkins, his former deputy, claiming that there had not been 'a shred of evidence' that Hollis had been disloyal at any time or in any way, was easily countered and only served to confirm the fact that Hollis had been interrogated as well as investigated.[5] Had there been no 'shred of evidence' why were the American and White Commonwealth security authorities warned of the danger that Hollis might have been a spy? Having retired, Furnival Jones and Simkins had probably been unaware of that highly secret event, for unless recalled for a specific purpose, former officers, however distinguished, are cut off from all information. I understand that even Sir

Dick White, who regards the Hollis case as 'contrived', has never seen the MI5 files on it. Others have since objected to my continuing inquiries into the Hollis affair on the grounds that he was 'acquitted' by Lord Trend, but Will Owen, the Labour M.P., had been acquitted by a jury of twelve and then admitted to MI5 that he had indeed been a spy, as a witness to that event, Leo Abse, has recorded.

While Hollis's supporters may have preferred to do little in public, I have been assured by a prime source that some of them were quickly active in private, briefing other writers to do what they could to denigrate my information. They were particularly concerned to undermine the evidence that Hollis could have been the MI5 spy called 'Elli' but were singularly unsuccessful, especially when the Canadian authorities unexpectedly released Gouzenko's testimony. In that connection there were even efforts to brand Gouzenko as a drunkard, which was entirely unfounded.[6]

As part of the inspired ploy it was suggested that the fact that three successive Directors-General of MI5, Sir Michael Hanley, Sir Howard Smith and Sir John Jones, had never bothered to reopen the Hollis case was strong evidence of the general belief in his innocence. That statement is not strictly correct because the Hollis case was discussed at length in the summer of 1977 when James Callaghan, then Prime Minister, called in Hanley, Sir Maurice Oldfield the MI6 chief, and the Cabinet Secretary Sir John Hunt, to discuss Soviet penetration and 'go over the ground again'. But what Director General in his right mind would want to reopen that can of worms once it had been officially sealed, unless there was some new and pressing reason for doing so?

To reduce the risk of a Parliamentary demand for a further inquiry into the Hollis case, the Prime Minister has seized every opportunity to suggest that it is too old to warrant time and effort, yet, as I write, the much older Philby case has been reopened.[7]

The latest apologia being bandied about by Hollis supporters is a theory – for which there is no evidence whatever – that he was framed to cover the treachery of others!

Among those very senior authorities who fear that Hollis was a spy are at least one former Director-General of MI5, a former Director of G.C.H.Q., and at least two former Directors of MI6. At a lower level are several former long-serving officers of both MI5 and MI6 and several women who served as ancillary staff. One of the latter has gone so far, recently, as to say that Hollis was definitely a Soviet agent, claiming to have ascertained, at higher level, that he had handed over some information to Soviet Intelligence.[8] In late 1982 five former members of the secret services were considering an offer to appear on a television programme about Hollis in which they were prepared to assert their belief that there had been a high-level spy inside MI5 in the 1960s and that Hollis was their chief suspect.[9] Peter Wright eventually did so on the 'World in Action' programme screened in Britain on 16 July 1984. In a long interview he confirmed the account of the Hollis case given in *Their Trade is Treachery*, and an account of the warning to the American and White Commonwealth security chiefs that Hollis may have been a Soviet agent which I had published in *The Times* on 12 December 1981. He claimed to be convinced that Hollis had been a spy, and said that seven of his former colleagues agreed with him while others were satisfied that there had certainly been a Soviet agent at high level in MI5 long after Blunt and Philby had left the secret services. Wright said that parts of Mrs Thatcher's statement to Parliament about my book had been false, and that she had been misled by those who briefed her.

Stephen Knight, an experienced and dependable researcher, questioned several MI5 officers, both retired and serving, about the Hollis case in connection with his recent book, *The Brotherhood*, which deals with various aspects of Freemasonry. He concluded: 'Few people in MI5 now doubt that Sir Roger Hollis was a Russian spy for nearly thirty years.'[10]

One senior retired MI5 officer who remains in touch with the organization has assured me that many in the headquarters in Curzon Street now incline to the opinion that Hollis was a spy and favour a further inquiry to try to settle the issue and, hopefully, remove the debilitating doubt. Further information of which I am unaware may have accrued, but Hollis's behaviour in the Gouzenko case seems to have contributed to that doubt. Though the case has been allowed to moulder through deliberate inaction some windfall event may yet settle it.

Perhaps those who just cannot bring themselves to believe that the head of MI5 could have spied for twenty-nine years without being caught should study the recent trial of Commander Dieter Gerhardt, the former commandant of the South African naval base at Simonstown who was convicted of spying for the Soviet Union for more than twenty years.[11] The gallant and treacherous Commander had not enjoyed the advantage of being inside a counter-espionage service where he could have monitored events that might have menaced him.

While most M.P.s welcomed the independent inquiry into security procedures announced by Mrs Thatcher, many were disappointed that it was to be carried out by the Security Commission, which was headed by a judge. They would have preferred some involvement of Parliament through completely trustworthy Privy Councillors, if only because judges inevitably approach issues with a legal mind, when intelligence and security matters demand a different approach. Because of the limitation on M.P.s' questions after the announcement there was widespread misunderstanding of the purpose of the inquiry and I had some difficulty in convincing M.P.s that it would not examine the Hollis case or any others disclosed in my book because its terms of reference had been framed to prevent that.

Eventually Lord Bridge, another Law Lord, and Lord Allen, formerly Permanent Secretary to the Home Office, were selected to assist Lord Diplock and quickly settled into their formidable task of seeking oral and written evidence from witnesses, who included myself. Among other suggestions, I strongly recommended the introduction of the polygraph as a routine instrument in the positive vetting process, citing the C.I.A.'s evidence for its value.

Meanwhile the initial impression, generated by the Prime Minister's statement, that the events described in *Their Trade is Treachery* were inaccurately or even falsely recorded was quickly eroded by a series of confirmations which has steadily continued. Through the subterfuge of giving details to newspapers which had the resources to pursue them, I was soon able to bring into the open names which I had been required to omit from the original text. The first of these was the identity of the recruited Soviet agent who had eventually exposed Blunt in 1963, Michael Straight, who has since written his own account of the circumstances, confirming what I had disclosed and adding more details. Graham Mitchell openly admitted that he had indeed been deeply suspect, had been interrogated and had been cleared.[12] A former woman MI5 officer, Joan Miller, confirmed that Driberg had indeed been employed by MI5, his agent-runner Maxwell Knight also being a homosexual and being 'crazy about him'. In spite of considerable publicity about Driberg's MI5 work, the matter has been studiously ignored by Parliament which, being a club, avoids criticism of its members, past and present, whenever possible.

The communism and Soviet allegiance of Bernard Floud, which had brought swift denials, has been amply confirmed, as has the initial recruitment by Floud of Jenifer Hart – again with silence from the deniers.[13]

The public exposure of Leo Long, whose treachery had been clearly indicated in my book, was fully reported by the media and led to a Parliamentary statement by Mrs Thatcher on 9 November 1981. She said that she was giving the statement only because Long

555

had publicly admitted his guilt, implying that she would not have done so had he kept his mouth shut. This meant that the immunity effectively dispensed by Hollis, which the Prime Minister clearly regarded as having been reprehensible, would have protected Long from official public censure in perpetuity, had he remained silent – an implication of interest to future traitors.

Later the admissions by Sir Dennis Proctor and Alister Watson that they had been interrogated by MI5 were also reported by the media.[14]

The fact that it was Hollis who interviewed Gouzenko, which many journalists attempted to deny, especially in Canada, was fully confirmed by Canadian as well as British authorities. So was the much disputed fact that Gouzenko had warned of the existence of a spy in MI5 with the code-name 'Elli' – by the unexpected publication of the Gouzenko transcripts.

The warning given to the White Commonwealth security agencies in the mid-1970s that Hollis might have been a spy was confirmed by the Canadian Solicitor-General. Most of those investigators who doubted that Hollis had been a Soviet agent now seem convinced that there was certainly a spy at high level during his later years in MI5. Indeed, a number of authors have reprinted much of the information disclosed in *Their Trade is Treachery*, as historical fact. My account of Philby's exposure by Flora Solomon has been confirmed in her own memoirs.

This book provides further confirmations of and substantial extensions to the previous information and more will arise soon from the delvings of academic historians who are researching the activities of some of the most damaging traitors because of their influence on international relations. The mass of additional information which has flowed to me over the past three years supports the general accuracy of the original disclosures and not one item of it militates against the official suspicions that Hollis was a spy.

The most impressive confirmation of the message which *Their Trade is Treachery* delivered, however, came with the submission of the Security Commission's report to Mrs Thatcher early in 1982, after nine months of solid effort.[15] It made many recommendations, most of them still secret, for improving the security system to prevent penetration by Soviet agents and stated that the Commission had paid particularly close attention to the penetration problem 'because of the circumstances which led to the Prime Minister's statement on 26 March 1981'.

The report, which would normally have generated many Parliamentary questions, or even a debate, had negligible impact because the Prime Minister chose to issue her statement about it right in the middle of the Falklands conflict, when her opponents and critics were concentrating all their political attention on that issue. That situation also enabled her to go back on her promise to Parliament to publish as full an expurgated version of the report as possible, which had been standard practice with comparable reports in the past. Her decision to issue only a thirteen-page White Paper, representing a small fraction of the report, would undoubtedly have provoked criticism with cries of 'cover-up!' from opposition M.P.s under normal circumstances.[16] Because of the overwhelming interest in the Falklands war she was never challenged about her statement in the White Paper that an expurgated text would have given 'a seriously misleading impression of the report'. This reason for withholding information from Parliament was new and established a precedent which could be used again.

The document was as uninformative as possible but under the heading 'Security and Intelligence' there was a bald statement that a number of changes in the recruitment and personnel security procedures for those engaged in the security and intelligence services (MI5, MI6 and G.C.H.Q.) had been recommended and were being implemented. The large number of improvements recommended and adopted hardly accorded with the Prime Minister's allegations that the book which had been responsible for them was inaccurate. They did not, however, include the introduction of the polygraph, for which I had pressed, an omission suggesting that the Commission lacked resolution because the same body, though under different leadership, was to take a different view only a year later.

Once again, officials who drafted the White Paper put the Prime Minister into an unnecessarily hazardous position. They included the statement, attributed to her: 'The Commission's report is generally reassuring: Lord Diplock and his colleagues take the view that the procedures, as they have applied since the Committee under Lord Radcliffe reported in April 1962, have worked well.' This seemed to be a dangerous hostage to fortune and, within two months, the Prime Minister was faced with the arrest of Geoffrey Prime, a long-term Soviet agent at G.C.H.Q. where, clearly, the 'procedures applied since 1962' had not worked well.

CHAPTER FIFTY-NINE

G.C.H.Q.'s Billion-Dollar Spy

THE security procedures in which Mrs Thatcher and her predecessors had placed such trust were shown to be devastatingly ineffective following the arrest of Geoffrey Arthur Prime on Official Secrets Act charges in July 1982. Then aged forty-four, Prime had been spying for the Soviet Union for at least fourteen years, nine of them inside the most sensitive of all secret intelligence departments, G.C.H.Q. Though never of high rank, Prime had such access to British and American secrets concerning the interception of Soviet intelligence that he inflicted damage officially estimated by the Pentagon as costing $1,000 million.[1] Further, he was yet another example of a long-time Soviet agent who was detected only as a result of a fluke incident after spying under circumstances which should have been subjected to the tightest possible security. In *Their Trade is Treachery*, published in the year before Prime's arrest, I stated the MI5 opinion that security arrangements at G.C.H.Q. were inadequate, with few checks at the gates to prevent espionage or sabotage and with people taking out secret papers against standing orders. Nothing was done until after Prime's arrest.

Prime had joined the R.A.F. in 1956 and, after taking a Russian-language course, was engaged on signals intelligence work at Gatow in Berlin, where he also learned German.[2] He was later to tell MI5 that, on his own initiative, he volunteered to spy for the Soviet Union, having taken an interest in the Soviet system, but at least one authority on the case suspects that he was recruited through sexual blackmail. Prime had a morbid sexual interest in young girls, which was, eventually to be the cause of his detection. However it occurred, Prime met two Soviet Intelligence officers, whom he knew as 'Igor' and 'Valya', in East Berlin. Either on his initiative, or theirs, he decided to resign from the R.A.F. and to offer his services to G.C.H.Q., which he joined in September 1968. Before leaving for Britain his controllers gave him an advanced course in espionage, involving the use of secret inks, one-time pads and microdots, and a code-name – 'Rowlands'. His kit was packed under the false bottom of a briefcase, together with a payment of £400.

At first Prime worked in a London out-station of G.C.H.Q. where he was able to discover much about secret methods and operations. In March 1976 he moved to the heart of G.C.H.Q.'s operations at Cheltenham, where he also gained deep insight into American interception activities because of the exceptionally close liaison with the U.S. equivalent, the much larger National Security Agency. Once again, the K.G.B. had been able to recruit a person of seemingly limited potential and then intrude him into an agency of extreme sensitivity.

Prime conveyed his material to Soviet Intelligence by means of letters to East Germany containing messages in invisible ink, by dead-letter boxes in Surrey, and through visits to Vienna, East Berlin and, probably, Eire, Rome and Cyprus. These visits, made under Soviet instructions in the guise of holidays, indicate the importance still being paid by the K.G.B. to the use of countries other than the target country for clandestine meetings, any regular reason for foreign travel being a huge advantage to a spy.

At the beginning of 1973 the world's most advanced reconnaissance satellite had been launched by the U.S. into stationary orbit 22,300 miles above the earth, where it could maintain surveillance on missiles being fired on test ranges in the Soviet Union. With an aerial 70 feet wide it was designed to pick up all the telemetry signals emitted by Soviet missiles while in flight. These signals emanate from devices fitted to various points on the missiles to inform the scientists on the ground about velocity, altitude, aerodynamic details and engine performance, which they must know to measure and improve range and accuracy. After intercepting the signals, the satellite, code-named 'Rhyolite', transmitted them to receiving stations, one of them being a joint G.C.H.Q./N.S.A. station at Menwith Hill in Yorkshire. So far as is known, the details of Rhyolite, and the quite extraordinary things it could do, were kept secret until 1975 when Prime was told about them as part of his work.

By the time Prime began to betray Rhyolite's secrets an improved version had been placed in orbit and the Russians had received another bonus – a young employee of an American electronics company involved in the Rhyolite project had begun to sell them details complementary to those supplied by the G.C.H.Q. traitor.[3] As a result Soviet scientists were able to feed false information into the satellite on such a scale and so convincingly that U.S. Intelligence was misled over several years about the true state of Soviet missile development. The Russians had already been running a successful disinformation programme to convince the West that they were in technological trouble and as a result had managed to gain a lead in the nuclear missile field which is largely responsible for the current N.A.T.O. effort to restore the balance. For any disinformation operation to continue there must be feedback of its effects and Prime was in a perfect position to accomplish that. He also was able to inform the K.G.B. when Soviet codes were being broken by G.C.H.Q.[4]

The American spy was caught and sentenced early in 1977 but Prime, who must have been very worried, continued to spy until September of that year when he decided to resign from G.C.H.Q. on the grounds of excessive strain, though he was not under suspicion of any kind. No security inquiry was made into his action in throwing away his career at the age of thirty-nine to become a wine salesman and, later, a taxi driver.

Though allegedly out of touch with secrets, Prime was summoned to Vienna by the K.G.B. in April 1981 when he said that he handed over reels of photocopied documents and notes which he had retained since leaving G.C.H.Q. Later that year, in November, he was summoned to East Berlin, which he should not have visited as a former employee still under the Official Secrets Act, and received £4,000 for past services.

Prime was responsible for a number of sexual offences against young girls and when the police were closing in on him early in 1982 he confessed to his wife that he was responsible and telephoned the police. When his house and personal effects were searched the police discovered his one-time pads and other evidence of his espionage activities. His wife, to whom he had also reported his espionage, had felt it her duty to alert the police about it after she had found envelopes addressed to East Berlin.

When first questioned Prime denied the espionage but later confessed and pleaded guilty on 10 November 1982, being sentenced to thirty-five years' imprisonment for the Official Secrets Act offences and three years for the sexual offences.

The Americans were incensed at this loss of their secrets and the damage it had caused. Only the chance fact that an American spy had been equally seriously involved prevented what might have been irrevocable injury to the joint effort of G.C.H.Q. and the N.S.A. The Prime Minister, who must have regretted her reassuring statement to Parliament, asked the Security Commission to undertake a thorough inquiry and it did so with vigour. Probably because younger people, who regarded the Commission's previous report following my book as far too complacent, had replaced some of the former members of the Commission its recommendations were to be more robust.

The Commission, which reported in a White Paper in May 1983, found that Prime had been positively vetted four times, lying successfully and naming referees who either knew little about him or were not prepared to reveal what they knew. During one week when the P.V. team had been carrying out inquiries which cleared him for access to Top Secret information, Prime was in a flat in East Berlin undergoing training in K.G.B. espionage techniques!

Prime had been able to remove secret documents to photograph them at home because spot checks had not been carried out at the G.C.H.Q. gates and it had not been practicable to ensure that all top secret papers had been returned to the security vault each evening. After Prime had lost his one-time pads in 1972 he had written for more to East Berlin and two very obvious foreigners had called at his sister's home and left another briefcase with a new spy kit and another £400 under the false bottom.

Because the Russians had not pressured Prime into staying at G.C.H.Q., and as they did not seem to have made as much use of him as they might, the Security Commission expressed its fear that they might have other sources inside G.C.H.Q. and at the time of writing inquiries into that possibility are still being conducted by MI5.[5]

The Security Commission made several recommendations for improving security at G.C.H.Q., the major one being the introduction of the polygraph on a pilot scale, a measure which the previous Security Commission inquiry had rejected. More than twenty years previously the Radcliffe Committee had suggested that the security authorities should build up a body of knowledge and experience about the polygraph to discover whether it could be valuable, but the recommendation was withheld from the published report and nothing whatever was done. Though the American security authorities had their own espionage problems associated with the Prime case they argued that as G.C.H.Q. was 'little more than an arm of the N.S.A.' the polygraph should be introduced there. Cabinet officials and various ministers opposed the machine as un-British and an unwarrantable invasion of privacy likely to cause trade union reaction which they would rather avoid, but when members of the Security Commission visited the U.S. to be advised about the polygraph's potential they returned deeply impressed on two counts. First, the evidence showed it to be a powerful deterrent to spies considering entry to secret departments and, secondly, the C.I.A. had an impressive list of confessions of disqualifying information provided by applicants, some of whom had admitted that they were trying to gain access to secret information for hostile purposes. Currently, the polygraph is to be used on a pilot scale in MI5 and MI6, as well as G.C.H.Q., responsibility for its operation being in the hands of MI5.

The British authorities explained to American representatives that they were severely limited regarding additional security precautions at G.C.H.Q. because it had never been admitted that the British Government intercepted the secret messages of foreign countries during peacetime and it would be unduly embarrassing to have to do so, especially for the Foreign Secretary, because he would also have to admit that G.C.H.Q. was run by the Foreign Office, which would rather not be associated, officially, with any form of intelligence-gathering or espionage.[7] As the Russians and every other nation of consequence knew the purpose of G.C.H.Q. there seemed to be little substance to this reason, save for the long-standing pretence that gentlemen do not read other people's communications. Effectively it prevented such security improvements as the de-unionization of G.C.H.Q., which the Americans wanted in view of serious disruption which had occurred as a result of union-inspired stoppages of work in 1979 and 1981.[8]

The publicity which had to be given to the Prime case as a result of his trial and the Security Commission's report on his activities made the pretence no longer tenable so the Government decided to ban union membership to all G.C.H.Q. staff, numbering some 10,000, including those in all out-stations.[9] Again, Whitehall's pathological dedication to unnecessary secrecy was to land the Government in serious political trouble and alienate the unions. The Government's security advisers urged ministers to make the minimum disclosure about G.C.H.Q. and as a result the ban was announced without any explanation about the disruptions which the unions had caused during 1979 and 1981, when serious events were in train such as the invasion of Afghanistan and the attempted assassination of President Reagan. Only when the unions had reacted strenuously, gaining public and media support in the process, did the Government decide to disclose the events. In the so-called interests of secrecy, the main reason of the ban – that the nation could not risk strike action during the run-up to a major military emergency – was never given. The advisers argued that any suggestion that the unions concerned might one day be in extremist left-wing hands would be too inflammatory. The Government and the nation was, therefore, subjected to sympathetic industrial action and the unions were enabled to adopt their pretence that the Government was claiming that trade unionists were potential traitors, which, as the union leaders knew, was entirely false. The maximum damage was also inflicted on relations between the Government and G.C.H.Q. staff.

The severity of the political consequences of the treachery of Prime and his American counterpart has been publicly recognized in statements by U.S. politicians. Senator Daniel Moynihan, while Vice-Chairman of the Senate Intelligence Committee, claimed that the discovery that the Russians had been able to cheat on the strength of their missile forces was largely responsible for American reluctance to sign a second treaty limiting strategic arms.[10] In April 1982 the U.S. Secretary of Defense, Caspar Weinberger, admitted that the Soviet Union had achieved superiority over the U.S. in intercontinental missiles, while its huge advantage in short-range missiles was having to be hurriedly countered by the deployment of cruise missiles and Pershing IIs.[11]

While the interrogation of Prime by MI5 and American security officers produced more information about Soviet espionage methods it did little to offset the colossal damage he had inflicted. Nor is there any certainty that Prime has told the whole truth about his treachery or what motivated it. The official damage assessment shows that neutralizing the advantage to the Russians will take many years and enormous investment. As recently as late 1983 an American project to launch an improved Rhyolite-type satellite was abandoned because of the fear that the Russians would still be able to 'spoof' it with the information supplied by Prime and his American counterpart. In addition, the injury to American trust in British security remains so serious that all the doubts raised by previous cases like those of Fuchs, Maclean, Burgess and Philby have been resurrected. The simultaneous treachery by the American spy helped to prevent a complete rupture of the G.C.H.Q./ N.S.A. relationship, as did the geographical fact that the U.S. needs listening bases in Britain to cover parts of the Soviet Union and Eastern Europe, but understandably the U.S. authorities and the American public are angry that yet another British spy betrayed American secrets.

The Potential Value of Oversight

The Security Commission excelled itself in the thoroughness of its inquiry into the Prime case and in the robustness of its report but it remained another 'stable-door-locking operation'. General security at G.C.H.Q. was shown to have been weak and irresolute, indicating a need for oversight by some outside body. Successive governments have ruled that each department must be responsible for its own security, and independent inquiries, like those of the Radcliffe

Committee in 1962, have endorsed that principle. Nevertheless, MI5 is charged with advising other departments on the nature and scale of the threats to their security and on defence measures against them. So that department shared some of the blame, especially as it failed to detect the Soviet agents who so blatantly delivered espionage equipment to the home of Prime's sister. (Inevitably Fifth Estate figures rose to MI5's defence claiming that it should be praised for catching Prime when it had had nothing whatever to do with his detection.[12] It only remains for some future prime minister to list the case as one of MI5's unsung triumphs.)

The fact that a character as weird and, in some ways, as inept as Prime should have been able to spy for fourteen years and then to have been detected only by the fluke circumstances of his sexual activities exposed disgraceful weaknesses across the whole security field, which the K.G.B. and G.R.U. will continue to exploit. What seems to be needed without further delay is some degree of oversight to ensure that security precautions have not only been introduced on paper but are being properly applied. The record shows that it is not safe to leave security entirely to the initiative of the departments. Whether the task should fall within the responsibilities of a general oversight body is a matter for debate but it would seem that the existence of some outside checking system could help to ensure that security procedures are rigorously applied before another terrible incident like the Prime treachery reveals that they are not.

Mrs Thatcher and her ministers could hardly have been advised more ineptly concerning the handling of the deunionizing of G.C.H.Q. The advice originated from intelligence chiefs, known in Whitehall as 'The Friends'. Commenting on it, a retired ambassador with much experience told me, 'The Friends should never be consulted in such circumstances because they will always give priority to their own cover.' It is not unreasonable to suggest that if ministers had access to the views of an independent oversight body less committed to unnecessary secrecy the case could have been presented more effectively and with less damage to the public interest.

CHAPTER SIXTY

Payment Deferred

In the early winter of 1982 MI5 and the Government were to be responsible for the conviction of a traitor who had spied for the Soviet Union over a period of about thirty years and, though previously exposed, had not only escaped prosecution but had openly boasted about his treacherous activities and his immunity to retribution.[1] This was Hugh Hambleton, by then a full professor in a Canadian university, whose recruitment by the K.G.B. and subsequent espionage in N.A.T.O. have been outlined in Chapter 29. He had moved back to Canada after securing his Ph.D. at the London School of Economics in 1964 and was to claim that he had been out of contact with the K.G.B until reactivated in 1967 by Colonel Rudolph Herrmann, a Czech-born professional K.G.B. officer who specialized in the reactivation of sleepers.[2] Through Hambleton's growing reputation as an economist, and his world-wide travel, he was able to continue his services, having been supplied with some of the most advanced espionage equipment. In 1975 he was smuggled into Moscow for clandestine discussions, when he met Andropov.[3]

Meanwhile Herrmann had moved into the U.S. as an 'illegal' operator to service other Soviet agents, organize dead-letter boxes and perform other subversive tasks. In the autumn of 1977, however, the F.B.I. found out his true role and he agreed to act as a double agent. In the course of debriefings he named Hambleton as a 'long-term and trusted Soviet agent' and revealed details of his treachery. In a joint operation by the F.B.I. and the R.C.M.P., code-named 'Red Pepper', Hambleton was put under surveillance and was filmed in contact with Soviet bloc agents.[4] His home and his mother's home, where he had hidden his transmitter and other equipment, were raided in November 1979 and, while he confessed to having assisted Soviet Intelligence, he claimed that he had not damaged Canadian security, though Canada is a member of N.A.T.O., on which he had spied.[5]

For reasons which have never been satisfactorily explained,

Hambleton was not prosecuted. The Canadian legal authorities may have decided that a case would not succeed under the weakly worded Canadian Official Secrets Act or they may have gone too far in offering Hambleton inducements which made him immune. The F.B.I. was so angry at his escape that, in March 1980, it issued a press statement revealing that Hambleton had been exposed by Herrmann.[6] The Canadians still declined to move even when Hambleton gave interviews describing how exciting his traitorous activities had been. In that same year he visited Britain and was interviewed by Special Branch, though no action was taken.

In June 1982 the R.C.M.P. learned that Hambleton planned to fly to Britain again and warned him that he might receive a 'hostile reception'.[7] Such was his confidence, however, that he completed the journey and was astonished when he was arrested. He was refused bail because of the fear that he might defect. His trial took place in late November and December and, after protesting his innocence, he admitted his guilt and was sentenced to ten years in prison. The charges related to the period between 1 January 1956 and 21 December 1961 and were stated to be within the jurisdiction of the Central Criminal Court. Hambleton had British as well as Canadian citizenship; without that, it might not have been possible to prosecute him.

The Trudeau Government has remained greatly embarrassed by the prosecution which, clearly, it should have carried out itself in view of the evidence and the admissions which Hambleton made. The F.B.I., on the other hand, was delighted and it is difficult to resist the suggestion that the Government took its resolute action to please the American authorities, especially in view of the damage to the image of British security inflicted by the Prime case. The case also served to demonstrate to the British public that, even if Hambleton had been given some degree of immunity in Canada, the days when that could be done so lightly in Britain – the Hollis days – were over.

In his defence, Hambleton claimed that he had been working as a double for French Intelligence but this was disproved. He also claimed that he had been working in collaboration with the R.C.M.P. security authorities but the evidence that he ever accomplished anything in that direction, apart from telling them what he wanted them to know, is meagre. On balance, therefore, and in view of the sentence there can be no doubt that he was a damaging spy over many years and, once again, was exposed only as a result of information lodged by a defector to an American agency.

MI5's reaction to the prosecution, which was pressed by the Attorney-General, is unknown, as is the possibility that new evidence about Hambleton's treachery both in Paris and in London had been secured prior to his arrest. If Hambleton had continued his treachery in London, as seems probable from the wording of the charge and the fact that the K.G.B. would be unlikely to neglect such a recently productive source, then the failure to detect him had been an MI5 responsibility.

The Potential Value of Oversight

The evidence suggests that no oversight body could have heard of Hambleton's treachery before 1980, when the F.B.I. made its public statement and he visited Britain and was questioned by Special Branch on behalf of MI5. It might have taken an interest from then on but, as Hambleton could not have been extradited under the Official Secrets Act, nothing could have been done before his chance return in 1982, when commendably quick action was taken. An oversight body might, reasonably, have been curious about Hambleton's complete confidence that he would not be arrested in Britain in spite of the warning given to him by the R.C.M.P.

CHAPTER SIXTY-ONE

A Minor with Major Access

THE newspaper headline 'Big Security Shake-up' has appeared over accounts of incompetence in the face of treachery at least twenty times in my writing career and did so again on 30 March 1984 following another report by the Security Commission, which had been almost continuously occupied since its 'reassuring' inquiry in 1981. The report, which had taken a year to compile, in spite of its brevity, dealt with the case of the youngest offender to be prosecuted under the Official Secrets Act, a lance-corporal in the Intelligence Corps, Philip Aldridge, who was nineteen at the time of his offence.[1]

Aldridge was gaoled for four years in January 1983 for abstracting a top secret document and trying to sell it to the Russians. At the time of his trial the security authorities claimed to have no idea just how sensitive the document had been because Aldridge misled them about it. When the truth was eventually established, the young lance-corporal became another textbook example of the axiom that what matters in the security world is not rank but access.

As a new recruit to the Intelligence Corps, Aldridge had been given positive vetting clearance under the routine restriction that, until he reached the age of twenty-one, he would be allowed to handle top secret documents only when under close supervision. Normally he was based at Aldershot but because the Defence Intelligence Staff (D.I.S.) at the Defence Ministry was overloaded with work during the Falklands campaign and in the period after it he was transferred for a fortnight to a section of it working in the Metropole building near Trafalgar Square in London. His job was to maintain a register of classified documents and he was also involved in the assured destruction of those copies which were no longer needed.As he was not quite twenty he should never have been left alone while tearing up documents and placing them in a specially secure bag for incineration but the more senior N.C.O.'s with whom he was working had not been warned about this restriction and probably assumed that Aldridge was over twenty-one. As a result the lance-corporal was allowed to work alone even when extremely sensitive papers were being processed.

Aldridge was cunning enough to appreciate his opportunity and, probably on his first day there, he abstracted seventeen pages of a copy of the weekly assessment of the intelligence position produced for the Prime Minister and other very senior ministers by the Joint Intelligence Committee. When he left the Metropole to return to Aldershot it was believed that the papers had been destroyed.

How Aldridge aproached the Russians has not been officially stated. He may have been foolish enough to visit the Soviet Embassy. He certainly sent a letter there and received a favourable response in the form of an advertisement placed in the *Daily Telegraph* on behalf of the Russians by a woman and reading, 'I love you Spider. Love Mum.'[2] The letter was, apparently, intercepted through a routine monitoring operation and telephone calls he probably made may have been tapped. His quarters at Aldershot were searched and his diary was passed to MI5 where it was found to contain Soviet Embassy telephone numbers. By the time the culprit was arrested he had destroyed the document and the security authorities took his word that it was of moderate consequence and had dealt with Exocet missiles, though Defence Ministry officials could not recall any document of that nature at the relevant time. Aldridge told the truth later possibly because he was troubled by his conscience but more likely because he wanted to improve his position in prison so that he could take an Open University course.[3]

The Security Commission's report was much more an indictment of security precautions at the Defence Ministry than of Aldridge. It makes it plain that officials of the D.I.S. attempted to play down the seriousness of the case and their own deficiences which had made the offence possible. Lack of control over Aldridge was only one of several security weaknesses which disturbed the Commissioners who criticized the department for 'a general laxity of approach' and were 'increasingly concerned about the state of security in the D.I.S. generally'. They were further disturbed by the suggestions of an internal Defence Ministry inquiry conducted into the Aldridge case that hopefully intended to forestall any more searching investigation by an outside body. The Commission therefore recommended that such an investigation should be carried out by MI5, which should aim at a comprehensive overhaul of the existing security arrangements.

MI5, rightly, was praised by the Commission for its prompt detection of Aldridge's treachery but a less clumsy and more mature operator might have been able to circumvent the routine monitoring of Soviet Embassy activities, and the extent of the improperly supervised access by young people to thousands of documents of the highest sensitivity alarmed the Commission.

The Prime Minister once again and, one imagines, somewhat wearily told Parliament that she had ordered a tightening of security throughout Government departments, the intelligence agencies and the armed forces.

The Russians appear to have derived no direct benefit from the episode but, indirectly, it may have reinforced their belief that young servicemen are worth cultivating and suborning because some of them have access to information of great interest to both the K.G.B. and G.R.U. It is probably a coincidence that, at the time of writing, seven young servicemen stationed in Cyprus have been charged with offences involving the communication of secret information to people believed to have been working for Soviet Intelligence. Soviet agents have targeted on servicemen for many years, even operating blindly in areas like Salisbury Plain, where there are many military establishments, offering lifts in cars and drinks in bars to curry friendships which might be exploited. Nevertheless a volunteer like Aldridge could whet their appetites and intensify their effort, for it was probably a surprise to them that such a young and inexperienced soldier could have had such interesting access.

The Defence Intelligence Staff works in very close liaison with that of the U.S. and other allies and the inefficiency in protective security was yet another bad advertisement for Britain.

The Potential Value of Oversight

The Aldridge case provided clear-cut evidence of apathy and even resignation to the inevitability of security offences within an extremely important department of the Defence Ministry. It also showed that such a department, which is crucially concerned with the gathering of intelligence, will excuse and conceal its incompetence concerning security precautions if it can. The wording of the Security Commission's report suggests that it was more appalled than it indicated, or was allowed to indicate. So an arrangement to allow any oversight body to question the Security Commissioners about aspects of their investigations into cases could be constructive.

Again, it required a serious breach of security for any improvement to be effected and the lack of confidence on the Security Commission's part was so great that it believed that only oversight by an outside body, MI5, would ensure that the required measures would be devised and put into practice. How much safer it might be if a standing outside body had the power and responsibility for overseeing such departments on a continuous basis. Without such an oversight body, however constituted, complacency and confidence in not being exposed will continue. And as the next chapter shows, the Defence Ministry is not the only department guilty of such calamitous failings.

CHAPTER SIXTY-TWO

Another 'Good Bottle Man'

THE final recommendation of the Security Commission on the Aldridge case was that MI5 'should conduct a comprehensive review of protective security arrangements' in the Defence Intelligence Staff of the Defence Ministry.[1] The wounded feelings of the servicemen and civilians in the D.I.S. at this public rebuke were to turn to broad smiles in the following month, April 1984, with the publication of sufficient details of the trial of an MI5 officer, Michael Bettaney, to show that the department most in need of such a review was MI5 itself.[2]

While the MI5 management was already only too aware, when the report on Aldridge appeared in March, that it was soon to face public castigation, it took some comfort from the Security Commission's remark that the counter-intelligence service had been seen at its best. That well-deserved compliment was to be quickly swamped, however, by the quite appalling revelations of the Bettaney case. Aldridge had removed one document; Bettaney had removed dozens. Aldridge tried to contact the Russians to sell his document; Bettaney was that most dangerous and most feared of all spies, an ideological 'mole' deep inside MI5. Not only had positive vetting and document security failed, Bettaney had been promoted to a far more sensitive position after clear evidence of drunkenness and instability, just as Maclean had in the Foreign Office more than thirty years previously.

Bettaney, who came from a working-class home in Stoke-on-Trent, had needed a more exacting faith and converted to Roman Catholicism at the age of sixteen, after taking instruction. Bright academically, he was accepted into Pembroke College, Oxford, in 1969 to read English, and after his first year was awarded a scholarship. A quiet student, he is remembered as an ardent Catholic; in fact, he considered becoming a priest. His known politics tended to be right wing and he joined the Officer Training Corps. He then began to read widely about the rise of the Nazis. Having no firm ideas about a career he approached the University

Appointments Board and was 'talent-spotted' as likely material for MI5. His tutor at Oxford was to describe him, after his arrest, as giving 'a strong impression of dependability and of being a man who was entirely trustworthy'.[3]

After securing a second-class degree and passing the Civil Service examination he was formally recruited to MI5, subject to a satisfactory positive vetting, in late 1973 but was required to wait until he reached the minimum age of twenty-five for an officer. He filled in the time by staying on at Pembroke to initiate some research and began to drink heavily on occasions. He lived in West Germany for a year, teaching part time and learning the language. He lived there with a priest from Eastern Europe who might have influenced him. After being positively vetted, he started work with MI5 in the autumn of 1975, when Sir Michael Hanley was Director-General. After basic training at the headquarters in Curzon Street he spent some time in F Branch, studying files on British communism, and was then posted to Ulster for counter-I.R.A. activities. Recalled to London in 1980 he was given a rather boring post on the training side and was to claim that he had become progressively disenchanted with MI5 as a whole. He was due for re-vetting, after his first five years' service, but has claimed that this was never completed as a result of some disagreement over the referees, whose names he had supplied.[4]

On 12 October 1982 Bettaney was fined after being arrested for being drunk and incapable in Oxford Street. According to newspaper reports he told the police, 'You can't arrest me I'm a spy', or, more likely, 'You can't arrest me, I work for MI5.' Bettaney was to claim that he had been to a joint MI5 and Foreign Office party where many of his colleagues had been drinking heavily. He was fined £10 and was to claim that he reported the incident to the MI5 management. I have never met a teetotal MI5 officer but have met several who were heavy drinkers, two of them having a drink problem, and if Bettaney had been attending an MI5 party the circumstances were probably regarded as extenuating. A few days later he was in court again and was fined for a railway fare offence but did not disclose this to MI5.[5]

The drunken episode did not prevent his planned transfer to the counter-espionage branch, Section K, where he could hardly have been more sensitively placed. The headquarters for his work, which was concerned with countering the activities of the K.G.B. and the G.R.U., were in an out-station in Gower Street.[6]

Bettaney was to say that the move fortified his determination to help the adversary because he could not work against the Russians but instead of resigning he continued to draw his salary and

573

became a traitor and agent in place. He marked various documents which crossed his desk and photocopied them later or took notes which he typed out at home. He photographed everything at home so that he would be able to supply his information in cassettes, which could be more easily secreted in dead-letter boxes. On at least one occasion, when he was night-duty officer at the Gower Street office, he took a camera into the building, against the rules, knowing that staff were never subject to search, and photographed documents there. MI5 has been castigated for this, and possibly rightly so, but if Bettaney was already under suspicion then the camera might have been condoned so that he could be observed using it through a hidden T.V. camera of the type used in the Mitchell case.[7]

All this was going on only a few months after Mrs Thatcher had told the House of Commons that the Security Commission's review following publication of *Their Trade is Treachery* had been 'generally reassuring' and that the threat from committed communists, such as Blunt and Philby, had receded. The danger of such complacent pronouncements was derisively demonstrated by Bettaney in a lecture he was required to give to recruits about the past penetrations of MI5 by Soviet agents. According to one recruit, he ended by assuring his audience, 'You can be sure from the lessons we have learnt that MI5 is not penetrated now.'

After some research inside MI5, Bettaney chose a K.G.B. officer posing as a diplomat, calling himself Arkady Gouk, as the person to approach and on 13 April 1983 he delivered a letter to his residence in Holland Park at midnight, probably knowing that no MI5 watchers were on duty there. The contents of the letter constituted a serious offence because they gave details of MI5's reasons for expelling three Soviet Intelligence officers in the previous month, including an account of how they had been detected. Gouk, no doubt, reported the letter to the Centre which reacted in the routine way concerning such a 'walk-in'. Fearing that Bettaney was an MI5 provocation to secure further deportations or an attempt to plant a double agent, the Centre advised no action but to await further developments. Bettaney therefore tried again, depositing another letter at Holland Park at midnight on 12 June containing a copy of a top secret document giving an MI5 assessment of the K.G.B. and G.R.U. effort being mounted in Britain, and its purposes. It also contained an arrangement for communication by dead-letter boxes. Again, presumably on instructions from the Centre, there was no response. After a further attempt by letter on 10 July 1983, when Bettaney later said that he feared he might be under surveillance, he continued to collect information for a further attempt at contact in Vienna.[8]

After collecting more than fifty documents giving the greatest detail of MI5's 'order of battle' and counter-espionage plans against both the K.G.B. and the G.R.U., Bettaney made plans to visit Vienna for a holiday, as Prime had done before him, and was to claim that he had discovered the names of K.G.B. agents to approach there. Presumably he told his superiors he intended to visit Vienna before he bought an air ticket to leave on 19 September, a date chosen because he was due for leave three days before. Had he managed to arrive there with his haul almost every officer in MI5 would have become 'Sovbloc Red', because there can be little doubt that the K.G.B. would have met him, in the safety of a foreign capital, and having realized that such material could never have been provided as 'chickenfeed' it would have accepted him and arranged for his regular control in London and wherever he might be posted. The possibility of another 'mole' in place for a further twenty-six years could hardly have been resisted.[9]

As will be seen, the evidence against Bettaney depended mainly on documents and copies of letters found in his home and his interpretation of them. Confessions by previous Soviet spies, like Fuchs, Philby and Blunt, have proved to be partly false and I regard Bettaney's account of his projected trip to Vienna as suspect. It could be that some message concerning a meeting there had been delivered to him from the K.G.B. which had chosen Vienna. As a fervent and unrepentant pro-Soviet communist, which Bettaney proved to be, he would have been required to avoid incriminating the K.G.B. in any way. The fact that Gouk remained in Britain during the trial is proof enough that he never met Bettaney but some message could have been delivered by a 'cut-out' or even by some coded radio programme from Moscow.

Bettaney's major treachery was foiled – so far as is known – by his arrest on 16 September but it remains a matter for wonder that if his objective was simply to pass on all the information that he could, he did not just deliver it through Gouk's letter box. It may be that the K.G.B. insisted on a meeting or that Bettaney was determined to make his mark with his new masters by personal contact.

Whether the MI5 management considered the possibility of offering the traitor immunity is not known. It probably did not, realizing that the Attorney-General, Sir Michael Havers, could not have countenanced it on political grounds after the furore over the immunities granted to Blunt and his accomplices. Because of the inevitable damage to MI5's reputation and to the morale of the Service, immunity would almost certainly have been considered in

Hollis's day.

Like most spies, Bettaney did not panic when arrested and was rather arrogant. In the interviews, which lasted four days, he disclosed what was hidden in his semi-detached home in Coulsdon, realizing that otherwise the police would tear it apart in their searches. With his assistance, copies of classified documents, and, it is believed, of the letters he had delivered to Gouk, were found in a cushion, an electric shaving box and a laundry cupboard.[10]

How he had been detected remains uncertain, though MI5 claims some credit for catching him early. His system of marking documents may have been spotted or he might have raised suspicion through his use of the photocopying machines over which there is stricter supervision, following Security Commission recommendations resulting from the *Their Trade is Treachery* inquiries. Once Bettaney became suspect he would have been under telephone and letter check and his house may have been entered and bugged. MI5 might have preferred to let the case run until Bettaney could be caught with a Soviet controller but it could not risk the trip to Vienna. It has been suggested that the K.G.B. 'blew' him to cause a problem for MI5 but it is unlikely that they would have done that before testing what he had to offer. The suggestion that a British spy inside the K.G.B. revealed him also seems unlikely, because to have prosecuted Bettaney without further evidence would have put that source at risk and such sources are too rare to be expendable. It is, of course, possible that the K.G.B. had an agent inside MI5 who was really a double, and that, when approached for a view about Bettaney, the agent informed the MI5 management.

When Bettaney appeared at the Old Bailey on 10 April he was the first MI5 officer to face prosecution and the first – so far as is known – to claim that he had become converted to communism while within the Service. After an opening statement by the Attorney-General the remainder of the trial, during which Bettaney appeared in the witness box, was held in closed session for two reasons. Firstly, highly secret evidence had to be discussed; to prevent leakages, the jury had been carefully vetted. Secondly, it had become clear that Bettaney's purpose in pleading not guilty, after making a confession covering 170 pages, was not to repudiate it but to use the trial as a platform for pro-Soviet and anti-British propaganda, directed against MI5 particularly. He would have stressed his own motives in working for 'peace', while alleging that MI5 was part of the Tory machinery working for war and grossly infringing civil liberties. The reality of this danger was proved by a damaging statement, which Bettaney was said to have written, read out by his lawyers after his conviction.[11] He claimed that he had been given an unfair trial when a comparable traitor in the country he professed to love so dearly would probably have been given no trial but would have been shot. A letter written by Bettaney and sent to the *Observer* from prison provided further evidence of his determination to blacken the Government and MI5.[12]

Being found guilty of all ten charges of which he had been accused under the Official Secrets Act, he was sentenced to a total of twenty-three consecutive years' imprisonment, the sentence being merited but also necessary to keep him out of contact with Soviet agents for a period long enough for the value of his knowledge to be eroded. Predictably, the Russians issued a lying statement denying that they had ever received anything from Bettaney.

A routine damage assessment satisfied the MI5 management that the traitor had been apprehended before he had done much more than limited damage – providing he had been telling the truth. The real injury he had inflicted was to the reputation of MI5 both at home and abroad and to morale within the Service.

Once again positive vetting had been shown to be of scant value and the re-vetting which might have exposed Bettaney's political conversion and drinking habits had been negligently applied.

Journalistic inquiries, of a type which had not been made when Bettaney had been recruited by MI5, showed him to be an unstable loner who was an occasional heavy drinker and had the usual bleat about 'society's unfairness', which seems to be an integral part of traitor's make-up. He was, as the judge told him, 'puerile, self-opinionated and dangerous'. So how could such a man have gained and sustained the confidence of his superiors?

The most disturbing aspect of the Bettaney case was the exposure of the fact that an officer of several years' service can become disillusioned, convert to pro-Soviet communism and transfer his services to the adversary in spite of the massive prison sentences given to some traitors in the past. The previous traitors, with the possible exception of Blake, had been recruited before entering the secret services and when very young.[13] Further, if Bettaney is to be believed, his was a case of auto-conversion, without being worked on by other communists with an eye to his recruitment to espionage. Such a person could not be detected during a first positive vetting. But Bettaney may have been lying and may have had communist friends.

A month after Bettaney's conviction, on 14 May, the K.G.B. officer who called himself Arkady Gouk and whom Bettaney had contacted by letter, was declared *persona non grata* and duly expelled. The Russians retaliated, however, by expelling the MI5 security officer at the British Embassy in Moscow. Whether or not the Foreign Office had been given further evidence against Gouk is not yet known.

The Security Commission, which at the time of writing is still investigating the case, will presumably consider the possibility that Bettaney was influenced or, perhaps, talent-spotted by somebody else in MI5. In that respect they may remind themselves of the statement by James Callaghan that in the late 1970s, after Bettaney had joined MI5, it was thought that some officers who had been recruited as Soviet agents might be in the process of passing out of the Service.[14] Such agents would have been required by the K.G.B. to nominate replacements. Whatever the cause and nature of Bettaney's conversion it must now be accepted that no officer can, in future, be considered as entirely immune to ideological ensnarement. The Government, and Mrs Thatcher in particular, had pinned their hope on the belief that the 'climate of treason' which had induced young men to spy for the Soviet Union in the 1930s had evaporated and that such cases could be forgotten as part of a poisoned past. Bettaney has shown that half a century later the simplistic attractions still exist and the present is poisoned too.

Supporters of Hollis will protest that it is invidious to make comparisons between him and Bettaney, a convicted spy, but the comparisons present themselves. Both were unremarkable products of Oxford and had a strong religious factor in their backgrounds. Neither had shown any left-wing leanings at Oxford and Bettaney's known behaviour disposes of the argument that if Hollis had been inclined to communism, while in China or later in MI5, there would have been discoverable evidence of it at Oxford, as there was with the Cambridge Ring. Both were remembered for drinking at Oxford and Bettaney might have qualified for Evelyn Waugh's description of a 'good bottle man'. Both became secretive and withdrawn and it seems that Bettaney found no difficulty in squaring his continuing religious belief with communist ideology. He has continued to attend Mass in prison while confirming to friends his faith in the Soviet system.

If Bettaney had managed to contact the K.G.B. in safety, and had then come under professional control, he might have continued in MI5, reaching the top management and retiring at sixty, after twenty-eight years of treachery, in the year 2010.

The Potential Value of Oversight

From what is known about the Bettaney case so far it would seem that precautions about document security, which MI5 is responsible for devising and for recommending to other secret departments, were not being put into effective use in the Service itself. This is reminiscent of how MI5 had failed to subject its own staff to positive vetting and suggests that the complacency concerning the possibility that MI5 might be penetrated had regenerated itself or had always existed. Would that have been the case if the MI5 management, which has remained a law unto itself, totally free from outside interference, had been subject to independent oversight and been constantly aware of that? The same question can be asked concerning Bettaney's second positive vetting if the Security Commission confirms that it was never satisfactorily completed.

Clearly, lessons learned from previous cases in other departments had not been applied in MI5, or, at least, had not been applied effectively. In spite of the Blunt affair and the continuing suspicion about Hollis, the MI5 management may have continued to consider it unthinkable that any of its colleagues could be or might become Soviet spies. An oversight body might ensure that the possibility is regularly thought about in future.

The camera incident provoked Bettaney to reveal that MI5 officers are never subjected to random searches. The Security Commission may recommend that they should be, just as G.C.H.Q. staff are liable to them following the Prime case. Oversight could ensure that this extra safeguard, likely to be regarded as insulting by some officers, is applied. Further reasons for the need for oversight over MI5 may emerge from the Security Commission's inquiry, but because of the secrecy surrounding the trial evidence and the circumstances of Bettaney's detection they may not become available for public comment.

CHAPTER SIXTY-THREE

The Outlook for Oversight

Mrs Thatcher's use of the Security Commission to carry out the inquiry which she instigated as a result of the publication of *Their Trade is Treachery* necessitated consultation with the leader of the opposition, Michael Foot, both before announcing the inquiry and after receiving its report. The implications of this consultation were considered by her Cabinet advisers and it was seen to carry advantages. The confidentiality of the consultations meant that Foot would be extremely restricted concerning anything he would want to say in Parliament or in public about the matter. As I have pointed out, there was great potential embarrassment for Foot, if the Prime Minister was subjected to searching questions by back-benchers, because of the disclosures about his friend, Driberg. Parliament's interest had been suppressed when the inquiry was instigated by the severe restriction of questions and again when the report was completed by Mrs Thatcher's announcement about it in the middle of the Falklands conflict. It therefore appeared to the public and to the media that Foot, having been made privy to the secret aspects of the inquiry, fully agreed with Mrs Thatcher's statements to Parliament, including her apparent assurance that Hollis had been cleared.

It so happened, however, that the Labour Party's National Executive Committee had set up a study group to look into the security services and this had already started work in July 1979. The membership included Michael Foot. Its long deliberations were published as a Labour Party discussion document in March 1983, shortly before the general election, and it contained some surprising statements about Hollis, suggesting that the Committee was far from satisfied with the Prime Minister's statement about him.[1]

The document's introduction stated, 'We have also taken note of the growing evidence of espionage cases covered up by the authorities – the most serious of which, concerning Sir Roger Hollis, the former Director-General of the Security Service itself, suggests that much of Britain's security efforts may have been in vain.' A few pages further on, under the heading 'The Security Service (MI5)', the document stated, 'Recently the Prime Minister revealed during a Parliamentary debate that a former Director-General of MI5, Sir Roger Hollis, had been inconclusively investigated as a suspected K.G.B. double agent. Although this required a year-long investigation by former cabinet secretary, Sir Burke Trend, the enquiry was entirely covered up – despite the devastating implications for British security as far as foreign powers are concerned.' The investigations had, of course, continued for at least nine years, and still continue, but the Labour Party document clearly disassociated itself from the Prime Minister's assurances', to which Foot had subscribed, on three counts: the inquiry into Hollis had been inconclusive; it had not been a routine matter to eliminate him from a general investigation; and it had been deliberately covered up.

I have tried to establish whether or not the Committee had access to any new information about the Hollis case and believe that they did not. The conclusions seem to have been reached mainly on the evidence supplied by my book and by other investigators covering the same field.[2]

The main purpose of the Labour Party's report, entitled *Freedom and the Security Services*, however, was to show the party faithful and the electorate in general what a Labour Government intended to do to bring the secret services under very firm legal control with an extreme degree of accountability to Parliament.

Under existing arrangements responsibility for MI5 rests with the Home Secretary, while the Foreign Secretary answers for MI6 and G.C.H.Q., with the Prime Minister intruding, when necessary, on specially important issues. They can call in the heads of the secret services if they wish but the extent to which they do so depends very much on the interest that the Home Secretary and Foreign Secretary choose to take in secret affairs. There has to be some liaison because their permission is required for certain operations, but the regular channel between the secret services and ministers is the Cabinet Secretary, who is the chief accounting officer for them. In this function he is assisted by a committee of high-level civil servants, which he chairs, and by a Co-ordinator of Intelligence, currently Sir Anthony Duff, located in the Cabinet Office. There are also secret committees chaired by the Prime Minister.

In response to any Parliamentary demand for a more effective system of supervision, reigning governments always claim that existing arrangements are adequate but nobody is really tasked to know what the secret services are doing and Cabinet secretaries are told no more than the secret service chiefs are prepared to tell them. There is, in fact, no effective oversight, for the Cabinet Secretary has far too many other responsibilities and the Co-ordinator is more concerned with the 'products' – the results of intelligence and security operations – than with processes. The knowledge available to ministers – and therefore to Parliament – is severely limited by the system, which has allowed the secret services to consume so much of their own smoke that, on occasions, they have been able to conceal the fact that there has been a fire.

The extent to which Parliament has accepted the reluctance of successive governments to inform them about secret service matters does little credit to M.P.s or peers, and very senior civil servants whom I have questioned have expressed astonishment at Parliament's passivity, though grateful for it when they were involved in secret affairs. For years Parliament has put up with a 'blocking arrangement' agreed to by ministers early in the life of a Parliament whereby the clerks are precluded from accepting many questions on security and intelligence issues.[3] Severe limitations are also imposed by the Speaker in his interpretation of custom and privilege. In January 1983, however, the giant stirred when a report of the Commons Liaison Committee courageously pointed out that existing select committees had the power to examine the work of the secret services and should do so because they would then become more accountable to Parliament and the committees' inquiries would be a spur to efficiency.[4] As expected, the Government scowled, but in my view, and that of very senior mandarins, some degree of oversight is inevitable, not only because of the growing demand for more open Government, especially since the Bettaney case, but because its advantages far outweigh its drawbacks. The potential advantages accrue in three areas: to the secret services themselves; to ministers; and to Parliament and the public.

Much would depend on the degree of oversight and the powers accorded to the oversight body, particularly regarding the thorny issue of access to information about operations, but the case evidence presented in this book supports the belief that effective oversight would improve the general efficiency and competence of the services. The size of the services is, rightly, held secret and a body with on-going experience and some permanent professional staff could help to ensure that they are large enough for their tasks and do not become too large. There is private argument, for instance, whether MI5 is big enough to cope with the threat from what Macmillan called 'the great hostile machine' of Soviet bloc espionage in view of its recently increased role in combating

582

terrorism in Ulster and elsewhere. An independent oversight body could be helpful in assuring governments, which tend to oppose expansion of MI5 for fear of being accused of running a 'secret police', that some increase is genuinely needed.

An oversight body could also play a constructive role in establishing adequate salaries, fringe benefits and career prospects, including trasfer to other Government departments for individuals whose cover has been broken or who are worn out by stress. While there has been frequent interchange between MI6 and the Foreign Office, it is now more limited and several officers have been only too happy to take jobs as clerks in the Parliamentary infrastructure. Salary scales and other factors governing recruitment are currently controlled by Treasury requirements which must conform to Civil Service scales and practice. It would seem to be significant that MI6, which has always paid better salaries than MI5, has consistently been able to attract better talent.

It seems doubtful that the cost-effectiveness of the secret services has ever been studied except, in a modest way, by the services themselves. The 'customers' – the various Government departments served by the secret services – tend to insist that they need everything that can be discovered instead of stipulating particular products and this has led to unnecessary extravagance. If they had to pay for their products out of their own votes, departments might be more selective. An oversight body might be empowered to keep an eye on cost-effectiveness.

There can be little doubt that incompetence on a scale which, one hopes, would not have been tolerated in other Government departments has flourished in the secret services. It should be possible to retire an incompetent chief early, but when a department is immune to oversight it is difficult to discern such a situation until a damaging scandal, like the Crabb affair, brings it to notice. One of the most disturbing results of my inquiries is the extent to which former officers criticize the secret services and individual managers after they have retired and feel free to talk. There might, perhaps, be some process whereby the oversight body could function as an ombudsman for the secret services so that glaring evidence of incompetence or suspected treachery could be reported to it in writing and in confidence. Interviews with the complainants should enable the oversight body to distinguish between those genuinely concerned and those with grudges. It was certainly wrong that de Mowbray could secure a review of the Hollis case only by knocking on the door of Number 10 Downing Street.

With access to secret service officers other than those belonging to the senior management an oversight body could check on the

583

state of morale, which is normally hidden through the blanket ruling that staff are forbidden to speak to anyone outside about any aspect of their work. MI5, MI6 and G.C.H.Q. are big bureaucracies where morale is a crucial component of efficiency, and much depends on leadership. Few of the staff in MI5 knew Hollis or believed that he had any interest in them, yet this was quite unknown to the governments of his day.

Recently the Franks Committee on the Falklands conflict was given oversight facilities which enabled it to draw the Government's attention to deficiencies in the intelligence system which might otherwise have continued.[5] Substantial changes were made as a consequence, providing further proof that when independent oversight is permitted shortcomings in the secret services are, almost invariably, revealed. An oversight body would provide such valuable surveillance on a continuing basis. It could also ensure that improvements to security procedures, such as those recommended by the Security Commission, have really been put into effect, for the Security Commission has no right of follow-up. Currently ministers assure Parliament that improvements are being practised but they have only the word of the secret services themselves and, with regard to positive vetting for example, spy cases have revealed some disregard of them.

The case evidence suggests that the mere existence of oversight could exert a deterrent effect, reducing slackness and the deliberate stifling of errors and disasters because of possible 'embarrassment'.

Cases of suspect M.P.s and peers might be treated to the greater satisfaction of the Security Service through the existence of oversight. If there was some Parliamentary representation on the body the Government might find it possible to abolish the immunity of M.P.s and peers to telephone tapping and other forms of surveillance which, in equity, they should not enjoy.

While the recent record of the secret services would savour of lack of resolve rather than excess of zeal – except for the K.G.B. expulsions – oversight might conceivably save them, one day, from the kind of trauma suffered by the C.I.A. after the revelations of the 1970s and, more recently, by the R.C.M.P. security service. Ultimately the British secret services will be required to operate within the law which, currently, they have to transgress, when making surreptitious entries for example, and an experienced oversight body could be helpful in advising on the necessary legislation and later in ensuring that the agencies work within it with sufficient freedom of action to perform their tasks and with the minimum of interference from outside influences.

Regarding potential benefits to ministers, one has only to study

Hansard to appreciate the problems presented to Harold Macmillan by a succession of spy cases. He was held responsible and, through misleading briefs, made the mouthpiece of statements which have subsequently been disproved. Mrs Thatcher has fared little better with the Blunt, Long, Hollis, Prime, Aldridge and Bettaney cases, and with more, possibly, to follow. Oversight would be a built-in deterrent to the preparation of misleading briefs and, in the knowledge that the truth was known elsewhere, ministers might be more restrained in going beyond their briefs. It could also benefit the nation if it prevented the misuse of ministers for the undeserved protection of the secret services and some of their officers.

The direct benefit to Parliament and the public would depend on the extent to which the oversight body was permitted by its constitution to report to them. There would, presumably, be at least an annual report and that, supplemented perhaps by reports on special issues, could go far to satisfy the demand for accountability and for acceptable reassurance that the secret services are in good shape. There should be less fear, and fewer allegations, that disasters were being concealed, with enhanced respect for the services as a consequence. Perhaps the most important function of oversight for Parliament would be in ensuring that it could not so easily be misled by ministers making facile use of secrecy as a means of protecting the secret services or themselves.

An oversight body might play a constructive role in the reduction of unnecessary secrecy in Whitehall, which is at the root of many security problems and has, so far, proved intractable, whatever ministers may claim about their concern for more open government. As James Callaghan stated in the Blunt debate, 'Secrecy allows incompetence and corruption to thrive', treachery being the form of corruption he had in mind. The record presented in this book shows that secrecy and cover up have been the most consistent enemies of efficiency in the services. That it still continues was glaringly demonstrated by the recent Government action in barring staff at G.C.H.Q. from union membership, as described in Chapter 59.

There are disadvantages with any new security procedure, and the one most volubly expressed in connection with oversight is the danger to the secrecy in which the services must function. The secret services, and ministers who have uncritically accepted their advice, insist that this danger is so severe as to neutralize any possible advantage. The most convincing answer to this blanket objection, which reflects little more than the secret services' hostility to any intrusion, is the experience of the U.S., where oversight on a scale unlikely to be accepted in Britain has been working effectively, with very few exceptions, for more than seven years.[6] An oversight body worthy of the name would need a full-time professional staff which would offer another area for Soviet penetration, as would the oversight body itself, but the U.S. experience has shown that this risk can be countered by security procedures.[7]

In discussions with American officials about the possible adoption of oversight, Cabinet Office officials and ministers have expressed their horror at the prospect because of the danger that a future extreme left-wing government might abuse the system.[8] This ignores the fact that such a government would bring in the necessary legislation anyway, especially if the present system is allowed to continue. In view of the swingeing legislation projected in the Labour Party discussion document of 1983, the present Government would be well advised to take some moderate action to forestall the necessity – or excuse – for measures which could be damaging to the services.

One of the greatest advantages from the introduction of oversight would be the improvement it would bring to American trust in British security which has been undermined again and again by Soviet penetrations over more than thirty years, the Prime and Bettaney cases being the most recent at the time of writing. The U.S. security authorities and the leading politicians who deal with them are convinced that oversight has exerted a most beneficial effect on the efficiency and effectiveness of their own secret services and would do the same for the British counterparts.[9] Among the advantages would be its deterrent effect on the creation of legends and the increased chance that case-deaths would be more rigorously investigated, making the detection of 'moles' more likely.

The importance of the Anglo-American relationship on the sharing of intelligence cannot be overestimated and Parliament, especially the Labour side, seems not to be properly aware of it, again, perhaps, because of unnecessary secrecy. If the value of the partnership was fully known to the public, through officially released information, the left-wingers would be less able to maintain their anti-American stance on defence. (A major part of the intelligence essential to Britain's survival as a free nation derives from reconnaissance satellites. Britain has none and no capability for launching any and is, therefore, entirely dependent on the U.S. for such information, which is freely given.)

The effectiveness of an oversight system would depend on its nature, which could take several forms. The House of Commons Liaison Committee called for the establishment of an all-party Select Committee on Security and Intelligence composed of Privy

Councillors selected from the Commons and the Lords.[10] Such a system, involving select committees of both Congress and Senate, has been operating in the U.S. since 1976, having been placed on a statutory basis since 1980. Under legislation the heads of the various intelligence departments, including the F.B.I., are required to keep both committees 'fully and currently' informed of all intelligence activities, including counter-intelligence, and must also furnish further information on request. In particular, they must report any 'signal failure' so that the committees can inquire into it and satisfy themselves as to its causes. From time to time the committees issue expurgated reports on intelligence and security matters. Their full-time professional staffs have facilities for monitoring 'performance' and have detected various weaknesses which have been rectified. I have been assured that, to date, the benefits of oversight have outweighed any disadvantages and that the services themselves now favour it, if only because it spares them from unfounded criticism.[11]

The Canadian Government is currently in the throes of establishing a civilian security service, subject to scrutiny and controls, following disclosures about excesses of zeal by security officers of the R.C.M.P. and the realization that ministers had been kept in ignorance of what was being done in the name of national security.[12] It has rejected oversight by any Parliamentary committee as posing too great a security risk and raising the danger that M.P.s on the committee might use secret information for party purposes. The Canadian Parliament has decided to establish a 'watchdog' body of three to five Privy Councillors, who may not be sitting politicians. This will be an oversight body with limited powers but sufficiently informed to report to Parliament about failures, excesses and cover-ups, though not in any detail that would infringe security. In addition, there will be a single inspector-general to monitor operations and to report to the responsible minister who, in Canada, is the Solicitor-General.[13]

The present British Government is equally likely to reject any oversight by a completely Parliamentary body. Insight into the Government's attitude to select committees was afforded to me recently by a senior minister when, through Labour intransigence over another issue, the re-formation of the committees was delayed for seven months after the 1983 general election. He told me that the Government was delighted because the committees were disliked as an intrusive nuisance. Any oversight body must be credible and it is not likely to be so, to either Parliament or the public, unless it has some Parliamentary membership.

Whatever form an oversight body may take it must consist of

people whose ability, impartiality and integrity are beyond dispute. This would surely rule out, on the grounds of partiality, any minister or civil servant who had previously been responsible for the secret services. A one-man-band arrangement, like the remit performed by Lord Wigg and later by Lord Trend, will not suffice. Wigg, who had been highly critical of the secret services, was quickly 'captured' by the security machine.

While access to operations should, probably, be limited, an oversight body should have sufficient powers for Parliament and the public to accept any assurance it gives as being based on the true facts. It would need a full-time staff of professionals responsible for the main liaison with the secret establishments. It would require the power to report directly to the Prime Minister and not through Cabinet Office officials. How much Parliament and the public would be told would depend on the Prime Minister, working with advisers, as happens now with such bodies as the Franks Inquiry into the Falklands conflict and the Security Commission.

As at present constituted, the Security Commission is no alternative as it is essentially a hindsight body, while an oversight body must be on-going. There is much to be said, however, in the current political climate, for an extension of the Security Commission's functions so that it could become an oversight body, at least for a pilot period. This might be more acceptable to the Government and could be proposed as its initiative. The Commission's terms of reference would have to be changed and it would require a small, permanent staff. Its membership could be widened to include Parliamentarians, perhaps from both the Commons and the Lords. The problem of its access to secret information and of its power to question members of the secret services have already been resolved with respect to hindsight inquiries into security breaches.

Given the political will, it should be possible to devise some system to provide an appropriate degree of accountability without overly interfering with ministerial responsibility or damaging the secrecy of the services, but I, and others whom I have consulted, expect a long struggle. The pressures on Mrs Thatcher to resist any improvement in accountability will be intense and it may be in her cautious nature to accede to them. I fear that we shall be assured, once again, that all is well, though we have been told that time and again when the record shows it to have been unfounded.

The best hope lies in the courage of Parliament which has the power if it can summon up the will to use it.

AUTHOR'S NOTE

Since this book was completed, Peter Wright, the former MI5 counter-intelligence officer, has not only confirmed publicly much of what appeared in *Their Trade is Treachery*, but has provided a 140-page document confirming and extending the rest. Entitled 'The Security of the United Kingdom against the Assault of the Russian Intelligence Service' the document, which deals with the Hollis case, the Mitchell case and several others, including those of Ellis and Watson, was delivered to Sir Anthony Kershaw, the Conservative M.P., in his capacity as chairman of the all-party Commons Select Committee on Foreign Affairs. Wright's purpose was to secure an official inquiry into the past penetration of MI5, MI6 and G.C.H.Q. to ensure that the possibility of current and future penetration is reduced to a minimum.

An examination of the document was requested by the Cabinet Secretary, Sir Robert Armstrong, and, as Sir Anthony Kershaw felt that he needed the Prime Minister's opinion before he could form a judgement on the issue, he handed it in. There can be little doubt that a copy was quickly passed to the MI5 management for its views and a statement as to whether there was anything new in it.

It seems likely that MI5 will claim that Wright's document contains nothing of consequence that was not already in *Their Trade is Treachery*, and that Mrs Thatcher will be advised that any further inquiry is unnecessary because the facts have already been examined by the Security Commission in 1981. As readers of this book will appreciate, however, the Security Commission did not examine the accounts of past penetration.

While other M.P.s may not be allowed to read Wright's dossier as such, I have been assured that this book contains his main points plus facts of which he has been unaware. So it should be possible for Parliamentarians to decide whether an inquiry into past penetrations would serve a useful purpose, and to press for it if that is their conclusion.

Prime sources have told me that the MI5 management will continue to oppose any inquiry because it would lower the morale of the serving members. For some years recruits have been assured that the service is 'clean' beyond all doubt, but the Bettaney case has demonstrated the complacency of that assertion. A full and honest statement on past penetration is likely to be far less damaging to morale than the exposure of further 'moles' who, according to Wright and other officers, are more likely to gain access to secret departments if the current attitude to the Soviet assault, past and present, is allowed to continue. If M.P.s feel sufficiently aggrieved by what has been exposed and are really concerned about the public disquiet, they could mount a demand for an inquiry and for future oversight which the Government would find irresistible.

Notes and Sources

THE entry 'Confidential information' implies that the source has requested anonymity, or that the author considers it to be in the source's best interests. Unless otherwise stated, the contact with the source has been direct.

Introduction (pages 3 - 7)
1   See Ronald Lewin, *Ultra Goes to War*, Hutchinson 1978
2   See J. C. Masterman, *The Double Cross System*, Yale University Press 1972
3   At least two MI6 officers spied for the *Abwehr*
4   K.G.B. - *Komitet Cosudarstvennoy Bezopasnosti* (Committee for State Security) G.R.U. — *Glavnoye Razvedyvatelnoye Upravlenie* (Chief Intelligence Directorate of the Soviet General Staff)
5   *The Rote Kapelle*, University Publications of America, Washington 1982

Chapter 1: A Soviet Agent Called Sonia (pages 8-13)
1   Ruth Werner (Sonia's pen-name), *Sonja's Rapport*, Verlag Neues Leben, Berlin 1982
2   Confirmed by Peter Wright on television (World in Action), 16 July 1984
3   Juergen Kuczynski, *Memoiren*, Aufbau-Verlag 1983 and various German biographical dictionaries on German exiles
4   Werner, *op cit*
5   Letters from Professor Stephen MacKinnon of Arizona State University who, with his wife, Jan, has written a detailed biography of Smedley
6   Werner, *op cit* Major-General C. A. Willoughby, *Shanghai Conspiracy*, Heinemann 1965. Otto Braun, *Chinesische Aufzeichnungen (1932-39)*, Dietz Verlag, Berlin 1975
7   Jan Valtin (Richard Krebs), *Out of the Night*, Alliance Book Corporation New York 1941
8   F.W. Deakin and G. R. Storry, *The Case of Richard Sorge*, Chatto and Windus 1966. Chalmers Johnson, *An Instance of Treason*, Heinemann 1965. Willoughby, *op cit*
9   Hans Otto Meissner, *The Man with Three Faces*, Evans Bros 1955
10 Chalmers Johnson, *op cit*
11 Deakin and Storry, *op cit*
12 Willoughby, *op cit*
13 Otto Braun, *op cit*
14 Willoughby, *op cit*. Letters from Harold Isaacs to the author. Also letters from Jack Tilton of the Shanghai Municipal Police
15 Letters to the author from Rewi Alley, who was a Factory Inspector in Shanghai from 1927-38

16 Letter from Professor MacKinnon
17 *Ibid*

Chapter 2: A 'Good Bottle Man' (pages 14-20)

1 Old volumes of *Who's Who* and theological references
2 *Oxford University Year Books*. Hollis read English
3 Letters to the author from Sir Harold Acton and Sir Dick White
4 Michael Davie, *The Diaries of Evelyn Waugh*, Weidenfeld and Nicolson 1976
5 Cockburn interview to *Daily Mail* reporter (unpublished) March 1981. Cockburn wrote in the *Daily Worker* under the name Frank Pitcairn. He died in December 1981
6 Letters from Dr P. G. Dickens, New College and James Railton, Secretary Oxford University Sports Centre
7 Confidential Hollis family source
8 Conversation with Merlyn Rees
9 See Werner, *op cit*
10 Confidential information
11 Letter from Sir Dick White
12 Letters from Sir Peter Macadam, B.A.T. chairman and B.A.T. employees
13 Letters from Isaacs and Alley
14 Alexander Foote, *Handbook for Spies*, Museum Press 1964. Sandor Rado, *Code-name Dora*, Abelard 1977
15 Confidential information
16 Werner, *op cit*

Chapter 3: An Unsuspected Communist Connection (pages 21-31)

1 Braun, *op cit*. Werner *op cit*
2 Willoughby, *op cit*. Ewert's career is summarized in Hermann Weber, *Die Wandlung des Deutschen Kommunismus*, Band 2, Stuttgart 1969. Also in *Geschichte der Deutschen Arbeiterbewegung Biographisches Lexikon*, Berlin 1970
3 Confidential information from former MI5 officer
4 Ian Angus, *Canadian Bolsheviks*, Vanguard, Montreal 1981
5 Gunter Nollau, *International Communism and World Revolution*, Hollis and Carter 1961
6 Valtin (Krebs), *op cit*
7 *Ibid*. Also Nollau, *op cit*
8 Theodore Draper, *American Communism and Soviet Russia*, Viking, New York 1960
9 Nollau, *op cit*. J. P. Harrison, *The Long March to Power*, Macmillan, London 1973
10 Jane Degras, *Comintern Documents 1956-65*, Royal Institute of International Affairs
11 John F. W. Dulles, *Anarchists and Communists in Brazil*, Austin, Texas, 1973
12 Robert J. Alexander, *Communism in Latin America*, Rutgers 1960
13 Werner, *op cit*
14 Braun, *op cit*
15 Ruth Werner, *Olga Benario*, Verlag Neues Leben, Berlin 1962
16 *The Times*, 26 November 1935. Also 17 March 1936
17 *The Times*, 18 July 1936. She was living at 181 Maida Vale W.9.
18 Werner, *Olga Benario*
19 Confidential information
20 Confidential information. Legal requirements inhibit further presentation of this evidence
21 Letter from Isaacs
22 Confidential information
23 Letter from Isaacs

24 Foote, *op cit*
25 Whittaker Chambers, *Witness*, André Deutsch 1953. Allen Weinstein in *Perjury*, Knopf, New York 1978, wrote, 'Chambers' precise reasons for becoming a communist in 1925 are unknown but this decision came during a period that included many elements of personal failure.'
26 Alex Orlov, *Handbook of Intelligence and Guerilla Warfare*, University of Michigan Press 1963
27 See *China Forum*, Shanghai (40 issues 1932-34) reprinted by Center for Chinese Research Materials, Washington 1976. Also, *About Shanghai, Guidebook for 1934*, reprinted by Oxford University Press 1983
28 Anthony Glees, 'The Hollis Letters', *The Times*, 3 April 1982
29 Confidential information
30 Werner, *Sonja's Rapport*

Chapter 4: Fully Trained Agent (pages 32-8)

1 *China Forum* reprints, Willoughby *op cit*. Nollau *op cit*. *Times* reports from Reuter, 19 August and 28 August 1931
2 Elisabeth Poretsky, *Our Own People*, Oxford University Press 1969
3 *China Forum* reprints, *North China Herald*, 13 July 1932 and various other references up to 23 September 1936
4 Werner, *Sonja's Rapport*
5 James Maxton, *Hansard*, 23 February 1932, Col. 216
6 Werner, *Sonja's Rapport*
7 *Times* 20 September 1932 and several subsequent reports
8 Otto Braun quoted in Mader, Stuchlek and Pehnert, *Dr Sorge Funkt aus Tokyo*, Mitautor 1966
9 Letter from Tilton
10 Letter from Isaacs
11 Werner, *Sonja's Rapport*. For Sorge's movements see Deakin and Storry, *op cit*. Chalmers Johnson, *op cit*
12 Werner, *Sonja's Rapport*
13 Irving S. Friedman, *British Relations with China 1931-39*, Institute of Pacific Relns. Inquiry Service New York 1940
14 Confidential information
15 Glees, 'The Hollis Letters' and private conversations
16 *Ibid*
17 Letter from *Times* staff
18 Werner, *Sonja's Rapport*
19 *Ibid*
20 *Ibid*
21 Sonia features a photograph of this medal, no. 944, in her memoirs

Chapter 5: A Strange Appointment (pages 39-43)

1 Letter from B.A.T. employee (Dick Price)
2 Glees, 'The Hollis Letters'
3 Confidential information
4 Letters from *Police des Etrangers*, Leyson and Montreux
5 Letters from B.A.T.
6 Werner, *Sonja's Rapport*
7 *Central Somerset Gazette*, 16 July 1937
8 Marriage certificate. Letter from Sir Duncan Oppenheimer
9 Family information through intermediary
10 Letter from Sir Dick White
11 *Ibid*
12 Confidential information

13 Correspondence between Guy Liddell of MI5 and Ray Atherton, U.S. Embassy, declassified 7 July 1982, no. 755014
14 Confidential information
15 Letter from Tilton
16 Letter from Sir Dick White
17 Stephen Knight, *The Brotherhood*, Granada 1984
18 Information from Dr Glees
19 Glees, 'The Hollis Letters'
20 Confidential information

Chapter 6: The Dangerous Dr Kuczynski (pages 44-53)

1 Information from senior R.S.S. source
2 *The Times*, 21 November 1981
3 *The Rote Kapelle*, C.I.A. Handbook
4 Juergen Kuczynski, *op cit*
5 Karl W. Fricke, *Die Staatssicherheit*, Verlag Wissenschaft und Politik, von Nottbeck 1982
6 Juergen Kuczynski, *op cit*. Other visitors to Paris included Burgess
7 *Ibid*
8 See Chapters 15 and 18. Also Juergen Kuczynski, *Dialog mit meinem Urenkel*, Aufbau Verlag 1983
9 Declassified 31 July 1983 with covering letter from Guy Liddell to Herschel Johnson, dated 26 December 1940
10 Juergen Kuczynski, *op cit*
11 *Ibid*
12 *Ibid*
13 Glees, *Exile Politics during the Second World War*, Oxford Historical Monographs, Clarendon Press 1982
14 Information from Mrs Joan Phipps
15 David Dilkes, *The Diaries of Sir Alexander Cadogan*, Cassell 1971
16 *Ibid*
17 Confidential information
18 Confidential information
19 Confidential information
20 Richard Deacon, *The British Connection*, Hamish Hamilton 1979
21 Mrs Edwards housed the Krivitskys in Montreal when they were hiding from Soviet vengeance under the name Thomas
22 Confidential information

Chapter 7: Swiss Interlude (pages 54-8)

1 Werner, *Sonja's Rapport*
2 Conversations with Mr and Mrs Copeman. Foote, *op cit*
3 Believed to be Brigitte, who used the surnames Lewis and Long
4 Communications from Swiss immigration authorities
5 *Ibid*
6 Foote, *op cit*
7 Drago Arsenijevic, *Genève appelle Moscou*, Lattès, Paris 1981
8 Foote, *op cit*
9 General Register Office. It has been stated that Beurton's name was really Brewer. This is incorrect and I can find no evidence that he or Sonia ever used that name
10 Foote, *op cit*. Werner, *Sonja's Rapport*
11 Confidential information
12 Werner, *Sonja's Rapport*
13 *Ibid* and Rado, *op cit*

14 Werner, *Sonja's Rapport*
15 Leopold Trepper, *The Great Game*, McGraw Hill, New York 1977
16 Werner, *Sonja's Rapport*. Anthony Read and David Fisher, *Operation Lucy*, Coward, McCann and Geoghegan, New York, 1981
17 Swiss records and Werner, *op cit*
18 *The Rote Kapelle*, C.I.A. Handbook
19 Werner, *Sonja's Rapport* and Swiss records

Chapter 8: Target – MI5 (pages 59-66)

1 Letter from Sir Eric St Johnston
2 Letter from Mrs MacPherson and subsequent conversations
3 Letter from Derek Tangye
4 Confidential information
5 Contemporary telephone book. Letters from Oxford University Estates Bursars
6 Hollis family information from an intermediary
7 *Ibid*
8 Werner, *Sonja's Rapport*
9 Confidential information
10 Juergen Kuczynski, *René Kuczynski* (biography), Aufbau Verlag, Berlin 1957. *Biographisches Handbuch der deutschsprachigen Emigration*, Band 1, Munich 1980
11 Letters from Academic Secretary, London School of Economics
12 Letters from Mrs Georgina Warrilow, Bodleian Library
13 *Ibid*
14 Letters from Senior Bursar's office, St Hugh's College
15 *Mrs Warrilow, loc cit*
16 Senior Bursar's office, *loc cit*
17 Juergen Kuczynski, *op cit*
18 *The Times*, 3 December 1947
19 Letters from National Institute of Economic and Social Research, which gave Dr Kuczynski a grant. Letters from Nuffield and other likely colleges
20 Werner, *Sonja's Rapport*
21 *Ibid*
22 See Chapter 9
23 Letter from Rev. A. C. Cox, son of Sonia's host, and subsequent conversations
24 See Chapter 39
25 Werner, *Sonja's Rapport*
26 Confidential information. According to *Rote Kapelle* (C.I.A. Handbook) G.R.U. agents were advised to secure lodgings in 'suburbs' not town centres
27 F.B.I. document dated 16 June 1950: memo from Hoover to the White House. Contrary to many statements, Kremer never controlled any of the Cambridge Ring, who were all separately controlled by the K.G.B.

Chapter 9: A British Bonus for Soviet Spies (pages 67-76)

1 Foote, *op cit* and Werner, *op cit*
2 Confidential information. Also Paul Wright, 'Radio Communication', December 1980
3 *Ibid*
4 *Ibid*
5 *Ibid*
6 Letter from Professor F. H. Hinsley
7 F. H. Hinsley, E. E. Thomas *et al.*, *British Intelligence in the Second World War*, Vol. 1 H.M.S.O. 1979

8 Bradley F. Smith, *The Shadow Warriors*, André Deutsch 1983. Also letters and discussions
9 Letters from Professor Hinsley and Sir Dick White
10 Letter from Professor Hinsley
11 Confidential information from R.S.S. source
12 Confidential information
13 *Ibid*
14 Confidential information. *The Times*, 21 November 1979
15 Werner, *Sonja's Rapport*
16 *Ibid* and F.B.I. document, *Foocase*, 17 March 1950, (Foocase was the file code for Fuchs) which states that Rolf had been 'arrested by the U.S. Army in Teheran and, after it had been determined that he was a Russian espionage agent, was turned over to the Russians'
17 Bradley Smith, *op cit*. David Dilkes, *op cit*
18 Foote, *op cit*
19 Bradley Smith, *op cit*. Joseph Persico, *Piercing the Reich*, Viking, New York 1979
20 Persico, *op cit*. *Rote Kapelle*, C.I.A. Handbook. Also see Chapter 13
21 Werner, *Sonja's Rapport*. Letter from Mrs Pamela Anderson (née Laski) and subsequent conversation. The site of 50a George Street is now part of a school in Middle Way
22 Researches at Clifton College
23 Conversation with Mrs Anderson
24 Werner, *Sonja's Rapport*
25 *Ibid*
26 See *Diplomatic Lists*. Evidence of Elizabeth Bentley, *Out of Bondage*, Devin-Adair, New York 1951
27 Weinstein, *op cit*

Chapter 10: In Post at Blenheim Palace (pages 77-80)

1 Letters from Derek Tangye and other former MI5 staff
2 Liddell, *op cit*
3 Various German biographies on the activities of exiles during the war
4 *Ibid*. The biographies wrongly state that Juergen Kuczynski was interned until 1941. In fact, he was released on 24 April 1940, (Kuczynski's *Memorien*)
5 Glees, *op cit* and numerous conversations
6 Confidential information
7 Letters from Tangye and other former MI5 staff
8 Letter from St Johnston
9 Conversations with Robertson and Mrs Morris
10 Conversations with people named
11 Letter from Fulford
12 Conversation with Mrs Phipps (Miss Miller). Letter from Colonel Eric St Johnston, who knew Knight. Declassified letter from Knight to Herschel Johnson, 5 June 1940, indicates the extent of his independence
13 Conversation with Mrs Phipps
14 *Ibid*
15 *Ibid*
16 Conversations with the two sources
17 Patrick Seale and Maureen McConville, *Philby*, Penguin 1978
18 Confidential information

Chapter 11: A Dubok in a Graveyard (pages 81-6)

1 Information provided by Gouzenko in letters and several conversations

2 Gouzenko mentioned the name Brown in a telephone conversation which he instigated on 21 September 1981. Later confirmed by Mrs Gouzenko
3 For Moscow control of duboks see David Dallin, *Soviet Espionage*, Oxford University Press 1956. *Report of the Royal Commission (Canada)* on Gouzenko revelations, 1946
4 Gouzenko letters and conversations
5 Confirmed by Peter Wright, *loc cit*
6 Werner, *Sonja's Rapport*
7 Confidential information
8 See *Their Trade is Treachery*, paperback, page 7, Sidgwick and Jackson, 1982
9 Research by Michael Chapman-Pincher
10 Letter from Mrs Gouzenko
11 *Ibid*

Chapter 12: The Two-Faced Dr Fuchs (pages 87-96)

1 Information collected by the author at the time of Fuchs's trial in 1950. U.S. Tripartite Talks Document, 19-21 June 1950, various F.B.I. documents
2 Letters from Mrs Ronald Gunn and Mr James Gunn
3 Letters from James Gunn
4 Letters from Gunn family
5 Letter from Sir Nevill Mott
6 F.B.I. document. Long memorandum from J. Edgar Hoover to the White House, dated 16 June 1950
7 *Ibid*
8 Margaret Gowing, *Independence and Deterrence*, Vol. 2 Macmillan 1974. Fuchs revealed his friendship with Kahle to a fellow-prisoner, Donald Hume: document in the author's possession.
9 Gowing, *op cit* and U.S. Tripartite Talks document, D.O.E. Archives.
10 U.S. Tripartite Talks document
11 Gowing, *op cit*
12 Fuchs' confessions to Sir Michael Perring and James Skardon. Also Hoover memorandum to White House, 16 June 1950
13 *Foocase*, F.B.I. document dated 17 March 1950. Also confidential information
14 Hoover memorandum to White House
15 Hoover memorandum to White House and confidential information
16 Hoover memorandum to White House. Letters from F.B.I. officer, Robert Lamphere. Confidential information
17 Gowing, *op cit*
18 *Ibid*
19 Confidential information
20 U.S. Tripartite Talks document
21 Hoover memorandum to White House. Confidential information. Letters from Lamphere
22 Dilkes, *op cit*. *Soviet Atomic Espionage*, Joint Committee on Atomic Energy report, U.S. Government Printing Office 1951. F. H. Hinsley, *op cit*
23 *Soviet Atomic Espionage* report
24 Bradley Smith, *op cit*
25 Gowing, *op cit*
26 Gowing, *op cit*. U.S. Tripartite Talks document. *Soviet Atomic Espionage* report
27 *Soviet Atomic Espionage* report. U.S. Tripartite Talks Document. Leslie R. Groves, *Now It Can Be Told*, Harper and Row, New York 1962
28 *Soviet Atomic Espionage* report. 'Raymond' was identified by Fuchs as Harry Gold
29 Gowing, *op cit*
30 Gowing *op cit*. U.S. Tripartite Talks document

31 U.S. Tripartite Talks document
32 Confidential information
33 *Soviet Atomic Espionage* report
34 Hoover memo to White House
35 Letter from Professor Robert Williams of Washington University, St Louis, who is researching an academic book on the Fuchs case. The London-based officer was John Cimperman. The treatment of the information by William Harvey at F.B.I. headquarters indicates some incompetence there
36 *Soviet Atomic Espionage* report
37 Gowing, *op cit*
38 Bradley Smith, *op cit*. Anthony Cave Brown, *The Last Hero, Wild Bill Donovan,* Michael Joseph 1982
39 Persico, *op cit*. Bradley Smith, *op cit*. Letters from Joseph Gould
40 Letters from Joseph Gould
41 Persico, *op cit*

Chapter 13: The Kuczynski Parachutists (pages 97-103)

1   Several letters from Joseph Gould
2   Juergen Kuczynski, *Memoiren*. Glees, *Exile Politics*
3   Glees, *op cit*
4   Invitation reproduced in Juergen Kuczynski, *René Kuczynski*
5   Glees, *op cit*
6   Bradley Smith, *op cit*. Hinsley, *op cit*. Confidential information
7   Persico, *op cit*. Letters from Joseph Gould
8   Werner, *Sonja's Rapport*
9   Letters from Joseph Gould
10 German biographies on German exiles
11 Werner, *Sonja's Rapport*
12 *Ibid*
13 Letter from Joseph Gould
14 Persico, *op cit*. Letters from Joseph Gould
15 Letter from Joseph Gould
16 *Ibid*
17 Persico, *op cit*. Letters from Joseph Gould
18 Werner, *Sonja's Rapport*. Juergen Kuczynski, *Memoiren*. Letter from Kenneth Galbraith
19 Werner, *Sonja's Rapport*
20 *Sunday Times*, 27 January 1980
21 U.S. Embassy paper on the Springhall case dated 4 August 1943, declassified 31 July 1983. *Daily Express* and *Daily Herald* reports of the case, 29 July 1943
22 Part of the Springhall document referred to in note 21
23 Foote, *op cit*
24 Confidential information
25 Richard Deacon, *The British Connection*, Hamish Hamilton 1979
26 Uren, *The Times*, 10 November 1981
27 Winston Churchill, *Closing the Ring*, (Vol. 5: *The Second World War*), Cassell 1951. Refers to a minute to Sir Alexander Cadogan *et al*
28 Letters and documents from Jack Tilton

Chapter 14: A Mole Called 'Elli' (pages 104-15)

1   Report of Royal Commission 1946, Ottawa, 27 June 1946
2   Information from Gouzenko confirmed by his wife
3   Cables from Sir William Stephenson. Confidential information. Nunn May has commonly been called Allan but the General Register Office record shows that he was named Alan

4   Information from Gouzenko and R.C.M.P. sources
5   Confirmed by Wright *loc cit*, Gouzenko and Mrs Gouzenko
6   Confidential information
7   Confirmed by Wright, *loc cit*. The message was deciphered in 1951
8   Confidential information
9   Philby, *My Silent War*, Macgibbon and Kee 1968
10   Confidential information
11   Cable from Sir William Stephenson. I have confirmed with others that Hollis 'did not like Americans'
12   Information from Gouzenko. Camp X was a secret training and communications centre located near Lake Ontario between Oshawa and Whitby
13   Conversation with Malcolm MacDonald. J. L. Granatstein, *A Man of Influence*, Deneau 1981. Malcolm MacDonald, *People and Places*, Collins 1969
14   Montgomery Hyde, *The Atom Bomb Spies*, Hamish Hamilton 1980. Hyde had access to the diaries of Mackenzie King
15   Report of Royal Commission
16   Letter from Mrs Gouzenko
17   Igor Gouzenko, *This was My Choice*, Palm, Montreal 1968
18   Conversation with Gouzenko. Letter from Mrs Gouzenko
19   Robert Bothwell and J. L. Granatstein, *The Gouzenko Transcripts*, Deneau 1982. Like 'Alex', 'Elli' has been commonly used because it is short and quickly transmittable.
20   Montgomery Hyde, *op cit*. Granatstein, *op cit*
21   Report of Royal Commission
22   Robert Kaplan, press interview, 26 March 1981, reported in *Toronto Star* on 27th
23   Conversations with Gouzenko. Letter from Mrs Gouzenko
24   *Ibid*
25   Letter from Mrs Gouzenko
26   Confidential information
27   Confidential information
28   Report of Royal Commission, Justice D. C. McDonald *et al.*, *Freedom and Security under the Law*, 1981
29   Bothwell and Granatstein, *op cit*
30   See Appendix A. Conversations with Gouzenko. Letters from Mrs Gouzenko
31   Letter from Mrs Gouzenko
32   Montgomery Hyde, *op cit*. Confirmed by confidential source
33   Letter from Mrs Gouzenko
34   Confidential information
35   Confidential information
36   Confidential information
37   Confidential information
38   Letter from Mrs Gouzenko

Chapter 15: The Return of Klaus Fuchs (pages 116-23)

1   Werner, *Sonja's Rapport*. Confirmed by on the spot inquiries
2   U.S. Tripartite Talks document. F.B.I. memorandum quoted by David C. Martin, *Wilderness of Mirrors*, Harper and Row, New York 1980. *Ottawa Gazette*, 2 May 1950
3   Gowing, *op cit*
4   F.B.I. document, Hoover to White House. *Soviet Atomic Espionage* report
5   Fuchs's confessions. Confidential information
6   When a copy of *The Traitors* was smuggled into prison for Fuchs to read, he said that he believed MI5 had helped the author with it to 'save their prestige'. Information from Fuchs's fellow-prisoner, Donald Hume

7 Werner, *Sonja's Rapport*
8 Report from Roger Hollis to T. E. Bromley at the Foreign Office, 10 September 1945. PRO. FO371c 4790/2069. Hollis's address was Snuffbox, Box 500, Oxford
9 F.B.I. document, Hoover to White House
10 Gowing, *op cit*. Confidential information
11 See Thomas Whiteside, *An Agent in Place*, Heinemann 1967
12 F.B.I. document, Hoover to the White House
13 Report from Chiefs of Staff dated 13 March 1947, PRO. CAB 21/2554
14 Juergen Kuczynski, *Memoiren*
15 Werner, *op cit*. Letter from Mr and Mrs Tom Greathead and conversations between the Greatheads and Michael Chapman-Pincher
16 Evidence from the Greatheads
17 Witnesses interviewed by Michael Chapman-Pincher
18 Confidential information from G.C.H.Q. source

Chapter 16: The 'Blowing' of Sonia (pages 124-31)

1 Confidential information
2 Confidential information
3 Glees, 'The Hollis Letters'
4 Philby, *op cit*
5 PRO FO371c 4790/2069
6 A. W. Cockerill, *Sir Percy Sillitoe*, Allen 1975, originally called *Cloak without Dagger*
7 PRO documents. See *The Times*, 2 April 1981
8 Foote, *op cit*. Confidential information
9 The MI5 term for such specially secret documents is 'Y-Boxed'
10 Werner, *Sonja's Rapport*. Berthe, aged sixty-seven, is buried at Great Rollright
11 Deacon, *op cit*. Confidential information
12 Deacon, *op cit*
13 *Ibid*
14 Confidential information. Much of what Foote told Frawley is in Foote, *op cit* (1964 edition)
15 Information from the Greatheads and other surviving witnesses
16 Confidential information
17 Werner, *Sonja's Rapport*
18 Smedley's death certificate, General Register Office
19 Confidential information
20 Sonia is said to have used the name Schultz in her early conspiratorial days in Germany – see *Rote Kapelle*, C.I.A. Handbook

Chapter 17: The Rise of Roger Hollis (pages 132-7)

1 Glees, *Hollis letters*. Confidential information
2 Confidential information
3 *Ibid*
4 Sir Martin Furnival Jones, *Evidence to Franks Committee* (Departmental Committee on Section 2 of the Official Secrets Act 1911). Vol. 3 H.M.S.O. 1972
5 Personal communication from Anthony Sillitoe
6 *Ibid*
7 Barrie Penrose and Simon Freeman, *Sunday Times*, 24 January 1982
8 Letter from Colonel Wild
9 Confidential information
10 Oxford University Calendars
11 Confidential information
12 Obituary of Henry Arnold, *The Times*, 14 July 1981

13 Confidential information. Michael Thwaites, *Truth Will Out*, Collins 1980
14 Confidential information. Thwaites, *op cit. The Bulletin* (Australia), 10 December 1966
15 Confidential information
16 Thwaites, *op cit*
17 Confidential information
18 U.S. Tripartite Talks document

Chapter 18: A Highly Suspect Escape (pages 138-54)

1 Werner, *Sonja's Rapport*. Information from Greatheads
2 Confidential information from British and American sources
3 See David C. Martin, *op cit* for a good account of this
4 Confidential information. Letters from Robert Lamphere. David C. Martin, *op cit*
5 Confidential information. Also see Montgomery Hyde, *op cit* (information from Sir Michael Perrin)
6 Confidential information. Gowing, *op cit*
7 Fuchs's confessions and evidence at his trial
8 Philby, *op cit*
9 *Soviet Atomic Espionage* report. Fuchs's trial transcript
10 Confidential information
11 Information from F.B.I. source
12 *Soviet Atomic Espionage* report
13 F.B.I. (*Foocase*) document dated 17 March 1950
14 Letter from Lord Shawcross
15 *Hansard*, 6 March 1950
16 F.B.I. Document. Hoover to White House dated 16 June 1950
17 Letters from Lamphere. Foote's book was first published in 1949
18 F.B.I. documents as dated. Letters from Professor Robert Williams
19 Document in author's possession
20 See Operation Farouche, Chapter 44
21 Information from Mrs Pamela Anderson (née Laski)
22 Letter from confidential source
23 Werner, *Sonja's Rapport*
24 A. S. Blank, Julius Mader, *Rote Kapelle gegen Hitler*, Verlag der Nation, East Berlin, 1979
25 Juergen Kuczynski, *Memoiren*. He visited Dobb
26 Juergen Kuczynski, *Dialog mit meinem Urenkel*, page 145, Aufbau Verlag, Berlin 1983
27 Information from Mrs Davenport
28 *Ibid*
29 *The Times*, 2 April 1981, report by Peter Hennessy
30 *Hansard*, 23 October 1950, statement by George Strauss, Supply Minister. *Soviet Atomic Espionage* report. *Daily Express* (Chapman Pincher), 27 October 1950, 26 February 1951
31 Confidential information
32 *Soviet Atomic Espionage* report. Gowing, *op cit*
33 Franks Report on the Official Secrets Act

Chapter 19: The Cambridge Conspiracy (pages 155-70)

1 Letters from Major-General Denis Moore and conversations. PRO documents Op. Rodeo WO216 799, WO216 801 and other relevant documents
2 See Mackenzie King diaries
3 Confidential information

4 Trevor Barnes, 'The Secret Cold War', *Historical Journal*, 25, 3 (1982)
5 *Ibid*
6 Letters from Robert Lamphere. F.B.I. note dated 19 June 1951, quoted in Montgomery Hyde, *op cit*
7 Often mis-spelled Klugman because there was a contemporary student of that name. Cambridge calendars list him as Klugmann
8 Confidential information
9 See Nikolai Tolstoy, *Stalin's Secret War*, Cape 1981. Writings of Margarete Buber-Neumann. Also see Malcolm Muggeridge, *Chronicles of Wasted Time*, Vol. 2, Collins 1973
10 Confidential information
11 Confidential information
12 Confidential information
13 Confidential information. Also see Whiteside, *op cit*, Werner, *Sonja's Rapport*
14 Confidential information
15 *The Times*, 21 November 1979
16 Confidential information
17 Evidence from various cases: e.g. Fuchs, Nunn May. Confidential confirmation. The Comintern (short for Communist International) was the worldwide communist organization formed in Moscow in March 1919 to promote world revolution
18 T. E. B. Howarth, *Cambridge Between Two Wars*, Collins 1978. Bruce Page *et al:*, *Philby*, André Deutsch, 1968. Seale and McConville, *op cit*
19 Confidential information
20 *Granta*, 7 March 1934
21 Foreign Office List
22 Letter from Robert Lamphere. Confidential confirmation
23 Michael Straight, *After Long Silence*, Collins 1983
24 Andrew Boyle, *The Climate of Treason*, Coronet 1980. Burgess obtained a First in Part One but an Aegrotat in his Finals – a note certifying that he had been too ill to achieve what had been expected of him
25 *The Times*, 21 November 1979
26 Information from Lady Llewelyn-Davies
27 Confidential information
28 Seale and McConville, *op cit*
29 *Ibid*
30 Confidential source. Burgess was to announce that he had worked for MI5 in his joint statement with Maclean in Moscow. See Chapter 23
31 Confidential source
32 Confidential information
33 The official was Bob Stewart
34 Sir John Masterman, *On the Chariot Wheel*, Oxford University Press 1975
35 Confidential information
36 Seale and McConville, *op cit*
37 Confidential information
38 Seale and McConville, *op cit*. Flora Solomon and Barnet Litvinoff, *Baku to Baker Street*, Collins 1984

Chapter 20: The Great Defection Legend (pages 171-203)

1 Foreign Office lists. The story that 'Henry' was a Mr Ernst Henry is incorrect. Ernst Henry was the pseudonym of a Russian journalist who was an Agitprop agent but never registered as a diplomat. He promoted communism and subversion openly, which would never have been allowed if he had been a controller
2 Juergen Kuczynski, *Memoiren*

3   Elizabeth Bentley, *op cit*
4   Gowing, *op. cit*. F.B.I. sources
5   Wilfrid Mann, *Was there a Fifth Man?*, Pergamon Press 1982. Also letters from Mann who, contrary to suggestions by Andrew Boyle, never met Maclean
6   Mann, *op cit*
7   Confidential information. Letters from Robert Lamphere who was in the F.B.I.'s security division
8   Letters from Robert Lamphere
9   *Ibid*
10   Confidential information
11   Letters from Lamphere. Lamphere insists that he 'pressed Patterson over and over to find out why there had not been more progress by MI5 in developing a list of suspects who were in the British Embassy at the pertinent period. He would tell me that he would inquire or that there was nothing new'
12   Confidential information
13   Goronwy Rees, *A Chapter of Accidents*, Chatto and Windus 1972
14   Cyril Connolly, *The Missing Diplomats*, Queen Anne Press 1952. Also conversations
15   Foreign Office lists. Cyril Connolly conversations. Connolly, op cit
16   Confidential information
17   See Roy Medvedev, *Washington Post*, 19 June 1983. Also newspaper reports from Moscow
18   Trumbull Higgins, *Korea and the Fall of MacArthur*, Oxford University Press 1960
19   Medvedev made the claim in the *Washington Post*. The Foreign Office has assured the author that Maclean was not on the list of delegates and Verne Newton, an American researcher, has confirmed that from the U.S. archives
20   Letter from Gordon W. Creighton and conversations
21   Conversations with the individual concerned
22   Wilfrid Mann, *op cit*
23   Confidential information
24   Confidential information. Also F.B.I. information quoted by David C. Martin, *op cit*
25   Letter from Lamphere
26   *Ibid*. Philby, in *My Silent War*, claims that the short-list of six suspects had been sent to him and that he discussed it with Sir Robert Mackenzie. If that is correct, then Philby must have been under instruction to avoid informing the F.B.I. or took the decision not to do so
27   Letter from Lamphere
28   White Paper: 'Report Concerning the Disappearance of Two Former Foreign Office Officials', H.M.S.O., 23 September 1955, Cmnd 9577
29   *Ibid*
30   Supplied by Burgess to Tom Driberg and used in his book, *Guy Burgess*, Weidenfeld and Nicolson 1956
31   Erich Kessler, a former acquaintance of Burgess, testified to an MI5 officer who visited him in Switzerland that Burgess once told him, 'I have such a friend in Donald Maclean that if ever I were in great difficulties, financial, for instance, he would go out of his way, forget his family, even, to help me'
32   Confidential information arising out of Blunt's interrogation
33   *Ibid*
34   Evidence of Vladimir Petrov, see page 214
35   Goronwy Rees, *op cit*
36   Information originating with Jack Hewitt
37   Confidential information
38   White Paper, see note 28 above

39 *Hansard*, 7 November 1955, col 1514
40 White Paper, see note 28 above
41 Cyril Connolly, *op cit* and conversations
42 Confidential information. Also information originating with Hewitt
43 *The Great Spy Scandal*, Daily Express Publications 1955
44 *Ibid*. Information from George Carver, former C.I.A. officer
45 Connolly, *op cit*
46 *Ibid. The Great Spy Scandal*, Daily Express Publications 1955
47 *Hansard*, 21 November 1979, col.402
48 Letter from Lamphere
49 Confidential information
50 Letter from Lamphere and conversation with George Carver
51 The letter described by Philby was not found in Burgess's effects. It may have been destroyed, but MI5 officers involved in the case doubt that it ever existed. In Boyle's *Climate of Treason* the letter is converted to a telegram, but Philby would have known that all telegrams are subject to security scrutiny and MI5 would, or should, have been looking for just such a clue
52 *Hansard*, 21 November 1979, col 402
53 *The Times* interview, 21 November 1979
54 *Hansard*, 26 March, 1981, col 1079
55 Blunt had been seconded for membership of the Travellers by Liddell in 1948
56 *The Times* interview, 21 November 1979
57 Goronwy Rees, *op cit*
58 Cyril Connolly, *op cit*. He gives the name as Ronald Styles. It seems that Mrs Maclean remembered it as Roger
59 *The Great Spy Scandal*, Daily Express Publications 1955
60 Evidence of Vladimir Petrov
61 Confidential information. Also see *The Times* interview, 21 November 1979
62 Confidential information derived from friends of Blunt. In his book, *Random Variables*, Collins 1984, Lord Rothschild describes how he gave Blunt the £100 to buy the painting in 1932. In 1984 it was to be valued at £500,000
63 Confidential information
64 Goronwy Rees, *op cit*
65 Communication from Anthony Sillitoe
66 *Daily Express*, 11 June 1951
67 Confidential information
68 Foreign Office source
69 Conversation with George Carver
70 *Ibid*
71 Confidential information
72 Evidence of Vladimir Petrov. Thwaites, *op cit*. Also see White Paper on the Burgess and Maclean defection
73 Peter Hennessy and Gail Brownfeld, 'Britain's Cold War Security Purge', *Historical Journal*, December 1982
74 *Ibid*
75 *Ibid*. M.O.D. Memorandum. Security Questionnaire Form PV 300. Press notice issued by H. M. Treasury for publication 12 March 1952
76 Confidential information
77 Confidential information

Chapter 21: Chief Liaison Officer – for the K.G.B. (pages 204-12)

1 Confidential information
2 Letters from John Read
3 *Ibid* plus additional information from confidential sources
4 Confidential information

5 Letter from John Read
6 Confidential information
7 Confidential information
8 Philby, *op cit*
9 Confidential information
10 Confidential information
11 Confidential information
12 Nicholas Elliott
13 Conversation with Otto John
14 Confidential information

Chapter 22: Second-in-Command (pages 213-19)
1 Letter to *Daily Express* Editor in my possession
2 The intermediary was the late Bernard Hill
3 Letter from R.C.M.P. source
4 Reproduced in *Their Trade is Treachery*, Sidgwick and Jackson 1981
5 Statement to Canadian Press, 27 March 1981
6 Thwaites, *op cit*
7 Confidential information
8 Sir William McMahon
9 Confidential information from R.C.M.P. source
10 Conversation with Gouzenko
11 Confidential source
12 *Ibid*
13 *Ibid*
14 *Ibid*
15 Colonel T. A. Robertson

Chapter 23: The 'Whitewash' Paper (pages 220-31)
1 Cmnd 9577
2 Confidential information. For inaccuracies about Burgess, see Goronwy Rees,
   op cit
3 *Hansard*, 7 November 1955, col. 1483
4 Letter from Michael Thwaites. The White Paper seems to have been
   published only because the Australian Government decided to publish a
   report on the Petrov defection
5 *Hansard*, 7 November 1955, col. 1599
6 *Hansard*, 25 October 1955
7 Seale and McConville, *op cit*
8 Confidential information
9 Conversation with Mr Macmillan at Birch Grove
10 See *The Great Spy Scandal*, Daily Express Publications 1955
11 Confidential information
12 *Ibid*
13 Information from Sir Maurice Oldfield
14 *Ibid*
15 Confidential information
16 Statement from a witness at the party
17 Cmnd 9715, 1956
18 Eleanor Philby, *Kim Philby, the Spy I Loved*, Hamish Hamilton 1968
19 See *Sunday Times*, 12 February 1956 and other papers that day. A likely
   explanation for the production of the two traitors is given by Douglas
   Sutherland in *The Fourth Man*, Secker and Warburg 1980
20 *Daily Express*, 27 February 1956

21 Tom Driberg, *Guy Burgess: A Portrait with Background*, Weidenfeld and Nicolson 1956
22 Confidential information. See *Their Trade is Treachery*, Sidgwick and Jackson 1981
23 *Daily Express*, 23 November 1956
24 For a review of the excellent television documentary-drama *An Englishman Abroad*, of a visit paid by the actress Coral Browne to Moscow and a meeting with Burgess, see *Daily Mail*, 3 December 1983

Chapter 24: Momentous Escapade (pages 232-7)

1 Confidential information
2 Information from Naval Intelligence source
3 Confidential information
4 Former MI10 source
5 Former MI6 source
6 Information from Lord Glendevon
7 *Hansard*, 14 May 1956, col. 1751. An excellent example of ministerial stone-walling
8 Confidential information
9 Bernard Hutton, *Commander Crabb is Alive*, Tandem 1968. Conversations with Mrs Pat Rose
10 *Ibid* and see Chapter 39

Chapter 25: In Control (pages 238-49)

1 Sir Martin Furnival Jones, Franks Report on the Official Secrets Act
2 Imperial Calendar 1956
3 Conversation with Mrs Betty Morris
4 Conversations with Mrs Patricia Stewart
5 E.g. those of Blake and Wennerstrom (see Whiteside, *op cit*)
6 Letter from Tangye. Statement by David Leigh, *Frontiers of Secrecy*, Junction Books 1980. (This information came from a relative of Hollis)
7 Confidential information
8 Letter from Professor R. V. Jones
9 *The Times*, 2 April 1960
10 Confidential information
11 *Ibid*
12 Josef Frolik, *The Frolik Defection*, Leo Cooper 1975. Deacon, *op cit. The Times*, 25 January 1974
13 Confidential information
14 *Ibid*
15 *Ibid*
16 Sir Dick White, *The Times* (obituary notice), 6 November 1973
17 Letters from the officer concerned, Colonel Basil Spurling

Chapter 26: A 'Pig' called 'Lavinia' (pages 250-7)

1 U.B. – *Urzad Bezpieczenstwa*. Much of the information in this chapter derives from confidential sources. David C. Martin, *op cit* also supplies prime source information from C.I.A.
2 A reliable account of the Portland Spy-Ring is given by Norman Lucas, *The Great Spy Ring*, Arthur Barker 1966. Lucas had excellent access to the Special Branch information
3 Confidential information
4 Lord Wigg, *George Wigg*, Michael Joseph 1972. *Hansard*, 7 May 1963, col 311
5 Confidential information

6 Gordon Lonsdale, *Spy*, Neville Spearman 1965. According to Eleanor Philby, *op cit*, Lonsdale's book was ghosted by Philby
7 Harry Houghton, *Operation Portland*, Hart-Davis 1972
8 Costello had been at Trinity College, Cambridge in the early 1930s and was in the New Zealand Legation in Moscow from 1944–50. He was in the New Zealand diplomatic service in Paris from 1950–5. He died 23 February 1964. The two 'diplomats' expelled in New Zealand were Andreev and Shtykov
9 Information from George Miller, a Russian-speaking student of Soviet affairs
10 *Hansard*, 23 March 1961, col. 584
11 *Hansard*, 13 June 1961, col. 211. Also 22 June, col. 1683
12 *Ibid*
13 Harold Macmillan, *At the End of the Day*, Macmillan 1973. *Hansard*, 23 March 1961, col. 586

Chapter 27: A 'Real Outsider' (pages 258-63)

1 Confidential information
2 Information from Lord George-Brown, see Chapman Pincher, *Inside Story*, Sidgwick and Jackson 1978
3 Confidential information
4 Information from Lord George-Brown
5 *Hansard*, 11 May 1961
6 Letter from Patrick Kelleher
7 Lord Harris of Greenwich. The Irish criminal was Sean Bourke
8 John Vassall, *Vassall*, Sidgwick and Jackson 1975
9 Deacon, *op cit*. For an Iron Curtain statement that Blake had been recruited before his service in Korea, see E. Gomori 'Clandestine Service C.I.A.', *Kozmosz*, Budapest 1979

Chapter 28: A Defector in Place? (pages 264-7)

1 Confidential information. Greville Wynne, *The Man from Moscow*, Hutchinson, 1967. Oleg Penkovsky, *The Penkovsky Papers*, edited by Frank Gibney, Collins 1965 (a compilation of documents and tape-recordings made available by the C.I.A.)
2 Confidential information
3 *Penkovsky Papers*. See Chapter 34
4 See *Their Trade is Treachery*
5 Confidential information

Chapter 29: A Spy in the Labour Party (pages 268-70)

1 See Chapter 26
2 Confidential information
3 See Chapman Pincher, *Inside Story*. Further confidential information
4 Information supplied by Lord George-Brown
5 See Chapter 60. Hambleton trial transcript
6 *Ibid*

Chapter 30: The Numbers Game (pages 271-4)

1 Report on Security Procedures in the Public Service, Cmnd 1681, 1962
2 See Anthony Courtney, *Sailor in a Russian Frame*, Johnson 1968, and various statements by him in Parliament
3 Confidential information from R.C.M.P. sources
4 Senior R.C.M.P. source. When Hollis retired, the Soviet Embassy staff numbered 142: 71 official envoys, 26 attachés, 37 clerks and 8 chauffeurs

Chapter 31: A Defector Called 'Kago' (pages 275-85)

1 Leo Abse, *The Times*, 26 October 1981. Abse, 'The Judas Syndrome', *Spectator*, 20 March 1982
2 Vassall, *op cit*
3 Confidential information
4 Confidential information
5 Nosenko's American code-name was Foxtrot. The K.G.B. has a list of male as well as female prostitutes used for seduction purposes
6 Conversation with Vassall
7 Vassall told the author that he hated the bookcase because it was 'out of keeping with my nice antiques'
8 Confidential information
9 See Edward J. Epstein, *Legend*, Hutchinson 1978. David C. Martin, *op cit*. Henry Hurt, *Shadrin*, Readers Digest Press 1981. Confidential information
10 Conversation with Vassall
11 *Daily Express*, 23 November 1962. See Chapman Pincher, *Inside Story*
12 Report of the Tribunal Appointed to Inquire into the Vassall Case and Related Matters, Cmnd 2009, 1963. *Hansard*, 7 May 1963, col 240
13 Conversation with Lord Carrington
14 Harold Macmillan, *op cit*
15 White Paper, published 7 November 1962. See *The Times*, 8 November 1982
16 See *Their Trade is Treachery*

Chapter 32: Philby's Defection (pages 286-304)

1 Confidential information from Foreign Office source
2 Confidential information
3 *Ibid*
4 Flora Solomon and Barnet Litvinoff, *op cit*
5 Private information from friends of Mrs Solomon. See also Seale and McConville, *op cit*
6 By Sir Dick White
7 Confidential information
8 Evidence from former MI5 officers
9 Evidence from MI6 and C.I.A. sources
10 Information from Nicholas Elliott
11 Tim Milne had been forbidden to publish his account of his association with Philby, at the time of writing
12 Philby claimed to have seen a photograph of Deutsch in the F.B.I. files, but checks showed that no such photograph existed before Philby had left Washington
13 Confidential information confirmed by C.I.A. source
14 Harold Macmillan, *op cit*
15 Eleanor Philby, *op cit*. In the late afternoon Philby had told his wife he had an appointment but would be back
16 Philby, *op cit*
17 *The Cheka*, Vol. 5, 1983
18 *Hansard*, 26 March 1981, col. 1079
19 Geoffrey McDermott writing in *New York Times*
20 *Hansard*, 1 July 1963, col. 33. Heath reacted to disclosures in the U.S. magazine, *Newsweek*
21 *Ibid*
22 Harold Wilson, *Labour Government, 1964-1970*, Weidenfeld and Nicolson and Michael Joseph 1971
23 Macmillan, *op cit*. Conversations with Harold Macmillan and Sir Harold Evans

24 See Derek Tangye, *The Ambrose Rock*, Michael Joseph 1982
25 Conversation with Otto John. John supplied accurate information about the impending plot to kill Hitler to be followed by a peace treaty. Also confidential information
26 Letter from Professor R. V. Jones. He wrote, 'What is certain is that from December 1941 Philby knew that one form of Enigma could be broken and anyone interested in cryptography would realise that if you could break one form you could break any other of comparable difficulty'
27 There have been claims in the Soviet Press that he holds the rank of brigadier, or even major-general
28 George Honigmann. Philby's decree absolute was dated 17 September 1946. A further inquiry into Lizi's activities was made after Philby was safely in Russia. One of his former MI6 colleagues was found to have lived with her for a while in London while knowing her communist and pro-Russian connections and had failed to report them. He was required to leave the service
29 Confidential information. Also see William Hood, *Mole*, Weidenfeld and Nicolson 1982. Hood, a former C.I.A. officer, tells how the C.I.A. interrogated Akhmedov, who repeatedly said, 'But you must know this. I went over it in detail with the British.' Checks showed that not only had Philby reported little but had derided Akhmedov as a source, as Hollis had derided Gouzenko
30 While large portions of the Russia Committee archives for 1948–50 are available at the Public Record Office, those for 1951 are still withheld. See Peter Hennessy, *The Times*, 28 July 1982
31 See Thomas Powers, *The Man who Kept the Secrets*, Weidenfeld and Nicolson 1979
32 *Ibid*
33 Letters from R.C.M.P. sources. Also see John Sawatsky, *Men in the Shadows*, Doubleday, Canada 1980. Also statement by former R.C.M.P. Commissioner, George McLellan on Canadian T.V.
34 Confidential information
35 Eleanor Philby, *op cit*. Conversation with Otto John. Confidential information from MI6 source
36 Information from MI6 sources
37 See Philby interview with Roy Blackman, *Daily Express*, 15 November 1967 Information from relative of Mr Greene

Chapter 33: The Mitchell Case (pages 305-16)

1 Confidential information. Also letter written by Jonathan Aitken to Margaret Thatcher on 31 January 1980. Conversation with Harold Macmillan
2 Confirmed by Peter Wright, *loc cit*
3 See David C. Martin *op cit*
4 *Hansard*, 26 March 1981, col. 1079
5 It has not been possible to discover where he lived while at Blenheim. By 1948, and probably before, he was back in London living in the Highgate area
6 The identities of some of these recruits are now known
7 See Hennessy and Brownfeld, *op cit*
8 Confidential information. Confirmed by Harold Macmillan
9 Known in the jargon as 'barium meals'
10 Information given to me by Colonel Lohan, a close friend
11 Sir Richard Way
12 Confidential information. Evidence that Coote had been a low-handicap golfer supplied by William Deedes, Editor, *Daily Telegraph*. Hollis, at his best, played off four
13 Conversation with Colonel Robertson

14   Confidential information from the R.C.M.P. and F.B.I.
15   Confidential information from senior R.C.M.P. source. Conversations with Lord Wigg

Chapter 34: The Profumo Affair (pages 317-36)

1   Cmnd 2152, September 1963
2   Witnesses were not required to give evidence under oath and were allowed to testify confidentially if they wished. In her book, *Nothing But...*, Christine Keeler states, 'Lord Denning was kind enough to believe half of what I said...'
3   Penkovsky, *op cit*
4   Denning Report
5   Conversations with Christine Keeler. Also Keeler, *op cit*
6   Conversations with Michael Eddowes and letters
7   Conversations with Christine Keeler
8   Christine Keeler, *op cit*
9   See Jane's *Weapons Systems*
10   Denning Report
11   Documents supplied by German Embassy
12   Personal examination of Eddowes' documents
13   Denning omitted any mention of Eddowes' evidence from his report
14   In *Nothing But...*, New English Library 1983, Keeler records how she was repeatedly grilled by Detective Sergeant Burrows and Inspector Herbert about the request to discover the nuclear weapons date, so they, at least were taking it seriously. 'My interrogation took place in a windowless room at the station with all the classic techniques of the Gestapo'
15   See note 34 below
16   Harold Macmillan, *op cit*. He records a visit from Hollis who told him that, according to Keeler, Ward had asked her to find out from Profumo some information concerning *atomic secrets*
17   One of the officers involved in the case described Ivanov as probably the most dedicated communist in his experience
18   Denning Report
19   *Ibid*
20   *Robert Kennedy*, posthumous book published by McCall's magazine, 20 October 1968
21   Confidential information from the officer concerned. A senior Foreign Office source claims that the first intimation MI5 had about the relationship between Profumo and Keeler was a monitored telephone call in which Ivanov claimed to have the same girlfriend as the War Minister
22   See *The Great Spy Scandal*, Daily Express Publications. The caller to Wigg is believed, in MI5, to have been the K.G.B. agent Victor Louis
23   The Profumo Debate, *Hansard*, 17 June 1963, col. 34
24   Mark Chapman-Walker
25   Profumo Debate, *op cit*
26   Denning Report
27   The writer was Wagstaffe ('Woods')
28   Denning Report. Also see Chapman Pincher, *Inside Story*, Sidgwick and Jackson 1978
29   *Hansard*, Security and the Denning Report, 16 December 1963, col. 974
30   Conversations with Eddowes and examination of his documents. In Parliament Macmillan was to deny that Dickinson said that the report would be on his desk but Eddowes made a contemporary record of the events
31   Profumo Debate, *op cit*
32   Lord Wigg, *op cit*

33 Letter from Dilhorne stating 'Tom Denning used so much of it that I could have successfully sued him for breach of copyright'

34 The documents have been obtained through the persistence of Michael Eddowes who showed me photostats on 2 August 1983. They show that the American concern about the possible leakage of nuclear secrets through Keeler's and Ward's connections was serious and it is hard to believe that the anglophile F.B.I. representative in London, John Minnick, did not tell MI5 about it. The F.B.I.'s interest had intensified when it realized that Ward had been responsible for sending an attractive woman called Maria (Mariella) Novotny to the U.S. to embroil President Kennedy in deviant sexual activities, in which she appeared to have had some success until she was summarily deported. It would be instructive to know if Denning was ever told of the American security interest in Keeler and Ward

Chapter 35: A Clutch of Curious Incidents (pages 337-41)

1 Confidential information
2 Transcript of Martelli trial
3 Confidential information. For evidence that 'Fedora' was a fake see Henry Hurt, *op cit*. The F.B.I.'s realization of 'Fedora's' duplicity was concealed until after Hoover died in 1972, still in office, aged seventy-seven. While MI5 was informed of the truth in 1978 it did not reach those retired officers who had been concerned with the Hollis case until the 'Fedora' fiasco became public in 1981. It is their view that the exposure of 'Fedora' as a fake is further serious evidence against Hollis. MI5 was never allowed to contact 'Fedora' directly and was never told of his true identity. He was definitely not Viktor Lessiovsky, as has been claimed. The most likely candidate seems to be Vladimir Chuchukin, a K.G.B. agent at the U.N. in New York fro 1962 to 1977
4 Sir John Masterman, *The Double Cross System*, Yale University Press 1972
5 Masterman, *On the Chariot Wheel*, Oxford University Press 1975
6 Confidential information

Chapter 36: The 'Blunden' File (pages 342-57)

1 Confidential information
2 See Hinsley, *op cit*
3 *Ibid*
4 Long confession. Statement by Prime Minister, *Hansard*, 9 November 1981, col. 40
5 Confidential information and Juergen Kuczynski, *op cit*
6 MI6 source
7 Wolfgang zu Putlitz, *The Putlitz Dossier*, Wingate 1957
8 Ellic Howe, *The Black Game*, Michael Joseph 1982
9 Confidential information and zu Putlitz, *op cit*
10 *Ibid*
11 *Ibid*
12 Conversation with Lady Llewelyn-Davies
13 *Ibid*
14 Nothing to do with 'M' of the Bond novels which referred to the head of MI6, not MI5
15 Conversation with Knight's assistant, Joan Miller
16 By René McColl
17 Confidential information. Also the Burgess and Maclean statement in Moscow, *op cit*

18 Kislytsin told Petrov that there was a special section of the K.G.B. archives to house the vast quantity of material supplied by Burgess and Maclean but some of this may have been supplied by Burgess and Blunt, jointly

19 Letter from Colonel Wild and conversations

20 Letter from Michael Howard to Colonel Wild

21 When Krivitsky gave evidence to the U.S. Senate Committee on oath he said there had been occasions when the Red Army and German Intelligence had co-operated on espionage and the exchange of military information. The Soviet Union also gave assistance to the German Navy. The German raider, *Komet*, had reached the Pacific from Germany via the north of the U.S.S.R. in 1940 with Soviet collusion, doing much damage to Allied shipping and not returning to Germany until November 1941 (Patrick Beesly, *Very Special Intelligence*, Hamish Hamilton 1977)

22 Wild recalled that General Montgomery once said to him, 'Why is it that whatever I do there is always a Panzer division there?'

23 Letter from Buckingham Palace

24 Information from Lady Llewelyn-Davies

25 This has been confirmed by an MI5 source, by friends of Blunt, by Blunt himself and by a Buckingham Palace source

26 Letter from Reginald G. Le Pla

27 Peter Allen, *The Crown and the Swastika*, Hale 1983. Walter Schellenberg, *The Schellenberg Memoirs*, André Deutsch 1956. The Duke also had a long and friendly talk with von Papen, Hitler's ambassador to Vienna on 4 February 1937

28 Peter Allen, *op cit*, for the most documented account

29 *Ibid*. Also see Dusko Popov, *Spy Counter-Spy*, Weidenfeld and Nicolson 1974. Professor Cameron Watt, who examined the German Foreign Ministry files, does not believe that Blunt's mission was concerned with any Windsor papers

30 Information from Verne Newton

31 Information from Buckingham Palace source

32 Conversation with Colonel Robertson

33 Confidential information

34 Sidney Hook, *Encounter*, December 1983

35 See David Leigh, *The Frontiers of Secrecy*, Junction Books 1980

36 Goronwy Rees, *op cit*

37 *Ibid*

38 Confidential information

39 *Hansard*, 21 November 1979, col 402

40 Confidential information

41 *Ibid*. Published in *Their Trade is Treachery*. Blunt later confirmed his chance meeting with Philby in a letter to the *Sunday Times*, 22 November 1981

42 The friend was James Cornford. Letters from Michael Straight. Confirmed by Straight in his book, *After Long Silence*, Collins 1983

43 *Ibid*

44 *Ibid*

45 F.B.I. reports to Hoover, subject Michael Whitney Straight, dated June, July and August 1963 and declassified in September 1983

46 Christine Keeler, *op cit*

Chapter 37: The Fixing of Blunt's Immunity (pages 358-74)

1 Information from former member of the staff of the Courtauld Institute. Copy of letter from Blunt giving Pennsylvania address and dated 14 August 1963 in author's possession

2 Confidential information

3 Letters from Michael Straight

4 Letters from Straight mentioning correspondence with Martin
5 Letters from Straight, and Straight, *op cit*
6 Information from Dr Glees
7 Letter from Michael Straight
8 *Hansard*, 21 November 1979, col. 402
9 *Hansard*, 9 November 1981, col. 40
10 Part of a group of F.B.I. documents entitled Michael Whitney Straight declassified in June 1983, File No. 100-61929, Sect. 1 and 2
11 Letter from Straight, and Straight, *op cit*
12 Information from the officer, who is now retired
13 After Blunt's confession the officer wanted to consult his minute in the file and found that it was missing. Later, in 1978, when Long's case was examined again, the minute was back in the file
14 Sir Isaiah Berlin
15 *Hansard*, 21 November 1979, col. 402
16 *Ibid*
17 *Ibid*. See also *Hansard*, 9 November 1981, col. 40
18 *Ibid*
19 *Ibid*
20 Maurice Crump, letter to *The Times*, 19 April 1984, followed by telephone conversations with the author
21 *Ibid*
22 Confidential information
23 *Hansard*, 21 November 1979, col. 402. Confidential information
24 Confidential information
25 *Hansard*, 21 November 1979, col. 402
26 Confidential information
27 *Hansard*, 21 November 1979, col. 402
28 Information from Michael Straight. Conversation with him in London
29 Adviser for the Queen's Pictures and Drawings
30 Statement to the author by the person concerned
31 Confidential information
32 *Hansard*, 21 November 1979, col. 402
33 Information from that associate
34 Letters from Michael Straight
35 *Hansard*, 21 November 1979 and 9 November 1981, col. 40
36 *Hansard*, 23 January 1964, col. 1274
37 Information from Lord Wigg

Chapter 38: The Interrogation of Leo Long (pages 375-8)

1 *Hansard*, 9 November 1981, col. 40
2 Confidential information
3 *Hansard*, 9 November 1981, col. 40
4 *Ibid*
5 Statements to newspapers and on television
6 *Hansard*, 9 November 1981, col. 40. A debate on Long was refused

Chapter 39: The Interrogation of Sir Anthony Blunt (pages 379-93)

1 Confidential information. See Chapter 20, note 1
2 Letter from Michael Straight
3 Andrew Wilson, *Observer*, 29 March 1981. Simon Freeman and Barrie Penrose, *Sunday Times*, 8 November 1981
4 *Ibid*
5 Information deriving from personal friends of Blunt
6 Letter from Miss Rosemary Leach, a former member of the Courtauld

7 In the B.B.C.'s *Timewatch* programme on 27 July 1983 Miss Fischer-Williams (Mrs Hart) admitted these statements, though having no knowledge that Floud was other than a communist
8 *Observer*, 8 November 1981. *Daily Mail*, 9 November 1981. Sir Dennis died in 1983
9 Ewen Montagu, *Beyond Top Secret Ultra*, Davies 1977. Montagu dedicates the book to 'the memory of Tommy Harris, the greatest deceptioneer of us all'
10 Confidential information
11 Former MI5 officers think that Harris could have helped Mrs Maclean out of a feeling of 'old comradeship' for her husband
12 Answer in Canadian Parliament to Mr Tom Cossitt dated 14 April 1980
13 Blunt, *The Times*, 21 November 1979
14 See Callaghan statement, *Hansard*, 21 November 1979
15 *Hansard*, 9 November 1981

Chapter 40: Big Fish Escapes as Small Fry (pages 394-401)
1 Letter from F.A.O. colleague of Cairncross (R. A. Bishop)
2 Confidential information
3 Information from G. K. Young, David Footman and others
4 Quoted by Ronald Lewin in *Ultra Goes to War*, Arrow 1980
5 Letter from David Footman
6 David Martin, *Patriot or Traitor*, Hoover Institution Press, Stanford 1978
7 *Ibid* and letters from David Martin
8 Confidential information
9 The names of all are known to me but cannot be given for legal objections
10 See *Daily Mail*, 23 June 1982, and subsequent reports
11 *Hansard*, 9 November 1981

Chapter 41: A Committee Called 'Fluency' (pages 402-8)
1 Confidential information confirmed from several sources
2 Over the last twenty-five years the K.G.B. has been increasing its use of this kind of slander against Western officials and politicians, backing it up with forged documents as part of the Kremlin's 'active measures' to destabilize democracies. (See *Soviet Active Measures*, Hearings before the Permanent Select Committee on Intelligence, House of Representatives, U.S. Government Printing Office 1982)
3 Confidential information from British and American sources
4 At White's residence in Queen Anne's Gate, London. In a recent letter Sir Dick, who believes Hollis to be innocent, has expressed his revulsion at the requirement to investigate his old friend
5 As officers of the Fluency Committee left the Service or were posted to other duties they were replaced
6 Confidential information
7 Sir Dick White
8 Mr Mitchell explained that after the *New Statesman* revealed that he was 'Peters', following the disclosures in *Their Trade is Treachery*, he had 'no option but to admit it'
9 Among those wrongly accused was Courtenay Young. The officer who walked out in protest in the late 1970s and who was described to me by a colleague as 'a great interrogator and brilliant agent-runner', has demanded an apology but without satisfactory result

Chapter 42: The Canadian Dimension (pages 409-20)

1 Many letters from R.C.M.P. officers. John Sawatsky's book *Men in the Shadows*, Doubleday 1980, is also an excellent source

2 There have been several references to 'Featherbed' in the Canadian Parliament, e.g. 15 April 1980 (statements by the Solicitor-General) and 26 June 1980

3 Wright's name was first published by Sawatsky in his book *For Services Rendered*, Doubleday 1982. To preserve his cover, though he has long been retired, I withheld it from *Their Trade is Treachery*

4 Sawatsky gives a detailed account of Bennett's life and service in *For Services Rendered*. I have checked and extended his information from prime sources

5 Confidential information. See Chapter 49

6 Sawatsky, *For Services Rendered*. See also *Daily Express*, 20 December 1982

7 See Operation Coverpoint

8 Confidential information

9 Morrison had been given the code-name 'Long Knife' when Sawatsky revealed the case in his book, *For Services Rendered*. The disclosure led to the attempted prosecution. The case was given wide publicity in the Canadian and British Press

10 See Chapman Pincher, *Their Trade is Treachery*

11 Sawatsky, *For Services Rendered*

12 Confidential information from British and R.C.M.P. sources

13 See *Their Trade is Treachery*. John Barron, *K.G.B.*, Corgi 1975

14 Confidential information. See David C. Martin *op cit*. Information deriving from Nosenko

15 Confidential information from R.C.M.P. source

16 Following disclosures about the Watkins case in *Their Trade is Treachery* the Canadian Press secured public statements from Canadian Government officials followed by a belated inquest in December 1981. This was fully reported in *The Citizen* (Ottawa), the *Globe and Mail* (Toronto) and other Canadian papers. On 19 May 1981, Robert Kaplan, the Solicitor-General, gave evidence about the circumstances of Watkins' death to the Justice and Legal Affairs Committee (see *Globe and Mail*, 28 May 1981)

17 Confirmed by official Canadian source

18 For the pathologist's testimony see *Globe and Mail*, 22 December 1981

19 Confidential information from R.C.M.P. sources

20 See F.B.I. document on H.A.R. Philby, Hoover to London Representative, dated 14 June 1966, in which Michael Straight is recorded as having named Norman as a member of the communist cell. Norman's name is blanked out but Straight has identified it for me. Full-scale biographies of Norman are being prepared by Professor James Barros of Toronto University's Department of Political Science (because of the impact of Norman's treachery on international affairs) and by Professor Roger Bowen of Colby College, U.S.

21 F.B.I. papers on Norman secured by Professor Barros

22 Professor Barros confirms that Pearson did all he could to protect Norman. Original information came from an R.C.M.P. source. For relationship between Norman and Pearson see also J. L. Granatstein, *A Man of Influence*, Deneau 1981

23 Professor Barros. Information about his behaviour in New Zealand from Mrs K. P. Kirkwood, widow of another Canadian diplomat who replaced Norman as High Commissioner in New Zealand in 1956. The K.G.B. was also receiving inside information about Korea from Donald Maclean (see Chapter 20)

24 Professor Barros's book

25 Bourdine has been widely and wrongly referred to as Borodin

26   See Chapter 60
27   R.C.M.P. sources
28   R.C.M.P. sources
29   By Robert Kaplan, see Chapter 53
30   From an R.C.M.P. witness to the event
31   See Chapter 50

Chapter 43: Hollis's Last Cases (pages 421-30)

1   A full account of the Bossard case is given in the Report of the Security
     Commission, June 1965, Cmnd 2722. Norman Lucas, *op cit* provides informa-
     tion from Special Branch sources
2   *Ibid*
3   *Ibid* and press reports of the case, e.g. Chapman Pincher, *Daily Express*, 11
     May 1965
4   See trial transcript, 10 May 1965 (Old Bailey) and *Daily Express*, 11 May
     1965. Also confidential information
5   Cmnd 2722
6   On 10 May 1965. Information from Dr Glees
7   Cmnd 2773, issued September 1965
8   Also dealt with in Cmnd 2722
9   *Ibid*
10   Various press reports on the case
11   Information from Lord Wigg
12   Information from Mr Macmillan at Birch Grove
13   Imperial Calendar for 1965. Salary of a Deputy Permanent Secretary
14   Information from a friend of the Hollis family
15   Information from a colleague of Miss Hammond
16   Press reports: *The Times*, 5 January 1968; *Evening Standard*, 9 February
     1968
17   Obituary notice, *The Times*, 6 November 1973. Written by Sir Dick White
18   Information from a guest at the dinner

Chapter 44: The 'Drat' Inquiry (pages 431-9)

1   Letters from Jack Tilton
2   Letters from John E. Bacon, Information and Privacy Co-ordinator, C.I.A.
3   Willoughby, *op cit*
4   Information from former C.I.A. officer
5   *Ibid*
6   Information from former Director-General of MI6. When I applied to the
     C.I.A. for information about Hollis the agency required a copy of his death
     certificate before a search could be started
7   Letters from some of these contemporaries. Also confidential information
8   Confidential information
9   It is remotely possible that more of Sonia's traffic may be discovered and
     interpreted but if this provides any evidence against Hollis there can be little
     doubt that it will be tightly held by the authorities
10   Confidential information
11   Letters and conversation with Gouzenko and Mrs Gouzenko
12   Letter from Gouzenko

Chapter 45: The Ellis Case (pages 440-56)

1   Ellis's early life has been described in some detail by William Stevenson in
     Intrepid's Last Case, Random House 1983. See also Montgomery Hyde, *Secret
     Intelligence Agent*, Constable 1982

2 Attempts have been made by Ellis's supporters to deny any involvement of Zilenski, who was born in 1914, on the grounds that he was too young, but at the most relevant time, 1938, he was twenty-four, two years older than Maclean when he began spying in the Foreign Office

3 For information about Skobline see Schellenberg, *op cit.* Gordon Brook-Shepherd, *The Storm Petrels*, Collins 1977

4 See *Their Trade is Treachery*, 'The "Klatt" Affair'

5 Stevenson, *op cit.* Montgomery Hyde, *Secret Intelligence Agent.* Confidential sources

6 See William Stevenson, *The Man Called Intrepid*, Macmillan 1976

7 Letter from Lord Lothian in Washington to Secretary of State Cordell Hull dated 6 September 1940

8 Dusko Popov, *op cit.* He has much to say about Ellis

9 F.B.I. document

10 Confidential information

11 See Schellenberg, *op cit.* S. Payne Best, *The Venlo Incident*, Hutchinson 1950

12 *Der Britische Nachrichtdienst*, found among captured German records. It had been prepared early in 1940

13 F.B.I. documents. Letters to Hoover entitled 'Dickie Ellis' dated October 1963 and 9 May 1956. While much is blanked out, the 9 May document states that the information is 'being referred to the attention of the Espionage Section'

14 William Branigan

15 Cables from Sir William Stephenson and telephone conversations

16 'Magic' intercept of a message sent from Berlin to Tokyo on 12 December 1940. It was not decoded until 19 August 1945, when it gave details of a British War Cabinet appreciation of the Far East situation by the Chiefs of Staff. (Wash NA SRNA 0020 RG457, PRO Kew CAB 65/8 and 66/10)

17 The merchant ship was the S.S. *Automeden* which was intercepted by the German raider, *Atlantis*. Before she was sunk she was boarded and her secret papers captured

18 Montgomery Hyde has recalled that Ellis was always complaining about being short of money. Conversations with the author

19 Confidential information. Also see Anthony Cave Brown, *The Last Hero*, Michael Joseph 1982

20 Letter from Sir William McMahon's office

21 Thwaites, *op cit*

22 Poretsky, *op cit*

23 Established by reference to agencies dealing with Interdoc. Confirmed by Stevenson, *Intrepid's Last Case*, who also records a letter from Ellis in which he states that, while doing his 'weeding job' he took the opportunity to 'slip a few bits of paper into the files'

24 Explanation of the law given in the House of Lords by Baroness Young, Minister for the Civil Service, to Lord Boyd-Carpenter

25 F.B.I. documents already cited

Chapter 46: The American Secret Behind the D-Notice Affair (pages 457-62)

1 See evidence in the Report of the Committee of Privy Councillors appointed to inquire into D-Notice matters. June 1967, Cmnd 3309

2 Information from Lord Wigg

3 *Hansard*, 28 February 1967, col. 274

4 See James Bamford, *Puzzle Palace*, Sidgwick and Jackson 1983, which is extremely informative and well documented on these matters

5 See Bamford, *op cit.* Also Senate hearings on National Intelligence Act 1980, pp. 254, 255, 261, *et seq*

6   See evidence of Privy Councillors Report
7   *Ibid*
8   Privy Councillors Report
9   Cmnd 3312, 1967
10 *Hansard*, 22 June 1967
11 Wilson, *op cit*. See also Marcia Williams (Lady Falkender), *Inside No. 10*, Weidenfeld and Nicolson 1972
12 See Chapman Pincher, *Inside Story*
13 *Daily News*, 22 July 1975. The report led to an investigation by a Congressional committee on individual rights
14 Bamford, *op cit*
15 *Ibid*

Chapter 47: Presents from Prague (pages 463-76)

1   Lord Wigg, *op cit*
2   Report of Security Commission, Cmnd 3856, 1968
3   Statement by Harold Wilson, *Hansard*, 17 November 1966, col. 635
4   Josef Frolik, *The Frolik Defection*, Leo Cooper 1975
5   Abse, *op cit*
6   Confidential information
7   The fitness to serve seems to depend on the Whips, who tend to overestimate their capacity for knowing about the private lives of M.P.s
8   Trial transcript and Frolik, *op cit*
9   August, who was a particularly informative defector, has not written his memoirs, though he planned to do so at one stage (see Chapman Pincher, *Inside Story* and *Their Trade is Treachery*). He did, however, give intriguing evidence concerning British M.P.s and trade union leaders to a Senate Judiciary Committee in Washington, which withheld most of it from its published report on 10 July 1976
10 See *Daily Telegraph*, 21 December 1981
11 Trial transcript. Newspaper reports for 17 June 1971 onwards
12 Confidential information. See *Their Trade is Treachery* for an account of Driberg's clandestine activities
13 *Ibid*
14 *Ibid*
15 See Tom Driberg, *Ruling Passions*, Quartet 1978
16 See *Inside Story*. Stonehouse gave his own version of his experiences with Czechs in the *News of the World*, March 1975. August made his allegations to the U.S. Senate Judiciary Committeee
17 *Hansard*, 17 December 1974, col. 1353
18 At the request of Sir Maurice Oldfield I gave a copy of the tape to MI6 and have a receipt for it from Sir Maurice. It went into the MI6 records but led to no further action
19 Information from a Privy Councillor who made a personal inquiry into this case
20 *The Times*, 20 October 1965; *Sunday Telegraph*, 3 July 1966
21 Confidential information. Confirmed by Frolik to Tom Mangold in B.B.C. interview
22 See *Freedom and Security under the Law*, Commission of Inquiry concerning certain activities of the R.C.M.P., Canadian Government Publishing Centre 1981
23 E.g. James Callaghan, *Hansard*, 15 December 1977, col. 912
24 Confidential information
25 Contemporary newspaper reports
26 Information from C.I.A. source

27 Jan Sejna, *We Will Bury You*, Sidgwick and Jackson 1982
28 See David C. Martin, *op cit*
29 Thomas Powers, *The Man Who Kept the Secrets*, Weidenfeld and Nicolson 1979
30 See Golitsin's recent book, *New Lies for Old*, Bodley Head 1984
31 Confidential information. Also statement by James Angleton: 'The unique contribution Golitsin has made to the security of several major Western allies has been recognized by them at the highest levels of government'

Chapter 48: The Interrogation of Sir Roger Hollis (pages 477-87)

1   Confidential information
2   *Ibid*
3   *Ibid*
4   Information from Sir Maurice Oldfield
5   Information from American sources critical of the British situation
6   Dr Glees article on the Hollis letters and subsequent conversations
7   Information from a source who has questioned the Hollis family
8   See *Archie*, a symposium edited by Patricia Clarke and David Footman, privately published 1966
9   Sir Dick White
10 Letters from Gouzenko and Mrs Gouzenko
11 See Eleanor Philby's book *The Spy I Loved*. Philby's previous wife, Aileen, appeared to have no inkling that Philby was working for the K.G.B.
12 Courtney, who had published a book about his disgrace by the K.G.B. (*Sailor in a Russian Frame*, Johnson 1968) spoke to the Monday Club on 16 December 1971 claiming that Hollis had 'allowed himself to be placed in a position which was wide open to the type of blackmail at which the K.G.B. is so adept'. See *Daily Express*, 17 December 1971

Chapter 49: A Belated Purge (pages 488-91)

1   Little was said about this in Parliament but the press publicity was immense. See papers for the last week of September 1971
2   See Edward Heath, *Hansard*, 21 November 1979, col. 468
3   See *Daily Express*, 30 September 1971
4   Confidential information from Ministry of Defence source
5   *Daily Express*, 31 August 1971 and 30 September 1971
6   Statement by Foreign Office officials
7   Information from Defence Intelligence source
8   Confidential information and conversations with Lord Kagan
9   Statement by Attorney-General Sir Peter Rawlinson in Parliament, 8 November 1971, col. 641. Also private conversation
10 Gouzenko put forward a five-point plan to encourage defectors by guaranteeing citizenship without undue delay for those who could prove their bona fides, lifelong physical protection from revenge squads, material security, assistance in finding employment and recognition of services
11 Many more K.G.B. and G.R.U. agents have been expelled from Britain and other Western nations since 1971. According to a U.S. State Department report, 147 were expelled from various countries in 1983 – three times as many as in the previous year

Chapter 50: Operation Gridiron (pages 492-9)

1   John Sawatsky's book, *For Services Rendered*, is a very full study of the Bennett case. I have checked all the material used in this chapter with prime R.C.M.P. sources and with British sources where relevant

2 Positive vetting was not used in Canada until the Royal Commission on Security published its report in 1968. A further two years elapsed before the R.C.M.P. adopted it
3 Minutes of Proceedings and Evidence of the Standing Committee on Justice and Legal Affairs, House of Commons (Canada), 24 November 1977, page 2; 30
4 See *For Services Rendered*

Chapter 51: The First K7 Report (pages 500-4)

1 Departmental Committee on Section 2 of the Official Secrets Act 1911, H.M.S.O. Cmnd 5104, September 1972
2 Mr Justice Caulfield at the Old Bailey in January 1971
3 *Hansard*, 7 May 1963, col. 327
4 *The Times* letters, 21 October 1981. See also my response *The Times* letters, 31 October 1981

Chapter 52: The Second K7 Report (pages 505-9)

1 Letters from Gouzenko and conversations
2 *Ibid*
3 Letter from Mrs Gouzenko. Confirmed by Peter Wright, *op cit*
4 Letter from Gouzenko
5 *Ibid*
6 Letter from Professor Granatstein
7 Death certificate, General Register Office
8 *The Times*, 6 November 1973
9 The *Sun*, 24 January 1974

Chapter 53: An Ultra-Secret Warning (pages 510-14)

1 Confidential information from British, Canadian and Australian sources
2 *Ibid*
3 *The Times*, Peter Hennessy, 3 April 1984
4 Information from Admiral of the Fleet Lord Hill-Norton
5 Information from Vice-Admiral Sir Louis Le Bailly
6 Reported in the Canadian press, e.g. *Toronto Star*, 27 March 1981
7 Various exchanges in the Canadian Parliament in March 1981. During one of them Trudeau recalled that 'Gouzenko had referred to a mole inside the British Intelligence Service, MI5'
8 Confidential information

Chapter 54: A Secret Verdict of 'Not Out!' (pages 515-25)

1 Information originally from a confidential source, since confirmed by events and information from various people concerned
2 Conversations with Lady Falkender
3 Sir Maurice Oldfield, for instance, told me that he intended to remain the chief of MI6 until he had fixed his successor to his satisfaction, which he did
4 *Hansard*, 26 March 1981, col. 1079
5 Confidential information
6 Information deriving from some of these witnesses
7 The attitude to Gouzenko's evidence is shown by a remark by a former very senior officer who told me that he was not impressed by Gouzenko's memories in extreme old age. Gouzenko was sixty-two at the time
8 See Philby, *op cit*. Confidential information from F.B.I. source
9 Including Privy Councillors
10 See *Hansard*, 26 March 1981, col. 1079

11 *The Times* leader, 28 March 1981
12 See Barrie Penrose and Roger Courtiour, *The Pencourt File*, Secker and Warburg 1978. Wilson was widely criticized for his approach
13 I.T.N., *News at One*, 27 March 1981
14 Conversation with Harold Wilson
15 Wilson offered the Kremlin almost £1,000 million worth of credit for trade deals
16 *Hansard*, 26 November 1975, col. 827. *Daily Express*, 27 November 1975. Roy Hattersley announced that seventy-one Soviet inspectors were, already attached to British firms. These included firms of interest to the K.G.B. such as Vickers, Swan Hunter, International Computers
17 Letter from Barrie Penrose
18 *Daily Express*, 29 July 1977. For Callaghan's meeting with security chiefs see *Hansard*, 21 November 1979, col. 506. Conversation with Merlyn Rees, who was Home Secretary at the time
19 Information from a member of the panel
20 In *Freedom and the Security Services*, published March 1983
21 See *Daily Express*, 23 April 1976. Written answer by Anthony Crosland, the Foreign Secretary, *Hansard*, 30 April 1976, col. 198. The Hungarian spies were not made 'Persona non grata'.
22 Markov was murdered in London in September 1978 apparently when standing in a bus queue, when he was prodded by a trick umbrella which implanted a pellet containing the exceptionally poisonous substance ricin

Chapter 55: The Public Exposure of Sir Anthony Blunt (pages 526-33)

1 Conversation with Lord Rawlinson
2 See Heath statement, Blunt Debate, *Hansard*, 21 November 1979, col. 460
3 Information from a researcher who interviewed several of these friends
4 See Chapter 39, Note 12
5 Conversation with Merlyn Rees
6 Andrew Boyle, *op cit*
7 *Hansard*, 15 November 1979, col. 477 (Archie Hamilton M.P.)
8 *Hansard*, 21 November 1979, col. 402
9 *Ibid*
10 *Hansard*, 9 November 1981, col. 40. The Prime Minister said, 'I can assure the House that a person suspected of an espionage offence would not now be interviewed by the Security Service on the basis that he need not fear prosecution unless the case had first been referred to the Attorney-General and permission had been given for the interview to be conducted on that basis'
11 *Hansard*, 21 November 1979, col 504
12 *Ibid*
13 *Ibid*
14 *Ibid*, col 502
15 Confidential information
16 Information from Blunt's solicitor
17 *Daily Telegraph*, 21 January 1984

Chapter 56: An Aladdin's Cave (pages 534-9)

1 Sir Martin Furnival Jones, evidence to the Franks Committee on the Official Secrets Act
2 Conversations with Jonathan Aitken who has previously confirmed, publicly the existence of the letter

3　An account of this remarkable operation was published in the *Bookseller*, 4 April 1981. Sidgwick and Jackson were awarded the annual Silver Trophy of the Publishers Publicity Circle for its promotion of the book (*Bookseller*, 16 January 1982)

4　Neither *The Times* nor the *Daily Mail* received any complaint from the D-Notice Committee's Secretary

5　See *Daily Express*, 24 March 1981

Chapter 57: A Flawed Announcement (pages 540-7)

1　*Hansard*, 26 March 1981, col. 1079

2　*Ibid*

3　*Ibid*

4　*Ibid*. See *Their Trade is Treachery*

5　See Driberg, *op cit*. Mervyn Stockwood, the former Bishop of Southwark, who was a friend of Driberg, told me that he induced him to remove the most unpleasant material from his autobiography!

6　Foot dismissed the information about Driberg's clandestine activities on the grounds that, had it been true, it would have leaked years ago. Others claimed that Driberg was incapable of keeping any secret. The truth was very different, as it had been with Burgess. Both were discreet regarding their espionage

7　*Freedom and the Security Services*, Labour Party, March 1983

8　*Hansard*, 26 March 1981, col. 1082

9　*The Times* letters, 4 and 8 April 1981

10　*Hansard*, 9 November 1981, col. 40

11　Letter from Lord Trend

12　The identity of the office is known to me and nobody could have been better placed to provide a full brief

13　*Freedom and the Security Services*, Labour Party, March 1983

Chapter 58: Aftermath (pages 548-57)

1　Mr Bob Cryer, *Hansard*, 27 March 1981

2　Statement from a professional American researcher. More recently (1984) American researchers have found evidence of the 'sanitizing' and removal of documents concerning Hollis

3　Leo Abse, *op cit*

4　One of a series published in Moscow in 1983. References have been made to it in the *Daily Telegraph*, 29 March 1983, in a dispatch by John Miller from Moscow. A copy of the book is in the author's possession

5　*The Times* letters, 21 October 1981, and my response, 31 October 1981

6　Part of a general campaign to brand Gouzenko as an unsavoury character – see *Toronto Sun*, 8 June 1982, for rebuttal. Also cable from Sir William Stephenson

7　Confidential information

8　Statement from the person concerned

9　The officers had been approached by Granada Television

10　Stephen Knight, *op cit*

11　For details of the Gerhardt case see *Daily Telegraph*, 30 December 1983

12　Statement to *Daily Telegraph*, 25 March 1981, reproduced in other papers, e.g. *Manchester Evening News*, 26 March 1981

13　See Chapter 39

14　Robert Bothwell and J.L. Granatstein, *op cit*

15　Security Commission Report, Cmnd 8540, May 1982

16　*Ibid*. I have been appraised of the complete report by someone who read it

Chapter 59: G.C.H.Q.'s Billion-Dollar Spy (pages 558-64)

1 Information from N.S.A. source
2 See report of the Security Commission, Cmnd 8876, May 1983. Opening speech of the Attorney-General, Queen v. Geoffrey Arthur Prime, Central Criminal Court. See also James Bamford, *op cit*
3 Two Americans working for the K.G.B. were Christopher John Boyce, who worked in the code room of T.R.W., the builders of Rhyolite, and Andrew Daulton Lee who sold the secrets. Both were given heavy prison sentences. See Bamford, *op cit*
4 Confidential information. E. J. Epstein, *Commentary*, July 1982, New York
5 Cmnd 8876 and confidential information
6 *Ibid*
7 Information from an official Washington source
8 For an accurate account of the background see *The Times*, Peter Hennessy, 26 January 1984. *Daily Telegraph*, Graham Paterson, 31 January 1984
9 The ban was announced by Sir Geoffrey Howe, the Foreign Secretary, on 25 January 1984. It caused a spirited reaction from trade unions but the ban was successfully imposed
10 The senator made his comments on the C.B.S. programme, *60 Minutes*
11 For an account of the Great Missile Deception see Chapman Pincher, *Time and Tide*, summer issue 1984
12 See for example the letter from Sir Patrick Reilly and my response, *The Times*, December 1982

Chapter 60: Payment Deferred (pages 565-7)

1 See *Toronto Sun*, 13 May 1980. Questions were asked probing Hambleton's apparent immunity to prosecution in the Canadian Parliament in 1980 and 1981 but produced no meaningful response
2 See F.B.I. press release concerning Herrmann and naming Hambleton as a 'Soviet agent', Washington, 3 March 1980
3 His own admission at his trial
4 The operation was named 'Red Pepper' by the Canadian Solicitor-General, Robert Kaplan, in the Canadian Parliament on 23 May 1980. 'Red Pepper' was discussed on the Canadian Broadcasting Corporation's *Current Affairs* T.V. programme, in which Hambleton appeared, on 8 June 1982
5 See *Daily Telegraph*, 8 December 1982. *Toronto Sun*, 13 January 1980
6 Referred to in Note 2 above
7 See *The Citizen*, Ottawa, 4 December 1982, which claimed that Kaplan, the Solicitor-General, had told him that the R.C.M.P. had been instrumental in ensuring that Hambleton would make his fateful journey to Britain

Chapter 61: A Minor with Major Access (pages 568-71)

1 Security Commission report, Cmnd 9212, H.M.S.O.
2 *Daily Telegraph*, 30 March 1984
3 Cmnd 9212

Chapter 62: Another 'Good Bottle Man' (pages 572-9)

1 Cmnd 9212
2 See opening statement by Sir Michael Havers, the Attorney-General, *The Times*, 11 April 1984
3 Dr David Fleeman, *The Times*, 11 April 1984. Cherwell, 4 May 1984
4 Report of a letter received from Bettaney in prison by the *Observer* (22 April 1984)
5 *Observer* letter, 22 April 1984, and various newspaper reports

6   *Ibid*
7   Havers' statement, *The Times*, 11 April 1984
8   *Ibid*
9   View of a professional intelligence officer
10 Havers' statement, *The Times*, 11 April 1984
11 *Daily Telegraph*, 17 April 1984
12 Confidential information
13 Vassall's evidence that George Blake had considered becoming a Catholic priest before embracing communism offers an interesting comparison
14 *Hansard*, 21 November 1979, col. 504

Chapter 63: The Outlook for Oversight (pages 580-8)

1   *Freedom and the Security Services*, Labour Party, March 1983
2   Chiefly Duncan Campbell
3   Letters from various M.P.s
4   House of Commons First Report from the Liaison Committee, session 1982-83, the Select Committee System, 19 January 1983 (see para 25)
5   Falkland Islands Review, Cmnd 8787, January 1983, H.M.S.O.
6   Oversight committees for both the Senate and Congress were created under the Intelligence Oversight Act of 1980, which placed on statute a process which had been in action since 1976. The Act requires the intelligence and security agencies to keep the two committees 'fully and currently informed'. For details see Calendar No.780, report No. 96-730. Also hearings before the Select Committee on Intelligence of the U.S. Senate, February, March and April 1980
7   Confidential information from American source. Efforts to penetrate the staff of the committee have been made by the K.G.B. but successfully countered to date, so far as is known
8   Confidential information from American source
9   When Director of Central Intelligence, in 1980, Admiral Stansfield Turner strongly supported oversight (Senate hearings in February 1980)
10 Liaison Committee report, see Note 4 above
11 Confidential information from American sources
12 The oversight question has been the subject of massive media coverage and lively debate over the past two years in Canada. A Commission of Inquiry headed by Mr Justice D.C. McDonald published a long and detailed report on the activities of the security section of the R.C.M.P. in August 1981 (Canadian Government Publishing Centre, Catalogue CP32-37/1981 2 IE). See also Senate Report on Canadian Security Intelligence Service, November 1983
13 Reports of Canadian Parliament for 21 June 1984. Also report in *Maclean's* news magazine, 9 July 1984

APPENDIX A

Igor Gouzenko's memorandum to the R.C.M.P. made at the request of MI5 on 6 May 1952

Supt. McClellan
R.C.M.P. H.Q.
Ottawa
6 May 1952

Dear Sir:

Regarding your request for information about the person in British MI5, here's what I remember, and what I think about the matter.

1. I forget the cover name. You mentioned it in your letter and that looks like it, but since I forget, I won't repeat it. However, the cover name is not so important in this case. Moscow quite often changed the cover names, and there is great probability that it had changed the cover name of the person in question during the last 10 years.

It seems to me that the cover name in this case was of female character. But of course it is not necessary that the person was a woman. There were some cases when Moscow gave male agents female cover names, and vice versa.

2. History: At the very first moment when I gave Canadian authorities information from a great number of other agents, I mentioned first of all three persons whom I considered to be of most importance:

a) A member of Parliament Fred Rose, in Canada; b) the assistant to Stettinius in the U.S. [ed. note: former Secretary of State Edward Stettinius]; c) a member of MI5 in Great Britain. In the case of Fred Rose there was documental evidence.

In the case of the assistant to Stettinius and the member of MI5, there were only my words. The case of the assistant to Stettinius was particularly weak. I repeated just what I had heard from cipher clerk Kulakov.

During the course of a general conversation with him in the cipher room of the embassy, when I expressed surprise at the amount of documental information which agents in Canada gave to Moscow, he said something in this line: "This is nothing – in the United States the assistant of Stettinius is working for us."

And then he added that such a person could not only supply vital information, but could even influence the foreign policy of the U.S. in favour of Moscow. I did not ask Kulakov for a name, and probably he did not know it. But I did not doubt his words – he had just come from Moscow where he was working in the cipher branch at Intelligence H.Q.

Now, in retrospect, this information about a certain assistant to Stettinius was really not much to go on. Stettinius, as I learned later from a U.S. magazine, had four or five assistants.

It took Whittaker Chambers to give the full name and all the particulars. The result of this was that eventually (five years later) one of the assistants of Stettinius (during the San Francisco conference), a certain Alger Hiss, was tried and convicted.

If there had been no Whittaker Chambers my words about the assistant to Stettinius would have been just words, and would have been met only with disbelief. How agents are sometimes powerful and influential can be seen from the fact that almost to the last moment Hiss enjoyed complete confidence and support from no less important a person than Secretary of State [Dean] Acheson.

Whittaker Chambers, who actually wanted to help his country, was ridiculed. Only the conviction of Hiss made high officials, including Acheson, reverse their opinions.

3. The case of the member of MI5 was, in my opinion much stronger and there was much more to go on than in the case of the assistant to Stettinius.

In the first place I was not told by somebody, *but saw the telegram myself* concerning this person. And then, as a second confirmation, I was told by Lieut. Lubimov.

With these two pieces of evidence there is not the slightest doubt in my mind that there was a Soviet agent inside MI5 during the period of 1942–43, and possibly later on.

4. Telegram: I saw it in the course of my work in the cipher branch of Intelligence H.Q. in Moscow during the latter part of 1942, or the beginning of 1943. I remember that I sat at the same table with Lieut. Lubimov who was, like me, a former student of the Architectural Institute, and who had been mobilized at the outbreak of war and sent, first to the Military Engineering Academy and then to cipher courses at the Intelligence Academy.

The telegram dealt with the description of a contact through a "dubok" – a hiding place for small objects etc. It was clear that the person mentioned, (and it was stated, I remember) was "one of five of MI".

It was evident that personal contact with the man from MI5 was avoided. The place of the "dubok" in that particular case was at some graveyard – in a split between stones of a certain tomb.

5. Lubimov's words: I must state that I now forget whether I deciphered the telegram myself or whether Lubimov did it and showed it to me as being interesting stuff. (We quite often showed each other interesting telegrams.)

But I remember that the telegram struck me as unusual and we had a short talk about it. It is more probable that Lubimov deciphered it, since he usually was working on telegrams from London. (He knew the English language better than anybody as he had an English tutor in childhood.)

624

In a short exchange of words, Lubimov said: "This man has something Russian in his background." I understood that he learned this from previous telegrams.

6. The words "something Russian" could be understood in different ways:

a) The man himself (White Russian of noble origin, etc.) or his relatives (wife, father, mother etc.) came from Russia or are Russian.

b) He could be 100 percent English but was in Russia (before the revolution of 1917, or during the 1919-21 civil war, or later on official duties, or as a tourist).

c) Or, less probable, he has some friends of Russian origin.

d) And, to stretch the words, he could have attended some Russian courses (language, history, etc.).

7. Total: a) (What I saw with my own eyes): the man was contacted not personally, but through a "dubok". This showed that Moscow took special precautions in dealing with him. A "dubok" contact might have taken place once a month, or even once every two months. The place of a "dubok" can be changed often.

b) (Words of Lubimov): Something Russian in his background.

8. Indirect but possible evidence: In 1944 (the latter part, or maybe the beginning of 1945) in the embassy. Zabotin received from Moscow a long telegram of a warning character. In it, Moscow informed that representatives of British "greens" (counter-intelligence) were due to arrive in Ottawa with the purpose of working with local "greens" (R.C.M.P.) to strengthen work against Soviet agents, and that such work would be definitely stepped up.

After that the telegram, in a most detailed way, went on to describe what precautions Grant (Zabotin) should take. In the main, his contacts with agents should be twice as rare as before (once a month, or once in two months) Also to split the big groups of agents (as in the Research Council group) and to put them on separate contacts.

To pay more attention, to be careful, and to give detailed instructions to agents in the way of conspiracy (if Communist, to stop attending party meetings; to stop political conversations in the place of work; to throw out all incriminating literature; to learn to avoid shadowing, etc.). The instructions took up two full pages.

Now it could be that Moscow just invented these representatives who were supposed to arrive in Ottawa, in order to make Zabotin more careful. On the other hand, it might be genuine, in which case it would mean that Moscow had an inside track in the British MI5.

This, of course, would be indirect evidence and you are in a good position to check it.

9. Who could possibly know the real name of the agent, or provide more particulars about him outside of Russia?

a) The Soviet military attaché in London.

b) His cipher clerk.

c) Contact man (however in the case of contact through a "dubok", the man who picked up the letters would not necessarily know who put them in the "dubok". For example, on several occasions Zabotin sent people to pick up stuff and they had not the slightest idea where it came from.

d) Maj.-Gen. Bolshakov – if he is still in the U.S. as a Soviet military attaché. Before that he was chief of First Intelligence H.Q. in Moscow, and he certainly knows about this agent.

10. The mistake in dealing with the matter: The mistake (in my opinion) was that the task of finding the agent was given to MI5 itself. I conclude this from the fact that on two occasions representatives of MI5 talked with me in Ottawa during the Royal Commission investigation.

The result, even beforehand, could be expected as nil. The same result would be found if the task of finding the assistant to Stettinius was given to the U.S. State Department. After "thorough and careful" investigation they would come up with a disarming smile and the suggestion that someone should visit a doctor.

This is work in the dark. If an agent is so powerful and has influence, he could make this work more dark, more complicated and fruitless. My humble suggestion is (and I think it is not too late yet) to entrust this job to some people outside of MI5 (Scotland Yard, active army men, etc.).

The best thing, in my opinion, would be to send this letter or a copy of it, to former Governor General Alexander who, at the present time, is defence Minister in Britain and MI5 is now under his jurisdiction. He is an energetic and serious man. Let him decide to whom to entrust the job.

Besides, he was in Ottawa during the Canadian spy trials and he would probably treat the information more seriously than anybody in England.

11. Suggestion as to how to get the best results: I am sure that if, during the last six years, British authorities had established a 24-hour, month-after-month check on the movements of members of the Soviet embassy, commercial attaché, military attaché, etc. – and a real check, not just token – they would have not just one, but dozens of agents in their hands by now.

Even contacts through "duboks" are still done by people. The favourite places for a dubok are telephone booths (behind the phone box); toilets (inside the water tank, as in the case of Nora who used the toilet in the dentist's office in Ottawa); some abandoned stone structure with plenty of splits between the stones – old fences, graveyards, etc.

In most cases all places are selected in such a way that access to them is easy but not conspicuous. So the people who will watch the contact men from the Soviet embassy should carefully examine the place which the contact man had just left (telephone booths, toilets, fences, etc.) and if something is found, wait there for the arrival of the agent to pick it up.

The secret is in persistency – watch every movement of the hands of the contact men.

Sometimes they may use a trick such as this: The contact man sits down on a bench in a casual and relaxed pose.

Unnoticed, he may pin a letter under the bench with thumb tacks, then, minutes later, leave the place. Agents may come half an hour later and pick it up. So those who are watching the agent's every movement – even the most unsuspicious and relaxed movements – should check them right away.

All this, of course, you know. But as far as I can see in London they don't practise it. Otherwise, they would have got some results long ago.

12. I might have forgotten some small details, but you have my previous statements and you can add whatever I may have missed.

Sincerely
IGOR GOUZENKO

APPENDIX B

Statement by Margaret Thatcher about *Their Trade is Treachery, Hansard,*
March 1981, col. 1079 *et seq*

Security

The Prime Minister (Mrs. Margaret Thatcher):
With permission, Mr. Speaker, I will make a statement about the security
implications of the book published today that purports to give a detailed
account of the investigations into the penetration of the Security Service
and other parts of the public service that were undertaken following the
defection of Burgess and Maclean in 1951.

The events into which those investigations were inquiring began well
over 40 years ago. Many of those named or implicated in this book as
having been the subject of investigation have died. Others have long since
retired. None of them is still in the public service.

The extent of penetration was thoroughly investigated after the defection of Burgess and Maclean, as indeed, the author of this book makes
clear. The book contains no information of security significance that is
new to the security authorities, and some of the material is inaccurate or
distorted. All the cases and individuals referred to have been the subject of
long and thorough investigation.

The investigations into the possibilities of past penetration have
inevitably extended widely. They have covered not only those suspected of
being guilty but all those who could conceivably fit the often inconclusive
leads available. The fact that somebody has been the subject of investigation does not necessarily, or even generally, mean that he has been
positively suspected. Many people have had to be investigated simply in
order to eliminate them from the inquiry.

The results of the investigations into Philby and Blunt are now well
known. There were good reasons for suspecting a few others, but as it was
not possible to secure evidence on which charges could be founded they
were required to resign or were moved to work where they had no access
to classified information. Many others were eliminated from suspicion.

Apart from the main allegation, to which I will come, I do not propose
to comment on the allegations and insinuations in this book. Nor can I say
which allegations are unsubstantiated or untrue – as some certainly are –
since by doing so I should be implicitly indicating those that were
suspected of having a degree of substance.

628

I must, however, comment upon the grave allegation that constitutes the main theme of the book – that the late Sir Roger Hollis, director general of the Security Service from 1956 to 1965, was an agent of the Russian intelligence service.

The case for investigating Sir Roger Hollis was based on certain leads that suggested, but did not prove, that there had been a Russian intelligence service agent at a relatively senior level in British counter-intelligence in the last years of the war. None of these leads identified Sir Roger Hollis, or pointed specifically or solely in his direction. Each of them could also be taken as pointing to Philby or Blunt. But Sir Roger Hollis was among those that fitted some of them, and he was therefore investigated.

The investigation took place after Sir Roger Hollis's retirement from the Security Service. It did not conclusively prove his innocence. Indeed, it is very often impossible to prove innocence. That is why, in our law, the burden of proof is placed upon those who seek to establish guilt and not on those who defend innocence. But no evidence was found that incriminated him, and the conclusion reached at the end of the investigation was that he had not been an agent of the Russian intelligence service.

This view was challenged, however, by a very few of those concerned, and in July 1974, Lord Trend, the former Secretary of the Cabinet, was asked to review in detail the investigations that had taken place into the case of Sir Roger Hollis and to say whether they had been done in a proper and thorough manner, and whether in his view the conclusions reached were justified. Lord Trend examined the files and records and he discussed the case with many of those concerned, including two people who considered that the investigation should be reopened.

Mr. Pincher's account of Lord Trend's conclusions is wrong. The book asserts that Lord Trend "concluded that there was a strong prima facie case that MI5 had been deeply penetrated over many years by someone who was not Blunt", and that he "named Hollis as the likeliest suspect". Lord Trend said neither of those things, and nothing resembling them. He reviewed the investigations of the case and found that they had been carried out exhaustively and objectively. He was satisfied that nothing had been covered up. He agreed that none of the relevant leads identified Sir Roger Hollis as an agent of the Russian intelligence service, and that each of them could be explained by reference to Philby or Blunt. Lord Trend did not refer, as the book says he did, to "the possibility that Hollis might have recruited unidentified Soviet agents into MI5". Again, he said no such thing.

Lord Trend, with whom I have discussed the matter, agreed with those who, although it was impossible to prove the negative, concluded that Sir Roger Hollis had not been an agent of the Russian intelligence service.

I turn next to the arrangements for guarding against penetration now and in the future.

All Departments and agencies of the Government, especially those concerned with foreign and defence policy and with national security, are targets for penetration by hostile intelligence services. The Security Service, with its responsibilities for countering espionage and subversion, is a particularly attractive target. Recent security successes, such as the expulsion of members of the Russian intelligence service from this country in 1971, would hardly have been achieved if the Security Service had been penetrated.

The Security Service exercises constant vigilance not only against the risk of current penetration but against the possibility of hitherto undetected past penetration, which might have continuing implications. But, however great our confidence in the integrity and dedication of those now serving in the Security Service, we need to make sure that the arrangements for guarding against penetration are as good as they possibly can be, both in this area and throughout the public service.

Existing security procedures were introduced during the years following the Second World War. Burgess, Maclean, Philby and Blunt were all recruited by the Russian intelligence service before the Second World War and came into the public service either before or during the war, well before existing security procedures were introduced.

It was in 1948 that the then Prime Minister announced the Government's intention to bar Communists and Fascists and their associates from employment in the public service in connection with work the nature of which was vital to the security of the state. This led to the introduction of what came to be known as the "purge procedure".

In 1952, the positive vetting procedure was instituted, with the object of establishing the integrity of civil servants employed on exceptionally secret work. In 1956, it was publicly declared that character defects, as distinct from Communist or Fascist sympathies or associations, might affect a civil servant's posting or promotion. In 1961, security procedures and practices in the public service were reviewed by an independent committee under the chairmanship of the late Lord Radcliffe.

The committee's report, published in 1962, contained an account of those procedures, and made various recommendations for modifying them, which the Government accepted. These procedures, as modified in 1962, are still in operation.

These arrangements have over the years substantially reduced the vulnerability of the public service to the threat of penetration and have served the interests of national security well. But it is 20 years since they were last subject to independent review. In that time the techniques of penetration and the nature of the risks may have changed. We need to make sure that our protective security procedures have developed to take account of those changes. I have therefore decided, after consultation with the right hon. Gentleman the Leader of the Opposition, to ask the Security Commission: "To review the security procedures and practices currently followed in the public service and to consider what, if any changes are required."

These terms of reference will enable the Security Commission to review, and to make recommendations as appropriate, on the arrangements and procedures used in all parts of the public service for the purposes of safeguarding information 'and activities involving national security against penetration by hostile intelligence services, and of excluding from appointments that give access to highly classified information both those with allegiances that they put above loyalty to their country and those who may for whatever reason be vulnerable to attempts to undermine their loyalty and to extort information by pressure or blackmail.

There are difficult balances to be struck here between the need to protect national security, the nature and cost of the measures required to do so effectively, the need for efficiency and economy in the public service, and the individual rights of members of the public service to personal freedom and privacy. The Security Commission will be able to consider how these balances ought to be struck in the circumstances of the present time, as it conducts its review and prepares its recommendations. It will be my intention to make its findings known to the House in due course, to the extent that it is consistent with national security to do so.

In conclusion, Mr. Speaker, I should like to emphasise once again that this statement arises out of a book that deals with investigations of matters and events that occurred many years ago. My concern is with the present and with the future. That is why I am asking the Security Commission to undertake the review that I have described.

Index

635

638